Florida

THE ROUGH GUIDE

Other available Rough Guides

Amsterdam • Andalucia • Australia • Barcelona • Berlin • Brazil
Brittany & Normandy • Bulgaria • California • Canada • Corsica • Crete
Czech & Slovak Republics • Cyprus • Egypt • England • Europe • France
Germany • Greece • Guatemala & Belize • Holland, Belgium & Luxembourg
Hong Kong • Hungary • Ireland • Italy • Kenya • Mediterranean Wildlife
Mexico • Morocco • Nepal • New York • Nothing Ventured
Pacific Northwest • Paris • Peru • Poland • Portugal • Prague • Provence
Pyrenees • St Petersburg • San Francisco • Scandinavia • Scotland • Sicily
Spain • Thailand • Tunisia • Turkey • Tuscany & Umbria • USA • Venice
Wales • West Africa • Women Travel • Zimbabwe & Botswana

Forthcoming
India • Malaysia & Singapore • World Music

Rough Guide credits

Text editor:	Greg Ward
Series editor:	Mark Ellingham
Editorial:	Martin Dunford, John Fisher, Jonathan Buckley, Jules Brown, Graham Parker
Production:	Susanne Hillen, Andy Hilliard, Gail Jammy, Vivien Antwi, Melissa Flack, Alan Spicer
Finance:	Celia Crowley
Publicity:	Richard Trillo

For their valued assistance on this edition, the author would like to thank Rachel O'Conner at the Florida Division of Tourism, everyone at the various Visitor Bureaux and Chambers of Commerce throughout the state, Cyn Zarco in Miami, Ellen Sarewitz for proof reading, Micromap Ltd for map revisions, and Pamela Main in the car and in the sea. On the home front, there was once Jack Holland and now there's also Greg Ward . . .

This second edition published 1993 by Rough Guides Ltd, 1 Mercer Street, London WC2H 9QJ.
Distributed by the Penguin Group:

Penguin Books Ltd, 27 Wrights Lane, London W8 5TZ
Penguin Books USA Inc., 375 Hudson Street, New York 10014, USA
Penguin Books Australia Ltd, 487 Maroondah Highway, PO Box 257, Ringwood, Victoria 3134, Australia
Penguin Books Canada Ltd, 10 Alcorn Avenue, Toronto, Ontario M4V 1E4, Canada
Penguin Books (NZ) Ltd, 182–190 Wairau Road, Auckland 10, New Zealand

Originally published in the UK by Harrap Columbus Ltd, 1991.
Previous edition published in the United States and Canada as *The Real Guide Florida*.
Typeset in Linotron Univers and Century Old Style to an original design by Andrew Oliver.
Printed in the UK by Cox & Wyman Ltd, Reading, Berks.

Illustrations in Part One and Part Three by Ed Briant. Basics illustration by Tommy Yamaha. Contexts illustration by Henry Iles.

384pp.
Includes index

A catalogue record for this book is available from the British Library.
ISBN 1-85828-074-5

Florida

THE ROUGH GUIDE

Written and researched by
Mick Sinclair

additional contributions by
Lin Gaskin, Steven Lansdell, Emilie Strauss,
Paul Whitfield and Cyn Zarco

THE ROUGH GUIDES

It will be difficult for us to paint as complete a picture of the vast land of Florida as we should like, because this region is as yet unexplored and unconquered, and its confines are still a mystery.

Garcilaso de la Vega *The Florida of the Inca*, 1605.

One of the wondrous things about Florida, Rudy Graveline thought as he chewed on a jumbo shrimp, was the climate of unabashed corruption. There was absolutely no trouble from which money could not extradite you.

Carl Hiaasen *Skin Tight*, 1990.

CONTENTS

Introduction vi

INTRODUCTION

The cut-rate package trips and photos of tanning flesh and Mickey Mouse that fill the pages of glossy holiday brochures ensure that everyone has an image of **Florida** – but not one that's either accurate or complete. Pulling 35 million visitors each year to its beaches and theme parks, the aptly nicknamed "sunshine state" is devoted to the tourist trade, yet – as contradictory as it may seem – it's also among the least-understood parts of the US, with a history, character and diversity of landscape unmatched by any other region. Beyond the palm trees and sands lie hikeable forests and canoeable rivers that the travel agent's pictures never reveal, and even the famed beaches themselves can vary wildly over a short distance – hordes of copper-toned ravers are often just a frisbee's throw from a deserted, pristine strand coveted by wildlife-watchers. The variations continue inland, where smart, modern cities are rarely more than a few miles from steamy, primeval swamps.

In many respects, Florida is still evolving. Socially and politically, it hasn't calmed since the earliest days of US settlement: stimulating growth has always been the paramount concern and currently, with a thousand people a day moving to the booming state, it's the fourth most populous place in the nation, with no signs of a slowdown. The changing demographics have begun eroding the traditional Deep South conservatism and are overturning the common notion that Florida is dominated by retirees. In fact, the new Floridians tend to be a younger breed, working energetically to shape not only Florida's future but the future direction of the whole US. Immigration from outside the US is increasing, too, with Spanish-speaking enclaves providing a reminder of geographic and economic ties to Latin America and the Caribbean – links almost as influential in raising the state's material wealth over the past decade as the arrival of huge domestic businesses, including sections of the film industry opting for central Florida in preference to Hollywood.

Florida does face problems, however, the most pressing of them being its growing reputation for crimes against (and even murders of) tourists. While the authorities are devising schemes to reduce such attacks, it is an inescapable fact that planeloads of visitors who have left their cares – and sometimes their common sense – at home, are an inviting target for the opportunist criminal. Statistically at least, the odds are astronomical against you becoming a victim, but you should be wary at all times and pay heed to the safety tips given in *Basics* and throughout the *Guide*. On the home front, the state's provision of houses, schools and roads struggles to keep pace with growth, levels of poverty in the rural areas can be severe, and in an increasingly multi-ethnic society where the traditional Anglo-American dominance is sometimes perceived as being under threat, racial tensions frequently surface. Allowing development that does not jeopardize the state's natural assets is another hot issue: surprisingly large amounts of land are under state or federal protection, and there are signs that the conservation lobby is gaining the upper hand. But uncontrolled expansion continues to pose major ecological problems – not least to the endangered Everglades.

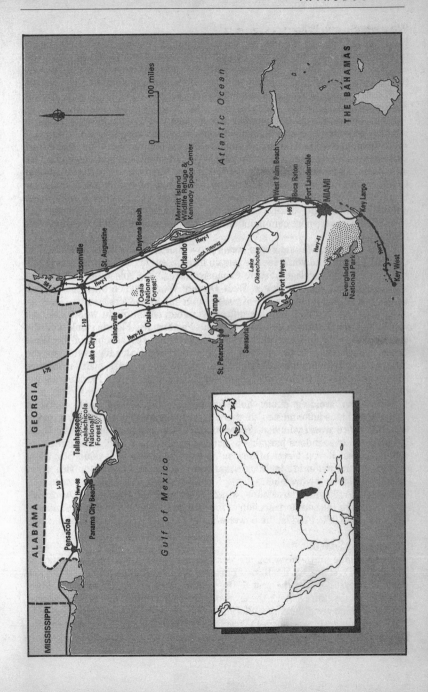

Where to Go and When

Heat-induced lethargy is no excuse not to get out and explore the different facets of Florida: the state is compact enough to be toured easily and quickly. The essential stop is **Miami**, where the addictive, cosmopolitan vibe is enriched by the Hispanic half of its population, and the much-photographed Art Deco district of **Miami Beach** provides an unmistakeable backdrop for the state's liveliest nightclubs.

From Miami, a simple journey south brings you to the **Florida Keys**, a hundred-mile string of islands of which each has something to call its own: be it sports fishing, coral-reef diving, or a unique species of dwarf deer. The single road spanning the keys comes to a halt at **Key West**, a blob of land that's legendary for its sunsets and anything-goes attitude. North from Miami, much of the **Southeast Coast** is a disappointingly urbanized strip – commuter territory better suited for living in than visiting. Alongside the busy towns, however, beaches flow for many unbroken miles and finally escape the residential stranglehold along the **Northeast Coast**, where communities often become subservient to the sands that flank them.

Whenever beachlife and ocean views grow stale, make a short hop inland to **Central Florida** and you'll see the terrain turn green: to cattle farms, grassy hillsides, and isolated villages beside expansive lakes. The sole upset to the rural idyll could hardly be any bigger: **Walt Disney World**, which practises tourism on the scale of the infinite, and – if you're in the mood – offers an ultra-clever fix of escapist fun. If you're not, the upfront commercialism might well encourage you to skip north to the deep forests of the **Panhandle**, Florida's link with the Deep South – or to the art-rich towns and sunset-kissed beaches of the **West Coast**, which should be savored while progressing steadily south to the **Everglades**. This massive alligator-filled swathe of sawgrass plain, mangrove islands and cypress swamp provides as definitive a statement of Florida's natural beauty as you'll encounter.

Other than avoiding public holidays and weekends in strongly touristed districts, and mosquito-infested southern areas in the height of summer, it makes little difference **when** you visit. Year-round, intense competition for your dollar gives rise to tremendous bargains in accommodation and food, although prices will be lowest if you travel off-season (see below). The best-value plan is to explore northern Florida in March and move south in April – or vice versa during October and November.

More recently, the devastation which resulted from **Hurricane Andrew's** sweep through the southern section of the state in August 1992 was a reminder to new arrivals that, in Florida, the power of nature should never be underestimated.

Climate and Seasons

Warm sunshine and blue skies are consistent facts of life in Florida, although technically the state is split into **two climatic zones**: subtropical in the south and warm temperate – like the rest of the southeastern US – in the north. More importantly for the visitor, these two zones determine the state's **tourist seasons**, which are different for Florida's southern and northern halves and have a big effect on costs (see above). Travellers used to northern European temperatures, however, will probably not be unduly concerned by the subtleties of the seasonal variations.

Anywhere **south of Orlando** experiences very mild winters (November to April), with pleasantly warm temperatures and a low level of humidity. This is the peak period for tourist activity, with prices at their highest and crowds at their thickest, and marks the best time to visit the inland parks and swamps. The southern summer (May to October) seems hotter than it really is (New York is often warmer) because of the extremely high humidity, only relieved by afternoon thunderstorms and Atlantic breezes. Lower prices and fewer tourists are the rewards for braving the mugginess, although mosquitoes can render the natural areas off-limits. Winter is the off-peak period **north of Orlando**, and while it's known for snow to fall in the Panhandle, in all probability the only chill you'll detect is a slight nip in the evening air. The northern Florida summer is when the crowds arrive, and when the days – and the nights – can be almost as hot and sticky as southern Florida.

The Florida Sun: Sunbathing and Sunburn

Any visitor with sensitive skin should bear in mind that Florida shares a latitude with the Sahara Desert; the power of the Florida **sun** should never be underestimated.

Time spent outdoors should be planned carefully at first, especially between 11am and 2pm, when the sun is at its strongest. A powerful **sunscreen** is essential; anything with an SPF of less than 25 is unlikely to offer the necessary protection. Light-colored, loose-fitting, lightweight clothes should protect any parts of your body not accustomed to direct sunlight. Wear a hat with a wide brim, carry sunglasses, and keep to the shaded side of the street. Drink plenty of **fluids** (but not alcohol) to prevent dehydration – public drinking-water fountains are provided for this purpose; iced tea is the best drink for cooling off in a restaurant.

AVERAGE DAYTIME TEMPERATURES (°F)												
	Jan	Feb	Mar	Apr	May	Jun	Jul	Aug	Sep	Oct	Nov	Dec
Miami	69	70	71	74	78	81	82	84	81	78	73	70
Key West	69	72	74	77	80	82	85	85	84	80	74	72
Orlando	60	63	66	71	78	82	82	82	81	75	67	61
Tampa	60	61	66	72	77	81	82	82	81	75	67	62
Tallahassee	53	56	63	68	72	78	81	81	77	74	66	59

HELP US UPDATE

Months of painstaking research in blistering heat has ensured that this second edition of *The Rough Guide to Florida* is as accurate and up-to-date as possible. Nonetheless, in Florida the changes come thick and fast: bars and hotels open and close, and last year's sleepy resort becomes this year's place to be.

Among the countless readers who enjoyed the first edition of this book on their Florida travels, the following people wrote to share their experiences. Their comments and suggestions were very much appreciated – and many of them received other *Rough Guides* as a reward: Victor Carlton, Phil Lawless, C Lane, Vivien Smallwood, Lesley Timpson, Mike Turner, Sue Grice, Mary & Colin Hall, Sam Levene, Anna Crago, D & J McLaggan, HF Harrison, M Jarvis & A Pitter, Linda Street, Mrs G Mowat, L Connolly, Mick Edwards & Helen Duff, Sue Swannie & David Cash, Mr Ken Cross, Steve Deutsch and Liette Robin.

Readers' opinions, ideas and updates to this second edition are very welcome. Please mark letters "Rough Guide Florida Update" and send to:

Rough Guides, 1 Mercer Street, London WC2H 9QJ,
or Rough Guides, 375 Hudson Street, 4th Floor, New York, NY 10014.

PART ONE

THE
BASICS

GETTING THERE FROM BRITAIN AND IRELAND

There's never been a better time for British travellers to go to Florida. Price wars between airlines on transatlantic routes are hotter than ever and many operators are tossing in car rental and accommodation for only a little over the regular airfare. Comparatively few airlines fly non-stop from the UK to Florida but many have one-stop links, and connections from other US airports are plentiful. Innumerable charter flights from all over the UK to major holiday centers such as Orlando throw up even more low-cost options.

FROM LONDON

Whenever and however you go, the most expensive time to fly is **high season**, between June and August and a week either side of Christmas;

April, May, September and October are slightly less pricey, and November to March is considered **low season** – cheaper still. It's important to remember, however, that high season in the UK is the low season – the least costly and least busy time – in south Florida, so the extra you might spend on a summer flight may be offset by cheaper deals once you're on the ground. Seasons in north Florida, however, match those of the UK. For more on the seasonal variations across Florida, see the Introduction.

Before **booking a flight**, shop around for the best price: scan the travel ads in the Sunday papers, London's *Time Out* and giveaway magazines, or phone the airlines or one of the agents mentioned below. The details we've given are the latest available, but are sure to have undergone at least subtle changes by the time you read them.

ROUTES

All **non-stop scheduled flights from London** to Florida land either at Miami or, less often, Orlando. The flight lasts around eight hours, leaving London around midday and arriving during the afternoon (local time). The return journey is slightly shorter, leaving in the early evening and flying through the night to arrive in London around breakfast time.

Many more routings use **direct one-stop flights** to Florida (a flight may be called "direct" even if it stops on the way, provided it keeps the same *flight number* throughout its journey). Obviously, these take a few hours longer than non-stop flights but can be more convenient (and

SCHEDULED FLIGHTS

The following carriers operate scheduled flights to Florida from London (all use **Gatwick** airport unless otherwise stated).

American Airlines Daily non-stop to Miami from Heathrow; one-stop flights to most other Florida airports, usually via Dallas.

British Airways Daily non-stop to Miami from Heathrow; 1–2 daily via Miami or Orlando to Tampa; 4 weekly non-stop to Miami; daily non-stop to to Orlando.

Continental Daily via Newark to most Florida airports.

Delta Daily non-stop to Miami

Northwest Daily via Boston to Orlando and (via Orlando) Miami.

United Daily non-stop to Miami from Heathrow.

USAir Daily via Charlotte to Miami, Orlando and Tampa.

Virgin Airlines 4–5 weekly non-stop to Miami; daily to Orlando.

sometimes cheaper) if you're not aiming specifically for Miami or Orlando. All the state's cities and large towns have airports – the other major one is Tampa – with good links from other US cities.

Alternatively, you could take a flight to **New York or another northern East Coast** city and travel on from there – this won't save any money overall but is an idea if you want to see more of the country before reaching Florida. Again, agents have the cheapest offers, with seats to New York on carriers such as *Air India* and *Kuwait Airlines* sometimes to be found for under £300.

TICKETS AND AGENTS

Of the various **ticket types** offered by airlines, the cheapest are, not surprisingly, **economy**

returns, which are bookable at any time and work out around £340 for a midweek flight in low season to £440 for a weekend flight in high season. Economy returns have no restrictions regarding length of stay, but a change of your return date after booking entails a penalty of between £35 and £50. Of other tickets, **standby** deals (tickets which you pay for in advance without specifying precise travel dates), and **APEX** returns, which have to be booked 14, 21 or 30 days in advance for a stay of at least a week, are £100–150 dearer than economy fares if bought directly from the airline. However, cut-rate APEX tickets are what you're likely to find offered by **agents** such as *STA Travel* or *Campus* (addresses below) who always have the lowest fares, with special reductions for students and anyone under 26.

AIRLINES AND AGENTS

AIRLINE ADDRESSES

Air India, 17–18 New Bond St, London W1 ☎071/493 4050

American Airlines, 15 Berkeley St, London W1 ☎081/572 5555

British Airways, 156 Regent St, London W1 ☎081/897 4000

Continental, Beulah Court, Albert Rd, Horley, Surrey RH6 7HZ ☎0800/776464

Delta, Victoria Plaza, Victoria Station, London SW1 ☎0800/414767

Kuwait Air, 16–20 Baker St, London W1 ☎071/486 6666

Northwest, Northwest House, Tinsley Lane, Crawley, West Sussex RH10 2TP ☎0345/747800

United, 192 Piccadilly, London W1 ☎0800/888555

USAir, Piccadilly House, Regent St, London SW1 ☎0800/777333

Virgin Atlantic, Sussex House, High St, Crawley, West Sussex RH10 1PH ☎0800/747747

LOW-COST FLIGHT AGENTS

Campus Travel, 52 Grosvenor Gardens, London SW1 ☎071/730 2101 *Also many other branches around the country.*

Council Travel, 28A Poland St, London W1 ☎071/437 7767

STA Travel, 86 Old Brompton Rd, London SW7 ☎071/937 9971 *Offices nationwide.*

Travel Cuts, 295 Regent St, London W1 ☎071/637 3161

SPECIALIST US FLIGHT OPERATORS

Globespan, PO Box 149, Glasgow G2 3EJ ☎041/332 6600 reservations ☎0737/773171

Falcon, Groundstar House, London Rd, Crawley, West Sussex RH10 2TB ☎071/221 6298 Also ☎021/666 7000, ☎061/831 7000 and ☎ 041/248 7911.

Unijet, "Sandrocks", Rockey Lane, Haywards Heath, W Sussex ☎0444/458181

North American Travel Club, Hayworth House, Market Place, Haywards Heath, West Sussex RH16 1DB ☎0444/415921

Jetsave, Sussex House, London Rd, East Grinstead, West Sussex RH19 1LD ☎0342/312033

MAJOR COURIER FIRMS

CTS Ltd ☎071/351 0300

DHL ☎081/890 9393

Polo Express ☎081/759 5838

Through an agent, provided your plans are flexible and you hunt around, you can often make savings of £100–200 on regular fares, bringing prices down to around £300–350 for a weekend flight in high season. Look out, too, for any short-term offers from the major airlines – which can cut fares to any east-coast US city to as low as £250 return.

Many agents and airlines offer **"open jaw"** deals whereby you fly into the US at one city and out through another: these won't save money if you're sticking to Florida but you could, for example, combine New York with Miami for around £380.

PACKAGES AND COURIER FLIGHTS

You can also pick up seats on **charter flights** through a number of **specialist operators** – excellent value, especially if you're travelling from somewhere other than London. They also offer fly-drive packages and all-inclusive flight-accommodation deals, and their brochures fill the shelves of high-street travel agents, or you can contact them at the addresses listed opposite.

Around £100 can be cut from the cheaper fares if you travel as a **courier**. Most of the major courier firms offer a cheap return flight as payment for delivering a package or documents (see the Yellow Pages, or the addresses opposite); a return to Miami can work out as little as £180. Normally, though, you're required to sacrifice your baggage allowance (only hand baggage is allowed) and fit in with tight restrictions on travel dates.

FROM ELSEWHERE IN BRITAIN

There are no non-stop scheduled flights to Florida from anywhere in Britain other than London, although *Northwest* has one of the cheapest APEX flights (from £420) on its four-times-a-week service from Glasgow via Boston to Orlando and Miami.

British Airways, through the charter airline *Britannia*, has a weekly non-stop flight from Manchester to Orlando. Other cheap flights are run by the specialist operators mentioned above from the UK's bigger regional airports. Most of these include accommodation, and prices are based on two or more people travelling together; flight-only deals tend to turn up at the last minute to fill unused seats, and you should scan high-street travel agents' windows for the latest offers. Even if the price you pay (typically, a return to Orlando or one of the busier coastal areas for £260–350) does include a hotel room, you don't, of course, have to use it.

FROM IRELAND

If you're under 26 or a student, the cheapest flights from Eire to Florida are through *USIT*, O'Connell Bridge, 19–21 Aston Quay, Dublin 2 (☎01/778 117), which offers a return fare of IR£420 with *Northwest* via London. It's not possible to fly non-stop from Eire to Florida although *Aer Lingus* and *Delta* have services from Dublin and Shannon via New York or Atlanta for IR£500–550.

INCLUSIVE HOLIDAYS

Packages – fly-drive, flight-accommodation deals and guided tours (or a combination of all three) – can be a good way of skirting potential problems once you're in Florida and they usually work out cheaper than arranging the same trip yourself. The drawbacks are the loss of flexibility and the fact that flight-accommodation schemes often use hotels in the mid-range to expensive bracket – cheaper accommodation is almost always readily available. There are a great many packages to choose from and your high-street travel agent will have plenty of brochures and information.

FLY-DRIVE

Fly-drive deals, which combine car rental with a flight booking, are extremely good value, and should certainly be considered before booking a flight and car rental separately. In fact, many airlines offer seven days' car rental at little, if any, extra cost above booking a flight to Florida with them. *British Airways*, for example, can set you up with a week's car rental and a return flight to Miami or Orlando for £315–£489 depending on season. If you're not aiming for these major centers, several American airlines have even cheaper deals based on smaller Florida cities.

The most obvious drawback of fly-drive deals is that the quoted prices are usually based on **four adults** sharing a car (and, obviously, each booking a flight with the airline involved); two people travelling together will often face a £20 surcharge. Scan a handful of brochures for the deal which suits you best – and be sure to read the small print.

TOUR OPERATORS

Airtours, Helmshore, Rossendale, Lancs BB4 4NB ☎0706/260000

AmeriCan Adventures, 45 High St, Tunbridge Wells, Kent TN1 1XL ☎0892/511894

Bon Voyage, 18 Bellevue Rd, Southampton, Hants SO1 2AY ☎0703/330332

British Airways Holidays, Atlantic House, Hazelwick Ave, Three Bridges, Crawley, West Sussex RH10 1NP ☎0293/572704

Contiki Travel, Wells House, 15 Elmfield Rd, Bromley, Kent BR1 1LS ☎081/290 6422

Enterprise, Groundstar House, London Rd, Crawley, West Sussex RH10 2HB ☎0293/560777

Greyhound, Sussex House, London Rd, East Grinstead, West Sussex RH19 ☎0342/317317

Premier, Westbrook, Milton Rd, Cambridge CB4 1YQ ☎0223/355977

TransAmerica, 3A Gatwick Metro Centre, Balcombe Rd, Horley, Surrey RH6 9GA ☎0293/774441

Trek America, Trek House, The Bullring, Deddington, Oxford OX15 0TT ☎0869/38777

Unijet, "Sandrocks", Rocky Lane, Haywards Heath, West Sussex RH16 4RH ☎0444/459191

Virgin Holidays, The Galleria, Station Rd, Crawley, West Sussex RH10 1WW ☎0293/617181

Renting a car for longer than seven days can usually be arranged with a minimum of fuss for as little as £23 per week for a subcompact (ideal for two people); around £33 for an intermediate vehicle.

Other important facts to consider when looking for a fly-drive deal are the unavoidable extra expenses such as the Collision Damage Waiver, the Florida surcharge and the cost of fuel, and the fact that under-25s may face problems renting a car in the US (although a pre-arranged booking should prevent this). For complete details on these matters and full car rental and driving facts, see "Getting Around".

FLIGHT AND ACCOMMODATION DEALS

There's really no end of **flight and accommodation packages** to all the major coastal areas and Orlando, and although you can always do things cheaper independently, you won't be able to do the *same* things cheaper – in fact the equivalent room booked by itself will probably be a lot more expensive. *STA Travel* (address on p.4) offers a package deal which includes flight and $15-a-night hostel accommodation (bear in mind

not every Florida town has a hostel, see "Accommodation").

Any number of tour operators offer other, costlier deals. Of these, *Virgin Holidays* has the cheapest and widest selection, averaging £400–500 per person for a week, inclusive of return flight and car hire. See also "Accommodation", p.26, for details of pre-booked accommodation schemes.

TOURING AND ADVENTURE PACKAGES

Geographical isolation and scorching summer temperatures mean that Florida tends to miss out on the specialist **touring and adventure trips** that cover much of the rest of the US. Nonetheless, *Trek America* is one UK-based company that does include Florida, offering 8- or 12-day tours (£318 and £425 respectively), which include transport, accommodation and a guide. Other operators worth contacting include *Contiki* and *AmeriCan Adventures*, whose brochures can be found in youth- and student-oriented travel outlets. Once you're in Florida, tours of much shorter length, often just a day or two, can usually be arranged on the spot – details are given throughout the Guide.

GETTING THERE FROM AUSTRALASIA

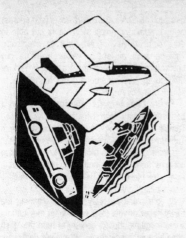

Travellers from Australia and New Zealand planning a trip to Florida are faced with two obvious alternatives: either to fly direct to Miami in Florida itself, or to take the cheaper option of only flying as far as the West Coast, and making their own•way cross-country. Our sections on "Getting There from the US and Canada" and "Getting Around" detail some of the possibilities for transcontinental overland trips.

Other than any charter deals, seasonal bargains and all-in-packages which may be on offer from high-street travel agents, the cheapest flights are available from specialists such as STA, whose offices are listed below.

From **Australia**, the best offer currently available to **Miami** is on *Northwest*, for AU$1760, from Melbourne, Sydney, Brisbane and Canberra. *Air New Zealand* has the lowest price to **Los Angeles** – AU$1290, from Melbourne, Sydney, Brisbane, Adelaide and Cairns – while **San Francisco** is reachable for $1320 on *Qantas* from the same set of cities.

From **New Zealand**, a return to **Miami** on *United Airlines* costs NZ$2279 from *STA*, at the time of writing (single NZ$1464); **Los Angeles** is NZ$1550 return on *Qantas* or *Air France*, and **San Francisco** is $1599 on *Air France*. All flights are from **Auckland**.

AIRLINES AND AGENTS IN AUSTRALASIA

Air New Zealand
Air New Zealand House,
Queen St, Auckland ☎09/357-3000

British Airways
64 Castlereagh St,
Sydney, NSW ☎02/258-3300
Dilworth Building, Queen St/Customs St,
Auckland ☎09/367-7500

Qantas
Qantas International Centre, International Square,
Sydney, NSW ☎02/236-3636

STA Travel
222–224 Faraday St, Carlton,
Melbourne 3053 ☎03/347-4711
1a Lee St, Railway Square,
Sydney, NSW 2000 ☎02/519-9866
10 High St,
Auckland ☎09/309-9723

GETTING THERE FROM THE US AND CANADA

Every major and most minor US airlines fly to Florida, where Miami is the main hub, closely followed by Orlando and Tampa. Of the bigger carriers, *Delta* and *American Airlines* (flying as *American Eagle*) have the best links with the state's many smaller regional airports.

Prices are similar no matter which airline you choose; variations in cost are more dependent on which day of the week you travel (midweek is always cheaper than weekends) and how flexible your plans are (you might save $100 by shortening or lengthening your trip by a day or so).

Booking directly with an airline tends to be expensive, although it is the best way to take advantage of any car rental and accommodation deals they may offer in conjunction with a flight (see "Packages", p.10). Price-wise, the best outlets for plane tickets are the specialist opera-

tors such as *STA* and *Council Travel* (see address below), primarily aimed at students but able to offer competitively priced fares to everybody. Through such an outlet, you're likely to pay upwards of $275 round trip from New York or Chicago to Miami; around $350 round trip to Miami from Los Angeles.

From **Canada**, *Air Canada* flies direct between Toronto and Montreal to Miami and Tampa; *American Airlines* flies non-stop from Toronto to Miami, Orlando and Fort Lauderdale, and from Vancouver to Miami; *Delta* has non-stop services from Toronto and Vancouver to Miami. Again, the place to find the lowest-priced fares is a specialist flight agent, such as *Travel Cuts*.

If your plans are very flexible, scanning the travel pages of your local newspaper may turn up some bargains; though be sure to read the small print — many seemingly attractive deals are dependent on two people travelling together and using specified hotel accommodation.

BY CAR

How feasible it is to **drive** to Florida naturally depends on where you live and how much time you have. If you're aiming for the tourist hot-spots like Orlando you may enjoy a few days passing through the relaxing scenery of the south east before and after your trip. From the north-east or midwest, reckon on around 26 hours of actual driving to get to Florida; from the West Coast you'll probably need 40 hours behind the wheel.

Don't even think about **renting** a car to drive to Florida: although rental rates within the state are low, crossing the state line in a rental car is prohibitively expensive.

BY TRAIN

A few years ago, the deregulation of the airline industry helped make domestic air travel as cheap as train travel. In an effort to win back business, ***Amtrak*** (contactable on a nationwide toll-free number ☎1-800/USA RAIL) has sharpened up its act all round: raising comfort levels, offering better food, introducing "Thruway" buses to link with its trains, and launching new services — most recently the Los Angeles–Miami *Sunset Limited* route.

MAJOR AIRLINE NUMBERS	
Air Canada	☎1-800/776-3000
American Airlines	☎1-800/433-7300
America West	☎1-800/247-5692
Canadian Pacific	☎1-800/426-7000
Continental	☎1-800/525-0280
Delta	☎1-800/221-1212
TWA	☎1-800/221-2000
United	☎1-800/722-5243
US Air	☎1-800/428-4322

Consequently, travelling to Florida by train can be enjoyable and relaxing, if not particularly inexpensive.

From **New York**, the *Silver Meteor* and the *Silver Star* traverse the eastern seaboard daily to Miami or Tampa (each train splits in half in Jacksonville before continuing), and the *Palmetto* charts a similar course from New York to Jacksonville. The fare is $153 each way, and the journey from New York takes around 30 hours. From **Los Angeles** to Miami, the *Sunset Limited* crosses the southerly reaches of the US in a three-day journey. The round-trip fare varies according to season from $254 to $421.

If you really can't bear to be parted from your car and you live within driving distance of Lorton, Virginia (just south of Washington DC), the **Florida Auto Train** will carry you and your vehicle to Sanford, near Orlando. The journey time is

17 hours and passenger fares range from $75 to $125; depending on its size, your car will cost a further $120–220.

All the above involve overnight travel. To spare yourself a restless night fidgeting in your seat, upwards of $50 will get you a "slumbercoach", essentially a narrow bed which pulls down from the wall; a "roomette", similar to a slumbercoach but with a private bathroom; or a fully-fledged "bedroom", more spacious than a roomette and with a few sticks of furniture.

BY BUS

Long-distance travel on *Greyhound* **buses** can be an endurance test but is at least the cheapest form of public transportation to the Sunshine State. Also, if you have the time and inclination to include a few stopovers on the way, you'll find

DISCOUNT AGENTS IN THE USA AND CANADA

COUNCIL TRAVEL OFFICES IN THE USA

Head office: 205 E 42nd St, New York, NY 10017	☎212/661-1450	1153 N Dearborn St, Chicago, IL 60610	☎312/951-0585
Other main offices at:		729 Boylston St, Suite 201, Boston, MA 02116	☎617/266-1926
530 Bush St, Suite 700, San Francisco, CA 94108	☎415/421-3473	2000 Guadalupe St, Suite 6, Austin, TX 78705	☎512/472-4931
3300 M St NW, 2nd Floor, Washington DC 20007	☎202/337-6464	1314 Northeast 43rd St, Suite 210, Seattle, WA 98105	☎206/632-2448

STA TRAVEL OFFICES IN THE USA

nationwide information	☎1-800/777-0112	166 Geary St, Suite 702, San Francisco, CA 94108	☎415/391-8407
Main offices at:		273 Newbury St, Boston, MA 02116	☎617/266-6014
48 E 11th St, New York, NY 10003	☎212/477-7166		
7202 Melrose Ave, Los Angeles, CA 90046	☎213/934-8722)	3730 Walnut St, Philadelphia, PA 19104	☎215/382-2928

TRAVEL CUTS OFFICES IN CANADA

Head Office: 187 College St, Toronto, ON M5T 1P7	☎416/979-2406	1 Stewart St, Ottawa, ON K1N 6H7	☎613/238-8222
Other main offices at:		2383 Ch Ste Foy, Suite 103, Ste Foy, Quebec, PQ G1V 1T1	☎418/654-0224
MacEwan Hall Student Centre, Univ of Calgary, Calgary, AB T2N 1N4	☎403/282-7687	Place Riel Campus Centre, Univ of Saskatchewan, Saskatoon, SA S7N 0W0	☎306/975-3722
12304 Jasper Ave, Edmonton, AB T5N 3K5	☎403/488-8487	501–602 W Hastings, Vancouver, BC V6B 1P2	☎604/681-9136
1613 rue St Denis, Montréal, PQ H2X 3K3	☎514/843-8511	University Centre, Univ of Manitoba, Winnipeg, MA R3T 2N2	☎204/269-9530

that *Greyhound* operates a more comprehensive service than do planes or trains (they also reach all but the smallest Florida towns). Scan your local•newspaper or call your local *Greyhound* station for the special fares which are periodically offered, and remember that midweek travel will usually be cheaper than travelling at weekends.

Regular one-way fares from New York or Chicago to Miami or Orlando are $176 and $171 respectively, and the trip takes something in excess of 30 hours). From Los Angeles, the one-way fare to either Miami or Orlando is $193 (with a journey time of 60-plus hours). Buying a round-trip tickets will shave around $20–40 off the above fares.

PACKAGES

Pick up the travel section of any newspaper and you'll see dozens of Florida **package deals** on offer. These come in all shapes and sizes, and are designed to appeal to a multitude of budgets and interests (golf enthusiasts, for example, are spoilt for choice). Most, however, simply offer a week or two in the Florida sun for a single price – from around $250–$400 per person per week depending on which part of the country you live in – inclusive of round-trip flights, accommodation and (in many cases) car rental.

Besides independent operators catering to specialist interests, package deals are also offered by most airlines and by *Amtrak*. Contact the nearest office for the latest details.

ENTRY REQUIREMENTS FOR FOREIGN VISITORS

VISAS

To enter the US for less than ninety days, British citizens need a **full UK passport** (not a British Visitor's Passport) and a **visa waiver form**, which can be provided either by travel agents, or by the airline during check in, or on the plane and must be presented to immigration on arrival. The same visa waiver form can be used by citizens of most European countries, provided their passports are up to date, although citizens of Eire, Australia and New Zealand must have a **non-immigrant visitor's visa** before arriving. To obtain a visa, fill in the application form available at most travel agents and send it with a full passport to the nearest US Embassy or Consulate. Visas are not issued to convicted criminals and anybody who owns up to being a communist, fascist or drug dealer. You'll need to give precise dates of your trip and declare that you're not intending to live or work in the US (if you are intending to do either of these things, see p.47).

IMMIGRATION CONTROLS

During the flight, you'll be handed an **immigration form** (and a customs declaration: see below), which must be filled out and, after landing, given up at immigration control. On the form you must give details of where you are staying on your first night (if you don't know write "touring") and the date you intend to **leave** the US. Part of the form will be attached to your passport, where it must stay until you leave, when an immigration or airline official will detach it.

In addition to the form, the officer will be interested in how you intend to support yourself during your stay. Particularly if you're intending to stay for more than a couple of weeks, you may be asked to show a return ticket and ample means of support: about $300–400 per week is considered sufficient, so it's wise to have a stash of travellers' checks and credit cards to flash (bring all you can muster even if you don't intend to use them). If you're **staying with friends**, you'll need to provide their address and phone number, which may be checked if the officer sees fit to do so. If you've written "touring" on the immigration form, you'll be asked where you intend to spend your first night. Saying "a hotel" or "a hostel" and giving a broad indication that you know how to find one, should suffice.

There are, of course, ways to bend the rules slightly. One popular method is to borrow enough money to get into the country, afterwards returning it using an international money order. It's sad but true to say that you stand the best chance of a problem-free entry if you happen to be English-speaking, white, well dressed, sober and polite to the officials. Remember, too, that the reason for all this red tape is that the land of plenty is terrified by the idea of foreigners coming to look for work there – so even if you are thinking of doing this, do not say so.

CUSTOMS

Customs officers will relieve you of your customs declaration and ask if you have any fresh foods. If you say "yes" you'll have to hand them over and probably won't get them back, certainly not in the case of meat or fruit; say "no" and they might decide to check your baggage anyway. You'll also be asked if you've visited a farm in the last month: if you have, you could well lose your shoes. The **duty-free allowance** if you're over 17 is 200 cigarettes and 100 cigars and, if you're over 21, a litre of spirits.

As well as foods and anything agricultural, it's also prohibited to carry into the country any articles from Vietnam, North Korea, Kampuchea or Cuba, obscene publications, lottery tickets, chocolate liqueurs or Pre-Columbian artefacts. Anyone caught carrying drugs into the country will not only face prosecution but be entered in the

US EMBASSY AND CONSULATES IN CANADA

Embassy:
100 Wellington St, Ottawa, ON K1P 5T1 ☎613/238-5335

Consulates:

Suite 1050, 615 Macleod Trail, **Calgary, AB** ☎403/266-8962	2 Place Terrace Dufferin, **Québec City, PQ** ☎418/692-2095
Suite 910, Cogswell Tower, Scotia Square, **Halifax, NS** ☎902/429-2480	360 University Ave, **Toronto, ON** ☎416/595-1700
Complex Desjardins, South Tower, **Montréal, PQ**	1095 West Pender St **Vancouver , BC** ☎604/685-4311

US EMBASSIES AND CONSULATES ELSEWHERE

AUSTRALIA
Moonhah Place,
Canberra ☎62/733 711

DENMARK
Dag Hammerskjöld Allé 24,
2100 Copenhagen ☎31 42 31 44

IRELAND
42 Elgin St, Ballsbridge,
Dublin ☎01/688 8777

NETHERLANDS Museumplein 19,
Amsterdam ☎020/790 321

NEW ZEALAND
29 Fitzherbert Terrace, Thorndon,
Wellington ☎4/722 068

NORWAY
Drammensveien 18,
Oslo ☎22 44 85 50

SWEDEN
Strandvägen 101,
Stockholm ☎08/783 5300

UK
5 Upper Grosvenor St,
London W1 ☎071/499 7010

3 Regent Terrace,
Edinburgh EH7 5BW ☎031/556 8315

Queens House, 14 Queen St,
Belfast BT1 6EQ ☎0232/228239

---

records as an undesirable and probably denied entry for all time.

EXTENSIONS AND LEAVING

The date stamped on the form in your passport is the **latest** you're legally entitled to stay. Leaving a few days after may not matter, especially if you're heading home, but more than a week or so can result in a protracted – and generally unpleasant – interrogation from officials, which may cause you to miss your flight and be denied entry to the US in the future and your American hosts and/or employer/s to face legal proceedings.

Although not a foolproof method, one of the simplest ways to stay on is to make a quick trip to the Bahamas: the least costly way to do this is as a $100 day-trip with *Seascape Ltd* (☎1-800/327-7400), one of many cruise companies operating between Miami and Fort Lauderdale to the Bahamas and the Caribbean – its ads are in all the local newspapers. When you re-enter the US, you may be searched, so make sure you don't have a US library card or anything else that might indicate you have an unofficial, semi-permanent US address; your diary may also be examined. All being well, you'll routinely have a new leaving date stamped in your passport.

Alternatively, you can do things the official way and get an **extension** before your time is up. This can be done by going to the nearest **US Immigration and Naturalization Service (INS)** office (in Miami at 7880 Biscayne Boulevard, ☎305/536 5741; other addresses will be under the "Federal Government Offices" listings at the front of the phone book). They will automatically assume that you're working illegally and it's up to you to convince them otherwise. Do this by providing evidence of ample finances and, if possible, an upstanding American citizen to vouch for your worthiness. Obviously you'll also have to explain why you didn't plan for the extra time initially – saying your money lasted longer than you expected, or that a close relative is coming over, are well-worked excuses.

HEALTH AND INSURANCE

HEALTH

If you have a serious **accident** while in Florida, emergency medical services will get to you quickly and charge you later. For emergencies or ambulances, dial ☎911 (or whatever variant may be on the information plate of the pay phone). If you have an accident but don't require an ambulance, we've listed casualty departments in the Guide; ditto for **dental treatment**.

Should you need to see a **doctor**, lists can be found in the *Yellow Pages* under "Clinics" or "Physicians and Surgeons"*. A basic consultation fee is $50–75, payable in advance. Medications aren't cheap either – keep receipts for all you spend and claim it back on your insurance policy when you return.

Many **minor ailments** can be remedied using the fabulous array of potions and lotions available in **drugstores**. Foreign visitors should bear in mind that many pills available over the counter at home need a prescription in the US and that local brand names can be confusing; ask for advice at the **pharmacy** in any drugstore.

Travellers from Europe do not require **inoculations** to enter the US.

INSURANCE

Though not compulsory, **travel insurance** is *essential* for **foreign travellers**. The US has no national health system and you can lose an arm

*Foreign visitors may prefer to contact their own consulates for advice; for the address of the solitary British Consulate in Florida, see p.36.

and a leg (so to speak) having even minor medical treatment. Insurance policies can be bought through any high-street travel agent or insurance broker, though the cheapest are generally *Endsleigh*, who charge around £35 for three weeks to cover life, limb and luggage (with a 25 percent reduction if you choose to forego luggage insurance). Their forms are available from most youth/student travel offices (though their policies are open to all), or direct from 97–107 Southampton Row, London WC1 (☎071/436 4451). Another good option in Britain is *Touropa*, 52 Grosvenor Gardens, London SW1W 0NP (☎071/730 2101), Elsewhere in the world, get in touch with your nearest *STA* or *Travel Cuts* office (addresses on p.4 and p.7).

On all policies, read the small print to ensure the cover includes a sensible amount for medical expenses – this should be at least £1,000,000, which will cover the cost of an air ambulance to fly you home in the event of serious injury or hospitalization.

American travellers should find that their **health insurance** should cover any health charges or costs; if you don't have any you can get adequate coverage either from a travel agent's insurance plan or from specialist travel insurance companies such as *The Travelers*. If you are unable to use a phone or if the practitioner requires immediate payment, save all the **forms** to support a claim for subsequent reimbursal. Remember also that time limits may apply when making claims after the fact, so promptness in contacting your insurer is highly advisable.

Not surprisingly, however, few if any American health insurance plans cover against **theft** while travelling, though most **renter's or homeowner's insurance** policies will cover you for up to $500 while on the road.

If you have anything **stolen** (including money), register the loss immediately at the nearest police station and make a note of the precinct number (addresses in the *Guide*, or under "Police" in the Emergency listings at the front of the phone book, or dial ☎911). They will issue you with a reference number to pass on to your insurance company – an accepted alternative to the full statement insurers usually require.

COSTS, MONEY AND BANKS

To help with planning your Florida vacation, this book contains detailed price information for lodging and eating throughout the region. Unless otherwise stated, the hotel price codes given (explained on p.26) are for the cheapest double room in high season, exclusive of any local taxes which may apply, while meal prices include food only and not drinks or tip. Naturally, as time passes after the publication of the book, you should make allowances for inflation.

Even when the exchange rate is at its least advantageous (see below), most visitors find virtually everything – accommodation, food, petrol, cameras, clothes and more – to be better value in the US than it is at home. However, if you're used to travelling in the less expensive countries of Europe, let alone in the rest of the world, you shouldn't expect to scrape by on the same minuscule budget once you're in the US.

Your biggest single expense is likely to be **accommodation**. Few hotel or motel rooms in cities cost under $30 – it would be more usual to pay something like $50 – and rates in rural areas are little cheaper. Although hostels offering dorm beds – usually for $12–15 – exist, they are not widespread and in any case they save little money for two or more people travelling together. Camping, of course, is cheap, ranging from free to perhaps $18 per night, but is rarely practical in or around the big cities.

As for f**ood**, ten dollars a day is enough to get you an adequate life-support diet, while for a daily total of around $20 you can dine pretty well. Beyond this, everything hinges on how much sightseeing, taxi-taking, drinking and socializing you do. Much of any of these – especially in a major city – and you're likely to be getting through upwards of $50 a day.

The rates for **travelling** around using buses, trains and even planes, may look cheap on paper, but costs soon mount up. For a group of two or more, renting a **car** can be a very good investment.

Sales tax of 6 percent is added to virtually everything you buy in shops, but it isn't part of the marked price.

TRAVELLERS' CHECKS

US dollar travellers' checks are the best way to carry money, for both American and foreign visitors; they offer the great security of knowing that lost or stolen checks will be replaced. You should have no problem using the better-known checks, such as *American Express* and *Visa*, in shops,

---

MONEY: A NOTE FOR FOREIGN TRAVELLERS

Regular upheaval in the world money markets causes the relative value of the **US dollar** against the currencies of the rest of the world to vary considerably. Generally speaking, one **pound sterling** will buy between $1.45 and $1.90; one **Canadian dollar** is worth between 76¢ and $1; one **Australian dollar** is worth between 67¢ and 88¢; and one **New Zealand dollar** is worth between 55¢ and 72¢.

Bills and coins

US currency comes in **bills** worth $1, $5, $10, $20, $50 and $100, plus various larger (and rarer) denominations. Confusingly, all are the same size and same green colour, making it necessary to check each bill carefully. The dollar is made up of 100 cents in **coins** of 1 cent (known as a **penny**), 5 cents (a **nickel**), 10 cents (a **dime**) and 25 cents (a **quarter**). Very occasionally you might come across **JFK half-dollars** (50¢), **Susan B. Anthony dollar coins**, or a **two-dollar bill**. Change (quarters are the most useful) is needed for buses, vending machines and telephones, so always carry plenty.

For **emergency phone numbers** to call if your checks (and/or credit cards) should be stolen, see p.36.

restaurants and gas stations (don't be put off by "no checks" signs, which only refer to personal checks). Be sure to have plenty of the $10 and $20 denominations for everyday transactions.

Major Florida banks – such as *Bank of America, Barnett, First Florida, Southeast* and *Sun* – will (with considerable fuss) change travellers' checks in **other currencies** and foreign currency. Commission rates tend to be lower at exchange bureaux like *Deak-Perera* and *Thomas Cook*, airport exchange offices can also be reasonable. Hotels rarely, if ever, change money.

Banking hours in Florida are generally 10am until 3pm Monday to Thursday and 10am to 5pm on Fridays.

PLASTIC MONEY AND CASH MACHINES

If you have a **Visa**, **Mastercard** (known elsewhere as **Access**), **Diners Club**, **Discover** or **American Express** card you really *shouldn't* leave home without it. Almost all stores, most restaurants and many services will take some kind of plastic. In addition, hotels and car rental companies will ask for a card either to establish your credit-worthiness, or as security, or both. Even in these dark days for credit buying, some people still get funny about cash.

With *Mastercard* or *Visa* it is also possible to **withdraw cash** at any bank displaying relevant stickers, or from appropriate automatic teller machines (**ATMs**). *Diners Club* cards can be used to cash personal checks at *Citibank* branches. *American Express* cards can only get cash, or buy travellers' checks, at *American Express* offices (check the Yellow Pages) or from the travellers' check dispensers at most major airports. Most **Canadian** credit cards issued by hometown banks will be honoured in the US.

Thanks to relaxation in interstate banking restrictions, American holders of ATM cards from out of state are likely to discover that their cards work in the machines of select Florida banks (check with your bank before you leave home). Not only is this method of financing safer, but at around only a dollar per transaction it's economical as well.

Most major credit cards issued by **foreign banks** are accepted in the US, as well as cash

dispensing cards linked to international networks such as *Cirrus* and *Plus* – though it's important to check the latest details with your credit card company before departing, as otherwise the machine may simply gobble up your plastic friend. Overseas visitors should also bear in mind that fluctuating exchange rates may result in spending more (or less) than expected when the item eventually shows up on a statement.

Each of the two main networks operates a toll-free line to let customers know the location of their nearest ATM; **Plus System** is ☎1-800/THE-PLUS, **Cirrus** is ☎1-800/4CI-RRUS.

EMERGENCIES

If you're flat broke and at your wits as to what to do, there are a few alternatives before making a meal of yourself to the local alligators.

Assuming you know someone who is prepared to send you money in a crisis, the quickest way is to have them take the cash to the nearest Western Union office (information on ☎1-800/325-6000 in the US, or ☎0800/833833 in the UK) and have it instantaneously **wired** to the office nearest you, subject to the deduction of ten percent commission. It's a bit cheaper to get a bank to transfer cash by cable, while if you have a few days' leeway, sending a postal money order, which is exchangeable at any post office, through the mail is cheaper still. The equivalent for foreign travellers is the **international money order**, for which you need to allow up to seven days in the international air mail before arrival. An ordinary check sent from overseas takes 2–3 weeks to clear.

It's also possible to transfer cash from any branch of **Thomas Cook** via telex to their branches in Miami, Fort Lauderdale, Orlando, Sarasota, St Petersburg or Tampa. The main Florida addresses are given in the Guide and they're all in local phone books. The actual transfer of funds is, again, instantaneous; the cost from Britain is £25.

British travellers in difficulties have the final option of throwing themselves on the mercy of the **British consulate** in Miami, at Suite 2110, 1001 S Bayshore Drive (☎305/374 1522), who will – in worst cases only – repatriate you (on arrival in the UK, you have to surrender your passport until you repay the cost of the flight), but will never, under any circumstances, lend you money.

COMMUNICATIONS: TELEPHONES AND POST

Visitors from overseas tend to be impressed by the speed and efficiency of communications in the US and for the most part, Florida conforms to this high standard. A laid-back attitude, however, is ingrained in certain areas (notoriously so in the Florida Keys) and can frustrate travellers who have yet to adjust to the local pace.

PHONES

Florida's **telephones** are run by several companies, the largest being *Southern Bell*, all of which are linked to the *AT&T* network.

Public telephones invariably work and are easily found – on street corners, in railway and bus stations, hotel lobbies, bars, restaurants – and they take 25¢, 10¢ and 5¢ coins. The cost of a **local call** from a public phone varies according to the actual distance being called. The minimum is 25¢ for the first three minutes and a further 10¢ for each additional three minutes – when necessary, a voice will come on the line telling you to pay more.

USEFUL NUMBERS

Emergencies ☎911; ask for the appropriate emergency service: fire, police or ambulance

Local directory information ☎411	**Directory enquiries**	
Long-distance	**for toll-free numbers**	☎1-800/555-1212
directory information ☎1 (Area Code)/555-1212	**Operator**	☎0

FLORIDA AREA CODES

305 Miami, the Florida Keys and the southern section of the Southeast Coast.

407 Orlando and surrounds and the central section of the East Coast.

904 Most of the Northeast Coast, North Central Florida, the northern parts of the West Coast and the Panhandle.

813 Most of the West Coast and parts of South Central Florida.

INTERNATIONAL TELEPHONE CALLS

International calls can be dialled direct from private or (more expensively) public phones. You can get assistance from the **international operator** (☎1-800/874-4000), who may also interrupt every three minutes asking for more money, and call you back for any money still owed immediately after you hang up. One alternative is to make a **collect call** (to "reverse the charges"); dialling ☎1-800/445-5667 will connect you with an operator in Britain. The **cheapest rates** for international calls to Europe are between 6pm and 7am, when a direct-dialled three-minute call will cost roughly $5.

In **Britain**, it's possible to obtain a free **BT Chargecard** (☎0800/800 838), using which all calls from overseas can be charged to your quarterly domestic account; from Florida, you contact the British operator via AT&T, and your call is charged at standard payphone rates.

The telephone code to dial **TO the US** from the outside world (excluding Canada) is 1.

To make international calls **FROM the US**, dial 011 followed by the country code:

Australia 61	**Germany** 49	**Netherlands** 31	**Sweden** 46
Denmark 45	**Ireland** 353	**New Zealand** 64	**United Kingdom** 44

More expensive are **non-local calls** ("zone calls"), to numbers within the same area code (commonly, vast areas are covered by a single code) but costing much more and sometimes requiring you to dial 1 before the seven-digit number. Pricier still are **long-distance calls** (ie to a different area code), for which you'll need plenty of change. If you still owe money at the end of the call, the phone will ring immediately and you'll be asked for the outstanding amount (if you don't cough up, the person you've been calling will get the bill). Non-local calls and long-distance calls are far cheaper if made between 6pm and 8am and calls from **private phones** are always much cheaper than those from public phones.

Making telephone calls from **hotel rooms** is usually more expensive than from a payphone (and there are usually payphones in hotel lobbies). On the other hand, some budget hotels offer free local calls from rooms – ask when you check in. An increasing number of phones accept **credit cards** – simply swipe the card through the slot and dial. Another way to avoid the necessity of carrying copious quantities of change everywhere is to obtain an **AT&T charge card** (information on ☎1-800/874-4000 ext 359), for which you have to have an American credit card.

Many government agencies, car rental firms, hotels and other services have **toll-free numbers**, for which you don't have to pay anything: these numbers always have the prefix ☎1-800. Some lines, such as ☎1-800/577-HEAT to get the latest on the Miami Heat basketball team, employ the letters on the push-button phones as part of their "number".

POST OFFICES AND MAIL SERVICES

Post offices are usually open Mon–Fri 9am–5pm and Sat 9am–noon and there are blue **mail boxes** on many street corners. Ordinary **mail within the US** costs 29¢ for a letter weighing up to an ounce; addresses must include the **zip code**, as well as the sender's address on the envelope. **Air mail** between Florida and Europe generally takes about a week to arrive. Postcards cost 40¢, aerograms are 45¢, while letters weighing up to half an ounce are 50¢.

Letters can be sent c/o **General Delivery** (what's known elsewhere as **poste restante**) to any post office in the country but *must* include the post office's zip code and will only be held for thirty days before being returned to sender – so make sure there's a return address on the envelope. If you're receiving mail at someone else's address, it should include "c/o" and the regular occupant's name; otherwise it, too, is likely to be returned.

PARCELS

Rules on sending **parcels** are very rigid: packages must be in special containers bought from post offices and sealed according to their instructions, which are given at the start of the Yellow Pages. To send anything out of the country, you'll need a **customs declaration form**, available from a post office.

TELEGRAMS AND FAXES

To send a **telegram** (sometimes called "a wire") don't go to a post office but to a *Western Union* office (listed in the Yellow Pages). If you have a credit card, you can phone and dictate your message. For domestic telegrams ask for a **mailgram**, which will be delivered to any address in the country the following morning. **International telegrams** are slightly cheaper than the cheapest international phone call: one sent during the day from Florida should arrive at its overseas destination the next morning.

Public **fax** machines, which may require your credit card to be "swiped" through an attached device, are found at photocopy centers and, occasionally, bookshops.

INFORMATION, MAPS AND THE MEDIA

everywhere – designed to promote local business interests but also holding local maps and information and with a positive attitude towards helping travellers. Most communities have local **free newspapers** (see below) carrying news of events and entertainment – the most useful of which we've detailed in the Guide.

Drivers entering Florida will find **Welcome Centers**, fully stocked with information leaflets and discount booklets, at two points: on Hwy-231 at Campbellton, near the Florida–Alabama border and off I-75 near Jennings, just south of the Florida–Georgia line. More convenient for arrivals on I-10 are the visitor information centers at Pensacola and Tallahassee, detailed later in the Guide.

For advance information on Florida, write to the Florida Division of Tourism at 126 W Van Buren Street, Tallahassee, Florida 32399-2000 (☎904/487-1407).

Once in Florida, you'll find most large towns have at least a **Convention and Visitors Bureau** ("CVB"; typically open Mon–Fri 9am–5pm, Sat 9am–1pm), with detailed information on the local area and piles of discount coupons for cut-rate food and accommodation though they can't actually book hotel or motel rooms. In addition there are **Chambers of Commerce** almost

MAPS

CVBs and Chambers of Commerce give away an excellent **free map** of the whole state (though the *Official Transportation Map* does not, as its name suggests, detail public transit routes). If you're planning to drive – or cycle (see "Getting Around" – through rural areas, use *DeLorme's* highly detailed 120-page *Florida Atlas & Gazetteer* ($12.95). The best commercially available **city plans** are published by *Rand-McNally* (see box).

USTTA AND FLORIDA TOURISM OFFICES OVERSEAS

US Travel and Tourism Administration (**USTTA**) offices are located all over the world, usually sharing the buildings of US embassies or consulates. They tend to provide fairly basic brochures; for detailed advice it's better to contact Florida direct.

UK
USTTA:
22 Sackville St, London W1X 2EA ☎071/495 4466
(telephone enquiries only).
Florida Division of Tourism:
18–24 Westbourne Grove,
London W2 5RH ☎071/727 1661
Answerphone only; leave your address and they'll send a large (but barely useful) brochure for £2.

AUSTRALIA
4 Cliff St, Milsons Point,
Sydney, NSW 2061 ☎612/957 3144

DENMARK
Dag Hammerskjöld Allé 24,
2100 Copenhagen ☎31 42 31 44

IRELAND and NORTHERN IRELAND
Queen's House, 14 Queen St,
Belfast BT1 6EQ ☎0232/228239

NETHERLANDS
Museumplein 19,
Amsterdam ☎020/790 321

NORWAY
Drammensveien 18,
Oslo ☎22 44 85 50

SWEDEN
Strandvägan 101,
Stockholm ☎08/783 53000

MAP AND TRAVEL BOOK SUPPLIERS

UK

Stanford's
12–14 Long Acre,
London WC2E 9LP ☎071/836-1321

The Travellers' Bookshop
25 Cecil Court,
London WC2N 4EZ ☎071/836-9132

UNITED STATES

The Complete Traveler Bookstore
199 Madison Ave,
New York, NY 10016 ☎212/685-9007
3207 Filmore St,
San Francisco, CA 92123 ☎415/923-1511

Elliot Bay Book Company
101 S Main St,
Seattle, WA 98104 ☎206/624-6600

Latitudes Map & Travel Store
Calhoun Square, 3001 Hennepin Ave S,
Minneapolis, MN 55408 ☎612/823-3742

Map Link
25 E Mason St,
Santa Barbara, CA 93101 ☎805/965-4402

Rand McNally
150 E 52nd St,
New York, NY 10022 ☎212/758-7488
595 Market St,
San Francisco, CA 94105 ☎415/777-3131
444 North Michigan Ave,
Chicago, IL 60611 ☎312/321-1751

The Savvy Traveller
50 E Washington St,
Chicago, IL 60602 ☎312/263-2100

Traveler's Bookstore
22 W 52nd St,
New York, NY 10019 ☎212/664-0995

CANADA

Open Air Books & Maps
25 Toronto St,
Toronto, ON M5R 2C1 ☎416/363-0719

AUSTRALIA

The Travel Bookshop,
20 Bridge St,
Sydney ☎241-3554

Local **hiking** maps are available at ranger stations in state and national parks either free or for $1–2 and some camping shops carry a supply. For travelling around more of the US, the *Rand McNally Road Atlas* is a good investment, covering the whole country plus Canada and Mexico.

Members of the *American Automobile Association (AAA)* and its overseas affiliates (such as both the AA and the RAC in Britain) can also benefit from their maps and general assistance. They're based at 1000 AAA Drive, Heathrow, FL 32746-5063 (☎1-800/336-4357); further offices all across the state are listed in local phone books.

MEDIA

NEWSPAPERS

The best-read newspaper in Florida is the *Miami Herald*, providing insightful coverage of state, national and world events; the *Orlando Sentinel* and *Tampa Tribune* are not far behind and, naturally enough, excel at reporting their own areas. **Overseas newspapers** are often a preserve of

specialist bookshops, though you will find them widely available in major tourist areas.

Every community of any size has at least a few **free newspapers**, found in street-distribution bins or just lying around in piles. It's a good idea to pick up a full assortment: some simply cover local goings-on, others provide specialist coverage of interests ranging from long-distance cycling to getting ahead in business – and the classified and personal ads can provide hours of entertainment. Many of them are also excellent sources for bar, restaurant and nightlife information and we've mentioned the most useful titles in the Guide.

TELEVISION

Florida's **TV** is pretty much the standard network sit-com and talk-show barrage you get all over the country, with frequent interruptions for hard-sell commercials.

If you're thinking of travelling elsewhere in the US, the *Rough Guide: USA* (Penguin; US $18.95, CAN $25.99, UK £12.99) is essential reading.

Game shows fill up most of the morning schedule; around lunchtime you can take your pick of any of a dozen daily soaps. Slightly better are the **cable networks**, to which you'll have access in most hotels and include the around-the-clock news of *CNN* and *MTV*'s non-stop circuit of mainstream pop videos.

Especially in the south, Spanish-language stations service the Hispanic communities.

RADIO

As with TV, Florida's **radio** stations offer few surprises, with the majority sticking to the usual commercial format of retro-rock, classic pop, MOR country, or easy-listening pap.

Except for news and chat and the occasional fire-and-brimstone preacher, stations on the AM band are best avoided in favor of the FM band, in particular the public and college stations on the air in Tallahassee, Gainesville, Orlando, Tampa and Miami, found on the left of the dial (88–92FM). These invariably provide diverse and listenable programming, whether it be bizarre underground rock or abstruse literary discussions and they're also good sources for local nightlife news.

GETTING AROUND

Travel in the surprisingly compact state of Florida is rarely difficult or time-consuming. Crossing between the east and west coasts, for example, takes only a couple of hours and even the longest possible trip – between the western extremity of the Panhandle and Miami – can be accomplished in a day. With a car you'll have no problems at all, but travelling by public transport requires adroit forward planning: cities and larger towns have bus links – and, in some cases, an infrequent train service – but many rural areas and some of the most enjoyable sections of the coast are sadly off-limits to non-drivers.

BY BUS

Buses are the cheapest way to travel. The only long-distance service is *Greyhound*, which links all major cities and many smaller towns. In isolated areas buses are fairly scarce, sometimes only appearing once a day, if at all – so plot your route with care. Between the big cities, buses run around the clock to a fairly full timetable, stopping only for meal breaks (almost always fast-food dives) and driver change-overs. *Greyhound*, though not luxurious, is bearable and it's feasible occasionally to save on a night's accommodation by travelling overnight and sleeping on the bus. Any sizeable community will have a *Greyhound* station; in smaller places the local post office or petrol station doubles as the stop and ticket office. In the Florida Keys, the bus makes scheduled stops but can also be flagged down anywhere along the Overseas Highway.

Fares – for example $37 one way between Miami and Orlando – are expensive but not staggeringly so and can sometimes be reduced by travelling on weekdays (except Fridays).

Remarkably, in 1993 *Greyhound* stopped publishing **timetables**, with the exception of condensed summaries of nationwide services – which obviously makes detailed route planning for Florida extremely difficult. The only toll-free information service is in Spanish (☎1-800/531-5332); otherwise information can be obtained from local terminals. The phone numbers for the larger *Greyhound* stations are given in the Guide.

It's handy to know that a fair-sized chunk of the Southeast Coast can be covered for very little money (if also very slowly) using **local buses**, which connect neighboring districts. It's possible, for example, to travel from Miami to West Palm Beach for under $3, but doing so takes all day and three changes of bus – the *Tri-Rail* (see below) covers the same route for even less.

BY TRAIN AND THE TRI-RAIL

A much less viable way of getting about is by **train** (run by *Amtrak*). Florida's railroads were built to service the boom towns of the Twenties and, consequently, some rural nooks have rail links as good as the modern cities. The actual trains are clean and comfortable but no route in the state offers more than two services a day. In some areas, *Amtrak* services are extended by buses, usable only in conjunction with the train.

Fares are not particularly cheap – $51 one way between Miami and Orlando is typical.

THE TRI-RAIL

Designed to reduce road traffic along the congested Southeast Coast, the elevated **Tri-Rail** system came into operation in 1989, ferrying commuters between Miami and West Palm Beach with twelve stops on the way. The single-journey flat fare is a very cheap $2.50; the only drawback is the fact that almost all services run during rush hours – meaning a very early start, or an early evening arrival.

> For Amtrak information: ☎1-800/USA RAIL
> For Tri-Rail information : ☎1-800/TRI RAIL

BY PLANE

Provided your plans are flexible and you use the special cut-rate fares which are regularly advertised in local newspapers, off-peak **plane** travel within Florida is not much more expensive than taking a bus or train – and will also, obviously, get you there quicker. Typical cut-rate one-way fares are around $60 for Miami–Orlando and $100 for Miami–Tallahassee; the full fares are much higher.

For toll-free airline numbers, see p.8.

DRIVING AND CAR RENTAL

As a major vacation destination, Florida is one of the cheapest places in the US in which to **rent** a car. Drivers are supposed to have held their licences for at least one year (though this is rarely checked); people under 25 years old may encounter problems and will probably be inflicted with high insurance premiums.

Car rental companies will also expect you to have a credit card; if you don't have one they may let you leave a hefty **deposit** (at least $200) but don't count on it. The likeliest tactic for getting a good deal is to phone the major firms' toll-free 800 numbers for their best rates – most will try to beat the offers of their competitors, so it's worth haggling.

In general the lowest rates are available at the airport branches – $99 per week for a subcompact is the standard budget rate (a week's rental is roughly equivalent to the price for four days). Always be sure to get free unlimited mileage and be aware that leaving the car in a different city to the one in which you rent it may incur

Car Rental Firms in the US	
Alamo	☎1-800/327-9633
American International	☎1-800/527-0202
Avis	☎1-800/722-1333
Budget	☎1-800/527-0700
Dollar	☎1-800/421-6868
Hertz	☎1-800/654-3131
National	☎1-800/227-7368
Rent-a-Wreck	☎1-800/535-1391
Snappy	☎1-800/669-4800
Thrifty	☎1-800/367-2277
USA Rent-a-Car System	☎1-800/872-2277
Value	☎1-800/468-2583

a **drop-off charge** of as much as $200 – although many firms do not charge drop-off fees within Florida.

Alternatively, a number of **local** companies rent out new – and not so new (try *Rent-a-Heap* or *Rent-a-Wreck*) – vehicles. They are certainly cheaper than the big chains if you just want to spin around a city for a day, but free mileage is not included, so they work out far more costly for long-distance travel. Addresses and phone numbers are in the Yellow Pages.

When you rent a car, read the small print carefully for details on **Collision Damage Waiver (CDW)**, a form of insurance which often isn't included in the initial rental charge but is well worth considering. This specifically covers the car that you are driving yourself – you are in any case insured for damage to other vehicles. At $9 to $12 a day, it can add substantially to the total cost, but without it you're liable for every scratch to the car – even those that aren't your fault. Some credit card companies (*AMEX* for example) offer automatic CDW coverage to anyone using their card; read the fine print beforehand in any case. You'll also be charged a **Florida surcharge** of $2 per day.

RENTING AN RV

Besides cars, Recreational Vehicles or **RVs** – those huge juggernauts that rumble down the highway complete with multiple bedrooms, bathrooms and kitchens – can be rented from around $300 per week for a basic camper on the back of a pickup truck. These are good for groups or families travelling together, but they can be quite unwieldy on the road.

Rental outlets are not as common as you might expect, as people tend to own their own RVs. On top of the rental fees you have to take into account mileage charges, the cost of gas (some RVs do twelve miles to the gallon or less) and any drop-off charges. In addition, it is rarely legal simply to pull up in an RV and spend the night at the roadside; you are expected to stay in designated RV parks – some of which charge $35 per night.

The *Recreational Vehicle Rental Association*, 3251 Old Lee Highway, Fairfax, VA 22030 (☎703/591-7130 or ☎1-800/336-0355) publishes a newsletter and a directory of rental firms. A couple of the larger companies offering RV rentals are *Cruise America* (☎1-800/327-7799) and *Go! Vacations* (☎1-800/845-9888).

ADVANCE PLANNING FOR OVERSEAS TRAVELLERS

Air passes

All the main American airlines (and *British Airways* in conjunction with *USAir*) offer **air passes** for visitors who plan to fly a lot within the US: these have to be bought in advance, and in the UK are usually sold with the proviso that you cross the Atlantic with the relevant airline. All the deals are broadly similar, involving the purchase of at least three **coupons** (for around £160; around £55 for each additional coupon), each valid for a flight of any duration in the US.

The **Visit USA** scheme entitles foreign travellers to a 30 percent discount on any full-priced US domestic fare, provided you buy the ticket before you leave home – but this isn't a wise choice for travel within Florida, where full-priced fares are very high.

Greyhound Ameripasses

Foreign visitors intending to travel virtually every day by bus (which is unlikely), or to venture further around the US, can buy a *Greyhound* **Ameripass**, offering unlimited travel within a set time limit, before leaving home: most travel agents can oblige. In the UK, they cost £50 (4-day), £85 (7-day), £125 (15-day) or £170 (30-day). *Greyhound*'s office is at Sussex House, London Road, East Grinstead, West Sussex RH19 1LD (☎0342/317317). Extensions can be bought in the US for the dollar equivalent of £12 a day.

The first time you use your pass, it will be dated by the ticket clerk (which becomes the commencement date of the ticket), and your destination is written on a page which the driver will tear out and keep as you board the bus. Repeat this procedure for every subsequent journey.

Amtrak rail passes

Rail travel can't get you around all Florida, but overseas travellers have a choice of three **rail passes**. The least expensive, the **East Region Pass**, available in 15- and 30-day forms, costs $158 ($178 June–Aug) and $209 ($229) respectively. Alternatively, the **National Pass** entitles you to travel throughout the US, again for 15 or 30 days, for a price of $208 ($308 June–Aug) or $309 ($389) respectively. By combining rail with some other form of travel, you could take advantage of the 30-day **Coastal Pass**, permitting unlimited train travel on the country's east and west coasts; this pass costs $179 ($199 June–Aug).

On production of a passport issued outside the US or Canada, the passes can be bought at *Amtrak* stations in the US. In the UK, you can buy them from *Amtrak*'s UK agent, Destination Marketing Limited, 2 Cinnamon Row, Plantation Wharf, York Place, London SW11 3TW (☎071/978 5212).

Car rental

UK nationals can **drive** in the US on a full UK driving licence (International Driving Permits are not always regarded as sufficient). Fly-drive deals are good value if you want to **rent** a car (see p.5), though you can save up to 60 percent simply by booking in advance with a major firm (*Holiday Autos* guarantee the cheapest rates). You can choose not to pay until you arrive, but make sure you take a written confirmation of the quoted price with you. Remember that it's safer not to rent a car straight off a long transatlantic flight; and that standard rental cars have **automatic transmissions**.

It's also easier and cheaper to book **RVs** in advance from Britain. Most travel agents who specialize in the US can arrange RV rental, and usually do it cheaper if you book a flight through them as well. A price of £400 for a five-berth van for two weeks is fairly typical.

Car rental firms in the UK

Alamo	☎0800/272 200	**Budget**	☎0800/181 181	**Hertz**	☎081/679 1799
Avis	☎081/848 8733	**Europcar**	☎081/950 5050	**Holiday Autos**	☎071/491 1111

American driving terms

Antennae	Aerial	*Parking brake*	Hand brake
Divided Highway	Dual carriageway	*Parking lot*	Car park
Fender	Bumper/Car wing	*Speed zone*	Area where speed limit decreases
Freeway	Limited access motorway	*Stickshift*	Gear stick/manual transmission
Gas(oline)	Petrol	*Trunk*	Boot
Hood	Bonnet	*Turn-out*	Lay-by
No standing	No parking or stopping	*Windshield*	Windscreen

ROADS

The best roads for covering long distances quickly are the wide, straight and fast **Interstate Highways**, usually at least six lanes and always prefixed by "I" (eg I-95) – marked on maps by a red, white and blue shield bearing the number. Even-numbered Interstates usually run east–west and those with odd numbers north–south.

A grade down are the **State** and **US highways** (eg Hwy-1), sometimes divided into scenic off-shoots such as Hwy-A1A, which runs parallel to Hwy-1 along Florida's east coast. There are a number of **toll roads**, by far the longest being the 318-mile **Florida Turnpike**; tolls range from 25¢ to $6 and are often graded according to length of journey – you're given a distance marker when you enter the toll road and pay the appropriate amount when you leave. You'll also come across **toll bridges**, usually charging 10–25¢ to cross, sometimes as much as $3.

Even major roads in cities are technically state or US highways but are better known by their local name. Part of Hwy-1 in Miami, for instance, is more familiarly known as Biscayne Boulevard. Rural areas also have much smaller **County Roads** (given as **Routes** in the Guide, such as Route 78 near Lake Okeechobee); their number is preceded by a letter denoting their county.

RULES OF THE ROAD

Although the law says that drivers must keep up with the flow of traffic, which is often hurtling along at 70mph, the official **speed limit** in Florida is 55mph (65mph on some Interstate stretches), with lower signposted limits – usually around 30–35mph – in built-up areas. A **minimum speed limit** of 40mph also applies on many Interstates and highways. There are no spot fines; if you get a ticket for **speeding**, your case will come to court and the size of the fine will be at the discretion of the judge; $75 is a rough minimum. If **the police** do flag you down, don't get out of the car and don't reach into the glove compartment as they may think you have a gun. Simply sit still with your hands on the wheel; when questioned, be polite and don't attempt to make jokes.

Apart from the obvious fact that Americans **drive on the right**, various rules may be unfamiliar to **foreign drivers**. US law requires that any **alcohol** be carried unopened in the boot of the car; it's illegal to make a **U-turn** on an Interstate or anywhere where a single unbroken line runs along the middle of the road; to **park on a highway**; and for front-seat passengers to ride without fastened **seatbelts.** At junctions, you can turn right on a red light if there is no traffic approaching from the left; and some junctions are **four-way stops**: a crossroads where all traffic must stop before proceeding in order of arrival.

It can't be stressed too strongly that **Driving Under the Influence (DUI)** is a very serious offence. If a police officer smells alcohol on your breath, he/she is entitled to administer a breath, saliva or urine test. If you fail, they'll lock you up with other inebriates in the "drunk tank" of the nearest jail until you sober up – and, controversially, in some parts of the state they're empowered to suspend your driving licence immediately. Your case will later be heard by a judge, who can fine you $200 or in extreme (or repeat) cases, imprison you for thirty days.

PARKING

Parking meters are common in cities; their charge for an hour ranges from 25¢ to $1. **Parking lots** charge up to $12 a day. If you park in the wrong place (such as within ten feet of a fire hydrant) your car is likely to be towed away or **wheel-clamped**; a sticker on the windscreen will tell you where to pay the $30 fine. Whenever possible, **park in the shade**; if you don't, you might find the car too hot to touch when you return to it – temperatures inside cars parked in the full force of the Florida sun can reach 140°F.

BREAKDOWN

If you **break down** in a rented car, there'll be an emergency number pinned to the dashboard. Otherwise you should sit tight and wait for the Highway Patrol or State Police, who cruise by regularly. Raising your car bonnet is recognized as a call for assistance, although women travelling alone should, obviously, be wary of doing this. Another tip, for women especially, is to rent a **mobile telephone** from the car rental agency – you often only have to pay a nominal amount until you actually use it, but having a phone can be reassuring at least and a potential life-saver should something go terribly wrong.

HITCHING

Where it's legal, **hitching** may be the cheapest way to get around but it is also the most unpredictable and potentially very dangerous, especially for women travelling alone. Small country roads are your best bet: in rural areas it's not uncommon for the locals to get around by thumb. One place *not* to hitch is Miami; not only is this illegal, but if you do take the risk, the chances are you'll be lucky to live to regret it. Anywhere else, observe the general common-sense rules on hitching: make sure you sit next to a door that's unlocked, keep your luggage within reach, refuse the ride if you feel unsure of the driver and demand to be let out if you become suspicious of his/her intentions.

Hitching is illegal not only in Miami but also on the outskirts of many other cities and is always prohibited if done by standing on the road (as opposed to beside it on the pavement or grass verge) or by a freeway entrance sign – rules which are enforced. On Interstates, thumb from the entrance ramps only. Another, slightly less risky, technique is to strike up a conversation with likely-looking drivers in roadside diners or gas stations. Safer still is to scrutinize the **"ride boards"** on university campuses, although drivers found this way will usually expect a contribution towards fuel costs.

CYCLING

Cycling is seldom a good way to get around the major cities (although some sections of Miami are well toured by bike), but many smaller towns are quiet enough to be pleasurably explored by bicycle, there are many miles of marked **cycle paths** along the coast and long-distance **bike trails** crisscross the state's interior. Cycling is gaining popularity among Floridians, too and a

free monthly magazine, *Florida Bicyclist*, is aimed at the growing band of devoted pedallers; find it on street corners, bookshops and bike shops.

Bikes can be **rented** for $8–15 a day, $30–55 a week from many beach shops and college campuses, some state parks and virtually any place where cycling is a good idea; outlets are listed in the Guide.

For **long-distance** cycling – anything over thirty miles a day – you'll need a good-quality all-terrain multi-gear bike, preferably one with wide touring tyres. For safety and visibility, wear a brightly colored **helmet** and cycling **gloves** (available from most bike shops). Keep your water-bottle filled and drink from it frequently to avoid dehydration and don't forget the power of the Florida sun.

The best **cycling areas** are in North Central Florida, the Panhandle and in parts of the Northeast Coast. By contrast, the southeast coastal strip is heavily congested and many south Florida inland roads are narrow and dangerous. Wherever you cycle, avoid the heaviest traffic – and the midday heat – by doing most of your pedalling before 10am.

For free biking **information** and detailed **maps** ($2–15) of cycling routes, write to the **State Bicycle Program**, Florida Department of Transportation, 605 Suwanee Street, Tallahassee, FL 32399-0450 (☎904/488-3111). You can get the same maps from most youth hostels; the Florida *AYH* also publishes the *AYH Bicycle Hospitality Directory*, a list of local cycling enthusiasts willing to host bike-mad visitors overnight (PO Box 533097, Orlando, FL 32853-3097).

ACCOMMODATION

Accommodation costs inevitably form a significant proportion of the expenses for any traveller in Florida, though as ever in the US you usually get good value for what you pay. If you're on your own, it's possible to pare costs by sleeping in dormitory-style hostels, where a bed can cost from $12 to $15. However, groups of two or more will find it little more expensive to stay in the far more plentiful motels and hotels, where basic rooms away from the major cities typically cost anything upwards of $30 per night. Many hotels will set up a third single bed for around $5–10 on top of the regular price, reducing costs for three people sharing. By contrast, the lone traveller will have a hard time of it: "singles" are usually double rooms at an only slightly reduced rate. Prices quoted by hotels and motels are almost always for the actual room rather for each person using it.

Motels are plentiful on the main approach roads to cities, around beaches and by the main road junctions in country areas. High-rise **hotels** predominate along the popular sections of the coast and are sometimes the only accommodation in city centres. In major cities **campgrounds** tend to be on the outskirts, if they exist at all.

Wherever you stay, you'll be expected to **pay in advance**, at least for the first night and perhaps for further nights too, particularly if it's high season and the hotel's expecting to be busy. Payment can be in cash or in dollar travellers' checks, though it's more common to give your credit card number and sign for everything when you leave. **Reservations** are only held until 5pm or 6pm unless you've told the hotel you'll be arriving late. Most of the larger chains have an advance booking form in their brochures and will make reservations at another of their premises for you.

Since cheap accommodation in the cities and on the popular sections of the coast is snapped up fast, always **book ahead** whenever possible, using the suggestions in this book.

MOTELS AND HOTELS

While **motels** and **hotels** essentially offer the same things – double rooms with bathroom, TV and phone – motels are often one-off affairs run by their owners and tend to be cheaper (typically $30–45) than hotels ($45–75), which are likely to be part of a nationwide chain. All but the cheapest motels and hotels have pools for guests' use and many offer cable TV and free local phone calls. Under $60, rooms tend to be similar in qual-

ACCOMMODATION PRICE CODES

It's a fact of Florida life that the plain-and-simple motel room which costs $30 on a weekday in low season is liable to cost two or three times that amount on a weekend in high season. To further complicate matters, high and low season vary depending on whether you're in north or south Florida (see Introduction), and some accommodations which depend on business travellers for their trade (such as those in downtown areas, distanced from the nearest beach) will actually be cheaper at weekends than on weekdays. Local events – such as a Space Shuttle launch on the Space Coast, or Spring Break in Panama City Beach – can also cause prices to increase dramatically.

Throughout the book, we've graded accommodation prices according to the cost of the least expensive double room throughout most of the year – but do allow for the fluctuations outlined above.

①	up to $30	④	$60–80	⑦	$130–180
②	$30–45	⑤	$80–100	⑧	$180+
③	$45–60	⑥	$100–130		

BED AND BREAKFAST AGENCIES

For a list of inns in various areas, contact one or several of the following:

A&A Bed & Breakfast of Florida Inc
PO Box 1316,
Winter Park, FL 32790 ☎407/628-3222

Bed & Breakfast East Coast
PO Box 1373,
Marathon, FL 33050 ☎305/743-4118

B&B Scenic Florida
PO Box 3385,
Tallahassee, FL 32315-3385 ☎904/386-8196

Bed & Breakfast of Volusia County
PO Box 573,
DeLeon Springs, FL 32028 ☎904/985-5068

Bed'n'Breakfast Central Gulf Coast
PO Box 9515,
Pensacola, FL 32513-3222 ☎904/438-7968

Florida Suncoast Bed & Breakfast
PO Box 12,
Palm Harbor, FL 33563 ☎813/784-5118

ity and features; spend $60–70 in rural areas, $80–100 in the cities and the room and its fittings get bigger and more luxurious, with additional facilities often including a tennis court, gym and a golf course. Paying over $150 brings all the above, plus a fabulous ocean view, *en-suite* jacuzzi and all imaginable upmarket trappings.

Alternatively, there are number of unexciting but dependable **budget-priced chain** hotels, which, depending on location, cost around $25–45; the cheapest are *Days Inn, Econo Lodge, Hampton Inns, Knights Inns* and *Red Carpet Inns*. Higher on the budgetary scale are the **mid-range chains** like *Best Western, Howard Johnson's* (now usually abbreviated to *HoJo's*), *TraveLodge* and *La Quinta* – though if you can afford their prices – usually $75–125 – there's normally somewhere nicer to stay.

On your travels, you'll also come across **resorts**, which are motels or hotels offering,

HOTEL DISCOUNT VOUCHERS

Many of the higher-rung hotel chains offer **pre-paid discount vouchers**, which in theory save you money if you're prepared to pay in advance. To take advantage of such schemes, British travellers must purchase the vouchers in the UK, at a usual cost of between £30 and £60 per night for a minimum of two people sharing. However, it's hard to think of a good reason to buy them; you may save a nominal amount on the fixed rates, but better-value accommodation is not exactly difficult to find in the US, and you may well regret the inflexibility imposed upon your travels. Most UK travel agents will have details of the various voucher schemes; the cheapest is the "Go As You Please" deal offered by *Days Inn* (☎0483/440480 in Britain).

besides a room, a restaurant, bar and private beach – on average these cost $70–110; and **efficiencies**, which are motel rooms adapted to offer cooking facilities – ranging from a stove squeezed into a corner to a fully equipped kitchen – usually for $10–15 above the basic room rate.

Since inexpensive diners are everywhere, very few hotels or motels bother to offer **breakfast**, although there's a trend towards providing free coffee (from paper cups) and sticky buns on a self-service basis from the lobby.

OTHER DISCOUNTS AND RESERVATIONS

During **off-peak periods** many motels and hotels struggle to fill their rooms and it's worth **haggling** to get a few dollars off the asking price. Staying in the same place for more than one night will bring further reductions. Additionally, pick up the many **discount coupons** which fill tourist information offices and welcome centers (see p.18) and look out for the free *Traveler Discount Guide*. Read the small print, though: what appears to be an amazingly cheap room rate sometimes turns out to be a per-person charge for two people sharing and limited to midweek.

When it's worth blowing a hunk of cash on somewhere really atmospheric we've said as much in the Guide. Bear in mind the most upscale establishments have all manner of services which may appear to be free but for which you will be expected to **tip** in a style commensurate with the hotel's status – see "Tipping" in "Directory".

BED AND BREAKFAST

Bed and breakfast in Florida is often a luxury. Typically, the bed and breakfast inns, as they're usually known, are restored buildings in the smaller towns and more rural areas – although the cities also have a few. Even the larger establishments tend to have less than ten rooms, sometmes without TV and phone but always with flowers, stuffed cushions and an almost overly contrived homely atmosphere; others may just be a couple of furnished rooms in someone's home.

While always including a huge and wholesome breakfast (five courses is not unheard of), prices vary greatly: anything from $45 to $200 depending on location and season; most cost between $60 and $80 per night for a double. Bear in mind, too, that most are booked well in advance, making it sensible to contact either the inn directly (details are given throughout the Guide), or one of the agents below, at least a month ahead – longer in high season.

Y'S AND YOUTH HOSTELS

At around $12 (a few dollars more for non-members) per night per person, **hostels** are clearly the cheapest accommodation option other than camping. There are two main kinds of cheap hostel-type accommodation in the US: YMCA/YWCA hostels (known as *"Ys"*) offering accommodation for both sexes, or in a few cases, women-only accommodation and official *AYH* youth hostels. In Florida, you'll find *AYH* **youth hostels** in Miami Beach, Daytona Beach, St Augustine, Fort Lauderdale, Orlando and St Petersburg. Miami Beach, St Petersburg and Clearwater Beach also have **privately run youth hostels**, of a similar standard and price.

Particularly if you're travelling in high season, it's advisable to **book ahead** through one of the specialist travel agents or international youth hostel offices. Some hostels will allow you to use a **sleeping bag**, though officially they should (and many do) insist on a **sheet sleeping bag**, which can usually be rented at the hostel. The maximum stay at each hostel is technically three days, though this is again a rule which is often ignored if there's space. Few hostels provide meals but most have **cooking** facilities and there's sometimes a curfew of around midnight: alcohol, smoking and, of course, drugs are banned.

The informative *American Youth Hostel (AYH) Handbook* ($5) is available from hostels in the US, or direct from the *AYH* national office: 733 15th Street NW, Suite 840, Washington DC 20005 (☎202/783-6161). Specific hostel information for Florida can be had from the *Florida Council*, PO Box 533097, Orlando, FL 32853-3097 (☎407/649-8761).

For **overseas hostellers**, the *International Youth Hostel Handbook* provides a full list of hostels. In Britain, it's available from the *Youth Hostel Association* headquarters/shop, at 14 Southampton Street, London WC2 (☎071/836 1036), where you can also buy a year's *IYHF* **membership** for £9 (£3 if you're under 18).

CAMPING

Florida **campgrounds** range from the primitive (a flat piece of ground that may or may not have a water tap) to others which are more like open-air hotels, with shops, restaurants and washing facilities. Naturally enough, prices vary accord to amenities, ranging from nothing at all for the most basic plots to up to $35 a night for something comparatively luxurious. There are plenty of campgrounds but often plenty of people intending to use them: take special care over plotting your route if you're camping during public holidays or weekends, when many sites will be either full or very crowded. By contrast, some of the more basic campgrounds in state and national parks will often be completely empty midweek. For camping in the wilderness, there's a nightly charge of $1.50 payable at the area's administrative office.

Privately run campgrounds are everywhere, their prices range from $8 to $35 and the best located are listed throughout the Guide; for a fuller list write for the free *Florida Camping Directory* to the **Florida Campground Association**, 1638 Plaza Drive, Tallahassee, FL 32308-5364 (☎904/656-8878).

State parks – there are over 300 in Florida – are often excellent places to camp; sites cost $8–17 for up to four people sharing. Never more than half the space is reserved, the rest goes on a first-come first-served basis (bear in mind that park offices close at sunset; you won't be able to camp there if you arrive later). **Reservations** can be made within two months of arrival by phone only and stays are limited to fourteen days. Reservations won't be held after 5pm unless previously arranged. If you're doing a lot of camping in state parks, get the two free leaflets, *Florida State Parks Camping Reservations Procedures* and *Florida State Parks Fees Schedule* from any state park office, or by writing to the **Department of Natural Resources**, Division of

Recreation and Parks, 3900 Commonwealth Boulevard, Tallahassee, FL 32399 (☎904/488-9872).

Similarly priced campsites exist in National Parks and National Forests – see the details throughout the Guide, or contact the **National Park Service**, PO Box 2416, Tallahassee, FL 32316 (☎904/222-1167) and the **US Forest Service**, Suite 4061, 227 N Bronough Street, Tallahassee, FL 32301 (☎904/681-7265).

However desolate it may look, much of undeveloped Florida is, in fact, private land and **rough camping** is illegal. For permitted rough camping, see "The Backcountry", p.37.

FOOD AND DRINK

Florida has a mass of restaurants, fast-food outlets, cafés and coffeeshops on every main street, all trying to outdo one another with their cut-price daily specials. In every town mentioned in this book, you'll find reviews of the full range of eating options.

Fresh fish and seafood are abundant all over Florida, as is the high-quality produce of the state's cattle farms – served as ribs, steaks and burgers – and junk-food is as common as anywhere else in the country. But the choice of what to eat is influenced by where you are. In the northern half of the state, the accent is on wholesome cooking – traditional Southern dishes such as grits, cornbread and fried chicken. As you head south through Florida, this gives way to the most diverse and inexpensive gathering of Latin American and Caribbean cuisines to be found anywhere in the US – you can feast on anything from curried goat to mashed plantains and yucca.

BREAKFAST

For the price (on average $3–5) breakfast is a good-value, very filling start to the day. Go to a **diner**, **café** or **coffeeshop**, all of which are very similar and usually serve breakfast until at least 11am (though some continue all day) – although there are special deals at earlier times, say 6–8am, when the price may be even less.

LUNCH AND SNACKS

The Florida workforce takes its lunch-break between 11.30am and 1.30pm, during which hours all sorts of low-cost **set menus** and all-you-can-eat specials are on offer – generally excellent value. Chinese restaurants, for example, frequently have help-yourself rice and noodles or dim sum feasts for $4–6 and many Japanese restaurants give you a chance to eat sushi much more cheaply ($6–8) than usual. Most Cuban restaurants and fishcamps (see "Restaurants", below) are exceptionally well priced all the time and you can get a good-sized lunch in one for $4–5. **Buffet restaurants** – most of which also serve breakfast and dinner – are found in most cities and towns; $6–8 lets you pig as much as you can from a wide variety of hot dishes. A chain version, *Shoney's,* turns up throughout the state.

As you'd expect, there's also **pizza**; count on paying $5–7 for a basic two-person pizza at national chains and local outlets. If it's a warm day and you can't face hot food, find a deli (see below) with a **salad bar**, where you can help yourself for $3. **Frozen yogurt** or **ice cream** may be all you feel like eating in the midday heat: look for the exotic versions made with mango and guava, sold by Cuban vendors.

SNACKS

For **quick snacks**, many **supermarket deli counters** do ready-cooked meals for $3–4, as well as a range of **salads** and **sandwiches**. Filled **bagels** are also common, while **street stands** sell hot dogs, burgers or a slice of pizza for around $1: in Miami **Cuban fast-food stands** serve crispy pork sandwiches and other spicy snacks for $2–3 and most shopping malls have ethnic fast-food stalls, often pricier than street stands but usually with edible and filling fare. Bags of fresh oranges, grapefruit and watermelons are often sold from the roadside in rural areas, as are **boiled peanuts** – a dollar buys a steaming bagful. Southern fast-food chains like *Popeye's Famous Fried Chicken* and *Sonny's Real Pit Bar-B-Q* and Mexican outlets such as *Taco Bell,* will take away your hunger for $3–4, but are only marginally better than the inevitable **burger chains**.

FREE FOOD AND BRUNCH

Some **bars** are used as much by diners as drinkers, who fill up on the free **hors d'oeuvres** laid out by a lot of city bars between 5 and 7pm

Monday to Friday – an attempt to nab the commuting classes before they head off to the suburbs – and sometimes by beachside bars to grab beach-goers before they head elsewhere for the evening. For the price of a drink you can stuff yourself silly on chilli, seafood or pasta.

Brunch is another deal to look out for: indulged in at weekends (usually Sunday) between 11am and 2pm. For a set price ($8 and up) you get a light meal (or even a groaning buffet) and a variety of complimentary cocktails or champagne. We've listed the most interesting venues as appropriate in the Guide.

DINING OUT

Even if it sometimes seems swamped by the more fashionable regional and ethnic cuisines, traditional **American cooking** is found all over Florida. Portions are big and you start with **salad**, eaten before the main course arrives. Unique to Florida, look out for **heart of palm** salad, based around the delicious vegetable at the heart of the sable palm tree. Main dishes are dominated by enormous **steaks**, **burgers**, piles of **ribs** or half a **chicken**. Vegetables include french fries or a baked potato, the latter commonly topped with sour cream and chives.

Southern cooking makes its presence felt throughout the northern half of the state. Vegetables such as **okra**, **collard greens**, **black-eyed peas** and fried **eggplant** are added to staples such as fried chicken, roast beef and **hogjaw** – meat from the mouth of a pig. Meat dishes are usually accompanied by **cornbread** to soak up the thick gravy poured over everything; with fried fish, you'll get **hush puppies** – fried corn balls with tiny bits of chopped onion. Okra is also used in **gumbo** soups, a feature of **cajun** cooking which originated in nearby Louisiana as a way of using up leftovers. A few (usually expensive) Florida restaurants specialize in cajun food but many others have a few cajun items (such as red beans and rice and hot and spicy shrimp and steak dishes) on their menu.

Don't be shocked to see **alligator** on menus: a certain number are culled each year, their tails deep-fried and served in a variety of styles – none of which affect the bland, chicken-like taste; or **frogs' legs**, which are a much less ecologically sound meal.

Regional **nouvelle cuisine** of the Californian kind is far too pretentious and expensive for the typical Floridian palate, although some restaurants in the larger cities do extraordinary and inspired things with local fish and the produce of the citrus farms, creating small but beautifully presented and highly nutritious affairs for around $40 a head.

Almost wherever you eat you'll be offered **Key Lime Pie** as a dessert, a dish which began life in the Florida Keys, made from the small limes that grow there. The pie is similar to lemon meringue but with a sharper taste. Quality varies greatly; take local advice to find a good outlet and your tastebuds will tell you why many swear by it.

FISH AND SEAFOOD

Florida truly excels with **fish and seafood** – which is great news for fish-eating vegetarians who are poorly catered for otherwise. Even the shabbiest restaurant is likely to have an excellent selection, although fish comes freshest and cheapest at **fishcamps**, rustic places right beside the river where your meal was swimming just a few hours before; a fishcamp lunch or dinner will cost around $5–9. **Catfish** tends to top the bill, but you'll also find **grouper**, **dolphin** (the fish not the mammal, sometimes known by its Hawaiian name, **mahimahi**), **mullet**, **tuna** and **swordfish**, any of which (except catfish, which is nearly always fried) may be boiled, grilled, fried or "blackened" (charcoal-grilled). Of **shellfish**, the tender claws of **stone crabs**, eaten dipped in butter, raise local passions during their mid-October to mid-May season; **spiny** (or **"Florida"**) **lobster** is smaller and more succulent than its more famous Maine rival; **oysters** can be extremely fresh (the best come from Apalachicola) and are usually eaten raw (though best avoided during summer, when they carry a risk of food poisoning) – many restaurants have special **"raw bars"**, where you can also consume meaty **shrimp**, in regular and jumbo sizes. One crustacean you can't eat raw is the very chewy **conch** (pronounced "konk"); abundant throughout the Florida Keys, it usually comes as fritters but tastes better in a chowder.

ETHNIC CUISINE

Florida's **ethnic cuisines** become increasingly exotic the further south you go. In Miami, **Cuban food** is extremely easy to find and can be very good value. Most Cuban dishes are meat based: frequently pork, less often beef or chicken, always fried (including the skin, which becomes a crisply

AMERICAN FOOD TERMS FOR FOREIGN TRAVELLERS

A la mode	With ice cream
Au jus	Meat served with a gravy made from its own juices
Biscuit	Scone
BLT	Bacon, lettuce and tomato toasted sandwich
Broiled	Grilled
Brownie	A fudgy, filling chocolate cake
Chips	Potato crisps
Cilantro	Coriander
Clam chowder	A thick soup made with clams and other seafood.
Cookie	Biscuit
Eggplant	Aubergine
English muffin	Toasted bread roll, similar to a crumpet
Frank	Frankfurter (hot dog)
(French) fries	Chips
Gravy	White lard-like sauce poured over biscuits for breakfast
Grits	ground white corn, served hot with butter, often a breakfast side dish.
Hash browns	Potato chunks or grated potato chips fried in fat
Hero	French-bread sandwich
Hoagie	Another French-bread sandwich
Home fries	Thick-cut fried potatoes
Jello	Jelly
Jelly	Jam
Muffin	Small cake made with bran and/or blueberries
Popsicle	Ice lolly
Potato chips	Crisps
Pretzels	Savory circles of glazed pastry
Seltzer	Fizzy/soda water
Sherbet	Sorbet
Shrimp	Prawns
Sub	Yet another French-bread sandwich
Soda	Generic term for any soft drink
Surf 'n' Turf	Restaurant serving fish and meat
Teriyaki	Chicken or beef, marinated in soy sauce and grilled
Zucchini	Courgettes

Cuban Specialties

Ajiaco criollo	Meat and root vegetable stew
Arroz	Rice
Arroz con leche	Rice pudding
Bocadillo	Sandwich
Chicarones de pollo	Fried chicken crackling
Frijoles	Beans
Frijoles negros	Black beans
Maduros	Fried plantains
Masitoas de puerca	Fried spiced pork
Morros y Christianos	Literally "Moors and Christians", black beans and white rice
Pan	Bread
Pan con lechon	Crispy pork sandwich
Piccadillo	Minced meat, usually beef, served with peppers and olives
Pollo	Chicken
Puerca	Pork
Sopa de mariscos	Shellfish soup
Sopa de plantanos	Meaty, plantain soup
Vaca	Beef
Tostones	Fried mashed plantains

Mexican Specialties

Burritos	Folded tortillas stuffed with re-fried beans or beef, and grated cheese
Chiles Rellenos	Green chillies stuffed with cheese and fried in egg batter
Enchiladas	Soft tortillas filled with meat and cheese or chilli and baked
Fajitas	Like tacos but a soft flour tortilla stuffed with shrimp, chicken or beef
Frijoles	Re-fried beans, ie mashed fried beans.
Guacamole	Thick sauce made from avocado, garlic, onion and chilli, used as a topping
Mariscos	Seafood
Nachos	Tortilla chips topped with melted cheese
Quesadilla	Folded soft tortilla containing melted cheese
Salsa	Chillies, tomato and onion and cilantro
Tacos	Folded, fried tortillas, stuffed with chicken, beef or (occasionally) cow's brains
Tamales	Corn meal dough with meat and chilli, wrapped in a corn husk and baked
Tortillas	Maize dough pancakes
Tostada	Fried, flat tortillas, smothered with meat and vegetables

crackling) and usually heavily spiced, served with a varying combination of yellow or white rice, black beans, plantains (a sweet-tasting tropical vegetable) and yucca – a potato-like vegetable completely devoid of taste. Seafood crops up less often, most deliciously in thick soups, such as *sopa de mariscos* – shellfish soup. Unpretentious Cuban diners serve a filling lunch or dinner for under $6, though a growing number of upmarket restaurants will charge three times as much for identical food. In busy areas, many Cuban cafés have street windows where you buy a thimble-sized cup of sweet and rich *Café Cubano* – Cuban coffee – for 50–75¢, strong enough to make your hair stand on end; the similarly priced *café con leche*, coffee with warm milk or cream, is strictly for the unadventurous and regarded by Cubans as a children's drink. If you want a cool drink in Miami, look out for roadside stands offering *coco frío* – coconut milk sucked through a straw directly from the coconut, for $1.

Although nowhere near as prevalent as Cuban cooking, foods from other parts of the Caribbean and Latin America are easily located around Miami: **Haitian** food is the latest craze, but **Argentinian**, **Colombian**, **Nicaraguan**, **Peruvian**, **Jamaican** and **El Salvadorean** restaurants also serve the city's diverse migrant populations – at very affordable prices.

Other ethnic cuisines turn up all around the state, too. **Chinese** food is everywhere and can often be very cheap, as can **Mexican**, although many Mexican restaurants are more popular as places to knock back margaritas than for eating in; **Japanese** is more expensive; **Italian** food is popular, but can be expensive once you leave the simple pastas and explore the more gourmet-inclined Italian regional cooking that's catching on fast in the major cities. **French** food, too, is widely available, though always pricey, the cuisine of social climbers and power-lunchers and rarely found outside the larger cities. **Thai**, **Korean** and **Indonesian** food is similarly city-based, though usually cheaper; **Indian** restaurants, on the other hand, are thin on the ground just about everywhere and often very expensive. More plentiful are well-priced, family-run **Greek** restaurants and a smattering of **Minorcan** places are evidence of one of Florida's earliest groups of European settlers.

Whatever and wherever you eat, **service** will always be enthusiastic and excellent. Foreign travellers should note that this is mainly due to the American system of **tipping**, on which the staff depend for the bulk (and sometimes all) of their earnings. You should always top up the bill by 15–20 percent; not to tip at all is severely frowned upon. Many (not all) restaurants accept **payment** in the form of credit/charge cards: if you use one, a space will be left to fill in the appropriate tip; travellers' checks are also widely accepted (see p.14).

DRINKING

While regular **bars** in the classic American image do exist in Florida – long, dimly lit counters with a few punters perched on stools before a bartender-cum-guru and tables and booths for those who don't want to join in the drunken bar-side debates – most drinking is done in restaurant or hotel lounges, at fishcamps (see "Eating"), or in **"tiki bars"**, open-sided straw-roofed huts beside a beach or hotel pool. Some beachside bars, especially in Daytona Beach and Panama City Beach, are split-level, multi-purpose affairs with discos and stages for live bands – and take great pride in being the birthplace of the infamous wet T-shirt contest (nowadays sometimes joined by G-string and "best legs" shows), an exercise in unrestrained sexism that shows no signs of declining in popularity among a predominantly late-teen and twenty-something clientele.

To **buy and consume alcohol** you need to be 21 and could well be asked for ID even if you look much older. **Licensing laws and drinking hours** vary from area to area, but generally alcohol can be bought and drunk in a bar, nightclub or restaurant any time between 10am and 2am. More cheaply, you can usually buy beer, wine or liquor in supermarkets and, of course, liquor stores, from 9am to 11pm Monday to Saturday and from 1pm to 11pm on Sundays. Note that it is illegal to consume alcohol in a car, on most beaches and in all state parks.

BEER

A small band of Florida **micro breweries** (tiny, one-off operations) create interesting beers, though rarely are these sold beyond their own bar or restaurant – such as the **Sarasota Brewing Company** in Sarasota. It's more common for discerning beer drinkers to stick to imported brews, best of which are the Mexican brands *Bohemia*, *Corona*, *Dos Equis*, *Superior* and *Tecate*. Don't forget that in all but the more pretentious

COCKTAILS

Bacardi	White rum, lime and grenadine – not the brand name drink	Margarita	The cocktail to drink in a Mexican restaurant, made with tequila, triple sec, lime juice and limes, and blended with ice to make slush. Served with or without salt. Also available in fruit flavors.
Bellini	Champagne with peach juice		
Black Russian	Vodka with coffee liqueur, brown cacao and coke		
Bloody Mary	Vodka, tomato juice, tabasco, worcester sauce, salt and pepper		
		Mimosa	Champagne and orange juice
Brandy Alexander	Brandy, brown cacao and cream	Mint Julep	Bourbon, mint and sugar
Champagne cocktail	Brandy, sugar and champagne	Negroni	Vodka or gin, campari and triple sec
Daquiri	Dark rum, light rum and lime, often with banana or strawberry	Pina Colada	Dark rum, light rum, coconut, cream and pineapple juice
Harvey Wallbanger	Vodka, galliano, orange juice	Screwdriver	Vodka and orange juice
		Silk Stocking	Gin, tequila, white cacao, cream and sugar
Highball	Any spirit plus a soda, water or ginger ale	Tequila Sunrise	Tequila, orange juice and grenadine
Kir Royale	Champagne, cassis		
Long Island Iced Tea	Gin, vodka, white rum, tequila, lemon juice and coke	Tom Collins	Gin, lemon juice, soda and sugar
Mai-Tai	Dark rum, light rum, cherry brandy, orange and lemon juice	Vodka Collins	Vodka, lemon juice, soda and sugar
Manhattan	Vermouth, whisky, lemon juice and soda	Whisky Sour	Bourbon, lemon juice and sugar
		White Russian	Vodka, white cacao and cream

bars, several people can save money by buying a quart or half-gallon **pitcher** of beer. If bar prices are a problem, you can stock up with **six-packs** from a supermarket at $2–4 for domestic, $4–6 for imported brews.

WINE AND HARD LIQUOR

If **wine** is more to your taste, try to visit one of the state's fast-improving **wineries**: several can be toured and their products sampled for free. One of the most successful is also one of the newest: *Chautauqua Vineyards*, in De Funiak Springs (see p.322). In a bar or restaurant, however, beside a usually threadbare stock of European wines, **California** wine is the most worth trying. *Cabernet Sauvignon* is probably the most popular, a light and easily drunk red; also widespread are the heavier reds – *Burgundy*,

Merlot and *Pinot Noir*. Among the whites, *Chardonnay* is very dry and flavorful and generally preferred to *Sauvignon Blanc* or *Fumé Blanc*, though these have their devotees. It's fairly inexpensive: a glass of wine in a bar or restaurant costs $1.50–2.50, a bottle $5–8. Buying from a supermarket is cheaper still – just $3–6 a bottle.

Hard liquor generally costs $1.50 a shot. **Cocktails** are extremely popular, especially rich fruity ones consumed while gazing over the ocean or into the sunset. Varieties are innumerable, sometimes specific to a single bar or cocktail lounge, though there are a few standards listed above, any of which will cost $2–5. Cocktails and all other drinks, come cheapest during **happy hours** (usually 5–7pm; sometimes much longer) when many are half-price and there might be a buffet thrown in.

PERSONAL SAFETY

No one could pretend that Florida is trouble-free, although outside of the urban centers, crime is often remarkably low-key. Even the lawless reputation of murder-a-day Miami is in excess of the truth, although several clearly defined areas are strictly off-limits. At night you should always be cautious – though not unduly frightened – wherever you are. All the major tourist areas and the main nightlife areas in cities are invariably brightly lit and well policed. By being careful, planning ahead and taking good care of your possessions, you should, generally speaking, have few real problems.

Foreign visitors tend to report that the police are helpful and obliging when things go wrong, although they'll be less sympathetic if they think you brought the trouble on yourself through carelessness*.

CAR CRIME

Even more than muggings on the street (see below), it's been crimes committed against tourists driving **rented cars** in Florida which have garnered headlines around the world in recent months and threatened the continued well-being of the state's number one industry.

Until April 1993, most Florida rental cars were given number plates with a "Y" or "Z" prefix,

*One way you might accidently break the law is by **jaywalking**. If you cross the road on a red light or anywhere except at an intersection, and are spotted by a cop, you're likely to get a stiff talking-to – and possibly a ticket, leading to a $20 fine.

making them easy to spot. Although the offending plates have been banned, you may still be offered a rental cars which has one; if so, insist that the company offer you a different car.

When driving, under no circumstances stop in any unlit or seemingly deserted urban area – and especially not if someone is waving you down and suggesting that there is something wrong with your car. Similarly, if you are "accidentally" rammed by the driver behind, do not stop immediately but drive on to the nearest well-lit, busy area and phone the emergency number (☎911) for assistance. Keep your doors locked and windows never more than slightly open (as you'll probably be using air conditioning, you'll want to keep them fully closed anyway). Do not open your door or window if someone approaches your car on the pretext of asking directions. Even if the person doing this looks harmless, they may well have an accomplice ready to **attack you from behind**. Hide any valuables out of sight, preferably locked in the boot or in the glove compartment (any valuables you don't need for your journey should left in your hotel safe).

Always take care when planning your route, particularly through urban areas and be sure to use a reliable map such as the ones we've recommended under "Information, Maps and the Media". Particularly in Miami, local authorities are making efforts to add directions to tourist sights and attractions to road signs, thereby reducing the possibility of visitors unwittingly driving into dangerous areas. Needless to say, you should always heed such directions, even if you think you've located a convenient short cut. . . .

STREET CRIME AND HOTEL BURGLARIES

After car crime, the biggest problem for most travellers in Florida is the threat of **mugging**. It's impossible to give hard and fast rules about what to do if you're confronted by a mugger. Whether to run, scream or fight depends on the situation – but most locals would just hand over their money.

Of course, the best thing is simply to avoid being mugged and there are a few basic rules worth remembering: don't flash money around; don't peer at your map (or this book) at every street corner, thereby announcing you're a lost stranger; even if you're terrified or drunk (or

LOSING YOUR PASSPORT

Few disasters create bigger headaches for foreign travellers than **losing your passport**. You can't get home without it, and it can be an extremely tough process to get a new one. The only **British Consulate** in Florida – which can (very grudgingly) issue passports – is in Miami at Suite 2110, S Bayshore Drive, Coconut Grove, FL 33131 (☎305/374-1522). Expect to spend around $40 on fees and waste at least a week.

both), don't appear so; avoid dark streets and never start to walk down one that you can't see the end of; and in the early hours stick to the roadside edge of the pavement so it's easier to run into the road to attract attention.

If the worst happens and your assailant is toting a gun or (more likely) a knife, try to stay calm: remember that he (for this is generally a male pursuit) is probably scared, too. Keep still, don't make any sudden movements – and hand over your money. When he's gone you'll be shocked, but try to find a cab to take you to the nearest police station. Here, report the theft and get a reference number on the report to claim insurance (see "Health and Insurance", p.13) and travellers' check refunds. If you're in a big city, ring the local *Travelers Aid* (their numbers are listed in the phone book) for sympathy and practical advice.

Another potential source of trouble is having your **hotel room burgled** while you're out. Some Orlando area hotels are notorious for this and many such break-ins appear to be inside jobs. Always store valuables in the hotel safe when you go out; when inside keep your door locked and don't open it to anyone you are suspicious of; if they claim to be hotel staff and you don't believe them, call reception on the room phone to check.

LOST TRAVELLERS' CHECKS

Lost travellers' checks are a common problem. You should keep a record of the numbers of your checks separately from the actual checks and, if you lose them, ring the issuing company on their toll-free number. They'll ask you for the check numbers, the place you bought them, when and how you lost them and whether it's been reported to the police. All being well, you should get the missing checks reissued within a couple of days – and perhaps an emergency advance to tide you over.

STOLEN TRAVELLERS' CHECKS/CREDIT CARDS EMERGENCY NUMBERS

Mastercard (*Access*) ☎ 1-800/336-8472
American Express (TCs) ☎ 1-800/221-7282; (credit cards) ☎1-800/528-2121
Diners Card ☎1-800/968-8300
Thomas Cook ☎1-800/223-7373
Visa ☎1-800/627-6811 or ☎1-800/227-6811

THE BACKCOUNTRY

Despite the common notion that Florida is entirely composed of theme parks and beaches, much of the state is wide-open undeveloped land, holding everything from scrubland and swamps to shady hardwood hammocks and dense forests streaked by gushing rivers. Hiking and canoe trails make the wilderness accessible and rewarding – miss it and you're missing Florida.

The US's protected backcountry areas fall into several potentially confusing categories. **State parks** are the responsibility of individual states and usually focus on sites of natural or historical significance. **National parks** are federally controlled, preserving areas of great natural beauty or ecological importance. Florida's three **national forests** are also federally administered but enjoy much less protection than national parks.

HIKING

Almost all state parks have undemanding **nature trails** intended for a pleasant hour's ramble; anything called a **hiking** or **backpacking trail** – plentiful in state and national parks, national forests and through some unprotected land as part of the 1300-mile **Florida Trail** (intended eventually to run the full length of the state) – requires more thought and planning.

Many hiking trails can be easily completed in a day, the longer ones have rough camping sites at regular intervals (see "Camping", below) and most periodically pass through fully equipped camping areas – giving the option of sleeping in

comparative comfort. The **best time** to hike is from late autumn to early spring: this avoids the exhausting heat of the summer and the worst of the **mosquitoes** (see "Wildlife", below) and reveals a greater variety of animals. While hiking, be extremely wary of the **poisonwood** tree (ask a park ranger how to identify it); any contact between your skin and its bark can leave you needing hospital treatment – and avoid being splashed by rainwater dripping from its branches. Be sure to carry plenty of drinking water, as well as the obvious hiking prerequisites.

In some areas you'll need a **wilderness permit** (free or $1) from the local park rangers' or wilderness administration office, where you should call anyway for maps, general information on the hike and a weather forecast – sudden rains can flood trails in swampy areas. Many state parks run **organized hiking trips**, details of which are given throughout the Guide. For general hiking information, write for the free *Backpacking in Florida State Parks* to the **Florida Department of Natural Resources**, 3900 Commonwealth Boulevard, Tallahassee, FL 32393 (☎904/488-1234) and to the **Florida Trail Association**, PO Box 13708, Gainesville, FL 32604 (☎1-800/343-1882).

CANOEING

One way to enjoy natural Florida without getting blisters on your feet is by **canoeing**. Canoes can be rented for around $12–15 a day anywhere where conditions are right: the best of Florida's rivers and streams are found in north Central Florida and the Panhandle. Many state and national parks have canoe runs, too and the **Florida Canoe Trails System** comprises 36 marked routes along rivers and creeks, covering a combined distance of nearly a thousand miles.

Before setting off, get a canoeing **map** (you'll need to know the locations of access points and any rough camping sites) and check **weather conditions** and the river's **water level**: a low level can expose logs, rocks and other obstacles; a flooded river is dangerous and shouldn't be canoed; coastal rivers are affected by tides. Don't leave the canoe to **walk on the bank** – this damages the bank and is likely to be trespassing. When a **motorboat** approaches, keep to the right and turn your bow into the wake. If you're **camping**, do so on a sandbar unless there are designated rough camping areas beside the river. Besides food, carry plenty of drinking water, a first-aid kit, insect repellent and sunscreen.

Several small companies run canoe trips ranging from half a day to a week; they supply the canoe and take you from the end of the route back to where you started. Details are given throughout the Guide; or look out for the free *Canoe Florida* leaflet, available from most state parks and some local tourist information offices. For more on the Florida Canoe Trails System, pick up the free *Florida Recreational Trails System Canoe Trails* (available from the **Department of Natural Resources**, address above).

CAMPING

All hiking trails have areas designated for **rough camping**, with either very limited facilities (a handpump for water, sometimes a primitive toilet) or none at all. Travelling by canoe (see "Canoeing", above) you'll often pass sandbars which can make excellent overnight stops. It's preferable to cook by stove, but otherwise start **fires** only in permitted areas – indicated by signs – and use deadwood. Where there are no toilets, **bury human waste** at least four inches in the ground and a hundred feet from the nearest water supply and campground. **Burn rubbish** carefully and what you can't burn, carry away. **Never drink** from rivers and streams, however clear and inviting they may look (you never know what unspeakable acts people – or animals – further upstream have performed in them), or from the state's many natural springs; **water** that isn't from taps should be boiled for at least five minutes, or cleansed with a iodine-based purifier, before you drink it. Always get advice, maps and a weather forecast from the park ranger's or wilderness area's adminstration office – often you'll need to fill in a wilderness permit, too and pay a $1.50-a-night **camping fee**.

WILDLIFE

Though you're likely to meet many kinds of **wildlife** on your travels, only mosquitoes and, to a much lesser extent, alligators and snakes, will cause any problems.

From June to November, **mosquitoes** are a tremendous nuisance and virtually unavoidable in any area close to fresh water. Through these

months, **insect repellent** (available for a few dollars in most camping shops and supermarkets) is essential, as is wearing long-sleeved shirts and long trousers. It's rare for mosquitoes to carry diseases, although during 1991 Florida was hit by an outbreak of **viral encephalitis**, a mosquito-borne disease which can cause paralysis and death. As each generation of mosquitoes dies out during the winter, it's unlikely that this will be repeated – at least not for many years.

The biggest surprise among Florida's wildlife is the apparent docility of **alligators** – almost always they'll back away if approached by a human (though this is not something you should put to the test) – and the fact that they now turn up all over the place, despite being decimated by decades of uncontrolled hunting. These days, not only is it unlawful to kill alligators (without a licence), but feeding one can get you two months in prison and a hefty fine: an alligator fed by a human not only loses its natural fear of people but comes to associate them with food – and lacks the brainpower to distinguish between food and feeder. The only truly dangerous type of alligator is a mother guarding her nest or tending her young. Even then, she'll give you plenty of warning, by showing her teeth and hissing, before attacking.

Like alligators, Florida's **snakes** don't go looking for trouble but several species know how to retaliate when provoked – which you're most likely to do by standing on one. Two species are potentially deadly: the **Coral Snake**, which has a black nose and bright yellow and red rings covering its body and usually spends the daylight hours under piles of rotting vegetation; and the **Cottonmouth Moccasin** (sometimes called the **Water Moccasin**), dark-colored with a small head, which lives around rivers and lakes. Less harmful, but still worth avoiding, are two types of **rattlesnake**: the easily identified **Diamondback**, whose thick body is covered in a diamond pattern, which turns up in dry, sandy areas and hammocks; and the grey-colored **Pygmy**, so small it's almost impossible to spot until it's too late. You're unlikely to see a snake in the wild and snake attacks are even rarer, but if **bitten** you should contact a ranger or a doctor immediately. It's a wise precaution to carry a **snakebite kit**, available for a couple of dollars from most camping shops.

For more on Florida's wildlife and its habitats, see "Natural Florida" in *Contexts*.

WOMEN'S FLORIDA

In the state that invented the wet T-shirt contest and which still promotes itself with photos of bikini-clad models draping themselves around palm trees, first-time visitors may be surprised to find women playing demanding and crucial roles in Florida life – in many respects a mark of the achievements of the women's movement over the last two decades. While the force of feminist politics has dissipated of late, the fact that women's bars, bookstores and support centers – if nothing on the scale of New York or the West Coast – are well established in the larger cities, indicates a continued commitment to female self-determination.

Equally, if not more, effective in this thoroughly capitalist society, are the growing number of women's business organizations seeking ways to further female career advancement and raise (if not destroy) the "glass ceiling" – the invisible sexist barrier halting movement up the corporate ladder. In Florida, some such groups have focused recent efforts on strengthening the female presence in that traditional arena of male-bonding and off-the-record deal-making: the golf course.

Practically speaking, a woman **travelling alone** in Florida is not usually made to feel conspicuous, or liable to attract unwelcome attention. Outside of Miami and the seedier sections of the other major cities, much of the state can feel surprisingly safe. But as with anywhere, particular care has to be taken at night. **Mugging** is nowhere near the problem it is in New York, but you can't relax totally – though a modicum of common sense can often avert disasters. Walking through unlit, empty streets is never a good idea and if there's no bus service (and you can afford it), take cabs – if not, an escort. It's true that women who *look* confident tend not to encounter trouble – those who stand around looking lost and scared are prime targets.

In the major urban centers, provided you listen to advice and stick to the better parts of town, going into **bars** and **clubs** alone should pose few problems: there's generally a pretty healthy attitude towards women who do so and your privacy will be respected. Gay and lesbian bars are usually a trouble-free and welcoming alternative.

However, **small towns** tend not to be blessed with the same liberal or indifferent attitudes towards lone women travellers. People seem to jump immediately to the conclusion that your car has broken down, or that you've suffered some terrible tragedy; in fact, you may get fed up with well-meant offers of help. If your **vehicle breaks down** in a country area, walk to the nearest house or town for help; on Interstate highways or heavily travelled roads, wait in the car for a police or highway patrol car to arrive. One increasingly available option is to rent a portable telephone with your car, for a small additional charge – a potential lifesaver.

Rape statistics in the US are outrageously high and it goes without saying that you should *never* **hitch** alone – this is widely interpreted as an invitation for trouble and there's no shortage of weirdos to give it. Similarly, if you have a car, be careful who you pick up: just because you're in the driving seat doesn't mean you're safe. Avoid travelling at night by public transport – deserted bus stations, if not actually threatening, will do little to make you feel secure – and where possible you should team up with a fellow traveller. There really is security in numbers. On *Greyhound* buses, follow the example of other lone women and make a point of sitting as near to the front – and the driver – as possible. Should disaster strike, all major towns have some kind of rape counselling service; if not, the local sheriff's office will make adequate arrangements for you to get help, counselling and, if necessary, get you home.

Specific **women's contacts** are listed in the city sections of the Guide, but for good back-up material get hold of *Places of Interest to Women* ($7; Ferrari Publications, PO Box 35575, Phoenix, AZ; ☎602/863-2408), a guide for women travelling in the US, Canada, the Caribbean and Mexico which is updated annually. And for more detailed country-wide info, read the annual *Index/Directory of Women's Media* (published by the Women's Institute for the Freedom of the Press, 3306 Ross Place NW, Washington DC 20008), which lists women's publishers, bookshops, theater groups, news services and media organizations and more, throughout the country.

GAY AND LESBIAN FLORIDA

With **?** thousand people a day moving into the state, it's inevitable that Florida's gay and lesbian communities will grow considerably in the urban areas over the next few years, becoming ever more organized and vocal. At present, however, it's a salient fact that the biggest gay and lesbian scene is in Key West, at the tip of the Florida Keys and as far as it is possible to get from the rest of the state. The island town's live-and-let-live tradition has made it a holiday destination favored by American gays and lesbians for decades and many arrivals simply never went home: instead, they've taken up permanent residence and opened guest-houses, restaurants and other businesses – even running gay and lesbian snorkelling and diving trips.

Elsewhere, Miami's fast-expanding network of gay and lesbian resources, clubs and bars – if not as ubiquitous as in New York or on the West Coast – is the major indication of what's to come. There are smaller levels of activity in the other cities and along developed sections of the coast (where the gay tourist dollar is recognized as being as good as anyone else's) a number of motels and hotels are specifically aimed at gay travellers. Predictably, attitudes to gay and lesbian visitors get progressively worse the further you go from the populous areas. Being open about your sexuality in the rural regions is likely to garner at least an ill-at-ease response, perhaps open hostility – the hell-and-damnation reaction to AIDS widespread in these parts certainly doesn't improve matters.

For a complete rundown on local **resources**, **bars** and **clubs**, see the relevant headings in individual cities. Of national and statewide **publications** to look out for, by far the best is the free *TWN* (*The Weekly News*), packed with news, features and ads for Florida's gay bars and clubs. Also worth a look are *Bob Damron's Address Book* (PO Box 11270, San Francisco, CA 94101; $12), a pocket-sized yearbook of nationwide listings of hotels, bars, clubs and resources, available from any gay specialist bookshop and *Gay Yellow Pages* (Ferrari Publications, PO Box 292, Village Station, New York, NY 100114; $8.95). Specifically lesbian publications are harder to find: the most useful is *Gaia's* Guide (132 W 24th St, New York, NY 10011; $6.95), a yearly international directory with a lot of US information.

DISABLED TRAVELLERS

Travellers with mobility problems or other physical disabilities are likely to find Florida – as with the US generally – to be much more in tune with their needs than any other country in the world. All public buildings must be wheelchair accessible and have suitable toilets, most city street corners have dropped kerbs and most city buses are able to "kneel" to make access easier and are built with space and handgrips for wheelchair users.

Provided they're given notice (at least a day, preferably more), domestic **airlines** within the US and most transatlantic airlines, can do much to ease a disabled person's journey and, if necessary, a helper will usually be permitted free travel.

On the ground, the major **car rental** firms can, given sufficient notice, provide vehicles with hand controls (though these are usually only available on the more expensive makes of vehicle); *Amtrak* will provide wheelchair assistance at its train stations, adapted seating on board and a 15 percent discount on the regular fare, all provided 72 hours notice is given; *Greyhound* buses, despite the fact that they lack designated wheelchair space, will allow a necessary helper to travel free.

In the **Orlando** area, *B.S. Mini Med* specialize in assisting disabled visitors. They provide wheelchair or stretcher transportation from Orlando airport to any Orlando accommodation for $75 and trips within the area – to the Disney parks and other attractions, for example – are charged at $20 plus $2 per mile (for the disabled traveller plus up to eight companions). The company are contactable at 551 Little River Loop, Suite 213, Altamonte Springs, FL 32714 (☎407/296-3460).

Many of Florida's hotels and motels are recently built and disabled access has been a major consideration in their construction. Rarely will any part of the property be difficult for a disabled person to reach and often several rooms are specifically designed to meet the requirements of disabled guests.

The state's major **theme parks** are also built with disabled access in mind and attendants are always on hand to ensure that a disabled person gets any necessary assistance – and derives maximum enjoyment from their visit. Even in the Florida wilds, facilities are good: most state parks arrange programmes for disabled visitors; the **Apalachicola National Forest** has a lakeside nature trail set aside for the exclusive use of disabled visitors and their guests; and, in the **Everglades National Park**, all the walking trails are wheelchair accessible, as in one of the backcountry camping sites.

For further information, get the free *Florida Services Directory for Physically Challenged Travellers* from the Florida Division of Tourism (see "Information, Maps and Media" for the address). For general information on travelling in the US, contact **SATH**, the Society for the Advancement of Travel for the Handicapped, 347 Fifth Avenue, Suite 610, New York, NY 10016 (☎212/447-7284).

TRAVELLING WITH CHILDREN

Travelling with kids in the United States is relatively problem-free; children are readily accepted – indeed welcomed – in public places across the country and probably nowhere more so than in Florida, where visiting families have long constituted a major part of the state's mighty tourist industry.

Hotels and **motels** almost without exception welcome children: those in major tourist areas such as Orlando often have a games room (usually of the computer kind) and/or a play area and allow children below a certain age (usually 14, sometimes 18) to stay free in their parents' room.

In all but the most formal **restaurants**, young diners are likely to be presented with a kids' menu – liberally laced with hot dogs, dinosaur burgers and ice-cream in various guises – plus crayons, drawing pads and assorted toys.

ACTIVITIES

Most large towns have at least one kid-aimed **museum** with plenty of inter-active educational exhibits – often sophisticated enough to keep adults, too, amused for hours. Virtually all museums and other tourist attractions have reduced rates for kids under a certain age.

Florida's **theme parks** may seem the ultimate in kids' entertainment but in fact are much more geared towards entertaining adults than most people expect. Only Walt Disney World's **Magic Kingdom** is tailor-made for young kids (though even here, parents are warned that some rides may frighten the very young); adolescents (and

adults) are likely to prefer Disney-MGM Studios or Universal Studios.

Away from the blockbusting tourist stops, **natural Florida** has much to stimulate the young. In the many state parks and in the Everglades National Park, park rangers specialize in turning formative minds on to the wonders of nature: with alligators, turtles and all manner of brightly colored birds lurking in abundance, this is surprisingly easy to do. A boat trip in dolphin-inhabited waters – several of these are recommended in the *Guide* – is another likely way to stimulate curiosity in the natural world.

On a more cautious note, adults should take great care not to allow young flesh to be exposed to the Florida sun for too long: even a few minutes' unprotected exposure can cause serious sunburn.

No matter how you go, once you get there be sure to take special care in keeping track of one another – it's no less terrifying for a child to be lost at Walt Disney World than it is for him or her to go missing at the mall. Whenever possible agree a meeting place *before* you get lost and it's not a bad idea, especially for younger children, to attach some sort of wearable ID card and for toddlers to be kept on reins.

A good idea in a major theme park is to show your child how to find (or how to recognize and ask uniformed staff to take them to) the "Lost Kids Area". This designated space not only makes lost kids easy to locate but provides supervision, plus toys and games to keeep them amused until you show up to claim them. Elsewhere, tell your kids to stay where they are and not to wander; if *you* **get lost**, you'll have a much easier time finding each other if you're not all running around anxiously.

GETTING AROUND

Children under two years old **fly** for free – though that doesn't mean they get a seat, a pretty major consideration on long-distance flights – and when aged from two to twelve they are usually entitled to half-price tickets.

Once you're in Florida, travelling **by bus** may be the cheapest way to go, but it's also the most discomforting for kids. Under-2s travel (on your lap) for free; ages 2 to 4 are charged 10 percent of the adult fare, as are any toddlers who take up a seat. Children under 12 years old are charged half the standard fare.

Even if you discount the romance of the railroad, **taking the train** is by far the best option for long journeys – not only does everyone get to enjoy the scenery, but you can get up and walk around, relieving pent-up energy. Children's discounts are much the same as for bus or plane travel. Recreational Vehicles (RVs) are also a good option for family travel, combining the convenience of built-in kitchens and bedrooms with freedom of the road (see "Getting Around" on p.22 for details).

Most families choose to travel **by car and** while this is the least problematic way to go it's worth planning ahead to assure a pleasant trip. Don't set yourself unrealistic targets if you're hoping to enjoy a driving vacation with your kids. Pack plenty of sensible snacks and drinks; plan to stop (ie don't make your kids make you stop) every couple of hours; arrive at your destination well before sunset; and if you're passing through big cities, avoid travelling during rush hour. Also, it can be a good idea to give an older child some responsibility for route-finding – having someone "play navigator" is good fun, educational and often a real help to the driver. If you're doing a fly-drive vacation, note that when **renting a car** the company is legally obliged to provide free car seats for kids.

SPORTS

Florida is as sports mad as the rest of the US, but what's more surprising is that collegiate sports are often, especially among lifelong Floridians, more popular than their professional counterparts. This is because Florida's professional teams are comparatively recent additions to the sporting scene and have none of the traditions and bedrock support that the state's college sides enjoy. Seventy thousand people attending an inter-college football match is no rarity. Other sports less in evidence include soccer, volleyball, greyhound racing and Jai Alai – the last two chiefly excuses for betting.

PROFESSIONAL SPORTS

BASEBALL

Until April 1993, when the **Florida Marlins** played their first game, Florida had no professional **baseball** side of its own. Now the Marlins play at the Joe Robbie Stadium, 16 miles north-west of downtown Miami (box office Mon–Fri 10am–6pm; ☎305/620-2578; tickets $10–15).

Many northern baseball teams, however, have long held their pre-season **spring training** (Feb and March) in the state – and thousands of their fans plan vacations so that they can watch their sporting heroes going through practice routines and playing in the friendly matches of the **Grapefruit League**. Much prestige is attached to being a spring training venue and the local community identifies strongly with the team that it hosts – in some cases the link goes back fifty years. Turn up at 10am to join the crowds watching the training (free); of the twenty-odd sides who come to train in Florida, you'll find the country's top teams at the following: the **LA Dodgers**, Holman Stadium, Vero Beach (☎407/569-4900); the **Boston Red Sox**, Chain O'Lakes Park, Winter Haven (☎813/293-3900); **Detroit Tigers**, Marchant Stadium, 2301 Lakeland Hills Blvd, Lakeland (☎813/682-1401); and the **Minnesota Twins**, Tinker Field, 287 S Tampa Ave, Orlando (☎407/849-6346).

FOOTBALL

Of the state's two professional **football** teams, the **Miami Dolphins** are easily the most successful, appearing five times in the Superbowl

and, in 1972, enjoying the only all-win season in NFL history. They too play at the Joe Robbie Stadium (see above; most tickets $30). By contrast, the **Tampa Bay Buccaneers** have fared only moderately well; they're based at 4201 Dale Mabry Highway (☎813/879-BUCS; tickets $15–35).

Much greater fervor is whipped up by the University of Florida's **Gators** (in Gainesville) and Florida State University's **Seminoles** (in Tallahassee), both of whom play ten-match seasons in the Southeast Conference – although the Seminoles are planning to join the rival Atlantic Coast Conference. A poor third among the college teams in terms of support but enjoying a record-breaking undefeated home run in 1991, the University of Miami's **Hurricanes** play in the National College League – which they've won on several occasions. Tickets are $18–35 for professional matches; $12–18 for college games. Further details are given in the Guide.

BASKETBALL

Both the state's two professional **basketball** teams are infants and yet to make much of a mark: **Miami Heat** joined the National Basketball Association (NBA) in 1988, followed two years later by **Orlando Magic**. Top among the college sides are Miami University's **Hurricanes**. Tickets for professional games cost $8–26; college games $6–16. Further details are given in the Guide.

PARTICIPANT SPORTS

WATER SPORTS

Even non-swimmers can quickly learn to **snorkel**, which is the best way to see one of the state's finest natural assets: the living coral reef that curls around its southeastern corner and on along the Florida Keys. Many **guided snorkelling trips** run to the reef and cost around $25 – details are given throughout the *Guide*. More adventurous than snorkelling is loading up with air-cylinders to go **scuba diving**. You'll need a **Certified Divers Card** to do this; if you don't already have one you'll be required to take a course which can last anything from one hour to a day and costs $50–100. Get details from any **diving shop**, always plentiful near good diving areas, who can also provide equipment, maps and general information.

When you snorkel or dive, observing a few **underwater precautions** will increase enjoyment and safety: wear **lightweight shoes** to avoid treading on jellyfish, crabs, or sharp rocks; *don't* wear any **shiny objects**, as these are likely to attract hungry fish – such as the otherwise harmless barracuda; **never dive alone**; always leave your boat by diving **into the current** – by doing this, the current will help glide you back to the boat later; always display the red and white **"diver down" flag**. And, obviously, never dive after drinking alcohol.

The same reefs that make snorkelling and diving so much fun cause **surfing** to be less common than you might expect and limited to a few sections of the east coast. Florida's biggest waves strike land between **Sebastian Inlet** and **Cocoa Beach** and surfing tournaments are held here during April and May. Lesser breakers are found at Miami's Beach's **First Street Beach**, Boca Raton's **South Beach Park** and around the **Jacksonville Beaches**. Surfboards can be rented from local beach shops for $8–10 a day.

Cutting a (usually) more gentle passage through water, many of the state's rivers can be effortlessly navigated by **canoe**; these can rented for around $12–15 a day from most state parks and riverside recreational areas.

Additionally, there are a number of long-distance canoe trails and several companies offering inclusive canoe trips; see "The Backcountry" (p.37) for more details.

FISHING

Few things excite higher passions in Florida than **fishing**: the numerous rivers and lakes and the various breeds of catfish, bass, carp and perch that inhabit them bring eager fishermen from all over the US and beyond. Saltwater fishing is no less popular, with barely a coastal jetty in the state not creaking under the strain of weekend anglers. The most sociable way to fish, however, is from a **"party boat"** – a boatload of people putting to sea for a day of rod-casting and boozing; these generally cost $25 and are easily found in good fishing areas. **Sportsfishing** – heading out to deep water to do battle with marlin, tuna and the odd shark – is much more expensive. In the prime sportfishing areas, off the Florida Keys and off the Panhandle around Destin, you'll need around $200 a day for a boat and a guide. To protect fish stocks, a highly complex set of **rules and regulations** governs where you can fish and what you can catch. For the latest facts, get the free *Florida Fishing Handbook* from the **Florida Game and Freshwater Fish Commission**, 620 Meridian Street, Tallahassee, FL 32399-1600 (☎904/488-1960).

FESTIVALS AND HOLIDAYS

Someone, somewhere is always celebrating something in Florida, although apart from national holidays, few festivities are shared throughout the region. Instead, there is a disparate multitude of local annual events: art and craft shows, county fairs, ethnic celebrations, music festivals, rodeos, sand-castle-building competitions and many others of every description. The most interesting of these are listed throughout the Guide and you can phone the visitor center in a particular region ahead of your arrival to ask what's coming up. For the main festivities in Miami and Miami Beach see p.117 and in Key West, p.137.

NATIONAL FESTIVALS

As with everywhere else in the US, the most important of the annual **national festivals and holidays** celebrated in Florida is **Independence Day** (July 4), when the entire state grinds to a standstill as people get drunk, salute the flag and partake of firework displays, marches, beauty pageants and more, all in commemoration of the signing of the Declaration of Independence in 1776. **Halloween** (October 31) has no such patriotic overtones – in fact it's not even a public holiday despite being one of the most popular yearly flings. Traditionally kids run around the streets banging on doors demanding "trick or treat" and get rewarded with pieces of candy; these days such activity is confined to rural areas, although you will find plenty of evidence of Halloween in cities, with waitresses liable to be disguised as witches or cats and hip city nightspots hosting everyone-dress-in-black specials. More sedate is **Thanksgiving Day** (last Thursday in November), the third big event of the year and essentially a domestic affair with relatives returning to the familial nest to stuff themselves with roast turkey in celebration of the first harvest of the Pilgrim Fathers and the start of the European colonization of North America.

The biggest holiday event to hit Florida is the annual **Spring Break**: a six-week invasion of tens of thousands of students seeking fun in the sun before knuckling down to their summer exams, which usually lasts from the latter part of February through March and early April. Times are changing, however: one traditional Spring Break venue, Fort Lauderdale, has successfully encouraged the students to go elsewhere; another, Daytona Beach, is planning to do likewise. Panama City Beach, though, welcomes the carousing collegiates with open arms and Key West – despite its lack of beach – is fast becoming a favorite Spring Break location. If you are in Florida during this time, it'll be hard to avoid some signs of Spring Break – a mob of scantily clad drunken students is a tell-tale sign – and at the busier coastal areas you may well find accommodation costing three times the normal price; be sure to plan ahead.

PUBLIC HOLIDAYS

On both Independence Day and Thanksgiving Day, shops, banks and offices will be closed for the day, as they will on most of the **other public holidays**: New Year's Day; Martin Luther King's Birthday (January 15); President's Day (third Monday in February); Memorial Day (last Monday in May); Labor Day (first Monday in September); Columbus Day (second Monday in October); Veteran's Day (November 11); and Christmas Day. Good Friday is a half-day holiday, although Easter Monday is a full-day holiday.

STAYING ON

Far from being the land of the "newly wed and the nearly dead" as many comedians have described the state, Florida's immaculate climate has persuaded people from all over the US and the rest of the world to arrive in search of a subtropical paradise. The following suggestions for finding work are basic and if you're not a US citizen represent the limits of what you can do without the all-important Social Security number (without which legally you can't work at all).

FINDING WORK

Since the federal government introduced fines of up to $10,000 for illegal employees, employers have become understandably choosy about whom they hire. Even the usual **casual jobs** – catering, restaurant and bar work – have tightened up for those without a **Social Security number**. If you do find work it's likely to be of the less visible, poorly paid kind – a washer-up instead of waiter. **Agricultural work** is always available on Central Florida farms during the October to May citrus harvest; check with the nearest university or college, where noticeboards detail what's available. There are usually no problems with papers in this kind of work, though it often entails working miles from major centers and is wearying "stoop" (continually bending over) labor in blistering heat. If you can stick it out the pay is often good and comes with basic board and accommodation.

House-cleaning and **baby-sitting** are also feasible, if not very well-paid options.

FINDING A PLACE TO LIVE

Apartment hunting in Florida is not the nightmare it is in, say, New York: accommodation is plentiful and not always expensive, although the absence of housing associations and co-ops means that there is very little really cheap accommodation anywhere except in country areas. Accommodation is almost always rented unfurnished so you'll have to buy furniture; in general, expect to pay $500–600 a month for a studio or one-bedroom apartment, $900–1200 per month for 2–3 bedrooms in Miami, Tampa or Orlando, a lot less in rural areas. Most landlords will expect one month's rent as a deposit, plus one month's rent in advance.

There is no statewide organization for accommodation so you'll have to check out the options in each place. By far the best way to find somewhere is to ask around – often short-term lets come up via word of mouth. Otherwise, rooms for rent are often advertised in the windows of houses and local papers have "Apartments For Rent" sections. In **Miami**, the best source is *New Times*, although you should also scan the *Miami Herald* classifieds. In **Tampa** and **Orlando** check out the *Tampa Tribune* and *Orlando Sentinel* respectively.

OPPORTUNITIES FOR FOREIGN STUDENTS

Foreign students wishing to study in Florida can either try the long shot of arranging a year abroad through their own university, or apply directly to a Florida university (being prepared to stump up the painfully expensive fees).

The Student Exchange Visitor Programme, for which participants are given a J-1 visa enabling them to take a job arranged in advance through the programme, is not much use since almost all the jobs are at American summer camps – of which the state has none. If you're interested anyway, organizations to contact **in the UK** include *BUNAC* (16 Bowling Green Lane, London EC1; ☎071/251 3472) or *Camp America* (37 Queens's Gate, London SW7; ☎071/589 3223).

DIRECTORY

ADDRESSES Though foreign visitors can find them confusing at first, American addresses are masterpieces of logic. Generally speaking, roads in built-up areas are laid out to a grid system, creating "blocks": addresses of buildings refer to the block, which will be numbered in sequence, from a central point, usually somewhere downtown; for example, 620 S Cedar will be six blocks south of this downtown point. In small towns and parts of larger cities, "streets" and "avenues" often run north–south and east–west respectively; streets are usually named (sometimes alphabetically), avenues generally numbered.

CIGARETTES AND SMOKING Smoking is now severely frowned upon in the US, although no government measures have been taken against tobacco advertising. It's possible to spend a month in Florida without ever smelling tobacco; most cinemas are non-smoking, restaurants are usually divided into non-smoking and smoking sections and smoking is universally forbidden on public transport – including almost all domestic airline flights. Work places, too, tend to be smoke-free zones, so employees are reduced to smoking on the street outside. Cigarettes are, however, still widely sold. A packet of twenty costs around $1.95, though most smokers buy cigarettes by the carton for around $12.

DATES In the American style, the date 6.9.94 means not September 6 but June 9.

DEPARTURE TAX None: airport tax is included in the price of your ticket.

DONATIONS Many museums request donations rather than an admission fee; usually you'll be expected to put $2 or so into the collection as you enter. If you don't, you won't be turned away but will suffer the indignity of being considered a complete cheapskate.

DRUGS Despite the widely accepted fact that much of the marijuana and cocaine consumed in the US arrives through Florida, the state's laws regarding possession of drugs are among the toughest in the country. Recreational drug use is by no means unheard of, but many people, even in the cities, view any kind of drug-taking as an attempt to turn the country over to Satan. Bluntly put, as a foreign visitor especially, it isn't worth the risk of being caught in possession of any illegal substance in any quantity whatsoever.

ELECTRICITY 110V AC. All plugs are two-pronged and rather insubstantial. Some travel plug adapters don't fit American sockets. British-made equipment won't work unless it has a voltage switching provision.

FLEA MARKETS Beside almost any major road junction, you'll find something touting itself as "Florida's Biggest Fleamarket". The genuinely big ones usually take place on Fridays and weekends, with hundreds of booths selling furniture, household appliances, ornaments, clothes; often hideous and always cheap.

FLOORS The *first* floor in the US is what would be the ground floor in Britain; the *second* floor would be the first floor and so on.

ID Should be carried at all times. Two pieces should suffice, one of which should have a photo: a passport and credit card(s) are your best bets.

HURRICANES Despite the much-publicized onslaught of Hurricane Andrew in August 1992, statistically it's highly improbable that a hurricane will hit during your visit and even if it does there will be plenty of warning – accurate tracking of potential hurricanes brewing around the Gulf of Mexico and the Caribbean from June to November (regarded as the hurricane season) being a feature of every TV weather bulletin. Local services are well equipped, most buildings are (supposedly) hurricane-proof, evacuation routes are signposted and even phone books carry tips on how to survive – and since Andrew,

Floridians have become much less blasé in their attitude to hurricanes. A more likely source of danger are thunderstorms; see below.

LAUNDROMATS All but the most basic hotels will wash laundry for you, but it'll be a lot cheaper (about $1.50) for a wash and tumble dry in a laundromat – found all over, including many hotels, motels and campgrounds. Take plenty of quarters.

LOTTERY Every few weeks, the state goes potty over the drawing of the winning six-sequence number in the Florida Lottery. Along with millions of others, you can buy as many tickets as you can afford (at a dollar a time) from any shop displaying the lottery sign. The prize sometimes reaches $17 million.

MEASUREMENTS AND SIZES The US has yet to go metric, so measurements are in inches, feet, yards and miles; weight in ounces, pounds and tons. Liquid measurements differ, too: American pints and gallons are about four-fifths of British ones. US clothing sizes can be calculated by subtracting two from British sizes; thus, a British women's size 12 is a US size 10. Shoe sizes are one and a half more than the equivalent British size.

PUBLIC TOILETS Don't exist as such in the city. Bars, restaurants and fast-food outlets are the places to go, although technically you should be a customer.

TAX Be warned that 6 percent sales tax is added to virtually everything you buy in a shop but isn't part of the marked price.

THUNDERSTORMS Subtropical southern Florida has frequent, very localized thunderstorms throughout the summer. Obviously, if possible you should shelter inside a building to avoid being struck by lightning (which, on average, kills eleven people a year). If you're caught in the open, stay away from metallic objects and don't make a dash for your car – most people who are struck are doing this. On the plus side, the air after a storm is refreshingly free of humidity.

TICKETS For music, theater and sports, use *Ticketmaster*, whose offices are plentiful and listed in the phone book and through whom you can buy tickets over the phone by giving your credit card number.

TIME Most of Florida runs on Eastern Standard Time, five hours behind GMT in winter. The section of the Panhandle west of the Apalachicola River, however, is on Central

---

FLORIDA TERMS

Barrier Island A long, narrow island of the kind protecting much of Florida's mainland from coastal erosion, comprising sandy beach and mangrove forest – often blighted by condos (see below).

Condo Short for "condominium", a tall and usually ugly block of (normally) expensive flats, common along the coast and in fashionable areas of cities. Many are rented out for holidays or owned as timeshares.

Cracker Nickname given to Florida farmers from the 1800s, stemming from the sound made by the whip used in cattle round-ups (or possibly from the cracking of corn to make grits). These days it's also a common term for the state's conservative ruralites: surly, insular types who prefer the company of wild hogs to people they don't already know.

Crackerbox Colloquial architectural term for the simple wooden cottage lived in by early Crackers (see above), ingeniously designed to allow the lightest breeze to cool the whole dwelling.

Florida Ice Potentially hazardous mix of oil and water on a road surface following a thunderstorm.

Hammocks Not open-air sleeping places but patches of trees. In the south, and especially in the Everglades, hammocks often appear as "tree islands" above the flat wetlands. In the north, hammocks are larger and occur on elevations between wetlands and pinewoods. All hammocks make excellent wildlife habitats and those in the south are composed of tropical trees rarely seen elsewhere in the US.

Intracoastal Waterway To strengthen coastal defences during World War II, the natural waterways dividing the mainland from the barrier islands (see above) were deepened and extended. The full length, along the east and southwest coasts, is termed the "Intracoastal Waterway".

Key Derived from the word "cay" – literally an island or bank composed of coral fragments.

No see'ems Tiny, mosquito-like insects; near-impossible to spot until they've already bitten you.

Snowbird Term applied to a visitor from the northern US coming to Florida during the winter to escape sub-zero temperatures – usually recognised by their sunburn.

Standard Time – one hour behind the rest of Florida. British Summer Time runs almost parallel to US Daylight Saving Time – implemented from the last Sunday in April to the last Sunday in October – causing a four-hour time gap for two weeks of the year.

TIPPING You really shouldn't depart a bar or restaurant without leaving a tip of *at least* 15 percent (unless the service is utterly disgusting): it causes a lot of embarrassment and nasty looks and a short paypacket for the waiter/waitress at the end of the week. About the same amount should be added to taxi fares – and round them up to the nearest 50¢ or dollar. A hotel porter should get roughly $1 per item for carrying your baggage to your room. When paying by credit or charge card, you're expected to add the tip to the total bill before filling in the amount and signing.

VIDEOS The standard format used for video cassettes in the US is different from that used in Britain. You cannot buy videos in the US compatible with a video camera bought in Britain.

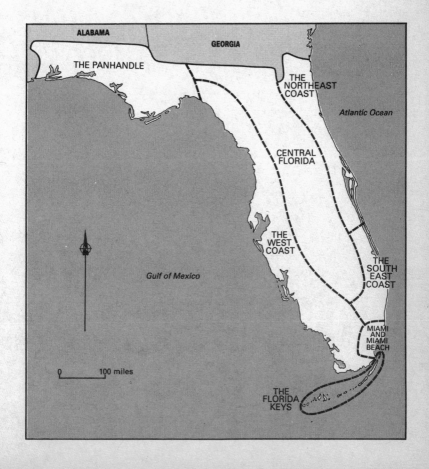

ALABAMA

GEORGIA

THE PANHANDLE

THE NORTHEAST COAST

Atlantic Ocean

CENTRAL FLORIDA

THE WEST COAST

THE SOUTH EAST COAST

Gulf of Mexico

MIAMI AND MIAMI BEACH

0   100 miles

THE FLORIDA KEYS

CHAPTER ONE

MIAMI AND MIAMI BEACH

You tell people you're from Miami and they duck.

Carl Hiaasen.

F ar and away the most exciting city in Florida, **Miami** is a stunning and often intoxicatingly beautiful place. Set beside the cool blue waters of Biscayne Bay, with its roads lined by lush tropical foliage, the state's major urban center – not much bigger than a suburban town – is awash with sunlight-intensified natural colors and a delicious scent of jasmine. An emergent city with a sharp, contemporary style (and some horrific social problems), there are moments, such as when the downtown skyline glows in the warm night and the beachside palm trees sway in the evening breeze, when a better-looking city is hard to imagine.

The climate and landscape may be near perfect, but it's people that make Miami unique. The antithesis of the traditional Anglo-American-dominated US metropolis, half of Miami's two-million population is Hispanic, of which the vast majority are Cubans. They form easily the most visible – and powerful – ethnic group in a city that's home to dozens from all over Latin America and the Caribbean. Spanish is the predominant language almost everywhere, and news from Havana, Caracas or Bogotá frequently gets more attention than the latest word from Washington. The city is no melting pot, however. Ethnic divisions and tensions are often appallingly clear. Since the black ghettoes first erupted in the Sixties, violent expressions of rage – most recently among Haitians and Puerto Ricans – have been a regular feature of Miami life.

HURRICANE ANDREW: SOME CONSEQUENCES

More than a year after **Hurricane Andrew** hit the city, damage and debris – ruined buildings, felled trees and more – was still visible in and around Homestead and parts of South Miami. At the time of writing, the main tourist sights and attractions in these areas were either fully or partially re-opened with normal service expected to be restored by the end of 1993. The opening hours and admission fees given in the *Guide* are the latest available prior to publication but are likely to have altered, if only slightly, by the time of your visit.

Key Biscayne was also severely affected by Hurricane Andrew and, at the time of writing, all of its hotels and several of its restaurants were closed for refurbishment. Again, such establishments were anticipating re-opening in the near future and the information in the *Guide* is given on the assumption that they will have done so.

For a fuller account of Hurricane Andrew, see "History" in *Contexts*.

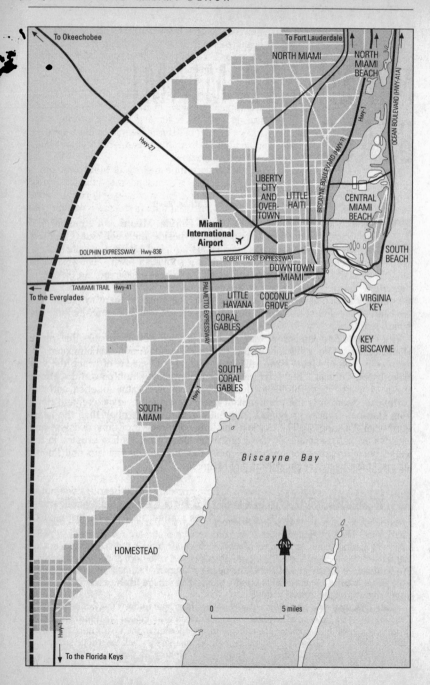

Some sections are still extremely dangerous, but Miami has cleaned itself up considerably since 1980, when it had the highest murder rate in the country. It has also grown rich as a key gateway for US–Latin American trade: globe-trotting brokers now fill a glut of expensively designed banks and financial institutions, rising to symbolize the city's rocketing fortunes. Strangely enough, another factor in Miami's revival has been *Miami Vice*, a cop show less about crime than designer clothes and fabulous subtropical scenery. In the viewer's mind Miami was full of both; in reality it already had the latter and quickly acquired the former as the newly restored Art Deco district of **Miami Beach** – a long and slender strip of land separating mainland Miami from the ocean – became a regular backdrop on the fashion pages of glossy magazines.

Obsessed with the future, Miami has very little history to look back on. A century ago it was a swampy outpost where a thousand mosquito-tormented settlers commuted by boat around a trading post and a couple of coconut plantations. The arrival of the railroad in 1896 gave Miami its first fixed land link with the rest of the continent, and literally cleared the way for the Twenties property boom which saw entire communities appearing almost overnight, forming the basis of the modern city.

In the Fifties, Miami Beach became a celebrity-filled resort area as – with much less fanfare – thousands of Cubans fleeing the successive regimes of Batista and Castro began arriving on mainland Miami. The Sixties and Seventies brought decline: retirees filled Miami Beach, and the Liberty City riot of 1980, marking a low point in Miami's black–white relations, severely damaged the tourist industry on which the city depended.

Since then, with the strengthening of Latin American economic links and a younger and more cosmopolitan breed of visitor energizing Miami Beach, the city is enjoying a surge of optimism and affluence – and, as Hispanic immigration into the US drastically alters the demography of the nation, today's Miami could well be a preview of tomorrow's US.

The area code for Miami and Miami Beach is ☎305.

Arrival and Information

However and whenever you arrive in Miami, grasping initial bearings will not be difficult. All points of entry are within a few miles of the center and public transit links are generally reliable. Numerous offices around the city dispense general tourist information and advice.

By Air

All passenger **flights** land at Miami International Airport, an ultra-modern complex six miles west of downtown Miami. Once through the gate, it's a simple matter to get across the city.

The main **car rental firms** (see "Driving and car rental," below) have desks close to the baggage reclaim area, and provide free transport to collect a vehicle. **Local buses** depart from several points beside the airport's concourse; take #7 to downtown Miami (a half-hour journey), or the "J" bus for the slightly longer journey to Miami Beach. You'll find the bus stop by looking for the "City Bus and Tri-

Rail Shuttle" signs opposite the airport's "E" departure gates. A short cab ride from the airport will deliver you to the Miami West *Greyhound* station, with links to other parts of Miami (see below) and beyond.

Quicker, if more expensive than public transit, the **Airporter**, **SuperShuttle** and **Red Top** minivans (grandly calling themselves "limos") run around the clock and will deliver you to any address in or around Miami for $8–15. Their representatives are easy to spot as you leave the baggage reclaim area. **Taxis** are in good supply, simply step into the nearest one outside the airport building. Fares are around $15 to downtown Miami, and $20 to Miami Beach.

By Bus

Of several **Greyhound** stations in Miami, the busiest is **Miami West**, near the airport at 4111 NW 27th Street (☎871-1810). Most *Greyhound* buses, however, including those to and from from Key West, also call at the **Downtown** station, 700 Biscayne Boulevard (☎372-7222). Fewer services use the city's other *Greyhound* stations: in **Homestead**, 5 NE Third Avenue (☎247-2040); in **Central Miami Beach**, 7101 Harding Avenue (☎538-0381); and in **North Miami Beach**, 16250 Biscayne Boulevard (☎945-0801). Local bus services are detailed on p.59.

By Train and Tri-Rail

The **train** station, 8303 NW 37th Avenue (☎1-800/872-7245), is seven miles north-west of downtown Miami with an adjacent Metrorail stop providing access to downtown Miami and beyond; bus #L stops here on its way to Central Miami Beach. The **Tri-Rail** (☎1-800/TRI-RAIL), the cheap commuter service along the southeast coast (see *Basics*), links directly with the Metrorail at 1149 E 21st Street, also seven miles northwest of downtown Miami. For more information on the Metrorail, see p.59.

By Car

Most of the major **roads** into Miami take the form of elevated expressways which – accidents and rush hours permitting – make getting into the city simple and quick, if potentially hair-raising. From the north, **I-95** (also called the **North South Expressway**) streaks over the downtown streets before joining **Hwy-1**, an ordinary road which continues through South Miami. Crossing the Everglades from the west coast, **Hwy-41** (also called the **Tamiami Trail**) enters Miami along SW Eighth Street, and you'll save time by turning off north along the **Florida Turnpike** (coming from the north and skirting the city's western periphery) to reach the **Dolphin Expressway (Hwy-836)**, which meets I-95 just south of downtown Miami. **Hwy-27**, the main artery from central Florida, becomes the **Robert Frost Expressway** close to the airport and intersects with I-95 just north of the downtown area. The slower, scenic coastal route, **Hwy-A1A**, enters the city at the northern tip of Miami Beach.

Information

Although Miami has no single office devoted to providing tourist information, several useful outlets for leaflets, free tourist magazines and general practical advice are dotted around the city. In **downtown Miami**, outside Bayside Marketplace, an information stand is open from 11.30am to 8pm (☎1-800/283-2707); at **Miami Beach**, the Miami Beach Chamber of Commerce, 1920 Meridian Avenue (Mon–Fri 9am–5pm, Sat 10am–4pm; ☎672-1270), is a good stop.

MIAMI MEDIA

TV Stations

4 WTVJ NBC   **10 WPLG** ABC   **23 WLTV** Spanish-language
6 WCIX CBS   **17 WLRN** PBS   independent
7 WSVN FOX   **33 WBFS** Independent

Radio Stations

WIOD 610 AM. All-talk: phone-ins, entertainment, sports, news.

WINZ 940 AM. All-news format with magazine shows, sports reports, weather and entertainment.

WDNA 89.5 FM. Innovative music shows.

WVUM 90.3 FM. University radio, dominated by British indie rock.

WLRN 91.3 FM. Alternative news, with educational, political and arts programming.

WTMI 93.1 FM. Classical music by day, jazz after midnight.

WLVE 93.9 FM. Pop, jazz and rock.

WZTA 94.9 FM. Classic Sixties rock.

WFLC 97.3 FM. MOR rock.

WEDR 99.1 FM. Soul music, with rap and disco.

WMXJ 102.7 FM. Rock, R&B and soul oldies.

WHQT 105 FM. Black dance music.

Useful **Chambers of Commerce** in other districts are detailed throughout the *Guide*. If you're spending time in Homestead, or just passing through to or from the Everglades or the Florida Keys, be sure to stop at the area's excellent Visitor Information Center, 160 Hwy-1 (daily 8am–6pm; ☎1-800/388-9669).

Any free **maps** you pick up are unlikely to be much use beyond very basic route-finding; it's worth spending $2.50 on the street-indexed *Trakker* map of Miami, available from most newsstands and many shops.

The Friday issue of Miami's only daily **newspaper**, the reputable *Miami Herald* (weekdays 35¢; Sunday edition $1) – also published in Spanish as *El Nuevo Herald* – carries comprehensive weekend entertainment listings. A better source for listings, however, is the weekly *New Times*, free from street machines and many restaurants and bars. Also free, and easily found around the South Beach, *Ocean Drive* carries handy basic info on the local cafés and clubs and the celebs who frequent them.

Getting Around

A small and easily navigated city, Miami seldom presents problems for getting around. It's a city designed for the car, but a comprehensive public transit system provides a sound alternative for daytime travel.

Driving and Car Rental

Driving around Miami is a piece of cake – and certainly the most practical way to get anywhere. Traffic in and out of Miami can be heavy, but the city's **expressways** (see "Arriving", above) will carry you swiftly from one area to another. Only use the ordinary streets and avenues for short journeys; they're often clogged by local traffic, and many districts have confusing one-way systems. Be wary of driving anywhere during **rush hour** (7–9am and 4–6pm), when traffic jams are likely.

MIAMI ADDRESSES: SOME ORIENTATION

Miami's street **naming and numbering system** takes some getting used to. The city splits into quadrants, divided by Flagler Street and Miami Avenue (which intersect downtown). **"Streets"** run east–west and **"avenues"** run north–south, their numbers getting higher the further you go from downtown Miami. **"Roads"** are less common and run northwest–southeast. Streets and avenues change their compass-point prefix when crossing into a new quadrant. For example, SE First Street becomes SW First Street after crossing Miami Avenue, and NW Second Avenue becomes SW Second Avenue after crossing Flagler Street.

In some areas the pattern varies, most obviously in Coral Gables where the streets have names instead of numbers and avenues are numbered in sequence from Douglas Avenue.

Driving between Miami and Miami Beach is straightforward using one of six causeways, each well marked and quickly accessed from the main arteries.

Other than finding a space – exceptionally difficult at night in Coconut Grove and the South Beach – **street parking** won't cause much difficulty. Parking **meters** are everywhere and usually require 50¢–$1 for the first hour, 50¢ for each additional hour. Parking at public **parks and beaches** is normally $2 per day; **parking lots** generally charge $2 an hour, $6 per day. Shopping mall parking lots seldom charge but may have a two-hour time limit.

Most of the major **car rental** companies have booking desks at the airport and provide free transportation to their nearby office to collect a car: *Alamo*, 3355 NW 22nd Street (☎1-800/327-9633); *Avis*, 2330 NW 37th Street (☎1-800/331-1212); *Budget*, 3901 NW 38th Street (☎1-800/527-0700); *Hertz*, 3755 NW 21st Street (☎1-800/654-3131); and *Thrifty*, 2701 Le Jeune Road (☎1-800/367-2277). Each charges around $25 a day, $150 a week. If you want to rent a car in another part of the city, call and ask for the nearest branch office – or just look in the phone book. Depending on the fine print, smaller firms can be cheaper; the pick of the bunch is *Value Rent-a-Car*, 2875 NW Le Jeune Road (☎1-800/327-4847), also with a desk at the airport – around $20 a day, $100 per week.

Public Transit

An integrated **public transit** network of buses, trains and a monorail run by *Metro-Dade Transit* covers Miami, making the city easy – if time-consuming – to get around by day; night travel is much harder.

Bus routes cover the entire city, most radiating out from downtown Miami. Frequencies vary greatly, but major areas are usually linked by at least two services an hour between 6am and 7pm on weekdays, fewer at weekends. On busy routes, such as Miami–Miami Beach, buses run until 10pm or 11pm; otherwise they finish around 7pm. The flat-rate single-journey **bus fare** is $1.25, payable on entry by dropping the exact amount in change (no bills) into a machine beside the driver. If you need to **transfer** to another bus, say so when you get on; the driver will give you a free transfer ticket which you hand over to the driver of the next bus. Transfer tickets are route- and time-stamped to prevent you lingering too long between connections, or taking a scenic detour (if you do so, you'll be charged the full fare again).

Considerably quicker – though much less comprehensive – than the buses, an elevated railroad called the **Metrorail** carries trains every five to fifteen minutes

---

MAJOR MIAMI BUS ROUTES

From downtown Miami to:

Coconut Grove #48.	Key Biscayne #B.
Coral Gables #24.	Miami Beach #C, #F, #K, #M or #S.
Little Havana #8.	Miami International Airport #7.

Greyhound within Miami

From downtown Miami to:

Homestead (3 daily; 1hr 15min)	Miami West (18 daily; 15–45min)
Miami Beach (18 daily; 25–45min)	North Miami Beach (18 daily; 20–45min)

---

from 5.30am to midnight along a single line between the northern suburbs and South Miami. Useful stops are Government Center (for the downtown area), Vizcaya, Coconut Grove and Douglas Road or University (for Coral Gables); the stations tend to be awkwardly situated, however, and you'll often need to use Metrorail services in conjunction with a bus. Single-journey **Metrorail fares** are $1.25; buy a token from the machines (insert five quarters) at the station and use it to get through the turnstile. **Transfers between buses and Metrorail** cost 25¢ from the bus driver or a Metrorail station transfer machine.

Downtown Miami is ringed by the **Metromover** (sometimes called the "People Mover"), a daytime monorail loop that doesn't cover much ground but gives a bird's-eye view of downtown Miami. The flat fare is 25¢, payable into the machines at the stations. Transfers to Metromover from Metrorail are free; to transfer from Metromover to Metrorail, insert $1 in coins into the turnstile between the respective platforms.

Also operated by Metro-Dade Transit and running between South Beach and downtown Miami, at 15-minute intervals between 7pm and 4am on Friday and Saturday and from noon to 4pm on Sunday, for $1.25, are the **Breeze minibuses**, mainly to intended to reduce traffic – and drunken driving – as revellers head to and from South Beach.

Over **long stays** involving regular public transit use, it's economical to buy a **Metropass**, which gives unlimited rides on all services for a calendar month. The *Metropass* costs $60 from any shops displaying the *Metro-Dade Transit* sign, and is on sale from the 20th of the month.

For **information** and free **route maps and timetables**, go to the *Transit Service Center* (daily 7am–6pm) inside the Metro-Dade Center in downtown Miami; or phone ☎638-6700 (Mon–Fri 6am–10pm, Sat & Sun 9am–5pm). Individual route maps and timetables can usually be found on buses.

Beside the official services, **privately run minibuses** (known as "Jitneys") link busy areas for a flat fare of $1. They generally pull up at regular bus stops, but can be waved down practically anywhere: look for the destination board on the front. Note that such buses are unregulated, and rarely insured to carry passengers – you travel on them very much at your own risk.

Taxis

Taxis are abundant, and at night are often the only way to get around without a car. **Fares** average out at $1.80 per mile, making the trip between the airport and Miami Beach – easily the longest journey you're likely to make – around $20, and

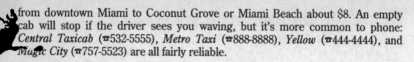

from downtown Miami to Coconut Grove or Miami Beach about $8. An empty cab will stop if the driver sees you waving, but it's more common to phone: *Central Taxicab* (☎532-5555), *Metro Taxi* (☎888-8888), *Yellow* (☎444-4444), and *Magic City* (☎757-5523) are all fairly reliable.

Cycling

You won't be able to see all of Miami by **cycling**, although Coral Gables and Key Biscayne are naturals for pedal-powered exploration, and a fourteen-mile cycle path runs through Coconut Grove and on into South Miami. Read the free leaflet, *Miami on Two Wheels*, available from the Greater Miami Convention and Visitors' Bureau (see "Information", above) for details.

You can **rent a bike** for $12–25 per day from several outlets: in Coconut Grove, *Dade Cycle Shop*, 3216 Grand Avenue (☎443-6075), or in Key Biscayne, *Key Biscayne Bicycle Rentals*, 260 Crandon Boulevard (☎361-5555). For cruising around Miami Beach, you can beat exorbitant hotel bike-rental charges by going to the *Miami Beach Cycle Center*, 923 W 39th Street (☎531-4161), or *Cycles on the Beach*, 713 Fifth Street (☎673-2055).

Walking and Walking Tours

Miamians find it strange that anybody should *want* to **walk** anywhere, but some of the city's more enjoyable areas are compact enough to cover on foot – although they are too far apart to walk between. For an informed and entertaining stroll, take one of **Dr Paul George's Walking Tours**, that look at the pasts and presents of a number of areas: downtown Miami, Coconut Grove, Coral Gables, Little Havana and the Miami Cemetery, among a long list. The walks last two to three hours and cost $13, details on ☎375-1625.

Elsewhere, you shouldn't miss the ninety-minute **Art Deco walking tour** of South Miami Beach. A perfect introduction to the area's phenomenal architecture, the tour begins each Saturday at 10.30am from the *Leslie Hotel*, 1244 Ocean Drive, and costs $6.

On Sundays at 10.30am, you can join a guided **bicycle tour** of the Art Deco district, costing $5 for the tour and $5 for the bike. The tour departs from *Cycles on the Beach* (see above; reservations ☎672-2014).

Guided Tours: by Bus, Boat and Helicopter

Scores of travel companies run **guided bus tours** around Miami's obvious points of tourist interest; usually these are overpriced ($25–40 for a day) and only mildly instructive, but, if you're tempted, pick up their leaflets from any hotel or Chamber of Commerce.

A cheaper and better option is the **Old Town Trolley Tour**: a 90-minute narrated shunt around the main sights of downtown Miami, Coconut Grove, Coral Gables, Little Havana and the Art Deco district. The trolley leaves from the Bayside Marketplace, close to the downtown area, every thirty minutes between 10am and 4pm daily; cost is $7.

If you prefer water to dry land – and the downtown skyline is undoubtedly most striking from across the water – several small craft moored along the jetty at the Bayside Marketplace offer **boat tours** around Biscayne Bay; departure times and prices (usually $20 per person for an hour) are chalked up. One of the longest established is *Bayside Cruises* (☎888-3002), whose 90-minute cruises depart daily at 1pm, 3pm, 5pm, 7pm and 9pm.

Accommodation

Competition is always fierce between Miami's providers of beds, and **finding a place to stay** is never difficult. The small size of the city means that you can stay just about anywhere and not feel isolated, though the lion's share of the **hotels** and **motels** are on **Miami Beach**: an ideal base for nightlife, beachlife – and seeing the city. Prices vary from $20 to $200 but you can anticipate spending $40–75 during the summer, and $60–85 during the winter (up to $100 or more per night in the ultra-chic South Beach hotels). Alternatives to hotels and motels are few. **Bed and breakfast inns** in South Miami offer a homely ambience at good rates but need to be booked far ahead, while **budget accommodation** is restricted to two **youth hostels** in Miami Beach and a **campground** which is miles out in the city's southwest fringe.

Away from Miami Beach, choice is reduced and costs are higher. **Downtown Miami** – good to visit by day but dull at night – has few affordable rivals to expense-account chain hotels; distinctive character and architecture make **Coral Gables** appealing, but its rooms are seldom cheap; the stylish high-rise hotels of **Coconut Grove** are a jet-setters' preserve; and in **Key Biscayne** you'll need $100 a night for the plainest oceanside room. Only in **South Miami**, unremarkable in itself but a feasible base if you're driving, will you find a good assortment of no-frills motels for $40–60 a night. The **airport** area hotels, one bargain among them, should only be considered if you've an inconveniently timed plane to catch.

Seldom will a **single** room be significantly cheaper than a **double**; in the few instances where it is, we've indicated it in the listings.

During the winter, it's highly recommended to reserve **ahead**, either directly or through a travel agent. Between May and October, however, you'll save by going for the best deals on the spot (though you may want to arrange your first night in advance). Don't be afraid to **bargain**; doing so often results in a few dollars being lopped off the advertised rate. The prices listed are for the winter, all will be lower during the summer.

Hotels and Motels

Downtown Miami

Hampton Inn-Downtown, 2500 Brickell Ave (☎1-800/HAMPTON). A generic but perfectly adequate chain motel, a mile from the center of downtown Miami. ④.

Howard Johnson, 200 SE Second Ave (☎1-800/654-2000). Very standard chain hotel but the lowest-priced rooms this close to the heart of downtown Miami. ⑤–⑦.

Inter-Continental Miami, 100 Chopin Plaza (☎1-800/327-0200). Wicker chairs and a Henry Moore sculpture improve the atmosphere of this multinational chain hotel. Very classy and comfortable. ⑧.

ACCOMMODATION PRICE CODES

All accommodation prices in this book have been coded using the symbols below. Note that prices are for the least expensive double rooms in each establishment.
For a full explanation see p.26 in *Basics*.

① up to $30	④ $60–80	⑦ $130–180
② $30–45	⑤ $80–100	⑧ $180+
③ $45–60	⑥ $100–130	

Marina Park, 340 Biscayne Blvd (☎1-800/528-1234). A bland exterior shields a personable interior, with views across the Port of Miami and the neighboring parks. ⑥–⑧.

Occidental Parc, 100 SE Fourth St (☎1-800/521-5000). A good choice, delectably positioned beside the Miami River. All rooms are suites with small kitchens. ⑥–⑦.

Omni International, 1601 Biscayne Blvd (☎1-800/THE-OMNI). Mostly utilized by business folk and wealthy Latin Americans on shopping trips to the expansive downstairs mall. ⑥–⑦.

Coconut Grove

Doubletree at Coconut Grove, 2649 S Bayshore Drive (☎1-800/528-0444). Elegant high-rise with cosy rooms and great views, just a quarter of an hour's walk from the area's cafés and bars. ⑦.

Grand Bay Hotel, 2669 S Bayshore Drive (☎1-800/327-2788). A glass of champagne on arrival is just the start; expense-account elegance throughout. ⑧.

Mayfair House, 3000 Florida Ave (☎1-800/341-0809). Luxury all-suite hotel, complete with rooftop swimming pool. ⑧.

Coral Gables

Biltmore Hotel, 1200 Anastasia Ave (☎1-800/727-1926). A landmark, Mediterranean-style hotel which has endured mixed fortunes since it began pampering the rich and famous in 1926. Show up to pace the echoey corridors and sink into the lobby armchairs even if you can't afford to stay here. ⑥–⑧.

Colonnade Hotel, 180 Aragon Ave (☎1-800/533-1337). Marble floors, oriental rugs and brass lamps fill this showpiece of Mediterranean Revival architecture. ⑤–⑥.

Gables Inn, 730 S Dixie Hwy (☎661-7999). Basic but clean and the cheapest in the area. ③.

Hotel Place St Michel, 162 Alcazar Ave (☎444-1666). Small and romantic hideaway just off the Miracle Mile, with Laura Ashley decor and copious European antiques. Rate includes continental breakfast. ⑤–⑦.

Riviera Courts, 5100 Riviera Drive (☎1-800/368-8602). Simple and homely pool-equipped motel, close to the University of Miami. ④.

Key Biscayne

Sheraton Royal, 555 Ocean Drive (☎1-800/334-8484). Upper bracket beachside hotel with all the amenities you can think of, and some good off-season reductions. ⑧.

Silver Sands Oceanfront Motel, 301 Ocean Drive (☎361-5441). Hardly a bargain, but the simple rooms are the cheapest on the island. ⑥.

Sonesta Beach Hotel, 350 Ocean Drive (☎1-800/SONESTA). High-rise resort with luxurious rooms, sports facilities, bars and a prime stretch of private beach. ⑧.

South Miami and Homestead

A1 Motel, 815 N Krome Ave (☎248-2741). Basic and clean, with some non-smoking rooms and a do-it-yourself laundry. ③–④.

Coral Roc, 1100 N Krome Ave (☎247-4010). Unexciting but fully functional motel. ③–④.

Everglades Motel, 605 S Krome Ave (☎247-4117). Slightly run-down in exterior appearance, but the rooms are okay and there's a coin-operated laundry for guests. ②–③.

Greenstone Motel, 304 N Krome Ave (☎247-8334). Simple and adequate motel in the heart of old Homestead. ③–④.

Hampton Inn, 124 E Palm Drive (☎1-800/HAMPTON). Unpretentious and friendly with good-sized rooms. ④.

Super 8, 1202 N Krome Ave (☎1-800/800-8000). Branch of a plain but cheap motel chain, with clean and reasonably priced rooms. ③.

South Miami Beach

Abbey Hotel, 300 21st St (☎531-0031). Good value, smart and intimate hotel that doesn't overemphasize its Art Deco pedigree. ④–⑤.

Cavalier Hotel, 1320 Ocean Drive (☎534-2135). Recently opened and completely revamped 1930s Art Deco hotel, now featuring neo-Moorish decor. ⑦.

Century Hotel, 140 Ocean Drive (☎674-8855). Stark, deconstructivist chic, right out of the pages of a design magazine. Home away from home for its predominantly fashion-industry clientele. ⑤–⑦.

Clay Hotel, 406 Española Way (☎534-2988). Vintage hotel which functions as the city's only youth hostel (see "Budget Accommodation", below), but has some private rooms. ①.

Colony Hotel, 736 Ocean Drive (☎673-0088). Beautifully refurbished Art Deco delight. ⑤–⑥.

Essex House, 1001 Collins Ave (☎532-3872). Warm atmosphere and one of the more tastefully restored Art Deco hotels. ④–⑥.

Lafayette, 944 Collins Ave (☎673-2262). Pleasant, airy rooms a short walk from the beach strip. ⑦.

Leslie, 1244 Ocean Drive (☎1-800/338-9076). Excellently located on the beachside Art Deco strip with striking interior design – bright colors and crookedly angled mirrors. The rooms are equipped with tape-player/radios as well as TVs. ⑤–⑥.

Marlin, 1200 Collins Ave (☎673-8770). Eleven costly but cosy suites, and a rooftop sun deck. One of the few South Beach hotels with room service. ⑧

Mermaid, 909 Collins Ave (☎538-5324). Cost-effective rooms – some with kitchenettes – in a Caribbean-style cottage. ③–⑤.

Park Central, 640 Ocean Drive (☎538-1611). Among the best of the Art Deco piles, retaining ceiling fans alongside regular air conditioning. ⑥–⑦.

Park Washington, 1020 Washington Ave (☎532-1930). Quiet and cosy, two blocks from the ocean, with a fridge in every spartan room. ④.

Raleigh, 1775 Collins Ave (☎534-6300). The 1990s refurbishment aped the original 1940s look, but added state-of-the-art electronics in every room. Probably the best run and currently the most glamorous hotel in South Beach. ⑥–⑧.

Ritz Plaza, 1701 Collins Ave (☎534-3500). The first Art Deco hotel with room service; also boasts an Olympic-sized pool. ⑦.

Waldorf Towers, 860 Ocean Drive (☎531-7684). Another Art Deco landmark, facing the ocean and right in the throng of the fashionable strip. ⑥.

Central Miami Beach

Alexander Hotel, 5225 Collins Ave (☎1-800/327-6121). Well-equipped suites, free champagne on arrival, mattresses adjusted to your desired firmness. You won't want to leave. ⑧.

Fountainbleau Hilton, 4441 Collins Ave (☎538-2000). Once the last word in glamor, now elaborately refurbished and seeking to regain its lost esteem; a staff of two thousand attends your every whim. ⑦–⑧.

The Golden Sands, 6910 Collins Ave (☎1-800/932-0333). Nothing flash and mostly filled by package-touring Europeans, but likely to turn up the cheapest deals in this pricey area. ③.

North Miami Beach

Beach Motel, 8601 Harding Ave (☎861-2001). Unelaborate motel whose plain rooms are a short trot from the Surfside beach. ③.

Blue Mist, 19111 Collins Ave (☎932-1000). The cheapest in Sunny Isles, its rooms are basic but most face the ocean. ③–④.

Marco Polo Resort, 19201 Collins Ave (☎1-800/432-3663). A hideous conglomeration of Moorish kitsch and Fifties Americana. Grotty rooms, sometimes offered at slashed rates. ④.

Paradise Inn, 8520 Harding Ave (☎865-6216). Neatly tucked into Surfside's main street and one of the best bargains around. ③.

At the Airport

Hampton Inn-Miami Airport, 5125 NW 36th St (☎1-800/HAMPTON). Branch of a good-value hotel chain, with some of the best rates in the airport area. ④.

Hotel MIA, Miami International Airport (☎1-800/327-1276). There's no excuse for missing your plane if you stay here; this stylishly designed and fully equipped hotel is located inside the airport. ⑥-⑦.

Miami Airways Motel, 5001 36th St (☎883-4700). Easily the cheapest in the area. ②.

Quality Inn, 2373 NW Le Jeune Rd (☎1-800/228-5151). Well-presented chain hotel with a beckoning pool. ④.

Budget Accommodation: Youth Hostels and Camping

Impeccably positioned in the heart of South Beach, the city's AYH **youth hostel**, *Hostel International of Miami Beach*, at the *Clay Hotel*, 1438 Washington Avenue (☎534-2988), has beds in small dorms for $10 ($13 for non-IYHA-members) with private singles and doubles also available; see "Hotels and Motels," above. Also in South Beach, the *Miami Beach International Travelers Hostel*, 236 Ninth Street (☎534-0268) offers beds in 4-person dorms for $12 per person.

Staying at either hostel is certainly preferable to **camping** at the horrendously located *Larry & Penny Thompson Memorial Campground*, 12451 SW 184th Street (☎232-1049), twelve miles southwest of downtown Miami and well away from any bus route; $18 per night; weekly $74.

Bed and breakfast

Miami has but one **bed and breakfast** option, the homely *Grandma Newton's*, 40 NW Fifth Avenue, South Miami (☎247-4413; ③), which has just five rooms, each priced around $50. At the time of writing, *Grandma Newton's* was closed due to hurricane damage, but it was expected to re-open by the autumn of 1993.

MIAMI

A diverse place despite its size, many of **Miami**'s districts are officially cities on their own, and each has a distinctive background and character. Some should be explored on foot, but you'll certainly need a car, or local buses, to travel between them. Remember that the mood can switch dramatically within a few blocks, making it easy to stray into hostile territory if you don't stay alert.

The obvious starting point is **downtown Miami**, the small bustling nerve center of the city, whose streets are lined by garishly decorated shops and filled by a startling cross-section of people – bringing a lively human dimension to an area overlooked by futuristic office buildings. Close to the **downtown area** are regions of marked contrast. Those to the north – with a few exceptions – are ugly and dangerous, and infamous for their outbreaks of violent racial unrest. To the south are the international banks that signify Miami's new wealth – and the state-of-the-art residential architecture that comes with it.

Beyond the environs of downtown Miami, the city spreads out in a broad arc to the west and south. The first of Miami's Cubans – who have reshaped the city substantially over the last two decades – settled a few miles west in (what became)

DOWNTOWN MIAMI

Freedom Tower

To Little Haiti & Greyhound Station

PORT BOULEVARD

To Bayside Marketplace

BISCAYNE BLVD

BISCAYNE BOULEVARD

NW5 ST.

NE5 ST.

NORTH MIAMI AVENUE

NE 1 AVENUE

NE 2 AVENUE

Metromover Monorail

NW 2 AVENUE

US Federal Courthouse

New Courthouse

Metro Dade Center

NE 2 ST.

Gesu Church

Historical Museum of Southern Florida

NW 1 ST.

NE 1 ST.

Dade County Courthouse

Alfred Du Pont Building

Main Public Library

Center for the Fine Arts

WEST FLAGLER STREET

EAST FLAGLER STREET

Metromover Monorail

Gusman Center for the Performing Arts

SW 1 ST.

SE 1 ST.

SW 1 AV.

SOUTH MIAMI AVENUE

SE 1 AVENUE

SE 2 AVENUE

SE 3 AVENUE

To Little Havana

SW 2 ST.

SE 2 ST.

SW 2 AVENUE

0   200 yards

To Brickell Avenue

Miami River

Miami River

Little Havana. This is still one of the most enjoyable and intriguing parts of Miami, rich with Latin American looks and sounds but far less solidly Cuban than it used to be. Immediately south, Little Havana's tight streets give way to the spacious boulevards of **Coral Gables**, whose tenderly worked Mediterranean architecture – a far cry from the cheap pastiches which proliferate elsewhere – is as impressive now as it was in the Twenties, when it set new standards in town planning. South of the downtown area, **Coconut Grove** is mounting a strong bid to become Miami's trendiest quarter: beautifully placed alongside Biscayne Bay with a plethora of neatly appointed streetside cafés to linger in – and ample remains from earlier times to fill your time more purposefully.

Beyond Coconut Grove and Coral Gables, **South Miami** is a lacklustre residential sprawl with few noteworthy aspects, fading into farming territory on Miami's southern edge, and into the barren expanse of the Everglades to the west. Given the choice, **Key Biscayne** is a better destination: a classy, secluded island community with some beautiful beaches, five miles off the mainland but easily reached by causeway.

Downtown Miami

Don't try to relax in **DOWNTOWN MIAMI**: humanity storms down its short streets, rippling the gaudy awnings of countless cut-price electronics, clothes and jewellery stores, easing up only to buy imported newspapers, or to gulp down a spicy snack and a glass of mango juice from a roadside fast-food stand.

Since the early Sixties, when newly released Cuban Bay of Pigs veterans came here to spend their US Government back pay, the predominantly Spanish-speaking businesses of the downtown square mile have reaped the benefits of any boost in South or Central American incomes. The recipients pour into Miami airport and move downtown in droves, seeking the goods they can't find at home. Minorities in the throng include dazed-looking Japanese and European tourists, clean-cut Anglo-Americans with local government jobs and street people of inde-terminate origin, dragging their worldly possessions with them. Only some solid US public architecture and whistle-blowing traffic cops remind you that you're still in Florida and not on the main drag of a seething Latin American capital.

The nerve-jangling (though by day relatively safe) streets, and the feeling they induce of being at the crossroads of the Americas, are reasons enough to spend half a day in downtown Miami, but there's also an excellent historical collection, a well-stocked library and an oddly art-filled old courthouse to investigate. Don't ignore, either, the many small Cuban cafés (see "Eating"); stopping for a quick *café Cubano* will revive your senses when the street melange becomes too much.

Along Flagler Street and the Metro-Dade Cultural Center

Nowhere makes a better first taste of downtown Miami than **Flagler Street**, by far the loudest, brightest, busiest strip, and long the area's center attraction. Start at the eastern end by glancing inside the 1938 **Alfred Du Pont Building**, no 169 E, now housing the *Florida National Bank* (go up to the first floor), whose fanciful wrought-iron screens, bulky brass fittings, and frescoes of Florida scenes epito-mize the decorative mood that gripped US architects at the end of the Depression.

Nearby, the even less restrained **Gusman Center for the Performing Arts**, no 174 E, began life in the Twenties as a vaudeville theater with all the exquisitely kitsch trappings you'd expect inside a million-dollar building designed to resemble a Moorish palace. The turrets, towers and intricately detailed columns remain (having been saved from the wrecker's ball in 1972), and a crescent moon still flits across the star-filled ceiling. Unfortunately, the only way to get a look at the inter-ior (the exterior is far less interesting) is by buying a ticket for a show: classical and contemporary music and dance are staged here from October to June. Make a night of it if you can; get show details from the ticket booth or on ☎372-0925.

Continuing on, four forbidding Doric columns mark the entrance to the **Dade County Courthouse**, no 73 W. Built in 1926 on the site of an earlier courthouse – and one-time public hangings – this was Miami's tallest building for fifty years, its night time lights showing off a distinctive ziggurat peak, and beaming out a warning to wrong-doers all over the city.

The Metro-Dade Cultural Center

Little inside the courthouse is worth passing the security check for (the juiciest cases are tried in the new US Courthouse; see "North of Flagler Street"), and you should cross SW First Avenue towards what looks like a giant air-raid shelter but turns out to be – once you ascend the entrance ramp off Flagler Street – the **Metro-Dade Cultural Center**. This was an ambitious attempt by the renowned architect Philip Johnson to create a post-Modern Mediterranean-style piazza, a congenial gathering place around which Miami could show itself a custodian of art and culture. The theory almost worked: superb art shows, historical collections and a major library frame the courtyard, but Johnson forgot the power of the south Florida sun. Rather than pausing to rest and gossip, most people scamper across the open space towards the nearest shade.

Facing the plaza, the **Historical Museum of Southern Florida** (Mon–Wed, Fri & Sat 10am–5pm, Thurs 10am–9pm, Sun noon–5pm; $4) combines shade with a comprehensive peek into the multifaceted past of south Florida. The section on the Seminole in particular has a strong collection of photographs and artefacts, revealing much about the native Americans' lifestyle (the Creek Indians began arriving in what was then Spanish-ruled Florida during the eighteenth century, fleeing persecution further north). More fine stuff covers the trials and tribulations of early Miami settlers, putting faces to names such as Tuttle and Brickell that crop up as street, park or bridge titles all over the city. The fluctuating fortunes of Miami Beach are also well chronicled: from the early days as a celebrities' vacation spot – with amusing photos of Twenties Hollywood greats – through the subsequent decline and the recent re-emergence of the Art Deco strip.

A few yards from the historical museum, the **Center for the Fine Arts** (Tues, Wed, Fri & Sat 10am–5pm, Thurs 10am–9pm, Sun noon–5pm; $5) has no permanent collection but showcases outstanding international travelling exhibitions. Directly opposite is the **Main Public Library** (Mon–Wed, Fri & Sat 9am–5pm, Thurs 9am–9pm, Sun 1–5pm; closed Sun in summer), which, beside the usual lending sections, has temporary exhibits on arty and literary themes and a massive collection of Florida magazines and books.

Adjoining the Cultural Center, the **Metro-Dade Center** (also called Government Center) chiefly comprises county government offices, but useful bus and train timetables can be gathered from the **Transit Service Center** (daily 7am–6pm) by the Metrorail entrance at the eastern side of the building.

North of Flagler Street

The tempo drops and the storefronts become less brash as you walk north of Flagler Street. A busy Hispanic procession passes in and out of the 1925 **Gesù Church**, 118 NE Second Street, a Catholic church whose Mediterranean Revival exterior and stylishly decorated innards make a pleasing splash, but otherwise nothing slows you down on the way to the Neoclassical **US Federal Courthouse**, 300 NE First Avenue (Mon–Fri 8.30am–5pm).

Finished in 1931, the building first functioned as a post office; Miami's then negligible crime rate required just one room on the second floor reserved for judicial purposes. The room did acquire a monumental **mural**, however: *Law Guides Florida's Progress*, by Denman Fink (the designer of much of Coral Gables, see p.75), a 25-foot-long depiction of Florida's evolution from swampy backwoods to modern state. If the courtroom's locked, ask a security guard to open it up. In 1985, David Novros, a fresco artist, was commissioned to decorate the building's medieval-style inner **courtyard**, to which his bold daubs of dark green and black, gradually giving way to bright reds, oranges and blues, make a lively addition.

By the late Sixties, Miami crime levels became too much for the old court-house to handle, and the building of a $22 million **New Courthouse** was started next door (main entrance on North Miami Ave; Mon–Fri 8.30am–5pm). A grue-some creation in concrete and glass, the major advantage of the new courthouse – other than size – over the old is that jurors can get in and out unobserved: "Getting them out without getting them dead," as one judge enthused.

Around Downtown Miami

A few polite parks and shopping precincts are within easy walking distance, but you'll need a car or a bus to make much progress **around downtown Miami**. To the north lies one of the most strongly defined ethnic areas in the city, although it borders a desolate, poverty-stricken district which you should take care to avoid. In total contrast, if you go south, an extraordinary line of swanky modern banks and spectacular apartments show off Miami's freshly found affluence. To the west, incidentally, only several miles of uninspired houses fill the gap between downtown Miami and Little Havana (described on p.71).

North of Downtown Miami

The Eighties saw the destruction of some decaying but much-loved buildings beside **Biscayne Boulevard** (part of Hwy-1) to make way for the **Bayside Marketplace** (Mon–Sat 10am–10pm, Sun noon–8pm), an oversized, overpriced, pink-colored shopping mall. Enlivened by mindlessly enjoyable street musicians and boasting some choice international food stands, the place is less hideous than might be expected, but is clearly aimed at tourists. If you're in the mood, a number of pleasure trips around the bay begin here (see "Guided tours" for more) – and, in case you've ever wondered, it was just to the south, on the yacht-filled marina of Bayfront Park of the Americas, that *Miami Vice*'s Sonny Crockett moored his floating home.

To the north of the Bayside Marketplace, endless lines of container-laden semis turning into Port Boulevard attest to the **Port of Miami**'s importance – now among the world's biggest cargo and cruise ship terminals. Just beyond, the perpetual flame of the *John Kennedy Memorial Torch of Friendship* symbolizes good relations between the US and its southern neighbors and guards the entrance to **Bicentennial Park**, filled with markers to various US-approved Central American luminaries.

Across Biscayne Boulevard, the **Freedom Tower**, originally the home of the now defunct *Miami News*, earned its current name by housing the Cuban Refugee Center from 1962. Most of those who left Cuba on the "freedom flights"* got their first taste of US bureaucracy here – a 1925 building modelled on a Spanish bell tower. Restoration has kept the doors closed for some years – the

---

* Between December 1965 and June 1972, ten empty planes a week left Miami and returned filled with Cubans – over 250,000 in total – allowed to leave the island by Fidel Castro. While US propaganda hailed them as "freedom fighters", most of the arrivals were simply seeking the fruits of capitalism, and, as Castro astutely recognized, any that were seriously committed to overthrowing his regime would be far less trouble-some outside Cuba.

Mediterranean features are more impressive from a distance, anyway – with plans afoot for the building to open up as offices topped by a gourmet restaurant.

Beyond the Freedom Tower, there's little more to see within walking distance, and you're on the fringe of some of the city's most impoverished – and dangerous – neighborhoods. Within reach, though, is the **City of Miami Cemetery**, on the corner of North Miami Avenue and NE Eighteenth Street, where used syringes litter the graves, anything valuable has been stolen, and the family vaults of early Miami bigwigs have had their doors torn off by the homeless seeking shelter. There are historical stories aplenty here, only safely heard on periodic **walking tours**; call ☎375-1625 for details.

Continuing North: Little Haiti and the Police Museum

About 170,000 **Haitians** live in Miami, forming one of the city's major ethnic groups – albeit far behind the Cubans in number. Roughly a third of them live in what's become known as **LITTLE HAITI**, a two-hundred-block area that centers on NE Second Avenue, north of 42nd Street (buses #9 or #10 from the downtown area). Aside from hearing Haitian Creole on the streets (almost all Miami's Haitians speak English as a third langauge, after Creole and French), you'll notice the brightly colored shops, offices and restaurants (Haitian food being the latest rage among Miami's food snobs; see "Eating"). The *Caribbean Marketplace*, 5927 NE Second Avenue (Tues–Sun 9am–8pm), is an entertaining attempt to sate tourists' curiosity – proffering a mouthwatering array of tropical fruits and Haitian delicacies, such as fried goat – though for more substantive insights into Haitian concerns, visit the **Haitian Refugee Center**, 32 NE 56th Avenue, where you'll quickly be informed as to why Haitians remain one of the more oppressed immigrant groups in Miami, most scraping their living as taxi drivers or hotel maids.

Close to Little Haiti (buses #3, #16 or #95 from downtown Miami), the **American Police Hall of Fame & Museum**, 3801 Biscayne Boulevard (daily 10am–5.30pm; $6), occupies the former local FBI headquarters and easily takes up a spare hour. Besides "Support your local police" suspenders, CIA baseball caps and the car from the film *Blade Runner*, the first floor is devoted to a somber memorial to slain police officers. Upstairs, there's a lot to dwell on: texts on gangsters; a dope addict's kit; an arsenal of weapons found on highways; the roadgang leg-irons still used in Tennessee; and moments of humor, too, including a signed photo of Keith Richards, a member of the museum's celebrity advisory board.

Without doubt, the Police Museum is ironically located: a shrine to law and order neighboring Liberty City and Overtown, scene of some of Miami's most desperate living.

Liberty City and Overtown

In December 1979, after a prolonged sequence of unpunished assaults by white police officers against members of the black community, a respected black professional, Arthur MacDuffie, was dragged off his motorbike in **LIBERTY CITY** and beaten to death by a group of white officers. Five months later, an all-white jury acquitted the accused: the following night, May 18, 1980, Miami – from Carol City to the north to Homestead to the south – was blazing. Reports of shooting, stone throwing and whites being dragged from their cars and attacked, and in some cases burned alive, were rife. The violence began on Sunday and roadblocks sealing off black districts stayed in place until Wednesday; a city-wide curfew lasted until Friday, and in the final tally eighteen were dead (mostly blacks killed by police and National Guardsmen), hundreds injured, and damage property was estimated at over $200 million.

Incredibly, the "worst racial paroxysm in modern American history" (not the first nor probably the last violent expression of Miami's racial tensions) signalled an upturn in Miami's broader fortunes, coming just as the city was establishing itself as a hub of Latin American finance, and about to became fashionable through *Miami Vice*. Even Liberty City (which, thanks to the national media, had given its name to the "Liberty City riot", although the trouble had been all over Miami) soon found a chic international fashion district (see "The Stores") springing up in the disused warehouses on its periphery – the western edge of Little Haiti. Miami's blacks have nonetheless remained at the bottom of the city's social heap. From the earliest days, "Coloredtown", as **OVERTOWN** was previously known, was divided by train tracks from the white folks of downtown Miami, and by the Thirties – when its jazz clubs thrilled multiracial audiences – conditions were so bad and overcrowding so extreme that Liberty City was built in an adjoining area to ease the strain.

In recent decades, Miami's black–white relations have been complicated by the extraordinary scale of Hispanic immigration, causing the city's Afro-Americans to miss out even on the menial jobs that elsewhere in the US are – unhappily – their traditional preserve, and leading to a unique form of political dispossession. This was borne out by the official snub delivered by the city's Cuban-American mayor, Xavier Suarez, to the visit of the ANC's deputy leader, Nelson Mandela, in June 1990. The incident, which stemmed from Mandela's refusal to denounce Fidel Castro, stimulated a well-organized **black boycott** of the city's lucrative tourist industry, causing black professional organizations around the US to cancel conventions planned for Miami. Dubbed the "quiet riot", the boycott had by July 1991 cost the city $12 million in lost revenue.

Needless to say, these areas (and certain parts of Coconut Grove, North Miami Beach and South Miami) are not only depressing but dangerous; you may find, particularly if you're white, that your very presence is seen as a provocation. If you do find yourself unwittingly driving through the area, keep your windows closed, doors locked, be wary when stopping at lights and do not leave your car.

If you've a serious interest in the Afro-American contribution to Miami and Florida, head for the **Black Archives History and Research Foundation of South Florida**, at 5400 NW 22nd Avenue (Mon–Fri 1–5pm; free; ☎636-2390), a resource center which also arranges guided tours through black historical areas.

South of Downtown Miami: the Miami River and Brickell Avenue

Fifteen minutes' walk south from Flagler Street, the **Miami River** marks the southern limit of downtown. If you're delayed in crossing by the drawbridge being raised to allow a ship through, glance towards the *Hotel Inter-Continental*, at the river's mouth, whose concrete modernity does nothing to suggest that Henry Flagler's *Royal Palm Hotel* stood there at the turn of the century. At the behest of Miami's biggest landowners, Flagler – a millionaire oil baron whose railroad opened up Florida's east coast and brought wealthy wintering socialites to his string of smart hotels – had extended the rail line here from Palm Beach. His luxury hotel and subsequent dredging of Biscayne Bay to accommodate cruise ships, did much to put Miami on the map. One landowner, William Brickell, ran a trading post on the south side of the river, an area now dominated by **Brickell Avenue**, beginning immediately across the SE Second Avenue bridge.

Running from here to Coconut Grove (see p.79), Brickell Avenue was *the* address in 1910s Miami, easily justifying its "millionaires' row" nickname. While the original grand homes have largely disappeared, money is still Brickell Avenue's most obvious asset: once over the bridge, you're facing a half-mile parade of **banks**, the largest group of international banks in the US. The impact of their tall, sheer-sided forms is softened by their sculpture-filled forecourts, fountains and palm trees. Far from being places to change a travellers' check, these institutions are bastions of international high finance. From the late Seventies, Miami emerged as a corporate banking center, cashing in on political instability in South and Central America by offering a secure home for Latin American money. Among it, it would be naive not to add, was a lot of dirty money that needed laundering: tales of dark-suited men depositing cash-filled suitcases are not without foundation.

The sudden rise of the Brickell banks was matched by new condominiums of breathtaking design a few blocks further along. These astronomically priced abodes (which you may recognize from the opening sequence of *Miami Vice*) include in their pastel-shaded midst the most stunning modern building in Miami: **the Atlantis**, at no 2025. First sketched on a napkin in a Cuban restaurant, and finished in 1983, the *Atlantis* crowned several years of innovative construction by a small architectural firm called Arquitectonica, whose style – attracting descriptions such as "beach blanket Bauhaus" and "ecstastic modernism" – fused post-Modern thought with a strong sense of Miami's bizarre architectural heritage. The building's focal point is a gaping square hole through its middle where a palm tree, a jacuzzi and a red-painted spiral staircase tease the eye. Unless you know someone who lives there, you can't go inside the *Atlantis*, which might be just as well: even its designers admit the interior doesn't live up to the exuberance of the exterior, and claim the building to be "architecture for 55mph" – in other words, seen to best effect from a passing car.

Little Havana

Unquestionably the largest and most visible ethnic group in Miami, the impact of **Cubans** on the city over the last three decades has been incalculable. Unlike most Hispanic immigrants to the US, who trade one form of poverty for another, Miami's first Cubans had already tasted affluence when they arrived en masse during the late Fifties and, rising quickly through the social strata, were soon enjoying more of the same here – and now wield considerable clout in the running of the city.

The initial home of the Miami Cubans was a few miles west of downtown Miami in what became **LITTLE HAVANA**, whose streets, if the tourist brochures are to be believed, are filled by old men in *guayaberas* (billowing cotton shirts) playing dominoes, and exotic restaurants whose walls vibrate to the pulsating rhythms of the homeland. Naturally, the reality is quite different: Little Havana's parks, memorials, shops and food stands all reflect the Cuban experience – and as such shouldn't be missed – but the streets are quieter than those of downtown Miami (except during the Little Havana festival in early March – see "Miami's Festivals"). Like their US peers, as soon as the early settlers acquired

CUBANS IN MIAMI: SOME BACKGROUND

Proximity to the Caribbean island has long made Florida a place of refuge for Cuba's activists: from José Martí in the 1890s to Fidel Castro in the early Fifties, the country's radicals arrived to campaign and raise funds, and numerous deposed Cuban statesmen have whiled away their exile in Florida.

During the mid-Fifties, when opposition to Cuba's Batista dictatorship – and the country's subservient role to the US – began to assert itself, a trickle of Cubans started arriving in a predominantly Jewish section of Miami called Riverside, moving into low-rent properties vacated as the extant community grew wealthier and moved out. The trickle became a flood when Fidel Castro took power; the area became **Little Havana**, Cuban businesses sprang up along SW Eighth Street, and Cubans began making their mark on Miami life.

Unsurprisingly, those who left Cuba were not peasants but the affluent middle classes with most to lose under communism. Regarding themselves as the entre-preneurial sophisticates of the Caribbean, stories are plentiful of high-flying Cuban capitalists who arrived penniless in Little Havana, took shit-shoveling jobs, and, over the course of two decades – aided by a formidable network of old ex-pats – toiled, wheeled and dealed their way steadily upwards to positions of power and influence (and not just locally, leading Miami Cubans also hold considerable sway over the US government's policy towards Cuba).

The second great Cuban influx into Miami was of a quite different social nature: the **Mariel boatlift** brought 125,000 islanders from the Cuban port of Mariel to Miami in May 1980. Unlike their worldly-wise predecessors, these arrivals were poor and uneducated, and a fifth of them were fresh from Cuban jails – incarcerated for criminal rather than political crimes. Bluntly put, Castro had called the bluff of the US administration and dumped his misfits on Miami. Only a few of them wound up in Little Havana: most "Marielitos" settled in Miami Beach's South Beach and proceeded to terrorize the local community, thereby becoming a source of embar-rassment to Miami's longer-established and determinedly respectable Cubans.

sufficient dollars, they gave up the tightly grouped, modest homes of Little Havana for fully fledged suburban living.

Seeing Little Havana

For all the powerful emotions stirred up by its politics, Little Havana doesn't have an awful lot to see; the appeal of the place is almost all atmosphere. On the graffi-tied streets, the prevailing mood is one of a community carrying on its daily busi-ness, and while the sights, smells and sounds are distinctly Cuban, many of the people you'll pass – at least those under fifty – are less likely to be Cuban than Nicaraguan or Colombian: the latest immigrant groups in Miami to use Little Havana as a first base.

Only the neighborhood's main strip, SW Eighth Street, or **Calle Ocho** (a direct Spanish translation), offers more than houses: on its course, tiny cups of sweet Cuban coffee are consumed from street-side counters, the odors of cigars being rolled and bread being baked periodically waft across the sidewalk, botan-ica shops sells *Santeria* (a Voodoo-like religion of African origin) ephemera beside six-foot-high models of Catholic saints, and you'll spot the only branch of *Dunkin' Donuts* to sell guava-filled doughnuts.

Exile Politics

However much Miami Cubans have prospered in the US, for many the "liberation" of their country is rarely far from their minds. Some older Cubans – driven by fanatical hatred of Fidel Castro and communism – still consider themselves to be in exile, though few would seriously think about giving up their comfortable lifestyles to return, whatever regime governs Cuba.

Within the complexities of Cuban exile politics, there's a major rift: one school of thought holds that the US sold Cuba out to the USSR, beginning when President Kennedy* withheld air support from the invading Brigade 2056 at the Bay of Pigs in 1961, and favors a violent overthrow of the communist regime with a return to the survival-of-the-fittest ethic of the old days. The more pragmatic line runs that, like it or not, the Cuban clock can't be turned back, and the only way for exiled Cubans to be usefully involved is to face up to the present situation and use their economic muscle to bring about changes.

Fuelled by a mix of *machismo* and hero-worship of early Cuban independence fighters, passions run high and action – usually violent action – has been prized more than words. In Miami, Cubans have been killed for being *suspected* of advocating dialogue with Castro. One man had his legs blown off for suggesting violence on the streets was counterproductive, and the Museum of Cuban Arts and Culture was bombed for displaying the work of Castro-approved artists.

While the atmosphere has calmed down lately, it's hard to see the feuding ending until the more fanatical factions die out, Castro himself expires, and Cuba emerges from the hardline communism which increasingly isolates it from the rest of the world.

---

* In 1978, the US government's House Select Committee on Assassinations listed a (still active) Miami-based Cuban "action group", Alpha 66, as having "the motivation, capability, and resources" to have assassinated President Kennedy, and various, if unsubstantiated, links to the alleged assassin, Lee Harvey Oswald.

Along Calle Ocho

The most pertinent place to begin seeing Little Havana is on Calle Ocho between Twelfth and Thirteenth avenues, where the **Brigade 2506 Memorial**, a simple stone inscribed with the brigade crest, topped by the Cuban flag and ringed by sculptured bullets, remembers those who died at the Bay of Pigs on April 17, 1961, during the attempt by a group of US-trained Cuban soldiers to invade the island and wrest control from Castro.

Depending on who tells the story, the action was either merely ill-conceived, or else highlighted the lack of commitment to Cuba by the US – to this day, sections of the Cuban community hate the then US president John Kennedy only slightly less than they hate Fidel Castro. Veterans of the landing, and many others, gather here on the anniversary: a strange sight of middle-aged men dressed in combat fatigues carrying assault rifles and making all-night-long pledges of patriotism.

A less emotionally charged local gathering place is a few yards away: the **Maximo Lopez Domino Park**, filling a corner of Fourteenth Avenue, to which entry to the open-air tables is (quite illegally) restricted to men over 55. This is one place where you really *will* see old men in *guayaberas* playing dominoes.

Besides discussing the fate of Cuba, the domino players might also be passing judgement on the **Latin Quarter**, described by city planners as an attempt to "create a world renowned showcase of Latin American culture", that's replacing a line of old buildings on the north side of Calle Ocho. Most Cuban objections to the scheme are to the name which doesn't, they claim, do justice to the Cuban influence in the area. More generally, the development seems destined to be a Hispanicized version of Bayside Marketplace (see "Around Downtown Miami"), with Spanish-style ceramics, plazas and fountains decorating pricey boutiques and eateries intended to woo tourists. As the fancy tilework of the Calle Ocho *McDonalds* proves, a fake-Hispanic wrapping doesn't guarantee the contents – the Latin Quarter might well be worth avoiding.

Further west, the peaceful greenery of **Woodlawn Cemetery**, between 32nd and 33rd avenues (daily sunset–dusk), belies the scheming and skulduggery that some of its occupants indulged in while alive. Two former Cuban heads of state lie here: Gerardo Machado, ousted from office in 1933, is in the mausoleum, while one of the playmakers in his downfall, Carlos Prío Socarras, president for four years from 1948, lies just outside. Also interred in the mausoleum (marked only by his initials) is **Anastasio Somoza**, dictator of Nicaragua until overthrown by the Sandinistas in 1979, and later killed in Paraguay. His niece, in a sharp indication of the linkage of Miami to Central American affairs, lives nearby and runs a restaurant.

Around Calle Ocho

With nondescript low-income housing to the north, and modest Spanish Revival Twenties bungalows to the south, the streets around Calle Ocho don't demand much of your time. One place which might detain you for a while, though, is the **Museum of Cuban Arts and Culture**, 1300 SW Twelfth Avenue (usually open Wed–Sun 1–5pm; $2; for latest opening times ring ☎858-8006), which suffered a bomb attack in 1989. Inside, a permanent stock of around two hundred paintings reflects the main historical currents in Cuban art – temporary shows of contemporary work have to be carefully chosen to avoid inflaming local passions and another possible bombing.

With little else to do, you might drop into the *La Esquina de Tejas* restaurant, 101 SW Twelfth Avenue, for a snack and to mull over the signed photos of Ronald Reagan on the walls. It was in this otherwise ordinary Cuban eatery that the re-election-seeking president took a well-publicized lunch in 1983, his advisors having realized the power of the Cuban vote in Miami. Four years later, George Bush called by for a swift *café Cubano* and a drawn-out photo-call. Aside from admiration of his right-wing domestic policies, Reagan's immense popularity among Miami Cubans was due in no small measure to his support for the Nicaraguan Contras, viewed as kindred spirits in the guerrilla struggle against communism (it's widely acknowledged that the Contras ran their anti-Sandinista operation from offices in Miami and trained for combat in the Everglades). The community's affection was demonstrated by the renaming of Twelfth Avenue as "Ronald Reagan Boulevard".

There's no point in actually going there (except for a sports event; see "Listings"), but from here you can see the rising hump of the 70,000-seat **Orange Bowl** stadium, about ten blocks north. The home of the Miami University *Hurricanes* is remembered despairingly by older Cubans as the place where, on a December night in 1962, John Kennedy took the Brigade 2056 flag and vainly promised to return it "in a free Havana".

Coral Gables

All of Miami's constituent cities are fast to assert their individuality, but none has a greater case than **CORAL GABLES**, south of Little Havana: twelve lusty square miles of broad boulevards and leafy streets lined by finely realized Spanish and Italian architecture; a cultured setting for a cultured community that makes the much more famous Art Deco district (see "South Beach") seem decidedly uncouth.

Whereas Miami's other early property developers built cheap and fast in search of a quick buck, Coral Gables' creator was a local man, **George Merrick**, more of an aesthete than an entrepreneur. In love with Mediterranean Europe, Merrick raided street names from a Spanish dictionary – by an unforeseen coincidence, many who live here now are wealthy, Spanish-speaking Cubans – and enlisted his artist uncle Denman Fink, and architect Phineas Paist, to plan the plazas, fountains and carefully aged stucco-fronted buildings defining his intended paradise.

Coral Gables land started selling overnight: in five years from the first sale in 1921, $150 million poured in, a third of which Merrick channelled into the biggest advertising campaign ever known. While Coral Gables quickly took shape, the Florida property boom ended as quickly and as spectacularly as it began (see "History" in *Contexts*, for the full account) and wiped Merrick out. He ran a fish-

---

CORAL GABLES: THE ENTRANCES

Merrick wanted people to know they'd arrived somewhere special as soon as they entered Coral Gables, and eight grand **entrances** were planned on the main access roads. Only four were completed before the bust. Of these, the most impressive are to the north, along a two-and-a-half-mile stretch of SW Eighth Street.

The million-dollar **Douglas Entrance** (junction with Douglas Road) was the most ambitious, consisting of a gateway and tower with two expansive wings of shops, offices and artists' studios. During the Sixties it was almost bulldozed to make room for a supermarket, but survived to become a well-scrubbed business area, still upholding Merrick's Mediterranean themes. Further west, the sixty-foot-high vine-covered **Granada Entrance** (junction with Granada Boulevard) allegedly resembles the entrance to the city of Granada in Spain. A better appetizer for Coral Gables is the **Country Club Prado Entrance** (junction with Country Club Prado), an expensive recreation of a formal Italian garden, bordered by freestanding stucco-and-brick pillars topped by ornamental urns and lamps hanging from fancy wrought-iron brackets.

The "Villages"

Driving (or cycling) around the less busy parts of Coral Gables, you'll catch glimpses of several **"Villages"**, small pockets of globe-spanning residential architecture intended to add diversity to the area's Mediterranean looks. These include the brightly colored roofs and ornately carved balconies of the **Chinese Village**, on the "5100" blocks of Riviera Drive, the timber-beamed town houses of the **French Normandy Village**, on Le Jeune Road, and the "400" blocks of Viscaya Avenue and, perhaps strangest of all, the twisting chimneys and scroll-work arches of the **Dutch South African Village**, also on the "400" block of Viscaya Avenue.

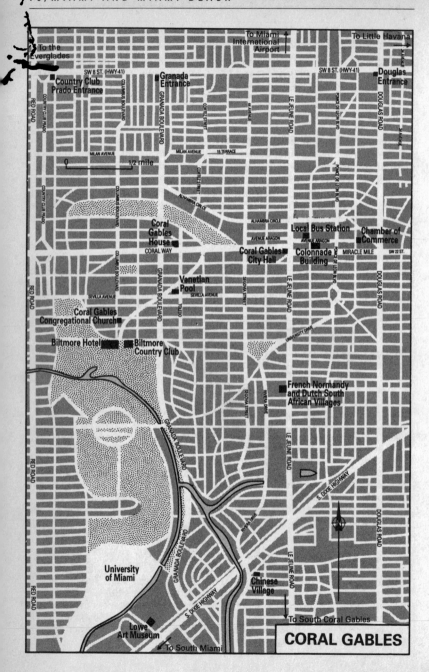

To Miami
International
Airport

To Little Havana

To the
Everglades

SW 8 ST. (HWY-41)

Country Club
Prado Entrance

Granada
Entrance

SW 8 ST. (HWY-41)

Douglas
Entrance

COLUMBUS BOULEVARD

GRANADA BOULEVARD

CORTEZ STREET

44 AVENUE

LE JEUNE ROAD

PONCE DE LEON BLVD

DOUGLAS ROAD

MILAN AVENUE

MILAN AVENUE

16 TERRACE

0   1/2 mile

ALHAMBRA CIRCLE

COUNTRY CLUB PRADO

ALHAMBRA CIRCLE

Coral
Gables
House

AVENUE ARAGON

Local Bus Station

Chamber of
Commerce

RED ROAD

AVENUE ARAGON

Coral Gables
City Hall

Colonnade
Building

MIRACLE MILE

SW 22 ST.

CORAL WAY

COLUMBUS BOULEVARD

GRANADA BOULEVARD

SEGOVIA STREET

LE JEUNE ROAD

PONCE DE LEON BLVD

DOUGLAS ROAD

Venetian
Pool

SEVILLA AVENUE

SEVILLA AVENUE

TOLEDO

Coral Gables
Congregational Church

UNIVERSITY DRIVE

Biltmore Hotel

Biltmore
Country Club

French Normandy
and Dutch South
African Villages

SEGOVIA STREET

HYLAN DRIVE

LE JEUNE ROAD

GRANADA BOULEVARD

S. DIXIE HIGHWAY

DOUGLAS ROAD

RED ROAD

RIVIERA DRIVE

LE JEUNE ROAD

University
of Miami

GRANADA BOULEVARD

Chinese
Village

LE JEUNE ROAD

To South Coral Gables

RED ROAD

S. DIXIE HIGHWAY

Lowe
Art Museum

To South Miami

CORAL GABLES

camp in the Florida Keys until that, too, was destroyed, by a hurricane, and wound up as Miami's postmaster until his death in 1942.

Coral Gables, however, was built with longevity as well as beauty in mind. Despite successive economic crises, it never lost its good looks and these days, boosted by a plethora of multinational companies moving into renovated office buildings, and a very image-conscious resident population, it is still a lovely place to explore.

The Miracle Mile and Around

Elaborate entrances apart, the best way into Coral Gables is along SW 22nd Street which, once across Douglas Road, becomes the **Miracle Mile**, conceived by Merrick as the centerpiece of his dream city's business district and still the preferred shopping place of community-conscious locals. It continues to bear the imprint of Merrick's vision, even if the occasional spot of mundane Art Deco makes a bizarre addition to the more fanciful Mediterranean trimmings.

Dominated by department stores, Latin American travel agents and a staggering number of bridal shops patronized by fussing Cuban matriarchs, the Miracle Mile (actually only half a mile long) becomes increasingly expensive and exclusive as you proceed west. Notice the arcades and balconies along its course, and the spirals and peaks of the **Colonnade Building**, no 133–169: now consumed by a smart hotel (see "Accommodation") and shops, it was completed in 1926 to accommodate George Merrick's land sales office. Which was a bit late as it turned out, with the property crash just a few months away.

Cut around the corner to collect info from the **Chamber of Commerce**, 50 Aragon Avenue (Mon–Fri 8.30am–5pm; ☎446-1657), and complete the Miracle Mile inside the grandly pillared **Coral Gables City Hall**, 405 Biltmore Way (Mon–Fri 8am–5pm), whose corridors are adorned by Twenties advertising posters boasting the charms of the "City Beautiful", and framed newspaper clippings verifying the property-acquiring mania of the time. There's also a caseful of oddments from the *Biltmore Hotel* (see below), which fall some way short of encapsulating the moneyed elegance that characterized Merrick's spa resort. On the third floor, gaze (from the landing) at Denman Fink's impressive blue and gold mural, decorating the interior of the bell tower.

About half a mile further west, along Coral Way – which, typically for a Coral Gables residential street, is quiet, pleasant and tree lined – the **Coral Gables House**, no 907 (Sun & Wed 1–4pm; $2), was George Merrick's boyhood home. In 1899, when George was 12, his family arrived here from New England to run a 160-acre fruit and vegetable farm – and, in the case of George's father, to deliver sermons at local Congregational churches. The farm was so successful that the house quickly grew from a wooden shack into a modestly elegant dwelling of coral rock and gabled windows (a combination that inspired the name of the future city, which grew up around the family farm). Understandably, the house highlights the Merrick family, rather than George's personal achievements, with many of their furnishings and portraits. The dual blows of the property crash and a citrus blight led to the gradual deterioration of the house, until restoration began in the Seventies. There's only enough inside to occupy half an hour, but it provides an interesting background on Coral Gables' founder, who lived here until 1916.

Along De Soto Boulevard

There's no reason to persist along Coral Way, which soon hits the airport area sprawl, so backtrack to the junction with De Soto Boulevard, which curls southwards to three of Merrick's most notable achievements.

While his property-developing contemporaries left ugly scars across the city after digging up the local oolitic limestone, Merrick had the foresight – and the help of Denman Fink – to turn his biggest quarry into a sumptuous swimming pool. The **Venetian Pool**, 2701 De Soto Boulevard (June–Aug Mon–Fri 11am–7.30pm, Sat & Sun 10am–4.30pm; rest of the year Tues–Fri 11am–4 or 5.30pm, Sat & Sun 10am–4.30pm; $4), a conglomeration of palm-studded paths, Venetian-style bridges and coral rock caves, opened in 1924. Despite the elaborate ornamentation, the pool was never aimed at the social elite. Admission was cheap and open to all, and even today, local residents get a special discount. Oddly, however, the pool is often deserted.

A short way on, Merrick donated the land on which arose the **Coral Gables Congregational Church** (Mon–Fri 8am–4pm), a bright Spanish Revival flurry topped by a barrel-tiled roof and enhanced by Baroque features. The building's excellent acoustics make it a popular setting for jazz and classical concerts; ask for details at the church office, just inside the entrance.

Merrick's crowning achievement – aesthetically if never financially – was the **Biltmore Hotel**, 1200 Anastasia Avenue, wrapping its broad wings around the southern end of De Soto Boulevard. The 26-storey tower of the hotel can be seen across much of low-lying Miami: if it seems similar to the Freedom Tower (see "Around Downtown Miami"), it's because they're both modelled on the Giralda bell tower of Seville Cathedral in Spain. The *Biltmore* was hawked as "the last word in the evolution of civilization", and everything about it was outrageous: 25-foot-high fresco-coated walls, vaulted ceilings, a wealth of imported marble and tile, immense fireplaces and custom-loomed rugs. To mark the opening in January 1926, VIP guests were brought in on chartered long-distance trains, dined on pheasant and trout, and given the run of the casino. Next day, they could fox hunt, play polo or swim in the US's largest pool – whose first swimming instructor was Johnny Weissmuller, future Olympic champion and the original screen Tarzan.

While high-calibre celebs such as Bing Crosby, Judy Garland and Ginger Rogers kept the *Biltmore* on their itineraries, the end of the Florida land boom and the start of the Depression meant that the hotel was never the success it might have been. In the Forties, many of the finer furnishings were lost when the hotel became a military hospital, and decades of decline followed. Things appeared rosier in 1986, when $40 million was lavished on a restoration programme with the aim of reopening the prestige hostelry. As it was, the company involved went bust and the great building remained closed until 1993. Now once again it functions as a hotel; you can step inside to admire the elaborate architecture, take afternoon tea for $10.50, or – best of all – join the free **historical tours** beginning at 1.30pm, 2.30pm and 3.30pm every Sunday in the lobby.

The neighboring **Biltmore Country Club** has fared better, its beaux-arts features having been painstakingly renovated. Poke your head inside for a closer look: the building is open to the public, though most people turn up to knock a ball along the lush fairways of the Biltmore Golf Course which, in the glory days of the hotel, hosted the highest-paying golf tournament in the world.

South of the Biltmore: Miami University and the Lowe Art Museum

One of the few parts of Coral Gables where Mediterranean architecture doesn't prevail is on the campus of the **University of Miami**, about two miles south of the *Biltmore*, whose dismal box-like buildings are filled by students more likely to have wealthy parents than healthy intellects. The sole reason to visit is the **Lowe Art Museum**, 1301 Stanford Drive (Tues–Sat 10am–5pm, Sun noon–5pm; $4), which features a strong stock of Renaissance and Baroque works, including a few El Grecos and some early works by Goya, although the innovative temporary exhibitions are often more spectacular.

South Coral Gables

Just as the Venetian Pool was a clever disguise for a quarry, so Merrick turned the construction ditches that ringed the infant Coral Gables into a network of canals, calling them the "Miami Riviera" and floating gondolas along them. The idea never really took off, although the placid waterways remain, running between the university campus and a secluded residential area on Biscayne Bay, just south of Coconut Grove (described below).

Dividing Coconut Grove and South Miami (see p.83), the **Matheson Hammock Park**, 9601 Old Cutler Road (6am–sunset; $2 parking fee), was a coconut plantation before becoming a public park in 1930. At weekends, thousands decant here to use the marina and take a dip in the man-made lagoon; the rest of the sizeable park is much less crowded, and the winding trails above the mangrove swamps could easily consume a few hours. Virtually next door, the **Fairchild Tropical Garden** (daily 9.30am–4.30pm; $7) turns the same rugged terrain into lawns, flowerbeds and gardens decorated by artificial lakes. If the landscaping doesn't seem too contrived, the tram ride ($1) is a good way to take in the hundred-acre site.

Coconut Grove

A stamping ground of down-at-heel artists, writers and lefties through the Sixties and Seventies, a business-led revitalization has turned today's **COCONUT GROVE** into a glitterati hangout. Art galleries, fashionable restaurants and towering bay-view apartments mark its central section – clear signs of a neighborhood whose fortunes are rising. But Coconut Grove, finely placed along the shores of Biscayne Bay, also retains much of value from its formative years. A century ago, a strange mix of Bahamian salvagers and New England intellectuals searching for spiritual fulfillment laid the foundations of a fiercely individual community, separated from the fledgling city of Miami by a dense wedge of tropical foliage. On arrival, it's soon apparent that Coconut Grove still likes to stress the distance between itself and the rest of Miami: cleaner and richer than ever, but continuing to fan the flames of liberalism – and boasting the best batch of **drinking and music locales** outside of Miami Beach.

North Coconut Grove

In 1914, farm machinery mogul James Deering followed his brother Charles (of Deering Estate fame, see "South Miami") to south Florida and blew $15 million on recreating a sixteenth-century Italian Villa within the jungle-like belt of vegeta-tion between Miami and Coconut Grove. A thousand-strong workforce completed his **Villa Vizcaya**, 3251 South Miami Avenue (daily 9.30am–5pm; $8), in just two years. The lasting impression of the grandiose structure is that both Deering and his designer (the crazed Paul Chalfin, hellbent on becoming an architectural legend) had more money than good taste: Deering's madly eclectic art collection, and the concept that the villa should appear to have been inhabited for 400 years, resulted in a thunderous clash of Baroque, Renaissance, Rococo and Neoclassical fixtures and furnishings, and even the landscaped **gardens**, with their fountains and sculptures, aren't spared the pretensions. Nonetheless, vulgarly stuffed as it is, Villa Vizcaya is one of Miami's more recherche sights, with many diverting details – Chinese figures casting shadows across the tearoom, and an overly English Georgian library, for instance – and is rightly one of the most visited. Don't be surprised, either, to discover brigades of beaming Cuban brides being photographed; the villa is a popular wedding reception spot. **Guided tours** leave frequently from the entrance loggia – dominated by a second-century marble statue of Bacchus – and provide solid background information, after which you're free to explore at leisure.

Straight across South Miami Drive from Villa Vizcaya, the **Museum of Science and Space Transit Planetarium** (daily 10am–6pm; $6) sets a different mood entirely. Filled with finger-friendly computers, it provides a lot of innocent fun, though a more forceful reason to visit is the wildlife at the museum's rear. Vultures and owls are among a number of permanently injured birds seeing out their days here, a variety of snakes are viewable at disturbingly close quarters – and the resident tarantulas don't mind being handled. The adjoining **planetar-ium** has the trips-around-the-cosmos shows you'd expect, making it a cool refuge on a hot day, and head-banging rock music laser shows most weekends. Get details from the ticket office (inside the museum) or phone ☎854-2222; shows usually cost $5.

Where South Miami Drive becomes Bayshore Drive, close to Mercy Hospital, a road to the left leads to the **Church of Ermita de la Curidad** (daily 9am–9pm), erected by Miami Cubans. A mural behind the altar traces the history of the island, and the conical-shaped church is angled to allow worshippers to look out across the bay – in the direction of Cuba.

Back on Bayshore Drive, for the next two miles or so you'll catch glimpses of raw oolitic limestone poking through the greenery on the inland side. It was on this ridge, known as **Silver Bluff**, that several early settlers established their homes, later joined by the well-heeled notables of 1910s Miami. A few of their houses still stand – none publicly viewable – and the area remains a preserve of the rich, with opulent abodes shielded from prying eyes by carefully maintained trees.

Central Coconut Grove

The suggestions of major money around Silver Bluff yield to blatant statements of wealth once you draw closer to central Coconut Grove. Bayshore Drive continues between expensive high-rise condos and jogger-filled landscaped parks. The marina on **Dinner Key**, entered by way of Pan American Drive, where turn-of-the-century settlers would enjoy a quiet waterside picnic, now sports lines of hundred-thousand-dollar yachts, and the neighboring **Coconut Grove**

Exhibition Center is usually consumed by top-of-the-range car and interior furnishing shows.

The gigantic Exhibition Center overshadows the more cheerful **Miami City Hall**, 3400 Pan American Drive (Mon–Fri 8am–5pm), a small and unlikely seat of local government. Believably, the blue-and-white-trimmed Art Deco building used to be an airline terminal: from the Thirties, passengers checked in here for a seaplane service to Latin America, and the sight of the lumbering craft taking off drew thousands to the waterfront.

Walking from the City Hall (inside which there's nothing worth viewing) across the Exhibition Center's parking lot brings you to a mildly appealing **historical collection** (11.30am–midnight; free) of photos and old radio parts from the seaplane times (which lasted until improvements to Latin American runways made sea landings unnecessary) on the ground floor of the *Havana Clipper* restaurant. Dinner Key also marked a landing point of another kind: Bay of Pigs veterans stepped ashore here after their release from Cuba in 1962; a small plaque in front of the City Hall records the fact.

It was at the Dinner Key Auditorium (a forerunner of the Exhibition Center) in 1969 that rock legend **Jim Morrison**, singer with the Doors, dropped his leather pants to expose himself during the band's first – and last – Florida show, causing Miami's police to clamp down on local rock clubs and bringing the band more notoriety than they knew what to do with.

At the time of the Morrison incident, Coconut Grove was the Haight-Ashbury of Miami, and **Peacock Park**, at the end of Bayshore Drive beside MacFarlane Road, was a notorious hippie haunt. More recently it's been cleaned up to fit the area's present smart and sophisticated image, with tennis courts and some peculiar abstract rock sculptures. The **Chamber of Commerce** (Mon–Fri 9am–5pm; ☎444-7270), on a corner of the park, has plenty of free leaflets and maps of the area.

Along Main Highway

At the end of MacFarlane Road you hit **Main Highway** and Coconut Grove as most Miamians think of it: several blocks of trendy cafés, galleries and boutiques. Though less enjoyable than Miami Beach's South Beach (see "Miami Beach"), it's a fine place for a stroll, if only to watch the neighborhood's affluent fashion victims going through their paces, and spill over into Grand Avenue to cruise the *CocoWalk*, on the corner with Virginia Street, an enjoyable collection of open-air restaurants and bars, and yet more stylish shops.

There's little to do other than eat, drink and pose (for where to do all three, see "Eating" and "Nightlife"). For a taste of sheer exclusivity drop into *Mayfair-in-the-Grove* (Mon, Thurs & Fri 10am–9pm, Tues, Wed & Sat 10am–7pm, Sun noon–5.30pm), at the corner of MacFarlane Road and Grand Avenue, a designer shopping mall whose zigzagging walkways – decorated by fountains, copper sculptures, climbing vines and Romanesque doodles in concrete – wind around three floors of expense-account stores.

The beige-and-white **Coconut Grove Playhouse**, 3500 Main Highway, opened in 1927 and still going strong with a mixed diet of Broadway blockbusters and alternative offerings, is the best of several examples of Mediterranean Revival architecture in the area, but warrants only a passing glance as you move on to the most enduring historic site in Coconut Grove, at the end of a path right across Main Highway from the playhouse.

· The tree-shaded track leads to a tranquil bayside garden and a century-old house known as the **Barnacle**, built by "Commodore" Ralph Middelton Munroe: sailor, brilliant yacht-designer and a devotee of the Transcendalist Movement (advocating self-reliance, a love of nature and a simple lifestyle). The Barnacle was ingeniously put together with local materials and tricks learned from nautical design. Raising the structure eight feet off the ground improved air circulation and prevented flooding, a covered verandah enabled windows to be opened during rainstorms, and a skylight allowed air to be drawn through the house; all major innovations which alleviated some of the discomforts of living all year in the heat and humidity of south Florida. More inventive still, when Munroe gained a family and needed more space, he simply jacked up the single-storey structure and added a new floor underneath. Only with the **guided tour** (Thurs–Mon at 10am, 11.30am & 1pm; $2) can you see inside the house, where many original furnishings remain alongside some of Munroe's intriguing photos of pioneering Coconut Grovers. The exterior, and the less compelling grounds, can be viewed any time between 8am and sunset.

Charles Avenue and Black Coconut Grove

The Bahamian settlers of the late 1800s, soon to provide the labor that went into building Coconut Grove and nearby areas, mostly lived along what became **Charles Avenue** (off Main Highway, close to the playhouse), in small, simply built wooden houses, much like the "conch houses" which fill Key West's Old Town (see Chapter Two). You'll find a trio of these still standing on the "3200" block, though be warned that they are on the edge of **Black Coconut Grove** (not a name you'll find on maps, but one which everyone uses), a run-down area stretching westwards to the borders of Coral Gables. The fact that such a derelict district exists within half a mile of one of the city's most fashionably upscale areas provides a stark reminder – as if it were needed – of Miami's racial divisions. Like all of Miami's black areas, white people should only approach with extreme caution; and not at all without a car.

South Coconut Grove

South of the playhouse, the outlook along Main Avenue soon reverts to expansive older homes set back from the street. A couple of easily found minor sites are the only reasons to stop – briefly as you pass through towards South Miami. After half a mile, you'll spy the *Ransom Everglades School*, 3575 Main Highway, founded in 1903 for boarding pupils who split the school year between the Adirondacks and here. Oddly enough, the main school room was a Chinese-style **pagoda** (Mon–Fri 9am–5pm; free), which still stands incongruously in the middle of what's now an upper-crust prep school. Inside the green-painted pine structure are a few amusing relics from the school's past.

A little further on, near the corner of Devon Road, the 1917 **Plymouth Congregational Church** (Mon–Fri 9am–4.30pm) has a striking vine-covered coral rock facade; remarkably, this finely crafted exterior was the work of just one man. Note, too, the 375-year-old hand-carved walnut main door, which looks none the worse for its journey from a monastery in the Spanish Pyrenees. Usually the church's only unlocked door is the one beside the parking lot, but check before trying at the luxuriously appointed church office, on the other side of Devon Road.

South Miami

South of Coral Gables and Coconut Grove, monotonous middle-class suburbs consume almost all of **SOUTH MIAMI**, an expanse of cosy but dull two-car family homes reaching to the edge of the Everglades, interrupted only by golf courses and a few contrived tourist attractions. Mini-malls, filling stations, cut-price waterbed outlets and bumper-to-bumper traffic are the star features of its primary thoroughfare, Hwy-1. You won't be able to avoid this route completely, but from South Coral Gables a better course is **Old Cutler Road**, which makes a pleasing meander through a thick belt of woodland between Biscayne Bay and the suburban sprawl. Cutting **inland** from Hwy-1 is an unrewarding ploy (and unthinkable without a car), since the four possible stops – three of them involving animals – are of minor importance.

Along Old Cutler Road: the Deering Estate

Long before modern highways scythed through the city, Old Cutler Road was the sole road between Coconut Grove and Cutler, a small town that went into terminal decline in the 1910s after being bypassed by the new Flagler railroad. A wealthy industrialist and amateur botanist, Charles Deering (brother of James, the owner of Villa Vizcaya; see "Coconut Grove"), was so taken with the natural beauty of the area that he purchased all of Cutler and, with one exception, razed its buildings to make way for the **Charles Deering Estate**, 16701 SW 72nd Avenue (Sat & Sun only 9am–5pm; $4), completed in 1922. Deering maintained the *Richmond Inn*, Cutler's only hotel, as his own living and dining quarters. Its pleasant wooden form now stands in marked contrast to the limestone mansion he raised alongside, whose interior – echoing halls, dusty chandeliers and checker-board-tile floors – is Mediterranean in style but carries a Gothic spookiness.

The buildings make a good starting point but impress less than the **grounds**, where signs of human habitation dating back 10,000 years have been found amid three hundred acres of pine woods, mangrove forests and tropical hardwood hammocks. **Free walking tours** outline the estate's background and nature (check departure times at the entrance); more adventurous **guided canoe tours** (Sat & Sun 9.30am & 1pm; $10) navigate the mangrove-fringed inlets. Night-time canoe trips are held under the full moon; ☎235-1668 for details.

Inland: the Monkey Jungle, Parrot Jungle, Metro Zoo, and the Gold Coast Railroad Museum

At the **Monkey Jungle**, 14805 SW 216th Street (daily 9.30am–5pm; $10.50), one of the few places of protection in the US for endangered primates, covered walkways keep visitors in closer confinement than the monkeys – a wide selection from Asia and Africa – and lead through a steamy hammock where several hundred baboons, orang-utans, gorillas and chimps move through the vegetation. In a similar vein, **Parrot Jungle**, 11000 SW 57th Street (9.30am–6pm; $10.50), has parrots, parakeets and macaws of rainbow plumage swapping squawks as they swoop across a gigantic aviary, happy to have escaped being press-ganged into riding bikes and walking tightropes for human amusement in the frequent "parrot shows".

A better place to view tamed wildlife – assuming you're not opposed to zoos in principle – is the **Metro Zoo**, 12400 SW 152nd Street (daily 9.30am–5.30pm; $8.25). Even so, while psychological barriers such as moats and small hills are employed instead of cages, it's hard to imagine that many animals enjoy baking heat and humidity any more than their audience; understandably, both tend to spend their time here pursuing shade and a cool drink. If you do come, the snow-white Bengal tigers are the prize exhibit.

The Gold Coast Railroad Museum

Sharing the zoo's entrance, but entirely free of kept animals, the **Gold Coast Railroad Museum** (Mon–Fri 10am–3pm, Sat & Sun 10am–5pm; $5) turns up a small but intriguing group of old locos which can be clambered aboard for a close inspection. Among them, the *Ferdinand Megellan*, a luxury Pullman car, was custom-built in 1928 for presidential use, complete with escape hatches and steel-armor plating. In it, Harry S Truman travelled 21,000 miles on his 1948 re-election campaign, giving three hundred speeches from the rear platform. Take your place in his footsteps and prepare to orate to passing lizards.

VISITOR INFORMATION

While in the vicinity, use the excellent **Visitor Information Center** (daily 8am–6pm; ☎1-800/388-9669 or ☎245-9180) on Hwy-1 close to the junction with Hwy-9336 (344th Street), which is piled high with information, and particularly strong on the Florida Keys and Everglades.

Continuing South: Homestead and Around

Suburbia yields to agriculture as you continue south along Hwy-1, where broad, fertile fields grow the fruit and vegetables destined for the nation's northern states. Aside from offering as good a taste of Florida farmlife as you're likely to find so close to its major city, the district can be a money-saving stop – see "Accommodation" – on the way to the Florida Keys (Chapter Two) or to the Everglades National Park (Chapter Six).

Closer in mood to the *The Waltons* than *Miami Vice*, **HOMESTEAD** is the agricultural area's main town but ranks as the least galvanizing section of Miami. Krome Avenue, just west of Hwy-1, slices through the center but, besides a few restored 1910s–1930s buildings (such as the Old City Hall, no 43 N), the only likely stop is the **Pioneer Museum**, no 826 (Nov–April daily 1–5pm; $1.50), where two yellow-painted train station buildings store photos and objects from Homestead's formative years – the end-of-the-line town was planned by Flagler's railroad engineers in 1904. To the rear, a 1926 caboose keeps moderately entertaining railroad mementoes.

Around Homestead

Time is better spent around Homestead than actually in it, with plenty to fill a day within a few minutes' drive of the town. And, if you want to gather your own dinner, keep an eye out for **"pick-your-own"** signs, where, for a few dollars, you can take to the fields and load up with peas, tomatoes or whatever crop is on offer.

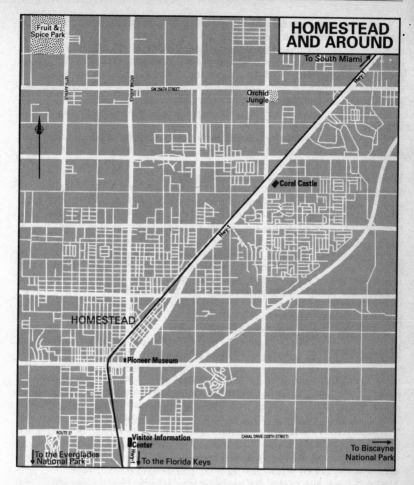

The Coral Castle

The one essential stop is the **Coral Castle** (daily 9am–6pm; $7.75), whose bulky coral rock sculptures stand beside Hwy-1 about six miles northeast of Homestead, at the junction with 286th Street. Remarkably, these fantastic creations, whose delicate finish belies their imposing size, are the work of just one man – the highly enigmatic **Edward Leedskalnin**. Jilted in 1913 by his sixteen-year-old fiancee in Latvia, Ed spent seven years working his way across Europe, Canada and the US before buying an acre of land just south of Homestead. Using a profound – and self-taught – knowledge of weights and balances, Ed somehow raised enormous hunks of coral rock from the ground, then used handmade tools fashioned from scrap to refine the blocks into chairs, tables and beds; odd furniture that suggest the castle was intended as a love nest to woo back his errant sweetheart (last heard of in 1980, still in Latvia).

You can wander around the slabs, and sit on the hard but surprisingly comfort-able chairs (in which Ed used to pass the day, reading), swivel a nine-ton gate with your pinkie and admire the numerous coral representations of the moon and planets that reflect Ed's interest in astronomy and astrology, as does the twenty-foot-high telescope with which he charted the earth's passage through space. But what you won't be able to do is explain how the sculptures were made. No one ever saw the secretive Ed at work, or knows how, alone, he could load 1100 tons of rock onto a rail-mounted truck, as happened when the pieces were moved here in 1936.

Sleeping on a bed of burlap-covered wood and working at a bench made from car running boards, Ed lived here until his death in 1951 – a mystery to the end.

The Fruit and Spice Park and Orchid Jungle

The subtle fragrances of the **Fruit and Spice Park**, 24801 SW 187th Avenue (daily 10am–5pm; $1), tickle your nostrils as soon as you enter. Rarely seen exot-ica such as the aptly named panama candle tree and the star fruit are the high-lights of a host of tropical peculiarities; at weekends the **guided tour** (1pm & 3pm; $1) is a sure way to initiate yourself into the secret lives of spices.

Avid horticulturalists will also relish a peek at **Orchid Jungle**, 26715 157th Avenue (daily 8.30am–5.30pm; $5), where an unbelievable variety of the famed flowers are grown and groomed, and where an enjoyable hammock trail reveals, besides more orchids, a rich array of ferns and bromeliads.

Biscayne National Park

If you're not going to the Florida Keys, make a point of visiting **Biscayne National Park** (daily 8am–sunset), at the end of Canal Drive (328th Street), east off Hwy-1 – and be prepared to strike out seaward. The bulk of the park lies beneath the clear ocean waters, where stunningly shaped living coral provides a habitat for shoals of brightly colored fish and numerous rock-hugging little crea-tures too delicate to survive on their own. For a full description of the wondrous world of the living coral reef, see "John Pennecamp State Park", in Chapter Two.

The lazy way to see it is on the three-hour **glass-bottomed boat trip** (daily at 10am & 1.30pm; $16.50; reservations ☎247-2400), but for a fuller encounter you should snorkel or scuba dive. Rent the gear from the **visitor center** (Dec–April Mon–Fri 8am–5pm, Sat & Sun 9am–5.30pm; rest of the year Mon–Fri 10am–4pm, Sat & Sun 10am–6pm; ☎247-7275), near the entrance at **Convoy Point**.

Another option is to visit the park's **barrier islands**, seven miles out. A tour boat leaves for **Elliot Key** from Convoy Point on Sundays between December and May at 1.30pm. Once ashore, besides calling at the **visitor center** (Sat & Sun 10am–4pm) and contemplating the six-mile hiking trail along the island's forested spine, there's nothing to do on Elliot Key except sunbathe in solitude.

Key Biscayne and Around

A compact, immaculately manicured community squeezed between two protec-tive stands of Australian pines and decorated by rows of coconut palms, **KEY BISCAYNE**, five miles off the Miami shore, is a great place to live – if you can afford it. Seeking relaxation and creature comforts away from life in the fast lane, the moneyed of Miami fill the island's upscale homes and condos: even Richard

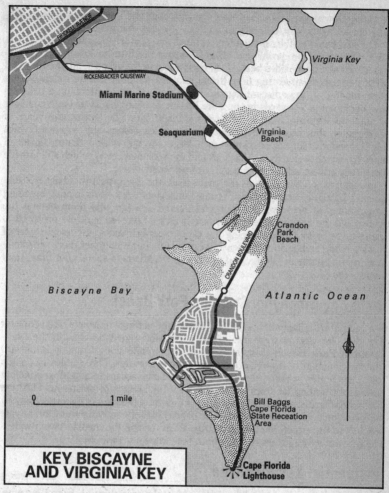

**KEY BISCAYNE
AND VIRGINIA KEY**

Nixon had his presidential winter house here, and singer Sting chose one of the luxury shorefront hotels for a recuperative pamper between tour dates. For all the wealth, Key Biscayne is a very visitable place: there are a couple of inviting beaches, a third within a state park, and a fabulous cycling path running the full length. Cheap eats and lodgings, though, are in predictably short supply.

Approaching Key Biscayne: Virginia Key and Around

Without a private yacht, the only way onto Key Biscayne is along **Rickenbacker Causeway** ($1 toll), a continuation of SW 26th Road just south of downtown Miami, which soars high above Biscayne Bay, allowing shipping to glide by underneath and giving a gasp-inducing view of the Brickell Avenue skyline (see

·"Around Downtown Miami"). Other than driving, you can cross the four-mile-long causeway by bike, bus (#B) or on foot – if you're energetic enough.

The first land you'll hit is the unexceptional and sparsely populated **VIRGINIA KEY**. On the left, the prominent **Miami Marine Stadium** makes the most of its waterfront setting: besides being seen from a seat in the grandstand, the rock and MOR performers appearing here throughout the summer can be watched from boats moored in the adjacent lagoon. More demanding of attention, a two-mile lane beginning a few yards beyond the Marine Stadium winds through a cluster of pines to **Virginia Beach** (daily 8am–sunset; cars $2). During the years of segregation, this was set aside for Miami's black community (chosen, cynics might presume, for its proximity to a large sewage works). Later, flocks of hippies became seriously laid-back around the secluded coves, which still provide a naturally private setting for (unofficial) **nude** sunbathing.

In contrast, on the right of the main road, the **Seaquarium** (daily 9.30am–6.30pm; $17.95) is a busy place. The most important work – formulating breeding programmes to preserve Florida's endangered sea life – is done behind the scenes and the Seaquarium's public face is as a marine-life park. Be prepared to spend three or four hours seeing the various performances: the usual roster of shark feeding and performing seals. It can be fun, but remember there are plenty more marine parks in Florida, and much more in Miami to spend your time – and money – on.

On to Key Biscayne: Crandon Park Beach

Not content with living in one of the best natural settings in Miami, the people of Key Biscayne also possess one of the finest landscaped beaches in the city – **Crandon Park Beach** (8am–sunset; cars $2), a mile along Crandon Boulevard (the continuation of the main road from the causeway). Three miles of golden beach fringe this grassy, palm-dotted park, and give access to a sandbar enabling knee-depth wading far from shore. Filled by the sounds of boisterous kids and sizzling barbecues each weekend, at any other time the park is disturbed only by the occasional jogger and a couple of holiday-makers straying from the private beaches of the expensive hotels nearby. Relax beside the lapping ocean waters and gaze out for manatees and dolphins, both known to swim by.

Residential Key Biscayne

Besides its very green, well-tended good looks, **residential Key Biscayne**, beginning with an abrupt wall of apartment buildings at the southern edge of Crandon Park Beach, has little to offer those who don't live there. You'll need to pass through, however, on the way to the much more rewarding Bill Baggs Cape Florida park (see below), and while doing so should make a loop along Harbor Drive, turning off along McIntire Drive. At no 485 W stands the former home of ex-president Richard Nixon, who picked up his *Miami Herald* here one morning in 1972 to read of a break-in at the *Watergate Hotel* in Washington; a seemingly insignificant event (only featured by the paper because two Miami Cubans were among those involved in the deed) at the time, but one which led to Nixon's resigning the presidency in disgrace two years later. On the same street, pick up general info at the **Chamber of Commerce**, 95 W (Mon–Fri 9am–5pm; ☎361-5207).

The Southern Tip: Bill Baggs Cape Florida State Recreation Area and Stiltsville

Crandon Boulevard terminates at the entrance to the **Bill Baggs Cape Florida State Recreation Area** (daily 8am–sunset; cars $3.25, pedestrians and cyclists $1), 400 wooded acres covering the southern extremity of Key Biscayne. An excellent swimming **beach** lines the Atlantic-facing side of the park, and a board-walk cuts around the wind-bitten sand dunes towards the **Cape Florida light-house**, built in the 1820s. Only with the ranger-led **tour** (daily except Tues at 9am, 10.30am, 1pm, 2.30pm & 3.30pm; $1) can you climb through the 95-foot-high structure, which was attacked by Seminole Indians in 1836 and seized by Confederate soldiers to disrupt Union shipping during the Civil War. It remained in use until 1878, and now serves as a navigational beacon.

Stiltsville

Looking out from the park across the bay, you'll spy the grouping of fragile-looking houses known as **Stiltsville**. Held above water by stilts from the Forties and Fifties, these wooden dwellings were built and occupied by fishermen, enrag-ing the authorities by being outside the jurisdiction of tax collectors. Stiltsville's demise has been signalled by a recent law forbidding repair work on the ramshackle structures; just one now has a full-time occupant, the others are occa-sionally used for parties. Hurricane Andrew demolished roughly half of Stiltsville – see what's left while you still can.

MIAMI BEACH

A long slender arm of land between Biscayne Bay and the Atlantic Ocean three miles offshore from Miami, **Miami Beach** was an ailing fruit farm in the 1910s when its Quaker owner, John Collins, formed an unlikely partnership with a flashy entrepreneur called Carl Fisher. With Fisher's money, Biscayne Bay was dredged, and the tons of muck raised from its murky bed provided the landfill which helped transform the wildly vegetated barrier island into the carefully sculptured landscape of palm trees, hotels and tennis courts that – by and large – it still is today.

In varying degrees, all twelve miles of Miami Beach are worth seeing – and its firm, crushed-coral-rock beach is excellent for sunbathing and swimming throughout – but only **South Beach**, a fairly small area at the southern end, will hold your attention for long. Here, rows of tastefully restyled Thirties Art Deco buildings have become the chic gathering places for the city's fashionable faces and the stamping ground of the more creative and unconventional elements in Miami life: it's no fluke that the leading-edge art galleries and nightclubs are found in this compact area. Heading north, **Central Miami Beach** was where Fifties screen stars had fun in the sun and helped cement Miami's international reputation as a glamorous vacation spot. Oddly enough, it's the monolithic hotels remaining from these times which give the area a modicum of appeal. Further on, **North Miami Beach**, despite splitting into several distinctive communities, has even less to kindle the imagination – a long way from the action and mostly over-run by package tourists – but makes a good back route if you're heading north from Miami towards Fort Lauderdale.

APPROACHING MIAMI BEACH: THE CAUSEWAYS & ISLANDS

The setting of countless *Miami Vice* car chases, the six **causeways** crossing
Biscayne Bay between Miami and Miami Beach offer striking views of the city, especially so at night when the illuminated downtown buildings twinkle over the bay's
dark waters. Some of the causeways also provide the only land access to artificial
residential islands, sheltering the rich and famous from unwanted attention.

Best pickings are along **MacArthur Causeway**, running from just north of
downtown Miami into Miami Beach's South Beach. A mile into it, **Watson Island
Park** holds the picnic-suitable **Japanese Garden**, bequeathed to the city by a
Japanese industrialist in 1961, where an eight-ton statue of Hotei – the Japanese
God of prosperity – holds pride of place. On subsequent islands are the former
homes of gangster Al Capone (Palm Island), author Damon Runyan (Hibiscus
Island) and actor Don Johnson (Star Island) – don't bother to make a house call; all
that can be seen are the most expensive burglar alarms in Miami.

South Beach

Occupying the southernmost three miles, the one genuinely exciting part of
Miami Beach is **South Beach**, filled with pastel-colored Art Deco buildings, up-
and-coming art galleries, modish diners, suntanned beach addicts and multinational swarms of photographers, TV and film crews zooming in on what has –
thanks to the visuals of *Miami Vice* and the fashion photography of Bruce Weber
(shooting nudes on the hotel roofs for the Calvin Klein *Obsession* campaign in
1986) – become the hottest high-style backdrop in the world.

Socially, South Beach is unsurpassed. By day, fine-bodied ravers soak up the
rays on the beach, and by night the ten blocks of Ocean Drive are the heart and
soul of the biggest party in Miami: chic terrace cafés spill across the specially
widened sidewalk amid a procession of fashion models, tropical-shirted existen-
tialists, wide-eyed tourists, tarot card readers and middle-aged trendies trying to
keep to keep up with the times. All the places worth showing yourself in are
listed under "Nightlife," and Ocean Drive is also the scene of the Miami Beach
cruise; see the box on p.93.

Not all South Beach is so sensuous. Just a few blocks from Ocean Drive, the
streets – and the streetlife – are much less photogenic, still bearing the scars of
the area's poverty-stricken Seventies, and the arrival in 1980 of the *Marielitos*,
Fidel Castro's gift to the US of Cuban criminals and misfits (see "Little Havana"
for more), many of whom ended up here. Provided you stick to the main streets
and exercise the usual caution, however, none of South Beach is unduly
dangerous.

The Art Deco District

As much as the beach and the social life, it's the **Art Deco district** that brings
people to South Beach, and none of them ever needs to ask directions. Art Deco
here is a smorgasbord rather a gourmet experience; there are no great buildings,
just a great number of them – in their hundreds between Fifth and 23rd streets –
built during the late Thirties in a style that became known as "Miami Beach Art
Deco".

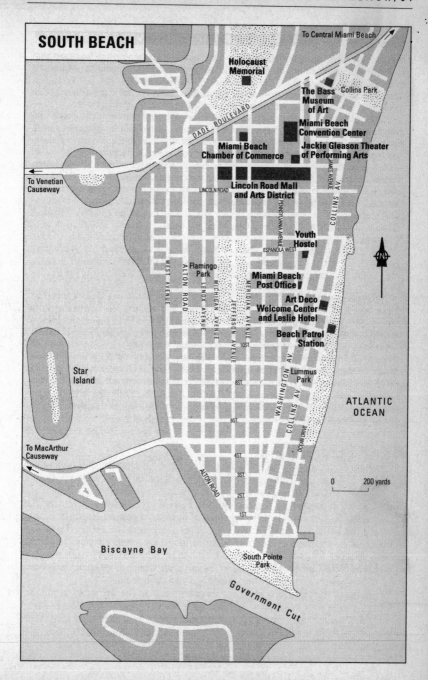

SOUTH BEACH

To Central Miami Beach

Holocaust
Memorial

Collins Park

The Bass
Museum
of Art

DADE BOULEVARD

Miami Beach
Convention Center

Miami Beach
Chamber of Commerce

Jackie Gleason Theater
of Performing Arts

To Venetian
Causeway

JAMES AVENUE

LINCOLN ROAD

COLLINS AV.

Lincoln Road Mall
and Arts District

PENNSYLVANIA AVENUE

Youth
Hostel

ESPANOLA WEST

Flamingo
Park

WEST AVENUE

ALTON ROAD

LENOX AVENUE

MICHIGAN AVENUE

MERIDIAN AVENUE

JEFFERSON AVENUE

Miami Beach
Post Office

Art Deco
Welcome Center
and Leslie Hotel

Beach Patrol
Station

N

Star
Island

10ST.

8ST.

WASHINGTON AV.

COLLINS AV.

Lummus
Park

ATLANTIC
OCEAN

To MacArthur
Causeway

6ST.

4ST.
3ST.
2ST.
1ST.

ALTON ROAD

OCEAN DRIVE

0   200 yards

Biscayne Bay

South Pointe
Park

Government Cut

ART DECO IN MIAMI BEACH

Art Deco's roots go back to the Paris of 1901, but as a building style it first took hold in the US during the Thirties. With it, the nation shook off the restraints of Classical revivalism and the gloom of the Depression. Thrilling and new, Art Deco architecture embraced technology, borrowing streamlined contours from the aerodynamic designs of futuristic cars, trains and planes. Simultaneously, Art Deco architecture could be playful and humorous, employing wacky ornamentation, vivid colors and utilizing new materials such as aluminium, chrome and plastic to heighten effect. Often derided as vulgar, Art Deco nonetheless became a symbol of a country emerging from economic catastrophe to become the first modern superpower.

In the late Thirties, a small group of architects built a lot – and fast – in Miami Beach. Employing the trademarks of Art Deco, they used local oolitic limestone and stucco to produce buildings that were cheap (and often cramped and uncomfortable) but instantly fashionable – defining the look of the US's fun and sun mecca with a style soon dubbed **"Miami Beach Art Deco"** (sometimes called **"Tropical Deco"**). Recognizable Florida motifs, such as herons, pelicans, blooming flowers and blazing sunsets, decorated facades and porches. Nautical themes were prevalent, too: windows resembled portholes, balconies stretched out like luxury liner sundecks, and any ungainly bulges on roofs were disguised as ship's funnels. Many of the buildings were painted stark white, sucking in the force of the Florida sun and reflecting it with matching intensity.

It's a sobering thought that Miami Beach almost lost all of these significant structures, which fell into decline from the late Fifties, as property developers sought to replace them with anonymous high-rise condos. In the mid-Seventies, the **Miami Beach Art Deco Preservation League** – whose first meeting drew just six people – was born with the aim of saving the buildings and raising awareness of their architectural and historical importance. The League's success has been dramatic – a major turning point was convincing the buck-hungry developers of the earning potential of such a unique area. The driving force of the movement, the late Barbara Capitman, also attempted a similar initiative in Opa-Locka, a socially blighted district in northwest Miami, nowadays better known for its crack dealers than its crazy, Arabesque architecture.

Seeing the Art Deco District

Painstaking restoration notwithstanding, little of the Art Deco district looks today quite like it did in the Thirties. Nowhere is the updating more apparent than in the colors – "a palette of Post Modern cake-icing pastels now associated with *Miami Vice*," according to the disgruntled Florida architecture chronicler Hap Hatton – which appeared in 1980 when local designer Leonard Horowitz started adorning the buildings. Furthermore, the details of restoration reflect the desires of the building's owners more than historical accuracy – and no money-spinning fashion shoot or TV commercial would look half as good with old Miami Beach as a backdrop. Not that there's anything wrong with what's happened: in its own right, 1990s Miami Beach Art Deco really is a sight to behold.

Examples of the Art Deco style are too numerous to list (or view) in full, but strolling around and keeping your eyes open reveals plenty. For a more structured investigation, take the ninety-minute **walking tour** ($6) leaving at 10.30am on Saturdays from the *Leslie Hotel*, 1244 Ocean Drive, or the **bicycle tour** ($10 including bike rental) which leaves at 10.30am on Sundays from *Cycles on the Beach*, 713 Fifth Street (reservations ☎672-2014).

The district's contemporary look should be assessed from Ocean Drive, where a line of revamped hotels have exploited their design heritage; their lobbies can be freely ventured into (and many are worth visiting for their bars and restaurants – see "Eating" and "Nightlife"). Among them, the *Park Central*, no 640, is a geometric *tour de force*, with octagonal windows, sharp vertical columns and a wrought-iron decorated stairway leading up the mezzanine level, which displays monochrome photos of Twenties Miami Beach. Nearby, a corner of the *Waldorf Towers*, no 850, is topped by an ornamental lighthouse. Just across the street in Lummus Park (the grassy patch that separates Ocean Drive from the beach), and more honestly redolent of the old days, stands the boat-shaped **Beach Patrol Station**, unmistakeable for its vintage oversized date and temperature sign, and still the base of the local lifeguards.

Just ahead are two buildings at the centre of the controversy which currently rages through South Beach: should the area's Art Deco buildings be decorated only in officially approved pastel colors, or should they be permitted much more vivid tones and be allowed to evolve a particularly 1990s South Beach style? The purple and orange frontage of the **Cardozo**, no 1300, and the intense yellow exterior of the **Leslie**, no 1244, were the recent work of Barbara Hulanicki, founder in the 1960s of London's scene-setting clothes store, *Biba*. Hulanicki's exuberant tones have upset many South Beach purists, but seem set to be the look of South Beach to come.

Walk at least once after dark along the beach side of Ocean Drive. This frees you from the crowds and enables a clear view of the Art Deco hotels' **neon illuminations**, casting shimmering circles and lines of vivid blues, pinks and greens around the contours of the buildings.

Away from the image-conscious trappings of Ocean Drive, perhaps the district's most enduring relic, an example of the less ornate Depression Moderne style, is the **Miami Beach Post Office**, 1300 Washington Avenue (lobby Mon–Fri 6am–6pm, Sat 6am–4pm). Inside, streaming sunlight brightens the murals sweeping around a rotunda; there can be few more enjoyable places to buy a stamp.

THE MIAMI BEACH CRUISE

A crawling bumper-to-bumper procession of horn-honking, passenger-swapping autos along Ocean Drive between Fifth and Fourteenth streets, the **Miami Beach cruise** – part unofficial street party, part pick-up exercise – takes place on Fridays and Saturdays from around 7pm to 4am, and on Sunday afternoons from noon to 7pm. Join in if you dare.

South of Fifth Street: South Pointe Park and Around

South of Fifth Street, a small and shabby area called **SOUTH POINTE** is being revamped by a major redevelopment project: more, it seems, to exploit the commercial potential of the location than to benefit the community. A marina and several restaurants have been added, and the luxury 26-storey *South Pointe Towers* leaps skyward from South Pointe Park (see below), dwarfing the stucco-fronted boxes in which most local people live. The best route through South Pointe is the shorefront boardwalk, beginning near the southern end of Lummus Park, and finishing by the 300-foot-long jetty lined with people fishing off **First Street Beach**, the only surfing beach in Miami and lively with tanned, athletic bodies even when the waves are calm. You can swim and snorkel here, too, but bear in mind that the big cruise ships frequently pass close by and stir up the current.

South Pointe Park

On its inland side, the boardwalk skirts **South Pointe Park** (daily 8am–sunset), whose handsome lawns and tree-shaded picnic tables offer a respite from the packed beaches. The park is a good place to be on Friday evenings when its open-air stage is at the center of enjoyable free events (look for posters around South Beach detailing the latest happening).

To while away some time, flop down on one of the seats on the southern edge of the park and look across **Government Cut**, a waterway first dredged by Henry Flagler at the turn of the century and now, substantially deepened, the route for large cruise ships beginning their journeys to the Bahamas and Caribbean. Busts permitting, you might also witness an impounded drug-running vessel being towed along by the authorities. Don't be surprised, either, to hear the neighing of horses: the Miami Beach police stable their steeds on the eastern side of the park.

The rest of South Beach: North along Washington Avenue

Running through South Beach parallel to Ocean Drive, much of **Washington Avenue** is lined by small, Cuban-run supermarkets (in which spoken English is a rarity), houses in need of a paint job and run-down retirement homes.

Española Way

Other than the Miami Beach post office (described above under "Seeing the Art Deco District"), nothing along Washington Avenue need delay you until you reach **Española Way**, between Fourteenth and Fifteenth streets. While Miami Beach is renowned for its Art Deco, the Mediterranean Revival architecture found across much of Miami is plentiful, too, and most evident on this slender street overhung by narrow balconies and striped awnings.

Completed in 1925, Española Way was grandly envisaged as an "artists' colony", but only the rhumba dance craze of the Thirties – said to have started here, stirred up by Cuban band leader Desi Arnaz* – came close to fitting the bill. Following South Beach's social climb, however, a group of browsable art galleries and art supply stores have revived the original concept; they now fill the first-floor rooms, while, above them, small top-floor apartments are optimistically marketed as "artist's lofts".

Lincoln Road Mall and the Lincoln Road Arts District

A short walk further, between Sixteenth and Seventeenth streets, the pedestrianized **Lincoln Road Mall** was considered the flashiest shopping precinct outside of New York during the Fifties, its jewellery and clothes stores labelled "the Fifth

---

* Arnaz (later to find wider fame as the husband of Lucille Ball) and his band often performed in the *Village Tavern*, inside the *Clay Hotel*, which is now the city's youth hostel; see "Accommodation".

Avenue of the South". Today, run-of-the-mill consumer durable stockists fill the section closest to Washington Avenue, and the interest has shifted a few blocks west to the **Lincoln Road Arts District**, around Lenox Avenue. Here, among a number of art galleries breathing life into what were, a few years ago, fairly seedy offices and shops, the studios (viewing hours are displayed on their doors) and showrooms of *South Florida Art Center, Inc.*, 810 Lincoln Road, will tune you into the burgeoning South Beach arts scene. A number of small cafés in the vicinity (see "Eating") also revel in the area's increasingly cultured mood.

The Jackie Gleason Theater of Performing Arts and the Miami Beach Convention Center

The first of two public buildings immediately north of Lincoln Road Mall, the 3000-seat **Jackie Gleason Theater of Performing Arts**, fronted by Pop artist Roy Lichtenstein's expressive *Mermaid* sculpture, stages Broadway shows and classical concerts, but is best known to middle-aged Americans as the home of wholesome entertainer Jackie Gleason's immensely popular TV show, which ran for twenty years from the Fifties.

On the far side of the theater, sunlight bounces off the shrill white exterior of the massive **Miami Beach Convention Center**, which occupies a curious niche in US political history. At the Republican Convention held here in August 1968, Richard Nixon won the nomination that would take him to the White House. Nixon counted his votes oblivious to the fact that Miami's Liberty City ghetto had just erupted into the first of its riots (see "Around Downtown Miami").

The Bass Museum of Art

A more likely place to spend an hour is a little further north at the **Bass Museum of Art**, 2121 Park Avenue (Tues–Sat 10am–5pm, Sun 1–5pm; $5, Tues donations), housed in a fetching coral-rock building within a sculpture-studded garden. The museum's contents – dominated by worthy European works, mostly from the fifteenth to seventeenth centuries with Rubens, Rembrandt and Dürer heading the cast – are a notch above what you'll find anywhere else in the state, and acclaimed Japanese architect Arata Isozaki is overseeing a major expansion, expected to be completed in 1995. For all that, few people come to Florida to see old European paintings, and, for anyone other than fine art buffs, the contemporary temporary exhibitions offer greater stimulation.

Central Miami Beach

North of 23rd Street, the energy of South Beach fades dramatically as you enter **CENTRAL MIAMI BEACH**. Collins Avenue charts a five-mile course through the area, between Indian Creek – across which are the golf courses, country clubs and secluded palatial homes of Miami Beach's seriously rich – and the swanky hotels on which the Miami Beach high-life centered during the glamorous Fifties. Strange as it may seem, casting an incredulous eye over a few of these often madly ostentatious accommodations is the root appeal of Central Miami Beach; its beach, linked by a long and lovely boardwalk stretching over a mile from 21st Street, tends to be less enticing – largely the preserve of families and older folk.

Seeing Central Miami Beach: Along Collins Avenue

The garbage-clogged **Collins Canal** defines the southern edge of Central Miami Beach, cut in the 1910s to speed the movement of farm produce through the mangrove trees which then lined Biscayne Bay. The canal's a dismal sight, but as it flows into the luxury yacht-lined Indian Creek the outlook improves, and along Collins Avenue you'll see the first of the sleek condos and hotels that symbolize the area.

Unlike their small Art Deco counterparts in South Beach, the later **hotels** of Central Miami Beach are massive monuments to the Fifties. When big was beautiful, these state-of-the-art pleasure palaces drew the international jet set by offering much more than mere accommodation: a price that few could afford also bought access to exclusive bars, restaurants and lounges where film and TV stars cavorted with other film and TV stars – as the rest of the US looked enviously on. The good times were short-lived. As everyone tried to cash in, cheap imitations of the pace-setting hotels formed an ugly wall of concrete along Collins Avenue; quality sank, service deteriorated and the big names moved on – quickly followed by the general public. By the Seventies, many of the hotels looked like what they really were: monsters from another time. As Miami's social star re-emerged through the Eighties, a revival got underway. Many of the polished-up hotels are now occupied by well-heeled Latin American tourists – along with grey-haired swingers from the US for whom Miami Beach will always be It.

The Fontainebleau

Prior to Central Miami Beach becoming a celebrities' playground, the nation's rich and powerful built rambling, shorefront mansions here. One such, the winter home of tyre-baron Harvey Firestone, was demolished in 1953 to make room for the **Fontainebleau Hotel**, 4441 Collins Avenue, a "dreamland of kitsch and consumerism" that defined the Miami Beach of the late Fifties and Sixties. Gossip-sheet perennials such as Joan Crawford, Joe DiMaggio, Lana Turner and Bing Crosby were *Fontainebleau* regulars, as was rebel crooner Frank Sinatra who, besides starting a scrambled-egg fight in the coffeeshop, shot many scenes here as the private-eye hero of the Sixties movie *Tony Rome*. Drop in for a look around the curving lobby, overhung by weighty chandeliers, and venture through the tree-coated grounds to the swimming pool, complete with rock grottoes and waterfalls to match.

If you can't face the toadying bellhops lurking in the lobby, one feature you shouldn't miss is on an exterior wall: approaching from the south, Collins Avenue veers left just before the hotel, passing beneath Richard Haas' 13,000-square-foot *trompe l'oeil* **mural**. Unveiled in 1986, it creates the illusion of a great hole in the wall exposing the hotel directly behind – one of the biggest driving hazards in Miami.

Further along Collins Avenue: More Hotels and Rich Homes

Truth be told, there's not much more to see in Central Miami Beach. For its place in local folklore, the *Fontainebleau* is easily the most tempting of the hotels, though you might snatch glances inside the *Shawnee*, no 4343, and the *Castle Beach Club*, no 5445, both Fifties survivors who've undergone stylized renovation, with marble floors, indoor fountains and etched glasswork. Meanwhile, the ultra-

THE HOLOCAUST MEMORIAL

At 1933–1945 Meridian Avenue in Central Miami Beach, it's hard not to be moved
by Kenneth Treister's **Holocaust Memorial**, completed in 1990. Depicting a
human hand reaching towards the sky with life-sized figures of emaciated and
tormented people attempting to climb its arm, the deeply emotive sculpture rises
from a lily pond in the centre of a plaza, around which are graphic images recalling
the Nazi genocide against the Jews.

swish *Alexander*, no 5225, has become a watering hole of Miami's present-day
smart set – don't try to sleep on the sofas.

Many of the rich people who live in Miami Beach have gracefully appointed
homes up pine-tree-lined drives on the other side of Indian Creek. Cross the
water with Arthur Godfrey Road and drive (or cycle) around the exclusive La
Gorce Drive and Alton Road for an eyeful of what money can buy.

Should the wealth become overpowering, your only escape is to move swiftly
on down Collins Avenue; not that what lies ahead is much of a pull. Surveying the
hotel-dominated scene stretching from here to North Miami Beach, an unrestrained Norman Mailer wrote in 1968: "Moorish castles shaped like waffle irons,
shaped like the baffle plates on white plastic electric heaters, and cylinders like
Waring blenders, buildings looking like giant op art and pop art paintings, and
sweet wedding cakes, cottons of kitsch and piles of dirty cotton stucco. . .".

North Miami Beach and Inland

Collins Avenue continues for seven uninspiring miles through **NORTH MIAMI
BEACH**, enriched only by a few noteworthy beaches and parks. Confusingly, due
to the dubious machinations of early property speculators, the four small communities that make up this northern section of Miami Beach lack a collective appella-
tion, and the area officially titled "North Miami Beach" is actually inland, across
Biscayne Bay.

Surfside and Bal Harbor

Untouched for years as big money developments loomed all around, the low-rise
buildings of **SURFSIDE** – the pleasant North Shore Park marks the community's
southern limit – evoke a moderately appealing old-fashioned mood, although the
community is in the throes of upward mobility and only the neighborhood **beach**,
between 91st and and 95th streets, will make you want to stick around; incidentally, it's one of the few in Miami Beach to allow topless sunbathing.

Directly north, **BAL HARBOR** is similar in size to Surfside but entirely different in character: an upscale residential area filled with the carefully guarded
homes and apartments of the some of the nation's wealthiest people. The exclusive *Bal Harbor Shops*, 9700 Collins Avenue, packed with outrageously expensive
designer stores, sets the area's snotty tone. A better place to spend time is
Haulover Beach Park, just to the north, whose sprawling vegetation backs onto
more than a mile of uncrowded beach – and there's a great view of the Miami
Beach skyline from the end of the pier.

Sunny Isles and Golden Beach

Beyond Haulover Park, **SUNNY ISLES** is as lifeless as they come: a place where European travel agencies dump their unsuspecting package tourists, who proceed to dominate the restaurants and tacky souvenir shops along Collins Avenue. You'll quickly get a tan on Sunny Isles' sands, but everything around is geared to middle-of-the-road tourism. Of passing interest, however, are some architecturally over-the-top hotels erected during the Fifties: along Collins Avenue, watch out for the camels and sheikhs guarding the *Sahara*, no 18335; the crescent-moon-holding maidens of the *Blue Mist*, no 19111; and the Moorish-Polynesian-Deco-Ultra-Bad-Kitsch style of the *Marco Polo*, no 19200.

By the time you reach **GOLDEN BEACH**, the northernmost community of Miami Beach, much of the traffic pounding Collins Avenue has turned inland on the 192nd Street Causeway, and the anachronistic hotels have given way to quiet shorefront homes. Public beach access here is negligible, and if you're not intending to leave Miami altogether (Collins Avenue, as Hwy-A1A, continues north to Fort Lauderdale), there's a bigger draw to be found directly inland.

Inland: the Old Spanish Monastery

Crossing the Sunny Isles Causeway (163rd Street) to the mainland leads into "North Miami Beach" – despite its name, a continuation of the depressed suburbs north of downtown Miami, and not an area to linger in. The only reason to come here is the last thing you'd expect: the **Old Spanish Monastery** (Mon–Sat 10am–5pm, Sun noon–5pm; $4), a twelfth-century monastery transported from Spain. Publishing magnate William Randolph Hearst came across the monastery in 1925, bought it for $500,000, broke it into numbered pieces and shipped it to the US – only for it to be held by customs, fearful that it might carry foot-and-mouth disease.

The demands of tax officials left Hearst short of ready funds, and the monastery lingered in a New York warehouse until 1952, when the pieces were brought here and reassembled as a tourist attraction. The job took a year and a half, done largely by trial and error thanks to the incorrect repacking of the pieces. Pacing the cloisters, as Cistercian monks did for 700 years, the uneven form of the buttressed ceilings and rough, honey-colored walls is clear, although the monastery – now used as an Episcopal church – is a model of tranquillity, its peacefulness enhanced by a lush garden setting. As you go in, look out for the photos in the entrance room showing the 11,000 boxes that contained the monastery when it came ashore – and a docker standing over them, scratching his head.

If you're not driving, **getting to the monastery** is relatively easy with buses #E, #H and #V from Sunny Isles, or #3 from downtown Miami; another possibility is to use the North Miami Beach *Greyhound* station, 16250 Biscayne Boulevard (☎305/945-0801). Each of these routes, though, leaves a nail-biting ten-minute walk through some very dodgy streets.

Continuing North: Towards Fort Lauderdale

The coastal route, Hwy-A1A (Collins Avenue) and the mainland Hwy-1 (Biscayne Boulevard) both continue into Hollywood, at the southern edge of the Fort Lauderdale area, fully described in Chapter Three. By **public transit**, you can travel north with *Broward County Transit* (☎305/357-8400) buses from the vast Aventura shopping mall on the corner of Lehman Causeway (192nd Street) and Biscayne Boulevard.

THE FACTS

Due perhaps to the cool night-time breeze that blows the humidity out of the subtropical heat, no one in Miami it seems can wait to get out and enjoy themselves. Entertainment listings are unfailingly the most-read section of any newspaper, and the very thought of not devoting evenings and weekends to hedonistic pursuits would bring many locals out in a rash.

Social **drinking** usually serves as a curtain-raiser on the night rather than an end in itself, seldom allowed to impinge on **eating** time: Miamians think nothing of eating out three times a day seven days a week, and the range of food on offer spans most of the world and suits all budgets – discovering and devouring Cuban cuisine being one of the joys of the city. Don't be surprised if the place where you had dinner doubles as a **live music** spot: restaurant back rooms feature significantly on a small but enjoyable local live music network, where reggae shines strongly. The city's effervescent **club** scene is fun to explore, too – set around South Beach's Art Deco strip are some of the hippest nightspots in the whole country. High-brow **arts** are steady rather than spectacular, with several orchestras, three respected dance groups and a diverse choice of drama at several medium-sized theaters. And if these don't appeal, you can burn up excess energy cruising the **shops**, not the country's greatest totems of consumerism but easily sufficient to slake a thirst for acquisition.

Miami is virtually impossible to **get around** at night without a car or taxi, although the bulk of the bars, live music spots and clubs are within walking distance of one another in South Beach. If you're staying in South Beach, you won't have to worry about parking lots or fret over the city's paucity of late-night buses; if you're not, you might use the *Breeze* minibuses to get there – and back – from downtown Miami (see p.59).

To find out **what's on**, read the listings in *New Times*, or in the Friday *Weekend* section of the *Miami Herald*. Make use, too, of the several **telephone hotlines** – see the box below – giving recorded information.

WHAT'S ON TELEPHONE HOTLINES

Call the following numbers for recorded information on what's happening in Miami.

Blues Hotline	☎666-MOJ	PACE Free Concert Hotline	☎681-1470
Folk Hotline	☎595-8042	WTMI Cultural Arts Line	☎550-9393
Jazz Hotline	☎382-3938	WSHE-FM Concert Hotline	☎581-7655
Movie Hotline	☎888-FILM	ZETA Link Concert Hotline	☎372-1442

Eating

With everything from the greasiest hotdog stand to the finest gourmet restaurant desperately vying for the tourist – as well as the local – dollar, **eating** in Miami is a buyer's market. All over the city, street stands, cafés and coffeeshops offer decent, filling **breakfasts** and all-day **budget food** (a good feed for under $5), and many restaurants dish up barely finishable **lunches** at remarkably low prices – $5–8 is about average. **Dinner** can be good value, too, rarely more than $10–15, and you don't need to be rich to indulge in the occasional blowout. Anywhere that serves breakfast is usually open at 6am or 7am, most restaurants do business between noon and midnight or 1am, some closing between lunch and dinner, and a few operating around the clock – see the box on p.102.

The big fast-food franchises and pizza chains are as plentiful here as elsewhere across the country, and typical **American** food, such as thick, juicy burgers and sizeable sandwiches, is easily found. Miami is too cosmopolitan for a single food style to be dominant, however, and only **seafood**, every bit as plentiful and good as you would expect so close to fish-laden tropical waters, is a common factor among the city's plethora of cuisines drawn from every corner of the Americas – and beyond.

So common all over the city that it hardly seems an ethnic cuisine at all, **Cuban** food is what Miami does best. A sizeable lunch or dinner in one of the innumerable small, family-run Cuban diners (always pleased to show off their culinary skills to non-Spanish-speaking customers) will cost an absurdly low $4–7, a fraction of the price of an identical meal at one of the fancier Cuban restaurants – mostly in Little Havana and Coral Gables – now being discovered by the nation's food critics. In Miami, though, **Haitian** cooking is the current rage, and the small but growing number of restaurants in Little Haiti, just north of downtown Miami, are, as you'd expect, the places to sample it. The city's strong Caribbean and Latin American elements are further acknowledged by **Argentinian**, **Jamaican**, **Nicaraguan** and **Peruvian** cooking, although, aside from Cuban food, for sheer quality and value for money it's hard to better the many **Japanese** outlets, most north of downtown Miami and a few in South Miami – all much cheaper than their European counterparts. **Chinese** and **Thai** places are abundant, too, as is low-cost **Italian** and **Mexican** food. By contrast, **Indian** food is having hard time taking root, despite a couple of commendable restaurants in Coral Gables in which to eat it.

The cost of dinner can be reduced by looking out for **early-bird specials**, when many restaurants knock a few dollars off the price of a full evening meal simply to get buns on seats from 5pm to 7pm. Be aware, too, of the **free food** offered at **happy hours** (see "Drinking") and the ample buffets that constitute Sunday **brunch** – see below.

Downtown and around

Aux Palmistes Chez Julie, 6820 NE Second Ave (☎759-8527). Where Little Haiti dances (see "Live Music") and dines on home-cooked fried pork, goat and fish. Closed Mon.

Big Fish, 55 SW Miami Ave Rd (☎372-3725). Lively lunch-only spot on the Miami River, with folding chairs, benches and picnic tables. Home-cooked fish sandwiches, fresh seafood chowder and more served. Closed Sun.

Bimini Grill, 620 NE 78th St (☎758-9154). Florida bayou-style food in a wooden shack on a river bank. Barbecued meats and Caribbean conch fritters are among the treats.

Brickell Delicatessen, 1101 Brickell Ave (☎374-3790). Open weekdays for fast breakfasting and lunching middle-management types. Good sandwiches, morning bagel and eggy dishes.

Chez Moi, 1 NW 54th St (☎756-7540). Not cheap, but a strong creole menu makes this Miami's top-ranked Haitian restaurant.

Dick Clark's American Bandstand Grill, at the *Bayside Marketplace*, 401 Biscayne Blvd (☎381-8800). Great collection of rock'n'roll memorabilia, from Fabian to the Beatles, to admire as you munch a charbroiled burger.

East Coast Fisheries, 360 W Flagler St (☎373-5516). Pick of the extensive seafood menu is the fish and chips for $8.95.

Firehouse Four, 1000 S Miami Ave (☎379-1923). Restored fire station usually frequented by three-piece suiters walking over from Brickell Avenue for pricey but good American and Continental fare. See "Drinking."

Gourmet Diner, 13900 Biscayne Blvd (☎947-2255). Always a line for a winning Continental daily menu.

Granny Feelgood's, 190 SE First Ave (☎358-6233). Delighting the discerning wholefood nibbler with lots of succulent nutty and fruity creations. Closed Sun.

Hiro, 17516 Biscayne Blvd (☎948-3687). Miami's only late-night sushi bar, and where the city's sushi chefs hang out after work. Open until 4am.

Joe's Seafood Restaurant, 2771 NW 24th St (☎638-8602). The dockside setting improves the otherwise only adequate seafood. Not to be confused with *Joe's Stone Crab* (see "Miami Beach").

Rita's Italian Restaurant, 7232 Biscayne Blvd (☎757-9470). Family-run Italian diner with check tablecloths, hearty portions and good prices – and an owner inclined to burst into song.

S & S Sandwich Shop, 1757 NE Second Ave (☎373-4291). Under the same ownership for nearly fifty years, proffering platefuls of meatloaf, turkey, stuffed cabbage, beef stew, shrimp creole or pork chops for less than $6. Counter service only. Closed Sun.

Shagnasty's Saloon & Eatery, 638 S Miami Ave (☎381-8970). Restaurant section of *Tobacco Road* (see "Drinking" and "Live Music"), its hamburgers, fries and sandwiches consumed by relaxing yuppies.

Shiroi Hana, 12460 NE Seventh Ave (☎891-5160). Excellent Japanese cuisine in roomy, comfortable setting. Extensive menu and polite clientele and staff.

Super Duper Sandwich Restaurant, 206 NE First Ave (☎374-5493). Biggest and busiest Cuban diner in downtown Miami. Closed Sun.

Tani Guchi's Place, 2224 NE 123 St (☎892-6744). Authentic, innovative and attractive Japanese food.

Las Tapas, at the *Bayside Marketplace*, 401 Biscayne Blvd (☎372-2737). Spanish bar and restaurant in Miami's zestiest shopping mall. Tapas served with sangria and a basket of bread.

Tark's, 13750 Biscayne Blvd (☎944-8275). Fast-and-fresh seafood: shrimp, Alaskan snow crab, stone crab claws, clams and oysters, all at picnic prices.

Trixie's, 3600 NE Second Ave (☎573-6799). Healthy all-natural foods served for breakfast and lunch. Very reasonably priced, and popular with the fashion designers who work nearby.

Two Guys Soul Food Restaurant, 3721 NW 167th St (☎624-5516). Soul food takeout: chitterlings, collard greens, conch, oxtail and beef stew.

Unicorn, at the *Waterways* mall, 3565 NE 207th St (☎933-8829). The city's most successful health food restaurant, with nutritious meals at sensible prices.

Little Havana

Ayestaran, 706 SW 27th Ave (☎649-4982). Long a favorite Cuban restaurant among those in the know, especially good value for its $5 daily specials.

La Carreta, 3632 SW Eighth St (☎444-7501). The real sugar cane growing around the wagon wheel outside is a good sign: inside, downhome Cuban cooking is served at unbeatable prices.

Casablanca Cafeteria, 2300 SW Eighth St (☎642-2751). Large family-style Cuban restaurant dispensing ample portions over two horseshoe-shaped counters, with an espresso bar opening onto the busy street.

Casa Juancho, 2436 SW Eighth St (☎642-2452). Pricey, but the tapas are good value at $6–8, and there's a convivial mood as strolling musicians serenade wealthy Cubans.

El Cid, 117 NW 42nd Ave (☎642-3144). A gargantuan Moorish-style castle where the staff dress as knaves and dioramas of freshly killed fowl greet you at the door. Lots of drinking, singing and eating with affordable Spanish and Cuban delicacies.

La Esquina de Tejas, 101 SW Twelfth St (☎545-5341). Where Reagan and Bush both solicited the Hispanic vote, and turning out dependable Cuban lunches and dinners – if the signed photos of Ronald don't put you off.

El Inka, 1756 SW Eighth St (☎845-0243). The city's oldest and best Peruvian restaurant, famed for its spicy meats and seafood, and doing extraordinary things with squid.

Hy-Vong, 3458 SW Eighth St (☎446-3674). Tiny dinner-only Vietnamese restaurant, a favorite of hip yuppies and Vietnam vets. No-frills, slow service, but damn good food. Closed Mon.

Las Islas Canarias, 285 NW 27th Ave (☎649-0440). Tucked away inside a drab shopping mall. Piles of fine, unpretentious Cuban food at unbeatable prices.

Malaga, 740 SW Eighth St (☎858-4224). Spanish and Cuban cuisine, specializing in fresh fish dishes, served inside or in the courtyard.

La Palacio de los Jugos, 5721 W Flagler Ave (☎264-1503). A handful of tables at the back of a Cuban produce market, where the pork sandwiches and shellfish soup from the takeout stand are the tastiest for miles.

Versailles, 3555 SW Eighth St (☎444-0240). Chandeliers, mirrored walls, a great atmosphere and wonderful inexpensive Cuban food.

Coral Gables

Café 94, 94 Miracle Mile (☎444-7933). With low-cost lunches and snacks, makes a fine pit-stop while exploring the area. Closed Sun.

Cheese Villa Café, 264 Miracle Mile (☎446-3133). Does a brisk trade in well-stuffed deli sandwiches and tasty soups.

El Corral, 3545 Coral Way (☎444-8272). An appealingly priced Nicaraguan eatery where anything that isn't beef isn't taken seriously – carnivores' heaven.

Darbar, 276 Alhambra Circle (☎448-9691). New Indian restaurant seeking to enlighten local tastebuds with a full selection of the basics, plus a few specialties. Closed Sun.

Doc Dammers' Bar & Grill, inside the *Colonnade Hotel*, 180 Aragon Ave (☎441-2600). Affordable eating in a spacious, old-style saloon; serving breakfast, lunch and dinner and offering a happy hour in its piano bar. See the "Happy Hours" box on p.105.

Hofbrau Pub & Grill, 172 Giralda Ave (☎442-2730). Three daily specials, but come for the Wednesday night $7-all-you-can-eat fish-fry. Closed Sun. See "Drinking".

House of India, 22 Merrick Way (☎444-2348). Quality catch-all Indian food including some excellently priced lunch buffets.

Marshall Majors, 6901 SW 57th Ave (☎665-3661). Very amenable neighborhood deli with great service and food.

Mykonos, 1201 Coral Way (☎856-3140). Greek food in an unassuming atmosphere: spinako-pita, lemon chicken soup, gyros, souvlaki and huge Greek salads.

Restaurant St Michel, in *Hotel Place St Michel*, 162 Alcazar Ave (☎444-1666). Outstanding French and Mediterranean cuisine amid antiques and flowers. Not cheap, but very alluring.

Victor's Café, 2340 SW 32nd Ave (☎445-1313). Mambo musicians secreted about the palms and fountains make for a lively meal but the Cuban food – while good – tends to be overpriced.

Yoko's, 4041 Ponce de Leon Blvd (☎444-6622). Intimate Japanese restaurant usually packed with students from the neighboring University of Miami.

Yuca, 148 Giralda Ave (☎444-4448). Currently the rave of food critics up and down the land, serving nouvelle Cuban cuisine in a deliberate gourmet-diner setting; great stuff, but don't budget for under $50 each.

24-HOUR EATS

These are places where you can get reasonably priced food all night. See the eating listings for fuller details. All five are in Miami Beach.

David's Coffee Shop, corner of Eleventh St and Collins Ave (☎534-8763).

Eleventh Street Diner, 1065 Washington Ave (☎534-6373). Fri and Sat only.

News Café, 800 Ocean Drive (☎538-6397).

Ted's Hideaway South, 124 Second St (no phone).

Wolfie's, 2038 Collins Ave (☎538-6626).

Coconut Grove

Big City Fish, inside *CocoWalk*, 3015 Grand Ave (☎445-2489). Mouthwatering seafood, gumbos and conch-fritters presented in a warehouse-like setting.

Café Tu Tu Tango, inside *CocoWalk*, 3015 Grand Ave (☎529-2222). A quirky and entertaining spot themed as an artist's garret; lengthy menu of good-quality food served in tapas-sized portions.

Captain Dick's Tackle Shack, 3381 Pan American Drive (☎854-5871). In the shadow of Miami City Hall and a great find in an otherwise expensive area: filling seafood and salads all at rock-bottom prices.

Fuddruckers, 3444 Main Hwy (☎442-8164). Where sides of beef hang from hooks before being turned into ultra-fresh burgers.

Grove Café, 3484 Main Hwy (☎445-0022). Succulent burgers to munch as you watch the Coconut Grove groovers swan by.

Hungry Sailor, 3064½ Grand Ave (☎444-9359). Pseudo-British pub creates moderately successful fish and chips and shepherd's pie, but does better with its conch chowder. See "Drinking" and "Live Music".

Mandarin Garden, 3268 Grand Ave (☎446-9999 or ☎442-1234). Very tasty, affordable Chinese food. The free parking is a big plus during traffic-jammed weekends.

Scotty's, 338 Pan American Drive (☎854-2626). Simple setting for tasty seafood and fish'n'chips consumed from marina-side picnic tables.

Señor Frog's, 3008 Grand Ave (☎448-0999). Broad selection of reasonably priced Mexican food, but most people come to gulp down margaritas.

Zanzibar, 3468 Main Hwy (☎444-0244). The burgers and omelettes may remove hunger pangs but the real attraction is people-watching from the outdoor tables.

Key Biscayne

Bayside Seafood Restaurant, 3501 Rickenbacker Causeway (☎361-0808). Variety of down-to-earth seafood dishes at bargain prices. See "Drinking" and "Live Music".

Beach House, 12 Crandon Blvd (☎361-1038). Gossipy locals' haunt for three square meals a day.

The Sandbar, at *Silver Sands Motel & Villas*, 301 Ocean Drive (☎361-5441). Tucked-away seafood restaurant offering easily affordable lunch or dinner a pebble's throw from crashing ocean waves.

Sunday's on the Bay, 5420 Crandon Blvd (☎361-6777). Marina seafood eatery catering to the boats and beer set. Very casual. See "Live Music".

South Miami

Anthony's, corner of 98th Ave & N Kendall Drive (☎595-8808). Above-average Italian meals.

Cami's Seashells, 6272 S Dixie Hwy (☎665-1288). Fast-food seafood restaurant. Half-lobster dinner specials at $6.95 bring folks in droves.

Fountain & Grill, at *Sunset Drugs*, 5640 Sunset Drive (☎667-1807). Large, clean and modern version of the traditional drugstore fountain diner. Noted for its grilled cheese sandwiches, burgers and meatloaf.

JJ's American Diner, 5850 Sunset Drive (☎665-5499) and 12000 N Kendall Drive (☎598-0307). Big burgers and sandwiches in a contemporary soda shop setting, complete with blaring rock'n'roll.

Never On Sunday, 9707 S Dixie Hwy (☎662-8739). Friendly joint serves cheap Greek and Italian dishes.

Old Cutler Inn, 7271 SW 168th St (☎238-1514). A neo-rustic country inn that's a neighborhood fave for its steaks and shrimps and for its delicious desserts.

Pars, 10827 SW 40th St (☎551-1099). Good Iranian food in a simple setting.

Sakura, 8225 SW 124th St (☎238-8462). Tiny sushi bar and restaurant that's always packed and gives good value.

Shorty's Bar-B-Q, 9200 S Dixie Hwy (☎665-5732). Sit at a picnic table, tuck a napkin in your shirt and graze on barbecued ribs and chicken and corn on the cob – pausing only to gaze at the cowboy memorabilia on the walls.

Su Shin, 10501 N Kendall Drive (☎271-3235). Great teriyakis, daily specials and sushi chefs with a sense of humor.

El Torito, at *The Falls* mall, 8888 Howard Drive (☎255-6506). Staff and decor are authentically Mexican and the food and the margaritas are a potent combination.

El Toro Taco, 1 S Krome Ave (☎245-5576). Excellent family-run Mexican restaurant, a gem in the center of Homestead.

Tropical Delite, 10865B Caribbean Blvd, at the *Caribbean Plaza* (☎235-5615). Dirt-cheap Jamaican home cooking: jerk chicken and goat curry among the favorites.

Wagons West, 13111 S Dixie Hwy (☎238-9942). Maximum cholesterol breakfasts and other unhealthy fare are avidly consumed in this always-crowded, budget-priced shrine to cowboys and the Wild West; sit at wagon-shaped booths and admire the Western memorabilia lining the walls.

Miami Beach

Aqua, 1400 Ocean Drive (☎534-5288). Arty but hearty sidewalk café, serving nouvelle cuisine for breakfast, lunch and dinner. The summertime prix-fixe dinner is usually good value.

Barrio, 1049 Washington Ave (☎532-8585). An unappealing nook but serving good Tex-Mex cuisine; on Monday nights, the waiters dress in drag.

Blue Star, at the *Raleigh Hotel*, 1775 Collins Ave (☎534-1775). An intimate restaurant patronized by the famous and the fashionable; expensive but divinely chic.

Caffè Cozzolino, 1627 Michigan Ave (☎672-2042). Good, inexpensive Italian food in a loft setting in the Lincoln Road arts district.

Caffè Milano, 850 Ocean Drive (☎531-3485). Fashionable café with a stylish yet relaxed atmosphere, worth sampling over a cappuccino or a snack.

Casona de Carlitos, 2232 Collins Ave (☎534-7013). Hearty Argentinian food and live pampas-synthpop music, lots of pasta Latin style and grilled red meat.

Cielito Lindo, 1626 Pennsylvania Ave (☎673-0480). Low-cost Mexican food is served with a smile in this cozy restaurant, handily placed just off Lincoln Road.

Crawdaddy's, 1 Washington Ave (☎673-1708). Chain restaurant designed in rustic fashion, with decent seafood and an excellent view of cruise ships sailing through Government Cut.

Dab Haus, 852 Alton Rd (☎534-9557). Locals and passing German tourists alike take a shine to the schnitzel and sauerbraten served at this folksy and inexpensive fill-up joint.

David's Coffee Shop, corner of Eleventh St and Collins Ave (☎534-8763). Low-priced Latin food served all day and all night to a crowd that's sleazy but discerning. See "24-Hour Eats".

Las Delicias de Alton Road, 1670 Alton Rd (☎531-7068). Cheap Cuban food living up to the establishment's name.

Don't Say Sandwich to Me, 1331 Washington Ave (☎532-6700). Besides the hangover breakfast special from 4 to 11am, serves every quick eat imaginable. Open 24 hours.

Eleventh Street Diner, 1065 Washington Ave (☎534-6373). All-American fare served around the clock on Fri and Sat; eat inside in cozy booths or outside on the terrace.

A Fish Called Avalon, 700 Ocean Drive (☎532-1727). Nouvelle seafood cuisine, an ocean-front setting and a fashionably peopled bar.

Joe's Stone Crab, 227 Biscayne St (☎673-0365). Only open from October to May when Florida stone crabs are in season; expect long lines of people waiting to pay $20 for a plateful of the succulent crustacean.

Larios on the Beach, 820 Ocean Drive (☎532-9577). Affordable and authentic Cuban food served in a Latin nightclub atmosphere – when the live band strikes up, the diners dance.

Lulu's, 1053 Washington Ave (☎532-6147). Deep-southern home cooking: fried chicken, greens, black-eyed peas and more, but you pay for the Elvis Presley memorabilia on the walls.

HAPPY HOURS

Almost every restaurant in Miami has a **happy hour**, usually on weekdays from 5 to 8pm, when drinks are cheap and come in tandem with a large pile of food – varying from chicken wings and conch fritters to chips and popcorn – from which you can stuff yourself for free, saving the cost of dinner later on. Watch for the signs outside or scan the numerous newspaper ads for the best deals – or try one of our listings, which are consistently among the best in the city.

Crawdaddy's, 1 Washington Ave, Miami Beach (☎673-1708). Cut-price oysters, shrimp and drinks in Miami Beach's most congenial happy hour.

Coco Loco's, in the *Sheraton*, 495 Brickell Ave near downtown Miami (☎373-6000). No better place to finish off a day downtown; the drinks are high but for a dollar you help yourself to a massive buffet.

Doc Dammers' Bar & Grill, inside the *Colonnade Hotel*, 180 Aragon Ave, Coral Gables (☎441-2600). Where the young (ish) and unattached of Coral Gables mingle after work to the strains of a pianist. See "Eating".

El Torito, in *The Falls* mall, 8888 Howard Drive, South Miami (☎255-6506). Happy hour drinks are 2-for-1 and there are free appetizers in this Mexican restaurant.

Firehouse Four, 1000 S Miami Ave, downtown Miami (☎379-1923). Happy hour in this 1923 former fire station is a riot of thirty-something yuppies pretending there's no economic recession.

Monty's Raw Bar, 2560 S Bayshore Drive, Coconut Grove (☎858-1431). Cheap drinks wash down the seafood, and tropical music complements the bay view at Coconut Grove's best happy hour.

Shagnasty's Saloon & Eatery, 638 S Miami Ave, near downtown Miami (☎381-8970). The hip yuppie's happy hour hangout, with free appetizers and many discounted drinks.

Mappy's, 1390 Ocean Drive (☎532-2064). Good cheap Cuban food lures beach bums and tourists, as does the fresh-squeezed-juice bar and the tropical milk shakes.

News Café, 800 Ocean Drive (☎538-6397). Utterly fashionable sidewalk café with extensive breakfast, lunch and dinner menu and front-row seating for the South Beach promenade.

Our Place Natural Foods Eatery, 830 Washington Ave (☎674-1322). Basic health food; low prices and a changing vegetarian menu.

Palace Bar & Grill, 1200 Ocean Ave (☎531-9077). One of the few trendy places for breakfast, opening for a party at 8am. Otherwise general inexpensive fare and good burgers.

Pineapples, 530 Arthur Godfrey Rd (☎532-9731). Fresh juices and vegetarian dishes and fabulous desserts.

Puerto Sagua, 700 Collins Ave (☎673-9569). Where local Cubans meet gringos over espresso coffee, beans and rice. Cheap, filling breakfasts, lunches and dinners.

Rascal House, 17190 Collins Ave (☎947-4581). Largest and loudest New York deli in town; huge portions and football stadium ambience.

Rolo's, 38 Ocean Drive (☎532-2662). Bleach-blonds and tanned Latin surfers breakfast here before surf's up. Also serves Cuban- and American-style lunches and dinners and stocks a formidable range of beers. See "Drinking".

Le Sandwicherie, 229 Fourteenth St (☎532-8934). French-style version of a Cuban sidewalk snack bar, with sandwiches to go or to stand and devour.

The Strand, 671 Washington Ave (☎532-2340). A place to see and be seen in; offering nouvelle and regular American food for trendy regulars and the slumming celeb.

Ted's Hideaway South, 124 Second St (no phone). Downbeat bar that proffers cheap fried chicken, steak and red beans and rice; see "Drinking".

Thai Toni, 890 Washington Ave (☎538-8424). Thai food at moderate prices in a fashionable hangout.

Titi's Tacos, 1321 Washington Blvd (☎532-3045). Fast, cheap and cheerful Mexican food.

Toni's New Tokyo Cuisine & Sushi Bar, 1208 Washington Ave (☎673-9368). Japanese cuisine for the American palate, such as South Beach roll – eel, salmon skin scallions, cucumber and masago – among many more curiosities.

Villa Deli, 1065 Alton Rd (☎538-4552). A transplanted New York deli serving the best hot pastrami for miles.

Wolfie's, 2038 Collins Ave (☎538-6626). Long-established deli drawing an entertaining mix of New York retirees and late-night clubbers – all served generous helpings by beehive-haired waitresses. Open 24 hours.

Brunch

Sunday **brunch** in Miami is usually a more upscale affair than its equivalents in New York or Los Angeles, with high-quality buffet food laid out in a stylish setting; the nosh is only occasionally accompanied by cheap drinks. Served from 11am to 2pm, brunch costs $5–30 depending on the quality of the food; again, check the newspapers for up-to-the-minute offers, or simply show up with a big appetite at one listed below – all in Miami Beach unless stated.

Brunch spots

Beach Villa Chinese Restaurant, at the *Beach Paradise Hotel*, 600 Ocean Drive (☎532-2679). Excellent dim sum brunch on Sat and Sun.

Biltmore Hotel, 1200 Anastasia Ave, Coral Gables (☎445-1926). Miami's most expensive brunch and served in the city's most historic hotel; overpriced but worth the indulgence just once.

Colony Bistro, 736 Ocean Drive (☎673-6776). Gourmet brunch served in a small but stylish sidewalk cafe; great for people-watching.

The Dining Galleries, at the *Fontainebleau Hotel*, 4441 Collins Ave (☎538-2000). Gargantuan buffet and doting service; also a sneaky way to glimpse the inside of this Fifties landmark hotel.

Grand Café, at the *Grand Bay Hotel*, 2669 S Bayshore Drive, Coconut Grove (☎858-0009). Fine food and lots of it in a very chic dining room – attracts the well-heeled glutton.

Sundays on the Bay, 5420 Biscayne Blvd, Key Biscayne (☎361-6777). The biggest and most enjoyable brunch in Miami; make a reservation to avoid waiting in line.

Drinking: Bars and Pubs

Miami's **drinking** is more commonly done in restaurants, nightclubs and discos than in the seedy **bars** so beloved of American film-makers. One or two dimly lit dives do capture the essence of the archetypal US bar, however and a handful of Irish and British **pubs** stock imported ales. But it's more in keeping with the spirit of the city to booze in restaurant lounges, the back rooms of music spots or at shorefront hotel bars. Most places where you can drink are open from 11am or noon until midnight or 2am, with 10pm to 1am being the liveliest hours.

Among the listings which follow, some are suited to an early evening tipple before moving on to dinner or a club; others – especially those in Coconut Grove and Miami Beach – make prime vantage points for watching the city's poseurs come and go; any will suffice if you just want to get tanked up. Prices are broadly similar, though the most pose-worthy places sometimes charge way above the average.

Downtown and around

Churchill's Hideaway, 5501 NE Second Ave (☎757-1807). A British enclave within Little Haiti, with soccer and rugby matches on video and UK beers on tap. See also "Live Music".

Firehouse Four, 1000 S Miami Ave (☎379-1923). By day filled by expense-account eaters (see "Eating"), in the evening Miami's oldest fire station makes a fine spot for a drink.

Tobacco Road, 626 S Miami Ave (☎374-1198). Crusty R&B venue (see "Live Music") which sees plenty of serious boozing in its downstairs bar.

Coral Gables

Duffy's Tavern, 2108 SW 57th Ave (☎264-6580). Pool tournaments and a large TV screen beaming sports events for the athletically minded drinker.

Hofbrau Pub & Grill, 172 Giralda Ave (☎442-2730). A fairly upscale dining place with a tavern-like atmosphere conducive to mellow imbibing.

John Martin's, 253 Miracle Mile (☎445-3777). Irish pub with occasional folk singers and harpists accompanying a good batch of imported brews. See "Live Music".

Coconut Grove

Fat Tuesday, inside *CocoWalk*, 3015 Grand Ave (☎441-2992). Part of a chain of bars famous for their fruit-flavored frozen daiquiris, which can be imbibed here while gazing over the milling crowds.

Hungry Sailor, 3064½ Grand Ave (☎444-9359). A would-be British pub with overpriced *Bass* and *Watneys* on tap, though the atmosphere is made by the nightly live reggae; see "Live Music".

Monty's Bayshore Restaurant, 2560 S Bayshore Drive (☎858-1431). Drinkers often outnumber the diners (see "Eating"), drawn here by the gregarious mood and the views across the bay.

Taurus, 3540 Main Hwy (☎448-0633). Old Coconut Grove drinking institution, with a burger grill on weekends and a nostalgic Sixties-loving crowd.

Tavern in the Grove, 3416 Main Hwy (☎447-3884). Down-to-earth locals' haunt with bouncy jukebox and easy-going mood.

Key Biscayne

Bayside Seafood Restaurant, 3501 Rickenbacker Causeway (☎361-0808). Friendly beer-drinking crowd beside the bay. See "Eating" and "Live Music".

The Sandbar, at *Silver Sands Motel & Villas*, 301 Ocean Drive (☎361-5441). The poolside tiki bar is a prime site for sucking cocktails as the ocean crashes close by.

Miami Beach

Clevelander, 1020 Ocean Drive (☎531-3485). The ultimate poolside sports bar, with pool tables, sports-tuned TVs and partially-clothed athletic physiques attacking the brews.

Irish House, 1430 Alton Rd (☎534-5667). Old neighborhood bar with two well-used pool tables.

The Island Club, 701 Washington Ave (☎538-1213). Stylishly oak-panelled tavern suited to lingering over a tipple; turns into a hip club on selected nights – see "Nightlife".

Mac's Club Deuce, 222 Fourteenth St (☎531-6200). Raucous neighborhood bar open until 5am, with a CD jukebox, pool table and a clientele that includes cops, transvestites, artists and models.

Penrod's Beach Club, 1 Ocean Drive (☎538-2604). A tri-level playpen by the sand for musclebound hunks and their bikini-wearing babes, drinking beer and smearing suntan oil. See "Live Music".

Rebar, 1121 Washington Ave (☎672-4788). The South Beach bar for the fashionably grungy.

Shabeen Cookshack, at the Marlin Hotel, 1200 Collins Ave. Slightly upmarket Jamaican-style watering hole gently throbbing to recorded reggae.

The Spot, 216 Española Way (☎532-1682). Trendy biker bar made famous by its former owner, actor Mickey Rourke.

Ted's Hideaway South, 124 Second St (no phone). Beer for a dollar a can and special reductions on draft when it rains outside; serves basic bar food around the clock. See "Food" and "24-Hour Food".

Nightlife: clubs and discos

Miami's **nightlife** has taken a profound turn for the better since the days when leggy cabaret shows were the high point of the action. Right now, in every sense except the literal one, Miami is a very cool place to dance, drink and simply hang out in **clubs** rated by the cognoscenti as among the hippest in the world. The appeal of the trendiest clubs – few in number and secreted about Miami Beach's South Beach, shifting their name and changing site frequently – may fade once their novelty wears off and too many people come looking for them, but, for the time being, an air of excitement and vibrancy hangs over the scene and there are plenty of fresh ideas to excite the most jaded clubber. Read *New Times* for the latest raves – or, better still, quiz any likely-looking groover that you encounter around the cafés and bars of South Beach. If you don't give a fig for fashion and just want to dance your legs off, there are plenty of mainstream **discos** – no different from discos the world over – where you can do just that. More adventurously, track down one of the city's **salsa** or **merengue** (a slinky dance music from the Caribbean) clubs, hosted by Spanish-speaking DJs.

Not surprisingly, Friday and Saturday are the busiest nights, but there's a decent choice on any night and some of the mainstream discos boost their midweek crowds by offering cut-price drinks, free admission for women and bizarre asides such as aerobics shows and amateur strip contests. Most places open at 9pm and hit a peak between midnight and 2am – although some continue until 7am or 8am and provide a free breakfast buffet for those who make it all the way through. Usually there's a **cover charge** of $4–10 and a **minimum age** of 21 (it's normal for ID to be checked). Obviously you should dress with some sensitivity to the style of the club, but only by turning up in rags at the smartest door are you ever likely to be turned away on account of your clothes. All the following are in Miami Beach unless stated otherwise.

Clubs and discos

Les Bains, 753 Washington Ave (☎532-8768). You'll need to look trendy to get past the doorman into this South Beach version of a upscale European disco. If you're too jaded to dance, try your hand at the blackjack table.

Bash, 655 Washington Ave (☎538-2274). Many revellers get no further than the garden, although there's an intimate bar and a beckoning dance floor in this club co-owned by Madonna's ex, Sean Penn and Simply Red's Mick Hucknall; no cover.

Cameo Theatre, 1445 Washington Ave (☎673-8679). Each night this Art Deco one-time movie theater sees different fare, from disco to punk to world beat. Attracts a young crowd; cover varies.

Club Manhattan, 6600 Red Rd, South Miami (☎666-1335). Reggae, rap and house music most nights; cover varies.

Disco Inferno, Sun at the *Cameo Theater*, 1445 Washington Ave (☎534-5533). Riproaring Seventies trash disco celebrating the Bee Gees, Village People, Chic and other greats of the genre; $7.

Fifth Street, 429 Lenox Ave (☎531-1910). Mixture of reggae, rap, funk and soul throughout the week; free–$6.

Island Club, 701 Washington Ave (☎538-1213). A cool spot to hang out and dance; mood varies from night to night; free. See "Drinking".

Third Rail, 727 Lincoln Ave (☎672-2995). Could be thrash, reggae or rock depending on the night. Some of the crowd never leave the pool table; cover varies.

Union Bar & Grill, 653 Washington Ave (☎672-9958). Pass through the rooms decorated as an English gentleman's club and you'll find a psychedelic disco room; usually no cover.

Warsaw Ballroom, 1450 Collins Ave (☎531-4555). The dingiest and busiest nightspot in town; Friday is exclusively gay (see "Gay and Lesbian Miami") but Saturday is "straight night" and Wednesday is a riotous "strip night"; cover $5–10.

Salsa and merengue clubs

Bonfire, 1060 NE 79th St, Little Haiti (☎756-0200). Smooth and very danceable salsa sounds Wed–Sun; $2–5.

Club Tipico Dominicano, 1344 NW 36th St, Little Havana (☎634-7819). Top merengue DJ hosting the sessions Fri–Sun; $5.

El Inferno, 981 SW Eighth St, Little Havana (☎856-5523). Popular local disco with Latin grooves Fri & Sat; $6.

Live Music

In a city that still goes crazy over the studio-based latin-pop of local girl Gloria Estefan, you might not expect to find a **live music** scene at all in Miami. In fact, an impressive number of **locales** – many of them poky clubs or the back rooms of restaurants or hotels – host bands throughout the week. It's often a matter of quantity over quality, however. Be they glam, goth, indie or metal, the city's **rock bands** tend to be pale imitations of the better-known US and European groups who periodically add Miami to their tour schedules. **Jazz** fans fare slightly better, there's a trustworthy **R&B** site and a very minor **folk** scene, but it's **reggae** that's most worth seeking out. Aside from acts flying in from Jamaica, the musicians among Miami's sizeable Jamaican population appear regularly at several small spots. Elsewhere, there's a rare chance to hear live **Haitian** music, but, less exotically, if you want to listen to country sounds you'll have to depart the city altogether. Other than for megastar performers (see below), to see a band you've heard of, expect to pay $6–15; for a local act, admission will be $2–5 or free. Most places open up at 8pm or 9pm, with the main band onstage around 11pm or midnight.

The most comprehensive music **listings** are in *New Times*, but if you can't decide where to go on a Friday night, go along to South Pointe Park (see "Miami Beach"), where there's entertainment and usually a **free concert**; look for the posters strewn all over South Beach.

Miami also gets its share of **big performances**: the top names in rock, soul, jazz, reggae and funk going through their paces at one of the big performance outlets listed in the box above – none of which has much atmosphere; tickets will be $18–35 from a branch of *Ticketmaster* (outlets all over the city; phone ☎358-5885 for the nearest), or over the phone by credit card.

BIG PERFORMANCE SPOTS

James L. Knight Center, 400 SE Second Ave, downtown Miami (☎372-0277).

Joe Robbie Stadium, 2269 NW 199th St, 16 miles northwest of downtown Miami (☎623-6262).

Miami Arena, 721 NW First Ave, downtown Miami (☎530-4400).

Sunshine Music Theater, 5555 NW 95th St, north of downtown Miami (☎741-7400).

Rock, jazz and R&B

Cameo Theater, 1445 Washington Ave (☎532-0922). The spot for weird and wonderful left-field arty happenings, poetry readings and interesting bands. Cover varies.

Churchill's Hideaway, 5501 NE Second Ave, Little Haiti (☎757-1807). Good place to hear local hopeful rock and indie bands; $4–6. See "Drinking".

Mango's Tropical Cafe, 900 Ocean Drive (☎673-4422). It's hard to stand still when the Brazilian and Cuban bands who play on this terrace strike up. Usually no cover.

Peacock Café, 2977 McFarlane Rd, Coconut Grove (☎442-8833). Back-room lounge features jazz, blues and occasional rock acts; cover varies.

Penrod's on the Beach, 1 Ocean Drive (☎538-5019). Straight-down-the-line rock bands most weekends for the boozing beach crowd. See "Drinking". Free before 10pm; later $3–6.

Scully's Tavern, 9809 Sunset Drive, South Miami (☎271-7404). Rock and blues bands playing for beer-drinking, pool-playing regulars; free.

Stephen Talkhouse, 616 Collins Ave (☎531-7557). Coffeehouse ambience that makes a comfortable setting for semi-established bands, of various musical persuasions.

Studio One 83, 2860 NW 183 St, Overtown (☎621-7295). Powerful rap, soul and reggae, but be wary of the location – a dangerous area north of downtown Miami; $5–15.

Tobacco Road, 626 S Miami Ave, downtown Miami (☎374-1198). Earthy R&B from some of the country's finest exponents. See "Drinking". Free–$6.

Washington Square, 645 Washington Ave (☎534-5019). Showcase for Miami's aspiring rock and glam acts, plus periodic indie-inspired fare; $2–10.

Reggae

Bayside Hut, 3501 Rickenbacker Causeway, Key Biscayne (☎361-0808). Bayside reggae jams on Fri & Sat; free.

Hungry Sailor, 3064½ Grand Ave, Coconut Grove (☎444-9359). Reggae bands fill the tiny corner stage of this attempted English pub almost every night; free–$3. See "Eating" and "Drinking".

Rockers Café, 216 Española Way (☎537-7701). Big names from Jamaica, top local talent and, without live bands, a rootsy reggae disco (see "Nightlife"); free–$20.

Sunday's on the Bay, 5420 Crandon Blvd, Key Biscayne (☎361-6777). Unlikely but lively setting for live reggae Thurs–Sun; free. See "Eating".

Folk

JohnMartin's, 253 Miracle Mile, Coral Gables (☎445-3777). Spacious Irish bar (see "Drinking") and restaurant with Irish folk music several evenings a week; free.

Our Place Folk Club, 830 Washington Ave (☎674-1322). Folk musicians and floor singers several nights a week in a wholefood eatery; free–$2. See "Eating".

Haitian music

Aux Palmistes Chez Julie, 6820 NE Second Ave, Little Haiti (☎759-8527). Great live Haitian music from 10pm to 4am on Fri & Sat; free–$5. See "Eating".

Obsession, 69 NE 79th St, Little Haiti (☎756-7575). Best place in Miami for the hottest Haitian sounds; $8–10.

CENTERS FOR CLASSICAL MUSIC AND PERFORMING ARTS

Colony Theater, 1040 Lincoln Rd, Miami Beach (☎673-1026).

Dade County Auditorium, 2901 W Flagler St, downtown Miami (☎547-5414).

Gusman Center for the Performing Arts, 174 E Flagler St, downtown Miami (☎372-0925).

Gusman Concert Hall, 1314 Miller Drive, University of Miami (☎284-2438).

Jackie Gleason Center of the Performing Arts, 1700 Washington Blvd, Miami Beach (☎673-7300).

Lincoln Theater, 55 Lincoln Rd, Miami Beach (☎673-3300).

Classical Music, Dance and Opera

The Miami-based New World Symphony (☎673-3331) gives concert experience to some of the finest graduate **classical** musicians in the US. Their season runs from October to April with most performances at the *Lincoln Theater* or the *Gusman Center for the Performing Arts*; tickets $10–30. For better-known names, look out for top-flight soloists guesting with the Miami Chamber Symphony (☎858-3500), usually at the *Gusman Concert Hall*; tickets $15–30.

The city's two major professional **dance** companies, the Miami City Ballet (☎532-4800) and the Ballet Theater of Miami (☎442-4840), appear at the *Gusman Center for Performing Arts*; tickets are $15–45, but the Miami City Ballet also holds cut-price work-in-progress shows at the Colony Theater for under $10. A third group is the Latin dance specialists, Ballet Flamenco La Rosa (☎672-0552), whose frenetic productions take place at the *Colony Theater*; tickets $10–20.

Opera is the poor relation of classical music and dance despite the efforts of the *Greater Miami Opera Association* (☎854-1643), which brings impressive names to varied programmes at the *Dade County Auditorium*; tickets $10–60.

Comedy

Whether it's the difficulty of finding jokes to span Miami's multicultural population, or simply the geographical distance from the country's stand-up comedy hotbeds of New York and Los Angeles, the city is very short of **comedy clubs**, although those it does have draw enthusiastic crowds and often comparatively big names. Admission will be $5–10; phone for show times.

Comedy Clubs

Coconut's Comedy Club, at *Howard Johnsons* hotel, 16500 NW Second Ave, North Miami (☎461-1161). Showcasing comic talent on the way up – or on the way down. Thurs only.

Improv Comedy Club, inside *CocoWalk*, 3015 Grand Ave, Coconut Grove (☎441-8200). One of the nationwide chain of Improv comedy clubs and the best place in Miami for comedy, despite the rather formal atmosphere. Reservations required.

Theater

It may be small, but Miami's **theater** scene is of an encouragingly good standard. Winter is the busiest period, although something of worth crops up almost every week on the alternative circuit. If you're fluent in Spanish, make a point of visiting one of the city's **Spanish-language theaters**, whose programmes are listed in the Friday *El Neuvo Herald*: *Bellas Artes*, 2173 SW Eighth St (☎325-0515), *Teatro Martí*, 420 SW Eighth St (☎545-7866), *Teatro Trail*, 3717 SW Eighth St (☎448-0592), are three of the best; tickets are $12–15.

Major and Alternative Theaters

Coconut Grove Playhouse, 3500 Main Hwy , Coconut Grove (☎442-4000). Comfortable and well-established mainstream theater that bucks up its MOR schedule with many interesting experimental efforts; $10–35.
Miami Actors Studio, 1150 SW 22nd St, Coral Gables (☎666-6992). Small showcase for the best of the city's acting talent, going through their paces in a mixed-bag of plays, usually Fri, Sat & Sun only; $5–10.
Minorca Playhouse, 232 Minorca Ave, Coral Gables (☎446-1116). Main base of the Florida Shakespeare Company, with Elizabethan drama throughout the year; $18–25.
New Theater, 4275 Aurora St, Coral Gables (☎595-4260). Sitting neatly between the mainstream and the alternative, a nice place for a relaxing evening; $8–18.
Ring Theater, at the University of Miami, 1312 Miller Drive (☎284-3355). Assorted offerings year-round from the drama students of Miami University; $5–18.

Film

Except for the **Miami Film Festival** (details on ☎444-FILM), ten days and nights of new films from far and wide each February at the *Gusman Center for Performing Arts*, Miami is barren territory for movie buffs. Most **movie theaters** are multiscreen affairs inside shopping malls showing first-run American features. Look at the *Weekend* section of the Friday *Miami Herald* for complete listings, call the *Movie Hotline* (☎888-FILM), or try *Omni 10*, in the *Omni* mall at 1601 Biscayne Boulevard; *Cinema 10*, in the *Miracle Center* mall, 3301 Coral Way; the 8-screen *AMC* in the *CocoWalk*, 3015 Grand Avenue; and *Movies at the Falls*, in the *The Falls* mall, 8888 Howard Drive; admission is $4–8.

For **arthouse**, **foreign-language** or simply fading monochrome **classics**, find out what's playing at the *Alliance Film/Video Project*, 927 Lincoln Rd (☎531-8504), or at Miami University's *Beaumont Cinema*, 1111 Memorial Drive (☎284-4177), both liable to have interesting movies for $2–5. Local **libraries** can be fruitful sources, too, as can the Tuesday screenings at the *Bass Museum of Art*, 2100 Collins Ave (☎673-7530) – newspaper listings carry the details.

Gay and Lesbian Miami

Miami's **gay** and **lesbian** communities are enjoying the city's boom times as much as anyone else, with a growing number of gay-owned businesses, bars and clubs opening up around the city. The scene, traditionally focusing on Coconut Grove, has recently gathered great momentum on South Beach. In either of these areas, most public places are friendly and welcoming towards gays and lesbians – although attitudes in other parts of Miami can sometimes be considerably less enlightened. The key sources of info are the free *TWN* (*The Weekly News*) and *Wire*, available from any of the places listed below and from many of the mixed bars and clubs around Coconut Grove and South Beach.

Resources

Gay Community Bookstore, 7545 Biscayne Blvd (☎754-6900). Copious stocks of books, magazines and newspapers of gay and lesbian interest.

Gay and Lesbian Community Hotline, phone ☎759-3661 for a recorded message which gives access – via touch-tone dialling – to more recorded info on gay bars and events, gay-supportive businesses, doctors and lawyers and much more.

Gay and lesbian bars, clubs and discos

Cheers, 5922 S Dixie Hwy, South Miami (☎667-4753). Cruisy, predominantly gay male bar with video room and pool tables under the stars; Monday is ladies' night, but women also drop in to the Friday disco.

On the Waterfront, 3515 NW S River Drive (☎635-5500). Latino and black gays dancing to salsa; Thurs is the best night.

Paragon, 1235 Washington Ave (☎534-1235). No place for the faint-hearted: the decadent *Paragon* has pulsating music, laser lights, no-shame male go-go dancers, drag queens and much much more; cover $5.

Sugars, 13705 Biscayne Blvd, North Miami (☎940-9887). Predominantly black gay club.

Uncle Charlie's, 3673 Bird Ave, South Miami (☎442-8687). Hardcore gay male bar, with music and much partying; women a rarity.

Warsaw Ballroom, 1450 Collins Ave, Miami Beach (☎1-800/9-WARSAW). While not exclusively gay (see "Nightlife"), this is the busiest and biggest gay disco in town.

Women's Miami

Though it lacks the extended networks of Los Angeles or New York, Miami is steadily becoming a better place for **women** seeking the support and solidarity of other women in business, artistic endeavor, or simply looking for a reliable and inexpensive source of medical care.

Women's organizations

Women's Caucus for Art Miami, 561 NW 32nd St (☎576-0041). Charitable organization striving to raise women's profile in the visual arts; membership open to men.

Women's Chamber of Commerce of South Florida, suite 310, 7700 SW 88th St (☎446-6660). Promoting women-owned and women-run businesses throughout south Florida.

Health care and counselling centers

A Women's Care, 68A NE 167th St (☎947-0885). Inexpensive private clinic specializing in abortions and offering complete gynecological services.

Eve Medical Center, 3900 NW 79th Ave (☎591-2288). Low-cost medical care and abortions in serene, supportive environment.

Miami Women's Healthcenter, at North Shore Medical Center, suite 301, 1100 NW 95th St (☎835-6165). Education, information, support and discussion groups, physician referrals, mammograms, seminars and workshops.

Planned Parenthood of Greater Miami, 11632 N Kendal Drive, South Miami (☎593-6363). Economical health care for men and women; including birth control supplies, pregnancy testing, treatment of sexually transmitted diseases and counselling.

Women's Resource & Counselling Center, 1108 Ponce de Leon Blvd (☎448-8325). Friendly clinic providing individual, marriage, group and family counselling, psychotherapy and assertiveness training.

The Stores

Shopping for the sake of it isn't the big deal in Miami that it is in some American cities, although there's plenty of opportunity for eager consumers to exercise their credit cards. Bizarre as it may seem, Miami leads the field in **shopping mall** architecture, blowing millions of dollars on environments intended subtly to soften the hard commercialism of the stores which fill them and several malls are worthy of investigation for this reason alone. These days, old-style **department stores**, such as the dependable *Macy's* and *Sears Roebuck & Co*, generally show up inside the malls, too, but Miami has one dignified survivor, *Burdines*, standing alone to show how shopping used to be done.

The closer you get to the beach, the wackier Miami's **clothes** shops become – look out for the zebra-print bikinis and Art Deco shirts. However, for quality togs at discounted rates the best places to try are the designer outlets of the **fashion district**, on Fifth Avenue between 25th and 29th streets, just north of downtown Miami, where you'll find classy outfits – mostly of Latin American origin – at slashed prices. With less finesse, there can be finds amid the discarded garb filling the city's **thrift stores**.

Unless you're existing on a shoestring budget – or are preparing a picnic – you won't need to shop for **food and drink** at all, although **supermarkets** like *Publix* and *Winn-Dixie*, usually open until 10pm, are plentiful – flip through the phone book to locate the nearest one. You can buy alcohol from supermarkets and, of course, from the many **liquor stores**, but if you're looking for quality grub or booze, only a few specialist suppliers will oblige.

Gun shops have long outnumbered **bookshops** in Miami, but large discount chains like *B. Dalton's* and *Waldenbrooks* have arrived, with branches throughout the city and there are also a few local outlets stocking reading material of quality. Some of the city's **record** shops make good browsing territory, too, their contents spanning everything from doo-wop rarities to the smoothest salsa hits.

The Malls . . . and Burdines department store

Aventura Mall, just north of 192nd St Causeway, North Miami Beach (☎935-4222). One of the largest air-conditioned malls in the state, boasting virtually every major department store: *Macy's*, *Sears*, *J C Penney*. Pick up a map on entry or you'll never find your way out.

Bal Harbor Shops, 9700 Collins Ave, Miami Beach (☎866-0311). Don't come to buy but to watch designer-shopping in a temple of upscale consumerism.

Bayside Marketplace, 401 Biscayne Blvd, near downtown Miami (☎577-3344). Squarely aimed at tourists but a good blend of diverse stores – selling everything from Art Deco ashtrays to bubblegum – beside the bay, with some excellent food stands.

Burdines, 22 E Flagler St, downtown Miami (☎577-2191). Run-of-the-mill clothes, furnishings and domestic appliances, but Miami's oldest department store – circa 1936 – is an entertaining place to cruise.

Dadeland Mall, 7535 N Kendall Drive, South Miami (☎665-6226). More top-class department stores and speciality shops in a totally enclosed, air-conditioned environment conducive to passionate shopping.

The Falls, 8888 Howard Drive, South Miami (☎255-4570). Sit inside a gazebo and contemplate the waterfalls and the rainforest that prettify suburban Miami's classiest set of shops.

Mayfair-in-the-Grove, 3000 Florida Ave, Coconut Grove (☎448-1700). The expensive stores take second place to the landscaped tropical foliage and the discreetly placed classical sculptures.

Clothes and Thrift Stores

Coral Gables Congregational Church Thrift Shop, 3010 De Soto Blvd, Coral Gables (☎445-1721). After viewing the church (see "Coral Gables"), drop into the interestingly stocked thrift store next door.

Decolectable, 233 Fourteenth St, Miami Beach (☎674-0899). Besides Art Deco furniture and ornaments, has a carefully chosen selection of the best of other people's cast-off attire.

Details at the Beach, 1149 Washington Ave (☎672-0175). Interesting clothing and furnishings in a store sure to delight interior designers.

Last Tango in Paradise, 1214 Washington Ave (☎532-4228). South Beach's best stock of vintage and retro clothing and accessories.

Miami Twice, 6562 SW 40th St (☎666-0127). Department store specialising in vintage clothing and accessories, also has some vintage furniture to drool over.

One Hand Clapping, 432 Española Way, Miami Beach (☎532-0507). Amid a wondrous assortment of antique junk, there are hats, dresses and scarves to delight the time-warped flapper.

Shimmy, 415 Española Way (☎673-3523). Has a counter displaying excellent silver jewellery imported from Mexico.

Tommy's at the Beach, 4568 Ocean Drive, Miami Beach (☎538-1717). Pricey but interesting collection of stylish, tropical-flavored designer beachwear and daywear.

Food and Drink

Epicure Market, 1656 Alton Rd, Miami Beach (☎672-1861). Tasty morsels for the gourmet palate and a mouthwatering array of hot foods for immediate consumption.

Estate Wines and Gourmet Foods, 92 Miracle Mile, Coral Gables (☎442-9915). Alongside the fine foods, an exquisite stock of wines chosen with the connoisseur in mind.

Books

Books & Books, 296 Aragon Ave, Coral Gables (☎442-4408) and 933 Lincoln Rd, Miami Beach (☎532-3222). Excellent stock of general titles but especially strong on art and design, travel and new fiction; also has author signings and talks: ☎444-POEM for the latest events.

Downtown Book Center, 247 SE First St, downtown Miami (☎377-9939). Large selection ranging from the latest blockbusters to esoteric and academic tomes.

Grove Antiquarian, 3318 Virginia St, Coconut Grove (☎444-5362). Quality used books and some valuable first editions spanning all subjects fill the shelves here, a relaxing oasis in the heart of lively Coconut Grove.

Records, CDs and Tapes

Lily's Records, 1260 SW Eighth St, Little Havana (☎856-0536). Unsurpassed stock of salsa, merengue and other Latin sounds.

KowTow Music, 1249 Washington Ave, Miami Beach (☎538-0938). Comprehensive selection spanning most musical tastes.

Yesterday & Today, 1614 Alton Rd, Miami Beach (☎534-8704). Dusty piles of blues, jazz, R&B and Sixties indie rarities.

Listings

Airlines *British Airways*, 354 SE First St (☎1-800/AIRWAYS); *Continental*, Airport Concourse "C" (☎1-800/525-0280); *Delta*, 201 Alhambra Circle (☎1-800/638-7333); *TWA*, Airport Concourse "G" (☎1-800/221-2000); *Virgin Atlantic*, 2655 Le Jeune Rd (☎1-800/862-8621).

Airport Miami International, six miles west of downtown Miami. Take local bus #7 from downtown Miami (an approximately half-hour journey), local bus #J from Miami Beach (around 40min), or a shuttle bus: *Airporter* (☎247-8874); *Red Top* (☎526-5764); *Super Shuttle* (☎871-2000). More details on p.55.

American Express Offices around the city: in downtown Miami, Suite 100, 330 Biscayne Blvd (☎358/7350); in Coral Gables, 32 Miracle Mile (☎446-3381); in Miami Beach, at *Bal Harbor Shops*, 9700 Collins Ave (☎865-5959).

Amtrak 8303 NW 37th Ave (☎1-800/872-7245).

Area Code ☎305.

Babysitting Central Sitting Agency: ☎856-0550.

Banks See "Money Exchange".

Bike rental See p.60.

Boat rental If the opening sequences from *Miami Vice* encouraged you to visit Miami, you might like to recreate them by skimming over Biscayne Bay in a motor boat. Equipped with 50hp engines, such vessels can be rented at hourly rates – beginning at $45 for one hour – from *Beach Boat Rentals*, 2380 Collins Drive, Miami Beach (☎534-4307).

Coastguard ☎535-4314.

Consulates *Denmark*, Suite 600, 2655 Le Jeune Rd (☎446-0020); *France*, 200 Biscayne Blvd (☎372-9541); *Germany*, Suite 2210, 100 N Biscayne Blvd (☎358-0290); *Netherlands*, in Houston, Texas (☎713/622-8000); *Norway*, Suite 525, 1001 North American Way (☎441-8780); *UK*, Suite 2110, 1001 S Bayshore Drive (☎374-1522).

Crisis Hotline ☎358-5357.

Dentists To be referred to a dentist: ☎667-3647.

Doctor To get a physician to visit you: ☎945-6325.

Emergencies Dial ☎911 and ask for relevant emergency service.

Everglades day trips In the absence of public transit, almost every tour operator in Miami offers half- or full-day trips ($20–35) to the Everglades, but seldom do these involve more than a quick gape at an alligator and an ecologically questionable air-boat ride – or even enter the Everglades National Park. Only *All Florida Adventure Tours* (☎1-800/33T-OUR3) and *Eco Tours Miami* (☎232-5398) run ecology-centered tours ($80 for a day) to the park and surrounding areas; unfortunately, they seldom have places for individual travellers. The Everglades are comprehensively detailed in Chapter Six.

Gay community hotline ☎759-3661.

Hospitals with emergency rooms In Miami: *Jackson Memorial Medical Center*, 1611 NW Twelfth Ave (☎325-7200); *Mercy Hospital*, 3663 S Miami Ave (☎854-4400). In Miami Beach: *Mt Sinai Medical Center*, 4300 Alton Rd (☎674-2121); *St Francis Hospital*, 250 W 63rd St (☎868-5000).

Laundromats Check the Yellow Pages for the nearest; handiest for South Beach is the 24-hr *Clean Machine*, 230 Twelfth St.

Library The biggest is *Metro-Dade County Public Library*, 101 W Flagler St (Mon–Sat 9am–6pm, Thurs until 9pm; Oct–May also Sun 1–5pm; ☎375-2665).

Lost and found For something lost on *Metro-Dade Transit*, phone ☎375-3366 (Mon–Fri 8.30am–4.30pm). Otherwise call the police.

Luggage consignment At the airport, some *Greyhound* terminals (phone to be sure) and the *Amtrak* station.

Money exchange At the airport and the following: *Barnett Bank*, 701 Brickell Ave (with 42 branches elsewhere; call ☎350-7143 for the nearest; *First Union National Bank*, 200 S Biscayne Blvd (☎789-5000); *Jefferson National Bank*, 301 Arthur Godfrey Rd (☎532-6451) and 18170 Collins Ave (☎935-6911); *Sun Bank*, 777 Brickell Ave (☎591-6000).

Parking fines $10, increasing to $22 if not paid within thirty days.

Pharmacies Usually open from 8am or 9am until 9pm or midnight. 24-hour pharmacies are *Eckard*, at 1825 Miami Gardens Drive (☎932-5740) and 9031 SW 107th Ave (☎274-6776); and *Walgreens*, 5731 Bird Rd (☎666-0757).

FESTIVALS

The precise dates of the festivals listed below vary from year to year; check the details at any tourist information office or Chamber of Commerce.

January

Mid *Art Deco Weekend*: on Ocean Drive in the South Beach; dwelling on the area's architecture with talks and free events.

Taste of the Grove: Pig it on food and free music in Coconut Grove's Peacock Park.

Late *Homestead Frontier Days*: home cooking and home-made arts and crafts at Harris Field in Homestead.

February

Early *Miami Film Festival*: latest US and overseas films premiered in downtown Miami's *Gusman Center for the Performing Arts*.

Mid *Coconut Grove Arts Festival*: hundreds of (mostly) talented unknowns display their works in Coconut Grove's Peacock Park and the nearby streets.

Late Miami Grand Prix: high-performance motor race which screeches around the streets of downtown Miami.

March

Early *Calle Ocho Festival*: massive festival of Cuban arts, crafts and cooking along the streets of Little Havana.

Carnival Miami: an offshoot of the *Calle Ocho* festival, with Hispanic-themed events across the city culminating in a parade at the Orange Bowl.

April

Early *Miracle Mile Festival*: parades and floats along Miracle Mile singing the praises of Coral Gables.

Coconut Grove Seafood Festival: an excuse to eat loads of seafood in Coconut Grove's Peacock Park.

June

Early *Goombay Festival*: a spirited bash in honor of Bahamian culture, in and around Coconut Grove's Peacock Park.

Art in the Park: arty stalls and displays in the Charles Deering Estate in South Miami.

August

First Sunday *Miami Reggae Festival*: celebration of Jamaican Independence Day with dozens of top Jamaican bands playing around the city.

September

Mid *Festival Miami*: three weeks of performing and visual arts events organized by the University of Miami, mostly taking place in Coral Gables.

October

Hispanic Heritage Festival: lasts all month and features innumerable events linked to Latin American History and culture.

Mid *Caribbean-American Carnival*: a joyous cavalcade of soca and calypso bands in Bicentennial Park.

November

Mid *Miami Book Fair International*: a wealth of tomes from across the world spread across the campus of Dade County Community College in downtown Miami.

December

30 *King Mango Strut*: a very alternative sort of New Year's Eve celebration, with part-time cross-dressers and clowns parading through Coconut Grove.

31 *Orange Bowl Parade*: mainstream climax of the New Year bashes all over the city, with floats, marching bands and the crowning of the Orange Bowl Queen at the Orange Bowl stadium.

Police Non-emergency: ☎595-6263.

Post offices In downtown Miami, 500 NW Second Ave; in Coral Gables, 251 Valencia Ave; in Coconut Grove, 3191 Grand Ave; in Homestead, 739 Washington Ave; in Key Biscayne, 59 Harbor Drive; in Miami Beach, 1300 Washington Ave and 445 W 40th St. All open Mon–Fri 8.30am–5pm, Sat 8.30am–12.30pm, or longer hours.

Rape hotline ☎549-7273.

Road conditions ☎470-5277.

Sports *Miami Dolphins*, Florida's oldest pro football team and the *Florida Marlins*, the country's newest professional baseball team, play at the Joe Robbie Stadium, sixteen miles northwest of downtown Miami: box office open Mon–Fri 10am–6pm; ☎620-2578; most seats are $30 for football and around $10–15 for baseball. The *Miami Heat* basketball team plays NBA matches at the Miami Arena, three miles north of downtown Miami: info on ☎577-HEAT; tickets $14–21. *Miami Freedom* plays soccer at Milander Park in Hialeah, seven miles northwest of downtown Miami: info on ☎888-0838; tickets $9.50. Miami University's football, basketball and baseball teams are all called the *Miami Hurricanes*: game and ticket (usually $5–13) info Mon–Fri 8am–6pm on ☎1-800/GO-CANES.

Thomas Cook In downtown Miami: 155 SE Third Ave (☎381-9525); in Coral Gables: suite 102, 901 Ponce de Leon Blvd (☎448-0269); in Miami Beach: at the *Fountainbleau*, 4441 Collins Ave (☎674-1907).

Ticketmaster Tickets for arts and sports events, payable by credit card: ☎358-5885.

Weather/surf information ☎661-5065.

Western Union Offices all over the city; call ☎1-800/325-6000 to find the nearest.

travel details

Trains
From Miami to Hollywood/Fort Lauderdale/Deerfield Beach/Delray Beach/West Palm Beach/Sebring/Winter Haven (2 daily; 20min/34min/52min/1hr 6min/1hr 40min/3hr 17min/3hr 56min); Ocala (1 daily; 5hr 37min); Tampa/St Petersburg (1 daily; 4hr 16min/4hr 51min); Washington/New York (2 daily; 22hr/29hr).

Tri-Rail
From Miami to Hollywood/Fort Lauderdale/Boca Raton/Delray Beach/West Palm Beach (5–15 daily; 16min/31min/1hr/1hr 7min/1hr 34min).

Buses
From Miami to Daytona Beach (9 daily; 8hr 55min–9hr 50min); Fort Lauderdale (19 daily; 1hr); Fort Myers (4 daily; 5hr 35min); Fort Pierce (9 daily; 4hr); Jacksonville (9 daily; 7hr 30min); Key West (3 daily; 4hr 30min); Orlando (7 daily; 6hr 45min); Sarasota (5 daily; 7hr 35min); St Petersburg (3 daily; 9hr 50min); Tampa (5 daily; 9hr 45min–10hr 35min); West Palm Beach (12 daily; 2hr 30min).

CHAPTER TWO

THE FLORIDA KEYS

F iction, films and folklore have given the **Florida Keys*** – a hundred-mile string of small islands running from the southeastern corner of the state to within ninety miles of Cuba – an image of sultry romance and glamorous intrigue that they don't really deserve. Throughout their length and especially for the first sixty-odd miles, fishing, snorkelling and diving dominate – admittedly with great justification – and are ruthlessly hawked at every opportunity. If you're not planning to indulge, not only will you feel left out of things but you'll be hard pushed to find much else to fill your time. Here and there the keys' idiosyncratic history rears its head, there are some stunningly untainted natural areas and a couple of highly worthwhile ecology tours, but these tend to be exceptions. Be absolutely sure, though, to visit the **Florida Reef**, a great band of living coral just a few miles off the coast: an exceptional sight, both for the multifarious forms and colors of the coral itself and for the dazzling assortment of creatures that live on it.

One of the better places to visit the reef is the John Pennecamp State Park, one of the few interesting features of **Key Largo**, the biggest of the keys and by far the dullest. Like **Islamorada**, further south, Key Largo is rapidly being populated by suburban Miamians, moving here for the sailing and fishing but unable to survive without shopping malls. Islamorada has some natural and historical points of note, however, as does the next major settlement, **Marathon**, which also, being at the center of the key chain, makes a useful short-term base. Thirty miles on, **the Lower Keys** get fewer visitors and less publicity than their neighbors. Don't dismiss them, though; in many ways these are the most unusual and appealing of the whole lot, home to a tiny species of deer, covered with dense forests – and, at Looe Key, possessing a tremendous embarkation point for trips to the Florida Reef.

However much you enjoy the other keys, they're really only stops on the way to **Key West**, the final dot of the North American continent before a thousand miles of ocean – the end of the road in every sense. Shot through with an intoxicating aura of abandonment, it's a small but immensely vibrant place. The only part of the keys with a real sense of the past, Key West was once – unbelievably – the richest town in the US and the largest settlement in Florida. There are old homes and museums to enjoy and plenty of congenial bars in which to while away the hours.

Key West also has a couple of small **beaches**, something noticeably missing – due to the reef – elsewhere. But the absence of sand and surf is easily made up for by the keys' **sunsets**: there's nothing to block the view of the fiery yellow disc

---

* A spelling variation on the word "cay", a key is a small island or bank composed of coral fragments. The Florida Keys are the largest grouping, but keys are common all along the state's southerly coastlines.

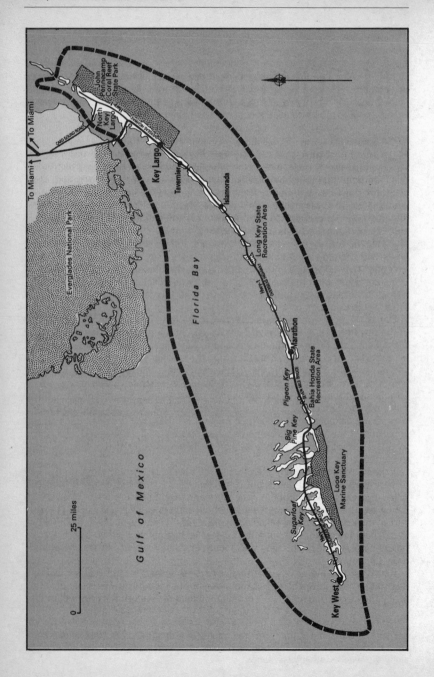

To Miami

To Miami

John
Pennecamp
Coral Reef
State Park

North
Key
Largo

CARD SOUND ROAD

OVERSEAS HWY

Key Largo

Tavernier

Islamorada

Everglades National Park

Long Key State
Recreation Area

Hwy 1

Florida Bay

OVERSEAS HIGHWAY

Pigeon Key

Marathon

SEVEN MILE BRIDGE

Bahia Honda State
Recreation Area

Big
Pine Key

Looe Key
Marine Sanctuary

Gulf of Mexico

Sugarloaf
Key

Hwy 1

Key West

25 miles

0

The area code for all numbers in this chapter is ☎305.

sinking into the horizon, bathing the sky in rich tones of red and orange. As one early visitor, the nineteenth-century ornithologist John James Audubon, rhapsodized: "a blaze of refulgent glory streams portal of the West and the masses of vapour assume the semblance of mountains of molten gold".

Practicalities

Travelling through the keys could hardly be easier as there's just one route all the way through to Key West: the **Overseas Highway (Hwy-1)**. The road is punctuated by **mile markers (MM)** – posts on which mileage is marked, starting with MM127 just south of Homestead (see Chapter One) and finishing with MM0 in Key West. Most motels and restaurants are strung along the highway, often using the mile markers as addresses. **Public transit** comprises three daily *Greyhound* buses between Miami and Key West (which can be hailed down anywhere on the route; see "Travel details" at the end of the chapter) and a skeletal local bus service in Key West.

Accommodation is abundant but is more expensive than on the mainland. During high season, from November to April, budget for *at least* $50–85 night, $35–55 the rest of the year, unless you're camping – well catered for along the keys.

Note that throughout this chapter, only the most basic **diving information** is given. Always take local advice before venturing into the water and see p.38 in *Basics*.

ACCOMMODATION PRICE CODES

All accommodation prices in this book have been coded using the symbols below. Note that prices are for the least expensive double rooms in each establishment. For a full explanation see p.26 in *Basics*.

①	up to $30	④	$60–80	⑦	$130–180
②	$30–45	⑤	$80–100	⑧	$180+
③	$45–60	⑥	$100–130		

North Key Largo and the John Pennecamp Coral Reef State Park

Assuming you're driving, the clever way to arrive in the keys is with Card Sound Road (Hwy-905A; $1.50 toll), which branches off Hwy-1 a few miles south of Homestead. Doing so avoids the bulk of the tourist traffic and, after passing through the desolate southeastern section of the Everglades, gives soaring views from Card Sound Bridge of the mangrove-dotted waters of Florida Bay (where a long wait and a lot of luck might bring a glimpse of a rare American crocodile) – and a first view of the keys as they all might have looked long ago, before commercialism took hold.

The bulk of **NORTH KEY LARGO**, where Hwy-905 touches ground, is free of development and human habitation is marked only by the odd shack amid a rich endowment of trees. Despite elaborate plans to turn the area into a city called Port Bougainvillea, with high-rise blocks and a monorail (a terrifying prospect ended by sudden bankruptcy), much of the land here is now owned and protected by the state. This may account for the scare stories about drug smugglers and practitioners of the Voodoo-like *Santeria*, seemingly designed to ward people off. In reality, there's no more drug smuggling here than anywhere else in the keys and the magic merchants come not to sacrifice innocent tourists but to gather weird and wonderful herbs for use in rituals. There's probably more danger from the exclusive *Ocean Reef Club*, whose golf course you'll spot after a few miles if you turn left where Hwy-905 splits; it's regarded by the FBI as the country's most secure retreat for very important people – watch out for nervous,

SWIMMING WITH DOLPHINS

Long before *Flipper*, the Sixties TV show, brought about a surge in their popularity, **dolphins** – marine mammals smaller than whales, and differentiated from porpoises by their beak-like snout – had been the subject of centuries of speculation and myth-making. The wildest notion suggests that dolphins once lived on land but became so disenchanted by the course of civilization at the time of Aristotle and Plato that they took to the sea, vowing to bide their time until humankind was ready to receive their wisdom. Whatever the truth, there's no dispute that dolphins are extremely intelligent, possessing brains similar in size to those of humans – and frequently resemble people in their behavior patterns. More remarkable, however, is the **dolphin language** of clicks and whistles, and their use of echolocation, a sonar technique enabling them to detect food in dark waters and, perhaps, to communicate with one another using "sound pictures".

The nets of tuna fishermen and other factors have reduced the world's dolphin population, but many live in Florida's waters and they are a common sight around the Florida Keys. Dolphins are also the star attraction of the state's many marine parks, although watching them perform leaps and somersaults in response to human commands gives just the merest inkling of their potential. By contrast, at the Dolphin Research Center (address below), the creatures are used in cancer-sufferer therapy and in the teaching of mentally handicapped children. The exceptional patience and gentleness shown by the dolphins (all of whom are free to swim out to sea whenever they want) in this work suggests that their sonar system allows them to make an X-ray-like scan of a body, detecting any abnormalities, and may even allow them to "see" emotions. Take a **tour** (Wed–Sun at 10am, 12.30pm, 2pm & 3.30pm; donation $5) of the research center to become better informed on these remarkable – and still barely understood – mammals.

The Dolphin Research Center is also one of three places in the Florida Keys where, by booking well ahead, you can **swim with dolphins**, $70 buying roughly twenty minutes in a large, open-air pool with the creatures. Be warned that seven-foot-long dolphins are disconcertingly large at close quarters and will lose interest in you long before you lose interest in them – they smell strongly of fish, too. If you have the chance, though, it's an unforgettable experience.

In Key Largo: *Dolphins Plus*, MM100 (☎305/451-1993).

In Islamorada: *Theater of the Sea*, MM84.5 (☎305/664-2431).

In Marathon: *Dolphin Research Center*, MM59 (☎305/289-1121).

armed men in dark suits. If you want to explore North Key Largo at length, you'll have to eat and sleep in Key Largo or Tavernier; see the listing below.

Continuing south, Hwy-905 merges with Hwy-1 (from the mainland) near MM109. Known from here on as the **Overseas Highway**, Hwy-1 is the main – and only – road all the way to Key West.

John Pennecamp Coral Reef State Park

Daily 8am–sunset; cars and drivers $3.75, 50¢ each passenger, pedestrians and cyclists $1.

The one essential stop as you approach Key Largo is the **John Pennecamp Coral Reef State Park** at MM 102.5. At its heart is a protected 78-square-mile section of living coral reef, part of the reef chain which runs from here to the Dry Turtugas, off Key West. Even globetrotting experts rate this as one of the most beautiful reef systems in the world, despite the substantial damage caused by decades of ecologically unsound tourism and irresponsible tampering with Florida's ecosystem*. Whether you do it here, which is one of the better spots, or elsewhere in the keys (such as Looe Key, see "The Lower Keys"), make sure you visit the reef – the eulogistic descriptions you'll hear are rarely exaggerations.

Seeing the Reef: practicalities

Since most of the park lies underwater, it's ideally seen underwater: if possible, take the **snorkelling tour** (9am, noon & 3pm; $24), or, if qualified, the **guided scuba dive** (9.30am & 1pm; $30). If you prefer to stay dry, a remarkable amount of the reef can be enjoyed on the two-and-a-half-hour **glass-bottomed boat tour** (9.30am, 12.30pm & 3pm; $15). Note that only during the summer are you likely to get a place on these tours simply by turning up at the park. To be sure, **reserve ahead** by calling ☎451-1621, or by dropping into *Sundiver Station*, MM103 (☎451-2220). If there's no room, try one of the numerous local diving shops: *American Diving Headquarters*, MM106 (☎1-800/322-3483) and *Captain Slate's Atlantis Dive Center*, at MM106.5 (☎451-1325), are just two which operate their own trips out to the reef – and cover a larger area than park tours – at broadly similar rates.

At the Reef

Only when you're **at the reef** does its role in providing a sheltered environment for a multitude of crazy-colored fish and exotic sea life become apparent. Even from the glass-bottomed boat you're virtually guaranteed to spot lobsters, angelfish, eels and wispy jellyfish shimmering through the current and shoals of silvery minnows stalked by angry-faced barracudas – and many more less easily identified aquatic curiosities.

Despite looking like a big lump of rock, the **reef**, too, is a delicate living thing, composed of millions of minute coral polyps extracting calcium from the sea water and growing from one to sixteen feet every 1000 years. Coral takes many shapes and forms, resembling anything from staghorns to a bucket – and comes in a paintbox variety of colors due to the plants, *zooxanthellae*, living within the

---

* Only a few decades ago, great sections of the reef were being dynamited or hauled up by crane to be broken and sold as souvenirs. These days, collecting Florida coral is illegal; any coral seen in tourist shops is likely to be imported from the Philippines.

coral tissues. Sadly, it's far easier to spot signs of death rather than life on the reef: the white patches show where a carelessly dropped anchor, or diver's hand, has scraped away the protective mucus layer and left the coral susceptible to lethal disease.

This destruction got so bad at the horseshoe-shaped **Molasses Reef**, about seven miles out, that the authorities sank two obsolete Coast Guard cutters nearby to lure divers away from the actual reef. In as much as the destruction has slowed, this plan worked and today you'll enjoy some great snorkelling around the reef and the cutters. If you prefer diving and **wrecks** appeal, head for **the Elbow**, a section of the reef a few miles northeast of Molasses, where a number of intriguing barnacle-encrusted nineteenth-century specimens lie: though the knowledge that they, like most of the keys' diveable wrecks, were deliberately brought here to bolster tourism in the Seventies lessens their allure – and you definitely won't find any treasure.

By far the strangest thing at the reef is not a natural sight at all but the *Christ of the Deep*, a nine-foot bronze statue of Christ intended as a memorial to perished sailors. The algae-coated creation, twenty feet down at Key Largo Dry Rocks, is a replica of Guido Galletti's *Christ of the Abyss*, similarly submerged off the coast of Italy – and is surely the final word in Florida's long-time fixation with Mediterranean art and architecture. The glass-bottomed boat trip, by the way, doesn't visit the Elbow or the statue.

Back on Land: the visitor center

Provided you visit the reef early, there'll be plenty of time left to enjoy the terrestrial portion of the park. The ecological displays at the **visitor center** (daily 8am–5pm) will whet your appetite for the trees, plants and wildlife found throughout the keys and following the mangrove and tropical hardwood hammock* **trails** within the park gives a practical insight into the region's transitional zones: the vegetation changes dramatically within an elevation of a few feet. More lazily, by renting a **canoe** ($6 per hour; $30 per day) you can idly glide around the park's mangrove-fringed inner waterways.

Key Largo and Tavernier

Thanks to the 1948 film in which Humphrey Bogart and Lauren Bacall grappled with Florida's best-known features – crime and hurricanes – almost everybody has heard of **KEY LARGO**. Yet the movie's title was chosen for no other reason than it suggested somewhere warm and exotic and the film, though set here, was almost entirely shot in Hollywood – hoodwinking countless millions into thinking that paradise was a town in the Florida Keys.

Recognizing a potential tourist bonanza, businesspeople here soon changed the name of their community from Rock Harbor to Key Largo (a title which until then had applied to the whole island, derived from *Cayo Largo* – Long Island – given by early Spanish explorers) and even today, tenuous links with Hollywood are maintained. At MM100, in the marina of the *Holiday Inn*, the tiny steam-

---

* Cropping up all over Florida, hammocks are pockets of woodland able to flourish where the ground elevation rises a few feet above the surrounding wetlands. For a fuller explanation, see "Natural History" in *Contexts*.

powered boat dragged by Bogart in another film, *The African Queen*, is moored (when it's not away on promotional tours) and the hotel's lobby displays a selection of stills of Bogart and co-star Katherine Hepburn acting their hearts out – in England and Africa.

Once you see the filling stations, bait-and-tackle shops, shopping plazas and fast-food outlets which dominate the real Key Largo, clutching at tourist-appeal straws becomes understandable: the place is totally boring. If arriving at the right time, turn right along any road off the Overseas Highway to enjoy the sunset; otherwise keep moving.

You only need travel ten miles before reaching the far more homely **TAVERNIER**, once the first stop on the Flagler railway (the keys' first link to the mainland, see "South of Marathon"), whose population centered on what are now the enjoyable open spaces of the **Harry Harris Park**, off the Overseas Highway along Burton Drive. Come by on a weekend and you could well find an impromptu party and free live music – locals sometimes drop by with their instruments for jam sessions – around the park's picnic tables.

Another reason to stop are the old buildings (a rarity in the keys, outside of Key West) of the **historic district**, between MM91 and MM92. Besides the plank walls and tin roofs of the turn-of-the-century Methodist Church (now functioning as a small Visitor Center) and post office, you'll see some of the "Red Cross buildings" erected after the 1935 Labor Day hurricane – which laid waste to a good chunk of the keys – with foot-thick walls of concrete and steel intended to withstand nature's fiercest poundings. Unfortunately, the use of seawater in the construction caused the walls to crumble, eventually leaving just these rusting steel frames.

Practicalities

Unless you've already called at the copiously stocked Visitor Information Center near Homestead (see Chapter One), pull up at the equally informative **Florida Keys Visitor Center**, 105950 Overseas Highway (daily 9am–6pm; ☎1-800/822-1088), for piles of brochures and money-saving vouchers.

Though there's not much else to stick around for, the high-quality snorkelling and diving in the Key Largo area may cause you to stay a couple of nights. Plenty of **motels** offer diving packages. Look for their signs or try: *Economy Efficiency*, 103365 Overseas Highway (☎451-4712; ②), with a two-night minimum; the beach cottages of *Sea Farer*, MM97.8 (☎852-5349; ③); or the *Hungry Pelican*, MM99.5 (☎451-3576; ③). Much more expensive, but a one-off, *Jules' Undersea Lodge*, at 51 Shoreland Drive (☎1-800/858-7119; ⑧), is a tiny "hotel", five fathoms deep. Book early and bear in mind that you must be a qualified diver.

Of many **campgrounds** in and around Key Largo, the cleanest and cheapest is the *John Pennecamp Coral Reef State Park* (☎451-1202; see above). The *Key Largo Kampground*, MM101 (☎451-1431), is a reasonable alternative but has no grass pitches.

As for **eating**, *Ganim's Kountry Kitchen*, 99696 Overseas Highway (☎451-2895), has cheap breakfasts and lunches; *Mrs Mac's*, MM99 (☎451-3722), provides bowls of ferociously hot chilli and other home-cooked goodies; or taste the fresh pasta and seafood at the *Italian Fisherman*, MM104 (☎451-4471). Key Largo has the keys' biggest and cheapest **supermarket**, the *Winn-Dixie* at the Waldorf Plaza Shopping Center, MM100; ideal for loading supplies for the journey ahead.

Assuming the bikers in leather jackets and tropical shorts don't frighten you off, check out the *Caribbean Club*, MM104 (☎451-9970), for a lively **drink**; if they do, *Coconuts*, the bar of the *Marina del Mar Resort*, MM100 (☎451-4107), is mellower.

Heading on: Islamorada and Around

Once over Tavernier Creek, you're at the start of a twenty-mile strip of islands encompassing Plantation, Windley and Upper and Lower Matecumbe keys, collectively known as **ISLAMORADA**. More than any other section of the keys, fishing is headline news here: tales of monstrous tarpon and blue marlin captured off the coast are legion and no end of smaller prey is easily hooked by total novices (and even former president George Bush, who regularly cast a rod in these waters, between crises).

Other than its state parks (see below), Islamorada is of short-lasting appeal if you've no interest in putting to sea: if you have, there's no problem renting fishing boats and guides or, much more cheaply, joining a fishing party boat from any of the local marinas. The biggest docks are at the *Holiday Isle*, 84001 Overseas Highway (☎1-800/327-7070) and *Bud 'n' Mary's*, MM80, which also sports a modest **Museum of Fishing** (Mon–Sat 10am–5pm; free).

There's notable **snorkelling** and **diving** in the area, too. Crocker and Alligator reefs, a few miles offshore, both have near vertical sides whose cracks and crevices provide homes for a lively variety of crabs, shrimps and other small, slow creatures which in turn attracted bigger, faster fish looking for a meal. Nearby, the wrecks of the *Eagle* and the *Cannabis Cruiser*, sunk while transporting the naughty weed (all of which has been removed), have families of gargantuan amberjack and grouper living around them. Get full snorkelling and diving details from the above marinas or any dive shop on the Overseas Highway.

On dry land, if the extortionate price doesn't deter you and you're not planning to visit any of the other marine parks in Florida, you might pass a couple of hours at the **Theater of the Sea**, MM84.5 (daily 9.30am–4pm; $11.75), whose sea lions, dolphins and half-dozen tankfuls of assorted fish and crustaceans are informally introduced by knowledgeable staff.

Otherwise, there's little in Islamorada to woo non-fisherfolk. The **Chamber of Commerce**, at MM82 (Mon–Fri 9am–5pm, closes for lunch; ☎1-800/FAB-KEYS), in a bright red railway guard's van, is packed with general info and will have the facts on the latest cut-rate accommodation deals (see below). Half a mile further south, the Art Deco **monument** marks the grave of 425 victims of the 1935 Labor Day hurricane, killed when a tidal wave hit their evacuation train. The unkempt state of the stone is perhaps an indication of modern keys dwellers' shrugged-shoulders attitude to the threat of a repeat disaster.

THE BACKCOUNTRY

With access to a boat, or sufficient money (around $200 a day) to rent one with a guide, Islamorada makes a good base for exploring the fish-laden waters and bird-filled skies of the **backcountry**. This is the term for the countless small uninhabited islands that fill Florida Bay, beginning about eighteen miles west and constituting the edge of the Everglades National Park – more fully described in Chapter Six. Ask at any Islamorada marina for more details.

Islamorada's state parks: Indian Key, Lignumvitae Key and Long Key

Three **state parks** at the southern end of Islamorada offer a broader perspective of the area than fishing and diving can provide. The **guided tours** to Indian Key and Lignumvitae Key are particularly fruitful, revealing, respectively a near-forgotten chapter of the Florida Keys' history and a virgin forest. Both tours begin by boat from Indian Key Fill at MM78. Departures (daily except Tues & Wed; $7) to Indian Key are at 8.30am and to Lignumvitae Key at 1.30pm. In winter, it's strongly advisable to **reserve a place**: ☎664-4815.

Indian Key

Just one of many small, mangrove-skirted islands off Lower Matecumbe Key, you'd never guess from the highway that **Indian Key** was once a busy trading center, given short-lived prosperity – and notoriety – by a nineteenth-century New Yorker called Jacob Houseman. After stealing one of his father's ships, Houseman sailed to Key West looking for a piece of the lucrative wrecking (or salvaging) business. Not trusted by the close-knit Key West community, he bought Indian Key in 1831 as a base for his own wrecking operation. In the first year, Houseman made $30,000 and furnished the eleven-acre island with streets, a store, warehouses, a hotel and a permanent population of around fifty. However, the income was not entirely honest: Houseman was known to lead donkeys with lanterns swinging from their necks along the shore to lure ships towards dangerous reefs and eventually lost his wrecking licence for salvaging from an anchored vessel.

In 1838 Indian Key was sold to physician-botanist Henry Perrine, who had been cultivating tropical plants here with an eye to their commercial potential. A Seminole attack in 1840 burnt every building to the ground and ended the island's habitation, but Perrine's plantings survived and today form a swath of flowing foliage – sisal, coffee, tea and mango plants, among the exuberant growths. Besides allowing ample opportunity to gawp at the plants, the two-hour **tour** takes you around the one-time streets, up the observation tower and past Houseman's grave – his body was brought here after he died working on a wreck off Key West.

Lignumvitae Key

You might set out not knowing a strangler fig from a gumbo limbo, but by the time you finish the three-hour **tour** of **Lignumvitae Key** you'll instantly recognize both, plus many more of a hundred or so species of tropical tree on this two-hundred-acre hammock. A further treat are the sizeable spiders, such as the Golden Orb, whose silvery web regularly spans the pathway. The trail through the forest was laid out by a wealthy early Miamian, W J Matheson, whose 1919 limestone **house** is the island's only sign of habitation and shows up the deprivations of early island living – even for the well-off. Curiously, the house blew away in the 1935 hurricane, but was found and brought back.

Long Key State Recreation Area

Daily 8am–sunset; cars $3.25, pedestrians and cyclists $1.

Many of the tree types found on Lignumvitae are spottable at **Long Key State Recreation Area**, MM67.5. The best thing to do here, though, is to rent a canoe and follow the simple **canoe trail** through the tidal lagoons, in the company of mildly amused wading birds. Details of **camping** in the park are on ☎664-4815.

Practicalities

Don't count on finding **accommodation** in Islamorada for under $50 a night, although price wars among the bigger hotels can ease the budget strain. The popular *Holiday Isle*, 84001 Overseas Highway (☎1-800/327-7070; ⑤), is just one place with good off-season deals; otherwise, the best bets are *Drop Anchor*, MM85 (☎664/4863; ④–⑥) and *Key Lantern*, MM82 (☎664-4572; ③). Check the rest at the Chamber of Commerce (address above). With a tent, use either Long Key State Park (see above) or the campervan-dominated *KOA* campground on Fiesta Key, MM70 (☎664-4922).

Provided you avoid the obvious tourist traps, you can **eat** well and fairly cheaply. *Manny & Isa's*, MM 81.5 (☎664-5019), serves high-quality, low-cost Cuban food; *Whale Harbor*, MM84 (☎664-4959), lives up to its name, proffering massive seafood buffets to devil-may-care gluttons; the ramshackle but justifiably pricey *Green Turtle Inn*, MM81 (☎664-9031; closed Mon), has glorious chowders.

When it comes to **nightlife**, many people get no further than the huge tiki bar at *Holiday Isle* (address above), which always throbs on weekends – if its insipid rock bands get on your nerves, investigate the nightly drinks specials at *Lorelei's*, MM102 (☎664-4656). Sample the much less touristy *Woody's*, MM102 (☎664-4335), for raunchy blues and boozing.

The Middle Keys: Marathon and around

Once over Long Key Bridge (standing alongside the old Long Key Viaduct, see "South Of Marathon", below), south of Long Key, you're into the **Middle Keys**, named for obvious reasons of geography and by definition making a sensible base for seeing the keys without uprooting yourself too often. The largest of several islands, Key Vaca – once a shantytown of railway workers – holds the nucleus of the area's major settlement, **MARATHON**, on first sight a town as commercialized and uninspiring as Key Largo, but with better features hidden from view a short way off the Overseas Highway.

SNORKELLING, DIVING AND FISHING

Around Marathon, **spearfishing** is permitted a mile offshore (there's a three-mile limit elsewhere), and many who don underwater gear have something in mind other than looking at the sea life; they're planning to skewer it. Assuming you don't want to join them, the choice locale for **snorkelling** and **diving** is around **Sombrero Reef**, marked by a 142-foot-high nineteenth-century lighthouse, whose nooks and crannies provide a safe haven for thousands of darting, brightly coloured tropical fish. *The Diving Site*, MM 53.5 (☎1-800/634-3935), is the pick of the local dive shops.

Marathon hosts four major **fishing tournaments** each year: you may fancy your chances but entering costs several hundred dollars and only the very top anglers participate. Being around during one, however, can be an insight into the Big Time Fishing mentality. If intrigued, turn up in early May (for tarpon); late May (dolphin, the fish not the mammal); early October (bonefish); or early November (sailfish). Get precise dates from the **Chamber of Commerce**, 3330 Overseas Highway (Mon–Fri 9am–5pm; ☎1-800/842-9580).

If you've not had your fill of tropical trees at Lignumvitae Key (see "Islamorada"), make a point of turning along 55th Street for **Crane Point Hammock** (Mon–Sat 9am–5pm, Sun noon–5pm; $4): its 63 steamy subtropical acres feature a hardwood hammock explorable with a **walking trail**. More substantial stuff is inside the hammock's **museum of natural history of the Florida keys**, where displays on the geology of the keys and an authoritative historical rundown – starting with the Caloosa Indians, who had a settlement on this site – justify a couple of hours. A large section of the museum is designed to introduce kids to the wonders of the keys' subtropical ecosystems.

For a closer look at the Florida Keys' natural life – and the problems it faces – take the waterborne **ecology tour** (selected days only, 10am & 2pm; ☎743-7000; $15) from the marina of the $200-a-night *Hawks Cay Resort* on Duck Key, reached by way of a causeway at MM61. Led by a radically minded local naturalist, the two-hour trip to an uninhabited island will leave you very knowledgeable about the make-up of the keys and the creatures who live in them – and surprisingly clued-up on algae; rather more interesting stuff than you might imagine.

With a less active time in mind, Marathon has a couple of small **beaches**. Sombrero Beach, along Sombrero Beach Road (off the Overseas Highway near MM50), is a slender strip of sand with good swimming waters and shaded picnic tables. Four miles north, the beach at Key Colony Beach, a man-made island dredged into existence during the Fifties for the purpose of building and selling pricey homes, is prettier and quieter.

Practicalities

If relaxation is a priority, spend a night or two at one of Marathon's well-equipped **resorts**, such as *Sombrero*, 19 Sombrero Boulevard (☎1-800/433-8660; ⑤–⑦), or *Banana Bay*, 4590 Overseas Highway (☎1-800/488-6636; ⑤–⑦). The least costly of the plentiful supply of cheaper **motels** are *Sea Dell*, 5000 Overseas Highway (☎1-800/648-3854; ③) and *Seaward*, 8700 Overseas Highway (☎743-5711; ③–④). Good deals can also be found at the *Flamingo Inn*, MM59 (☎289-1478; ④). The only **campground** permitting tents is *Knights Key Park*, MM47 (☎743-9954).

Despite the commercial conformity of Marathon's main drag, there are several friendly places to **eat**. *Herbie's*, 6350 Overseas Highway (☎743-6373), is justly busy on account of its inexpensive seafood; *Porky's Too BBQ*, MM45 (☎743-6637), provides platefuls of beef and chicken; quality Italian dishes come in the simple setting of the *Village Café*, at the Gulfside Village Plaza, 5800 Overseas Highway (☎743-9090). The *Grassy Key Dairy Bar*, MM58.5 (☎743-3816), cooks up a different cuisine each night, always good and competitively priced.

Marathon goes to sleep early; the only place with a suspicion of **nightlife** is the tiki bar of *Bacchus by the Sea*, 725 11th Street (☎743-6106), which is also the prime vantage point for watching alcohol-tinged sunsets.

South of Marathon: the Overseas Railroad, the Seven Mile Bridge and Pigeon Key

In 1905, Henry Flagler, whose railway opened up Florida's East Coast, undertook to extend its tracks to Key West. The **Overseas Railroad**, as it became known (though many called it "Flagler's folly"), was a monumental task that took seven years to complete and was marred by appalling treatment of workers.

Bridging the Middle Keys gave Flagler's engineers some of their biggest headaches. North of Marathon, the two-mile-long Long Key Viaduct (see above), a still-elegant structure of nearly two hundred individually cast arches, was Flagler's personal favorite and widely pictured in advertising campaigns. Yet a greater technical accomplishment was the **Seven Mile Bridge** to the south, linking Marathon to the Lower Keys. At one point, every US-flagged freighter on the Atlantic was hired to bring in materials – including special cement from Germany – while floating cranes, dredges and scores of other craft set about a job that eventually cost the lives of 700 laborers.

Once the trains started rolling (doddering over the bridges at 15mph), passengers looked out over an incredible panorama: a broad sweep of sea and sky etched in shifting tones of blue, black, turquoise and green, sometimes streaked by luscious red sunsets or darkened by approaching storm clouds.

The Flagler bridges were strong enough to withstand everything that the keys' volatile weather could throw at them. But the calamitous 1935 Labor Day hurricane tore up the railway and the bridges were adapted to accommodate a road: the original Overseas Highway. Tales of hair-raising bridge crossings (the road was only 22 feet wide), endless tailbacks as the drawbridges jammed – and the roadside parties which ensued – are part of keys folklore. The later bridges, such as the $45-million **new Seven Mile Bridge** opened in the early Eighties, certainly improved traffic flow but also ended the mystique of travelling the old road – and its walls are just high enough to hide the fabulous view.

The old bridges, with mid-sectional cuts to allow shipping to pass but otherwise intact, now make extraordinarily long fishing piers and jogging strips. A section of the former Seven Mile Bridge also provides the only land access to **PIGEON KEY**, a 1908 railway work camp, utilized until recently by the University of Miami for marine science classes. Its six original wooden buildings are in the process of being restored and a railway museum is also planned for the site. All of which could make an educational side trip; check the present state of things on ☎743-6040.

The Lower Keys

Starkly different to their northerly neighbors, the **Lower Keys** are quiet, heavily wooded and predominantly residential. Uniquely aligned north–south and built on a limestone rather than (like the preceding keys) a coral base, these islands have a flora and fauna that's very much their own, a lot of it tucked away miles from the Overseas Highway – like many of the local people, drawn here by the lack of rampant tourism and easily found seclusion. Most visitors speed right through on the way to Key West, just forty miles further, but linger here if you can and savor the understated character. The main settlement is Big Pine Key, where the **Lower Keys Chamber of Commerce**, at MM 31.9 (Mon–Fri 9am–5pm, Sat 9am–3pm, ☎1-800/872-2411), is packed with area info.

Bahia Honda State Recreation Area

Daily 8am–sunset; cars $3.25, pedestrians and cyclists $1.

While not officially part of the Lower Keys, the first place of consequence you'll hit after crossing the Seven Mile Bridge is **Bahia Honda State Recreation**

Area, one of the keys' prettiest spots. The northeasterly section of the park rings a lagoon with a beckoning natural **beach** and two-tone ocean waters that invite a dip. While here, ramble the **nature trail**, looping from the shoreline through a hammock of silver palms, geiger and yellow satinwood trees, passing rare plants such as dwarf morning glory and spiny catesbaea. Bird life, too, can be special. Watch for white crowned pigeons, great white herons, roseate spoonbills and giant ospreys (whose bulky nests are plentiful throughout the Lower Keys, often atop telegraph poles).

The southern end of the 300-acre park holds more good swimming waters, opportunities for snorkelling and diving (be warned that the currents hereabouts can be very swift) – and some excellent windsurfing; rent equipment from the marina's dive shop. You'll also notice the two-storey **Flagler Bridge**. The unusually deep waters here (Bahia Honda is Spanish for "deep bay"), made this the toughest of the old railway bridges to construct and widening it for the road proved impossible: the solution was to put the highway on a higher tier. It's actually far safer than it looks and there's a fine view from the top of the bridge over the Bahia Honda channel towards the forest-coated Lower Keys.

Big Pine Key and Around

The big pine trees on **BIG PINE KEY** are less of a draw than the little **Key deer**, who enjoy the freedom of the island – don't feed them and be especially cautious when driving. The deer, each no bigger than a large dog, arrived long ago when the keys were still joined to the mainland; they provided food for sailors and Key West residents for many years, but hunting and the destruction of their natural habitat led to near extinction by the late Forties. The **National Key Deer Refuge** was set up here in 1954 to safeguard these delightfully tame animals – one refuge manager went so far as to burn the cars and sink the boats of poachers – and their population has now stabilized at around 400.

Pick up factual background on the deer from the **refuge headquarters** (Mon–Fri 8am–5pm; ☎872-2239), at the western end of Watson Boulevard, off Key Deer Boulevard. To see them, driving along Key Deer Boulevard or turning east onto No Name Key should turn up at least a few; they often amuse themselves in domestic gardens. Your chances are best in the cooler temperatures of early morning or late afternoon.

Also on Key Deer Boulevard, the **Blue Hole** is a freshwater lake with a healthy population of soft-shelled turtles and at least one alligator, who now and then emerges from the cool depths to sun himself – parts of the lakeside path may be closed if he's staked out a patch for the day. Should the gator get your adrenaline pumping, calm down on the shortish **nature trail**, a quarter of a mile ahead along Key Deer Boulevard.

Moving on: the rest of the Lower Keys

An even calmer atmosphere prevails over the Lower Keys south of Big Pine Key, despite the efforts of property developers. The **TORCH KEYS**, so-named for their forests of torchwood – used for kindling by early settlers – may as well be swiftly bypassed on the way to **RAMROD KEY**, where Looe Key Marine Sanctuary is a terrific coral reef viewing site and to Sugarloaf Key, holding an oddball slice of keys' history.

Perhaps the most expensive thing you'll see anywhere in the keys, if not all of Florida, is the balloon-like "aerostat" hovering over **CUDJOE KEY**. With a budget of $16 million, it was used by the US government to beam TV images of American-style freedom – baseball, sit-coms, soap operas – to Cuba. Called *TV Marti*, the station was (ironically perhaps) named after the late-1800s Cuban independence fighter, José Martí. In July 1993, the Clinton administration decided to end the broadcasts; the future of the aerostat is uncertain.

Looe Key Marine Sanctuary

Keen underwater explorers shouldn't think twice about zooming in on **Looe Key Marine Sanctuary**, clearly signposted from the Overseas Highway on Ramrod Key. Named after the wreck of *HMS Looe*, a British frigate which sank here in 1744, this five-square-mile protected reef area is in every part the equal of the John Pennecamp Coral Reef State Park (see "North Key Largo"). The crystal-clear waters and the spur and groove formation of the reef create sights of miraculous diversity: big brain coral, complex tangles of elkhorn and staghorn coral, tall coral pillars rising towards the surface and soft corals like purple seafans and sea whips providing softer shadings. The incumbent marine life, a multitude of gaily striped and patterned fish, rays and octopus, adds to the unforgettable undersea spectacle.

The **sanctuary office** (Mon–Fri 8am–5pm; ☎872-4039) can provide free maps and information. You can only visit the reef itself on a trip organized by one of the many diving shops throughout the keys; the nearest is the neighboring *Looe Key Dive Center* (☎1-800/942-5397).

Perky's Bat Tower

On **SUGARLOAF KEY**, fifteen miles from Ramrod Key, the 35-foot **Perky's Bat Tower** stands as testimony to one man's misguided belief in the benefits of bats. A get-rich-quick book of the Twenties, *Bats, Mosquitoes and Dollars*, led Richter C. Perky, a property speculator who had recently purchased the island, into thinking bats would be the solution to the keys' mosquito problem. With much hullaballoo, he erected this brown cypress lath tower and dutifully sent away for the costly "bat bait" (probably bat shit) which he was told would lure an army of bats to the tower. It didn't work: no bat ever showed up, the mosquitoes stayed healthy and Perky went bust soon after. The background story is far more interesting than the actual tower, but if the tale tickles your fancy, view it from the bumpy road just beyond the sprawling *Sugarloaf Lodge*, at MM17.

Practicalities

For what they offer, **motels** in the Lower Keys are expensive. *Looe Key Reef Resort*, MM27.5 (☎872-2215; ③), is ideal for visiting the marine sanctuary, or there's *Parmer's Place*, MM28.5 (☎872-2157; ④). **Campgrounds** are plentiful but tents are accepted only at *Big Pine Key Fishing Lodge*, MM33 (☎872-2351) and *Seahorse*, MM31 (☎872-2443). Three **bed and breakfast inns**, along Long Beach Drive on Big Pine Key, make cosy alternatives – but book early: *Deer Run*, MM32.5 (☎872-2015; ⑤), *Barnacle*, MM32.5 (☎872-3298; ⑤) and *Casa Grande*, 33MM (☎872-2878; ④).

The best place to **eat** in the Lower Keys is *Mangrove Mama's*, at MM20 on Sugarloaf Key (sometimes closed Tues or Thurs and usually throughout Sept;

☎745-3030), for its rustic atmosphere, great seafood and home-baked bread. Otherwise, on Big Pine Key, *Island Jim's*, MM31.3 (☎872-2017), has good stuff from breakfast through to dinner, or grab a sandwich from *Dip N'Deli*, MM31 (☎872-3030).

Nightlife is not a strong card; when locals want to live it up they go to Key West. Take a shot at the *No Name Pub*, at the eastern end of Watson Boulevard on Big Pine Key (☎872-9115), for its varied beers and occasional live bands; the *Looe Key Reef Resort* (see above) for weekend drinking; or, if desperate, something bland but time-filling might be found in the lounge of the *Cedar Inn*, MM31 (☎872-4031).

Key West

Much closer to Cuba than mainland Florida, **KEY WEST**'s links with the rest of the US often seem very tenuous indeed. Famed for their tolerant attitudes and laid-back lifestyles, the 30,000 islanders seem adrift in a great expanse of sea and sky and – despite the million tourists who arrive each year – the place resonates with an anarchic and very individual spirit that hits you the instant you arrive. Locals (known as *conchs* – after the giant sea snails eaten by early settlers – if they've spent their lives here, or *freshwater conchs* if they've moved in) ride bicycles, shoot the breeze on street corners and wave and smile at complete strangers. The narrow thoroughfares and alleyways are a blaze of tropical T-shirts, garish hats and extravagant shorts. Even in tourist shops, king-sized cigarette papers and hash pipes are sold next to beachware and sunscreen – and no one turns a hair.

Yet as wild as it may at first appear, Key West today is far from being the drop-outs' and misfits' mecca that it was just a decade or so ago. Much of the sleaziness of that time has been brushed away through a steady process of restoration and revitalization – it takes a lot of money to buy a house here now – setting the course for the smooth-edged advent of a sizeable vacation industry. Not that Key West is anywhere near losing its special identity: it's still resolutely non-conformist and your ears will be argued off if you dare suggest otherwise. The liberal manners have stimulated a large influx of **gay** people, estimated at one in five of the population, who are not only out of the closet but taking a big role in running the place and sinking thousands of dollars into its future.

There's plenty to enjoy over a few days, even if many of the well-hyped "attractions" are less than they're cracked up to be and the endless tales of drug-runners, Ernest Hemingway (one of a number of writers who have lived here) and the landing of gigantic fish, need to be taken with a pinch of salt. The sense of isolation from the mainland – much stronger here than on the other keys – and the comraderie of the locals, is best appreciated by adjusting to the mellow pace and joining in: amble the streets, make meals last for hours and pause regularly for refreshment in the numerous bars. Give it a chance and Key West can be a deliciously seductive place.

Some history

Piracy was the main activity around Key West – first settled in 1822 – before Florida joined the US and the navy established a base here. This cleared the way for a substantial **wrecking industry**, with millions of dollars being earned through lifting people and cargo off shipwrecks along the Florida Reef, making Key West the wealthiest city in the US by the mid-nineteenth century.

The subsequent building of reef lighthouses sounded the death knell for the wrecking business, but Key West continued to prosper. Many **Cubans** arrived with cigar-making skills and migrant Greeks established a lucrative sponging enterprise (the harvesting of highly absorbent sea sponges, formed from the skeletons of tiny marine creatures, which were the forerunners of today's synthetic sponges). Industrial unrest and a sponge blight drove these businesses northwards (to Tampa and Tarpon Springs respectively) and left Key West ill-prepared to face the **Depression**. By the early Thirties, its remaining inhabitants – die-hard conchs resisting any suggestion that they move to the mainland – were living on fish and coconuts, finally declaring themselves bankrupt in July 1934. Under Roosevelt's New Deal, Key West was tidied up and readied for tourism, but the 1935 Labor Day hurricane blew away the Flagler railway – Key West's only land link to the outside world.

Eventually it was an injection of naval dollars during World War II and the geographical good fortune to be the US military's eyes and ears on communist Cuba, that saved Key West and provided the backbone of its economy until the **tourists** finally started arriving in force through the Eighties.

Far from being swamped by outsiders, however, the community was quick to assert itself. In April 1982, when the US border patrols began stopping all traffic leaving the keys and searching and questioning drivers in pursuit of drugs and illegal aliens, locals proclaimed the town to be the capital of the **"Conch Republic"**. Partly intended as an excuse for a booze-up, this declaration of UDI (followed immediately by surrender and a request for foreign aid) typically made a political point in a humorous way and symbolized the community's zealously maintained social, as well as geographic, separation from the mainland.

Arrival, Information and Getting Around

The Overseas Highway is the only road into Key West, and it runs through the bland eastern section of the island into the much more interesting Old Town. On the way you'll pass the unmissable **Welcome Center** on North Roosevelt Boulevard (daily 9am–5pm; ☎296-4444), though if you don't feel like stopping here, press on and use the **Greater Key West Chamber of Commerce**, 402 Wall Street (daily 8.30am–5pm, ☎294-2587), for free tourist pamphlets and discount vouchers.

A number of easily found **free publications** list current events: *Solares Hill* (monthly) is the most informative but look out for *Island Life* (weekly), *The Conch Republic* (monthly) and the gay-oriented gossip sheet, *What's Happening* (weekly).

Driving around the narrow, pedestrian-busy streets of the Old Town is more trouble than it's worth; better to see the area by **walking**. If you're planning to venture further afield, **rent a bike** from *Adventure Scooter & Bicycle Rentals*, at 708 and 925 Duval Street, or from the youth hostel (see "Accommodation").

Remarkably, there is a **bus service** (☎292-8164) on Key West: two routes, one clockwise and the other anticlockwise, loop around the tiny island roughly every fifteen minutes between 7am and 9am and 2.30pm and 5.30pm.

If you're pushed for time, take a ninety-minute narrated spin around the main sights with either the *Conch Tour Train* (leaving every 20–30min from Mallory Square 9am–4pm; $12) or the *Old Town Trolley* (board at any of the marked stops around the Old Town; every 30min 9am–4.30pm; $14).

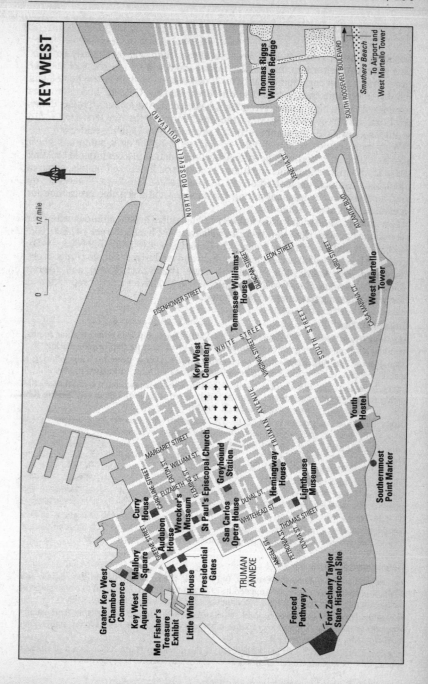

KEY WEST

N

0   1/2 mile

Thomas-Riggs Wildlife Refuge

SOUTH ROOSEVELT BOULEVARD

Smathers Beach

To Airport and West Martello Tower

NORTH ROOSEVELT BOULEVARD

VENETIA ST.

LEON STREET

DUNCAN STREET

West Martello Tower

CASA MARINA CT.

LAIRD STREET

ATLANTIC BLVD.

EISENHOWER STREET

WHITE STREET

Tennessee Williams' House

VIRGINIA STREET

SOUTH STREET

Key West Cemetery

TRUMAN AVENUE

Youth Hostel

MARGARET STREET

EATON ST.

WILLIAM ST.

ELIZABETH ST.

FLEMING ST.

CAROLINE STREET

GREENE STREET

Greyhound Station

St Paul's Episcopal Church

DUVAL ST.

Hemingway House

Lighthouse Museum

Southernmost Point Marker

Curry House

Audubon House

Wrecker's Museum

San Carlos Opera House

WHITEHEAD ST.

THOMAS STREET

Mallory Square

Greater Key West Chamber of Commerce

Key West Aquarium

Mel Fisher's Treasure Exhibit

Little White House

Presidential Gates

TRUMAN ANNEXE

ANGELA ST.

PETRONIA ST.

DUVAL ST.

Fenced Pathway

Fort Zachary Taylor State Historical Site

Accommodation

Accommodation costs in Key West are always high and particularly so from November to April, when the simplest motel room will be in excess of $90 per night. Prices drop considerably at other times but, other than at the hostel, you should expect little change from $50 wherever you stay. Genuine budget options are limited to pitching a tent or renting a basic cottage at *Jabour's Trailor Court*, 223 Elizabeth Street (☎294-5723), or the small dorms of the *Key West Hostel*, 718 South Street (☎296-5719; members $14.25, non-members $17.50; weekly $90).

With more money to spend, take advantage of Key West's numerous guest houses, which offer **bed and breakfast** accommodation in a century-old building at a price no higher than the much less atmospheric hotels and motels, some of which are unattractively located on the approach roads into town. Wherever you stay, a reservation is essential during the summer and a sensible precaution for weekends stays at any other time.

Gay and lesbian visitors are unlikely to encounter hostile attitudes wherever they choose to stay. However, the *Curry House*, 806 Fleming Street (☎1-800/633-7439; ④–⑤) and the *Rainbow House*, 525 United Street (☎1-800/749-6696; ④–⑤), are guest houses which are exclusively male and exclusively female respectively. Elsewhere, *Big Ruby's*, 409 Applerouth Lane (☎296-2323; ④–⑤) and *Cypress House*, 601 Caroline Street (☎1-800/525-2488; ③–④), have earned a reputation as classy and relaxing gay-oriented accommodations.

Guest Houses

Angelina Guest House, 302 Angela St (☎294-4480). Simple but well-priced regular rooms; spending a little more brings kitchenettes and suites, good value for four people sharing. ④.

Blue Parrot Inn, 916 Elizabeth St (☎1-800/231-BIRD). Dating from 1884 and offering a heated pool and continental breakfast, as well as comfortable, nicely furnished rooms. ⑥.

Curry Mansion Inn, 511 Caroline St (☎294-5349). The high price buys a night amid the quality antiques which furnish and decorate this landmark Victorian home; see "Seeing Key West" for an account of its distinguished past. ⑦–⑧.

Duval House, 815 Duval St (☎294-1666). The lower-priced rooms are here are very good value; extra spending brings a four-poster bed and a balcony overlooking the grounds. ⑤–⑦.

Eden House, 1015 Fleming St (☎1-800/533-KEYS). Wicker furnishings and a fish-filled pool add to the appeal of this thoughtfully renovated and fully modernized 1924 building, making it one of Key West's most relaxing hideaways. The cheaper rooms share a bathroom; the priciest have jacuzzis. ④–⑦.

Simonton Court, 320 Simonton St (☎1-800/944-2687). A choice of regular rooms in the main house or well-equipped cottages spread through the grounds. ⑤–⑦.

Wicker House, 913 Duval St (☎296-2475). The least costly of Key West's guest houses comprises four restored "conch" houses in which the cheaper rooms lack air-conditioning (ceiling fans are installed) and TVs, though there is a communal jacuzzi. ③–⑤.

Hotels and Motels

La Concha Holiday Inn, 430 Duval St (☎1-800/745-2191). Now a link in the *Holiday Inn* chain, this characterful hotel first opened in 1925 and has been refurbished to retain some of its Twenties style; a bigger plus for most guests is the large swimming pool. ⑥–⑦.

Hampton Inn, 2801 N Roosevelt Blvd (☎1-800/426-7866). Branch of a reliable (and usually low-cost) hotel chain with spacious rooms, a bar and a jacuzzi. The rates are far higher than most *Hampton Inns*, however. ⑦.

Sea Shell Motel, 718 South St (☎296-5719). If the adjoining youth hostel is full or doesn't appeal, this offers standard motel rooms at the lowest rates in the neighborhood. ④.

Southern Cross, 326 Duval St (☎1-800/533-4891). Key West's oldest hotel offers no-frills rooms; get one at the rear if you want to avoid the night-time hubbub along Duval Street. ⑤.

Southernmost Motel, 1319 Duval St (☎1-800/354-4455). The rooms at the US's most southerly motel are decked out in tropical shades; the poolside tiki bar is the ideal place to meet other guests before taking the ten-minute walk to the heart of Key West. ⑤.

La Terraza de Marti, 1125 Duval St (☎296-6706). Better known locally as "La-Te-Da", The rooms face a beckoning pool, and the tree-studded hotel complex includes several bars, discos and a classy restaurant (see "Eating"). Well placed for the town and very popular with gay visitors. ⑥–⑦.

Tilton Hilton, 511 Angela St (☎294-8694). Key West's cheapest hotel but otherwise one with little to recommend it. The rooms are very basic; be sure to see yours before paying for it. ③.

Seeing Key West: along Duval Street

The square mile of the **Old Town** contains virtually everything that you could want to see and is certainly the best place for imbibing Key West's finest feature: its atmosphere. Tourists are plentiful around the main streets but the relaxed, casually hedonistic mood that draws many to Key West affects everybody, whether they've been here twenty years or twenty minutes. All of the Old Town can be seen on foot in little more than a day, though you should allow at least two or three – dashing about isn't the way to enjoy the place.

Anyone who saw Key West two decades ago would now barely recognize the main promenade, **Duval Street**. Teetering just on the safe side of seedy for many years, much of the street's been transformed into a well-manicured tourist strip of boutiques and beachwear shops catering to the vacationing middle-aged of Middle America. Duval Street, however, busy around the clock with its screwball nature bubbling just below the surface, is never boring and cuts a mile-long swathe right through the Old Town – making it easy to regain bearings after exploring the side streets.

Other than shops and bars, few places on Duval Street provide a break from tramping the pavement. One is the **Wrecker's Museum**, 322 Duval Street (daily 10am–4pm; $2), which gives some background to the industry on which Key West's earliest good times were based: salvaging cargo from foundering vessels.

KEY WEST FESTIVALS

January–April *Old Island Days*. Tours, talks, concerts, flower shows and art festivals, all celebrating Key West's history.

April *Conch Shell Blowing Contest*. Ear-numbing music played on the shells of the creatures from which Key Westers take their nickname.

Late April *Conch Republic Celebration*. A party in Mallory Square with a symbolic raising of the Conch Republic flag, commemorating the declaration of the keys' independence from the US in 1982 (see "Some history").

July *Hemingway Days*. Literary seminars, writers' workshops, daft trivia competitions, arm-wrestling and lookalike contests to commemorate Ernest Hemingway, Key West's best-known ex-resident.

Late October *Fantasy Fest*. A gay-dominated version of Mardi Gras with outrageous costumes paraded all night long along Duval Street.

Get **precise dates** on all of these from the Chamber of Commerce or Welcome Center (addresses above).

In the days before radio and radar, wrecking crews simply put out in bad weather and sailed as close as they dared to the menacing reefs, hoping to spot a grounded craft. Judging by the choice furniture that fills the house, Captain Watlington, the wrecker who lived here from the 1830s, did pretty well. On the top floor, modern cartoons recount several Key West folk tales, including the dunking in the sea of a preacher who dwelled too long on the evils of drinking.

A few blocks on, **St Paul's Episcopal Church**, at no 401, is worth entering briefly for its rich stained-glass windows. If overwhelmed by piety, you might scoot around the corner for a look at the **Old Stone Methodist Church**, 600 Eaton Street, the oldest church in Key West, put up in 1877 and long enjoying the shade of the giant Spanish laurel tree in its front yard.

The San Carlos Opera House and the Southernmost Point

At 516 Duval Street, the **San Carlos Opera House** (daily 9am–5pm; $3) has played a leading role in Cuban exile life since it opened (on a different site) as the San Carlos Institute in 1871. Financed by a $100,000 grant from the Cuban government, the present building dates from 1924; across its grounds are spread soil from Cuba's six provinces and a cornerstone was taken from the tomb of legendary Cuban independence campaigner, José Martí. Following the break in diplomatic ties between the US and Cuba in 1961, the building fell on hard times – and was briefly used as a cinema, much to the annoyance of local Cubans – until it was revived by a million-dollar restoration project. Now, besides staging opera in its acoustically excellent auditorium and maintaining a well-stocked research library, it holds a commendable account of Key West history and Cuban life in the town.

You'll know when you get near the southern end of Duval Street because, whether it's a house, motel, filling station or restaurant, everything advertises itself as "the Southernmost . . .". Accurately, the **southernmost point** in Key West and consequently in the continental US, is to be found at the intersection of Whitehead and South streets. Many visitors derive great pleasure from having their photo taken by the daft-looking buoy that marks the spot; if you're not one of them, forget it.

Mallory Square and Around

In the early 1800s, thousands of dollars' worth of salvage was landed at the piers, stored in the warehouses and flogged at the auction houses on **Mallory Square**, just west of the northern end of Duval Street. The square's present-day commerce is based on tourism and little remains from the old times. By day, the square is a plain souvenir market, with overpriced ice cream, trinkets and T-shirts. But return at night for the **sunset celebration**, when buskers, jugglers, fire-eaters and assorted screw-loose types create a merry backdrop to the sinking of the sun. The celebration, which began in the Sixties as a hippie excuse for a smoke-in, is lively and fun, though it, too, has become very tourist-oriented.

Key West Aquarium and Mel Fisher's Treasure Exhibit

More entertaining than the square during the day is the small gathering of sea life inside the adjacent **Key West Aquarium**, 1 Whitehead Street (daily 10am–6pm, winter until 7pm; $6), where ugly creatures such as the porcupine fish and longspine squirrel fish leer out from behind glass and sharks (the smaller kinds such as lemon, blacktip and bonnethead) are known to jump out of their open tanks during the **guided tours** which begin at 11am, 1pm, 3pm and 4.30pm. If you intend to eat conch, a rubbery crustacean sold as fritter or chowder all over Key West, do so before examining the live ones here; they're not the world's most appetizing creatures.

In the wild, the aquarium's fish might make their homes around the remains of sunken galleons which plied the trade route between Spain and its New World colonies a few centuries ago, oblivious to the efforts of humans to bring up the booty that went down with them. In **Mel Fisher's Treasure Exhibit**, 200 Greene Street (daily 9.30am–5pm; $5), little more than a gangplank's length from the aquarium, you'll get a good look at skilfully crafted decorative pieces, an intensely impressive emerald cross, a liftable gold bar and countless vases and daggers alongside the obligatory cannon, pulled up from two seventeenth-century wrecks. As engrossing as the collection is, it's really a celebration of an all-American rags-to-riches story. Now the high priest of Florida's many treasure seekers, Fisher was running a surf shop in California before he arrived in the sunshine state armed with ancient Spanish sea charts. In 1985, after years of searching, he discovered the *Nuestra Señora de Atocha* and *Santa Margarita*, both sunk during a hurricane in 1622, forty miles southeast of Key West – they yielded a haul said to be worth millions of dollars. Among matters you won't find mentioned at the exhibit are the raging dispute between Fisher and the state and federal governments over who owns what and the ecological upsets that uncontrolled treasure-seeking has caused the keys.

The Truman Annexe and Fort Zachary Taylor

The old naval storehouse which contains the Fisher trove was once part of the **Truman Annexe** (daily 9am–8pm; free), a decommissioned section of a naval base established in 1822 to keep a lid on piracy around what had just become US territory. Some of the buildings subsequently erected on the base, which spans a hundred acres between Whitehead Street and the sea, were – and still are – among Key West's most distinctive – for example, the dreamy Romanesque-revival-style Customs House (across Front Street from the Mel Fisher Treasure Exhibit).

The most famous among them, however, was the comparatively plain **Little White House**, which earned its name by being the favorite holiday spot of President Harry S Truman, who first visited in 1946 (and after whom the annexe was named). The president allegedly spent his vacations playing poker, cruising Key West for doughnuts and swimming – during which time, due to the primitive plumbing, no one in the house was allowed to flush the toilet. The house, by the junction of Caroline and Front streets, is now a **museum*** recording, with an immense array of memorabilia, the Truman years (daily 9am–5pm; $6).

---

* The new museum is part of a dramatic metamorphosis affecting the entire annexe following its purchase for $17.25 million in 1986 by a young, post-Modern property developer called **Pritam Singh**. Remembered by some Key West residents as a scruffy hippie, Singh, who visited Key West in his long-haired youth and later adopted the Sikh religion, has won plaudits for his public- and environment-friendly building schemes all over the US. His plans for the Truman Annexe are an ambitious blend of preservation, rehabilitation and development; the intention is for mixed-income housing, shops and restaurants to appear amid what should be a carefully thought out historical site. How it will finally shape up is anyone's guess, but the project is a refreshingly far cry from Florida's traditional hit-and-run property scams.

In 1986, the new owner of the annexe made a lot of friends early on by throwing open the weighty **Presidential Gates** on Caroline Street, which previously only parted for heads of state and by encouraging the public to walk or cycle around the complex. Get the free **walking guide** from the well-signposted sales office and embark on a building-by-building tour – only the exteriors, as yet, are viewable.

The annexe also provides access, along a fenced pathway through the operating naval base, to the less interesting **Fort Zachary Taylor State Historical Site** (daily 8am–sunset; cars $3.25, pedestrians and cyclists $1.50), built in 1845 and later assisting in the blockade of Confederate shipping during the Civil War. Over ensuing decades, the fort simply disappeared under sand and weeds. Excavation work has gradually revealed much of historical worth, though the full importance is hard to comprehend without joining the 45-minute **guided tour** (daily at noon & 2pm). Most locals pass by the fort on the way to the best **beach** in Key West – a place yet to be discovered by tourists, just a few yards beyond.

Along Whitehead Street

A block west of crowded Duval Street, much quieter **Whitehead Street** has a trio of tourable sights and, with its mix of rich and poor homes, reveals a more down-to-earth side of Key West.

On the corner with Greene Street, the **Audubon House** (daily 9.30am–5pm; $5) was the first of Key West's once-elegant Victorian homes to get a thorough renovation – its success encouraged a host of others to follow suit and sent property prices soaring. It's a neat and tidy job, but unforgivably steals the name of a man who had nothing at all to do with the place. Famed ornithologist John James Audubon spent few weeks in Key West in 1832, scrambling around the mangrove swamps (now protected as the Thomas Riggs Wildlife Refuge, see p.143), looking for the bird life he later portrayed in his highly regarded *Birds of America* portfolio*. Yet Audubon's links with this house go no further than the well-observed lithographs which decorate the walls and staircase; the property belonged to a wrecker called John Geiger. Geiger and his wife took in many children from shipwrecks and broken marriages alongside their own twelve-strong brood and their enormous stock of family photos provides the only flicker of authentic history in the house, otherwise loaded with drab nineteenth-century furniture.

The Hemingway House
It may be the biggest tourist draw in Key West, but to the chagrin of Ernest Hemingway fans, guided tours of the **Hemingway House**, 907 Whitehead Street (daily 9am–5pm; $6), deal more in fantasy than fact. Although Hemingway owned this large, vaguely Moorish-style house for thirty years, he lived in it for barely ten and the authenticity of the furnishings – a motley bunch of tables, chairs and beds much gloated over by the guide – is hotly disputed by Hemingway's former secretary.

Already established as the nation's foremost hard-drinking, hunting- and fishing-obsessed writer, Hemingway bought the house in 1931, not with his own money but with an $8000 gift from the rich uncle of his then wife, Pauline.

---

* Curiously, Audubon was as interested in shooting birds as drawing them, and considered it a bad day in Florida if he didn't bag at least a hundred.

Originally one of the grander Key West homes, built for a wealthy nineteenth-century merchant, the dwelling was seriously run down by the time the Hemingways arrived. It soon acquired such luxuries as an inside bathroom and a swimming pool and was filled with an entourage of servants and housekeepers. Some of the writer's most acclaimed work was produced in the deer-head-dominated study (in an outhouse which Hemingway entered by way of a home-made rope bridge): the short stories, *The Short Happy Life of Francis Macomber* and *The Snows of Kilimanjaro* and the novels, *For Whom the Bell Tolls* and *To Have and Have Not*; the latter an interesting though hardly inspired description of Key West life during the Depression. Divorced from Pauline in 1940, Hemingway boxed up his manuscripts and moved them to a back room at the original *Sloppy Joe's* (see "Nightlife"), before heading off for a house in Cuba with his new wife, journalist Martha Gellhorn.

To see inside the house (and the study), the half-hour **guided tour** is compulsory, but afterwards you're free to roam at leisure and play with some of the fifty-odd cats. The story that these are descendants from a feline family here in Hemingway's day is yet another dubious claim: the large colony of inbred cats which Hemingway once described were in Cuba.

The Lighthouse Museum and the Bahama Village

From the Hemingway House, you'll easily catch sight of the **Lighthouse Museum**, 938 Whitehead Street (daily 9.30am–5pm; $4), simply because it *is* an 86-foot lighthouse; one of Florida's first, raised in 1847. The still-working light is of more value to shipping than visitors, however: there's a tiny collection of lighthouse junk and drawings at ground level and the boring climb to the top of the tower reveals a view better enjoyed from the top-floor bar of the *La Concha* hotel (see "Nightlife").

The narrow streets around the lighthouse constitute the so-called **Bahama Village**, immediately striking for its lack of tourists and glossy restoration jobs. Most of the squat, slightly shambolic homes – some of them once small cigar factories – are lived in, mainly, by poorly-off Bahamians and Cubans of African descent.

Caroline and Greene streets, the Dockside Area and Margaret Street

Turn right at the northern end of Duval Street along Caroline or Greene streets and you'll come across numerous examples of the late-1800s **"conch houses"**, built in a mix-and-match style that fused elements of Victorian, Colonial and Tropical architecture, raised on coral slabs and rounded off with playful "ginger-bread" wood trimming. Erected quickly and cheaply, conch houses were seldom painted, but many here are bright and colorful, evincing their recent transformation from ordinary dwellings to hundred-thousand-dollar winter homes.

In strong contrast to the tiny conch houses, the grand three-storey **Curry House**, 511 Caroline Street (daily 10am–5pm; $5), was the abode of William Curry, Florida's first millionaire. Inside, amid a riot of Tiffany glass and mahogany panelling, are a heady stash of strange and stylish fittings – from an antique Chinese toilet bowl to a Frank Lloyd Wright-designed lamp – added to boost the appeal of the $150 bed and breakfast accommodation on offer and making for an amusing ferret through the premises.

The dockside area

The rest of the **dockside area**, between Williams and Margaret streets, has been spruced up into a shopping and eating strip called **Land's End Village**, with a couple of enjoyable bars (see "Nightlife"). One with more than drinking to offer is *Turtle Kraals*, in business as a turtle cannery until the Seventies when harvesting turtles became illegal. There are tanks of touchable sea life inside the restaurant and, just along the short pier, a grim gathering of the gory machines used to slice and mince green turtles – captured off the Nicaraguan coast – into a delicacy known as *Granday's Fine Green Turtle Soup*. Apart from pleasure cruisers and shrimping boats, you might catch a fleeting glimpse from the docks of a naval hydrofoil – vessels of unbelievable speed employed on anti-drug-running missions from their base a mile or so along the coast.

Margaret Street and around

Leaving the waterfront and following Margaret Street for five blocks leads to the **Key West Cemetery** (daily sunrise–6pm; free; guided tours Sun at 10am & 4pm; $5; make a reservation on ☎296-3913), an unghoulish place of above-ground vaults (a high water table and solid coral rock prevents the traditional six-feet-under interment). Despite the lack of celebrity stiffs, the numerous mildly witty inscriptions, "I told you I was sick" being just one, encourage a casual stroll around – and suggest that the relaxed Key West attitude to life also extends to death.

Unlike his more flamboyant counterparts, Key West's longest residing literary notable, playwright **Tennessee Williams** – whose forte was steamy evocations of Deep South life such as *A Street Car Named Desire* and *Cat on a Hot Tin Roof* – kept a low profile during his 34 years here (he arrived in 1949) and his modest white clapboard **house**, at 1431 Duncan Street, a fifteen-minute walk from the cemetery, does much the same.

The rest of Key West

Outside the compact Old Town, there isn't a lot more of Key West. Most of the eastern section of the island – encircled by the North and South sections of Roosevelt Boulevard – is residential and decidedly boring. That said, Key West's longest beach is here, as are several minor points of botanical, natural and historical interest.

At the southern end of White Street, **West Martello Tower** is one of two Civil War lookout points complementing Fort Zachary Taylor (see above). In complete variance to the original military purpose, it's now filled by the intoxicating colors and smells of a **tropical garden** (Wed–Sun 9.30am–3.30pm; free). Though it makes a nice outdoor break, a more time-worthy target is the Tower's sister fort, East Martello – see below.

From the tower, Atlantic Avenue quickly intersects with South Roosevelt Boulevard, which skirts on one side the lengthy but slender **Smathers Beach** – the weekend parade ground of Key West's most viewable physiques and a haunt of windsurfers and parasailors – and on the other side, the forlorn-looking salt ponds of the **Thomas Riggs Wildlife Refuge**. From a platform raised above the refuge's mangrove entanglements, you should spot a variety of wading birds prowling the grass beds for crab and shrimp. Quiet and tranquil, save for the roar of planes in and out of the nearby airport, the refuge is not the busiest place in

Key West; to get inside you have to phone the Audubon House (☎294-2116) to learn the combination of the locked gate.

Half a mile further, just beyond the airport, the **East Martello Tower and Museum** (daily 9.30am–5pm; $3) is the second of the two Civil War lookout posts. The solid, vaulted casements now store a very viewable assemblage of local history, plus the wild junk-sculptures of a legendary Key Largo scrap dealer, Stanley Papio and the Key West scenes created in wood by a Cuban-primitive artist called Mario Sanchez. There are displays, too, on local writers and memorabilia from many movies shot in Key West. Its old houses and dependable climate have made it a popular location: in recent years, the final scenes of Sydney Pollack's *Havana* were shot here and *Crisscross* found Goldie Hawn running amok in the Old Town.

A short distance from the tower, South Roosevelt Boulevard meets the end of the Overseas Highway which crosses over onto the unexciting Stock Island before continuing (as Hwy-1) on its thousand-mile journey to the Canadian border. Staying on Key West, South Roosevelt Boulevard becomes North Roosevelt Boulevard and loops back towards the Old Town, passing a characterless neighborhood dominated by chain hotels, very ordinary restaurants and the Chernobyl-like chimneys of the local power station.

Eating

With abundant inexpensive **restaurants** and **snack stands** along the main streets, it's easy to eat cheaply and well in Key West. For special occasions, there are also several upmarket outlets serving delectable French, Italian and Asian cuisine. Fresh **seafood** is, not surprisingly, a feature of most menus, as is **conch fritter**, a Key West speciality which you should make the effort to sample at least once. Don't say no, either, to the local conch chowder.

Restaurants and take-away food

A&B Lobster House, 700 Front St (☎294-2536). Overlooking the town's harbor, there could hardly be a more scenic setting for indulging in fresh seafood or sampling the offerings of the raw bar.

Antonia's, 615 Duval St (☎294-6565). Excellent northern Italian cuisine served in a formal though friendly environment; dinner only – expensive but worth it.

Around the World, 627 Duval St (☎296-2115). Dishes drawn from every corner of the globe; if nothing appeals tuck into the sizeable salads and be sure to sample the extensive selections of wines and beers.

Bo's, 429 Duval St (☎294-9272). Over-the-counter fish'n'chips and conch fritters, claimed to be the cheapest in town.

Cafe des Artistes, 1007 Simonton St (☎294-7100). Pricey but tremendous tropical-French cuisine, utilizing the freshest local seafood, lobster and steak.

Camille's, 703 Duval St (☎296-4811). Laid-back lunches and dinners but best patronized for their locally acclaimed breakfasts. A great, low-cost way to start the day.

Croissants des France, 816 Duval St (☎294-2624). Crepes, soups and freshly baked goods served for breakfast or lunch, plus mouthwatering cream cakes and pastries for that decadent snack.

Dim-Sum, 613 Duval St (☎294-6230). Thai, Indonesian and Burmese specialties are the core of an exotic Asian menu; don't expect dinner to be less than $20.

Duffy's Steak & Lobster House, 1007 Simonton St (☎296-4900). As the name suggests, an immense selection of steak and lobster dishes, all at very appealing prices.

Key West Cookie Company, 621 Duval St (☎294-3969). Not only freshly baked cookies to nibble in the street, but also inexpensive daily lunch specials and the best *cafe con leche* – Cuban coffee with milk – between Miami and Havana.

Mangoes, 700 Duval St (☎292-4606). Eat indoors or outdoors under huge umbrellas; seafood and a variety of vegetarian dishes created with a Caribbean slant.

Siam House, 829 Simonton St (☎292-0302). Authentic Thai cuisine served with care in a near-authentic Thai setting. Great food, friendly staff and very reasonable prices.

South Beach Seafood & Raw Bar, 1405 Duval St (☎294-2727). Casual ocean-front dining at its best with the seafood selections; large portions of chicken, beef and ribs are also on offer.

Yo Sake, 722 Duval St (☎294-2288). Choose from the extensive range of traditional Japanese dishes, sample the sushi bar, or choose one of the daily specials – usually excellent value.

Nightlife

The anything-goes nature of Key West is exemplified by the **bars** which make up the bulk of the island's **nightlife**. Gregarious, rough and ready affairs, often open until 4am and offering a cocktail of yarn-spinning locals, revved-up tourists and (often) live country, folk or rock music, the best bars are grouped around the northern end of Duval Street, no more than a few minutes' stagger from one another.

Bars and Live Music Venues

Bull & Whistle Bar, 224 Duval St (no phone). Features the best of the local musicians each night. Check the list on the door to see whose playing – or just turn up to drink.

Captain Tony's Saloon, 428 Greene St (☎294-1838). This rustic fisherman's saloon was the original *Sloppy Joe's* (see below), a noted hang-out of Ernest Hemingway. Live music of various kinds nightly.

Full Moon Saloon, 1200 Simonton St (☎294-9090). Another laid-back bar which offers live music – be it blues, jazz, reggae or rap – Thurs–Sat until 4am.

Green Parrot Bar, 601 Whitehead St (☎294-6133). A Key West landmark since 1890, this bar draws local characters to its pool tables, dartboard and pinball machine and offers live music at weekends.

Havana Docks, at the *Pier House Hotel*, 1 Duval St (☎296-4600). An upmarket bar offering unparalleled patio views of the sunset accompanied by the lilting strains of a tropical island band. Inside, there's more live music – usually jazz or Latin – Wed–Sat.

Crazy Daizy's, at *La Concha Holiday Inn*, 430 Duval St (☎296-2991). Watch the sunset from the hotel's seventh-floor *Top* bar then descend to this ground-floor room to enjoy the Spectrelles re-creating the all-girl vocal group sounds of the Sixties.

Margaritaville, 500 Duval St (☎292-1435). Owner Jimmy Buffett – a Florida legend for his rock ballads extolling a laid-back life in the sun – occasionally pops up to join the live bands who play here nightly.

Sloppy Joe's, 201 Duval St (☎294-5717). Despite the memorabilia which hang on the walls and the crowds who pack the place nightly, this enjoyable bar – with live music nightly – is not the one made famous by Ernest Hemingway's patronage; for which, see *Captain Tony's Saloon*, above.

Turtle Kraals, Lands End Village, end of Margaret St (☎294-2640). Locals drop in for a drink here and there's also mellow music from a guitar and vocal duo on Fri and Sat nights.

Two Friends, 512 Front St (☎296-3124). A small and friendly bar with live jazz nightly except Mon.

Viva Zapata, 903 Duval St (☎296-3138). You might start your evening at the happy hour in this lively Mexican restaurant, which most locals use as a drinking spot and snack on the complimentary nachos.

Predominantly Gay Bars and Venues

Tolerant manners ensure that the above bars get plenty of **gay** customers (even if not all tourists leave their redneck attitudes on the mainland), but Key West also has a few specifically gay male hangouts.

The Copa, 623 Duval St (☎296-8521). A busy, progressive gay club with an enjoyable garden bar and, Wed–Sun, a pulsating disco with an excellent floor light show and often live entertainment; cover charge varies.

Eight-O-One Bar, 801 Duval St (☎294-4737). Step in off the street to the downstairs bar or continue up to the rooftop level for a great view over Duval Street and beyond; live entertainment three nights a week.

La-Te-Da, 1125 Duval St (☎294-8435). The various bars and discos of this hotel complex have long been a favorite haunt of local and visiting gays; the tea dance craze reached its zenith here in the late 1980s.

Key West Listings

Airport Four miles east of the Old Town on South Roosevelt Blvd (☎296-5439). No public transit link to the Old Town; a taxi will cost $8–9.

Bike rental From *Adventure Scooter & Bicycle Rentals*, at 708 and 925 Duval St and the *Youth Hostel*, 718 South St (☎296-5719).

Books The *Key West Island Bookstore*, 513 Fleming St, is packed with the works of Key West authors and keys-related literature.

Buses Local info: ☎292-8164.

Car rental Only worth considering if you're heading off to see the other keys. All companies are based at the airport: *Alamo* (☎294-6675); *Dollar* (☎296-9921); *Hertz* (☎294-1039); *Thrifty* (☎296-6514).

Dive shops Diving and snorkelling trips and equipment rental, can be arranged all over Key West. Try *Captain Corner's*, Zero Duval St (☎296-8865), or *Reef Raiders*, 109 Duval St (☎294-3635).

Ecology tours Dan McConnell, based at *Mosquito Coast Island Outfitters*, 1107 Duval St (☎294-7178), runs six-hour tours filled with facts on the ecology and history of the keys; $48.15 per person.

Greyhound, 615½ Duval St (☎296-9072); find it by turning right by the fire station off Simonton Street.

Late food shops *Owls*, 712 Caroline St, is open until 11pm; *Sunbeam Market*, 500 White Street, never closes.

Library 700 Fleming Ave; book sale on the first Saturday of each winter month.

Hospitals 24-hour casualty department at *Lower Florida Keys Health System*, 5900 Junior College Rd, Stock Island (☎294-5531).

Post office 400 Whitehead St (Mon 8.30am–5pm, Tues–Fri 9.30am–5pm, Sat 9.30am–noon; ☎294-2257; zip code 33040).

Reef trips The glass-bottomed *Fireball* makes six to seven trips a day from the northern tip of Duval Street to the Florida Reef; cost is $17.12 for the two-hour trip (☎296-6293). For snorkelling and diving, see "Dive shops", above.

Supermarket *Fausto's Food Palace*, 522 Fleming St (Mon–Sat 8am–8pm, Sun 8am–6pm).

Taxi Unlikely to be necessary except to get to the airport (see above); try *Five* (☎296-6666) or *Friendly Cab* (☎292-0000).

Water sports Jet-skiing, waterskiing and parasailing are all possible using outlets set up alongside Smathers Beach whenever conditions are right. For more details phone *Sunset Watersports* (☎296-5545) or *Watersports on the Atlantic* (☎294-2696).

Beyond Key West

A dot of land, seventy miles west of Key West in the Gulf of Mexico, is the last place you'd expect to find the US's largest nineteenth-century coastal fortification, but **Fort Jefferson** (daily during daylight hours), which rises mirage-like in the distance as you approach, is exactly that. Started in 1846 and intended to protect US interests on the Gulf, the fort was never finished, despite building work lasting thirty years. Failing to see a battle, Fort Jefferson served as a prison, but intense heat, lack of fresh water, outbreaks of disease and savage weather made the fort as unpopular with its guards as it was with its inmates; in 1874, after a hurricane and the latest yellow fever outbreak, it was abandoned.

Following the signposted **walk** around the fort and viewing the odds and ends in the small **museum**, won't take more than an hour – and spare time should be allocated to **swimming and snorkelling**: get a free map of the best locations from the park ranger's office, by the entrance.

Garden Key, on which the fort stands and the neighboring reef islands, make up the **Dry Tortugas**, named by the sixteenth-century Spaniard, Ponce de León, for the large numbers of turtles he found here (the "dry" was added later to warn mariners of the islands' lack of fresh water). After the fort fell into disuse, the entire area was designated a wildlife sanctuary to protect the nesting grounds of the snooty tern – unusual among terns for choosing to lay its eggs in scrubby vegetation and bushes. From early January, many of the black-bodied, white hooded birds show up to find home-building sites on Bush Key, and, with binoculars, they – plus a number of other winged rarities – are easily spied from the fort.

Getting to the Fort – and staying there

The only way to **get to the fort** without your own boat is by air with *Key West Seaplane* from *Murray's Marina*, 5603 Junior College Road, Stock Island (☎294-6978; $139 half-day, $239 full day). Avid bird-watchers sometimes **camp** at Fort Jefferson, though this, given the lack of amenities, is obviously not something to do on a whim – details on the *Key West Seaplane* number, above.

travel details

Three daily *Greyhound* buses run between Miami and Key West. Scheduled stops are listed below although the bus can be waved down anywhere on the route – stand by the side of the Overseas Highway and jump about like a maniac when you see the bus coming.

Scheduled stops are in North Key Largo (Central Plaza, 103200 Overseas Highway; ☎451-

6280); Islamorada (*Burger King*, MM82; ☎852-4266); Marathon (6363 Overseas Highway; ☎743-3488); Big Pine Key (MM30.2; ☎872-4022); Key West (615 ½ Duval St; ☎296-9072).

From Miami to North Key Largo/Islamorada/ Marathon/Big Pine Key/Key West (3 daily; 1hr 55min/2hr 20min/3hr 20min/3hr 50min/4hr 30min.

CHAPTER THREE

THE SOUTHEAST COAST

S
tretching from Miami's northern fringe along almost half the state's Atlantic shoreline, the 130-mile **Southeast Coast** is the sun-soaked Florida of popular imagination, with golden tans being perfected on palm-dotted beaches while warm ocean waves lap idly against silky-soft sands. Darkening this vision of paradise, however, is the fact that roughly half the region is the fastest-growing residential area in the state, with pressure for living space often leaving once pristine and spectacular ocean strips walled by unappealing high-rises. While you can drop your beach towel without a worry just about anywhere, don't spend all your time on the Southeast Coast doing nothing but bronzing. Take the trouble to explore some of the towns and seek out the undeveloped, protected sections, where you'll experience the Florida coastline as nature intended it.

The first fifty-odd miles of the Southeast Coast – **the Gold Coast** – are deep within the sway of Miami, back-to-back conurbations often with little to tell them apart. That said, the first and largest, **Fort Lauderdale**, is certainly distinctive: the reputation for rowdy beach parties – stemming from its years as a student Spring Break destination – is well out of date; the town has cultivated a cleaner cut, sophisticated image of late, aided by a top-rate art museum and an ambitious downtown improvement project. Further north, diminutive **Boca Raton** also has a style of its own: Mediterranean Revival architecture has been its hallmark since the Twenties, and it possesses some of the Gold Coast's finest beaches. Unconventional architect Addison Mizner shaped Boca Raton, but is best remembered for his work in **Palm Beach** – an essential place to see: inhabitated almost exclusively by multi-millionaires and perhaps the poshest place on earth, yet accessible even to the most impecunious day-tripper.

North of Palm Beach, the population thins and natural Florida asserts itself forcefully throughout the **Treasure Coast**. Here, rarely crowded beaches flank long, pine-coated barrier islands such as **Jupiter Island** and **Hutchinson Island**, whose miles of untainted shoreline are quiet enough for sea turtles to come ashore and shyly lay their eggs.

ACCOMMODATION PRICE CODES

All accommodation prices in this book have been coded using the symbols below. Note that prices are for the least expensive double rooms in each establishment. For a full explanation see p.26 in *Basics*.

①	up to $30	④	$60–80	⑦	$130–180
②	$30–45	⑤	$80–100	⑧	$180+
③	$45–60	⑥	$100–130		

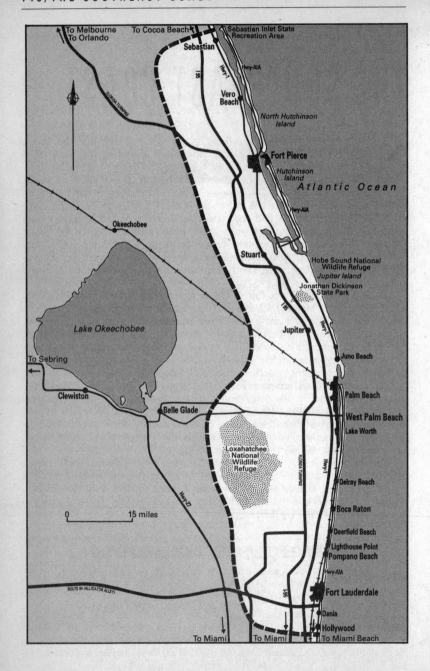

By car, the scenic route along the Southeast Coast is **Hwy-A1A**, which sticks wherever possible to the ocean side of the **intracoastal waterway**, formed when the rivers dividing the mainland from the barrier islands were joined and deepened during World War II to reduce the threat of submarine attack, and much loved by modern Florida's boat owners. When necessary, Hwy-A1A turns inland and links with the much less view-worthy **Hwy-1**. The speediest road in the region, **I-95**, runs about ten miles west of the coastline, splitting the residential sprawl from the wide-open Everglades – only worthwhile if you're in a hurry.

Although most **buses** keep to Hwy-1, the Southeast Coast is good news for non-drivers. Frequent *Greyhound* connections link the bigger towns, and a few daily services run to the smaller communities. Local buses, plentiful from the edge of Miami to West Palm Beach, are nonexistent in the more rural Treasure Coast. Along the Gold Coast, there's the further option of the dirt-cheap *Tri-Rail* rush hour service, while *Amtrak* has two daily **trains** running as far north as West Palm Beach.

THE GOLD COAST

The widely admired beaches and towns occupying a fifty-mile commuter corridor north from Miami make the **Gold Coast** – named for the booty washed ashore from sunken Spanish galleons – one of the most heavily populated and tourist-besieged parts of the state. The sands sparkle, the nightlife can be fun, and many communities have an assertively individualistic flavor – but if you're seeking peace and seclusion, look elsewhere.

Hollywood and Dania

From Miami Beach, Hwy-A1A runs through undistinguished Hallandale before reaching **HOLLYWOOD** – founded and named by a Californian – with a generous beach and a more cheerful persona than the better-known and much larger Fort Lauderdale, ten miles north. Allocate an hour to the pedestrian-only **Broadwalk**, parallel to Hwy-A1A (known here as Ocean Drive), whose snack bars and skateboarders enliven a casual amble, and the **Art and Culture Center of Hollywood**, 1650 Harrison Street (Tues–Sat 10am–4pm, Sun 1–4pm; $2), which offers a chance to browse the works of emergent Florida artists.

It was in Hollywood, incidentally, that rap group **2 Live Crew** was arrested for obscenity in June 1990; the group was acquitted, but not before the case became an anti-censorship *cause célèbre* across the country. If you stick around to sample Hollywood's nightlife, however, you'll find plenty to enjoy but little at music's cutting edge. Solid jazz and R&B are the staple fare of *Club M*, 2037 Hollywood Boulevard (☎925-8396), raunchy rock and roll prevails at the *J & S Lounge*, 5709 Johnson Street (☎966-6196), and country sounds fill the *Southern Fox Tavern*, 6019 Johnson Street (☎961-8964).

Modestly priced **motels** line Hollywood's oceanside streets. For good value try the *Stardust*, 915 N Ocean Drive (☎923-5531; ③), or the *Dolphin*, 342 Pierce Street (☎922-4498; ④). As usual, you'll save a few dollars by staying inland, where the *Shell Motel*, 1201 S Federal Highway (☎923-8085; ②–③) has the best rates.

> The area code for Hollywood, Dania and Fort Lauderdale is ☎305.

Ocean Drive continues north into **DANIA**, whose prime asset isn't the grouping of pseudo-English antique shops along Hwy-1 but the pine trees and sands of the **John U Lloyd Beach State Recreational Area** (daily 8am–sunset; cars $3.25, pedestrians and cyclists $1), on a peninsula jutting across the entrance to the shipping terminal of Port Everglades. An enjoyable short nature trail winds around the park's mangrove, seagrape and guava trees and, if you're around between July and September, ask at the gate (or phone ☎923-2833) about the Thursday night **fireside talks** given by park rangers – an atmospheric initiation into Florida's coastal ecology.

With more time to spare, visit the **Museum of Archeology**, 481 S Federal Highway (Mon–Sat 10am–4pm, Sun 1–4pm; $2), which will persuade any doubters that Florida was inhabited long before *Miami Vice*. In a large and diverse collection, including much from Africa and Egypt, a very strong pre-Columbian section is marked by copious Tequesta Indian artefacts unearthed locally.

Towards Fort Lauderdale: by boat, car or bus

Without luggage to weigh you down, call the *Water Taxi* (☎565-5507) to ferry you from the recreational area to any dockable part of Fort Lauderdale – see "Fort Lauderdale" for more details. Otherwise, without a car, you'll need to use **local bus** #1, or the pricier *Greyhound* (at 1707 Tyler Street in Hollywood; ☎922-8228) to continue north.

Fort Lauderdale

A thinly populated riverside trading camp at the turn of the century, and popular during the Twenties when its mangrove swamps were fashioned into slender canals, seven well-publicized miles of palm-shaded white sands and a low-budget Hollywood film later conspired to turn mild-mannered **FORT LAUDERDALE** into a town with a global reputation for rumbustious beachlife.

From the Thirties, inter-collegiate swimming contests began bringing the nation's youth here; a fact seized upon by the 1960 teen-exploitation movie, *Where The Boys Are*, which instantly made Fort Lauderdale the US's number one Spring Break venue, drawing hundreds of thousands of students to a six-week pre-exam frenzy of underage drinking and lascivious excess. By the late Seventies, the students were also bringing six weeks of traffic chaos and a reputation for rowdiness which hindered the town's chances of attracting regular tourists. Fighting back, the local authorities began a negative advertising campaign across the country's campuses, and enacted strict laws to restrict boozing and wild behavior around the beach.

Subsequently, the students turned their attentions to Daytona Beach (see Chapter Four), leaving Fort Lauderdale dominated by a mix of wealthy retirees and affluent yuppies, desperate to play down the beach party tag and play up the town's settler-period history. It's not an unpleasant place at all (with a flourishing gay scene, see "Gay Fort Lauderdale"), despite being a long way from the social inferno you might have been led to expect.

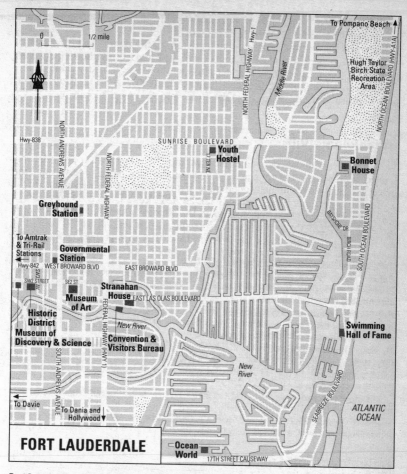

FORT LAUDERDALE

Arrival, Getting Around and Information

Known as Federal Highway, Hwy-1 ploughs through the center of **downtown Fort Lauderdale**, three miles inland from the coast. Just south of downtown, **Hwy-A1A** veers oceanwards off Hwy-1 along SW Seventeenth Street and runs through **beachside Fort Lauderdale**. All the long-distance public transport terminals are in or near downtown: the *Greyhound* **bus** station is at 515 NE Third Street (☎764-6551), while the **train** and *Tri-Rail* stations are two miles west at 200 SW 21st Terrace (☎464-8251), and linked to the center by buses #9, #10 and #81.

The handiest service of a thorough **local bus** network (☎357-8400) is #11, which runs twice hourly along Las Olas Boulevard between downtown Fort Lauderdale and the beach. Get **timetables** from Governmental Center, at the corner of Andrews Avenue and Broward Boulevard. Along the beach strip – Hwy-A1A between NE 41st Street and 17th Street Causeway – the **Wave Lane Trolley**

(☎768-0700) runs at half-hourly intervals, usually through the afternoon and evening until 10pm or midnight, for a flat fare of $1.

More expensive than the buses – but more fun – is the **Water Taxi** (☎565-5507), a small boat which will pick up and deliver you almost anywhere along Fort Lauderdale's many miles of waterfront; single journeys are $5, all-day tickets $13.

While downtown, gather the latest tourist information from the **Convention and Visitors Bureau**, 200 E Las Olas Boulevard (Mon–Fri 8.30am–5pm; ☎765-4466).

Accommodation

Although accommodation options in downtown Fort Lauderdale are relatively limited, scores of **motels** are clustered between the intracoastal waterway and the ocean and can be exceptionally good value. If money is tight, the well-equipped *Sol Y Mar*, 2839 Vistamar Street (☎556-1023), an **AYH hostel**, has beds for $12 ($15 non-members). The closest **campground** is *Easterlin County Park*, 1000 NW 38th Street (☎776-4466), three miles north of downtown, reached with bus #14.

Admiral's Court, 21 Hendricks Isle (☎1-800/248-6669). A good peaceful choice, nestled beside a canal in one of Fort Lauderdale's most exclusive residential areas, The Isles (see "Around Las Olas Boulevard and the Beach"). ②–③.

Bahia Cabana Beach Resort, 3001 Harbor Drive (☎1-800/922-3008). If you came to Fort Lauderdale looking to party, look no further than this tropically themed hotel, restaurant and bar complex, where the fun seldom stops before 2am. ⑤.

Bermudian Waterfront, 315 N Birch Rd (☎467-0467). North of the center but handy for the sea. As well as the regular economically priced rooms, there are also some 1- and 2-bedded suites with fully equipped kitchens. ②/⑤–⑥.

By-Eddy Apartment Motel, 1021 NE 13th Ave (☎764-7555; ③). Reasonably priced downtown rooms; outside of winter you'll need to book for a week.

Pillars Waterfront Motel, 111 N Birch Rd (☎467-9639). Relaxing and quiet motel not far from the ocean, complete with pool. ②–③.

Riverside Hotel, 620 E Las Olas Blvd (☎1-800/325-3280; ⑤–⑥). Elegant, comfortable, well-placed but over-priced downtown option.

Southern Shores, 3017 Bayshore Drive (☎1-800/827-6232). Relatively tranquil motel with its own pool, between the sea and the waterway. ②–③.

Downtown Fort Lauderdale

Anonymous bank buildings and tall glass-fronted offices make a uninspiring initial impression, but **downtown Fort Lauderdale** has an outstanding modern art museum and a number of restored early buildings to usefully occupy several hours. Lately, too, there's been a multi-million-dollar effort to prettify the district, with parks and promenades linked by the pedestrian-only **riverwalk** along the north bank of the New River, culminating at the state-of-the-art Museum of Discovery and Science.

The Museum of Art

In a cornerless post-modern structure, the **Museum of Art**, 1 E Las Olas Boulevard (Tues 11am–9pm, Wed–Sat 10am–5pm, Sun noon–5pm; $3.25; guided tours Tues noon & 6.30pm, Wed–Fri noon, Sat & Sun 2pm; free) provides ample space and light for the best art collection in the state, with a pronounced emphasis on modern painting and sculpture. The strongest exhibits are drawn from the museum's vast hoard of works under the banner of **CoBrA**, a movement begin-ning in 1948 with a group of artists from Copenhagen, Brussels and Amsterdam (hence the acronym), and typified by bright expressionistic canvases combining playful innocence with deep emotional power. Important names to look for include Asger Jorn, Carl Henning-Pedersen and Karel Appel, though many later adherents of the genre also produced formidable works – there's plenty of them here to admire and enjoy.

The Historic District and the Stranahan House

The modern buildings of downtown Fort Lauderdale do little to suggest the community's past. For a quick look at some that do, walk a few blocks west from the Art Museum to the clearly marked **Historic District**, where a couple of elderly structures can be toured. Of these, the 1907 **King-Cromartie House** (Tues–Fri noon–5pm, Sat 10am–5pm, Sun noon–5pm; $2), though a far from luxu-rious dwelling, held many then futuristic fixtures – among them the first indoor bathroom in Fort Lauderdale, gleefully pointed out by the period-attired tour guides. Around the corner, the three-storey **New River Hotel** served as Fort Lauderdale's first hotel, and is currently awaiting a refit job after housing the fore-runner of the Science Center (see above). To give perspective on the old build-ings, and the town's general past, the **Historical Society Museum**, 219 SW Second Avenue (Tues–Sat 10am–4pm, Sun 1–4pm; $2), mounts informative tempo-rary displays and stocks plenty of historical books and takeaway pamphlets.

A few minutes' walk east stands a more complete reminder of early Fort Lauderdale life: the carefully restored **Stranahan House** (guided tours Wed–Fri & Sat 10am–4pm; $3), behind *Wooley's* supermarket on Las Olas Boulevard. Erected in 1901 with high ceilings, narrow windows and wide verandahs, the building is a fine example of the Florida frontier style and served as the home and trading post of a turn-of-the-century settler, Frank Stranahan. **Guided tours** of the interior outline the story of Stranahan, a dealer in otter pelts, egret plumes and alligator hides, which he purchased from Seminole Indians trading along the river. Ironically, Stranahan, financially devastated by the late-Twenties Florida property crash, later drowned himself in the same waterway.

The Museum of Discovery and Science

Directly west from the Historic District, and marking the end of the Riverwalk, the gleaming **Museum of Discovery and Science** (Mon–Sat 10am–5pm, Sun noon–5pm; $6) is among the newest and best of Florida's growing number of child-oriented science museums. Kidless adults shouldn't think twice about coming (though they should aim to avoid weekends and school holidays, when the place is packed), however, because the exhibits present the basics of science in numerous ingenious ways and with dozens of entertaining interactive computer exhibits. You can even pretend to be an astronaut, rising in an air-powered chair to re-align an orbiting satellite, or make a simulated trip to the moon.

Around Las Olas Boulevard and the Beach

Leave downtown Fort Lauderdale for the beach along **Las Olas Boulevard**, lined first by trendy shops, art galleries and restaurants, and then by **The Isles** – well-tended residential canal-side land where householders park their cars on one side of their mega-buck properties and moor their luxury yachts on the other.

Once across the arching intracoastal waterway bridge, about two miles on, you're within sight of the ocean and the mood changes appreciably: where Las Olas Boulevard ends, **beachside Fort Lauderdale** begins – T-shirt, sunscreen and swimwear shops are suddenly everywhere.

Along the seafront, **Ocean Boulevard** bore the brunt of Spring Break partying until the clean-up of the Eighties (see above). Only a few beachfront bars suggest the carousing of the past, although the sands, flanked by graciously ageing coconut palms, are by no means deserted or dull – and still get a fair number of whooping students each spring. Since the bulk of Fort Lauderdale's accommodation is here, you'll have no difficulty exploring the beach, the bars, and a few other items of interest in either direction along the main strip.

South along Ocean Boulevard

A short way south of the Las Olas Boulevard junction, the **Swimming Hall of Fame**, 501 Seabreeze Boulevard (Mon–Sat 10am–5pm, Sun 11am–4pm; $4), salutes aquatic sports with a collection even dedicated non-swimmers will enjoy. The two floors are stuffed with medals, trophies and yellowing press cuttings pertaining to the musclebound heroes and heroines of swimming, diving and many more obscure watery activities.

For a few hours of solitude, thread through the residential streets a mile further south to the placid **South Beach Park**, a restful spot at the tip of Fort Lauderdale's coastline. Nearby, a rainy day is the only excuse for visiting **Ocean World**, 1701 SE Seventeenth Street (daily 10am–6pm; $10.95), a very average Florida marine park with the usual ball-chasing sea lions and dolphins, and tanks of motley sea creatures.

North along Ocean Boulevard

In the midst of the high-rise hotels and apartment blocks that now dominate the beachside area, Fort Lauderdale's pre-condo landscape is dramatically expressed by the jungle-like 35-acre grounds of the **Bonnet House**, a few minutes' walk off Ocean Boulevard at 900 Birch Road (guided tours only; May–Nov Tues & Thurs 10am, 11am & 1pm, Sun 2pm; $7). The house and its surrounds – including a swan-inhabited pond and resident monkeys – were designed by Chicago muralist Frank Clay Bartlett and completed in 1921. **Tours** of the vaguely plantation-style abode highlight Bartlett's eccentric passion for art and architecture – and for collecting ornamental animals, dozens of which fill virtually all of the thirty rooms.

SAWGRASS MILLS

Consumerism enters a new dimension twelve miles west of Fort Lauderdale at 12801 W Sunrise Boulevard, where **Sawgrass Mills** (Mon–Sat 10am–9pm, Sun 11am–6pm), a gathering of over 200 designer-name stores selling their wares at less than retail prices, draws South Florida shoppers and bargain-seeking tourists by the thousand.

Even if you don't intend to buy anything, simply exploring this tropically themed, mile-long mall – where the Big Names include *Sak's Fifth Avenue*, *Levi* and *Macy's* – can be mind-boggling. Not having a car is no excuse not to come: the **Sawgrass Mills Beach Shuttle** operates on weekdays between beachside Fort Lauderdale and Sawgrass Mills for $4 each way (details ☎1-800/FL-MILLS).

Another green pocket is nearby: beside Sunrise Boulevard, the tall Australian pines of the **Hugh Taylor Birch State Recreation Area** (daily 8am–sunset; cars $3.25, pedestrians and cyclists $1) form a shady backdrop for canoeing on the park's mangrove-fringed freshwater lagoon – a good way to perk yourself up after a morning spent prostrate on the beach.

Eating

Fort Lauderdale has many affordable, enjoyable places to **eat**, featuring everything from exotic Asian creations to homely conch chowder. The restaurants are grouped in different sections of the town, however, and without a car travelling between them can be difficult.

Bread of Life, 2388 N Federal Hwy (☎565-RICE). Excellent health-food restaurant, north of downtown.

Coconuts, 429 Seabreeze Blvd (☎467-6788). Unadventurous but dependable meat and seafood in a pleasant waterfront setting.

Egg & You, 2621 N Federal Hwy (☎564-2045). No-frills diner fare, and all-day breakfasts, on Hwy-1 heading north from Fort Lauderdale.

Ernie's BBQ Lounge, 1843 S Federal Highway (☎523-8636). The scruffy but likeable *Ernie's*, south of downtown, is a local legend for its glorious conch chowder (add sherry to taste).

The Floridian, 1410 E Las Olas Blvd (☎463-4041). Downtown coffee shop with a certain flair, serving breakfast, lunch and dinner to an eclectic and interesting crowd.

Franco & Vinny's Mexican Cantina, 2870 E Sunrise Boulevard (☎565-3839). Mexican favorites at giveaway prices near the beach.

Japanese Village, 716 E Las Olas Blvd (☎763-8163). Good but pricey Japanese food in central location.

Shirttail Charlie's, 400 SW Third Ave (☎463-FISH). Quality seafood and steaks beside the river in the heart of town. In season, alligator and stone crabs feature on the extensive menu.

Shooters, 3033 NE 37th Avenue (☎566-2855). Popular beach-area restaurant, drawing big crowds for its generous portions of seafood, thick burgers and satisfyingly large salads.

Southport Raw Bar, 1536 Cordova Rd (☎525-CLAM). Boisterous local bar offering succulent crustaceans and well-prepared fish dishes.

Sukhothai, at *Gateway Plaza*, 1930 E Sunrise Blvd (☎764-0148). Tasty, moderately spiced Thai dishes.

Tina's Spaghetti House, 2110 S Federal Highway (☎522-9943). On the periphery of downtown, *Tina's* has been dishing up low-priced Italian cooking for four decades.

Drinking, Live Music and Nightlife

Some of the restaurants above, particularly *Shooters* and the *Southport Raw Bar*, are also notable **drinking** spots. Other promising libation locations near the beach are the *Parrot Lounge*, 911 Sunrise Lane (☎563-1493), an easy-going bar specializing in over-sized pitchers of beer; *Elbo Room*, 241 S Atlantic Avenue (☎463-4615), once a Spring Break favorite but now an ideal place for an evening drink as the ocean breeze ruffles your hair. Inland, try *Shakespeare's Pub & Grille*, 1015 NE 26th Street (☎563-7833), a pseudo-English pub with dart board, decent beer and steak and kidney pies.

Live music is never far away. To find out who's playing where, pick up the free *XS* magazine, or pull the *"Showtime"* segment out of the Friday edition of the local *Sun-Sentinel* newspaper. Reliable venues include *Mombassa Bay*, 3051 NE

32nd Avenue (☎565-7441), for reggae and R&B; *O'Hara's Pub*, 722 Las Olas Boulevard (☎524-2801), a stylish jazz venue; *Musicians Exchange*, 729 W Sunrise Boulevard (☎764-1912), a less formal space for jazz and rock; and *The Edge*, 109 SW Second Avenue (☎525-9333), which periodically showcases cult indie bands.

Fort Lauderdale's two progressive **nightclubs** are *The Edge* (see above) and *Squeeze*, 2 S New River Drive (☎522-2068). If you're seeking the drunken hedonism of Spring Break, however, you might prefer the regular drink specials and bikini contests at the *Baja Beach Club*, 3200 N Federal Highway (☎568-0330).

Gay Fort Lauderdale

Fort Lauderdale has been one of **gay** America's favorite holiday haunts for years. Predictably, the local conservatism of recent years has caused the scene to quieten, although there's still plenty to delight vacationing gays.

Accommodation

Fort Lauderdale has a couple of comfortable **guest houses** aimed at gay men: *Midnight Sea*, 3016 Alhambra Street (☎463-4827; ④), and *The Palms on Las Olas*, 1760 E Las Olas Boulevard (☎1-800/858-5182; ④–⑤). *Big Ruby's*, 908 NE 15th Avenue (☎523-RUBY; ④), has a predominantly gay male clientele but women are also welcome; the *Mermaid Inn*, 725 N Birch Road (☎1-800/749-3953; ③–⑤), is exclusively for women. Of the **mixed** motels, try *Surf & Sand*, 3009 Sebastian Street (☎761-9544; ③–⑤), or the *Oasis*, 1200 S Miami Road (☎523-3043; ②–③), whose inland location keeps its prices down.

Bars and Clubs

Gay bars and clubs in Fort Lauderdale fall in and out of fashion; read the statewide free weekly newspaper, *TWN*, for the latest in-spots. Usually among the pacesetters are: *Cathode Ray*, 1105 E Las Olas Boulevard (☎462-8611), a video bar that steadily warms up as the evening wears on; *The Copa*, 915 Middle River Drive (☎463-1507), a long-running dance club that draws all ages; *Club Caribbean*, 2851 N Federal Highway (☎566-7471), which has a lively Sunday afternoon tea dance; *The Hideaway*, 2022 NE Eighteenth Street (☎566-8622) a cruisey bar; and the *Phoenix*, 502 E Sunrise Avenue (☎764-6163), which is more upmarket and also welcomes lesbians.

Inland from Fort Lauderdale

Away from its beach and downtown area, Fort Lauderdale is dismal suburbia all the way to the Everglades. Most people only pass through to reach "Alligator Alley" – the familiar name for I-75 which speeds arrow-straight towards Florida's West Coast (a hundred miles distant, see Chapter Six).

An exception to prevailing factories, housing estates and freeway interchanges is **DAVIE**, twenty miles from the coast on Griffin Road (take bus #9 from downtown), surrounded by citrus groves, sugar cane and dairy pastures. Davie's 40,000 inhabitants are besotted with the Old West: jeans, plaid shirts and stetsons are the order of the day, and there's even a hitching post (for tethering horses) outside the *McDonalds*. Davie's cowboys' origins go back to the 1910s settlers who came here to herd cattle and work the fertile black soil. If you're charmed by the attire, stock up in *Grifs Western*, 6211 SW 45th Street (☎587-9000), a leading purveyor of boots, hats and saddles; otherwise simply turn up for the **rodeo**, held most Fridays at 8pm at the indoor **Rodeo Complex**, 6549 SW 45th Street (☎797-1145). A smaller rodeo takes place most Wednesday evenings.

Like its counterparts elsewhere in the state, the **Seminole Native Village** (Mon–Sat 10am–4pm, Sun 10am–1pm; $3), a mile south of Davie on Hwy-441, is depressing – showing a native American culture reduced to flogging plastic tomahawks and staging alligator-wrestling shows for tourists. Here, though, some sensitivity can be found in the paintings by Guy LaBree, a local white man who spent time on Seminole reservations during his childhood and whose work is intended to pass legends and history on to younger Seminole generations. More predictably, it's the bingo hall across the road from the village that attracts most white people: laws against high-stakes bingo don't apply to Indian reservations, and you can win $100,000 or more. You can buy your fill of tax-free cigarettes, too.

Twelve miles north of Davie, **Butterfly World**, 3600 W Sample Road (Mon–Sat 9am–5pm, Sun 1–5pm; $7.95), stocks, as its name suggests, a massive collection of butterflies. Many of the creatures are raised here from unappealing larvae – which you'll see in the laboratory – and flap out their short lives around the nectar-producing plants inside several aviaries. Spotting Ecuadorian metalmarks, Malay sulpurs and their equally exotic peers, will keep amateur lepidopterists amused for hours.

North from Fort Lauderdale

With a car, stay on Hwy-A1A **north from Fort Lauderdale**: it's a far superior route to Hwy-1 and passes through several sedate beachside communities. Bus #11 runs this way as far as Atlantic Avenue in **POMPANO BEACH** – one of the bigger towns with a moderately noteworthy ocean strip – but, if you're independently mobile, press on.

Three miles further, Hwy-A1A crosses the Hillsboro Inlet, whose 1907 lighthouse gives its name to the posh canal-side community of **LIGHTHOUSE POINT**. There's nothing of importance here except *Cap's Place*, 2765 NE 28th Court (☎941-0418), which, awkwardly, can only be reached from the inland side of the intracoastal waterway; follow directions from NE 24th Street. The food – fresh seafood at affordable prices – is one reason to come, but the fact that the restaurant doubled as an illegal gambling den during the Prohibition era is another: Franklin D Roosevelt, Winston Churchill and the Duke of Windsor, remembered by fading photos, are just three of those who have relaxed in the company of owner Cap Knight, a one-time rum-runner who still presides over the restaurant.

More offbeat history is attached to **DEERFIELD BEACH**, four miles on. As Hwy-A1A twists to the right, you'll catch a glimpse of the triangular **Deerfield Park Island** in the intracoastal waterway. During the Thirties, the island was almost purchased by Al Capone, who, along with his gangster colleagues, frequented the *Riverview Restaurant*'s casino, underneath the Hillsboro Boulevard Causeway at 1741 Riverview Road. Capone's property bid was thwarted by his arrest for tax evasion, and the island, left untarnished by development, is occupied today by a contingent of racoons and armadillos. Its two **walking trails** are reachable only with the free ferry from the *Riverview* on Wednesday and Saturday mornings; call ☎305/428-3463 for times.

Into Boca Raton

Directly north of Deerfield Beach, Hwy-A1A and Hwy-1 both enter Palm Beach County, the latter becoming the stars-and-stripes-decorated **Blue Memorial Highway**: "a tribute to the armed forces that have served the United States of America", confirming the conservatism of the region. There's plenty of money around, too, much of it in the county's southernmost town, **BOCA RATON** (literally "the mouth of the rat"), populated by golf-mad retirees and the top executives of the numerous hi-tech industries – most famously computer giant IBM – headquartered locally. More noticeably, Boca Raton has an over-abundance of Mediterranean Revival architecture, a style prevalent here since the Twenties and kept alive by strict building codes. The town's new structures are compelled to use arched entrance ways, fake bell towers and red-tiled roofs whenever possible – it may be too contrived for comfort but certainly stands out. Other than the architecture, mostly observable in downtown Boca Raton around Hwy-1, the town has some under-acknowledged beaches and parks.

Downtown Boca Raton

The origins of Boca Raton's Spanish-flavored architecture, which you see all over the **downtown** area, go back to **Addison Mizner**, the "Aladdin of architects" who furnished the fantasies of Palm Beach's fabulously wealthy (see "Palm Beach") through the Twenties. Unable to give reign to his megalomaniacal desires elsewhere, Mizner swept into Boca Raton on the tide of the Florida property boom, bought 1600 acres of land and began selling plots of a future community "beyond realness in its ideality". Envisaging gondola-filled canals, a luxury hotel and a great cathedral dedicated to his mother, Mizner's plan was nipped in the bud by the economic crash and he went back to Palm Beach with his tail between his legs.

Bankruptcy notwithstanding, the few buildings Mizner completed left an indelible mark on Boca Raton. His million-dollar *Cloister Inn* grew into the present **Boca Raton Resort and Club**, a pink palace of marble columns, sculptured fountains and carefully aged wood (the centuries-old effect induced by the hobnail boots of Mizner's workmen) that still claims the 160-foot-wide Camino Real – carrying traffic between Hwy-A1A and downtown Boca Raton – as its private driveway. With $200-a-night rooms, the resort is an upper-crust gathering place best viewed on the **guided tours** ($4) run by the Boca Raton historical society between December and April; check the times on ☎395-8655.

For its part, the historical society resides in a more accessible Mizner work: the dome-topped **Old Town Hall**, 71 N Federal Highway (Mon–Fri 9am–5pm), built in 1927. The society's library, detailing the Mizner times and the rest of Boca Raton's past, is worthy of scrutiny; turn left along the corridor as you enter. Nearby, the **old railroad depot**, at the junction of Dixie Highway and SE Eighth Street, is another seminal Mizner-era building but without much allure: the depot (the *Count de Hoernle Pavilion*) is only opened for wedding receptions and meetings, and a couple of post-Mizner streamlined locos stand outside.

The well-heeled of present-day Boca Raton remember Mizner with **Mizner Park**, off Hwy-1 between Palmetto Park Road and Glades Road, not a park at all but one of several stylish open-air shopping malls which have improved downtown Boca Raton in recent years. Decorated by palm trees and waterfalls, and packed with haute couture stores and several affordable places to eat (see

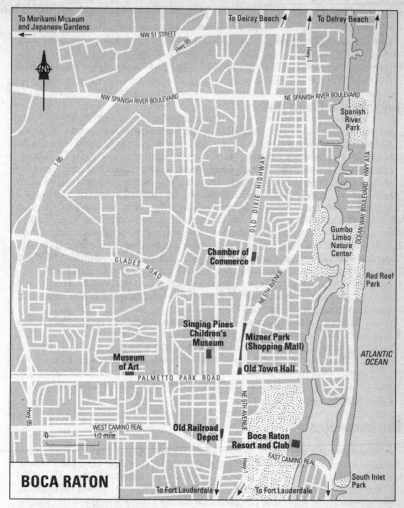

To Morikami Museum and Japanese Gardens

NW 51 STREET

Hwy-95

To Delray Beach

To Delray Beach

Hwy-1

N

NW SPANISH RIVER BOULEVARD

NE SPANISH RIVER BOULEVARD

Spanish River Park

I-95

OLD DIXIE HIGHWAY

OCEAN WAY BOULEVARD

HWY A1A

Gumbo Limbo Nature Center

GLADES ROAD

Chamber of Commerce

NE 5TH AVENUE

Red Reef Park

Singing Pines Children's Museum

Mizner Park (Shopping Mall)

Museum of Art

Old Town Hall

ATLANTIC OCEAN

PALMETTO PARK ROAD

NE 5TH AVENUE

Hwy-95

WEST CAMINO REAL

0 1/2 mile

Old Railroad Depot

Boca Raton Resort and Club

Hwy-1

EAST CAMINO REAL

South Inlet Park

BOCA RATON

To Fort Lauderdale

To Fort Lauderdale

"Practicalities"), Mizner Park is also set to be home to the grandly titled but actually rather small **International Museum of Cartoon Art**, due to open in 1994.

To escape the Mizner influence altogether, go to the beaches (see below) or turn west into Palmetto Park Road for the **Singing Pines Children Museum**, 498 Crawford Boulevard (Tues–Sun noon–4pm; $1), a Cracker cottage – the simple abode of early Florida farmers – built of driftwood and stocking entertaining remnants from the pioneer days, alongside kids' exhibitions. A mile further, the **Museum of Art**, 801 W Palmetto Road (Mon–Fri 10am–4pm, Sat & Sun noon–4pm; $3), has benefited from fortuitous donations and inspired curatorship to become one of Florida's finest small art museums. Besides staging and arranging travelling shows of high standard and featuring leading Florida artists in temporary exhibitions, the museum's permanent stock includes the Mayers Collection of drawings by modern masters – Degas, Matisse, Picasso and Seurat are among those represented – and a formidable trove of African art. Deserving of its growing reputation, the museum is moving in 1995 to a four-acre site – the futuristic **Boca Raton Museum Center** – at 700 Banyan Trail, near I-95 (call ☎395-2500 for the latest details).

Beachside Boca Raton

An air of secrecy hangs over Boca Raton's four **beaches**: all are open to the public but, walled-in by tall rows of Australian pine, they're not easily stumbled upon by accident and long-distance travellers are often outnumbered by choosy Floridians.

The southernmost patch, **South Inlet Park**, is the smallest and quietest of the quartet – often deserted in midweek, save for a few people fishing along its short jetty. To reach it, watch for a track turning sharply right off Hwy-A1A, just beyond the Boca Raton Inlet. **South Beach Park**, a mile north, is a surfers' favorite, although the actual beach is a fairly tiny area of coarse sand. **Red Reef Park**, a mile further, is far better for sunbathing and swimming; activities which should be combined with a walk around the **Gumbo Limbo Nature Center** (Mon–Sat 9am–4pm; donation), directly across Hwy-A1A, whose wide boardwalks take you through a tropical hardwood hammock and the mangrove forest beside the intra-coastal waterway. Keep your eyes peeled for ospreys, brown pelicans and the odd manatee lurking in the warm waters. During June and July, the center runs night sea-turtle-watching tours (details ☎338-1473).

Boca Raton's most explorable beachside area, however, is **Spanish River Park** (daily 8am–sunset; cars $2, pedestrians and cyclists free), a mile north of Red River Park: fifty acres of vivid vegetation and high-rise greenery, most of which is only penetrable on secluded trails through shady thickets. Aim for the 65-foot observation tower for a view across the park and much of Boca Raton. The adjacent beach is a slender but serviceable strip, linked to the park by several tunnels beneath Hwy-A1A.

Practicalities

The **Chamber of Commerce**, 1800 N Dixie Highway (Mon–Fri 9am–5pm; ☎395-4433), supplies the usual info. Don't expect a long list of budget diners and motels; nothing comes cheap in these parts. For a good-value breakfast, attack the buffet (served until 10am) at the otherwise forgettable *HoJo's*, 1001 S Federal Highway (☎391-6142). At *Mizner Park*, the *Bavarian Colony Deli* (☎393-3989), the slightly dearer *L&N Seafood* (☎750-3580) and *Ruby Tuesday's* (☎392-5705) are all worth trying. There's more choice a mile or two further north: barbecued ribs and steaks at *Tom's Place*, 7251 N Federal Highway (☎997-0920), and tasty sea fare at *The Seafood Connection*, 6998 N Federal Highway (☎997-5962).

The cheapest **motels** near the beaches are *Shore Edge*, 425 N Ocean Boulevard (☎395-4491; ③), and *Ocean Lodge*, 531 N Ocean Boulevard (☎395-7772; ③). You'll save money by sleeping inland at the *Econo Lodge*, 32899 N Federal Highway (☎1-800/624-3606; ②).

The area code for Boca Raton and Delray Beach is ☎407.

Inland from Boca Raton: The Morikami Museum and Japanese Gardens

South Florida might be the last place you'd expect to find a formal Japanese garden complete with Shinto shrine, teahouse and a museum recording the history of the Yamoto, but ten miles northwest of Boca Raton at the **Morikami Museum and Japanese Gardens**, 4000 Morikami Park Road (Tues–Sun noon–5pm; $4.25), are all three. They are reminders of a group of Japanese settlers who came here intending to grow tea and rice and farm silkworms, but finished up selling pineapples until a blight killed off the crop in 1908.

The colony is remembered by artefacts and photographs within the Morikami's older set of buildings. Across the beautifully landscaped grounds, the newer portion of the museum stages themed exhibitions drawn from an enormous archive of Japanese objects and art and has user-friendly computers ready to impart information about various aspects of Japan and Japanese life. A traditional **tea-house**, assembled here by a Florida-based Japanese craftsman, is periodically used for tea ceremonies.

North towards Palm Beach

The shoulder-to-shoulder towns **north of Boca Raton** are minor delays on the way towards Palm Beach; most have a nice patch of beach, and a couple are putting their modest histories on display, but none should be considered lengthy stops. Usefully if you're not driving, the local *CoTrans* **bus** #1S, between Boca Raton and West Palm Beach, runs through them hourly.

Delray Beach

Five miles north of Boca Raton, **DELRAY BEACH** justifies a half-day's visit: its powdery sanded municipal **beach**, at the foot of Atlantic Avenue, is rightly popular, and is one of the few in Florida to afford a view of the Gulf Stream – a cobalt blue streak of warm water about five miles offshore, snaking northwards to temper the climate of northwest Europe.

Nipping a short way **inland** along Atlantic Avenue, you'll find more to pass the time: on the corner with Swinton Avenue, an imposingly voluminous 1913 school house forms part of **Old School Square** (Tues–Fri 11am–3pm, Sun 1–4pm; free), a group of buildings restored and transformed into a cultural center. The spacious ground floor of the former school hosts temporary art exhibitions, though a peek upstairs reveals several one-time classrooms still furnished by desks and black-painted walls used to avoid the exorbitant cost of slate blackboards. Within sight, just across NE First Street, the **Cason Cottage** (Tues–Fri 10am–3pm; free), erected in 1920 for Dr John Cason, part of an illustrious local family, warrants a look for its simple woodframe design – based on pioneer-era Florida architecture.

Delray Beach makes a sensible **lunch** stop. Near Hwy-1, *The Sundy House*, 106 S Swinton Avenue (☎278-2163), provides lunch and pots of tea in an antique-filled 1902 home; at the municipal beach, *Boston's on the Beach*, 40 S Ocean Boulevard (☎278-3364), serves fresh seafood. The *Bermuda Inn*, 64 S Hwy-A1A (☎276-5288; ⑤), is the cheapest beachside **accommodation**.

Lake Worth

Pressing on by car, Hwy-A1A charts an evocative course along twenty-odd miles of slender barrier island, ocean views on one side and the intracoastal waterway – plied by luxury yachts and lined with opulent homes – on the other. As ever, Hwy-1 is duller, but whichever way you come, make a quick stop at **LAKE WORTH** (not to be confused with the actual lake of the same name which divides Palm Beach from West Palm Beach), ten miles north of Delray Beach, for the entertaining clutter of the **Historical Museum**, 414 Lake Avenue (Mon–Fri 8.30am–12.30pm; free). Plant-filled bathtubs, artily arranged rusting tools and pics aplenty from bygone decades are all infectiously doted over by the museum's curator.

Otherwise, there's nothing to hinder progress to Palm Beach (with Hwy-A1A), or West Palm Beach (with Hwy-1), just a few miles straight ahead.

Palm Beach

A small island town of palatial homes, pampered gardens and streets so clean you could eat your dinner off them, **PALM BEACH** has been synonymous for nearly a century with the kind of lifestyle only limitless loot can buy. A bastion of conspicuous wealth whose pomposity – banning laundry lines, for example – knows no bounds, Palm Beach is, for all its faults, irrefutably unique and no one can stop you tramping about in the shadows of the mind-bogglingly rich and famous, even if you don't share their pretensions.

The nation's nobs began wintering here in the 1890s, after Standard Oil magnate Henry Flagler brought his East Coast railway south from St Augustine and built two luxury hotels on this then secluded, palm-filled island. Throughout the Twenties, Addison Mizner began a vogue for Mediterranean architecture, covering the place with arcades, courtyards and plazas – and the first million-dollar homes. Since then, corporate tycoons, sports aces, jet-setting aristocrats, rock stars and CIA directors have flocked here, eager to become part of the Palm Beach elite and enjoy its aloofness from mainland – and mainstream – life.

Summer is very quiet – and easily the least costly time to stay overnight – but the place gets into motion between November and May. The winter months see a whirl of elegant balls, fund-raising dinners and charity galas; local residents give more to tax-deductible causes in a year than most people earn in a lifetime. Winter also brings the polo season – watching a chukka or two being the one time Palm Beach denizens show themselves in the less particular environs of West Palm Beach (on the mainland), where the games are held.

Even by walking – much the best way to view the moneyed isle – you'll get the measure of Palm Beach in a day. Either drive in along Hwy-A1A from the south, or arrive on foot using one of the two bridges over Lake Worth from West Palm Beach, the nearest bus and train stop.

Approaching Palm Beach: the South of the Island

Near-neighbors like to think otherwise, but Palm Beach as a byword for wealth, extravagance and exclusivity begins about five miles north of the town of Lake Worth on Hwy-A1A, by the junction with Southern Boulevard. Here, the **Palm Beach Bath and Tennis Club** is the first of the community's strictly members-

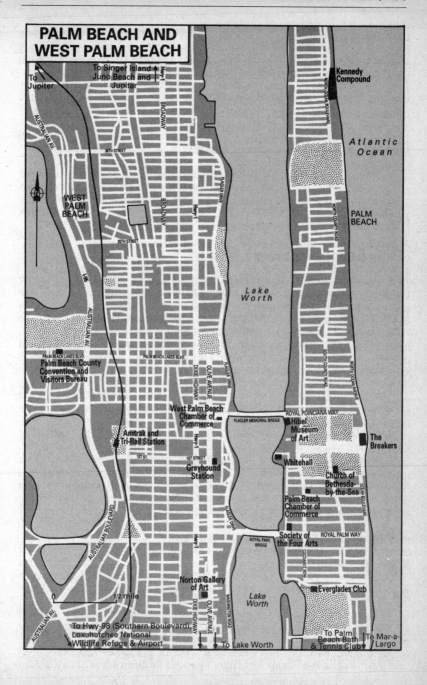

PALM BEACH AND WEST PALM BEACH

To Jupiter

To Singer Island, Juno Beach and Jupiter

Kennedy Compound

AUSTRALIAN AV.

BROADWAY

Hwy-1

36TH STREET

FLAGLER DRIVE

WEST PALM BEACH

BROADWAY

Hwy-1

NORTH COUNTY ROAD

NORTH OCEAN BOULEVARD

Atlantic Ocean

PALM BEACH

25TH STREET

I-95

Lake Worth

AUSTRALIAN AV.

PALM BEACH LAKES BLVD.

PALM BEACH LAKES BLVD.

Palm Beach County Convention and Visitors Bureau

DIXIE HIGHWAY

OLIVE AVENUE

FLAGLER DRIVE

SOUTH COUNTY ROAD

NORTH OCEAN AVENUE

West Palm Beach Chamber of Commerce

FLAGLER MEMORIAL BRIDGE

ROYAL POINCIANA WAY

Hibel Museum of Art

The Breakers

Amtrak and Tri-Rail Station

Hwy-1

1ST ST.

1ST STREET

Whitehall

Greyhound Station

Church of Bethesda-by-the-Sea

Palm Beach Chamber of Commerce

OCEAN BOULEVARD

AUSTRALIAN BOULEVARD

FLAGLER DRIVE

ROYAL PARK BRIDGE

Society of the Four Arts

ROYAL PALM WAY

0   1/2 mile

Norton Gallery of Art

DIXIE HIGHWAY

OLIVE AVENUE

WASHINGTON ROAD

Lake Worth

COCONUT ROW

Everglades Club

AUSTRALIAN AV.

To Hwy-98 (Southern Boulevard), Loxahatchee National Wildlife Refuge & Airport

To Lake Worth

To Palm Beach Bath & Tennis Club

To Mar-a-Largo

only watering holes; its arched windows give sweeping ocean views – passers-by see just the club's guarded entrance. Likewise for the next couple of miles, the high-class homes beside this busy two-lane highway (a bad place to cycle or walk, or even stop your car) are shielded from prying eyes by walls of hedges.

You should have no trouble, however, spotting the red-roofed Italianate tower topping **Mar-a-Largo**, finished in 1926, the $8-million winter abode of breakfast cereal heiress Marjorie Merriweather-Post, the queen of Palm Beach high society for nearly forty years. On Merriweather-Post's death in 1973, Mar-a-Largo's 118 rooms and eighteen-acre grounds were willed to the US government – who couldn't afford the upkeep; instead, "Florida's most sybaritic private residence" was sold to property tycoon Donald Trump.

Further on, close to the Via La Selva turning, a sprawling property once owned by John and Yoko Lennon can just be glimpsed. Hardly a place to enhance the ex-Beatle's anti-establishment credentials, it earlier belonged to turn-of-the-century multi-millionaire Cornelius Vanderbilt. Half a mile north, Hwy-A1A becomes Ocean Boulevard as it enters the town of Palm Beach.

Palm Beach: the town

The main residential section of Palm Beach – **the town** – is where you should spend most of your time. Start by strolling by the designer stores and high-class art galleries of **Worth Avenue**, marking the southern boundary, to which locals head if they're short of a $500 dinner jacket or ballgown, or need to sink a couple of million bucks into an inflation-proof painting. Cruised by Rolls Royces, Mercedes and Jaguars, and filled by some of the most upmarket shops and restaurants anywhere in the US, most of the people you'll see on Worth Avenue, particularly between May and November when the socialites socialize elsewhere, are camera-wielding tourists and immaculately groomed shop staff.

Other than expense-account acquisition, the most appealing aspect of the street is its architecture: stucco walls, crafted Romanesque facades and narrow passageways leading to small courtyards where miniature bridges cross non-existent canals and spiral staircases climb to the upper levels. On the top floor of one of the courtyard buildings, *Via Mizner*, on the corner with Hibiscus Avenue, sits the former pied-à-terre of the man responsible for the Mediterranean look replicated all over Palm Beach – the flamboyant architect, **Addison Mizner**.

Explore the rest of the town along Cocoanut Row or County Road, but first go to Worth Avenue's western end to gawp at the vessels moored on Lake Worth: rows of ocean-going yachts with more living space than most people's homes.

Along Cocoanut Row

Four blocks from its junction with Worth Avenue, **Cocoanut Row** crosses Royal Palm Way, close to the stuccoed buildings of the **Society of the Four Arts** (Mon–Sat 10am–5pm, Sun 2–5pm; free), which hosts art shows and lectures of an impressive standard from December to April, and whose **library** (May–Oct Mon–Fri 10am–5pm; Nov–April Mon–Sat 10am–5pm) is highly browsable.

Half a mile further along Cocoanut Row, you'll notice the white Doric columns fronting **Whitehall** (Tues–Sat 10am–5pm, Sun noon–5pm; $5), the most overtly ostentatious home on the island: a $4-million wedding present from Henry Flagler to his third wife, Mary Lily Kenan, whom he married (after controversially persuading the Florida legislature to amend its divorce laws) in 1901. Like

PALM BEACH'S ARCHITECT: ADDISON MIZNER

A former miner and prize-fighter, **Addison Mizner** was an unemployed architect when he arrived in Palm Beach in 1918 to recuperate following the recurrence of a childhood leg injury. Inspired by the medieval buildings he'd seen around the Mediterranean, Mizner, financed by the heir to the Singer sewing machine fortune, built the **Everglades Club** at 356 Worth Avenue. Described by Mizner as "a little bit of Seville and the Alhambra, a dash of Madeira and Algiers", the Everglades Club was the first public building in Florida in the Mediterranean Revival style, and fast became the island's most prestigious social club.

The success of the club, and the house he subsequently built for society bigwig Eva Stotesbury, won Mizner commissions all over Palm Beach as the wintering wealthy decided to swap suites at one of Henry Flagler's hotels for a "million-dollar cottage" of their own.

Brilliant and unorthodox, Mizner's loggias and U-shaped interiors made the most of Florida's pleasant winter temperatures, while his twisting staircases to nowhere became legendary. Pursuing a lived-in-since-medieval-times look, Mizner used untrained workmen to lay roof tiles crookedly, sprayed condensed milk onto walls to create an impression of centuries-old grime and fired shotgun pellets into wood to imitate worm holes. By the mid-Twenties, Mizner had created the Palm Beach Style – which Florida architecture buff Hap Hattan called "the old world for the new rich". Mizner later fashioned much of Boca Raton, for which see p.158.

many of Florida's first luxury homes, Whitehall's interior design was created by pillaging the great buildings of Europe: among the 73 rooms are an Italian library, a French salon, a Swiss billiard room, a hallway modelled on the Vatican's St Peter's and a Louis XV ballroom. All are richly stuffed with ornamentation but – other than mutual decadence – lack any aesthetic cohesion. Flagler was in his seventies when Whitehall was built, 37 years older than his bride and not enamored of the banquets and balls she continually hosted. He often sloped off to bed using a concealed stairway, perhaps to ponder plans to extend his railway to Key West – a display on the project fills his former office. From the 110-foot hallway, informative but not compulsory 45-minute **free guided tours** depart continuously and will leave you giddy with the tales – and the sights – of the earliest Palm Beach excesses.

Whitehall was built beside Flagler's first Palm Beach resort, the *Royal Poinciana Hotel*: a six-storey, Colonial-style structure of 2000 rooms which became the world's largest wooden building on completion in 1894. Other than a small plaque marking the spot, not a trace remains of the hotel whose hundred-acre grounds spread to what's now Royal Poinciana Way. Here, on the corner with Cocoanut Row, you'll find *Poinciana Place*, a soulless grouping of estate agents' and art dealers' offices, but also the location of the **Hibel Museum of Art**, 150 Royal Poinciana Way (Tues–Sat 10am–5pm, Sun 1–5pm; free). Forget Warhol and Rothko, the most commercially successful artist in the US is **Edna Hibel**, a seventy-year-old resident of Singer Island (just north of Palm Beach – see "Singer Island and Juno Beach") whose works fill this deep-carpeted gallery. Inspired by "love", Hibel has been churning out coy, sentimental portraits, usually of Asian and Mexican women bearing expressions of serenity, since the late Thirties, often working seven days a week to meet demand. Make a call, though, if only to admire the unflappable devotion of the guides, and to figure out why Hibel originals change hands for $50,000.

Along County Road

In terms of things to see, **County Road** is the poor relation of Cocoanut Row – to which it runs parallel – though it shouldn't be missed completely. On it, two blocks north of Worth Avenue, Mizner's Mediterranean Revival themes are maintained by the Palm Beach's very tidy local administration offices and bank buildings. By contrast, the 1926 **Church of Bethesda-by-the-Sea**, a fifteen-minute walk further, is a handsome imitation-Gothic pile replacing the island's first church (see "The North of the Island"): the large stained-glass windows depict Christianity around the world, but ignore them and walk instead through the echoing cloisters to the **Cluett Memorial Gardens** (daily 8am–5pm; free), a peaceful spot in which to take a stone pew and tuck into a picnic lunch.

A little further north, County Road is straddled by the golf course of **The Breakers**, erected in 1926 and the last of Palm Beach's swanky resorts. Inside, the lobby is filled with tapestries, chandeliers and huge fireplaces, and the *Alcazar Lounge* – to the right as you enter – has a case of photos and sundries from the hotel's past. If possible, be in the lounge at 3pm on a Wednesday, when a **free guided tour** departs on an instructive toddle around the premises.

The North of the Island

The limited points of interest beyond Royal Poinciana Way are best viewed from the three-mile **Lake Trail**, a cyclists' and pedestrians' path skirting the edge of Lake Worth, almost to the northern limit of the island. A bicycle is the ideal mode of transport here: rent one from *Palm Beach Bicycle Trail Shop*, 223 Sunrise Avenue (☎407/659-4583).

Most locals use the trail as a jogging strip, and certainly there's little other than exercise and fine views across the lake to make it worthwhile. Keep an eye out, though, for "Duck's Nest", the oldest remaining home in Palm Beach, built in 1891, and the original **Church of Bethesda-by-the-Sea**, dating from 1889. Serving a congregation of early homesteaders across a 125-mile stretch of coast, all of whom had to get here by boat, the shingled church is now a private house, but easily spotted by the clockface hanging from its short tower.

The lake trail expires a few minutes' pedal south of the Lake Worth Inlet, a narrow cut separating Palm Beach from the high-rise-dominated Singer Island; to get to the inlet – for a sight of the neighboring island and a modest feeling of achievement – weave on through the short residential streets.

For variation, cycle back to central Palm Beach along Ocean Drive (take care as there's no marked bike path) which passes the two-acre **Kennedy Compound***, at 1095 N Ocean Boulevard, bought by Joe Kennedy – father of John, Robert and Edward – in 1933. The Kennedys never fully integrated into ultra-conservative Palm Beach life – not feeling welcome at the Everglades Club, Joe upset the establishment by joining the rival Palm Beach Country Club – and it's said that few Palm Beach tears were shed in 1963 when John (then President) was assassinated. Various Kennedys still use the place, sometimes sneaking out for the 7am Sunday Mass at St Edward's Church, near the junction with Royal Poinciana Way.

---

* The Kennedy Compound was at the center of the most recent scandal to rock Palm Beach: the arrest on charges of sexual battery (Florida's legal term for rape) of William Kennedy Smith, the nephew of Senator Edward Kennedy, in April 1991.

The area code for Palm Beach is ☎407.

Practicalities

In a town that often fights shy of tourists, the **Chamber of Commerce**, 45 Cocoanut Way (Mon–Fri 9am–5pm; ☎655-3282) is a welcome provider of free maps and reliable **information**.

You'll need plenty of money to **sleep** in Palm Beach: comfort and elegance are the key words, and rates of $200 per night are not uncommon. *Palm Beach Historic Inn*, 365 S County Road (☎832-4009; ③–⑤), is a bed and breakfast spot with the best rates in town, but you'll need to book early. Otherwise, to save money, come between May and December, when the lowest prices on the island are found at *The Chesterfield*, 363 Cocoanut Row (☎1-800/CHESTR-1; ⑥), the *Colony*, 155 Hammon Avenue (☎1-800/521-5525; ⑥), the *Heart of Palm Beach*, 160 Royal Palm Way (☎1-800/525-5377; ⑥), and *The Plaza Inn*, 215 Brazilian Avenue (☎1-800/832-8666; ⑥). Obviously, it's far cheaper to stay outside Palm Beach and visit by day – easily done from West Palm Beach even without a car; see below.

Encouragingly, you can **eat** relatively cheaply. *TooJay's*, 313 Poinciana Place (☎659-7232), is a top-notch bakery and deli where scrumptious omelettes cost under $6; *Green's Pharmacy*, 151 N County Road (☎233-4443), has a steady supply of diner fare; and *Hamburger Heaven*, 314 S County Road (☎655-5277), dispenses delicious ground-beef burgers. A more expensive option, at between $10 and $15 a throw, is *Testa's*, 221 Royal Poinciana Way (☎832-0992), which serves exquisite seafood and pasta. If these are closed, or you just want picnic fare, use the *Publix* supermarket at 265 Sunset Avenue. If money is no object – and you're dressed to kill – make for *Café L'Europe*, 150 Worth Avenue (☎655-4020); spend less than $50 each in this super-elegant French restaurant and you'll still be hungry.

Thrift stores

Amazingly high-class clobber, some of it discarded after only a single use, turns up in Palm Beach's **thrift stores**, although the prices are above normal thrift-store levels. Peruse *The Church Mouse*, 374 S County Road (☎659-2154), *Goodwill Embassy Boutique*, 210 Sunset Avenue (☎832-8199), or *Thrift Store Inc*, 231 S County Road (☎655-0520), and be ready to spend.

West Palm Beach and Further Inland

Founded to house the workforce of Flagler's Palm Beach resorts, **WEST PALM BEACH** has long been in the shadow of its glamorous neighbor across the lake. Only during the last two decades has the town gained some life of its own, with smart new office buildings, a scenic lakeside footpath – and less seemly industrial growth sprouting up on its western edge. Above all, West Palm Beach holds the promise of accommodation and food at a lower price than in Palm Beach. Without a car, you'll need to pass through it on your way to the rich island: *CoTrans* buses from Boca Raton and *Greyhound* services stop here (details below), leaving a few minutes' walk to Palm Beach over one of the Lake Worth bridges

Other than basic needs, just the classy collections of the **Norton Gallery of Art**, 1451 S Olive Avenue (Tues–Sat 10am–5pm, Sun 1–5pm; $5 donation suggested), a mile south of the downtown area, provide reason to linger. Together with some distinctive European painting and drawing, from Gauguin, Klee, Picasso and others, the gallery boasts a solid grouping of twentieth-century American works: Mark Tobey's study of stifling urban motion, *The Street*, and Stuart Davis' *New York Mural* impress most. Among a sparkling roomful of Far Eastern pieces are seventh-century sculpted buddhas, absorbingly complex amber carvings and a collection of 1500–500 BC tomb jades.

Information and Public Transit

The **Chamber of Commerce**, 401 N Flagler Drive (Mon–Fri 8.30am–5pm; ☎833-3711), and the **Palm Beach County Convention and Visitors Bureau**, 1555 Palm Beach Lakes Boulevard (Mon–Fri 8.30am–5pm; ☎471-3995), have stacks of free leaflets, and can answer questions on the whole Palm Beach county area. The West Palm Beach **train** (☎1-800/872-7245) and *Tri-Rail* (☎1-800/TRI RAIL) station is at 201 S Tamarind Avenue and is linked by regular shuttle buses to the downtown area. Most *CoTrans* **bus** (☎233-1111) routes converge at the junction of Olive Avenue (Hwy-1) and First Street; the *Greyhound* station is at 100 First Street (☎833-0825).

Sleeping, Eating and Nightlife

Most budget chain **motel** prices in West Palm Beach are inflated. The best deals are at *Queens Lodge*, 3712 Broadway (☎842-1108; ③), *Parkview Motor Lodge*, 4710 S Dixie Highway (☎1-800/523-8978; ③–④), or *Mt Vernon Motor Lodge*, 310 Belvedere Road (☎1-800/545-1520; ③).

Go to *Robinson's Pastry Shop*, 215 Clematis Street (☎833-4259), for wonderful fresh-baked snacks and sandwiches; pricier meals with lakeside views, can be had at *Speakeasy*, 104 Clematis Street (☎833-EASY). The *Speakeasy* mutates into an interesting reggae-flavored **disco** after dark, and the *Respectable Café*, 518 Clematis Street (☎833-9999), is also good for an evening **drink** and live music.

Inland from West Palm Beach

By car, West Palm Beach makes a good access point for the **Loxahatchee National Wildlife Refuge** (daily 30min before sunrise to 30min after sunset; cars $3, passengers $1), whose 200 square miles of sawgrass marshes are marginally penetrable on two easy **walking trails** from the **visitor center** (☎407/734-8303) – one through a Cypress hammock, the other a boardwalk over the marshes to an observation tower. On either, you'll probably see a few snakes and alligators and get a firm impression of what undeveloped inland Florida is all about – and how incredibly flat it is. Get there by travelling west along Hwy-80 for about five miles, then turn south along Hwy-441; the well-signposted main entrance is twelve miles ahead.

African and Asian, rather than Floridian, wildlife is the star attraction of **Lion Country Safari** (daily 9.30am–5.30pm; last vehicles admitted 4.30pm; $11.95), off Hwy-80 six miles west of the southbound Hwy-441 turning. Lions, elephants, giraffes, chimpanzees, zebras and ostriches are among the creatures roaming a 500-acre plot where human visitors are confined to their cars. It's awkward to reach and expensive to visit, but if you can't leave Florida without photographing a flamingo, *Lion Country Safari* could well be for you.

Venturing **further inland** to the Lake Okeechobee area (described in Chapter Five) is only sensible if you want to stare at sugar cane or go fishing: Hwy-80 from West Palm Beach runs the forty miles to the lakeside Belle Glade, a route traversed by *CoTrans* bus #10 – but not a good place to be without independent transportation.

THE TREASURE COAST

West Palm Beach marks the northern limit of Miami's hinterland, and the end of the Southeast Coast's heavily touristed sections. Aside from some small and uninvolving towns, the next eighty miles – dubbed the **Treasure Coast** simply to distinguish it from the Gold Coast – missed out entirely on the expansion seen to the south and to the north, leaving wide open spaces and some magnificent swathes of quiet beach that attract protective lovers of natural Florida and a small band of well-informed tan-seekers.

Singer Island and Juno Beach

Out of West Palm Beach, Hwy-A1A swings back to the coast at **SINGER ISLAND**, a familiar name to anyone who's read Charles Willeford's novel *Sideswipe*: the author's Miami homicide cop, Hoke Moseley, holes up here for a few weeks before boredom drives him back south. The beaches are perfectly adequate but the place lacks life and is predominantly residential, with no budget-range accommodation.

This trend continues for the next few miles of golf courses and planned retirement communities, but one good stop is **JUNO BEACH**, where Hwy-A1A follows a high coastal bluff and, with luck, you'll find a path down to the uncrowded sands.

Alternatively, keep going until you reach the beachside **Loggerhead Park**, also the site of the **Children's Museum** (Tues–Sat 10am–3pm, Sun noon–3pm; free), intended for kids but allowing adults to brush up on their knowledge of marine life in general and sea turtles in particular. There's a turtle hatchery here, and displays on the life cycles of the world-weary-looking creatures. The only time turtles give up the security of the ocean is between June and July, when they steal ashore to lay eggs under cover of darkness. This is one of several places along the Treasure Coast where expeditions are led to watch them; get the details at the museum or on ☎407/626-8280.

Jupiter and Jupiter Island

Splitting into several anodyne districts around the wide mouth of the Tequesta River, **JUPITER**, directly north of Juno Beach, was a rum-runners' haven during the time of Prohibition; these days it's better known as the home town of Florida's favorite son, actor Burt Reynolds, markers to whom are everywhere. The first is the *Jupiter Theater* where Hwy-A1A meets Indiantown Road. Founded by the man himself in 1979, the theater is the base of one of Florida's better professional companies. Nearby, the Reynolds-owned *Backstage* restaurant, 1061 Indiantown Road (☎407/747-9533), serves expensive gourmet lunches and dinners beneath walls covered by pics of Burt, Burt's wife and Burt's celebrity friends. Anyone on a Burt pilgrimage will also enjoy a walk through Burt Reynolds Park, near the town center beside Hwy-1, where the **Loxahatchee Historical Museum** (Tues–Fri 10am–3pm, Sat & Sun 1–4pm; $3), daringly perhaps, describes pioneer life on and around the Tequesta River long before Burt's time.

The only other thing in Jupiter to merit consideration is the red-brick **lighthouse**, a nineteenth-century beacon on the north bank of the Jupiter inlet, with a small **museum** (Sun afternoons only; free) at its foot. The lighthouse can be seen from Beach Road, the route Hwy-A1A takes back to the coast after looping through the town. This route skirts the **Jupiter Inlet Colony** – a rich person's billet whose roads are guarded by photo-electric beams, enabling police to check any suspicious traffic cruising the dead-end streets – before heading north along Jupiter Island.

Jupiter Island

Two miles into **JUPITER ISLAND** on Hwy-A1A, pull up at the **Blowing Rocks Preserve** (daily 6am–5pm; donation), where a limestone outcrop covers much of the beach and powerful incoming tides are known to drive through the rocks' hollows, emerging as gusts of spray further on. At low tide, it's sometimes possible to walk around the outcrop and peer into the rock's sea-drilled cavities.

Seven miles further north, the shell-strewn Hobe Sound Beach marks the edge of **Hobe Sound National Wildlife Refuge**, which occupies the remainder of the island. With spectacular success as a nesting ground for sea turtles, the refuge is also rich in birdsong, tweeting scrub jays being among the tuneful inhabitants. To find out more about the flora and fauna, call at the small **interpretive center** (Mon–Fri 9–11am & 1–3pm; ☎407/546-2067), on the mainland where Hwy-A1A meets Hwy-1.

Inland: the Jonathan Dickinson State Park

Two miles south of the Hobe Sound interpretive center on Hwy-1, the **Jonathan Dickinson State Park** (daily 8am–sunset; cars $3.25, pedestrians and cyclists $1) protects a natural landscape quite different from what you'll see at the coast. Step up to the observation platform atop **Hobe Mountain**, an 86-foot-high sand dune, and survey the pines, the palmetto (a stumpy, tropical palm fan) flatlands and the mangrove-flanked course of the winding Loxahatchee River. The intrepid can make a nine-mile hike along the **Kitchen Creek trail**, starting from the park's entrance and finishing up at some basic campgrounds within a cypress hammock. Get hiking maps from the entrance office, and be aware that campground space must be booked ahead of arrival: phone ☎305/546-2771. Cabins, at $50 a night, are also available.

Anyone less adventurous should rent a canoe and paddle along the Loxahatchee River – don't be put off by the preponderance of alligators – to the **Trapper Nelson interpretive center**, named after a Quaker washed ashore near here in 1697. Another way to get there is by taking the two-hour **Loxahatchee River Cruise** (twice daily except Tues; $9; reservations ☎407/746-1466).

Stuart and on to Hutchinson Island

Another long barrier island lies immediately north of Jupiter Island. To reach it (with either Hwy-1 or Hwy-A1A), you'll first pass through **STUART**, a neat and tidy town on the south bank of the St Lucie River. Stuart has a number of century-old wooden buildings proudly preserved on and around Flagler Avenue – pick up a **free walking guide** from the **Chamber of Commerce**, 400 S Federal Highway (Mon–Fri 9am–5pm; ☎305/287-1088) – and a *Greyhound* station at 757 SE Monterey Road (☎407/287-7777), but not much else keep you engaged. There is a **bike rental** outlet, however, *Pedal Power*, 1211 SE Port St Lucie Boulevard (☎407/335-1310), which you'll need (if you don't have a car) to make progress along Hwy-A1A, over the intracoastal waterway and to Hutchinson Island (although there isn't a cycle path until you reach Jensen Beach – see below).

Hutchinson Island

Largely hidden behind thickly grouped Australian pines, several beautiful beaches line the twenty-mile-long **HUTCHINSON ISLAND**: watch carefully for the public access points. It would be hard, however, to miss **Stuart Beach**, facing Hwy-A1A as it arrives from the mainland: a low-key, brown-sanded strand where locals are far more prevalent than tourists – a fine venue for a few hours of ray absorption.

Close by, the **Elliot Museum** (daily 1–4pm; $2.50) gathers a sizeable hotch-potch of mechanical objects and ornaments, few of which seem to have much to do with inventor Sterling Elliot, whom the place is intended to commemorate. A talented inventor active from the 1870s, Elliot's creations displayed here include an automatic knot-tier and the first addressing machine, while his quadricycle – a four-wheeled bicycle – solved many of the technical problems hindering the development of the car. So it's hard to fathom why much of the museum is given over to reconstructed turn-of-the-century shops, Victoran fashion accessories and a hangar full of vintage cars.

A mile south, **Gilbert's House of Refuge** (Tues–Sun 1–4pm; $1) is a better stop: a convincingly restored refuge for wrecked sailors, one of five erected along Florida's east coast during the 1870s. Furnished in spartan Victorian style, the rooms of the refuge are best understood with the commentary of the **free guided tour** (starting when you're ready, every day except Saturday). There's more evidence of the refuge's importance in the entrance area – lifeboat equipment, ship's logs and a modern weather station – along with reminders of the building's more recent function as a sea turtle hatchery.

Pushing on, roughly halfway along the island, **Jensen Beach** has the only road to the mainland between Stuart and Fort Pierce, and a small but enjoyable beach. If you feel like sticking around, the *River's Edge*, 2625 NE Indian Drive (☎407/334-4759; ③), beside the intracoastal waterway, makes a practical base. Jensen Beach also marks the start of a **cycle path** which continues – passing one of Florida's two nuclear power stations (which, if you're interested, has a visitor center with interactive exhibits pertaining to energy production) – to the Fort Pierce Inlet, which divides Hutchinson Island in two. To reach the northern half (known as North Hutchinson Island), you'll need to pass through the area's biggest town, Fort Pierce.

Fort Pierce

A number of rustic motels, bars and restaurants grouped along Hwy-A1A beside a more than adequate beach make the first taste of **FORT PIERCE** a favorable one. Unfortunately, the bulk of the town (looped through by Hwy-A1A), two miles away across the intracoastal waterway, has considerable social problems, and tourism plays second fiddle to processing and transporting the produce of Florida's citrus farms. The convivial coastal section makes an amenable base for island exploration, but the mainland town has only a few features likely to dent your day.

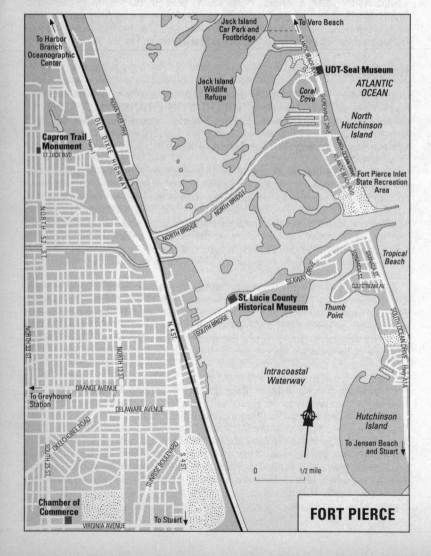

The Historical Museum

Beside Hwy-A1A, close to the intracoastal waterway bridge, the **St Lucie County Historical Museum** (Tues–Sat 10am–4pm, Sun noon–4pm; $2) keeps a cogent assembly of relics. Among them are a full-sized Seminole Indian chickee (an open-sided, palm-thatched hut) and a solid account of the Seminole Wars, including the 1835 fort from which Fort Pierce took its name, and a re-creation of *Chubbs* general store, the hub of the turn-of-the-century town. Outside the museum, a 1907 cracker cottage can be given a once-over; note the tall ceilings and plentiful windows allowing the muggy Florida air to circulate in the days before air conditioning.

Downtown Fort Pierce and Around

Entering **downtown Fort Pierce**, your gaze is held by a sewage treatment works and the towers of a cement factory, their industrial greyness contrasting strongly with Hutchinson Island's raging greenery. Hwy-A1A quickly escapes oceanwards to North Hutchinson Island. If you have time in hand, don't bother with the downtown area but make an excursion a few miles north along Hwy-1.

The Capron Trail Monument and Indian River Drive
A couple of miles north of downtown Fort Pierce, Hwy-1 crosses St Lucie Boulevard, and a left turn along here leads to a memorial (by the junction with 25th Street) recalling the nineteenth-century soldiers who inched their way from here towards Fort Brooke – the site of present-day Tampa. Their machetes hacked out the **Capron Trail**; one of the first east–west cross-Florida routes. Driving back, stay on St Lucie Boulevard as it crosses Hwy-1 and turn left along **Indian River Drive**, where gracious, rambling wooden homes dating from the early 1900s line the intracoastal waterway.

Harbor Branch Oceanographic Center
Five miles further north on Hwy-1, the **Harbor Branch Oceanographic Center** (guided tours Mon–Sat 10am & 2pm; $3) is a phenomenally well-equipped deep-sea research facility funded by the *Johnson & Johnson* baby powder empire. The diving vessels developed and used here are way ahead of anything the US Navy possesses; **tours** take you aboard whichever of them may be in dock, and around the museum's racks of pickled deep-sea creatures, whose strange shapes might surprise even Jacques Cousteau. Tours begin from the **reception center** (Mon–Fri 10am–4pm; free), where stunning underwater pictures set the mood. You'll also get the chance to eat in the research center's canteen: a good feed for $4.

Practicalities

The Fort Pierce **Greyhound** station (☎461-3299) is six miles from downtown near the junction of Hwy-70 and the Florida Turnpike; a cab (☎461-7200) from here to the beach will cost around $12. If you're arriving on a late, or leaving on an early, *Greyhound* bus, you'll find a group of ordinary but inexpensive lodging

The area code for Fort Pierce and Vero Beach is ☎407.

and eating options close to hand. The former include *Days Inn* (☎468-3260; ③) and *Econo Lodge* (☎465-8600; ②–③), and the latter the buffet food of *Shoney's* (☎466-4066).

Otherwise, sleeping (with the exception of camping) and dining are best done close to the beach, two miles east of downtown Fort Pierce. Most **motels** are geared up for stays of several nights and many rooms include cooking facilities: try the well-equipped *Seaway Inn*, 1920 Seaway Drive (☎461-3787; ④), or the more basic *Dockside Inn*, 1152 Seaway Drive (☎461-4824; ②–③). There are further choices along Seaway Drive and the northern part of Ocean Drive; ask on the spot for the best deals. For **camping**, go inland to the Savannahs, a sizeable square of reclaimed marshland beside the intracoastal waterway, seven miles south of downtown Fort Pierce on Route 707 (☎468-1515).

Food options include the unpretentious *Captain's Galley*, 825 N Indian River Drive (☎466-8495), for traditional breakfasts and solid lunches; the more refined *Mangrove Matties*, 1640 Seaway Drive (☎466-1044), serves sizeable salads and sandwiches.

You can get general **information** from the **Chamber of Commerce**, 2200 Virginia Avenue (Mon–Fri 8.30am–5pm; ☎461-2700).

North Hutchinson Island

Consuming the southern tip of **NORTH HUTCHINSON ISLAND**, the **Fort Pierce Inlet State Recreation Area** (daily 8am–sunset; cars $3.25, pedestrians and cyclists $1), to the right as you arrive on Hwy-A1A, overlooking the Fort Pierce Inlet and the community's beach, makes a scenic setting for a picnic – as well as a launch site for local surfers. A mile north, a footbridge from the car park of the **Jack Island Wildlife Refuge** leads onto the mile-long Marsh Rabbit Run, a boardwalk trail cutting through a thick mangrove swamp to an observation tower on the edge of the Indian River. Among bird life to watch out for are great blue herons and ospreys.

Concern for the environment is not something shared by the **UDT-SEAL Museum** (Tues–Sat 10am–4pm, Sun noon–4pm; $2), on Hwy-A1A between the recreation area and the wildlife refuge, dedicated to the US Navy's frogman demolition teams who've been exploding sea-mines and beach defences since the Normandy landings. During World War II, the UDTs (Underwater Demolition Teams) trained on Hutchinson Island – like most of Florida's barrier islands, it was off-limits to civilians at the time. The more elite SEALs (Sea Air Land) came into being during the Sixties, the US equivalent of Britain's SAS. Some practical stuff covers the technicalities of establishing beachheads, though jingoism is predictably apparent – anyone who can't keep doubts over US foreign policy to themselves should steer clear.

Vero Beach and Around

For the next fourteen miles, Australian pines mar Hwy-A1A's ocean view until North Hutchinson Island imperceptibly becomes **Orchid Island** and you reach **VERO BEACH**, the area's sole community of substance and one with a pronounced upmarket image. It makes an enjoyable hideaway, however, with a fine group of beaches centering on Ocean Drive, parallel to Hwy-A1A. There's little to tempt you from the sands, but it's worth taking the trouble to view the *Driftwood Resort*, 3150 Ocean Drive, a Thirties hotel, now time-share apartments, erected from a jumble of driftwood, fleamarket finds and pieces of Palm Beach mansions demolished to avoid taxes.

Vero Beach Practicalities

Three miles from the coast, **inland Vero Beach** has a *Greyhound* station, 905 Hwy-1 (☎562-6588), and the local **Chamber of Commerce**, 1216 21st Street (Mon–Fri 9am–5pm; ☎567-3491). At the beach, exceptions to pricy **accommodation** are the *Riviera Inn*, 1605 S Ocean Drive (☎234-4112; ③–④), and *Sea Spray Gardens*, 965 E Causeway Boulevard (☎231-5210; ③–④), both with great deals off-season. The cost-effective place for **meals** is the *Beachside Restaurant*, 3125 Ocean Drive (☎334-4477).

North of Vero Beach: Sebastian Inlet

Tiny beachside communities dot the rest of the island, but you'll find most activity around the **Sebastian Inlet State Recreation Area** (daily 8am–sunset; cars $3.25, pedestrians and cyclists $1), sixteen miles north of Vero Beach. Roaring ocean breakers lure surfers here, particularly over Easter when contests are held, and anglers cram the jetties for the east coast's finest fishing. Without a board or a rod, you can keep amused by viewing the treasure salvaged from an eighteenth-century Spanish fleet stricken by a hurricane at the **McLarty Treasure Museum** (Wed–Sun 10am–4.30pm; $1), a couple of miles south of the actual inlet, and by keeping an eye out for the endangered bird life making sorties from the nearby Pelican Island, the oldest wildlife refuge in the country and off-limits to humans.

Beyond Sebastian you reach the outskirts of the Space Coast, covered in Chapter Four.

travel details

Trains
From Hollywood to Fort Lauderdale/Delray Beach/West Palm Beach (2 daily; 12min/42min/1hr 6min).

Tri-Rail
From Hollywood to Fort Lauderdale/Boca Raton/Delray Beach/West Palm Beach (5–15 daily; 12min/39min/48min/1hr 11min).

Buses
From Fort Lauderdale to Boca Raton/Delray Beach (4 daily; 50min/1hr 10min); Fort Pierce (12 daily; 2hr 50min); Stuart (4 daily; 3hr 15min); Vero Beach (5 daily; 3hr 55min); West Palm Beach (12 daily; 2hr).

From Hollywood to Fort Lauderdale (16 daily; 10–30min); Walt Disney World (1 daily; 5hr 1min).

From West Palm Beach to Belle Glade (1 daily; 1hr 5min); Fort Pierce (7 daily; 1hr 30min); Stuart (6 daily; 1hr); Tampa (1 daily; 6hr); Vero Beach (5 daily; 1hr 50min).

CHAPTER FOUR

THE NORTHEAST COAST

Substantially free of commercial exploitation, with washed-up shark's teeth sometimes more plentiful than people on its beaches, the 190 miles of Florida's **NORTHEAST COAST** are tailor-made for leisurely exploration. You'll often feel like doing nothing more strenuous than settling down beside the ocean, but throughout the region evidence of the forces that have shaped Florida – from ancient native American settlements to the launch-site of the Space Shuttle – is easy to find and worth exploring. When planning your trip, remember that the Northeast Coast's tourist **seasons** are the reverse of those of the Southeast Coast: the crowded time here is the summer, when accommodation will be scarcer and more expensive than during the quieter winter period.

Besides sharing a shoreline, the towns of the Northeast Coast have surprisingly little in common. Those making up the **Space Coast**, the first area you reach from the south, primarily service the hordes passing through to visit the **Kennedy Space Center**, the birthplace of the nation's space exploits and literally the launching pad of recent history's most spectacular events. Its public image is unrelentingly positive, but the Space Center makes a good call, as does the wildlife refuge which surrounds it. Each March and April, a different kind of blasting-off has traditionally occurred seventy miles north of the Space Coast at **Daytona Beach**, a small town with a big beach which, until a recent bout of soul searching, happily hosted the drunken legions of college kids indulging in the legendary excesses of the Spring Break holiday. Although the local authorities are discouraging the event, teenaged carousing can still be found at this time. If that appeals to you, don't think twice about coming; if it doesn't, Daytona at any other time is mellower – and its beach is just as huge.

Along the northerly portion of the coast, the plentiful evidence of Florida's early European landings is nowhere better displayed than in comprehensively restored **St Augustine**, where sixteenth-century Spaniards established North America's earliest foreign settlement. In addition to the fascinations of the town itself, the surrounding coast is attractive, too, part of a divine strand stretching to the **Jacksonville Beaches**, twenty miles north, where lying in the sun and tuning into the sprightly local nightlife will decadently waste a few days. Just inland, the city of **Jacksonville** is less appealing; struggling to shrug off its grey and industrial image, it merits only a cursory investigation as you strike out

---

ACCOMMODATION PRICE CODES

All accommodation prices in this book have been coded using the symbols below.
Note that prices are for the least expensive double rooms in each establishment.
For a full explanation see p.26 in *Basics*.

①	up to $30	④	$60–80	⑦	$130–180
②	$30–45	⑤	$80–100	⑧	$180+
③	$45–60	⑥	$100–130		

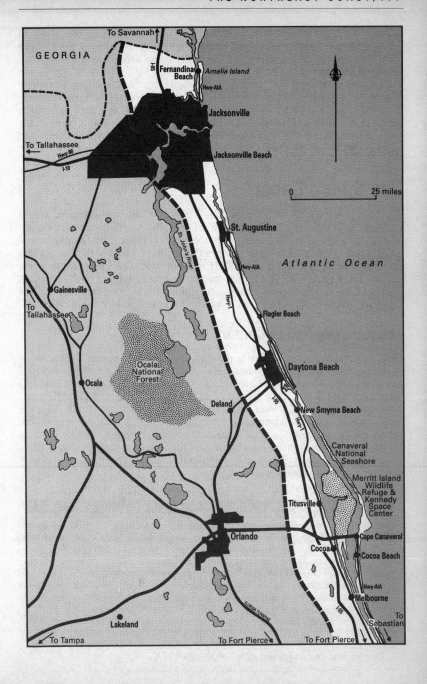

towards the state's northeastern extremity. Here, overlooking the coast of Georgia, slender **Amelia Island** is fringed by gorgeous silver sands, has a quirky Victorian-era main town, and is under the beady eye of dollar-crazed developers – arrive before they do.

The **road network** is very much a continuation of the Southeast Coast's system: Hwy-A1A hugs the coastline, **Hwy-1** charts a less appealing course on the mainland, and is a lot slower than **I-95**, which divides the coastal area from the eastern edge of Central Florida. *Greyhound* **buses** are frequent along Hwy-1 between the main towns, though the only **local bus services** are in Daytona Beach and Jacksonville. Forget the **train** – only Jacksonville has a station.

The Space Coast

The barrier islands which dominate the Treasure Coast (see Chapter Three) continue north into the so-called **SPACE COAST**, the base of the country's space industry and site of the Kennedy Space Center, occupying a flat, marshy island bulging into the Atlantic just fifty miles east of Orlando. Many of the visitors who flock here are surprised to find that the land from which the Space Shuttle leaves earth is also a sizeable wildlife refuge, framed by several miles of rough coastline. Except for the beach-oriented communities on the ocean, the towns of the Space Coast are uninteresting, chiefly of use as low-cost overnight stops or meal breaks.

The Kennedy Space Center

Justifiably the biggest attraction in the area, the **Kennedy Space Center** is the nucleus of the US space programme: it's here that space vehicles are developed and tested, and where they're blasted into orbit. Confusingly, the first launches were from the US Air Force base on Cape Canaveral (renamed Cape Kennedy between 1963 and 1973), from which unmanned satellites still lift off. After the space programme was expanded in 1964, the center of activity became Merritt Island, positioned between Cape Canaveral and the mainland, directly north of Cocoa Beach. There's no excuse not to visit the Space Center: it's a solid documentation of US achievements and proof positive that success in space is closely tied to the nation's sense of well-being.

THE KENNEDY SPACE CENTER: PRACTICAL INFO AND TIPS

The only **public entry roads** into the Kennedy Space Center are Hwy-405 from Titusville, and Route 3 off Hwy-A1A between Cocoa Beach and Cocoa: on either approach, follow signs for **Spaceport USA** (daily 9am–6pm or later; free), which holds the museum, Rocket Garden and *IMAX* film theater.

Arrive early to avoid the crowds, which are thinnest on weekends and during May and September. If you take one of the narrated bus tours ("Red" for the Space Center; "Blue" for Cape Canaveral; each two hours long; $7), **buy tickets** for them – and for the film ($4) – from the ticket pavilion as soon as you arrive.

To **see a launch** from the Space Center, phone ☎407/452-2121 between 8am and 4pm to reserve a free pass. Be aware, though, that almost as much of a launch can be seen from anywhere within a forty-mile radius of the Space Center.

For launch dates and times: ☎1-800-SHUTTLE.

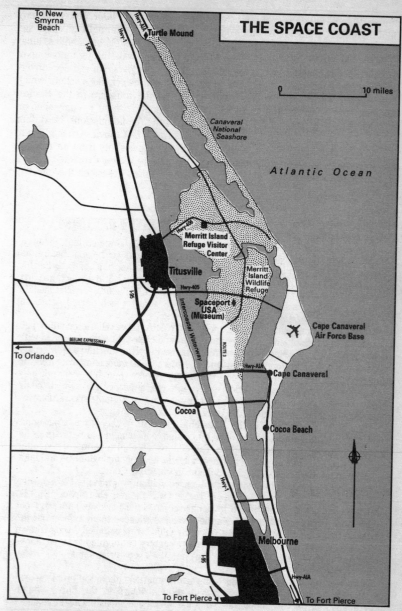

THE SPACE COAST

To New Smyrna Beach

Turtle Mound

0   10 miles

Canaveral National Seashore

Atlantic Ocean

Merritt Island Refuge Visitor Center

Titusville

Merritt Island Wildlife Refuge

Spaceport USA (Museum)

Cape Canaveral Air Force Base

Beeline Expressway

To Orlando

Cape Canaveral

Cocoa

Cocoa Beach

Melbourne

To Fort Pierce

To Fort Pierce

Seeing Spaceport USA

Everything at **Spaceport USA** is within easy walking distance of the car park, as
is the departure point for the bus tours. The **museum** will keep anyone with the

faintest interest in space exploration entertained for a good hour. Except for any mention of the Challenger or other disasters, everything you might expect to see is here: actual mission capsules, space suits, detailed models of satellites, lunar modules and the Viking craft used on Mars, a full-sized walk-through mock-up of the Space Shuttle, and a lot more – much of it surprisingly small and deceptively simplistic in appearance. The same applies to the firework-like rockets which launched the early space shots, standing outside the museum in the **Rocket Garden**. They're far daintier than the famously gigantic Saturn V – only seen on the "Red" bus tour (see below) – which launched the Apollo missions. Next door to the museum, the **Galaxy Theater** alternates two *IMAX* movies – using 70mm film projected onto a five-storey screen. With dramatic shots from an orbiting Space Shuttle, *The Dream Is Alive* is enjoyable despite Walter Cronkite's cringe-inducing commentary; the other film, *The Blue Planet*, describes the effect of human meddling on the Earth's ecosystem.

AMERICANS IN SPACE: THE BACKGROUND

The growth of the Space Coast started with the "**Space Race**", which followed President John Kennedy's declaration in May 1961 to "achieve the goal, before the decade is out, of landing a man on the moon and returning him safely to Earth". This statement came in the chill of the Cold War, when the USSR – which had just put the first man into space, following upon their launch of the first artificial satellite in 1957 – appeared scientifically ahead of the US, a fact which dented American pride and provided great propaganda for the Soviets.

Money and manpower were pumped into **NASA** (National Aeronautics and Space Administration), and the communities around Cape Canaveral expanded with a heady influx of boffins and would-be astronauts. The much-hyped Mercury programme helped restore prestige, and the later Apollo moonshots captured the imagination of the world. The moon landing by Apollo 11 in July 1969 not only turned the dreams of science fiction writers into reality faster than anybody could have predicted, but also meant for the first time – and in the most spectacular way possible – the US had overtaken the USSR.

Through the Seventies, as the incredible expense of the space programme became apparent and seemed out of all proportion to its benefits, pressure grew for NASA to become more cost-effective. The country entered a period of economic recession and NASA's funding was drastically slashed; unemployment – unthinkable in the buoyant Sixties – threatened many on the Space Coast.

After the internationally funded Skylab space station programme, NASA's solution to the problem of wasteful one-use rockets was the reusable **Space Shuttle**, first launched in April 1981, able to deploy commercial payloads and carry out repairs to orbiting satellites. The Shuttle's success silenced many critics, but the *Challenger* disaster of January 1986 – when the entire crew perished during take-off – not only sent a deep sense of loss around the country but highlighted the complacency and corner-cutting which had crept into the space programme after many accident-free years.

More recently, despite numerous satisfactory missions, technical problems and stringent safety procedures have caused serious delays to the Space Shuttle programme, and served to illustrate what a colossal accomplishment the manned moon landings actually were – and how remote the possibility is that their like will ever be seen again.

The Bus Tours

The only way to see the rest of the Merritt Island space complex without seriously breaching security is with the **"Red" bus tour**. This first crosses the "crawlerway" – the huge tracks along which the Space Shuttles are wheeled to the launch pad – on the way to the 52-storey-high **Vehicle Assembly Building** where the shuttles (like Apollo and Skylab before them) are assembled and fitted with their payloads. Unfortunately, you can't go in but, with luck, a door may be open and you'll get a slight sense of the enormous innards of what, in terms of volume, is among the world's largest structures, so high that special air conditioning is fitted to prevent clouds forming inside.

With further luck, a Space Shuttle will be in place for take-off when the bus takes a loop around the **launch pad** – no different in reality from what you've seen on TV, and no more interesting than any other large pile of scaffolding if a shuttle isn't present (obviously, when a countdown is underway there are no bus tours – see the box on p.178 for launch-watching tips). Besides a nose-to-nozzle inspection of a Saturn V rocket, the most impressive part of the bus tour is, perversely, also the most contrived: a simulated Apollo countdown and take-off watched from behind the blinking screens of a realistically mocked-up control room.

Only serious space buffs should take the **"Blue" bus tour**, a much less spectacular trip around the Cape Canaveral Air Force base. The site was developed by the US War Department in the Forties for guided missile testing, pioneering Mercury and Gemini missions blasted off from here, and it's still used for sending weather and communications satellites into orbit.

Merritt Island Wildlife Refuge

NASA doesn't have Merritt Island all to itself, but shares it with the **Merritt Island National Wildlife Refuge** (daily 8am–two hours before sunset; free), which allows alligators, armadillos, racoons and bobcats – and one of Florida's greatest gatherings of bird life – to live out their primeval existence beside some of the world's most advanced technology.

Even if you're only coming for a day at the Space Center, it would be a shame to pass up such a spectacular place – although it has to be said that Merritt Island, on first glance, looks anything but spectacular, comprising acres of saltwater estuaries and brackish marshes, interspersed by occasional hammocks of oak and palm, and by pine flatwoods where a few bald eagles construct ten-foot-thick nests. Winter is the **best time to visit**, when the island's skies are alive with tens of thousands of migratory birds from the frozen north, and when mosquitoes are nowhere to be found. At any other period, and especially in summer, the island's Mosquito Lagoon is worthy of its name; bring ample insect repellent.

Seeing the Refuge

Seven miles east of Titusville on Route 402, the six-mile **Black Point wildlife drive** gives a solid introduction to the basics of the island's ecosystem. Pick up the extremely informative free leaflet at the entrance, which describes specific stops along the route, including one from which you'll spot a couple of bald eagle nests, and another by the mudflats where kingfishers, gulls and terns are likely to be swooping on their dinner.

Be sure to do some walking within the refuge, too. Off the wildlife drive, the five-mile **Cruickshank trail** weaves around the edge of the Indian River; if the whole length is too strenuous, go as far as the observation tower, a few minutes' walk from the car park. For a more varied landscape, drive a few miles further east along Route 402 – branching from Route 406 just south of the wildlife drive – passing the **visitor center** (Mon–Fri 8.30am–5pm; Sat & Sun 9am–5pm; closed Sun April–Oct; ☎867-0667), and tackle the half-mile **Oak Hammock trail**, or the two-mile **Palm Hammock trail**, both accessible from the same car park.

The Canaveral National Seashore
A slender, 25-mile-long beach dividing Merrit Island's Mosquito Lagoon from the Atlantic Ocean, the **Canaveral National Seashore** (same hours as the Wildlife Refuge) begins at **Playlinda Beach** on Route 402, five miles east of the refuge's visitor center. The National Seashore's entire length is top-notch beachcombing and surfing territory. You can swim here, too, if you dare; the current is strong and jellyfish are plentiful. Except when rough seas and high tides submerge it completely, you should take a wind-bitten ramble along the palmetto-lined path to **Klondike Beach**, north of Playlinda Beach, totally wild and often coated by intriguing shells and, in summer, marked by the tracks left by sea turtles crawling ashore at night to lay eggs.

At the northern tip of the National Seashore, on **Apollo Beach** (only reachable by road from New Smyrna Beach, eight miles north, see "Heading North: New Smyrna Beach", below), the easily sighted **Turtle Mound**, a fifty-foot heap of oyster shells, provided a home for Surruque Indians over several generations and was marked on maps by Florida's first Spanish explorers, being visible several miles out to sea. You can walk to the top of the mound, for a view over Merrit Island and the NASA launch pads, within a few minutes.

Cocoa Beach

Unquestionably the best base from which to see the Space Coast, **COCOA BEACH** is just a few miles south of the Kennedy Space Center on a ten-mile-long strip of shore washed by some of the biggest waves in Florida – making the town a favored haunt of surfers. Major (and minor) surfing contests are held here during April and May, and throughout the year the place has a perky, youthful feel. At weekends you'll often come across free music in the beachside parks and beside the pier, and a walk around the *Harrods*-sized *Ron Jon Surf Shop*, 4151 Atlantic Avenue (☎799-8888) – packed with surfboards (rental is $8 per day), kites, sunglasses, sunscreen, extrovert beach attire and open 24 hours a day – demonstrates the prime concerns of the community.

Cocoa Beach comprises just the beach and a few residential streets off Atlantic Avenue (Hwy-A1A) so, other than getting stuck into the beachlife and making a trip to the Kennedy Space Center, there's not an awful lot to do.

Information and Transportation
The Cocoa Beach **Chamber of Commerce** has a desk inside the *Holiday Inn*, 1300 N Atlantic Avenue (Mon–Fri 9am–5pm; ☎459-2200), though a better place to check any cut-price accommodation and dining offers is the Cocoa Beach **Welcome Center**, 1399 N Atlantic Avenue (daily 9am–5.30pm, later in summer; ☎783-8811). **Public transportation** is non-existent in Cocoa Beach, but the

The area code for Cocoa Beach and the Space Coast is ☎407.

Cocoa Beach Shuttle (☎784-3831) runs to and from Orlando airport for $17 one way; call to be collected. To get around the beach area, hire a **bike** from the *Ron Jon Surf Shop* (address above), for $5 an hour or $30 a week.

Accommodation

Motel bargains are rare in Cocoa Beach. You can expect prices to be highest during February, July and August – and during Space Shuttle launches. The lowest rates are with *Motel 6*, 3701 N Atlantic Avenue (☎783-3103; ②), *Econo Lodge*, 5500 N Atlantic Avenue (☎1-800/446-6900; ②), and the *Wakulla Motel*, 3550 N Atlantic Avenue (☎783-2230; ③). For a longer stay, try the Cape Colony resort, 1275 N Atlantic Avenue (☎783-2252; ⑤), especially good value for several people sharing. The tent-friendliest **campground** is *Jetty Park*, 400 E Jetty Road (☎783-7222), five miles north. To relax in $100-a-night style, stay at *Sea Esta Suites*, 686 S Atlantic Avenue (☎1-800/872-9444; ⑥), whose price includes home-cooked breakfasts and supper.

Eating and Nightlife

Many inland restaurants strive to undercut each other, resulting in some good **eating** deals if you have the transportation to reach them; see "The Inland Towns" for suggestions, and scan free magazines (found in motels and at the Chamber of Commerce) such as *Restaurant Dining Out* for money-saving coupons. Close to the beach, the options are fewer. Open around the clock, the Fifties-style *Herbie K's Diner*, 2080 N Atlantic Avenue (☎783-6740), is as interesting for its after-hours social life as its juicy burgers; for simple basics go to *Lynn's Restaurant*, 26 N Orlando Avenue (☎783-3301); and for great oysters and a $5 lunch buffet, head for *Rusty's Raw Bar*, 2 S Atlantic Avenue (☎783-2401). For dinner, *The Pier House* (☎783-7549), on the pier, has a quality menu especially strong on seafood.

Nightlife is most enjoyable if you start early at one of the beachside **happy hours**: try *Spinnaker's*, also part of the pier complex (☎783-7549), or *Desperados*, 301 N Atlantic Avenue (☎784-3363). Later, the *Pig and Whistle*, 801 N Atlantic Avenue (☎799-0724), with TV soccer and overpriced bitter, is a refuge for home-sick Brits; *Coconuts*, 2 Minuteman Causeway (☎784-1422), has drinking and **live** sounds on the beach; and *Cape Sierra*, 8625 Astronaut Boulevard (☎799-9996), is a glittery **disco** enjoyed by a varied crowd, often with live bands of yesteryear.

The Inland Towns: Melbourne, Cocoa and Titusville

Travelling by *Greyhound* is the only excuse for passing through the Space Coast's sleepy inland towns. Strung along Hwy-1, each provides housing for space indus-try employees and not much else – except the promise of accommodation and food cheaper than at the beach.

Melbourne

The southernmost town is the pretty but dull **MELBOURNE**, forty miles north of Vero Beach (see p.174). Neither the art collections of the **Brevard Art Center and Museum**, 1463 Highland Avenue (Tues–Sat 10am–5pm, Sun noon–5pm; $2), nor the routine technical displays of the **Space Coast Science Center**, 1510

Highland Avenue (Tues–Sat 10am–5pm, Sun noon–5pm; $3), will hold you here very long. Melbourne's **restaurants** might, however: go to *The Luncheon Suite*, 1900 Harbor City Boulevard (☎984-7112), for sandwiches and burgers, or *Mac & Jean's Diner*, 1085 N Wickham Road (☎254-8818), for a buffet feed. *Greyhound* **buses** stop at 460 S Harbor City Boulevard (☎723-4323). For an **overnight stay**, use the *Econo Lodge*, 420 S Harbor City Boulevard (☎723-5320; ②–③).

Cocoa

In Cocoa, thirty miles north of Melbourne, and eight miles inland from Cocoa Beach, the cobblestoned pavements of **Old Cocoa Village**, filling several small blocks south of King Street (Hwy-520), make for a relaxing stroll. Among the twee antique shops and boutiques, seek out the *Porcher House*, 434 Delannoy Avenue (Tues–Fri 10am–1pm; $1), a grand Neoclassical abode of 1916 vintage.

Many of the buildings in Old Cocoa Village date from the early years of the century, but for a more solid view of the town's origins, head a few miles west to the **Museum of History and Natural Science**, 1463 N Highland Avenue (Tues–Sat 10am–4pm, Sun 1–4pm; $2), whose displays recount Cocoa's birth as a trading post, the first settlers arriving in the 1840s by steamboat and mule. There's a respectable display on Florida wildlife, too, and some informative leaflets which you'd do well to take away and scrutinize if you're heading for the Merritt Island Wildlife Refuge (see above).

It's worth making a quick stop at the **Astronaut Memorial Space Center**, 1519 Clearlake Road (Mon–Fri 10am–4pm, Sat 10.30am–4pm; $3), not for the Center's run-of-the-mill science exhibits but for **Space Shuttle Park** beside the car park: an unintentional antidote to the pizzazz of the Kennedy Space Center. You'll stumble over various bits of space hardware, including – incredibly – an Apollo command module with its cobweb-covered interior strewn with bare wires and plugs: a bizarre fate for something which, not long ago, was at the frontier of space science.

The *Greyhound* station is at 302 Main Street (☎636-3917); without a car, **getting to Cocoa Beach** involves a $12 taxi ride (☎636-7017). In Cocoa itself, **eat** at *Julie's Cafe*, 405 Delannoy Avenue (☎631-2800), where sizeable steak or seafood portions come at a bargain "early-bird" price from 5pm to 7pm; alternatively, *Cafe Margaux*, 222 Brevard Avenue (☎639-8343), is a stylish spot for a pasta lunch. Small and uninviting **motels** line Cocoa Boulevard; you might well feel more comfortable – and won't be spending more than you have to – by opting for the *Econo Lodge* at no 3220 N (☎632-4561; ②).

Titusville

If you don't visit the Kennedy Space Center, you'll at least get a great view of the towering Vehicle Assembly Building from **TITUSVILLE**, twenty miles north of Cocoa. All that's commendable about the town is the ease of access to the Space Center (on Hwy-405) and the Merritt National Wildlife Refuge (with Hwy-402). On the way to either place, don't be encouraged to visit the **Astronaut Hall of Fame** (daily 9am–5pm; $6.95), a tame celebration of the Mercury astronauts and an audiovisual show in a facsimile Space Shuttle.

The *Greyhound* station is at 20 N Washington Avenue (☎267-8760). For **food**, head for the under-$5 lunch dishes at *Ping On*, 407 Cheney Highway (☎269-2503), or the seafood of *Dixie Crossroads*, 1475 Garden Street (☎268-5000). Inexpensive **motels** are plentiful along Washington Avenue (Hwy-1); *South Wind*, no 1540 (☎267-3681; ②–③), and *Siesta* no 2006 (☎267-1455; ②–③), are just two.

Heading North: New Smyrna Beach

After the virgin vistas of the Canaveral National Seashore, the tall beachside hotels of **NEW SMYRNA BEACH**, thirty miles north of Titusville on Hwy-1, create a misleading first impression of a likeably low-key beach community, where the sea – protected from dangerous currents by offshore rock ledges – is perfect for **swimming**. To reach the beach (or the northern section of the National Seashore, see above), you have to pass through the inland section of the town, before swinging east on Hwy-A1A. Before aiming at the beach, take heed of the town's unusual **history**. A wealthy Scottish physician, Andrew Turnbull, bought land here in the mid-1700s and, bizarrely, set about creating a Mediterranean colony, recruiting Greeks, Italians and Minorcans, offering them fifty acres of land each in return for seven years' labor on his plantation. The colony didn't last: bad treatment, language barriers, disease and financial disasters hastened its demise, and many of the settlers moved north to St Augustine (see p.193).

The immigrants worked hard, however (by most accounts, they had little choice), laying irrigation canals, building a sugar mill and commencing work on what was to be a palatial abode for Turnbull. Close to Hwy-1, the **ruins** of the mill (at the junction of Canal Street and Mission Road) and his unfinished house (at Riverside Drive and Julia Street) are substantial enough to merit a look, and the nearby **Chamber of Commerce**, 115 Canal Street (Mon–Fri 9am–5pm; ☎1-800/541-9621), has a handy historical leaflet, as well as the usual local information.

Greyhound **buses** call at 502 N Orange Street (☎428-8211); if you want to stay over, the cheapest **motels** are both on Hwy-1 (locally called Dixie Freeway): *Smyrna Motel*, no 1050 N (☎428-2495; ②), and *Shangri-La*, no 805 (☎428-8361; ②).

Continuing north from New Smyrna Beach, Hwy-A1A joins with Hwy-1 for ten miles before splitting off oceanwards near Ponce Inlet, five miles south of mainland Daytona Beach.

Daytona Beach

The consummate Florida beach town, with rows of airbrushed-T-shirt shops, amusement arcades, wall-to-wall motels and bar-room G-string contests passing for high culture, **DAYTONA BEACH** owes its existence to twenty miles of light brown sand where the only pressure is to strip off and enjoy yourself. For decades, Daytona has been invaded each March and April by half-a-million college kids going through the **Spring Break** ritual of underage drinking and libido liberation, and by thousands of leather-clad motorcyclists arriving for the early March **Bike Week** races at the Daytona International Speedway. While the bikers look set to continue coming, Daytona has recently – and very controversially – decided to end its love affair with the nation's students, and to emulate Fort Lauderdale (see Chapter Three) in cultivating a more refined image.

Just how quickly Spring Break at Daytona Beach becomes a thing of the past remains to be seen, but its demise may at least give the town a chance to reveal its truer nature: a small, medium-paced, down-to-earth resort, with just a day's worth of things to see beyond its famous sands.

The area code for Daytona Beach and New Smyrna Beach is ☎904.

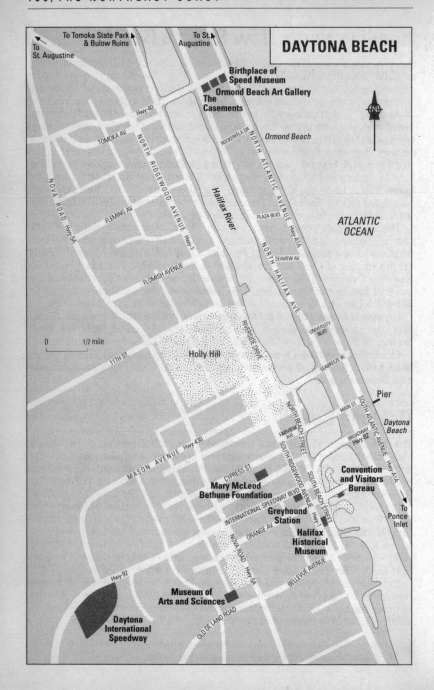

DAYTONA BEACH

To Tomoka State Park
& Bulow Ruins

To
St. Augustine

To St.
Augustine

Birthplace of
Speed Museum
Ormond Beach Art Gallery
The
Casements

ROCKERFELA DR.

Ormond Beach

N

Hwy 40

TOMOKA AV.

NOVA ROAD Hwy-5A

NORTH RIDGEWOOD AVENUE Hwy-1

Halifax River

FLEMING AV.

PLAZA BLVD.

NORTH ATLANTIC AVENUE Hwy-A1A

ATLANTIC
OCEAN

SEAVIEW AV.

NORTH HALIFAX AVE.

FLOMISH AVENUE

RIVERSIDE DRIVE

UNIVERSITY BLVD

0   1/2 mile

11TH ST.

Holly Hill

SEABREEZE BL.

Pier

MAIN ST.

SOUTH ATLANTIC AVENUE Hwy-A1A

Daytona
Beach

MASON AVENUE Hwy-430

FAIRVIEW AVE

NORTH BEACH STREET

BROADWAY Hwy-92

CYPRESS ST.

Mary McLeod
Bethune Foundation

SOUTH RIDGEWOOD AVENUE

Convention
and Visitors
Bureau

INTERNATIONAL SPEEDWAY BLVD

Greyhound
Station

To
Ponce
Inlet

ORANGE AV.

SOUTH BEACH STREET

Halifax
Historical
Museum

NOVA ROAD Hwy-5A

BELLEVUE AVENUE

Hwy-92

Museum of
Arts and Sciences

OLD DE LAND ROAD

Daytona
International
Speedway

It wasn't students or bikers who first paid attention to Daytona's long, straight and firm beach, but pioneering auto enthusiasts such as Louis Chevrolet, Ransom Olds and Henry Ford, who came here during the early 1900s to race their proto-type vehicles beside the ocean. The land speed record was regularly smashed, five times by millionaire British speedster Malcolm Campbell who, in 1935, roared along at 276mph. As a legacy of these times, Daytona is one of the few Florida towns where **driving on the beach** is permitted: pay $3 at any beach entrance, stick to the marked track, observe the 10mph speed limit, park at right-angles to the ocean – and be wary of high tide.

Arriving, Getting Around and Information

As Ridgewood Avenue, **Hwy-1** steams through **mainland Daytona**, passing the *Greyhound* station, at no 138 S (☎253-6576). By car, you should keep to **Hwy-A1A** (known as Atlantic Avenue), which enters **Beachside Daytona** – filling a narrow slither of land between the ocean and the Halifax River (part of the intracoastal waterway) a mile from the mainland.

Local buses (☎761-7700) connect mainland and beachside Daytona, although there are no night or Sunday services. The bus terminal is at the junction of Palmetto Avenue and International Speedway Boulevard (which in some sections still has signs giving its former name, Volusia Avenue) in mainland Daytona. At the beach, there's also a "trolley" (actually a vintage bus) running along the central part of Atlantic Avenue. A **taxi** between the mainland and the beach will cost around $7: cab companies include *AA Cab* (☎253-2522) and *Yellow* (☎252-5536).

Don't leave mainland Daytona without calling at the **Convention and Visitors Bureau**, 126 E Orange Avenue (Mon–Fri 9am–5pm; ☎1-800/845-1234), for reams of free **information**.

BUSES BETWEEN DAYTONA BEACH AND ORLANDO AIRPORT

Usefully, if you're enjoying yourself at the beach but have to fly home from Orlando, the **Daytona-Orlando Transit Service** (*DOTS*) operates shuttle buses every 90 minutes between 4.30am and 9pm from the corner of Nova Road and 11th Street to Orlando airport. On request, the buses also make stops in Deland and Sanford. The one-way fare is $20 ($36 round trip). For details and reservations, call ☎1-800/231-1965.

Beachside Daytona

Without a doubt, the best thing about Daytona Beach *is* the **beach**: a seemingly limitless affair – 500 feet wide at low tide and, lengthways, fading dreamily into the heat haze. Although it lives up to its racy reputation during the student mate-seeking season of Spring Break, frankly the beach doesn't have much to offer during the rest of the year, beyond developing your tan, taking the occasional ocean dip and strutting narcissistically about. Even the **pier**, at the end of Main Street, isn't up to much, holding two characterless bars and the *Space Needle* ($2), a cable-car-like conveyance which zaps you from one end to the other, over the heads of patient anglers.

Nearby, Main Street and Seabreeze Boulevard have better bars and cafés (see "Eating" and "Nightlife"), but for more diverse pursuits – such as rambling around sand dunes, climbing an old lighthouse or discovering Daytona's history – you need to head twelve miles south to Ponce Inlet, three miles north to Ormond Beach or cross the Halifax River to the mainland.

South to Ponce Inlet

Travelling south along Atlantic Avenue (buses #17A or #17B; only the former goes all the way to Ponce Inlet), small motels and fast-food dives give way to the towering beachside condos of affluent Daytona Beach Shores. As you approach **PONCE INLET**, four miles ahead, the outlook changes again, this time to single-storey beach homes and large sand dunes.

Here, at the end of Peninsula Drive – parallel to Atlantic Avenue – the 175-foot-high **Ponce Inlet Lighthouse** (daily 8am–sunset; $3) illuminated the treacherous inlet giving seaborne access to New Smyrna Beach (see p.185) from the late 1800s until 1970. Stupendous views make climbing the structure worthwhile, and the outbuildings hold surprisingly engaging artefacts from the early days of the lighthouse and mildly interesting displays on US lighthouses in general. The scrub-covered dunes that neighbor the light are also enjoyable, and several **nature trails** scratch a path through them to a (usually) deserted **beach**; pick up a map from the **ranger station** at the end of Riverside Drive.

Once you've trekked up an appetite, drop into *Lighthouse Landing* (see "Eating"), beside the lighthouse, whose cheap seafood is brought ashore at the adjoining marina.

North to Ormond Beach

In 1890, planning to bring his East Coast railway south from St Augustine, oil baron Henry Flagler bought the local hotel, built a beachside golf course and helped give **ORMOND BEACH**, three miles north of Main Street (buses #1A or #1B), a refined tone that it retains to this day. Millionaires like John D Rockefeller wintered here, and the car-potty fraternity of Ford, Olds and Chevrolet used Flagler's garage to fine-tune their autos before powering them along the beach.

Facing the Halifax River at the end of Granada Boulevard, Flagler's **Ormond Hotel** lasted, albeit in increasingly dilapidated form, until 1993, when it was demolished to much public sadness.

Less depressingly, **the Casements** (Mon–Fri 9am–5pm, Sat 9am–noon; free), a three-storey villa on the other side of Granada Boulevard which was bought by Rockefeller in 1918, is in fine fettle. **Guided tours** of the house (which, oddly enough, now holds displays of Hungarian folklore and Italian ceramics) run every thirty minutes from 10am, and tell you much more than you need to know about Rockefeller and his time here – mostly spent playing golf and pressing dimes into the hands of passers-by.

Also on Granada Boulevard, the **Birthplace of Speed Museum**, no 160 (Tues–Sun 1–5pm; $1), makes a convenient stop, though it contains only pictorial records of the early Daytona speed merchants and a few replicas of their machines. Nearby, at no 78, the Polynesian-style **Ormond Beach Art Gallery** (Tues–Sat 1–5pm; free) puts on reasonable temporary art shows – if they don't appeal, the galleries' jungle-like **gardens**, with shady pathways winding past fish-ponds to a gazebo, just might.

Mainland Daytona

When you're tired of the beach, or nursing a bad case of sunburn, cross the river to **mainland Daytona**, where several waterside parks and walkways contribute to a relaxing change of scene and three museums will keep you out of the sun for a few hours.

Near the best of the parks, on Beach Street, a few turn-of-the-century dwellings have been tidied up and turned into office space. One serves as the **Halifax Historical Museum**, at no 252 S (Tues–Sat 10am–4pm; $2), capturing – with an absorbing stock of objects, models and photos – the frenzied growth of Daytona and Halifax County. Amid the fine stash of historical fall-out, don't ignore the immense wall paintings of long-gone local landscapes.

One former Daytona resident referred to in the museum is better remembered by the **Mary McLeod Bethune Foundation**, a couple of miles north at 640 Second Avenue. Born in 1875 to freed slave parents, Mary McLeod Bethune was a lifelong campaigner for racial and sexual equality, founding the National Council of Negro Women and serving as a presidential advisor. In 1904, against the odds, she founded the state's first black girls' school here – with savings of $1.50 and five pupils. The white-framed **house** (Mon–Fri 9am–4pm; free), where Bethune lived from 1914 until her death in 1955, contains the scores of awards and citations she received, alongside furnishings and personal effects, and sits within the campus of the large community college which has grown up around the original school.

If you're keen on prehistory, stop off at the **Museum of the Arts & Sciences**, 1040 Museum Boulevard (Tues–Fri 9am–4pm, Sat & Sun 9am–5pm; $3), a mile south of International Speedway Boulevard (buses #6 and #7 pass close), to scrutinize the bones and fossils dug up from the numerous archeological sites in the area. These include the ferocious-looking reassembled remains of a million-year-old giant ground sloth. The other sections of the constantly expanding museum are intriguingly diverse. A stash of American paintings, furnishings and decorative arts from the seventeenth century onwards illuminates early Anglo-American tastes; a major African collection carries domestic and ceremonial objects from thirty of the continent's cultures; and Cuban paintings spanning two centuries (donated by Cuba's former dictator, Batista, who spent many years of exile in a comfortable Daytona Beach house), which provide a glimpse of the island nation's major artistic movements.

West to Daytona International Speedway

About three miles west along International Speedway Boulevard (bus #9) stands the ungainly configuration of concrete and steel which has done much to promote Daytona's name around the world: the **Daytona International Speedway**, home of the Daytona 500 stock-car meeting, and a few other less famous races. When high speeds made racing on Daytona's sands unsafe, the solution was this 150,000-capacity temple to high-performance thrills and spills, which opened in 1959.

Though it can't capture the excitement of a race (for details of which, see the box overleaf), the guided minibus **tour** (daily 9am–5pm except on race days; $3) is the only way to get in without buying a race ticket, and to witness the sheer size of the place and the remarkable gradient of the curves, which help make this the fastest racetrack in the world – 180mph is not uncommon.

DAYTONA SPEED WEEKS

The Daytona Speedway hosts eight major race meetings each year, starting in early February with the **Rolex 24**: a 24-hour race for GT prototype sports cars. A week or so later begin the qualifying races leading up to the biggest event of the year, the **Daytona 500** stock-car race in mid-February. Tickets (see below) for this are as common as Florida snow, but many of the same drivers compete in the **Pepsi 400**, held on the first Saturday in July, for which tickets are much easier to get. As well as cars, the track is also used for motorcycle races: **Bike Week**, in early March, sees a variety of high-powered clashes, and the **Daytona Pro-Am** races at the end of October include numerous sprints and a three-hour endurance test.

Tickets (the cheapest are $20–25 for cars, $10–15 for bikes) for the bigger events sell out well in advance, and it's also advisable to book accommodation for those times at least six months ahead.

For **information** and ticket details: ☎904/253-6711.

North to Tomoka State Park and the Bulow Ruins

At the meeting point of the Halifax and Tomoka rivers, just off Hwy-1 six miles north of Volusia Boulevard (bus #3, then a mile's walk), the attractive **Tomoka State Park** (daily 8am–sunset; cars $3.25, cyclists and pedestrians $1) has several hundred acres of marshes and tidal creeks, bordered by magnolias and moss-draped oaks. It's ripe for exploration by canoe (rental in the park), or slightly less effectively by foot along the raised boardwalks.

A fascinating recent addition to the park, the **Fred Dana Marsh Museum** (9.30am–4.30pm; admission included in park entrance fee) details the life and work of the man who, in the 1910s, was the first artist in the US to create large-scale murals depicting "the drama and significance of men at work". In the 1920s, Marsh also designed a then (and in some ways still) futuristic home for himself and his wife in Ormond Beach. Just north of Granada Boulevard on Hwy-A1A, the house can still be seen (no public admission) as, in the park, can Marsh's immense sculpture, *The Legend of the Tomokie*.

Take full advantage of the park by camping overnight (see "Accommodation"), which leaves time to visit the **Bulow Plantation Ruins** (daily 9am–5pm; free), five miles north: the scant and heavily vegetated remains of an eighteenth-century plantation, destroyed by Seminole Indians. A rough, mile-long loop road leads to it off Route 201.

Accommodation

From mid-May to November, scores of small **motels** on South Atlantic Avenue slash their rates to $20–30 a double, cheaper for two people sharing than staying at the youth hostel (see below). These rates go up by $10–15 from December to February, and soar to $60 during March and April (although the demise of Spring Break may serve to stabilize prices between December and mid-May). The choice is almost limitless but any of the following make good beach bases: *Travelers Inn*, no 735 (☎253-3501; ②–③); *Daytona Shores Inn*, no 805 (☎253-1441; ①–③); *Ocean Hut*, no 1110 (☎258-0482; ②–③); *Robin Hood*, no 1150 (☎252-8228; ②–③); *Islander*, no 1233 (☎258-5631; ①–③); *Cove*, no 1306 (☎1-800/828-3251; ②–③); and *Catalina*, no 1400 (☎255-4588; ②–③).

Prices rise steadily as you move north along Atlantic Avenue towards Ormond Beach, where the *Econo Lodge-on-the-Beach*, 295 S Atlantic Avenue (☎1-800/847-8111; ③–⑤), and the *Driftwood Beach Motel*, 657 S Atlantic Avenue (☎677-1331; ②–④), have appealing rates.

Bed and breakfast in Daytona means turning your back on the ocean and heading mainland. The choices are the homely *Coquina Inn*, 544 S Palmetto Avenue (☎252-4969; ④–⑥), and the jacuzzi-equipped *Live Oak Inn*, 444–448 S Beach Street (☎1-800/253-4465; ⑤–⑦).

The Youth Hostel and Camping

Big, lively and superbly positioned for the beach, the **youth hostel**, 140 S Atlantic Avenue (☎258-6937), charges members $12, others $15. The nearest **campgrounds** are less ideally placed: *Nova Family Campground*, 1190 Herbert Street (☎767-0095), ten miles south of mainland Daytona (bus #17B); and *Tomoka State Park* (☎677-3931), four miles north of mainland Daytona (bus #3, see above).

Eating

Major appetites can be satisfied for modest outlay at several buffet restaurants: *Kay's Coach House*, 734 Main Street (☎253-1944), *Shoney's*, 2558 N Atlantic Avenue (☎255-9054), and *Checkers*, 219 S Atlantic Avenue (☎239-0010), all of which have buffet breakfasts. Later in the day, *Shoney's* offers help-yourself lunches and dinners, *Checkers* has an all-you-can-eat dinner session, as does the *Manor Buffet*, 747 Ridgewood Avenue (☎253-3359).

If you're watching the calories, forego the buffet blow-outs in favor of regular diner food offered by the *Main Street Cafe*, 819 Main Street (☎257-2323), and the *Seabreeze Cafe*, 316 Seabreeze Boulevard (☎258-0510).

Slightly pricier but with a greater lunch or dinner choice are *Julian's*, 88 S Atlantic Avenue (☎677-6767), a dimly lit mock-Tahitian lounge with a large and good menu; *Lighthouse Landing*, beside the Ponce Inlet lighthouse (☎761-9271), strong on fresh seafood; *Brewsters*, 4511 S Atlantic Avenue (☎760-0810), for seafood or burgers beside the ocean; *Aunt Catfish's*, 4009 Halifax Drive, a few miles south of Daytona in Port Orange (☎767-4768), which has mighty portions of ribs and seafood prepared to traditional Southern recipes; if a desire for Japanese food hits, head for one of the two branches of *Sapporo*, 501 Seabreeze Boulevard (☎257-4477) and 3340 S Atlantic Avenue (☎756-0480).

Nightlife

The full effect of the curtailing of Spring Break on Daytona's **nightlife** remains to be seen, but even without the annual invasion of party-crazed students, the town seems likely to retain its reputation as one of the best spots on Florida's east coast for making merry when the sun goes down. The nucleus of the beachside action is *HoJo's Party Complex*, 600 N Atlantic Avenue (☎255-4471; $3–10), with bars, discos, live rock and reggae and ceaseless wet T-shirt competitions. There's more rabble-rousing at *Razzles*, 611 Seabreeze Boulevard (☎257-6236), *Ocean Deck*, 127 S Ocean Boulevard (☎253-5224), *701 South*, 701 S Atlantic Avenue (☎255-8431), and *Waves*, inside the *Marriot*, 100 N Atlantic Avenue (☎254-8200). Danceable **nightclubs** with a less collegiate crowd are the *Checker Café*, 219 S Atlantic Avenue (☎255-0251), and *Coliseum*, 176 N Beach Street (☎257-9982).

Simply for a **drink**, the *Boothill Saloon*, 318 Main Street (☎258-9506), and *Froggies*, 800 Main Street (☎253-0330), can be enjoyable, but if you find their biker clientele threatening, alternatives are *The Oyster Pub*, 555 Seabreeze Boulevard (☎255-6348), where the beer is helped down by dirt-cheap oysters and a loud jukebox, and *The Spot*, part of the *Coliseum* complex (see above). For **live music**, look to *The Other Place*, 642 S Atlantic Avenue (☎672-2461), in the Ellinor Village shopping center *Rockin' Ranch*, 801 S Nova Road (☎673-0904), or the cavernous *Finky's*, 640 N Grandview Avenue (☎255-5059), which features country combos and square dancing.

North from Daytona Beach

Assuming you don't want to cut twenty miles **inland** along I-4 or Hwy-92 to DeLand and the Orlando area (see Chapter Five), keep on Hwy-A1A northwards along the coast towards St Augustine – as usual, *Greyhound* buses take the duller Hwy-1. The first community you'll encounter is **FLAGLER BEACH**, fourteen miles from Daytona Beach, comprising a few houses and shops, a pier – and a very tempting beach. Nearby, at the **Flagler Beach State Recreation Area** (daily 8am–sunset; cars $3.25, cyclists and pedestrians $1), a good cross-section of coastal bird life can be spotted, particularly at low tide when freshly exposed sands provide a feast for swift beaks.

Continuing, soon after passing the blazing blooms of **Washington Oaks State Gardens** (daily 8am–sunset; cars $3.25, pedestrians and cyclists $1), you can't mistake **Marineland** (daily 9am–6pm; $12.85), Florida's original sea-creature theme park, whose crumbling Streamline Moderne architecture straddles the road. Instantly the state's biggest tourist draw when it opened in 1938, the subsequent imitations, and the far superior Sea World (see Chapter Five), have reduced Marineland to a shadow of its former self. Dreary shows such as the penguin feed, consisting of fish being shoved into penguin mouths while a barely audible list of penguin facts is recited, explains the often paltry crowds – only the jumping dolphins make the steep entry price remotely worthwhile.

Hwy-A1A crosses a narrow inlet three miles beyond Marineland onto **ANASTASIA ISLAND**, close to the Spanish-built seventeenth-century **Fort Matanzas**. Never conquered, partly due to the sixteen-foot-thick walls and the surrounding moat, even today, the fort is accessible only by **ferry** (departures daily every 15min, 9am–4.30pm; free), but, compared to what lies ahead in history-packed St Augustine, it's of minor appeal.

A better stop might be the **St Augustine Alligator Farm** (daily 9am–5.30pm; $7.95), a few miles further. A vividly colored Toco Toucon (a tropical bird) shrieks at visitors as they enter, and there's a wildlife-infested walk-through swamp. But time your visit to coincide with the "alligator show" (usually twice a day; phone ☎904/824-3337 for exact times), when a keeper drags an alligator around by its tail to demonstrate how the creature expresses anger: it bellows loudly, arches its back and displays a gaping jaw. It's heart-stopping stuff – not least when the handler, sitting on the creature's back, nervously puts his fingers between the gator's teeth.

Once past the Alligator Farm, you're well within reach of St Augustine, whose old center is just across Matanzas Bay, three miles ahead.

St Augustine

With the size and even some of the looks of a small Mediterranean town, there are few places in Florida as quickly engaging as **ST AUGUSTINE**, the oldest permanent settlement in the US and one with much from its early days still intact. St Augustine's eminently strollable narrow streets are lined by carefully renovated reminders of Florida's European heritage and the power struggles that led up to statehood, with plenty to fill a day or two. For variation, just across the small bay on which the town stands are two alluring lengths of beach.

Ponce de León, the Spaniard who gave Florida its name, touched ground here in 1513, but it wasn't until Pedro Menéndez de Avilés put ashore on St Augustine's Day in 1565 that settlement began, with the intention of subduing the Huguenots based to the north (at Fort Caroline, see "The Jacksonville Beaches"). Repeated battles with the British began when Sir Francis Drake's ships razed St Augustine in 1586, but Spanish control was only relinquished when Florida was ceded to Britain in 1763, by which time the town was established as an important social and administrative center – soon to become the capital of East Florida.

Spain regained possession twenty years later, and kept it until 1821 when Florida joined the US. Subsequently, Tallahassee became the capital of a unified Florida, and St Augustine's fortunes waned. A railway and a posh hotel stimulated a turn-of-the-century tourist boom, but otherwise expansion bypassed St Augustine – a fact which inadvertently made possible the restoration programme, starting in the Thirties. This has turned the otherwise quiet, residential community into a magnificent historical showcase.

Arrival and Information

From Anastasia Island, **Hwy-A1A** crosses over Mantanzas Bay into the heart of St Augustine; **Hwy-1** passes a mile west along Ponce de Leon Boulevard. The *Greyhound* station, 100 Malaga Street (☎829-6401), is a fifteen-minute walk from the center.

St Augustine is best seen **on foot**, but if you're in a hurry, the **sightseeing train** (tickets from 170 San Marco Avenue; daily 8am–5pm; $9) makes an hour-long narrated circuit of the main landmarks. St Augustine has no public transportation, though not having a car won't cause any problems in the town itself. Getting to the beaches means either a two-mile hike, renting a **bike** from *Buddy Larsen's*, 130 King Street (☎824-2402), or calling a **taxi** (☎824-8161).

After a few hours of hard exploration, **harbor cruises**, leaving five or six times a day from the City Yacht Pier, near the foot of King Street, make a relaxing break; the 75-minute guided trip around the bay costs $7.

The **visitor center**, 10 Castillo Drive (daily 8.30am–5.30pm; ☎825-1000), has the usual tourist brochures and discount coupons, shows a free film on the history of the town and can fill you in on the numerous local festivals, ranging from torch-lit processions (third Sat in June) to chowder tastings (last weekend in Oct).

The area code for St Augustine and Jacksonville is ☎904.

Accommodation

St Augustine attracts plenty of visitors, most of whom make short stays between May and October, when costs are $10–20 above the winter rates. The Old Town (see below) has many restored inns to indulge in **bed and breakfast**: *Carriage Way*, 70 Cuna Street (☎829-2467; ③–④), *Cordova House*, 16 Cordova Street (☎825-0770; ③–④), and *Kenwood Inn*, 38 Marine Street (☎824-2116; ③–④), are the best priced. To cut costs considerably, use the **youth hostel**, 32 Treasury Street (closed noon–5pm; ☎829-6163; ①), members $10, others $13, with a third night for half price.

Alternatively, cheap **motels** ring the Old Town. The least expensive is the *American Inn*, 42 San Marco Avenue (☎829-2292; ①); further along the same road are *Lantern Lodge*, no 137 (☎824-3321; ①), and *Equinox*, no 306 (☎824-0131; ①). Across the bay from the Old Town but well within striking distance, you'll find the waterside *Anchorage Motor Inn*, 1 Dolphin Drive (☎829-9841; ②–③), and *Lion Motel*, 420 Anastasia Boulevard (☎824-2831; ②–③).

Costs are usually higher **at the beaches**, but the laid-back *Vilano Beach Motel*, 50 Vilano Road (☎829-2651; ②), is a great base for enjoying the North Beach; to the south, the busier St Augustine Beach has more family-oriented weekly rented apartments than motels, though the small *Sea Shore*, 2370 Hwy-A1A (☎471-3101; ②–④), and *Seaway*, 2375 Hwy-A1A (☎471-3466; ②–④) are reliable.

The best place to **camp** is the *Anastasia State Recreation Area* (☎471-3033), four miles south off Hwy-A1A (see "The Beaches").

The Old Town

St Augustine's historic area – or **Old Town** – along St George Street and south of the central plaza, holds well-tended evidence of the town's Spanish period. Equally worthwhile are the lavish structures remaining from the turn-of-the-century resort times, along King Street, just west of the plaza. Deceptively, while St Augustine is small there's a lot to see: an early start, around 9am, will give you a lead on the tourist crowds and should enable a good look at almost everything inside a day.

The Castle

Given the fine state of the **Castillo de San Marcos** (Mon–Sat 8.45am–4.45pm, Sun 8.45am–6pm; free; times of free 20-min talks on the fort and local history are indicated in the courtyard), on the northern edge of the Old Town beside the bay, it's difficult to credit that the fortress was started in the late 1600s. The longevity is due to the design: a diamond-shaped rampart at each corner maximized fire-power, and fourteen-foot-thick coquina (a type of soft limestone found on Anastasia Island) walls reduced vulnerability to attack – as British troops found when they waged a fruitless fifty-day siege in 1702.

Inside, there's not a lot to admire beyond a small museum and echoing rooms – some of them with military and social exhibits – but venturing along the 35-foot-high ramparts gives an unobstructed view over the low-lying city and its waterborne approaches, which the castle protected so successfully.

Along St George Street

Leaving the castle, the little eighteenth-century **City Gate** marks the entrance to **St George Street**, once the main thoroughfare and now a tourist-trampled pedes-

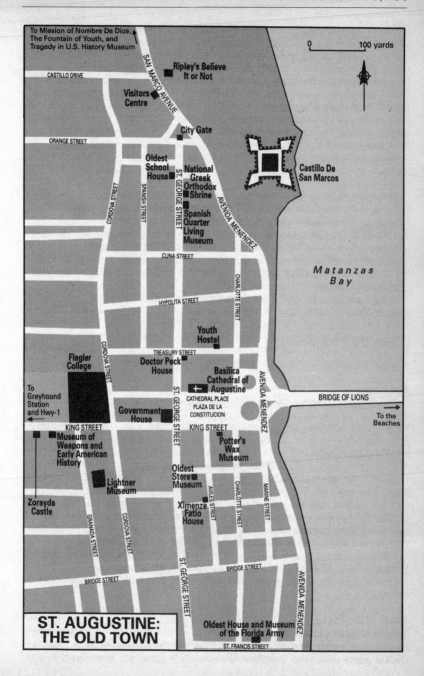

To Mission of Nombre De Dios,
The Fountain of Youth, and
Tragedy in U.S. History Museum

0   100 yards

CASTILLO DRIVE

SAN MARCO AVENUE

Ripley's Believe
It or Not

Visitors
Centre

ORANGE STREET

City Gate

Castillo De
San Marcos

Oldest
School
House

National
Greek
Orthodox
Shrine

CORDOVA STREET

SPANISH STREET

ST. GEORGE STREET

AVENIDA MENENDEZ

Spanish
Quarter
Living
Museum

CUNA STREET

CHARLOTTE STREET

Matanzas
Bay

HYPOLITA STREET

Youth
Hostel

TREASURY STREET

Doctor Peck
House

Flagler
College

CORDOVA STREET

Basilica
Cathedral of
Augustine

AVENIDA MENENDEZ

To
Greyhound
Station
and Hwy-1

CATHEDRAL PLACE
PLAZA DE LA
CONSTITUCION

BRIDGE OF LIONS

Government
House

ST. GEORGE STREET

KING STREET

To the
Beaches

KING STREET

Museum of
Weapons and
Early American
History

Potter's
Wax
Museum

Oldest
Store
Museum

Lightner
Museum

GRANADA STREET

CORDOVA STREET

AVILES STREET

Ximenze
Fatio
House

CHARLOTTE STREET

MARINE STREET

Zorayda
Castle

BRIDGE STREET

BRIDGE STREET

ST. GEORGE STREET

AVENIDA MENENDEZ

ST. AUGUSTINE:
THE OLD TOWN

Oldest House and Museum
of the Florida Army

ST. FRANCIS STREET

trianized strip – but home to plenty of genuine history. At no 14, the **Oldest School House** (summer daily 9am–8pm; rest of the year daily 9am–5pm; $1.75) still has its original red cedar and cypress walls and tabby floor (a mix of crushed oyster shells and lime, common at the time) from the 1700s. These minor architectural points are the main interest: the building only became a school some years later, thereby inadvertently becoming, as the staff are quick to point out, the oldest wooden schoolhouse in the US. Pupils and teacher are now unconvincingly portrayed by speaking wax models. Further along, at no 41, an unassuming doorway leads into the petite **National Greek Orthodox Shrine** (daily 9am–5pm; free), where taped Byzantine choirs, icons and candles are side-by-side with hard-hitting accounts relating the experiences of Greek immigrants to the US – some of whom settled in St Augustine from New Smyrna Beach (see p.185) in 1771.

More directly relevant to the town, and taking up a fair-sized plot at the corner of St George and Cuna streets, the **Spanish Quarter Living Museum** (daily 9am–5pm; $5) includes eight reconstructed homes and workshops. Volunteers disguised as Spanish settlers go about their daily tasks at spinning wheels, anvils and foot-driven wood lathes. Careful, accurate and not at all bad, the museum should be visited either early in the day or during an off-peak period; crocodile lines of camera-wielding tourists substantially lessen the effect. The main entrance is through the Triay House at no 29.

For a more intimate look at local life during a slightly later period, head for the **Doctor Peck House**, at no 143 (Mon–Sat 10am–4pm, Sun 1–4pm; $2). Thought originally to have been the Spanish treasury, by the time of the British takeover in 1763 this was the home of a physician and his gregarious spouse, who turned the place into a high society rendezvous. The Pecks' furnishings and paintings, plus the enthusiastic spiel of the guide, make for an enjoyable tour.

The Plaza

In the sixteenth century, the Spanish king decreed that all colonial towns had to be built around a central plaza, and St Augustine was no exception: St George Street runs into **Plaza de la Constitucion**, a marketplace from 1598, nowadays attracting shade-seekers and the occasional wino. On the north side of the plaza, the **Basilica Cathedral of St Augustine** (Mon–Fri 5.30am–5pm, Sat & Sun 5.30am–7pm; free) adds a touch of grandeur, although it's largely a Sixties remake of the late eighteenth-century original. Periodic **guided tours** (times are sometimes pinned to the door) revel in the painstaking details of the rebuilding – and the undistinguished stained-glass windows. Slightly more worthwhile, the ground floor of **Government House** (daily 10am–4pm; $2), on the west side of the plaza, keeps small displays of objects from the city's various renovation projects and archeological digs. In contrast, on the south side of the square, seeking shelter from a thunderstorm might be the sole justification for entering **Potter's Wax Museum** (summer daily 9am–8pm; winter 9am–5pm; $4.50), populated by effigies of people you may have heard of but probably won't recognize.

South of the Plaza

Tourist numbers lessen as you cross south of the plaza into a web of quiet, narrow streets with as much antiquity as St George Street. At 4 Artillery Lane, the **Oldest Store Museum** (summer Mon–Sat 9am–5pm, Sun 10am–5pm; rest of the year Mon–Sat 9am–5pm, Sun noon–5pm; $3.50) does an excellent job at recreating a general store of the 1880s, filled to the rafters with the produce of the time: curious foods and drinks, fiery medicinal potions and oversized consumer essentials such as apple peelers, cigar molders and wooden washing machines.

Close by, at 20 Aviles Street, the **Ximenze Fatio House** (March–Aug Mon, Thurs, Fri & Sat 11am–4pm, Sun 1–4pm; free) was favored by travellers who predated the town's first tourist boom, drawn by the airy balconies added to the original structure, which was built in 1797 for a Spanish merchant. Though the upper floor is a bit rickety, a walk around is safe and quick in the company of a guide who points out illuminating details.

More substantial history is unfurled a ten-minute walk away at the **Oldest House**, 14 St Francis Street (daily 9am–5pm; $5), occupied from the early 1700s (and, indeed, the oldest house in the town) by the family of an artillery hand at the castle. The second floor was grafted on during the British period, a fact evinced by the bone china crockery belonging to the incumbent, one Mary Peavitt, whose disastrous marriage to a hopeless gambler provided the basis for a popular historical novel, *Maria*, by Eugenia Price (if you're interested, the gift shop has copies). A smaller room, meanwhile, shows the pine-stripped "sidecar" style made popular by the arrival of Flagler's railway: it copies the decor of a train carriage.

Entered through the back garden of the house, the **Museum of the Florida Army** (entry included with admission to the Oldest House; same hours) is as riveting as it sounds, giving an inkling, mainly with old uniforms, of the numerous conficts which have divided Florida over the years. Anybody you might see striding by in modern military garb, incidentally, probably belongs to the Florida National Guard, whose headquarters are across the street.

West of the Plaza: along King Street

A walk west from the plaza along **King Street** bridges the gap between early St Augustine and its turn-of-the-century tourist boom. You'll soon notice, at the junction with Cordova Street, the flowing spires, arches and red-tiled roof of **Flagler College**. Now utilized by liberal arts students, it was – as the *Ponce de Leon Hotel* – an exclusive winter retreat a hundred years ago of the nation's rich and mighty. The hotel was an early attempt by entrepreneur Henry Flagler to exploit Florida's climate and coast, but as he developed properties further south and extended his railway, the *Ponce de Leon* fell from favor – not helped by a couple of freezing winters.

You can **walk around** the campus and the ground floor of the main building (daily 10am–3pm) to admire the Tiffany stained glass and the painstakingly restored painted ceiling in the dining room.

In competition with Flagler, the eccentric Bostonian architect, Franklin W Smith – seemingly obsessed with poured concrete and Moorish design (see the Zorayda Castle, below) – built a rival hotel of matching extravagance directly opposite the *Ponce de Leon*. He eventually sold it to Flagler, who named it the *Alcazar*. Fronted by a courtyard of palm trees and fountains, the building now holds the **Lightner Museum** (daily 9am–5pm; $4), where you could easily pass an hour poring over the Victorian cut glass, Tiffany lamps, antique music boxes and more. Much of it was acquired by publishing ace Otto C Lightner from once-wealthy estates hard hit by the Depression.

Why anybody should attempt to recreate the Alhambra in St Augustine is unclear, but Franklin W Smith (see above), a pioneering architect who'd been wowed by the Moorish architecture he'd seen in Spain, built a copy of a wing of the thirteenth-century palace here, at a tenth of the original size. In 1913, forty years after the **Zorayda Castle**, 83 King Street (daily 9am–5.30pm; $4), was finished, a well-heeled Egyptian consul purchased it to store his ankle-deep carpets and treasures from all points east: a 2300-year-old Sacred Cat Rug, said to put a curse on anyone who stands on it (which is perhaps why it hangs on the wall), and a divinely detailed gaming table inlaid with sandalwood and mother-of-pearl, are just two. As a giant folly stuffed with unanticipated gems, the Zorayda Castle has much charm; only the 25¢-test-your-sex-appeal machine by the exit shatters the mood.

In stark relief, just across the Zorayda's car park, a shack holds the **Museum of Weapons and Early American History** (summer daily 10am–8pm; rest of the year 10am–6pm; $2). Reading the small collection of Civil War diaries gives an interesting personal view of the struggle, but this one-room cache will mainly appeal to survivalist types, with plenty of tools to shoot, stab and batter foes to death.

North of the Old Town: San Marco Avenue and Around

Leading away from the tightly grouped streets of the Old Town, the traffic-bearing **San Marco Avenue**, beginning on the other side of the city gate from St George Street, passes the sites of the first Spanish landings and settlements and some remains of the Timuacua Indians who greeted them. A couple of other potential stops are of much less relevance to the town – but might be good for a laugh.

People either love or loathe them, but if you've never been inside one of the country's several **Ripley's Believe It or Not** collections, you shouldn't pass up the chance. This one, at 19 San Marco Avenue (June–Labor day daily 9am–9pm; rest of the year 9am–6pm; $7.50), isn't the biggest or best, but whether it's a grandfather clock made from clothes pegs, the Lord's Prayer printed on the head of a pin or a toothpick model of the Eiffel Tower – among the stacks of oddities discovered by Ripley as he travelled around the world in the Twenties and Thirties – each object seems stranger than the last, and it can be hard to tear yourself away.

Half a mile further along San Marco Avenue, don't be discouraged by the dull, modern church that now stands in the grounds of **Mission of Nombre de Dios** (summer daily 7am–8pm; rest of the year 8am–6pm; donation requested), a sixteenth-century Spanish mission*. A pathway leads to a 208-foot-tall stainless steel cross, glinting in the sun beside the river on the spot where Menéndez landed in 1565. Soon after, Father Francisco Lopez de Mendoza Grajales celebrated the first Mass in North America, recording that "a large number of Indians watched the proceedings and imitated all they saw", which was a bit unfortunate since the arrival of the Spanish signalled the beginning of the end of the Indians. A side-path takes a mildly interesting course around the rest of the squirrel-

---

*Established by Spanish settlers, **missions** were intended as communities to convert native Americans to Christianity, simultaneously exploiting their labor and seeking to earn their support in possible confrontations with rival colonial powers.

patrolled lawns, passing a few relics of the mission, on the way to a small, ivy-covered re-creation of the original chapel.

Besides the prospect of finding gold and silver, it's said that Ponce de León was drawn to Florida by a belief that the fabled life-preserving "fountain of youth" was located here. Rather tenuously, this fact is celebrated at a mineral spring very near the point where he landed in 1513, in a park at the end of Williams Street (off San Marco Avenue) touted as **The Fountain of Youth** (daily 9am–5pm; $4), about half a mile north of the old mission site. It's unlikely, however, you'll live forever after the drinking the fresh-from-the-earth water handed to you in a small beaker as you enter the springhouse, and the expansive acres of the park have far more significance as an archeological site. Many Timucua Indian relics have been unearthed, and you'll also come across some of the wiry plants which were the base of the "Black Drink", a thick, highly potent concoction which helped the Timucuans achieve mystical states – not pleasing the Spanish, remains of whose settlement have also been found here.

Williams Street also holds the morbid and depressing **Tragedy in US History Museum**, at no 7 (daily 9am–sunset; $4), where even self-confessed ghouls won't get much pleasure from looking at President Kennedy's assassination car and the ambulance that took him to hospital, or the bed of his (alleged) assassin, Lee Harvey Oswald. Here, too, are the tangled remains of Jayne Mansfield's death car, the bullet-spattered vehicle of Bonnie and Clyde, a collection of sickeningly racist correspondence and sundry testaments to human cruelty, including an imported Spanish jail cell still containing the bones of an unfortunate inmate.

The Beaches

If you've reached St Augustine with Hwy-A1A you'll need no introduction to the fine **beaches** which lie just a couple of miles from the Old Town. Few other people do either, especially on weekends when the bronzers, beachcombers and water-sports addicts descend in droves.

Across the bay, **St Augustine Beach** is family terrain, but here you'll also find the **Anastasia State Recreation Area** (daily 8am–sunset; cars $3.25, cyclists and pedestrians $1), offering a thousand protected acres of dunes, marshes, scrub and a wind-beaten group of live oaks, linked by nature walks – though most people come here to catch a fish dinner from the lagoon. In the other direction (take May Street, off San Marco Avenue), **Vilano Beach** pulls a younger crowd and marks the beginning of a dazzling strand continuing for twenty undeveloped miles all the way to Jacksonville Beach (see below).

Eating and Nightlife

The tourist throng on and around St George Street usually makes eating in the old town pricier than it should be, particularly for dinner. Early in the day, however, get a coffee or **breakfast** from *Cuzzin's Sandwich Shoppe*, 124 St George Street (☎829-8967); or cross south of the plaza to *Café Camacho*, 11 Aviles Street (☎824-7030), for cut-rate breakfasts and good-sized **lunches**. Also worth a lunch break are *Bayfront Delights*, 1 King Street (☎829-0159), a self-service bakery with seafood salads and sandwiches; the *Café Alcazar*, 25 Granada Street (☎824-7813), in the antique mall behind the Lightner Museum, for stylish snacks; and *Scarlett O'Hara's*, 70 Hypolita Street (☎824-6535), for tasty soups and salads.

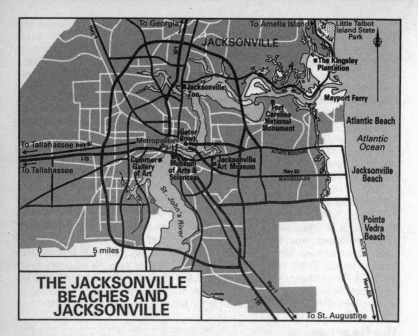

Most of the above are closed for **dinner** (though *Scarlett O'Hara's* does excellent fried crayfish suppers), and an evening meal for under $15 in the Old Town takes some finding. *The Chimes*, 12 Avenida Menendez (closes at 10pm; ☎829-8141), and *San Marco Grille*, 123 San Marco Avenue (☎824-2788), may oblige; otherwise head across the bay. On Anastasia Boulevard, *El Toro Con Sombrero*, no 10 (☎842-8852), is a rowdy bar with Mexican food, jumping until 1am; *O'Steen's*, no 205 (☎829-6974), serves fish and shrimp until 8.30pm; and the *Gypsy Cab Company*, no 828 (☎824-8244), has Greek, Italian and Cajun food in an Art Deco setting.

Nightlife
Try to exhaust yourself during the day because St Augustine has limited **nightlife**. In the Old Town, have a **drink** at the tavern-like *White Lion*, 20 Cuna Street (☎829-2388); among the floor-singers and (taped) Gregorian chant at *Monk's Vineyard*, 56 St George Street (☎824-5888); during the 5–7pm happy hours at *Scarlett O'Hara's* (see "Eating"); or squeeze into the compact *Milltop*, 19 St George Street (☎829-2329). You could also sip a cocktail overlooking the ocean from the deck bar of *Panama Hatties*, 2125 S Hwy-A1A (☎471-2255).

Onward: the Jacksonville Beaches

However good the beaches around St Augustine may be, they're just the start of an unblemished coastal strip running northwards for twenty miles alongside Hwy-A1A, with nothing but the ocean on one side and the swamps and marshes of the Talamato River (the local section of the intracoastal waterway) on the other. The scene begins to change when you near the sculptured golf courses and half-million-dollar homes of **PONTE VEDRA BEACH** – one of the most exclusive communities in northeast Florida. Despite laws to the contrary, there is only one public access point to the beach in Ponte Vedra (off Ponte Vedra Boulevard, which splits from Hwy-A1A near Mickler Landing) but it's worth finding: the crowd-free sands are prime beachcombing terrain, retreating tides often leaving shark's teeth among the more common ocean debris.

Four miles on, **JACKSONVILLE BEACH** is much less snooty: an affable beachside community whose residents relax here and commute to work in the city of Jacksonville, twelve miles inland. The damage inflicted by a hurricane in 1976 perhaps accounts for the uncluttered feel, although a current nine-block-wide redevelopment scheme may alter the cheery seaside mood. As it is, the place is inexplicably neglected by tourists outside of the summer months. The **pier** is the center of activity, and a fried-fish sandwich from its snack bar is the right accompaniment for observing novice surfers grappling with modest-sized breakers.

Cross Atlantic Boulevard, three miles north of the pier, and you're in the slightly more commercialized **ATLANTIC BEACH**, primarily of importance for its restaurants and nightlife (see below). Just north of Atlantic Beach, downbeat Mayport is dominated by its naval station, berth to some of the biggest aircraft carriers in the US Navy. It's best seen through a car window on the way to the Mayport ferry, crossing the St Johns River, and the barrier islands beyond (see "Towards Amelia Island").

Off the Beaches

Only two things are likely to drag you away from the beaches. The **American Lighthouse Museum**, 1011 N Third Street (Tues–Sat 10am–5pm; free), has a moderately time-filling collection of paintings, drawings, photos, plans and models of lighthouses and ships. Further away, a few miles inland on Girvin Road (off Atlantic Boulevard), the **Fort Caroline National Monument** (daily 9am–5pm; free) offers a more historical interlude: a small museum details the significance of the restored Huguenot fort here, which stimulated the first Spanish settlement in Florida (see "St Augustine"). Another reason to come is the great view from the fort across the mile-wide St Johns River and its ocean-going freighters.

Sleeping, Eating and Nightlife

In winter there'll be plenty of bargains, but during the summer be ready to spend $40–55 for a basic **motel** room, and book ahead. *Ocean View*, 60 Ocean Boulevard Drive (☎246-9514; ②–③), *Surfside*, 1236 N First Street (☎246-1583; ②–③), and *Golden Sands*, 127 S First Avenue (☎249-4374; ②–③), have the lowest rates. If you don't mind staying six miles inland, save a few dollars by using the *Econo Lodge*, 2300 Philips Highway (☎1-800/446-6900; ②), near the junction of I-95 and Hwy-90. With a tent, you can **camp** at the *Kathryn Hanna Park*, 500 Wonderwood Drive (☎249-2316), just south of Mayport.

For **eating**, *Beach Hut Café*, 1281 S Third Street (☎249-3516), and *Ellen's Kitchen*, 1824 S Third Street (☎246-1572), are basic, reliable and cheap. Slightly more costly are the fancy variations on deli staples at the *Sun Dog Diner*, 207 S Atlantic Boulevard (☎241-8221), or the health-conscious cuisine of *Heaven on Earth*, 363-14 Atlantic Boulevard (☎249-6252).

Nightlife is strong: *Pier 7*, 401 N First Street (☎246-6373), is a vibrant disco with big crowds and drink specials; *Einstein A Go Go*, 327 N First Street (☎249-4646), is a studeny showcase for alternative sounds and poetry readings; and *Baja Beach Club*, 222 Ocean Front (☎246-7701), hosts anything from Acid House raves to wet T-shirt contests. To escape the beach scene, head for *Palm Valley Bridge Restaurant & Lounge*, on Route 210 by the intracoastal waterway (☎285-1364), which has live bands most weekends and is always good for a drink.

Inland: Jacksonville

With long-established lumber and coffee industries, and the deep St Johns River making it a major transit point for seaborne cargo, **JACKSONVILLE** has traditionally been a place of hard work, expecting pleasure-seeking visitors to stick to the beaches, twelve miles east, and has long been suspicious of anything liable to upset its stability – even scaring the home-seeking US film industry off to California in the 1910s. Lately, with a growing white-collar sector easing the blight of years of heavy industry, there have been efforts to heighten Jacksonville's appeal with parks and riverside boardwalks, but the sheer size of the city – at 841 square miles, the second largest in the country – lessens its character and makes it an impossible nut to crack without a vehicle. For all that, Jacksonville is not an unwelcoming place, and will sufficiently consume a day – even if you spend most of it strolling the riverside downtown.

Downtown Jacksonville

Leaning on local businesses to divert some of their profits into area improvement schemes, an enlightened city administration has helped make **downtown Jacksonville** much less the forbidding forest of corporate high-rises that it initially looks. The St John's River snakes through the city center, dividing downtown Jacksonville in two. Not much on either bank can seriously interrupt a waterside walk.

The North Bank

Within four blocks of Bay Street on the **north bank** of the river, you'll find the few structures that survived the 1901 fire – which claimed much of early Jacksonville – and some of the more distinctive buildings from subsequent decades. These are best examined with the aid of the free *Downtown Walking* leaflet from the Convention and Visitors Bureau. Two notables are the heavily restored **Florida Theater**, 128 E Forsyth Street, which opened in 1927 and become a center of controversy thirty years later when Elvis Presley's pelvic thrusts shocked the city's burghers; and the **Morocco Temple**, 219 N Newnan Street, built by Henry John Kluthco, a classically minded architect who arrived to rebuild Jacksonville after the 1901 fire but later converted to Frank Lloyd Wright-inspired Modernism and erected this sphinx-decorated masterpiece in 1912.

The South Bank

To cross to the **south bank** of the river, take the *River Taxi* ($2 one way; $3 round trip) from the dock beside the gleaming *Landing* shopping mall, between Water Street and the river, and you'll be dropped next to a mile-long pathway

---

THE SKYWAY MONORAIL

For an overview of downtown Jacksonville, take the **Skyway monorail** (Mon–Thurs 6.30am–9pm, Fri 6.30am–10pm, Sat 9am–10pm; 25¢) from the corner of Bay and Pearl streets to the Conference Center, a five-minute journey at eye-level to the high-rise offices. The service is planned to be extended to cover more of the city.

---

called the Riverwalk. A westerly trot along this brings you first to the **Jacksonville Historical Center** (Mon–Sat 11am–6pm, Sun noon–6pm; free), a brief but interesting "walk-through" account of the city's origins and growth. Next comes the forgettable **Maritime Museum** (daily except Tues 11am–4pm; free), marking the city's ship-building industry with models and drawings of sea-going vessels, followed by the oversized **Friendship Fountain** (best seen at night when colored lights illuminate its gushing jets). Finally, the **Museum of Science and History** (Mon–Fri 10am–5pm, Sat 10am–6pm, Sun 1–5pm; $6) holds educational hands-on exhibits, primarily aimed at kids. Adults may prefer the hi-tech trips around the cosmos on offer in the planetarium, admission included.

Beside the museum, dwarfed by neighboring office towers, the tiny **St Pauls Episcopal Church** is a hundred-year-old example of the "Carpenter Gothic" building style. Don't bother going inside – the church is now used for secular purposes – but read the plaque outside recalling naturalist William Bartram, who passed this way in the 1750s and briefly described "Cow-ford", as Jacksonville was then known, in his journal – see "Books" in *Contexts*.

Out from Downtown Jacksonville

With a car, it's easy to zip between the likely points of call scattered about this nebulous city, but it's much harder – and frankly not worth the effort – to do the same thing by bus. A good scrutiny of the art collections will take up an afternoon, but if you feel like being outside, make for Metropolitan Park, or – especially with kids along – the extensive acreage of the zoo.

Jacksonville Art Museum and the Cummer Gallery

In this city of commerce and industry, you might not expect much from the **Jacksonville Art Museum** (Tues, Wed & Fri 10am–4pm, Thurs 10am–10pm, Sat noon–5pm, Sun 2–5pm; $3), which you'll find at 4160 Boulevard Center Drive, three miles from downtown Jacksonville and half a mile from the #BH 2 bus stop (from the downtown area, use the weekdays-only "riverside Shuttle" bus). However, the sizeable stock of ancient Chinese and Korean porcelain turns many knowledgeable heads, and the smaller selection of pre-Columbian objects shouldn't be missed. The museum's main purpose, though, is to provide support and studios for local artists; frequently the workspaces are open to the public – details from the reception desk. There's more art across the city, just south of the Fuller Warren river bridge, in the **Cummer Gallery of Art**, 829 Riverside Drive (Tues–Fri 10am–4pm, Sat & Sun 2–5pm; free), inside the former home of the wealthy Cummer family. The spacious rooms and sculpture-lined corridors, however, suggest the collection is more extensive than it really is. Despite the roster of prominent European names from the thirteenth to nineteenth centuries – with solid rather than brilliant representations of their work – the American art is the strongest feature: Edmund Gredcen's smokey cityscape *Brooklyn Bridge East*

River and Martin Heade's *St Johns River* are particularly evocative. Afterwards, take a stroll through the flower-packed gardens, which reach down to the river.

The Gator Bowl and Metropolitan Park

From all over Jacksonville you can see the floodlights of the 82,000-seat **Gator Bowl**, scene of the Florida–Georgia college football clash each November (an excuse for 48 hours of city-wide drinking and partying; tickets for the actual match are notoriously hard to get) and other less hysteria-inducing games throughout the season. Outside of match days, the main reason to visit is the neighboring **Metropolitan Park**, a plot of riverside greenery which has enjoyable free events most weekends – and some big free rock concerts during spring and autumn. In midweek, it's often deserted and makes a fine spot for a quiet riverside picnic. The "Northside Connector" bus stops close.

Jacksonville Zoo

Previously a sad place of restrictive cages and poorly utilized space, **Jacksonville Zoo** (daily 9am–5pm; $4) is fast developing into one of the best around, giving its inmates plenty of space to prowl, pose and strut. A justifiable source of pride are the white rhinos, seldom bred in captivity, who live in the seven-acre "African veldt". The zoo is on Hecksher Drive, just off I-95 north of downtown Jacksonville; bus #NS 10 stops outside – but only on weekends.

Information and practical details

In downtown Jacksonville, the **Convention and Visitors Bureau**, 3 Independent Drive (Mon–Fri 8am–5pm; ☎798-9148), has plenty of tourist leaflets and discount vouchers, and is an easy walk from the *Greyhound* station at 10 Pearl Street (☎356-5521). Some *Greyhound* services also stop in the grey surburbia of South and West Jacksonville – don't get off at either. The **train** station is an awkward six miles northwest of downtown at 3570 Clifford Lane (☎1-800/872-7245), from which a **taxi** (☎345-5511) downtown will cost around $8. The **local bus service** (☎630-3100) is geared to ferrying locals to and from work, by-passing many useful places and closing down early.

By bus, the journey between the **beaches** and downtown Jacksonville takes around fifty minutes with #**BS 1** (along Atlantic Boulevard), #**BS 2** (along Beach Boulevard) or #**BS 3** (from Mayport). There's also the **"Beaches Flyer"**, a quicker rush-hour service along Beach Boulevard.

Accommodation

The city's far-flung layout causes the cheapest **motels** to be around the perimeter, bothersome to get to and from without a car. The best prices are at the chain hotels near the airport, nine miles north of downtown Jacksonville: *Days Inn*, 1181 Airport Road (☎741-4000; ②–③), *Airport Motor Inn*, 1500 Airport Road (☎741-4331; ②), and *Red Roof Inn*, 14701 Airport Entrance Road (☎741-4488; ②). Downtown, beds are primarily for expense account holders: the *Hospitality Inn*, 901 N Main Street (☎355-3744; ③), is the cheapest among them. Scenically sited on the south bank of the river, the *Marina*, 1515 Prudential Drive (☎396-5100; ⑤), might be worth a flutter. Another cosy option is the **bed and breakfast** at *The House on Cherry Street*, 1844 Cherry Street (☎384-1999; ④), about three miles south of downtown.

Eating

On downtown Jacksonville's north bank, *Chow Down II*, 4 E Bay Street (☎353-2469), and *Akel's Deli*, 130 N Hogan Street (☎356-5628), offer **snacks** and quick **lunches**. Eating in the *Landing* mall is slightly pricier, though tempting: *Founder's Food Hall* is a lively fast-food emporium; *Fat Tuesday* offers spicy cajun lunches (☎353-1229); and *Harry's Oyster Bar* (☎353-4927) has a generous seafood menu. On the south bank, *Worman's Deli*, 1712 San Marco Boulevard (☎396-6592), and *The Loop*, 2014 San Marco Boulevard (☎384-7301), have good-priced general menus. More adventurously, the *Filling Station*, 1004 Hendricks Avenue (☎398-3663), concocts healthy lunches.

The pick of the city's many stylish **dinner** restaurants is the *Wine Cellar*, 1314 Prudential Drive (☎398-8989), where a well-prepared fish or meat meal costs upwards of $15.

Nightlife and Moving On

Nightlife in Jacksonville is a pale shadow of the rave-ups at the beach (see "The Jacksonville Beaches"), but check out the *Milk Bar*, 128 W Adams Street (☎356-MILK), likely to have anything from house and reggae sounds to live bands and 25¢-beer nights, and *Carib*, 43 W Monroe Street (☎359-0134), which has reggae and calypso sounds at weekends.

Jacksonville's position near Florida's northern border means you have to make a decision about where to **head next**. Swinging westward along I-10 takes you into northern Central Florida (see Chapter Five) and on towards the Panhandle (Chapter Seven); an appealing alternative – if only for a day trip – are the barrier islands, especially Amelia Island, thirty miles northeast along the coast, though these are only reachable by car.

Towards Amelia Island

From Jacksonville, Hwy-105 will take you along the north side of the St Johns River towards the islands marking Florida's northeast corner. A better route, though, is Hwy-A1A from the Jacksonville beaches, which crosses the river with the tiny **Mayport ferry** (roughly every 30min 6.50am–10.30pm; cars $1.50, cyclists and pedestrians 50¢). During the enjoyable short voyage pelicans swoop overhead to feed off the nearby shrimping boats.

The Kingsley Plantation and Little Talbot Island

Near the ferry's landing point, Hwy-A1A combines with Hwy-105 and soon passes the tree-lined driveway of the **Kingsley Plantation** (daily 9am–5pm; free; guided tours at various times; details on ☎251-3537; $1), centerpiece of which is the elegant riverside house bought in 1817 by a hunchbacked Scotsman called Zephaniah Kingsley. The house, and its 3000 acres, were acquired with the proceeds of slavery, of which Kingsley was a fanatical advocate and leading international dealer, amassing a fortune through the import and export of Africans. The restored plantation reveals the plight of the forced arrivals, and much about Kingsley's wife: a Madagascan woman who ran the plantation and lived in extravagant style – perhaps compensating for her years as Kingsley's servant.

One mile ahead, Hwy-A1A runs through **Little Talbot Island State Park** (daily 8am–sunset; cars $3.25, cyclists and pedestrians $1), which consumes almost the whole of a thickly forested 2500-acre barrier island. The park has two tree-shaded, ocean-facing picnic areas, but with a bit more energy, explore the superb four-mile **hiking trail**, winding through a pristine landscape of oak and magnolia trees, wind-beaten sand dunes and a chunk of the park's five-mile-long beach. If you're smitten by the natural charms and want to save the bother of finding accommodation on Amelia Island (see below), use the **campground** (☎251-3231) on the northwestern side of the park, beside the Fort George River.

Amelia Island

Most first-time visitors to Florida would be hard pushed to locate **AMELIA ISLAND**, which perhaps explains why this finger of land, thirteen miles long and never more than two across, at the state's northeastern extremity, is so peaceful and only modestly commercialized, despite the unbroken silver swathe of Atlantic beach gracing its eastern edge. Matching the sands for interest, Fernandina Beach, the island's sole town, was a haunt of pirates before transforming itself into an outpost of Victorian high society – a fact proven by its immaculately restored old center.

Some parts of the island are being swallowed by upmarket resorts (much of the southern half is taken up by the *Amelia Island Plantation*, a golf and tennis resort with private walking and biking trails, expensive restaurants and $200-a-night rooms), but you needn't think twice about coming – provided you have a car. In Fernandina, at least, they still concern themselves more with the size of the shrimp catch than with pandering to tourists.

Fernandina Beach

Hwy-A1A runs right into the effortlessly walkable town of **FERNANDINA BEACH**, whose Victorian heyday is soon apparent in the restored buildings lining the short main drag, Centre Street. The English spelling reflects bygone political to-ing and fro-ing: the Spanish named the town but the British named the

---

SOME AMELIA ISLAND HISTORY: THE EIGHT FLAGS

The only place in the US to have been under the rule of eight flags, Amelia Island was visited by Huguenot settlers in 1562. The Spanish came and founded a mission, which was destroyed in 1702 by the British, who returned forty years later to govern the island (naming it in honour of King George II's daughter). The ensuing Spanish administration was interrupted by the US-backed "Patriots of Amelia Island", who ruled for a day during 1812; the Green Cross of the Florida Republic flew briefly in 1817; and, oddest of all, the Mexican rebel flag appeared over Amelia Island the same year. US rule has been disturbed only by Confederate occupancy during 1861.

These shifts reflect the ebb and flow of allegiances between the great sea-trading powers, as well as the island's geographically desirable location: for many years offering harborage for ocean-going vessels outside US control but within spitting distance of the American border.

streets. Beside the marina, at the western end of Centre Street, you'll spot the vintage train carriage which houses the useful **visitor center** (Mon–Fri 9am–5pm; ☎261-3248).

Remarkably given the present-day calm, President James Monroe described Fernandina as a "festering fleshpot", after the 1807 US embargo on foreign shipping caused the Spanish-owned town to become a hotbed of smuggling and other illicit activities as ways were sought to circumvent the ban. The acquisition of Florida by the US in 1821 didn't diminish Fernandina's importance – this time as a key rail terminal for freight moving between the Atlantic and the Gulf of Mexico.

The Museum of History – and walking around Centre Street

The obvious place to gain insights into the town is the **Museum of History**, 233 S Third Street (Mon–Fri 11am–3pm, donation) – once the town jail – whose scattering of memorabilia is backed up by photographs and maps. The 45-minute **guided tour** of the museum is excellent (Mon–Sat at 11am & 2pm, donation), as are the longer **historical walks** (Mon & Thurs at 3pm from the visitor center; $4) which feature many of the old buildings on and around Centre Street.

Even if you miss the tours, **walking around** on your own is far from dull. Centre Street and the immediate area are alive with Victorian-era turrets, twirls and towers, plus many notable later buildings. Among them, the **St Peter's Episcopal Church**, on the corner with Eighth Street, was completed in 1884 by New York architect Robert S Schuyer, whose name is linked to many local structures. Perhaps eager to experiment, he never used the same style twice. The Gothic used for the church is a long way from the heavy-handed Italianate of the **Fairbanks Folly**, at the corner of Seventh and Cedar streets, which Schuyer finished for a newspaper editor who had commissioned it as a surprise for his wife: it was; she hated it and refused to step over the threshold.

The Beach

Well suited to swimming and busy with beach sports, the most active of the island's **beaches** is at the eastern end of Fernandina's Atlantic Avenue, a mile from the town center. If you don't mind a long hike with sand between your toes, you can walk along the beach to Fort Clinch State Park, three miles north (see below).

North to Fort Clinch State Park

After Florida came under US control, a fort was built on Amelia's northern tip, three miles from Fernandina, to protect seaborne access to Georgia. The fort now forms part of **Fort Clinch State Park** (daily 8am–sunset; cars $3.25, pedestrians and cyclists $1), and provides a home for a gang of Civil War enthusiasts pretending that they're Union soldiers of 1864, the only time the fort saw action. An atmospheric way to see the fort is with the soldier-guided **candle-lit tour** (offered most Fridays and Saturdays during the summer; $2; reservations essential: ☎261-4212). With the pseudo Civil War garrison moaning about their work and meager rations, the tour may sound like a ham job, but in fact it is a convincing, informative – and quite spooky – hour's worth.

The rest of the park can hardly be overlooked: by road, you need to go through several miles of it before reaching the fort, passing an animal reserve (from which overgrown alligators often emerge, so if you do fancy a spot of hiking, stick to the marked **nature trail**), and a turning for the **beach**, where legions of crab-catchers cast their baskets off a long fishing jetty. From the jetty, there's an immaculate view of Cumberland Island (only accessible with ferries from St Marys, on the Georgia mainland), a Georgian nature reserve famed for its wild horses – if you're lucky, a few will be galloping over the island's sands. Less inspiringly, you might also catch a glimpse of a nuclear-powered submarine gliding towards Cumberland Sound and the massive Kings Bay naval base.

Accommodation

The cheapest accommodation is a few miles south of Fernandina along Fletcher Avenue, with four **motels**: *Surf Inn*, no 3199 (☎261-5711; ②–③), the *Seaside Inn*, no 1998 (☎261-0954; ②–③), *Ocean View*, no 2801 (☎261-0193; ③), and *Beachside*, no 3172 (☎261-4236; ②–③). Should these be full, the next-best budget bet is *Shoney's Inn*, 2707 Sadler Road (☎277-2300; ③–④).

With a bit more cash, savor Fernandina's historic atmosphere by staying in one of the town's antique-filled **bed and breakfast inns**: the *Bailey House*, 28 S Seventh Street (☎261-5390; ④–⑤), and the *1735 House*, 584 S Fletcher Avenue (☎261-5878; ④), do much to evoke the past. More unusually, a far-in-advance booking might secure the $125-a-night *Lighthouse*, 748 Fletcher Avenue (☎261-5878; ⑥), which really *is* a small lighthouse, with space for four people.

Eating and Nightlife

For its size, the island has an exceptionally good number of places to **eat**, the bulk of them on and around Fernandina's Centre Street. *Marina*, 101 Centre Street (☎261-5310), is a convivial seafood-based restaurant and gossip parlor; the Chinese food of the *Bamboo House*, 614 Centre Street (☎261-0508), can be inexpensively sampled from the lunchtime buffet; an all-you-can eat lunch is also offered at *Cousin's Pizza & Pasta*, 927 S Fourteenth Street (☎277-4611).

A touch more expensively, *Brett's Waterway Cafe*, at the Fernandina Harbor Marina at the end of Centre Street (☎261-2660), has generous American meals and great views; and *Surf*, 3199 S Fletcher Avenue (☎261-5711), delivers tasty seafood beside the ocean. For a slap-up gourmet dinner, try the classy *Beech Street Grill*, corner of Eighth and Beech streets (☎277-3662).

You'll also find a limited menu of plain and simple dishes at the *Palace Saloon*, 117 Centre Street (☎261-6230), though you might prefer to save your visit to what's claimed to be the oldest **bar** in Florida – built in 1890 – for a night-time drink, not least because few other places warrant an after-dark investigation.

travel details

Trains
From Jacksonville to Miami (2 daily; 8hr 45min); Orlando/Tampa (2 daily; 3hr 5min/4hr 49min); Tallahassee/Pensacola (1 daily; 4hr 15min/8hr 50min).

Buses
From Cocoa to Daytona Beach (6 daily; 3hr 40min); Jacksonville (6 daily; 5hr 35min); Melbourne (5 daily; 30min); New Smyrna Beach (4 daily; 1hr 45min); Titusville (5 daily; 30min).

From Daytona Beach to Jacksonville (9 daily; 1hr 45min); Orlando (11 daily; 1hr 5min); St Augustine (3 daily; 1hr 5min).

From St Augustine to Jacksonville (3 daily; 45min).

From Jacksonville to Miami (11 daily; 9hr 15min); Orlando (5 daily; 3hr 15min); St Petersburg (8 daily; 8hr 45min); Tallahassee (5 daily; 2hr 54min); Tampa (8 daily; 6hr 35min).

CHAPTER FIVE

CENTRAL FLORIDA

Most of the broad and fertile expanse of **Central Florida**, stretching between the east and west coasts, was self-absorbed farming country when vacation-mania first struck the beachside strips; only as an afterthought to growing citrus and raising cattle were adventurous visitors ferried by steamboat along the region's rivers and across its gushing springs. Over the last two decades, this picture of tranquillity has been shattered: no section of the state has been affected by modern tourism more dramatically.

In the middle of the region, as contradictory as it may seem, the most visited part of Florida is also one of the ugliest: an ungodly clutter of freeway interchanges, motels, billboards and jumped-up tourist sights, arching around the otherwise affable small city of **Orlando**. The blame for the vulgarity lies with Orlando's near-neighbor, **Walt Disney World**, which since the Seventies has sucked millions of people into the biggest and cleverest theme park complex ever created – inadvertently sparking off a tourist-dollar chase of Gold Rush magnitude on its outskirts. The Disney parks are every bit as polished as their reputation suggests, but their surrounds are no advert for Florida and it's a tragedy that many visitors see no more of the state than this aggressive commercialism.

Encouragingly, the rest of Central Florida is markedly less brash. The slow-paced towns of **South Central Florida** make excellent low-cost bases for cruising the Orlando circuit – provided you're driving – and offer plenty of relaxed diversions in their lake-filled vicinity. Much the same can be said of **North Central Florida**, where tiny villages, far more prevalent than towns, still hold the century-old homes of Florida's pioneer settlers. The biggest surprise here, however, is **Gainesville**, an outpost of learning and liberalism with one of the state's two major universities – a welcome sight so deep in rural surrounds.

Since Walt Disney World redefined the geography of the region, **getting around** Central Florida by **car** has become generally easy and quick – but take time to leave the charmless freeways and journey down some of the multitude of minor routes linking the lesser towns and villages. Non-drivers will find that many of the smaller centers have good *Greyhound* **bus** connections, and some even see twice-daily **trains**. Car-less visitors wanting to get to the Disney parks are dependent on the local **shuttle buses** (see "Getting Around", below).

ACCOMMODATION PRICE CODES

All accommodation prices in this book have been coded using the symbols below. Note that prices are for the least expensive double rooms in each establishment. For a full explanation see p.26 in *Basics*.

①	up to $30	④	$60–80	⑦	$130–180
②	$30–45	⑤	$80–100	⑧	$180+
③	$45–60	⑥	$100–130		

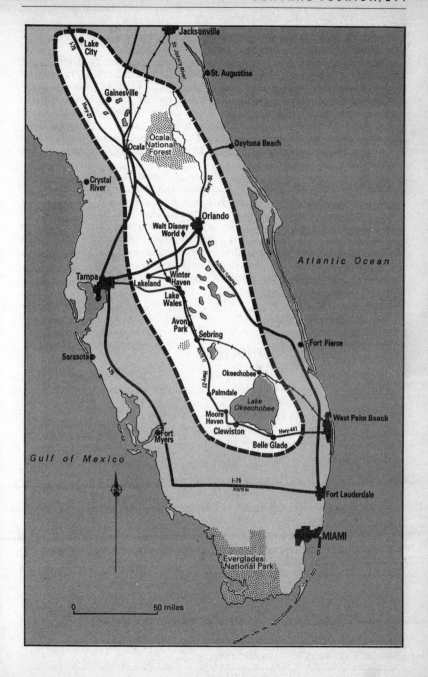

ORLANDO AND AROUND

An insubstantial city in the heart of peninsular Florida that doesn't unduly knock itself out to attract tourists, it's ironic that **Orlando**, a quiet farming town twenty years ago, now has more people passing through its environs than any other place in the state. Reminders of the old Florida are easy to find in and immediately north of Orlando, although most people get no closer to Orlando's heart than a string of motels along Hwy-192, fifteen miles south, or **International Drive**, five miles southwest – a long, brand new boulevard of mid-range hotels, shopping malls and restaurants, so short of character it could be molded from plastic.

The reason for these apparent anomalies is, of course, **Walt Disney World**, a group of state-of-the-art theme parks southwest of Orlando, and pulling 25 million people a year to a previously featureless 43-square-mile plot of scrubland. It's possible to pass through the Orlando area and not visit Walt Disney World, but there's no way to escape its influence: even the road system was reshaped to accommodate the place and, whichever way you look, billboards tout more ways to spend your money. Amid a plethora of fly-by-night would-be tourist targets, only **Universal Studios** and **Sea World** offer serious competition to the most finely realized concept in escapist entertainment anywhere on earth.

> The area code for the Orlando area is ☎407

Arrival and Information

The region's international **airport** is nine miles south of downtown Orlando. Shuttle buses run from the airport to any hotel or motel in the Orlando area for $10–15. If you're headed for downtown Orlando use local bus #11, or #42 for International Drive (both buses depart from the airport's "A Side" concourse, very 60min between around 6am and 9pm). A taxi to downtown Orlando, International Drive or the motels on Hwy-192 will cost around $40.

Arriving by **bus** or train, you'll wind up in downtown Orlando at the *Greyhound* terminal, 555 N Magruder Avenue (☎843-7720), or the **train station**, 1400 Slight Boulevard. Other train stops in the area are in Winter Park (150 Morse Boulevard) and Kissimmee (111 Pakin Avenue).

Giveaway magazines such as *See Orlando* and *Best Read Guide*, strewn wherever you look, are packed with handy facts, but a better source of reliable **infor-**

▐ ORLANDO AREA ORIENTATION: THE MAJOR ROADS ▐

The major cross-Florida **roads** form a web-like mass of intersections in or around Orlando and Walt Disney World: **I-4** passes southeast–northwest through Walt Disney World and continues in elevated form through downtown Orlando; **Hwy-192** (the **Irlo Bronson Memorial Highway**) crosses I-4 in Walt Disney World and charts an east–west course fifteen miles south of Orlando; **Hwy-528** (the **Beeline Expressway**) stems from I-4 between Walt Disney World and Orlando bound for the east coast; and the **Florida Turnpike** cuts northwest–southeast between Walt Disney World and Orlando.

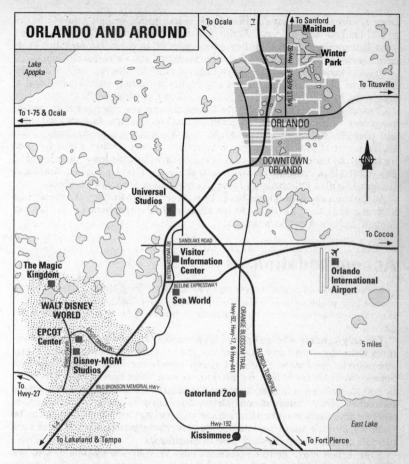

mation is the **visitor information center**, 8445 International Drive (daily 8am–8pm; ☎363-5871), where you should pick up the free *Official Visitor's Guide to Orlando*, plus any of hundreds of leaflets and discount coupons. Nearer, if you're using the motels along Hwy-192, and equally well stocked, is the **Kissimmee-St Cloud CVB**, no 1925 (daily 8am–6pm; ☎1-800/333-KISS).

Getting Around

With most routes operating from 6am to 7.30pm, **local buses** (☎841-8240) converge on the downtown Orlando terminal between Central and Pine streets. You'll need **exact change** (75¢) for the buses if you pay on board, but without it you can buy a ticket from the terminal's information booth. **Useful bus routes** are #1 to Loch Haven and Winter Park; #11 to the airport (a 45-min journey); and #8 to International Drive, where you can catch a shuttle bus (see below) to Walt

Disney World and the area's other major tourist parks, or link with #42 to the airport (an hour-long journey). At the time of writing, a free (or inexpensive) bus – the **International Drive Trolley** – was expected to come into operation year-round along International Drive, between Sea World and Universal Studios.

Orlando **taxis** are expensive: rates begin at $2.25 for the first mile with $1.30 for each additional mile, but for non-drivers they're the only way to get around at night – try *Town & Country* (☎828-3035) or *Yellow Cab* (☎699-9999).

Cheaper than taxis are the **shuttle buses**, minivans or coaches run by private companies connecting the main accommodation areas, such as International Drive and Hwy-192, with Walt Disney World, Sea World and Universal Studios. You should phone at least a day ahead to be picked up, and confirm a time to come back. You pay the driver on board. By a couple of dollars, the least costly is *Rabbit Bus* (☎291-2424), charging $8 return to Walt Disney World, $5 to Sea World and Universal Studios. Otherwise try *Mears Transportation Service* (☎423-5566).

All the main **car rental** firms have offices at or close to the airport; competition is strong and rates are good, so phone around (the numbers are in "Getting Around" in *Basics*) for the best deals.

Accommodation

You'll need to be mobile wherever you stay in the far-flung Orlando area, so price should be a greater consideration than location when looking for **accommodation**. If you're dependent on public transport, however, downtown Orlando is the place to be.

The only genuinely budget-priced accommodations are two hostels in **downtown Orlando**: a quiet area that also has, like neighboring **Winter Park**, several atmospheric old hotels. Scores of cheap motels are lined **along Hwy-192** between Walt Disney World and Kissimmee; many offer special rates which can be yours simply by picking up a discount coupon at one of the information offices mentioned above. **International Drive**, dominated by pricey chain hotels, is where you're likely to end up if you come on a package trip – but bargains can be found by showing up on spec during the slow winter periods. Campgrounds are plentiful on and around Hwy-192 close to **Kissimmee**.

More expensively, there's accommodation in Walt Disney World, too; see "Walt Disney World" for details.

Downtown

Harley Hotel, 151 E Washington St (☎352-0008). An historic, now completely modernized hotel overlooking Lake Eola. ④.

Orlando International Youth Hostel, 227 N Eola Drive (☎843-8888). In an atmospheric residential area, with beds in small dorms for $12 (non-members $15), or single and double private rooms under $30. ①.

Young Women's Community Club, 107 E Hillcrest St (☎425-2502). Women aged 16–54 who are AYH members can get a dorm bed here for $10; the facilities include a pool and small gym. ①.

Winter Park

The Fortnightly Inn, 377 E Fairbanks Ave (☎645-4440). A night or two at this personable 5-room bed and breakfast inn makes a relaxing break from the rampant commercialism of the Orlando area. ④–⑤.

Langford Resort Hotel, 300 E New England Ave (☎644-3400). For facilities and service, the price is reasonable and the location – a leafy Winter Park side street – is great. ⑤.

Park Plaza Hotel, 319 Park Ave (☎647-1072). A Twenties gem stuffed with wicker furniture and brass fittings; be sure to book early. Continental breakfast is included. ⑤.

International Drive and Around

Days Inn Lakeside, 7335 Sand Lake Rd (☎351-1900). An enormous branch of the nationwide chain in a winning lakeside location, with a small beach and three pools. ③–④.

The Floridian, 7299 Republic Drive (☎1-800/445-7299). A mid-sized hotel with an easygoing mood and nicely furnished rooms. ④–⑤.

Gateway Inn, 7050 Kirkman Rd (☎1-800/432-1179). Good-sized rooms, two pools and free shuttle buses to the major theme parks make this good base for non-drivers concentrating on the big attractions. ④–⑤.

Heritage Inn, 9861 International Drive (☎1-800/447-1890). Plain rooms at modest rates, a pool and a breakfast buffet are reasons for staying in this somewhat kitsch shrine to Southern Victoriana; also has live jazz some evenings. ③–④.

The Peabody Orlando, 9801 International Drive (☎1-800/PEABODY). Twenty-seven storeys of luxury rooms primarily aimed at delegates using the massive Orange County Convention Center, across the street. If money's no object and you like your in-room luxuries, and access to a fitness center and floodlit tennis courts, this one's for you. ⑧.

Radisson Inn and Aquatic Center, 8444 International Drive (☎345-0505). Speed-swimming records have been set at the Olympic-sized pool here, though with relaxation more in mind you'll find the spacious rooms and the location, directly opposite the restaurants of the Mercado Mediterranean Mall (see "Eating"), to be a winning combination. ⑤–⑥.

Red Roof Inn, 9922 Hawaiian Court (☎352-1507). Unelaborate but perfectly serviceable budget-range base, with a pool and a coin-op laundromat. ②–④.

Sonesta Villa Resort Orlando, 10000 Turkey Lake Rd (☎352-8051). All rooms are suites with full cooking facilities, and are spread across a ninety-acre lakeside site. ⑤–⑦.

Along Hwy-192

A1 Motel, 4030 W Hwy-192 (☎1-800/231-9196). A medium-sized motel which, being closer to downtown Kissimmee than Walt Disney World, is able to shave a few dollars off the rates of its counterparts a few miles west. ①–②.

Best Western Kissimmee, 2261 E Hwy-192 (☎1-800/944-0062). A good place to be with kids; there's a games room and play area, plus two pools. ②–③.

Casa Rosa, 4600 W Hwy-192 (☎1-800/432-0665). A generally quiet and relaxing motel with mood-enhancing Mediterranean-style architecture. ①.

Flamingo Inn, 801 E Hwy-192 (☎1-800/780-7617). The prices aren't the lowest to be found, but you can rely on the place being clean, tidy and well run; for in-room feasts, microwave ovens are available for $2 a day. ②–③.

Gemini, 4624 W Hwy-192 (☎1-800/648-4148). Offers free coffee and a free shuttle bus to the main theme parks, also has kitchenettes and microwave ovens. ①–②.

Golden Link, 4914 W Hwy-192 (☎1-800/654-3957). A comparatively large motel, with heated pool, a self-service laundromat and rentable refrigerators. ①–②.

Larson's Lodge Kissimmee, 2009 W Hwy-192 (☎1-800/624-5905). Another good place for kids; the rates might be a touch higher than others in the vicinity but under-18s stay for free in their parents' room and facilities include a games room, tennis court and jacuzzi. ②.

Maple Leaf Motel, 4647 W Hwy-192 (☎396-0300). Several people sharing a room will find the special offers here very attractive; cable TV, a pool and coin-op laundromat are among the features. ①.

Olympic Inn, W 4669 Hwy-192 (☎1-800/523-8729). One of the bigger motels in the area, offering a pool, a coin-op laundromat and cable TV, as well as great-value special rates even in high season. ①.

Camping: Kissimmee

Numerous serviceable **campgrounds** stand beside Hwy-192 close to **Kissimmee**. Suited to tents are *Twin Lakes*, 5044 Hwy-192 (☎396-8101), and the *KOA*, 4771 Hwy-192 (☎1-800/247-2728), which also has **cabins** for $25 and free shuttle buses to Walt Disney World. For a more peaceful setting, choose a site beside Lake Tohopekaliga, where the pace is leisurely and more fuss is made about fishing than visiting Mickey Mouse: try *Merry "D" RV Sanctuary*, 4261 Pleasant Hill Road (☎933-5837), or *Richardson's Fish Camp*, 1550 Scotty's Road (☎846-6540).

Orlando

Despite enormous expansion over the last decade, **ORLANDO** remains impressively free of the gross commercialism that surrounds it. Away from the small group of high-rise banks and offices in the downtown area, the bulk of the city comprises smart residential areas enhanced by parks and lakes. Historical leftovers and art collections spread through several sections will diversely fill a day – and, for anyone whose knowledge of the state begins and ends with theme parks, will give at least a brief taste of genuine Florida living. Usefully for non-drivers, bus #1 from downtown Orlando links the key areas.

Downtown Orlando

Except to sample the artificial charms of Church Street Station (see "Nightlife"), or to stay at the two hostels (see "Accommodation"), few visitors come to **DOWNTOWN ORLANDO** at all, which, despite the half-dozen corporate towers in its midst, is still redolent, in size and mood, of the tobacco-chewing cow-town that it used to be. Everything of consequence in the tiny district can be covered on foot within an hour.

Begin with a dawdle along **Orange Avenue**, mostly patrolled by lunch-seeking office workers, which passes beneath the Egyptian touches of the late-Twenties *First National Bank*, on the corner with Church Street, and, a few blocks north, the early Art Deco of *McCrory's Five and Dime* building and the Kress Building. Pre-dating the Twenties structure, some of the wooden homes built by Orlando's first white settlers stand around **Lake Eola**, a ten-minute walk east of Orange Avenue. Many are undergoing expensive restoration as their owners strive to become bed-and-breakfast moguls. There's a good view of the houses from the oak-filled park which rings the placid lake, overlooked by elevated freeways. Linger here to contemplate the city's first hundred years – and the fact that Orlando's early black inhabitants didn't live in these leafy environs but were consigned to a much less picturesque district west of the railway line, parallel to Orange Avenue; still today, very much the wrong side of the tracks.

Loch Haven Park and Leu Gardens

A large lawn squeezed between two small lakes, **Loch Haven Park**, three miles north of downtown Orlando, holds three buildings of varied content. The **Orlando Museum of Art** (Tues–Thurs 9am–5pm, Fri 9am–7.30pm, Sat 10am–5pm, Sun noon–5pm; suggested donation $3) is likely to take up at least an hour: a perma-

ORLANDO: DOWNTOWN ORLANDO, WINTER PARK AND MAITLAND

nent collection of pre-Columbian pieces backs up the usually excellent temporary exhibitions of modern American painting, culled from the finest collections in the world and arranged to illustrate a particular artistic genre.

Across the park, the small **Orange County Historical Museum** (Mon–Sat 9am–5pm, Sun noon–5pm; $2) is more liable to jog the memories of elderly locals than excite out-of-towners, although the artefacts and photos, re-created hotel lobbies and grocer's shops help form a picture of the time when, far from being a global tourist mecca, Orlando epitomized the American frontier town. If you have kids, study the history while they roam the adjacent **Science Center** (Mon–Thurs 9am–5pm, Fri 9am–9pm, Sat noon–9pm, Sun noon–5pm; $4), where hands-on exhibits explain the fundamentals of physics to formative minds.

Leu Gardens

A mile east of Loch Haven Park, **Leu Gardens**, 1730 N Forest Avenue (daily 9am–5pm; $3, including a tour of Leu House) was purchased by a green-fingered Orlando businessman in 1936 to show off plants collected from around the world. After seeing and sniffing the orchids, roses, azaleas and the largest camellia collection in the eastern US, take a trip around **Leu House** (guided tours only; on the hour Mon 1–3pm, Tues–Fri 10am–3pm, Sat & Sun 1–3pm), a nineteenth-century farmhouse bought and lived in by Leu and his wife, now maintained in the simple but elegant style of their time and laced with family mementoes.

Winter Park

A couple of miles northeast of Loch Haven Park, **WINTER PARK** has been socially a cut above the rest of the city since being launched in the 1880s as "a beautiful winter retreat for well-to-do people". For all its obvious money – a mix of new yuppie dollars and old wealth – Winter Park is a very likeable place, with a pervasive sense of community and a scent of California-style New Age affluence.

On Fairbanks Avenue, which brings traffic from Loch Haven into Winter Park, stand the hundred-year-old Mediterranean Revival buildings of **Rollins College**, the oldest college in the state and a tiny, if highly regarded, seat of liberal arts education. Other than neat landscaping, the campus has just one thing in its favor: the **Cornell Museum of Fine Art** (Tues–Fri 10am–5pm, Sat & Sun 1–5pm; free), which offers a staid bundle of modest nineteenth-century European and American paintings but does better with temporary shows, and an eccentric collection of old watch keys.

You'll find a more complete art collection a mile east of the college on Osceola Avenue, at the **Palosek Foundation**, no 633 (Oct–June Wed–Sat 10am–noon & 1–4pm, Sun 1–4pm; free): the former home of Czech-born sculptor Albin Palosek, who arrived penniless in the US in 1901 and did little more for the next fifty years than win big-money commissions, eventually channelling his profits into creating this house and studio which carries more than two hundred of his technically accomplished, realist pieces. Without a sculptor's eye for detail, however, you might derive greater pleasure from the Morse Museum.

Along Park Avenue: the Morse Museum and boat tours

Winter Park compounds its upmarket status along its showcase street, **Park Avenue** (which meets Fairbanks Avenue close to Rollins): a row of top-of-the-range outfitters, jewellers and spick-and-span restaurants. Should window-shopping and fine dining lack appeal, drop into the **Morse Museum of American Art**, just off Park Avenue at 133 Wolbourne Avenue (Tues–Sat 9.30am–4pm, Sun 1–4pm; $2.50), which houses the collections of Charles Hosmer Morse, one of Winter Park's founding fathers. The major exhibits are drawn from the output of Louis Comfort Tiffany – a legend for his innovative Art Nouveau lamps and windows that furnished high-society homes around the turn of the century. Great creativity and craftsmanship went into Tiffany's work: he molded glass while still soft, imbuing it with colored images of water lilies, leaves and even strutting peacocks. After this brilliant, priceless stuff, the Norman Rockwell paintings, and the museum's other possessions, seem rather pale.

To discover why people who can afford to live anywhere chose Winter Park as a home, take the **scenic boat tour** from the dock at 312 E Morse Boulevard (departures every 30min daily Mon–Sat 10am–4.30pm; $5.50) – an hour-long voyage over wood-shrouded lakes and their moss-draped connecting canals: a picture-postcard view only otherwise available from the rolling back lawns of big-buck waterside homes.

Maitland

Luscious sunsets over another body of water, Lake Sybelia, directly north of Winter Park in **MAITLAND**, inspired a young artist called André Smith to buy six acres on its banks during the Thirties. With the financial assistance of Mary Bok (wealthy widow of Edward Bok; see "South Central Florida"), Smith established what's now the **Maitland Art Center**, 231 W Packward Avenue (Mon, Wed & Fri 10am–4.30pm, Tues & Thurs 10am–8pm, Sat & Sun noon–4.30pm; free), a collection of stuccoed studios, offices and apartments grouped around garden courtyards, decorated by Aztec-Mayan murals and bas-reliefs. Smith invited other American artists to spend working winters here but his abrasive personality scared many potential guests away. The colony continued in various forms until Smith's death in 1959, never becoming the aesthetes' commune he hoped for. There are temporary exhibitions and a permanent collection, but it's the unique design of the place that demands a visit. While here, spare a thought for Smith's ghost, which, according to a number of local painters and sculptors who claim to have felt its presence, dispenses artistic guidance.

A few steps from the art center is the **Maitland Historical Museum and Telephone Museum**, 212 W Packward Avenue (Tues, Fri & Sun 2–4pm; free). The front rooms of the combined museums hold an ordinary gathering of ageing photos and household objects, but the back room is filled with wonderful vinta~~ telephones, commemorating the day in 1910 when a Maitland grocer laun~ the area's first exchange by installing telephones in the homes of his cus~ enabling them to place orders from their armchairs.

The only other thing to make you dally in Maitland is **Audubon** ~aviary Audubon Way (Tues–Sat 10am–4pm; donation), the headquarters~ health – a Society, Florida's oldest and largest conservation organizatic~ primarily an educational center and gift shop, but the s~ contains injured or orphaned birds of prey that are being n~ chance to see vultures, eagles, falcons and more, close u~

Eating

Given the level of competition among restaurants to attract hungry tourists, **eating** in Orlando is never difficult and need not be expensive. In **downtown Orlando**, however, the choices are comparatively limited although the need to satisfy a regular clientele of lunch-breaking office workers means prices are low. With a car, you might also investigate the local favorites dotted around downtown. Affluent **Winter Park** promises more variety, generally with higher standards and prices, though it does have a few serviceable low-cost diners.

Tourist-dominated **International Drive** holds a greater range – if much less atmosphere. The culinary hot-spots are the gourmet ethnic restaurants, but strict-budget travellers will relish the opportunity to eat massive amounts at one of several buffet restaurants – all for less than they might spend on a tip elsewhere. Buffet eating reaches its ultimate expression along **Hwy-192**, where virtually every buffet restaurant chain has at least one outlet, leaving the discerning glutton spoilt for choice.

Discount coupons in tourist magazines bring sizeable reductions at many restaurants, and also at the "Show Restaurants", where $30 per head not only buys a multi-course feed and (usually) limitless beer, wine and soft drinks, but also entertainment ranging from cavorting Ninja warriors to medieval knights jousting on horseback.

Downtown

Good Times Diner, 301 W Church St (☎246-1950). Glossy re-creation of a 1950s diner, with frothy milkshakes, thick burgers and an oldies jukebox.

Ha Long, 120 N Orange St (☎648-9685). The lunch buffet at this Vietnamese restaurant is the best deal for miles; there's also a lengthy dinner menu.

Jungle Jim's, inside Church Street Market, 55 W Church St (☎872-3111). Local branch of a fast-expanding chain where servers emerge from behind pseudo-jungle decor bearing enormous burgers and Mexican-style dishes; most nutritious, though, are the gigantic salads.

Le Peep, 250 S Orange Ave (☎849-0428). Ideal for a quick bite, with sandwiches, soups, pancakes and more.

Petit Four, 702 N Orange Ave (☎647-0897). An emporium of fresh-baked delights: the featherweight pastries and cakes make decadent snacks.

Around Downtown

El Bohio Cafe, 5756 Dahlia Drive (☎282-1723). One of two local outlets (with *Vega's*, see below) for generous portions of well-priced Cuban food.

Vinh's, 1231 E Colonial Drive (☎894-5007). Hole-in-the-wall Vietnamese restaurant which offers good food at giveaway prices for lunch and dinner.

Lilia's Philipine Delights, 3150 S Orange Avenue Drive (☎851-9087). A mouthwatering selection of Filipino dishes, though unfortunately the quality varies. If you're seriously hungry, go for the whole pig.

Vega's Cafe, 1835 E Colonial Drive (☎898-5196). Friendly Cuban diner with great-value ~~hes~~.

The Park

Avenue and ?, 252 Park Ave (☎628-8651). Well-prepared lunches – the salads are huge – ~~ide or on the terrace.~~

~~~p,~~ 109 Lyman Ave (☎644-5948). Turn the corner off fashionable Park ~~dependable budget-priced coffee shop.~~

Maison de Crepe, Hidden Garden Shops, off Park Ave (☎647-4469). Some people come here solely for the feather-light crepes, but the lunches and dinners are inventive and tasty.

Max's Bagel & Deli Emporium, 327 Park Ave (☎740-8600). Just the place to pretend you're in New York: the bagels come with a variety of toppings, while the deli counter has more filling items.

Park Avenue Grill, 358 Park Ave (☎647-4556). A fairly standard American menu but the window seats are excellent vantage points for people watching.

Power House, 111 Lyman Ave (☎645-3616). Order a vitamin-packed fruit juice to raise your energy level; or sample one of the flavorful soups.

Winter Park Diner, 1700 W Fairbanks Ave (☎644-2343). In business longer than most people can remember, and still serving generous portions of classic diner food at prices to please.

International Drive and Around

Bergamo's, Mercado Mediterranean Mall, 8445 International Drive (☎302-3805). Good-quality but slightly expensive freshly prepared pasta and seafood dishes; dinner only.

Butcher Shop Steakhouse, Mercado Mediterranean Mall, 8445 International Drive (☎363-9727). Bigger steaks and chops than you've ever seen in your life; carnivores who arrive hungry will leave happy.

Cricketers Arms, Mercado Mediterranean Mall, 8445 International Drive (☎254-0686). Fish and chips, pies and pasties, complement a range of imported ales and lagers at this inexpensive nook.

Florida Bay Grille, 8560 International Drive (☎352-6655). Don't come here for big portions; the focus is on carefully prepared seafood and meat dishes intended to delight the discerning diner.

José O'Day's, Mercado Mediterranean Mall, 8445 International Drive (☎363-0613). Not the best Mexican food you'll ever taste but the portions are large and filling, and the atmosphere is enjoyable.

Ming Court, 9188 International Drive (☎351-9988). Chinese cuisine of an exceptionally high standard makes this the best dining spot on International Drive; not as costly as you might expect.

Morrison's Cafeteria, 7440 International Drive (☎351-0051). Low-cost self-service eating; load your tray from an immense array of hot dishes, desserts and drinks.

Passage to India, 5532 International Drive (☎351-3456) and 845 Sand Lake Road (☎856-8362). Indian cuisine served in less spicy forms than is the norm in Europe; *thali* is a house speciality but the lunchtime buffet offers best value.

Ponderosa Steakhouse, 6362, 8510 & 14407 International Drive (☎352-9343; ☎354-1477; ☎238-2526). The biggest appetites will be fully satisfied here, where sizeable buffets – with plenty for non-meat eaters to enjoy – are laid out for breakfast, lunch and dinner.

Sizzler, 9142 International Drive (☎351-5369). Substantial breakfast buffet from 7am to 11am; lunch or dinner brings ample steak or seafood, plus an all-you-can-eat salad bar.

Western Steer, 6315 International Drive (☎363-0677). Breakfast, lunch and dinner buffets; the latter features five hot courses, as well as soups, salads, vegetables, fruit and ice cream, in limitless supply.

Along Hwy-192

Black-eyed Pea, 5305 W Hwy-192 (☎397-1500). Large portions of Southern-style cooking – catfish, fried chicken and much more – served for lunch and dinner.

Farmer's Family Buffet, 4320 W Hwy-192 & 5051 W Hwy-192 (☎396-2700; ☎396-6532). Cost-effective buffet eating. Both branches serve lunch and dinner, but only the 4320 location is open for breakfast.

Kettle, 7777 W Hwy-192 (☎396-4280). Consistently one of the lowest-priced dinner buffets in the area.

Key W Kool's, 7225 W Hwy-192 (☎396-1166). As a break from buffets, sample the seafood or steaks served for lunch or dinner in this tropically themed restaurant; or show up for the two-dollar breakfast.

Ponderosa Steakhouse, 5771 & 7598 Hwy-192 (☎397-2477; ☎396-7721). A gigantic buffet offered all day. Three other branches on International Drive, see above.

Sizzler, 7602 W Hwy-192 (☎397-0997). Most substantial breakfast buffet in the vicinity; also on International Drive, see above.

Western Sizzlin, 5073 Hwy-192 (☎397-1881). By a whisker, the cheapest breakfast and lunch buffets on this buffet-restaurant-lined strip. Also serves dinner.

Show Restaurants

Asian Adventure, 5225 International Drive (☎351-5655). Acrobats, magicians and Ninja warriors provide the entertainment as you munch a five-course Chinese dinner.

Capone's Dinner & Show, Mercado Mediterranean Mall, 8445 International Drive (☎397-2378). Give the secret password and enter this Prohibition-era speakeasy for a Twenties-style song-and-dance revue and an Italian-food buffet.

King Henry's Feast, 8984 International Drive (☎1-800/883-8181). Knights duel and jesters amuse as a five-course meal is served and drinks are quaffed from tankards.

Mardi Gras, Mercado Mediterranean Mall, 8445 International Drive (☎1-800/883-8181). Comedians, leggy dancers and a Dixieland jazz band combine in a showbizzy re-creation of a New Orleans nightclub during the Mardi Gras festival; the food is cajun style.

Medieval Times, 4510 Hwy-192 (☎1-800/229-8300). Knights swordfight and joust on horseback as you tuck into a feast inside a replica eleventh-century castle.

Sleuth's Dinner Show, 7508 Republic Drive (☎363-1985). If you know red herring isn't a seafood dish, you're well on the way to solving the murder mystery played out in this Agatha-Christie-like set as you eat.

Nightlife

Nightlife in Orlando isn't much to write home about. Although there are exceptions, the choice tends to be between big, brassy discos or restaurant-cum-bars with live music.

Downtown Orlando

Beacham's Blue Note, 54 N Orange Ave (☎843-3078). Stylish supper bar with live jazz and blues of impressive pedigree.

Church Street Station, 129 W Church St (☎422-2434). Don't let the crowds who flock here nightly fool you into thinking this complex of bars, restaurants and 1890s-style music hall, *Rosie O'Grady's*, merits the $15.95 admission fee. Once inside, you'll also have to pay well over the odds for drinks.

Dekko's, 46 N Orange Ave (☎648-8727). Top-notch disco, complete with pulsating laser lights and a split-level dance floor; draws curious tourists and dance-crazy locals.

Howl at the Moon Saloon, 55 W Church St (☎841-9118). You'll find it hard to concentrate on your drink as duelling pianists whizz through a singalong selection of rock and roll classics and songs from the shows.

Winter Park

Crocodile Club, inside *Bailey's Restaurant*, 118 W Fairbanks Ave (☎647-8501). Youthful but upmarket disco, popular with Rollins College students and trendy Winter Park ravers.

Shooters, 4315 N Orange Blossom Trail (☎298-2955). Lively locals' favorite for its food, drinks and live music (four nights a week) in a pleasant waterside setting.

International Drive, Hwy-192 and Around

Bennigan's, 6324 International Drive (☎351-4435). Sprawling sports bar with extended happy hours.

Crazy Horse Saloon, 7050 Kirkham Rd (☎363-6071). Rowdy country and bluegrass music; lots of drinking and high spirits.

Cricketers Arms, Mercado Mediterranean Mall, 8445 International Drive (☎254-0686). English ales, European lagers and the latest soccer scores – and sometimes the matches themselves on giant TV screens.

Fat Tuesday, Mercado Mediterranean Mall, 8445 International Drive (☎351-5311). Just the place to initiate yourself into the joys of the frozen daiquiri, available in many different flavors. Most evenings there's also live music.

Little Darlin's Rock and Roll Palace, 5770 W Hwy-192 (☎239-2823). Step through the giant jukebox to a hangar-like dance floor reverberating to the sounds of the Fifties and Sixties.

JJ Whispers, 5100 Adanson St (☎629-4474). High-tech disco complex which also includes a comedy club, *Bonkerz!*.

Sullivan's, 1108 S Orange Blossom Trail (☎843-2934). Live country music and square-dancing; draws a friendly and enthusiastic crowd.

North from Orlando

Back-to-back residential areas dissolve into fields of fruit and vegetables north of Orlando's city limits. Around here, in slow-motion towns harking back to Florida's frontier days, farming still has the upper hand over tourism. Though it's easy to skim through on I-4, the older local roads connecting the major settlements have far more atmosphere.

Sanford and Mount Dora

A position on the south shore of Lake Monroe, fifteen miles north of Maitland on Hwy-92 (also known as Hwy-17), allows **SANFORD** to grab its share of tourist dollars with riverboat cruises (from $20, details on ☎1-800/423-7401) from the marina on N Palmetto Avenue. For a more solid impression of the modestly sized town – and the turn-of-the-century lawyer and diplomat who created it – dip inside the **Shelton Sanford Memorial Museum**, 520 E First Street (Tues–Fri 11am–4pm free). Once called "Celery City" on account of its major agricultural crop, Sanford hasn't had a lot going for it since the boom years of the early 1900s, a period lovingly chronicled in the museum. For even more relics of the halcyon days, collect a self-guided tour map from the **Chamber of Commerce**, 400 E First Street (Mon–Fri 9am–5pm; ☎407/322-2212), and venture around 22 buildings of divergent classical architecture in the adjacent old downtown district, most of them now doing business as drugstores and insurance offices.

On the way back to Hwy-92 at Sanford's southwest corner, the **Seminole County Historical Museum**, 300 Bush Boulevard (Mon–Fri 9am–1pm, Sat & Sun 1–4pm; free), carries an multitude of objects from all over the county – including an intriguing selection of multi-cure medicine bottles. Alternatively, rake around **Flea World** (Fri, Sat & Sun 8am–5pm), at the end of Bush Boulevard by the Hwy-92 junction, a large-scale attempt to sell items that nobody in their right mind would ever buy.

To see a Victorian-era Florida village at its most self-consciously quaint, take Route 46 west of Sanford for seventeen miles and feast your eyes on the picket fences, wrought-iron balconies and fancy wood-trimmed buildings which make-up **MOUNT DORA**. The **Chamber of Commerce**, 341 Alexander Street (Mon–Fri 9am–5pm; ☎904/383-2165), has a free guide to the old houses and the inevitable antique shops that now occupy many of them.

Cassadaga

A village populated by spiritualists conjures up images of weirdos in forbidding mansions, but the few hundred residents of **CASSADAGA**, just east of I-4, ten miles north of Sanford, are disappointingly normal citizens in normal homes, offering contact with the spirit world for a very down-to-earth fee (commonly $30 for a half-hour session). A group of northern spiritualists bought this 35-acre site in 1875 and they quickly caught the imagination of Florida's early settlers – a time when contacting the Other Side was a lot easier than communicating with the rest of the US.

Throughout the year seminars and lectures cover topics ranging from UFO cover-ups to out-of-body travelling: the **Andrew Jackson Davis Building**, on the corner of Route 4139 and Stevens Street (Mon–Sat 9.30am–5pm, Sun noon–4pm; ☎904/228-2880), is the main information center and doubles as a psychic bookshop. Even if you don't stop, take a drive through what must rank as the state's oddest community.

DeLand and Around

Intended to be the "Athens of Florida" when founded in 1876, **DELAND**, four miles north of Cassadega, west off I-4, has turned out a commonplace central Florida town. It does, however, boast one of the state's oldest educational centers: the red-brick facades of the **Stetson University**, on Woodland Boulevard, have stood since the 1880s, partly funded by the profits of the cowboy hat of the university's title. Pick up a free tour map from the easily found DeLand Hall for a walk around the vintage buildings. Also on the campus, on the corner of Michigan and Amelia avenues, the **Gillespie Museum of Minerals** (summer Mon–Sat 9am–4pm; closed in winter; free) displays Florida quartz, calcite and limestone, and gemstones gathered from all over the world.

Assuming you're not rushing towards the east coast (Daytona Beach is twenty miles away on Hwy-92 or I-4; see Chapter Four), or making haste for the Ocala National Forest, less than ten miles east on Route 44 (see "North Central Florida"), **canoeing** provides a reason to hang around the DeLand area. Organized trips (around $13 a day) on the region's many rivers are arranged at *Katie's Wekiva River Landing* (☎407/628-1482), five miles west of I-4 on Route 46. For general information, use DeLand's **Chamber of Commerce**, 366 N Woodland Boulevard (Mon–Fri 9am–5pm; ☎1-800/749-4350).

North from DeLand: DeLeon Springs and Barberville

Ten miles north of DeLand on Hwy-17, watching tens of thousands of gallons of water emerging for the first time into daylight makes **DeLeon Springs State Recreation Area** (daily 8am–sunset; cars $3.25, pedestrians and cyclists $1) an indefinably pleasurable place – much to the amusement of central and northern Florida residents, for whom springs are a common sight. As well as swimming, canoeing and picnicking in and beside the actual spring, you can make your own pancakes in the *Old Spanish Sugar Mill Restaurant* (☎904/985-4212), a timbered diner beside the park.

Seven miles further on Hwy-17, the tiny crossroads community of **BARBERVILLE** celebrates the rural Florida it personifies with the **Pioneer Settlement for the Creative Arts** (Mon–Fri 9am–4pm, Sat 9am–2pm; $2.50), a turn-of-the-century train station and general store, with an assembly of pottery wheels, looms, milling equipment and other tools put to use in demonstrations of traditional handicrafts on a worthy but informative 45-minute guided tour.

South from DeLand: Blue Spring and Hontoon Island

The naturally warm waters at **Blue Spring State Park** (daily 8am–sunset; cars $3.25, pedestrians and cyclists $1), seven miles from DeLand on Hwy-17, close to Orange City, attract almost as many manatees as tourists each winter, the most-loved of Florida's endangered creatures swimming here from the cooler waters of the St Johns River. Aside from staking out the manatees from the observation platform (and watching a 20-minute slide show describing their habits), there's also the chance to see around **Thursby House** (Thurs–Sun 11am–4pm; $1), a large frame dwelling built by pioneer settlers in 1872. **Accommodation** in the park includes a $16-per-night campground and $55-a-night cabins which sleep up to four people (☎904/775-3663).

From Blue Spring, you can almost catch sight of **Hontoon Island**, a striking dollop of wooded land set within very flat and swampy terrain. Without a private boat, Hontoon Island is reachable only with the sporadic free **ferry** running daily from 9am to an hour before sunset from a landing stage on Route 44 (the continuation of DeLand's New York Avenue). Unbelievably, the island once held a boat-yard and cattle ranch, but today is inhabited only by the hardy souls who decide to stay over in one of its rustic **cabins** (reservations ☎904/775-3663; ②).

South from Orlando

Not much fills the rough acres directly **south from Orlando**, although one of the area's oldest and, in its way, most amusing destinations sits on what's called the "Orange Blossom Trail" (known variously as Hwy-92, Hwy-17 and Hwy-441), which runs the sixteen miles between Orlando and Kissimmee.

Gatorland Zoo

Fourteen miles south of Orlando, with an oversized wooden alligator mouth for an entrance, **Gatorland Zoo**, 14501 S Orange Blossom Trail (daily, summer 8am–8pm, winter 8am–6pm; $10.95), has been giving visitors since the Fifties a close look at the state's most feared and least understood animal. Surprisingly lazy beasts, the residents of the zoo (actually a working farm, licensed to breed alligators for their hides and meat) only show signs of life at the organized feeding – at 10am, then roughly every following two hours – when hunks of chicken are suspended from a wire and the largest alligators, using their powerful tail muscles, propel themselves out of the water to grab their dinner: a bizarre spectacle of heaving animal and ferociously snapping jaws. Take a look, too, at the **snake pit**, occupied by some of Florida's most deadly reptiles: coral snakes, copperheads, cottonmouth moccasins and diamond back rattlesnakes – none of whom you'd enjoy meeting in the wild, but a handy recognition exercise in case you do.

Kissimmee

A country-bumpkin counterpart to the modern vacation developments that ring it, KISSIMMEE, at the end of Orange Blossom Trail, has most of its fun during the Wednesday lunchtime cattle auctions at the **Livestock Market**, 805 E Donegan Avenue, and lays on the drab **Neighborhood Shops**, 815 Main Street (Mon–Sat 10am–5pm), a cluster of half a dozen turn-of-the-century homes mostly converted into gift shops, for souvenir-seeking tourists. The **motels** close to the town on Hwy-192 (see "Accommodation") make Kissimmee a cheap place to be, however, and even without a car getting about is relatively simple: **trains** stop at 111 Pakin Avenue, *Greyhound* **buses** at 16 N Orlando Avenue (☎407/847-3911), and **shuttle bus** links to the major Orlando area attractions are frequent.

To kill time in Kissimmee, take a walk around the forty-foot obelisk called **Kissimmee Monument of States**, on Monument Avenue. With stone slab and rock fragments, each particular to an American state, affixed to its garishly painted concrete blocks, the monument went up in 1943 to honour the former president of the local All-States Tourist Club, who – one might deduce from the state of the thing – no longer commands the respect he once did.

Walt Disney World

As significant as air conditioning in making the state what it is today, **WALT DISNEY WORLD** turned a wedge of Florida cow fields into one of the world's most lucrative vacation venues within ten years. Bringing growth and money to central Florida for the first time since the citrus boom a century ago, the immense and astutely planned empire (and Walt Disney World really *is* an empire) also pushed the state's media profile through the roof: from being a down-at-heel and slightly seedy mixture of cheap motels, retirement homes and clapped-out alligator zoos, Florida suddenly became a showcase of modern international tourism and in doing so, some would claim, sold its soul for a fast buck.

Whatever your attitude to theme parks, there's no denying that Walt Disney World is the pacesetter: it goes way beyond Walt Disney's original "theme park" – Disneyland, which opened in Los Angeles in 1955 – delivering escapism at its most technologically advanced and psychologically brilliant in a multitude of ingenious guises across an area twice the size of Manhattan. In a crime-free environment where wholesome all-American values hold sway and the concept of good clean fun finds its ultimate expression, Walt Disney World often makes the real world – and all its problems – seem like a distant memory.

Here, litter is picked up within seconds of being dropped, subtle mind-games soften the pain of queueing, the special effects are the best money can buy, and employees grin merrily as snotty-nosed kids puke down their legs. It's not cheap, forward planning is essential, and there are times when you'll feel like a cog in a vast machine – but Walt Disney World unfailingly, and with ruthless efficiency, always delivers what it promises.

Costs* may come as a shock, especially to families (who should note that Walt Disney World as a whole is much less geared to kids than might be expected),

---

*Walt Disney World's ticket prices are frequently raised by a few cents: the theory is that regular small increases won't put people off as much as less frequent big rises. Remember to add Florida's 6 percent sales tax to all prices quoted here.

When brilliant illustrator and animator Walt Disney devised the world's first theme park, California's **Disneyland** – which brought to life his cartoon characters, Mickey Mouse, Donald Duck, Goofy and the rest – he left himself with no control over the hotels and restaurants which quickly engulfed it, preventing growth and racking off profits Disney felt were rightly his. Determined that this wouldn't happen again, the Disney corporation secretly began to buy up 27,500 acres of central Florida farmland, and by the late Sixties had acquired – for a comparatively paltry $6 million – a site a hundred times bigger than Disneyland. With the promise of a jobs bonanza for Florida, the state legislature gave the corporation – thinly disguised as the Reedy Creek Improvement District – the rights of any major municipality: empowering it to lay roads, enact building codes, and enforce the law with its own security force.

Walt Disney World's first park, the **Magic Kingdom**, opened in 1971; predictably based on Disneyland, it was an equally predictable success. The far more ambitious **EPCOT Center**, unveiled in 1982. represented the first major break from cartoon-based escapism: millions visited, but the rose-tinted look at the future received a mixed response. Partly due to this, and some cockeyed management decisions, the Disney empire (Disney himself died in 1966) faced bankruptcy by the mid-Eighties.

Since then, clever marketing has brought the corporation back from the abyss – though the wisdom of the opening of EuroDisney in France in 1992 has yet to be determined – and it now steers a tight and competitive business ship, always looking to increase Walt Disney World's 100,000 daily visitors and stay ahead of its rivals. The recently opened Disney-MGM Studios, for example, aims to put a dent in Universal Studios' trade (see p.235), while Pleasure Island's nightclubs are clearly intended to compete with downtown Orlando's Church Street Station (see p.222). It may trade in fantasy, but where money matters, the Disney corporation's nose is firmly in the real world.

but the admission fee allows unlimited access to all the shows and rides in the particular park – and you'll need *at least* a day per park to go on everything in each of the three main ones. There's a strict embargo on bringing **food and drink** into the parks, where restaurants and snack bars – each as clinically themed as the parks – are plentiful but pricey. Only in Pleasure Island is alcohol served.

Seeing Walt Disney World: the Main Parks

Walt Disney World's three main theme parks are quite separate entities. The **Magic Kingdom** is the Disney park everyone imagines, where Mickey Mouse mingles with the crowds and the emphasis is on fantasy and fun – very much the park for kids. Recognizable for its giant, golfball like geosphere, **EPCOT Center** is Disney's attempted celebration of science and technology, coupled to a very Disneyfied trip around various countries and cultures: boring for young kids, it's a sprawling area that involves a lot of walking. The newest and most easily assimilated of the three, **Disney-MGM Studios**, suits almost everyone; its special effects are enjoyable even if you've never seen the movies they're based on, and the Backstage Tour, despite moments of tedium, at least visits *real* studios – reality being a rare commodity in Walt Disney World.

Doing justice to all three parks will take at least four days – one day should be set aside for rest – and you shouldn't tackle more than one on any single day. If you only have a day to spare, pick the park that appeals most and stick to it: day tickets are only valid for one location anyway.

When to Visit

While EPCOT Center in particular absorbs crowds easily, try to avoid the peak times. The **busiest periods** of Walt Disney World's main parks are from mid-February to August, and from Christmas Day to New Year's Day. The slowest months are January, September, October and November. The **busiest day** is Tuesday, with Friday and Sunday the least crowded.

Provided you **arrive early** at the park (8am is a good time) you'll easily get through the most popular rides before the mid-afternoon crush, when queues can become very long. If you can't arrive early, don't show up until 5 or 6pm, which still leaves time to do plenty before the place shuts up. Each park has regularly updated noticeboards showing the latest **waiting times** – seldom more than an hour, often ten minutes or less – for each show and ride.

Opening Times and Tickets

Each of the parks is **open** daily from 9am to 11pm between February and August, and from 9am to 9pm for the rest of the year, with extended hours on holidays. A **one-day ticket** costs $35 (children under ten $28; children under three free) from any park entrance, and allows entry to one park only, with unlimited passouts.

For seeing more than two of the parks, spread your visits over four or five days using one of the **passports**, which permit entry to all three parks and free use of the shuttle buses around the complex. **Four-day passports** cost $125 (children $98); **five-day passports** cost $170 (children $135). There's also a $190 **year-long passport**, strictly for fanatics.

As obvious as it may sound, if you arrive by car be sure to follow the signs to the park you want to visit and use its **parking lot** (fee $4). The lots are enormous, so make at least a mental note of where exactly you're parked – and save hours of embarrassed searching later on.

A complex **transportation system** uses buses and a monorail to cover Walt Disney World, linking the hotels and parking lots with the main attractions.

Disney Information: ☎407/824-4321

The Magic Kingdom

Anyone who's been to Disneyland in LA will recognize much of the **Magic Kingdom**. Like the original Disney theme park, it divides into four sections – **Adventureland**, **Tomorrowland**, **Fantasyland** and **Frontierland** – although these divisions become fairly meaningless once you're inside the park. Some rides are identical to their Californian forebears, some are greatly expanded and improved – and a few are much worse. And, like its older relative, the only way to deal with the place is enthusiastically: jump in with both feet and go on every ride you can.

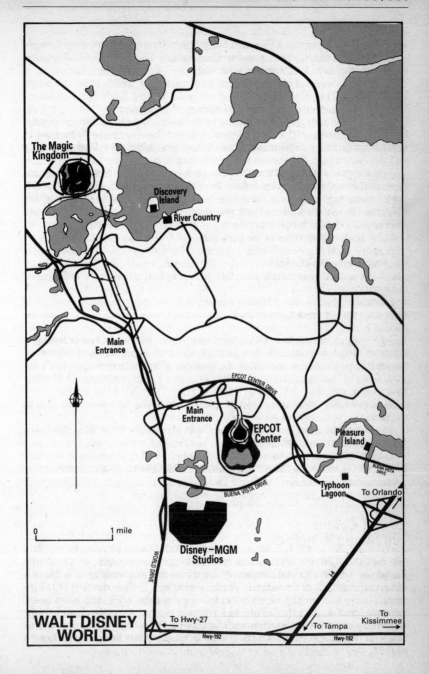

The Magic
Kingdom

Discovery
Island

River Country

Main
Entrance

EPCOT CENTER DRIVE

Main
Entrance

EPCOT
Center

Pleasure
Island

BUENA VISTA
DRIVE

BUENA VISTA DRIVE

Typhoon
Lagoon

To Orlando

0   1 mile

WORLD DRIVE

Disney–MGM
Studios

**WALT DISNEY
WORLD**

← To Hwy-27

Hwy-192

To Tampa →

To
Kissimmee →

Hwy-192

The Park

From the main gates, the unprepossessing **Main Street USA**, lined by souvenir shops and food-stands, leads towards **Cinderella's Castle**, a pseudo-Rhineland palace which might look like the most elaborate ride in the park but which, in fact, serves to conceal the electronics and machinery which drive the whole extravaganza. The castle does provide an easily spotted landmark for visitors, however, who are certain to lose their bearings at some point.

If you arrive early, beat the queues by immediately heading for the popular thrills-and-spills rides. The most nerve-jangling of these is **Space Mountain**, in essence an ordinary switchback but one where total darkness makes every jump and jolt unexpected. The ride may last less than three minutes but many people breath a sigh of relief once it's over. The park's newest ride, **Splash Mountain** (memorably satirized in an episode of *The Simpsons*), is another glorified switch-back, employing water to great effect. In a similar but less frenetic vein, **Big Thunder Mountain Railroad** puts you aboard a runaway train hurtling through gold-rush California, with explosions and earthquakes along the way.

Many of the other rides in the park rely on "AudioAnimatronic" characters – impressive vocal robots of Disney invention – for their appeal. The robots are at their most effective in **Pirates of the Caribbean**, a boat-ride through a pirate attack on a Caribbean island complete with drunken debauchery and general mayhem.

Elsewhere, the **Haunted Mansion** is worth a wait, as much for the duration of the ride – one of the longest in park – as for the clever special effects, from the sliding ceiling in the entrance room to the macabre goings-on as your "doom buggy" passes through a spook-filled cemetery. Almost as entertaining is **20,000 Leagues Under the Sea** (actually about six inches down in an artificial lagoon); keep your nose pressed to the porthole of the submarine and you'll see all manner of curious creatures pass by as Captain Nemo commentates. Heading in the other direction, **Mission to Mars** is a banal simulated journey to the Red Planet; the most impressive moment comes when you feel your seat change shape as the g-force increases.

The Magic Kingdom does show its age with **Mr Toad's Wild Ride** and **Snow White's Adventures**; although these creaky low-tech amusements are still very popular with young kids, they wouldn't be out of place in a fairground. Another long-term survivor is **The Enchanted Tiki Birds**, with hundreds of AudioAnimatronic tropical birds and Tiki-god statues singing and whistling their way through a programme of South Seas musical favorites.

EPCOT Center

Even before the new Magic Kingdom opened, Walt Disney was developing plans for **EPCOT Center**, or Experimental Prototype Community of Tomorrow, conceived in 1966 as a real community experimenting and working with the new ideas and materials of the technologically advancing US. The idea failed to shape up as Disney had envisaged: EPCOT didn't open its gates until 1982, when global recession and ecological concerns had put paid to utopian notions based on the infallibility of science. One drawback of this park is simply its immense size: twice as big as the Magic Kingdom and, ironically given its futuristic themes, very sapping on mankind's oldest mode of transportation – the feet.

The Park

EPCOT's 180-foot-high **geosphere** (unlike a semi-circular geodesic dome, the geosphere is completely round) provides information desks and souvenir shops and sits at the heart of the **Future World** section of the park, which keeps close to EPCOT's original concept of exploring the history of, and possible advances to be made in, agriculture, transport, energy and communications.

Future World divides into seven pavilions – each corporately sponsored, so don't expect to learn anything about alternative energy sources or global warming – and each has its own rides, films and interactive computer exhibits. The **Wonders of Life** pavilion has the best of the rides with **Body Wars**, a brief but exciting flight-simulator trip through a human body. While here, be sure to catch the entertaining **Cranium Command**, in which an AudioAnimatronic character is detailed to control the brain of a 12-year-old all-American boy.

Close by, **Horizons** holds a mildly amusing ride through the possible (but unlikely) lifestyles of the future, although **World of Motion** is completely forgettable, and you should concentrate instead on beating the queues which often stretch outside **Universe of Energy**: a celebration of the harnessing of the earth's energy which includes a ride through the the the dinosaur-roamed primeval forests where today's fossil fuels originated.

In the **Journey Into Imagination** pavilion, only diehard Michael Jackson fans will find his 3D cinematic portrayal of *Captain EO* at all entertaining; by contrast **The Living Seas**, the world's largest artificial saltwater environment, occupied by a multitude of dolphins, sharks and sea lions, has far greater appeal – not least for the chance to climb inside a massive diving suit.

Arranged around a forty-acre lagoon, the **World Showcase** section of EPCOT attempts to mirror the history, architecture and culture of eleven different nations. Each is presumably chosen for the ease of replicating an instantly recognisable landmark – Mexico has a Mayan Pyramid, France an Eiffel Tower – or stereotypical scene, such as the UK's pub, Germany's Bavarian village, and Morocco's inevitable bazaar. The elaborate reconstructions show careful attention to detail; highlights include the Viking longboat ride through **Norway**, **Japan**'s cultural museum, and the *Wonders of China* film. The most crowded place, though, is usually **The American Adventure** inside a replica of Philadelphia's Liberty Hall, where AudioAnimatronic versions of Mark Twain and Benjamin Franklin recount 200 somewhat sanitized years of US history in under half an hour.

Disney-MGM Studios

When the Disney corporation began making films and TV shows for adults – most notably *Who Killed Roger Rabbit* – they also, with an eye on the popularity of the Universal Studios tour in California, set about devising a theme park to entertain adults as much as kids. Buying the rights to the gem-filled Metro-Goldwyn-Mayer (MGM) oeuvre of films and TV shows, Disney acquired a vast repertoire of instantly familiar images to mold into shows and rides. Opening in 1990, Disney-MGM Studios served to mute the opening of Florida's Universal Studios (see p.235), and at the same time found an extra use for the real film studios based here – the people you'll see laboring over storyboards on the Backstage Tour aren't there for show: they are genuinely making films.

The Park

The first of several highly sanitized imitations of Hollywood's famous streets and buildings – causing much amusement to anyone familiar with the seedy state of the originals – **Hollywood Boulevard** leads into the park, its length brightened with reenactments of famous movie scenes, strolling film star lookalikes and the odd Muppet.

If you manage to arrive early, avoid a long wait in the sun later in the day by going straight on the two-hour **Backstage Tour**, visiting film production facilities, venturing around Disney's animation studios, and leaving eardrums rattled by the exploding Catastrophe Canyon: the tour's interest level goes up and down but you won't feel you've had your money's worth if you miss it. The same applies to the **Indiana Jones Stunt Spectacular**, re-creating – and explaining – many of the action-packed set pieces from the Spielberg films.

Wrong turnings and collisions with asteroids make **Star Tours**, a flight-simulator trip to the Moon of Endor piloted by *Star Wars* characters R2D2 and C-3PO, the most physical ride in the park by a long way – passengers' seatbelts are carefully checked before lift-off. For laughs go to **Superstar Television**, which plucks volunteers from the crowd to read the news, appear in *The Lucy Show* or team up with *The Golden Girls* – one place in Walt Disney World where the fun is spontaneous. Also good fun is **Jim Henson's MuppetVision 3D**, a three-dimensional movie whose special effects put you right inside the Muppet Show.

MGM's only stinker is **The Great Movie Ride**, repaying a (usually) long queue with a short ride through a few scenes from movie classics, such as *Casablanca* and *The Wizard of Oz*, with the leading roles taken by AudioAnimatronic robots. Finding out that the John Wayne character is wearing the real actor's belt buckle is, believe it or not, one of the highlights.

The Rest of Walt Disney World

The poor relations of Walt Disney World's major parks, several other Disney-devised amusements are intended to keep people on Disney property as long as possible, and offer therapeutic relaxation to those suffering theme-park burn-out.

Discovery Island

In Bay Lake, near the Magic Kingdom. Summer daily 10am–7pm; winter 10am–6pm; adults $8.50, children $4.75.

In **Discovery Island**, Disney plays God and attempts to re-create the world, erecting a "natural" habitat for a gorgeous variety of bird life, including strutting peacocks, gliding swans and a flamingo-filled lagoon, reached by prettily land-scaped trails. Despite the steep admission price (it makes economic sense to combine it with River Country, see below), if you're not seeing any real Florida wildlife in the real Florida wilds, you'll enjoy this a lot.

River Country

At the Fort Wilderness Resort (see "Walt Disney World accommodation", below). Summer daily 9am–8pm; winter 10am–5pm; adults $13.25, children $10.50.

River Country is a rustic version of Typhoon Lagoon (see below) built around the **Ol' Swimming Hole**, with fewer and less exciting slides – and no wave machines – but scoring well with its high-speed, corkscrewing descents from Whoop-'N-Holler Hollow; and the enjoyable inner-tube-cruised **White Water**

Rapids. With a small beach and a nature trail leading to a shady cypress hammock, River Country is more relaxing than Typhoon Lagoon and is a good place to unwind between touring the main parks.

Typhoon Lagoon

Just south of Pleasure Island (see "Disney nightlife"). Daily 10am–5pm; adults $20.50, children $16.50.

Typhoon Lagoon consists of an imaginatively constructed "tropical island" around a two-and-a-half-acre lagoon, rippled every ninety seconds by artificial waves: bodysurf the breakers, skim over them with a raft (rent one as soon as you arrive; $1 an hour, two-hour minimum), or plunge into them from **Humunga Kowabunga**, a pair of speed-slides fifty feet up the "mountain" beside the lagoon. There are several smaller slides, too, and the saltwater **Shark Reef** where snorkellers fearful of the open seas can explore a "sunken ship", and be sniffed by real (but not dangerous) nurse and bonnethead sharks. When you're exhausted, take an inner tube (provided at the start point) and float around **Castaways Creek**, a half-hour meander through grottoes and caves, only interrupted by a sudden drenching from a tropical storm.

The bad points are lengthy waits for the faster slides – it's best to come on a Tuesday or a Friday, avoiding the very busy weekends – and the inconveniently placed lockers for which you have to pay (50¢) each time you use them. Unlike the major parks, you can bring **food** to Typhoon Lagoon, but no alcohol or glass containers.

Walt Disney World Accommodation

If you want to be in Walt Disney World even when you're asleep, you'll be relieved to find a growing number of Disney-owned **hotels** within the Walt Disney Work complex. Predictably, each hotel follows a particular theme to the nth degree, and, also predictably, prices are much higher – sometimes above $300 per night – than you'll pay elsewhere. Three Disney hotels, however, are specifically intended for the less affluent visitor, averaging $80–90 a night.

Each hotel occupies its own landscaped plot, usually encompassing several swimming pools and a beach beside an artificial lake, and has several restaurants and bars. The Disney hotels are located in several areas and transport, be it by boat, bus or monorail, is complimentary between them and the main theme parks. Disney guests can also use theme park car parks for free. The standard of service should be excellent; if it isn't, complain like fury and you'll probably be treated like royalty through the remainder of your stay.

At quiet times, rooms may be available at short notice, but with Disney hotels pitching themselves at convention-goers as much as vacationers you may turn up on spec to find that there is no space at all, even in 1000-room properties such as the *Contemporary Resort*. To be assured of a room, you should book as far ahead – nine months is not unreasonable – as possible.

Reservations can be made through a single phone number: ☎407/W DISNEY.

Disney Village Resort Area

Dixie Landing Resort. A moderately priced, Southern-themed hotel, with rooms in the "manor house" or in the "bayou cottages" set in the grounds. ④–⑤.

Port Orleans Resort. Gaze from your wrought-iron balcony across the mini New Orleans re-created in this resorts' courtyard. ④–⑤.

EPCOT Resort Area

Caribbean Beach Resort. Disney's first attempt to create a "budget-priced" hotel still works rather well; the rooms at this plushly landscaped property are located in one of five lodges, each of which has its own pool. ④–⑤.

The Dolphin. Disney's latest and greatest hotel, topped by a giant sculpted dolphin, decorated in dizzying pastel shades and with reproduction artworks from the likes of Matisse and Warhol. ⑧.

The Swan. Intended as a partner to the *Dolphin*, from which it's separated by an artificial lake and beach, and likewise whimsically decorated and equipped with every conceivable luxury. ⑧.

The Yacht and Beach Club. Turn-of-the-century New England is the cue for these twin hotels, complete with clapboard facades and miniature lighthouse. Amusements include all manner of water-borne activities and a croquet lawn. ⑧.

Magic Kingdom Area

Contemporary Resort. The Disney monorail runs right through the center of this hotel, which takes its design ideas from the futuristic fantasies of the Magic Kingdom's Tomorrowland. ⑧.

The Grand Floridian Beach Resort. Gabled roofs, verandahs and crystal chandeliers are among the frivolous variations on early Florida resort architecture at this elegant and relaxing base. ⑧.

Polynesian Village Resort. An effective, if tacky, imitation of a Polynesian beach hotel; the concept is most effective if you spend your time on the lakeside beach under the shade of coconut palms. ⑤.

Fort Wilderness Resort and Campground. Hook up your RV or pitch your tent for $35–46, or rent a six-berth trailer for around $160 – a good deal for larger than usual groups.

Disney nightlife: Pleasure Island

From around 9pm, each Walt Disney World park holds some kind of closing time bash, usually involving fireworks and fountains. For more solid night-time entertainment, the corporation devised **Pleasure Island**, exit 26B off I-4, a remake of an abandoned island, whose pseudo-warehouses are the setting for a mixture of vaguely enjoyable themed bars and nightclubs. Walking around Pleasure Island is free, as is the live open-air music, but drinks are dear and to go inside any of the nightclubs – which are open from 7pm until 2am – you'll need a $13.95 **ticket** from one of the booths at the entry points, which lets you wander in and out of them all (assuming you're over 21 and have the ID to prove it).

The only shows taking place to a timetable are at the *Comedy Warehouse* – whose comedians really are funny and not afraid to send up Mickey Mouse – starting roughly half-hourly. If you're waiting for the curtain to go up, have a drink and lend an ear to the country and bluegrass music inside the *Neon Armadillo*, a Southwestern-style saloon, or check out the competent but unoriginal rock bands at *ZXFR Rock and Roll Beach Club*. Of the rest, *Mannequins Dance Palace* is a swish disco that doesn't get cracking until midnight; the less ostentatious *8Trax* spins exclusively 1970s' music.

The most original – and most enjoyable – place on Pleasure Island is the **Adventurers Club**, loosely based on a 1930s' gentlemen's club and furnished with a motley collection of face masks (some of which unexpectedly start speaking), deer heads and assorted fleamarket furniture. Between scheduled shows, actors and actresses move surreptitiously (despite their period attire) among the throng and strike up loud and unusual conversations with unsuspecting audience members.

Universal Studios

Half a mile north of Exit 30B off I-4. Daily, winter 9am–7pm, longer hours in summer. $31 per day; two-day ticket $49.

Year-round fine weather, a varied cast of natural landscapes and none of the union rules restricting film-making in California, have helped Florida gain the favor of the US movie industry. All the predictions suggest that Florida will be the US moving-image capital of the next century, and the opening of **UNIVERSAL STUDIOS** in June 1990 did nothing to dampen the speculation.

Obviously a sequel to the long-established and immensely popular Universal Studios tour in Los Angeles, Florida's Universal, like its competitor Disney-MGM, is a working studio, filling over 400 acres with the latest in TV and movie production technology and already turning out major features such as Ron Howard's *Parenthood*, *Psycho IV* and a bunch of tedious sitcoms – with the prospect of many more to come.

As a theme park, however, Universal is still struggling to justify the hype which surrounded its opening. Overall, the rides are more spectacular than those at Disney-MGM, with less emphasis on movie nostalgia – but the park has a less homely feel and only the very energetic will be able to take in the whole place inside a day.

The Park

Street sets replicating New York, Los Angeles and San Francisco – look for the dirt and chewing gum painted onto the walls and pavements – create a striking backdrop to the park, which is arranged around a large lagoon: the scene of the night-time **Dynamite Stunt Spectacular**.

For sheer excitement, nothing in the park compares to **Back to the Future**, a bone-shaking flight-simulator time trip from 2015 to the Ice Age. Next best is **Ghostbusters**, for its finely judged mix of audience participation (don't let it be you who has to hold the slime) and inventive special effects as the deliberately over-acting cast encourage you to buy a *Ghostbusters* franchise.

Moving on, neither the rickety **Earthquake – The Big One**, a ride into an 8.3 Richter-scale earthquake aboard a San Francisco subway train, nor the six-ton version of King Kong in **Kongfrontation**, which attacks your cable car amid cracks of thunder and lightning high above New York's East River, is particularly memorable – or worth a lengthy wait. Similarly, **ET's Adventure** is a rather dull ride on pretend bicycles to ET's home planet, although ET speaking your name (which was earlier programmed into a computer) as you leave is a pleasing touch.

Obviously less fun for kids but often more enjoyable than the rides, are the attempts to demystify TV and film production techniques. **Alfred Hitchcock: The Art of Making Movies**, explores some of the outrageous camera angles and visual tricks employed by Hitchcock to send shivers down the spines of millions. Apart from some rather tame efforts to frighten, the tour includes intriguing glimpses of some of Hitch's better films, a few scenes from the 3D version of *Dial M for Murder*, and a group of actors playing out crucial scenes – including the shower one from *Psycho* – using a witless audience member.

Stress rather than horror is the theme of the amusing **Murder, She Wrote**, where an episode of the whodunit blockbuster, with a member of the public as executive director, illustrates different production and post-production processes – and, again using audience members – is often hilarious to boot.

A more relaxing time might be expected at **The FUNtastic World of Hanna-Barbera**, although the excellent simulated cartoon chase from the creators of *The Flintstones* and *Yogi Bear* will have you shaking in your seat; afterwards, using the interactive computers, you can create your own cartoon audio effects – bangs, whoops and crashes – to your heart's content.

Sea World

6227 Sea Harbor Drive. Daily, winter 9am–7pm, longer hours in summer. $31.95.

It may have as many souvenir shops as fish but **SEA WORLD** is the cream of Florida's sizeable crop of marine parks and as such shouldn't be missed. To see it all and get value for money, you'll need to allocate a whole day, and be certain pick up the free map and show schedule at the entrance.

The big event is the **Shamu** show – twenty minutes of un-whale-like tricks performed by a playful killer whale. With substantially less razzamatazz, plenty of smaller tanks and displays around the park explain more than you need to know about the undersea world. Among the highlights, the **Penguin Encounter** attempts to re-create Antarctica with scores of the waddling birds scampering over a make-believe iceberg; the occupants of the **Dolphin Pool** assert their advanced intellect by flapping their fins and drenching passers-by; and **Sharks!** includes a walk through a glass-sided tunnel, offering the closest eye-contact you're ever likely to have with a shark and live to tell the tale.

Most impressive of all, however, at least for thrills and spills, is **Mission Bermuda Triangle**, a simulated dive to the five-mile deep Puerto Rican Trench where some of the mysteries of the Bermuda Triangle – a region with an usually high number of ship disappearances and plane crashes – are examined and (perhaps) explained.

Finally, if you've never been lucky enough to see a manatee in the wild, don't leave Sea World without taking in **Manatees: the Last Generation?**, where a few of the endangered creatures can be witnessed and the threat faced by their species is outlined in no uncertain terms.

Other attractions around Orlando

The Orlando area's small-time entrepreneurs are nothing if not inventive. No end of tacky, short-lived would-be attractions spring up each year and a large number of them swiftly sink without trace. The list opposite represents the best – or just the longest-surviving – of the thousand-and-one little places to visit around Orlando.

Elvis Presley Museum

5770 Hwy-192. Daily 10am–11pm; $4.

Clothes, guitars, guns and art owned by the legendary Memphis hip-shaker, put together as an excuse for a large souvenir shop.

Flying Tigers Warbird Air Museum

231 Hoagland Blvd, next to Kissimmee airport. Daily Mon–Sat 9am–5.30pm, Sun 9am–5pm; $6.

The main hangar contains battle-weary Tiger Moths, Mustangs and assorted bombers and biplanes in various states of repair – all being commercially restored.

Mystery Fun House

5767 Major Blvd. Daily 10am–9pm; $7.95.

The real mystery of this unprepossessing collection of distorting mirrors, moving floors and talking furniture is why more people don't ask for their money back. You can, at least, get there and back free on the shuttle bus which cruises International Drive with "Mystery Fun House" loudly emblazoned on its side.

Reptile World Serpentarium

5705 Hwy-192, just east of St Cloud. Tues–Sun 9am–5.30pm; $3.75.

A research center for the production of snake venoms, which are sold to hospitals and similiar institutions who in turn produce anti-venoms. Visitors are treated to a caged collection of poisonous and non-poisonous snakes from around the world, and demonstrations of venom extraction at 11am, 2pm and 5pm.

Ripley's Believe It or Not!

8201 International Drive. Daily 10am–11pm; $8.95.

A model of the world's tallest man, a chunk of the Berlin Wall and a Rolls Royce built from a million matchsticks, are among the innumerable oddities and curiosities packed into this seemingly lop-sided building.

Terror on Church Street

135 S Orange Ave. Tues–Thur & Sun 7pm–midnight; Fri & Sat 7pm–1am; $10.

The price may be high, but this combination of live actors, hi-tech special effects and imaginative audiotracks, all intended to scare people out of their wits, sometimes works surprisingly well.

Wet'n'Wild

6200 International Drive. Summer daily 9am–9pm, shorter hours in winter; $18, half-price after 3pm.

Water slides, chutes, rapids and wave machines, just the job for a day's splashing about when the thermometer soars.

Xanadu

4800 Hwy-192. Daily 10am–10pm; $4.95.

Supposedly the home of the future, equipped with some innovative and ecologically sound ideas, although whether anyone would ever want to live in this grossly designed cross between a teapot and an igloo is debatable, and the admission price is excessive.

SOUTH CENTRAL FLORIDA

Unfortuitously trapped between the holiday haunts of Orlando and the beaches of the Tampa Bay area, the main towns of **South Central Florida** haven't been done any favors, either, by decades of phosphate mining which have left their surrounds pockmarked with craters. Improvement is coming, however. Many of the unsightly holes have been turned into lakes (joining a large number of natural ones), and the prospect of boating, waterskiing and fishing on them is attracting visitors from the grip of Orlando. More interestingly, several of the region's small towns were big towns around the turn of the century and are keen to flaunt their pasts – and near them are several refreshingly under-hyped attractions which were bringing tourists to Florida when Walt Disney was still in kneepants.

Lakeland and Around

A logical place to begin touring the region, **LAKELAND**, fifty miles southwest of Orlando along I-4, plays the suburban big brother to its even more rural neighbors, providing sleeping quarters for Orlando and Tampa commuters, who emerge at weekends to stroll the edges of the town's numerous lakes, or to ride over them in hideous swan-shaped paddle-boats.

Aided by its busy railway terminal, Lakeland's fortunes rose in the Twenties' and a number of its more important buildings have been maintained as the **Munn Park Historic District** on and close to Main Street – pay special heed to the 1927 *Polk Theater*, 124 S Florida Avenue, and the restored balustrades, lampposts and gazebo-style bandstand on the promenade around Lake Mirror, at the east end of Main Street. A few minutes' walk from the town center, the generous size of the **Polk County Museum of Art**, 800 E Palmetto Street (Tues–Sat 10am–4pm, Sun noon–4pm; free), suggests Lakeland is striving to heighten its cultural profile: the spacious galleries air the latest innovative pieces by rising Florida-based artists on a temporary basis.

A stronger draw, and something no one would anticipate in such a tucked-away community, is the largest single grouping of buildings by **Frank Lloyd Wright**, who redefined America's architectural thinking throughout the Twenties and Thirties. Maybe it was the rare chance to design an entire communal area that appealed to Wright – the fee he got for converting an eighty-acre orange grove into **Florida Southern College**, a mile southwest of Lakeland's center, certainly didn't; the financially strapped college paid on credit and got its students to do the laboring.

Much of the integrity of Wright's initial concept has been lost: buildings have been crudely adapted and used for other than their intended purposes, and newer structures have distorted the overall harmony. Even so, the campus is an inventive statement and easily assessed using the free **maps** provided in boxes along its covered walkways. Interestingly, Wright's contempt for air conditioning caused him to erect thick masonry structures to shield the students from the Florida sun, and his desire to merge his work with the natural environment allowed for the creeping vegetation of the orange grove (now given way to lawns) to wrap around the buildings and provide further insulation.

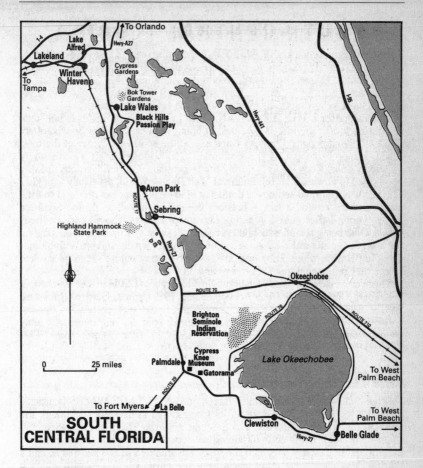

To Orlando

Lake Alfred

Lakeland

Hwy-A27

To Tampa

Winter Haven

Cypress Gardens

Bok Tower Gardens

Lake Wales

Black Hills Passion Play

Avon Park

ROUTE 17

Sebring

Highland Hammock State Park

Hwy-27

Okeechobee

ROUTE 70

ROUTE 78

ROUTE 710

Brighton Seminole Indian Reservation

Cypress Knee Museum

Palmdale

Gatorama

ROUTE 29

Lake Okeechobee

To West Palm Beach

0   25 miles

To Fort Myers

La Belle

Clewiston

To West Palm Beach

Hwy-27

Belle Glade

SOUTH CENTRAL FLORIDA

Practicalities

Get a descriptive **walking tour map** of the historic district from the **Chamber of Commerce**, 35 Lake Morton Drive (Mon–Fri 9am–4.30pm; ☎813/688-8551). For **eating**, the *Reececliff*, 940 S Florida Avenue (☎813/686-6661), a spartan diner in business since 1934, has ridiculously cheap – if rather small – breakfasts and lunches; the *Cabbage Rose*, 235 N Kentucky Ave (☎813/683-0772), serves decent lunches in the twee environs of an antique shop; more down to earth is the *Silver Ring*, 801 Tennessee Avenue (☎813/687-3283), with sizeable Cuban sandwiches. If you're around on a Friday, grab a bowl of homemade black bean soup from *Julio's*, 213 N Kentucky Avenue (☎813/686-1713).

Lakeland doesn't have any nightlife worth waiting around for, but if you're looking for **accommodation** before pressing on, make use of the atmospheric *Lake Morton Bed & Breakfast*, 817 South Boulevard (☎813/688-6788; ③), or inexpensive motels such as *Passport Inn*, 740 E Main Street (☎813/688-5506; ②–④), or *Scottish Inn*, 244 N Florida Avenue (☎813/687-2530; ②).

Lake Alfred, Winter Haven and Cypress Gardens

The sole reason to visit **LAKE ALFRED**, fifteen miles east of Lakeland on Hwy-17 (also known as Hwy-92), is to rummage about inside the **junk and antique shops** lining Haines Boulevard. While bargains may be few, students of Americana are in for a treat as they sift through the vintage Coke signs, old kitchen tools, yellowing family albums, and moth-eaten moose heads.

Like Lake Alfred, **WINTER HAVEN**, seven miles south, struggles to hold onto its passing traffic; the motels (see below) lining Cypress Gardens Boulevard are due to the long-popular **Cypress Gardens**, at the southeast corner of the town (daily, winter 9am–6pm, later in summer; $24). Gouged from a sixteen-acre swamp by dollar-a-day laborers during the Depression, Cypress Gardens makes a good place to unwind after the tumult of Walt Disney World, especially with kids. The neatly landscaped setting – a profusion of towering cypress trees and colorful plants arching around a lake – bolsters the patient mood, as do the Southern Belles: young ladies attired in antebellum hooped skirts who sit and fan themselves while being relentlessly photographed. Besides syncopated waterskiing on the lake, the gardens also have a selection of alligator, snake and bird exhibitions, plus Hug Haven, where baby creatures – such as tiny pumas – can be stroked before they're big enough to bite your hand off.

There are snack bars and restaurants inside Cypress Gardens, but it's cheaper to **eat** in the *Ranch House Motor Inn* coffeeshop, 1911 Cypress Gardens Boulevard (☎813/294-4104), purveyors of gooey breakfasts, bounteous lunches and evening booze-ups. The *Ranch House* is also a good spot for an **overnight stay** (reservations on ☎1-800/366-5996; ②–③), as is *Ye Olde English Motel*, 1901 Cypress Gardens Boulevard (☎813/324-5998; ②–③).

Lake Wales and around

Fourteen miles southeast of Winter Haven on Hwy-27, **LAKE WALES** is a lackadaisical town with more of note on its fringes than in its center, although the **Lake Wales Depot Museum**, 325 S Scenic Highway (Mon–Fri 9am–5pm, Sat 10am–4pm; free), holds an entertaining collection of train parts, remnants from the turpentine industry on which the town was founded in the late 1800s, and a Warhol-like collection of crate labels from the citrus companies with which it prospered during the early 1900s.

At the museum, confirm directions to **Spook Hill**, an optical illusion that's been turned into a transparently bogus "legend", but one which would be a shame to miss (conveniently, it's on the way to Bok Tower Gardens, see below). By car, cross Central Avenue from the museum and turn right into North Avenue, following the one-way system. Just before meeting Hwy-17A, a sign indicates the spot to brake and put your vehicle into neutral: as you do so, the car appears to slide uphill. Looking back from the junction makes clear the difference in road gradients which creates the effect.

Bok Tower Gardens

"A more striking example of the power of beauty could hardly be found, better proof that beauty exists could not be asked for", opined landscape gardener William Lyman Phillips upon visiting **Bok Tower Gardens** (daily 8am–6pm; $3, last admission 5pm) in 1956. As sentiment-drenched as it may sound, Phillips' comment was spot-on. Whether it's the effusive entanglements of ferns, oaks and palms, the bright patches of magnolias, azaleas and gardenias, or just the sheer novelty of a slope (this being the highest point in peninsula Florida), Bok Tower Gardens, two miles north of Lake Wales on Hwy-17A, is one of the state's most lush and lovely places.

Not content with winning the Pulitzer Prize for his autobiography in 1920, Dutch-born office-boy turned author and publisher **Edward Bok** resolved to transform the pine-covered Iron Mountain (as this hump is named) into a "sanctuary for humans and birds", in gratitude to his adopted country for making his glittering career possible. President Coolidge, one of Bok's many famous friends, showed up to declare it open in 1929.

Marvellous though they are, these 128 acres would be just a glorified botanical garden were it not for the intensely phallic **Singing Tower**, two hundred feet of marble and coquina rising sheerly above the branches, poetically mirrored in a swan- and duck-filled lake. Originally intended to conceal the garden's water tanks, the tower carries finely sculptured impressions of Florida wildlife on its exterior and fills its interior with a 53-bell carillon: richly timbred chimes resound through the garden every half-hour. Only the 3pm recital is "live" (all the others are recordings), but you can discover more about its workings in the **visitor center**, which fills an old cracker cottage near the garden's entrance.

A portion of the grounds is left in its raw state, allowing wildlife to roam – and be surreptitiously viewed through the glass front of a wooden hut – and a twenty-minute passage to be hacked along the **Pine Ridge trail**, through the pine trees, saw-edged grasses and wild flowers that once covered the entire hill.

Chalet Suzanne

In 1931, gourmet cook and world traveller Bertha Hinshaw, recently widowed and made penniless by the Depression, moved to an isolated site two miles north of Lake Wales, beside Hwy-17, to open a restaurant called **Chalet Suzanne**. Armed with self-devised recipes and tremendous powers of culinary invention – adding chicken livers to broiled grapefruit, for instance – Bertha had created what's now among the most highly rated meal stops in the country, one that's still run by her family.

Aside from the food (a multi-course lunch or dinner costs upwards of $40; reservations on ☎813/676-6011), the quirky architecture grabs the eye: drunkenly angled buildings painted in clashing pinks, greens and yellows, topped by twisting towers and turrets. You're free to wander through the public rooms – whose furnishings are as loopy as the architecture – even if you're not stumping up for a meal or staying in one of the luxurious guest rooms (⑤–⑧).

The one sensible structure is the soup cannery, where *Romaine* soup – another of Bertha's creations – begins its journey to the nation's gourmet food shops. While here, don't be frightened by low-flying aircraft: a small runway beside the cannery is where corporate execs and freeloading food critics breeze in by private plane for a slap-up meal.

Lake Kissimmee State Park

Nineteenth-century Floridian farming techniques might not seem the liveliest subject in the world, but the 1876 Cow Camp section of **Lake Kissimmee State Park** (daily 8am–sunset; cars $3.25, pedestrians & cyclists $1), fifteen miles east of Lake Wales off Route 60, is an enjoyable and instructive re-creation of a pioneer-era cattle farm, complete with park rangers playing the parts of "crackers" (the nickname of the state's early cattle farmers), and tending genuine cows and horses.

Elsewhere in the park, an observation point above Lake Kissimmee can be utilized for bird- and alligator-spotting; to get closer to the water, rent a canoe ($10 per half-day) from the marina.

South from Lake Wales: along Hwy-27

The section of Hwy-27 which runs **south from Lake Wales** is among Florida's least eventful roads: a four-lane snake through a landscape of gentle hills, lakes, citrus groves and fast-asleep retiree-dominated communities. Busy with farm trucks, the highway itself is far from peaceful, but provides an interesting backwoods course if you're making for either coast: smaller roads branch off towards Fort Myers, on the west coast, and, after Hwy-27 twists around the massive Lake Okeechobee, to the big centers of the southeast coast.

Avon Park, Sebring and Around

Two miles along Hwy-27 from Lake Wales stands the purpose-built amphitheater which stages the **Black Hills Passion Play**, a dramatic re-creation of the last week in the life of Christ, five times weekly between mid-February and mid-April. Seats cost $6 to $12 and are quickly snapped up. If intrigued, get more information on ☎813/676-1495.

Twenty miles further, **AVON PARK** acquired its name from an early English settler born in Stratford-on-Avon; for information on her, and a sprightly documentation of the community's general history, call in at the **Avon Park Museum**, 3 N Museum Avenue (usually 10am–2pm; free). Once you've worn out the museum, leave Avon Park with Route 17, tracing a ten-mile path around a series of lakes to **SEBRING**, whose unusual semicircular street-plan was devised by its founder, George Sebring: he planted an oak tree here in 1912 to symbolize the sun and declared that all the town's streets would radiate out from it. They still do, and Route 17 passes the small park now enclosing the great tree just prior to reconnecting with Hwy-27.

As quiet as can be for eleven months of the year, Sebring's tranquillity is shattered each March when tens of thousands of motor-racing fans pack its motels and restaurants, arriving for a twelve-hour endurance contest, the **12 Hours of Sebring**, held at a race track about ten miles east – if you're passing through then, plan accordingly.

Well away from the sound of revving engines, the orange grove and cypress swamp trails inside **Highlands Hammock State Park**, six miles west of Sebring on Route 634 (daily 8am–sunset; cars $3.25, pedestrians and cyclists $1), add up to a well-spent afternoon. Keep an eye out for the white-tailed deer who make their homes here, and try to time your visit to join the informative ranger-guided **tram tour** (for times, call ☎813/385-0011).

Further homage is paid to cypress trees just beyond Palmdale, forty miles south of Sebring, at the **Cypress Knee Museum** (daily 8am–sunset; $2), which stocks some of the most lifelike specimens of Cypress Knees – a lumpy growth on the tree which enables its submerged roots to breath. Close by, **Gatorama** (daily 8am–6pm; $4.50) is a working alligator farm, licensed to keep thousands of the toothy creatures for public viewing and for turning into handbags, boots and food – if you've already visited Orlando's Gatorland Zoo (see "South from Orlando"), this is more of the same.

Off Hwy-27 at Palmdale, Route 29 runs west to La Belle, from which Hwy-80 continues thirty miles to Fort Myers (see Chapter Six); Hwy-27 ploughs on around the southern edge of Lake Okeechobee.

Around Lake Okeechobee

The hamlets and tiny towns on the edge of **Lake Okeechobee** – a body of water which covers more than 750 square miles but is rarely more than fifteen feet deep – are proud agricultural communities growing fat from the "muck" (the technical term for the extremely fertile black soil found here), and by catering to the thousands of anglers who pursue the large-mouth bass, freshwater catfish and speckled perch (or "crappie") which populate the lake. Traditionally, the lake's waters have drained slowly south to nourish the Everglades after the summer rains, but the disruption caused to this cycle by extensive "reclaiming" of land for citrus, vegetables and sugar cane is one of the hottest environmental issues in Florida – and the reason why local farmers and ecologists are at each others' throats.

Points of scenic beauty are few: often the lakes' clear blue waters are obscured by levees, and grassy marshes stretch up to a mile offshore – great for spotting wading birds but not much else. The settlements are unexciting, too – better news are the secluded fishcamp restaurants which dish up fish as fresh as you've ever tasted it, and do a good sideline in frogs' legs and alligator tails; look for their handwritten signs beside the road.

The East Side of the Lake: Along Route 78

Leaving Hwy-27 just west of Moore Haven, Route 78 charts a 34-mile course along the eastern side of the lake, passing through Fisheating Creek, where the aptly named *Hideaway Restaurant* makes a good stop, and continuing into the treeless expanse of Indian Prairie, part of the 35,000-acre **Brighton Seminole Indian Reservation**. Although they live in houses rather than traditional Seminole chickees, the several hundred native Americans resident here stay close to long-held beliefs – handicrafts may be offered from the roadside, but you won't find any of the tacky souvenir shops common to reservations in more populous areas. On this side of the lake, **accommodation** is limited to several well-equipped **campgrounds**, the best of which are *Aruba Camp Resort* (☎813/946-1324), ten miles from Moore Haven on Route 78, which is dominated by RVs but also offers low-cost motel-type rooms, and *Twin Palms Resort* (☎813/946-0977), seventeen miles further.

Continuing on Hwy-27: Clewiston, Belle Glade and around

From Moore Haven, Hwy-27 is walled by many miles of sugar cane – half of all the sugar grown in the US, in fact – harvested between March and November by Jamaican laborers who are flown in, housed in hostels and notoriously underpaid for their physically demanding – and dangerous – work. Many in Florida, particularly the 43,000 locally employed in the sugar industry, seem content to turn a blind eye to the scandalous treatment of the migrants. Their plight is not a subject wisely brought up in **CLEWISTON**, fourteen miles from Moore Haven, dominated by the US Sugar Corporation and through the company's multi-million dollar profits enjoying the highest per capita income in the country – or in **BELLE GLADE**, twenty miles east, which has the biggest sugar mill in the country. A sad place of potholes and trailer parks, Belle Glade is worth pausing in for the **Laurence E Will Museum** (Mon–Fri 10am–6pm, Sat 10am–5pm; free), which documents the rise of this archetypal pioneer town, and the 1928 hurricane which whipped up the lake and flooded Belle Glade, leaving two thousand dead – an emotive sculpture in the park beside the museum remembers the tragedy.

Places to stay are relatively plentiful, though squarely aimed at fishing folk – if that's not your scene you may as well stay away: on Torrey Island, two miles west of Belle Glade on Route 717, *J-Mark Fish Camp* has motel rooms (☎407/996-5357; ②), and the *Belle Glade Marina & Campground* (☎407/996-6322) has lots of campervan space and a tent area.

Just outside Belle Glade, Hwy-27 swings south towards Miami (Chapter One), eighty miles distant, while Hwy-441 cuts forty miles to West Palm Beach (Chapter Three).

NORTH CENTRAL FLORIDA

Millions of people each year hammer through **North Central Florida** towards Orlando, almost all of them oblivious to the fact that a few miles east of the unrelentingly ordinary I-75 are the villages and small towns that typified Florida before the arrival of interstate highways and made-to-measure vacations. The region has just two appreciably sized towns, one of which holds a major university, and a terrain which varies from rough scrub to resplendent grassy acres lubricated by dozens of natural springs. Giving it a few days won't waste your time or break your budget: costs here are extremely low.

> The area code for North Central Florida is ☎904

Ocala and Around

Known throughout the US for the champion runners bred and trained at the thoroughbred horse farms occupying its green and softly undulating surrounds, **OCALA** itself is a town without much to shout about – though it makes an agreeable base for seeing more of the immediate area. The **Chamber of Commerce**, 110 E Silver Springs Boulevard (Mon–Fri 8.30am–5pm; ☎629-8051), can supply local facts, issue walking maps of the town's mildly interesting historic districts and tell you which of the **horse farms** are open for free tours. Better use of a day, however, is visiting the two contrasting museums on either side of the town, or the huge natural spring which has been pulling the crowds for years.

The Garlits and Appleton museums
Ten miles from Ocala, near Exit 67 off I-75, the **Don Garlits Museum of Drag Racing** (daily 10am–5pm; $7.50) parades dozens of low-slung drag-racing vehi-

cles, including the "Swamp Rat" machines which propelled local legend Don Garlits to 270mph over the drag tracks during the mid-Fifties. Yellowing press cuttings and grainy films chart the rise of the sport, and a subsidiary display of Chevys, Buicks and Fords – and the classic hits pumped out by a Wurlitzer jukebox – evoke an *American Graffiti* atmosphere.

An outstanding assembly of art and artefacts sits on the other side of Ocala, inside the **Appleton Museum of Art**, 4333 E Silver Springs Boulevard (Tues, Wed, Fri & Sat 10am–4.30pm, Thurs 10am–8pm, Sun 1–5pm; $3). Spanning the globe and 5000 years, the exhibits, collected by a wealthy Chicago industrialist, go together with remarkable cohesion, and there's barely a dull moment over two well-filled floors. Early Rembrandt etchings, a Rodin *Thinker* cast from the original mold and paintings by Jules Breton amid an exquisite stock of nineteenth-century French canvases, are admirable enough, but the handicrafts are really special: look for the Turkish prayer rugs, the brightly colored Naxco ceramics, the wooden Tibetan saddle and the massed ranks of "Toggles" – Japanese *netsuke* figures carved from ivory.

Silver Springs

Five miles east of the Appleton Museum on Silver Springs Boulevard, **Silver Springs** (daily 9am–5.30pm, longer hours in summer; $21.95) has been winning admirers since the late 1800s when Florida's first tourists came by steamboat to stare into the spring's deep, clear waters. Silver Springs makes a nicely mellow half-day, though the admission fee is questionably high considering the proliferation of springs all across central and northern Florida – some of them just a few miles east in the Ocala National Forest (see overleaf). What you pay for, in fact, is not the spring but the imported animals – monkeys, deer, giraffes, llamas and some hot-looking Scottish highland cattle – who now live around it. Take the **glass-bottomed boat tour** over the spring, and the bumpy **jeep safari** and smooth **river cruise** through the wildlife areas – all included in the admission price. Pass a few minutes, too, inspecting the **Antique Car Collection**, highlight of which is the Mercedes formerly owned by Maria Von Trapp, inspiration of *The Sound of Music*; seeing the car is as exciting as seeing the film.

Ocala Practicalities

Motels line Silver Springs Boulevard between Ocala and Silver Springs: the *Fairways Motel* (no 2829; ☎622-7503; ②–③), *Horne's Motor Lodge*(no 3805; ☎629-0155; ②–③) and *Silver Springs* (no 4121; ☎236-4243; ②–③) are all worth trying. For comparative luxury, the *Seven Sisters Inn*, 820 SE Fort King Street (☎867-1170; ④–⑤), offers bed and breakfast in a picturesque Queen Anne House. The only local **campground** to allow tents is the *KOA* (☎237-2138), five miles southwest of Ocala on Route 200.

You'll seldom spend more than $5 for a filling **meal** in the town, with a wide selection along E Silver Springs Boulevard. For hearty all-American food, go to the *Stage Stop Restaurant* (no 5131; ☎236-2501) or *Morrison's Cafeteria* (no 1600; ☎622-7447). Slightly more expensively, *Richard's Place* (no 316; ☎351-2233) does tasty things with vegetables; for something meaty and out of the ordinary, sample the large helpings of bratwurst and schnitzel at the *German Kitchen* (no 5340; ☎236-3055).

Ocala National Forest

Translucent lakes, bubbling springs and a splendid 65-mile hiking trail bring week-end adventurers to the **Ocala National Forest**, five miles east of Silver Springs on Route 40. Steer clear of the busy bits, and you'll find plenty to savor in seclusion – alternatively, if you only have time for a quick look, take a spin along Route 19 (meeting Route 40, 22 miles into the forest), running north–south in the shade of overhanging hardwoods near the forest's eastern edge.

Juniper, Alexander and Salt Springs

For undemanding nature, with swimming, canoeing (rent on the spot, for $15 per half-day), very gentle hiking – and lots of other people, especially on weekends and holidays – thrown in, the forest has three warm-water springs which fit the bill; and each of them has an campground. The easiest to reach from Silver Springs is **Juniper Springs** (info: ☎625-3147), twenty miles ahead on Route 40, particularly suited to hassle-free canoeing with a seven-mile marked course. **Alexander Springs** (info: ☎669-3522), on Route 445 about ten miles southeast of Juniper Springs, has good canoeing, too, and its see-through waters are perfect for snorkelling and scuba-diving.

To the north of the forest, reachable with Route 314 or Route 19, the most devel-oped site – it even has a petrol station and laundromat – is **Salt Springs** (informa-tion ☎685-2048). Despite the name, the springs here pump up 52 million gallons of freshwater a day, and the steady 72°F temperature stimulates a semi-tropical

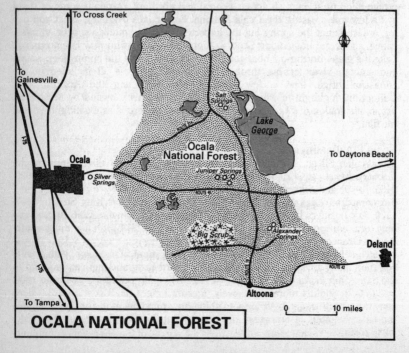

OCALA NATIONAL FOREST

INFORMATION ON THE OCALA NATIONAL FOREST

The **visitor information center** (daily 9am–5pm; ☎625-7470), just inside the forest on Route 40, has maps and general info. The latest **camping updates** are available by phoning the camping areas at Juniper, Alexander and Salt springs (see below). For specialist hiking tips, call at one of the **district ranger offices** – the northern and southern halves of the forest are administered respectively by the **Lake George Ranger District**, Route 2, Silver Springs (☎625-2520), and the **Seminole Ranger District**, 1551 Umatilla Road, Eustis (☎357-3721).

surround of vividly colored plants and palm trees. Swimming and canoeing are as good here as at the other two springs, but people come mainly for the fishing, casting off in anticipation of catfish, large-mouthed bass and speckled perch.

The Ocala Hiking Trail
The 65-mile **Ocala hiking trail** runs right through the forest, traversing many remote, swampy areas, and passes beside the three springs mentioned above. Very **basic campgrounds** appear at regular intervals (be warned that these are closed during the mid-Nov to early Jan hunting season). At the district rangers' offices (see the above box), pick up the excellent leaflet describing the trail, written with the novice backpacker in mind.

However keen you might be, you're unlikely to have the time or stamina to tackle the entire trail, though one exceptional area that merits the slog required to get to it is **Big Scrub**, a imposingly severe landscape with sand dunes – and sometimes wild deer – moving across its semi-arid acres. The biggest problem at Big Scrub is lack of shade from the scorching sun, and the fact that the nearest facilities of any kind are miles away – don't come unprepared. Big Scrub is in the southern part of the forest, seven miles along Forest Road 573, off Route 19, twelve miles north of Altoona.

North from Ocala

From the monotonous I-75, you'd never guess that the thirty-odd miles of hilly, lakeside terrain just to the east contain some of the most distinctive and insular villages in the state. Beyond the bounds of public transport, they can be reached only by driving; head north from Ocala with Hwy-301.

Cross Creek and the Rawlings Home
Native Floridians often wax lyrical about Marjorie Kinnan Rawlings, author of *The Yearling*, the tale of a Florida farmer's son's coming-of-age, and *Cross Creek*, describing the daily activities of country folk in **CROSS CREEK**, about twenty miles from Ocala on Route 325 (off Hwy-301). Leaving her husband in New York, Rawlings spent her most productive years – the Thirties – writing and tending an orange grove here; a time inaccurately re-created in Martin Ritt's 1983 film, *Cross Creek*.

The restored **Rawlings Home** (Thurs–Mon 10–11.30am & 1–4.30pm; guided tours on the half-hour; $1) gives an eye-opening insight into the toughness of the "cracker" lifestyle, but more surprising is the refusal of the self-reliant community

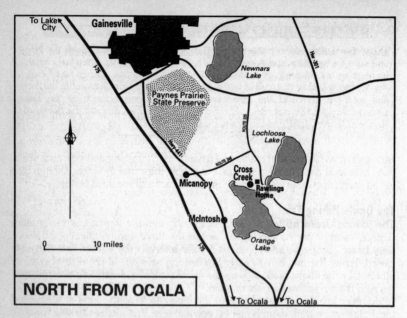

NORTH FROM OCALA

to cash in on their literary associations – and even the *Yearling Restaurant* (☎466-3033) isn't as overpriced as it could be. The menu, based on Rawlings' recipe book, *Cross Creek Cookery*, includes catfish, alligator tail, cooter (soft-shelled turtle) and other stomach fillers enjoyed by her neighbors – often more through necessity than choice. Lunch will set you back about $7.

Micanopy, McIntosh and Paynes Prairie

Four miles north of Cross Creek, Route 346 branches off to meet Hwy-441 just outside **MICANOPY**: a voguish vacation destination during the late 1800s, of late making efforts to win back visitors by turning itself, and many of its century-old brick buildings, into antique and craft shops. They're okay for a quick browse but if it's a weekend, much better to travel a few miles south along Hwy-441 to another village, **MCINTOSH**, whose 400-strong population spend their rest days dressing up in Victorian costumes, to escort visitors on tours of their restored homes.

In contrast to such conviviality, the marshy landscapes of the **Paynes Prairie State Preserve** (daily 8am–sunset; cars $3.25, cyclists and pedestrians $1), filling a broad sweep of land between Micanopy and Gainesville, can't help but strike a note of foreboding. It's an eerie place in many ways, though one well stocked with wildlife: cranes, hawks, waterfowl, otters, turtles and various wading birds all make homes here, as do many alligators. Ranger-led walks, hikes and horse-rides (reservations: ☎466-3397) uncover the fascinating natural history of the area – and some of the social history: habitations have been traced back to 10,000 BC. Without a guide, you can bone up on the background at the **visitor center** (Wed–Sun 9am–5pm), four miles from Micanopy off Hwy-441, and peer into the moody wilderness from the nearby **observation tower**.

Gainesville and Around

Without the University of Florida, **GAINESVILLE**, 35 miles north of Ocala, would be just another slow-paced rural community nodding off in the Florida heartland. As it is, the daintily sized place, once called Hogtown, is given a boost by its 40,000 students, who bring a lively, liberal spirit and account for the only decent nightlife in Central Florida outside Orlando. This, combined with a few low-key targets in and around the town, and plentiful cheap accommodation, make Gainesville a deserving base for a day or two.

On a sadder note, Gainesville hit the national headlines for all the wrong reasons in August 1990 when the bodies of five murdered and mutilated students were discovered in off-campus apartment blocks. Incredibly, despite the incarceration of a suspect, two similar killings took place in June 1991, and these horrific crimes are likely to haunt Gainesville for some time to come.

The Town and the University

Credible sights are few in Gainesville's quiet center, where most of the people you'll see are office workers going to or from work or nipping out to lunch. At the junction of University Avenue and NE First Street you'll spot the **Clock Tower**, an undramatic relic culled from Gainesville's nineteenth-century courthouse; inside are the clock workings and some photos from the old days. If these whet your historical appetite, explore northwards along Third Street, which reveals many of the showcase homes of turn-of-the-century Gainesville – Queen Anne, Colonial and various Revival styles dominate – and the palm-fronted **Thomas Center**, 306 NE Sixth Avenue (Mon–Fri 9am–5pm, Sat & Sun 1–4pm; free), once a plush hotel and restaurant, which now hosts small-scale art and historical exhibitions.

The old buildings are easily tracked down with the *Historic Gainesville* brochure issued by the **Visitors and Convention Bureau**, at 10 SW Second Avenue (Mon–Fri 8.30am–5pm; ☎374-5231). From the town center, it's an easy fifteen-minute walk along University Avenue to the university; though if you're feeling very lazy, take a bus (any number from #1 to #10) from beside the Clock Tower. The *Greyhound* station is centrally placed, at 516 SW Fourth Avenue (☎376-5252).

The University of Florida

Most of Gainesville's through-traffic passes half a mile west of the town center along Thirteenth Street (part of Hwy-441), from which the **University of Florida (UF)** campus stretches three miles west from its main entrance by the junction with University Avenue. Call at the **information booth**, facing SW Second Street, for a free map, without which it's easy to get lost in the expansive grounds.

After it opened in 1906, the university's early science alumni gave Florida's economy a leg-up by pioneering the state's fantastically successful citrus farms. These days, the curriculum is broader based and modern buildings dominate the campus, although the first you'll see are the red-bricked "Collegiate Gothic" structures favored by US turn-of-the-century academic institutions. In the center of the campus, styled in imitation of the Collegiate style, the 1953 **Century Tower** serves as a navigational aid and a time-keeping device – its electric bells issue a nerve-shattering clarion every hour.

Beyond the tower, the 73,000-seat **Florida Field** stadium – home of the Gators football team and a monument to the popularity of college sports in Florida – can hardly be missed, and neither can the adjacent **O'Connel Center**, an indoor sports venue, entering which is akin to walking into a giant balloon. It's not too much of an architectural simplification to say that air keeps the O'Connel building's roof up – feel the pressure change as you push through the swing doors. Aside from staging evening volleyball and basketball games, and entertaining design buffs, the building offers only a cool, refreshing breather.

A couple of other places also offer quick respites from the sun. The temporary shows in the **University Gallery** (Mon–Sat 9am–5pm, Sun 1–5pm; free), inside the Fine Arts Building, capture the best student art, while nearby, on Museum Road, the **Florida Museum of Natural History** (Tues–Sat 10am–4pm, Sun 1–4pm; free) is much larger but disappointing, with shallow displays and texts on Florida's prehistory and wildlife. The best feature is the Object Gallery's pull-out drawers, containing some weird and wonderful (dead) insects.

Back outdoors, walk about a mile west along Museum Road to the tidy University Garden, where a concealed footpath leads to **Lake Alice**, overlooked by a wooden observation platform gradually losing its battle against the surrounding vegetation. You could come here for a picnic, but the roar of insects, the constant scampering of lizards and the knowledge that alligators are plentiful, means keeping your guard up as you gaze over the sizeable lake.

Accommodation
Although Gainesville has rows of low-cost **motels** a couple of miles out of the center along SW Thirteenth Street, be warned that they fill quickly when the Gators are playing at home. The closest tent-friendly **campground** is ten miles south at the Paynes Prairie State Preserve (see above; ☎466-3397).

Bambi, 2119 SW 13th St (☎1-800/34BAMBI). Slightly nearer to downtown than most of the inexpensive motels. ②.
Comfort Inn, 2435 SW 13th St (☎373-6500). One of the newer budget options. ②.
Econo Lodge, 2469 SW 13th St (☎1-800/424-4474). Reliable chain motel. ②.
Gainesville Lodge, 413 W University Ave (☎376-1224). Much the most convenient place to stay, near downtown Gainsville and the campus. ②.

Eating
Gainesville is not a difficult place in which to find a good meal, with plenty of restaurants around the town center and the university.

Emiliano's Café, 7 SE First St (☎375-7381). Fresh-baked delights and substantial Costa Rican-style lunches.
Café Saigon, 101 SE Second St (☎375-6612). Very affordable Vietnamese meals.
Skeeter's, 2601 NW 13th St (☎373-5597). $2 early-bird breakfast specials and mountainous low-cost buffets for lunch and dinner. Folksy singers on Sundays.
Snuffy's, 1017 W University Ave (☎376-8899). Gourmet burgers, steaks and fresh seafood.

Nightlife
The town's students keep a bright **nightlife** in motion, live rock music being especially easy to find. For **what's on details**, check the *Scene* section of Friday's *Gainesville Sun*, or the free *Moon* magazine, found in most bars and restaurants.

Full Circle, 6 E University Ave (☎377-8080). The hippest of Gainesville's clubs. Comics and acoustic acts early in the week, and house, acid, techno and classic disco grooves on Thursday to Sunday nights.

The Hardback Café, 232 SE First St (☎372-6248). The best of the live music venues, attracting left-field acts at weekends and assorted painters and poets on other nights.
Lilian's, 112 SE First St (☎372-1010). Live bands and a 2–8pm happy hour.
Market Street Pub, 120 SW First St (☎377-2927). Brews its own beer and provides acoustic country and bluegrass music to help it down.
Richenbacher's, 208 W University Ave (☎375-5356). Live rock or reggae bands nightly and a 4–8pm happy hour.

Around Gainesville

Three places close to Gainesville will help flesh out a day. Two of them are neighbors and served by local buses; the third can only be reached by car – unless you're feeling energetic and **rent a bike** from *Chain Reaction Bicycles*, 1630 W University Avenue ($5 per hour or $12 per day; ☎373-4052).

Kanapaha Botanical Gardens and the Fred Bear Museum

Flower fanciers shouldn't miss the 62-acre **Kanapaha Botanical Gardens** (Mon, Tues & Fri 9am–5pm, Wed, Sat & Sun 9am–sunset; $1.50), five miles southwest of central Gainesville on Route 24, reachable with bus #1. The summer months more than most are a riot of color and fragrances, although the design of the gardens means there's always something in bloom. Besides vines and bamboos, and special sections planted to attract butterflys and hummingbirds, the highlight is the herb garden, whose aromatic bed is raised to nose-level to encourage sniffing.

Across the road from the gardens, a signpost points to the **Fred Bear Museum** (Wed–Sun 10am–6pm; $2.50): a mass of mounted, skinned and stuffed animals, and some (such as the elephant's ear table with hippo legs) turned into furniture. Many of the unfortunate creatures were caught and killed by Fred Bear himself, who runs the adjoining archery factory: not a place for animal lovers.

The Devil's Millhopper

Of thousands of sinkholes in Florida, few are bigger or more spectacular than the **Devil's Millhopper** (daily 9am–sunset; cars $2, pedestrians and cyclists $1; free guided tour Sat 10am), seven miles northwest of Gainesville, off 53rd Avenue. Formed by the gradual erosion of limestone deposits and the collapse of the resultant cavern's ceiling, the lower reaches of this 120-foot-deep bowl-shaped dent have a temperature significantly cooler than the surface, allowing species of alpine plant and animal life to thrive. A winding boardwalk delivers you into the thickly vegetated depths.

North of Gainesville

Travelling north of Gainesville puts you in easy striking distance of the Panhandle (Chapter Seven) to the west, and Jacksonville, the major city of the Northeast Coast (Chapter Four). Uncertain of which way to turn, relax for a few hours at **Ichetucknee Springs** (daily 8am–sunset; cars $3.25, pedestrians and cyclists $1), the birthplace of the Ichetucknee River, whose chilled waters lend themselves to canoeing or inner-tube rafting along a six-mile course. Weekdays, when beavers, otters and the odd turtle share the river, are the best time to come; weekend crowds scare much of the wildlife away. The springs are 35 miles north of Gainesville, on Route 238.

There's no point in stopping in the unremarkable Lake City, thirteen miles north of the springs, as a couple of more fulfilling short breaks are within a few minutes' drive. Don't bother, though, with the **Osceola National Forest**, east of Lake City, the smallest of the state's three federally protected forests, mostly visited by hardened fishermen bound for its Ocean Pond.

The Stephen Foster State Culture Center

Twelve miles north of Lake City, off Hwy-41, the **Stephen Foster State Culture Center** (daily 8am–sunset; cars $3.25, pedestrians and cyclists $1) offers a tribute to the man who composed Florida's state song, *Old Folks At Home*, immortalizing the waterway ("Way down upon the S'wanee river. . .") which flows by here on its 250-mile meander from Georgia's Okefenokee Swamp to the Gulf of Mexico. As it happens, Foster never actually saw the river but simply used "S'wanee" as a convenient Deep South-sounding rhyme. Besides exploring Florida's musical roots, the center has a sentimental display about Foster, who penned a hatful of classic American folk songs including *Camptown Races, My Old Kentucky Home* and *Oh! Susanna* – instantly familiar melodies which ring out through the oak-filled park from a belltower – before dying penniless in New York in 1863, aged 37.

The Olustee Battlefield Site

The **Olustee Battlefield Site**, thirteen miles west of Lake City beside Hwy-90 (daily 9am–5pm; free), is a sure sign you're approaching the Panhandle, a Confederate power base during the Civil War. The only major battle of the conflict in Florida took place here in February 1864, when 5000 Union troops pressing west from Jacksonville squared up to a similar-sized Confederate force. The five-hour battle, which left 300 dead, nearly 2000 wounded and both sides claiming victory, is marked by a monument and an interpretive center (closed Tues & Wed), and by a trail around the respective troop positions – hard to imagine the carnage that took place in what's now, as then, an otherwise peaceful pine forest.

travel details

Trains

From Orlando to Kissimmee/Lakeland/Tampa (2 daily; 18min/1hr 28min/2hr 17min); Winter Park/ Sanford/DeLand/Jacksonville (2 daily; 15min/ 38min/58min/3hr 12min).

From Winter Haven to Sebring/West Palm Beach/Fort Lauderdale/Miami (2 daily; 38min/2hr 9min/3hr/4hr 2min).

Buses

From Orlando to Fort Pierce/West Palm Beach/ Fort Lauderdale/Miami (7 daily; 2hr 25min/4hr/ 5hr 20min/5hr 55min); Kissimmee (2 daily; 40min);

Ocala/Gainesville/Tallahassee (4 daily; 1hr 30min/2hr 50min/5hr 30min); Sanford/DeLand/ Daytona Beach/Jacksonville (4–6 daily; 35min/ 1hr/2hr 35min/3hr 30min); Winter Haven/ Lakeland/Tampa (5 daily; 1hr 5min/1hr 35min/3hr 15min).

From Clewiston to Belle Glade/West Palm Beach (1 daily; 30min/1hr 35min).

From Lakeland to Winter Haven/Cypress Gardens/Lake Wales/Avon Park/Sebring/West Palm Beach (1 daily; 30min/45min/1hr 5min/3hr 5min/3hr 30min/5hr).

CHAPTER SIX

THE WEST COAST

I n three hundred miles from the state's southern tip to the border of the Panhandle, Florida's **WEST COAST** embraces all the extremes. Buzzing, youthful towns neighbor placid fishing hamlets; mobbed holiday strips are just minutes from desolate swamplands. Surprises are plentiful: search for a snack bar and you'll stumble across a world-class art collection; doze off on an empty beach and you'll wake to find it packed with shell-collectors. The West Coast's one constant is proximity to the Gulf of Mexico – and sunset views rivalled only by those of the Florida Keys.

The heavily populated **Tampa Bay area**, midway along the coast, is the obvious first stop if you're arriving from Central Florida. The West Coast's largest city, **Tampa** probably won't detain you long, although it has more to offer than its power-dressers and corporate towers initially suggest, not least a long-established Cuban community.

Directly across the bay, **St Petersburg** once took pride in being the archetypal Florida retirement community: lately it has recast itself in a younger mold and is riding high on its acquisition of a major collection of works by surrealist artist Salvador Dali. For the mass of visitors, though, the Tampa Bay area begins and ends with the **St Petersburg Beaches**, whose miles of sea, sun and sand are undiluted vacation territory – but also a useful base for exploring the Greek-dominated community of **Tarpon Springs**, just beyond.

Far from the beach crowds, and indeed far from beaches, the **Big Bend** consumes the coast **north of Tampa**. No settlement numbers more than a few thousand amid the area's dead-flat marshes, large chunks of which are wildlife refuges with little public access. Within the scattered communities, it's easy to discover evidence of busier times: from a prehistoric site of sun-worship at **Crystal River**, to the long-defunct railway that made **Cedar Key** a thriving cargo port over a century ago.

A string of barrier-island beaches runs the length of the Gulf **south from Tampa**. The mainland towns which provide access to them have a lot in their favor, too: **Sarasota**, the first of any size, is the custodian of a fine-arts legacy passed down by a turn-of-the-century circus boss; further south, Thomas Edison was one of a number of scientific pioneers who took a fancy to palm-studded **Fort Myers**, which neighbors **Sanibel** and **Captiva** – two atmospheric islands justify-

---

ACCOMMODATION PRICE CODES

All accommodation prices in this book have been coded using the symbols below. Note that prices are for the least expensive double rooms in each establishment.
For a full explanation see p.26 in *Basics*.

①	up to $30	④	$60–80	⑦	$130–180
②	$30–45	⑤	$80–100	⑧	$180+
③	$45–60	⑥	$100–130		

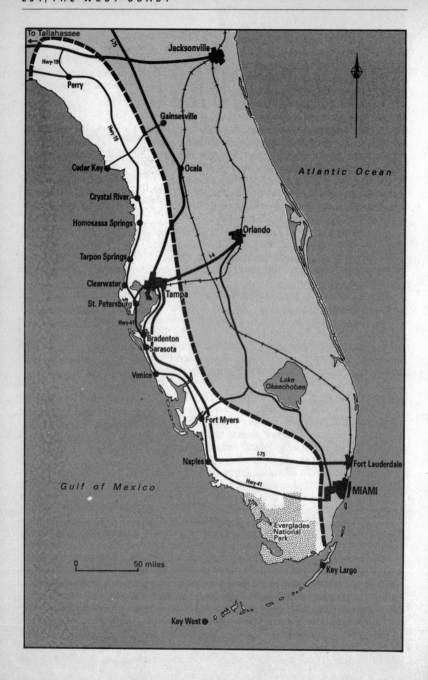

To Tallahassee
Hwy-19
I-75
Jacksonville
Perry
Gainsesville
Hwy 19
Cedar Key
Ocala
Crystal River
Homosassa Springs
Tarpon Springs
I-4
Orlando
Clearwater
Tampa
St. Petersburg
Hwy-41
Bradenton
Sarasota
Venice
Lake Okeechobee
Fort Myers
I-75
Naples
Hwy-41
Fort Lauderdale
MIAMI
Everglades National Park
Key Largo

Atlantic Ocean

Gulf of Mexico

0   50 miles

Key West

ing a few days' relaxed discovery. As you pass through, take the opportunity to strike inland: the southwest coast backs onto the **Everglades**, a vast expanse whose swamps and prairies are brimming with natural life. The window on it all is the **Everglades National Park**, spreading east almost to the edge of Miami; explorable on simple walking trails, by canoeing, or by spending the night at backcountry campgrounds with only the alligators for company.

Getting around

The West Coast is easy to get around. The region's **major roads**, and **I-4** from Central Florida, converge close to Tampa. From Tampa through the Big Bend, **Hwy-19** is the only route, served by two daily *Greyhound* **buses** in each direction. **Hwy-41** connects the main southwest coast settlements, and is often known as the **Tamiami Trail**, a nickname from its time as the only road link crossing the Everglades between Tampa and Miami; these days it's superseded for speed by the bland **I-75**. *Greyhound* services number five daily each way through the southwest coast, and a few towns are also connected by *Amtrak* buses from Tampa. The bigger centers have adequate **local bus services**, though the barrier islands and the Big Bend towns rarely have any public transport.

THE TAMPA BAY AREA

The geographic and economic nerve center of the region with a population almost on a par with that of Miami, the **Tampa Bay area** is easily the busiest and most congested part of the West Coast. People do live here for reasons other than work, however, and there's no reason to stay clear. The wide waters of the bay provide a scenic backdrop for Tampa itself, a stimulating city, while the barrier-island beaches along the coast let the locals swap metropolitan bustle for luscious sunsets and miles of glistening sands, which are also lapped up by large number of holiday-makers.

The area code for the Tampa Bay area and the south West Coast is ☎813

Tampa

TAMPA is a small city with an infectious upbeat mood; you'll only need a day to explore it thoroughly but you'll depart with a lasting impression of a city on the rise. The West Coast's undisputed business hub, it has been one of the major benefactors of the recent flood of people and money into Florida – and lavishes an impressive amount on a high-brow cultural diet envied by many larger communities. In spite of this, and the international airport that brings them to its doorstep, Tampa gets scant regard from many arrivals who aim for Busch Gardens, a theme park on the city's outskirts, and the Gulf coast beaches half an hour's drive west – missing out totally on one of Florida's most youthful and energetic urban communities.

Tampa **began** as a small settlement beside Fort Brooke, a US Army base built to keep an eye on local Seminole Indians during the 1820s. Staying tiny, isolated and insignificant until the 1880s, when the railway arrived and the Hillsborough

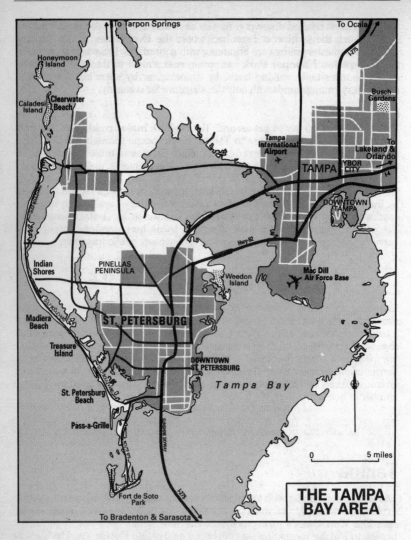

THE TAMPA BAY AREA

River – on which the city stands – was dredged to allow sea-going vessels to dock, Tampa became a booming port and simultaneously acquired a major tobacco industry as thousands of Cubans moved north from Key West to the new cigar factories of neighboring Ybor City. The Depression saw off the economic surge, although the port remained one of the busiest in the country and tempered the decline Tampa endured during the postwar decades. While the social problems that blight any US city are evident, there seems little to stand in the way of Tampa's continued emergence as a forward-thinking and financially secure community.

Regardless of the deals being struck in its towering office blocks, downtown Tampa is surprisingly quiet and compact, where the art museum and *Tampa Bay Hotel*, one of the few reminders of times gone by, form the basis of a three-hour ramble. Downtown Tampa may lack atmosphere and history, but there's plenty of both three miles northeast in **Ybor City**, whose Latin American character originated with migrant cigar workers; it now boasts myriad markers to the heady days of Cuban independence struggles. With more time to spare, Hyde Park contains the homes of Tampa's wealthiest early settlers, and it's worth venturing out to **Busch Gardens** or the **Museum of Science and Industry**, or into the wild, open country which appears remarkably quickly just north of the busy city.

Arrival, information and getting around

The city's **airport** (☎870-8700) is five miles northwest of downtown Tampa. Local bus #30 (see below) is the least costly connection; more expensive but potentially more convenient are the *Central Florida Transit* minivans (☎276-2730), which depart every thirty minutes throughout the day, costing $10. If you're heading for St Petersburg or the St Petersburg Beaches (see p.267 and p.270), use the around-the-clock *Limo Inc* buses (☎572-1111), whose representatives have desks in the baggage reclaim area; flat fare to any coastal accommodation is $25. **Taxis** (the main firms are *United*, ☎253-2424, and *Yellow*, ☎253-8871) are abundant but expensive: to downtown Tampa or a Busch Boulevard motel costs $12–15; to St Petersburg or the St Petersburg Beaches, $35–45. All the major **car rental** companies have desks at the airport.

Long-distance public transport terminates in downtown Tampa: *Greyhound* **buses** at 610 Polk Street (☎229-2174), and **trains** at 601 Nebraska Avenue (☎221-7600). The main routes **by car** into Tampa are I-275 and I-4 (intersecting with I-75, ten miles east of the city), which converge a few miles north of downtown Tampa. Be warned that downtown Tampa has a fiendish one-way system.

Local buses

Although downtown Tampa and Ybor City are easily covered on foot, to travel between them – or to reach Busch Gardens or the Museum of Science and Industry – without a car, you'll need to use **local buses** (☎254-HART), whose routes fan out from Marion Street in downtown Tampa. **Useful numbers** are #8 to Ybor City; #5, #18 or #39 to Busch Gardens; #44 (from University Square Mall) to the Museum of Science and Industry; and #30 to the airport. Only rush-hour commuter buses run **between Tampa and the coast**: #100 to St Petersburg and #200 to Clearwater. Alternatives are the numerous daily *Greyhound* buses or the twice-daily *Amtrak* bus.

Information

In downtown Tampa, collect vouchers, leaflets and general information from the **visitor information center**, 111 Madison Street (Mon–Sat 9am–5pm; ☎1-800/44-TAMPA). In Ybor City, visit the **Ybor City Chamber of Commerce**, 1513 Eighth Street (Mon–Fri 9am–5pm; ☎248-3712). Opposite Busch Gardens, the **Tampa Bay Visitor Information Center**, 3601 E Busch Boulevard (daily 10am–6pm; ☎985-3601) has local and state-wide informations. For **nightlife** listings, read the free *Creative Loafing* and *Tampa Tonite*, buy the Friday edition of the *Tampa Tribune*, or call the free *Nightlife* phone service on ☎854-8000.

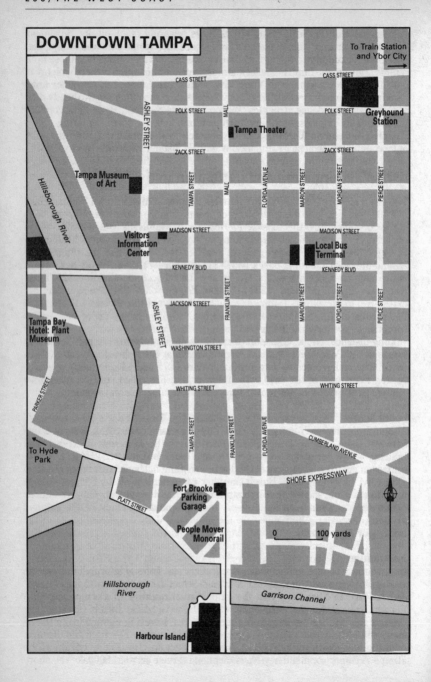

DOWNTOWN TAMPA

To Train Station
and Ybor City →

CASS STREET · CASS STREET

POLK STREET · POLK STREET · Greyhound Station

ASHLEY STREET

Tampa Theater

ZACK STREET · ZACK STREET

Tampa Museum of Art

TAMPA STREET · MALL · FLORIDA AVENUE · MARION STREET · MORGAN STREET · PIERCE STREET

Hillsborough River

Visitors Information Center

MADISON STREET · MADISON STREET

Local Bus Terminal

KENNEDY BLVD · KENNEDY BLVD

JACKSON STREET

ASHLEY STREET

FRANKLIN STREET · MARION STREET · MORGAN STREET · PIERCE STREET

Tampa Bay Hotel: Plant Museum

WASHINGTON STREET

WHITING STREET · WHITING STREET

PARKER STREET

TAMPA STREET · FRANKLIN STREET · FLORIDA AVENUE

CUMBERLAND AVENUE

To Hyde Park

SHORE EXPRESSWAY

Fort Brooke Parking Garage

PLATT STREET

People Mover Monorail

0   100 yards

Hillsborough River

Garrison Channel

Harbour Island

Accommodation

Except for the area around Busch Gardens, Tampa is not generously supplied with low-cost **accommodation**, and you're likely to save money by sleeping in St Petersburg or at the beaches, and treating the city as a day trip.

The cheaper **motels** are all on E Busch Boulevard close to Busch Gardens: *Garden View* (no 2500; ☎933-1921; ②), *Econo Lodge,* (no 1701; ☎933-7681; ②–③), *Economy Inn* (no 1810; ☎1-800/527-0605; ②), and *Golden Key* (no 2523; ☎933-6760; ②–③) are the best of a substantial bunch.

Any of the above makes a reasonable base for seeing the city by car; if you're dependent on buses, however, and downtown Tampa and Ybor City are your main interests, choice is much more limited. Several **bed and breakfast inns** are planning to open in Ybor City – check the latest by phoning the Chamber of Commerce (see "Information"). Until they do, you'll need to use one of the downtown business-traveller-aimed hotels, such as the convenient *Riverside,* 200 N Ashley Drive (☎223-2222; ④–⑥).

Other than the site at the Hillsborough River State Park (see "Around Tampa"), the only local **campground** where tents are welcome is the huge *Tampa East Green Acres,* at 12720 Hwy-92 (☎659-1004), a dispiriting twelve miles northeast of the city and useless without personal transport.

Downtown Tampa

Downtown Tampa's current prosperity is demonstrated by its upright office towers; aside from riverside warehouses in various states of dilapidation and renovation around the northern end of the pedestrianized **Franklin Street** (once the compact district's pulsating main drag and still the best place to get your bearings), recalling the city's past is largely left to text-bearing plaques detailing everything from the passage of sixteenth-century explorer Hernando de Soto to the site of Florida's first radio station. The single substantial relic of bygone days is the **Tampa Theatre**, 711 Franklin Street, one of the few surviving "atmospheric theaters" erected by Mediterranean-mad designer John Eberson during the Twenties. When silent movies enthralled the masses, Eberson's cinemas heightened the escapist mood: ceilings became star-filled skies, balconies were chiselled into Moorish arches, gargoyles leered from stuccoed walls, and replica Greek and Roman statuary filled every nook and cranny. Having fallen on hard times with the arrival of TV, the Tampa Theatre is enjoying a new lease of life as the home of the Tampa Film Club, sporting a full programme of very viewable movies – a $4 ticket for one (see "Nightlife") is the only way to gain access to the splendidly restored interior.

None of the contemporary buildings in downtown Tampa better reflects the city's striving for cultural articulacy than the **Tampa Museum of Art**, on the banks of the Hillsborough River at 601 Doyle Carlton Drive (Tues–Sat 10am–5pm, Sun 1–5pm; free guided tours at noon & 1pm). Incongruous as it may seem, the highly regarded museum specializes in classical antiquities and twentieth-century American art: selections from the permanent modern stock are cleverly blended with loaned pieces from the cream of recent US painting, photography and sculpture. A third gallery is devoted to major travelling exhibitions, often of an excellent standard.

Continuing south, you'll feel like an insignificant speck at the feet of the city's tallest structures: for a better view of them – and their surrounds – take the short monorail ride (from the terminal on top of the Fort Brooke Parking Garage on Whiting Street; 25¢ each way) to **Harbor Island**, a large shopping mall on a small island dredged from the Hillsborough Bay.

Across the river: the Tampa Bay Hotel

From Harbor Island you can't fail to spot the silver minarets, cupolas and domes glinting through the trees on the far side of the river, sprouting from the main building of the University of Tampa – formerly the **Tampa Bay Hotel**, a fusion of Moorish, Turkish and Spanish building styles financed to the tune of $2 million by steamship and railway magnate, **Henry B Plant**. The structure is as bizarre a sight in today's Tampa as it was on its opening in 1891, when its 500 rooms looked out on a community of just 700 souls. Be sure to make a closer inspection: walk across the river on Kennedy Boulevard and climb down the steps leading into Plant Park.

Plant had been buying up bankrupt railways since the Civil War and steadily inching his way into Florida to meet his steamships unloading at Tampa's harbor. Like Henry Flagler, whose tracks were forging a trail along Florida's east coast and whose posh resorts in St Augustine (see Chapter Four) were the talk of US socialites, Plant was wealthy enough to put fantasies of creating the world's most luxurious hotel into practice without worrying unduly about the cost. While the *Tampa Bay Hotel* boosted the prestige of the town, Plant's boast to "turn this sandheap into the Champs Élysées, the Hillsborough into the Seine", was never realized, and the hotel stayed open for less than ten years. Lack of care for the fittings (the hotel was only used during the winter months and left to fester during the scorching summer), and Plant's death in 1899, hastened its transformation from the last word in comfort to a pile of musty, crumbling plaster. The city authorities bought the place in 1905 and halted the rot, leasing the building to the fledgling Tampa University 23 years later.

In a wing of the main building, the **Plant Museum** (Tues–Sat 10am–4pm, Sun noon–4pm; $3) has several rooms holding what's left of the hotel's furnishings: not a welcome sight for purists, the clutter of Venetian mirrors, elaborate candelabras, ankle-deep rugs, Wedgewood crockery and intricate teak cabinets were the fruits of a half-million-dollar shopping expedition undertaken by Plant and his wife across Europe and Asia. Note the reassembled *Rathskellar*, a gentleman's social room previously in the hotel basement (now a student snack bar, see below) complete with German wine cooler, card and billiard tables and the final room which reveals Mrs Plant's affection for vulgarly sized ornamental swans.

A few strides from the museum, the former lobby is a popular rendezvous point for the university's two thousand students, who display their tans from the hotel's old wicker chairs surrounded by its antique French statuary. You can roam around much of the building at will, but the details only fall into place on the **free guided tour**, departing from the lobby at 1.30pm on Tuesdays and Thursdays (Sept–May only). After the tour, call into the *Rathskellar*, which looks nothing like its forebear re-created in the Plant Museum but has cheap food and, from 4pm, beer.

Hyde Park

If they don't ensconce themselves in a bay-view condo, Tampa's yuppies snap up the old wooden homes of **Hyde Park**, a mile southwest of downtown Tampa just off Bayshore Boulevard. Attracted by the glamor of the newly opened *Tampa Bay*

Hotel, well-heeled 1890s arrivals raised several blocks in the architectural modes that defined the wealthier sections of turn-of-the-century American towns: a mish-mash of Mediterranean, Gothic, Tudor and Colonial revival jobs, interspersed with Queen Anne cottages and prairie-style bungelows – rocking-chair-equipped porches being the sole unifying feature. Such complete blasts from the past are rare in Tampa and, provided you're driving (they don't justify a slog around on foot), the old homes are easy to appreciate on a twenty-minute drive on and around Swann and Magnolia avenues and Hyde Park and South boulevards. Even Tampans who prefer up-to-date living quarters descend on Hyde Park to lay waste to their wages in the fashionable stores of *Olde Hyde Park Village*, beside Snow Avenue, where several classy restaurants offer affordable refreshment; see "Eating", below.

Continuing south from Hyde Park, incidentally, brings you to the gates of **Mac Dill Air Force Base**. This, the nerve center of US operations during the 1991 Gulf War, was where the Queen knighted General "Stormin' Norman" Schwarzkopf later the same year.

Ybor City

In 1886, as soon as Henry Plant's ships (see above) ensured a regular supply of Havana tobacco into Tampa, cigar magnate Don Vincente Martinez Ybor cleared a patch of scrubland three miles northeast of present-day downtown Tampa and laid the foundations of **YBOR CITY**. Around 20,000 migrants, mostly Cubans drawn from the strife-ridden Key West cigar industry, joined by a smattering of Spaniards and Italians, settled here, creating an enclave of Latin American life and producing the top-class hand-rolled cigars that made Tampa the "Cigar Capital of the World" for forty years. Mass-production, the popularity of cigarettes and the Depression proved a fatal combination for skilled cigar makers: as unemployment struck, Ybor City lost its *joie de vivre*, and while the rest of Tampa expanded, its twenty tight-knit blocks of cobbled streets and red-brick buildings became surrounded by drab and dangerous low-rent neighborhoods.

Over the last few years, efforts to mold Ybor City into a tourist attraction have brought improvements and saved many older buildings from dereliction. As yet, visitors are too few to over-commercialize the place: shops still sell hand-rolled cigars, the smells of newly baked Cuban bread and freshly brewed coffee are never far off, and many relics from the eventful past remain. Taking their cue from the craftsmen who created the Spanish ceramics decorating many neighborhood structures, new faces are beginning to appear, too, opening arts and crafts galleries and helping make Ybor City one of Tampa's trendiest – and most enjoyable – quarters.

Walking around Ybor City

The Latin roots are instantly apparent and explanatory background texts adorn many buildings, but Ybor City's sights are never dramatic and its mood is surprisingly subdued. Take it in by leisurely strolling the ten blocks of Seventh and Eighth avenues east of Thirteenth Street: the heart of this individual yet very small community. The **Ybor City State Museum**, 1818 Ninth Avenue (Tues–Sat 9am–noon & 1–5pm; $1), offers just enough to help you grasp the main points of Ybor City's creation and its multi-ethnic make-up. Enormous wall photographs show the cigar rollers at work: thousands sat in long rows at bench-tables on a

25¢-per-cigar piece-work rate, cheering or heckling the *lector* (or reader) who recited the news from Spanish-language newspapers. Like the museum, the six restored **cigar workers' houses**, a few yards along on Ninth Avenue (one is open for a walk-through tour; hours as the museum; free), are more worthy than riveting, demonstrating the unelaborate turn-of-the-century domestic arrangements.

There's more activity in the factory where the cigar-rolling actually took place, now called **Ybor Square**, 1901 Thirteenth Street (Mon–Sat 9.30am–5.30pm, Sun noon–5.30pm), and converted into a collection of tourist-aimed shops and restaurants. A peek inside this cavernous structure – its three storeys supported by sturdy oak pillars – complements the museum's photos, however, and you should pause at one of the snack bars for an invigorating Cuban coffee. If you're not afraid to smoke it, you might even purchase (for a dollar) a hand-rolled cigar from *Tampa Rico* on the first floor.

Standing on the factory's iron-work steps in 1893, the famed Cuban poet and independence fighter José Martí spoke to thousands of Ybor City's Cubans, calling for pledges of money, machetes and manpower for the country's anti-Spanish pro-independence struggles*. It's estimated that expatriate Cuban cigar workers contributed ten percent of their earnings, most of which was spent on the illicit purchase and shipment of arms to rebels in Cuba. A stone marker at the foot of the steps records the event and, across the street, the **José Martí Park** remembers Martí with a statue.

From the earliest days, each of Ybor City's ethnic communities ran its own social clubs, published newspapers and even organized a medical insurance scheme which led to the building of two hospitals. The hospitals still function today, as do several of the social centers. Stepping inside one (opening hours vary wildly) reveals patriotic paraphernalia and sometimes, in the basement, men-only dens of dominoes and drinking: if you can, call into *Centro Español*, corner of Seventh Avenue and Fifteenth Street, *El Circulo Cubano*, 2010 Fourteenth Street, or *Centro Austriano*, 1913 Nebraska Avenue, for a look at Ybor City life that most visitors miss. One Ybor City institution out-of-towners invariably do find is the *Columbia* restaurant, 2117 Seventh Avenue (see "Eating"). Now filling a whole block, the *Columbia* opened in 1905 as a humble coffee stop for tobacco workers; inside, wall-lining newspaper cuttings recount its rise and rise.

Around Tampa

The collar of suburbia around downtown Tampa contains few reasons to stop. Hereabouts, though, the city's cheapest motels cluster around a theme park – **Busch Gardens** – ranking among the state's top tourist attractions. While as enjoyable as any of its ilk, you might be inclined to skip the park and divide your attentions between the **Museum of Science and Industry** and (provided you're driving; it's unreachable by public transport) the 3000 pristine acres of the

---

*A few years after Martí's speech, Tampa became the embarkation point for the US's Cuban Expeditionary Forces, with thousands of US soldiers housed in tents waiting to join the Spanish-American War. On January 1, 1899, the Spanish pulled out of Cuba and the US also withdrew – not without retaining a lot of power and influence – and Cuba acquired its independence.

Hillsborough River State Park. On the way, don't be tempted by the Seminole Indian Village (5221 N Orient Road), part of a Seminole reservation where a token collection of native American arts and crafts is on sale to tourists and high-stakes bingo is played.

Busch Gardens
3000 E Busch Boulevard. Daily, winter 9.30am–6pm; longer hours in summer; $27.95.

Incredible as it may seem, most people are drawn to Tampa by a theme park re-creation of colonial-era Africa in the grounds of a brewery. In glossing over the questionable tarting up of a period of imperial exploitation in the name of enter-tainment – and the garden's subtitle, "The Dark Continent", caused justifiable outrage within the local black community – **Busch Gardens** brazenly reshapes world history just as much as its arch rival, Walt Disney World. It costs a packet and is as tacky as hell, but if you do come you'll need to stick around all day to get your money's worth, go on everything in the park (all the rides are included in the admission fee) – and learn to love the kitsch without dwelling on its implications.

Traversable on foot or by pseudo-steam train, the 300-acre gardens divide into several areas. You'll first enter *Morocco*, where Moroccan crafts are sold at un-Moroccan prices, snake-charmers and belly dancers weave through the crowds, and the Mystick Sheiks Marching Band blast their trumpets into the ears of passers-by. Follow the signs to *Nairobi* and you'll find small gatherings of alliga-tors, crocodiles and monkeys in varying states of liveliness, and the animal hospital and petting zoo inhabited by cute and cuddly child-pleasing creatures. Directly ahead in *Timbuktu*, animals are less in evidence than amusements; a hair-raising switchback and a simulated ride through a desert sandstorm impress-ing most. If the Ubanga-Banga bumper cars in the *Congo* don't hold lasting appeal, gird your loins for the swirling raft trip around the Congo River Rapids – which may encourage you to cross Stanleyville Falls on a roller-coaster, the best feature of neighboring *Stanleyville*. The biggest single section of the gardens, the *Serengeti Plain*, roamed by giraffes, buffalos, zebras, antelopes, black rhino and elephants, is the closest the place gets to showing anything genuinely African; see the beasts from the all-too-brief monorail ride. After all this, retire to the *Hospitality House* of the *Anheuser-Busch Brewery*, purveyors of *Budweiser* to the masses and owners of the park, where the beer is free but limited to three drinks per person.

The Museum of Science and Industry
4801 E Fowler Avenue. Sun–Thurs 9am–4.30pm, Fri & Sat 9am–9pm; $5.50.

Two miles northeast of Busch Gardens, the **Museum of Science and Industry** will entertain adults with a couple of hours to kill as much as kids with all day to spare. Intended to reveal the mysteries of the scientific world, the hands-on displays and machines are hard to resist. Among the major exhibits, a hurricane demonstration allows begoggled participants to the feel the force of the strongest winds known, and a massive walk-through pinball machine lets you follow the ball along 700 feet of track. The most demanding item, the *Challenger Learning Center*, is so sophisticated a simulation of a space station mission that to use it requires advance booking (at least two weeks ahead; phone ☎1-800/444-MOSI) and a morning of instruction.

Hillsborough River State Park

12 miles north of Tampa on Hwy-301. Daily 8am–sunset; cars $3.25, pedestrians and cyclists $1.

Beneath a shady overhang of live oaks, magnolias and sable palms, the **Hillsborough River State Park** holds one of the state's rare instances of rapids – outside of a theme park – as the Hillsborough River tumbles over limestone outcrops before pursuing a more typical meandering course. Rambling the sizeable park's walking trails and canoeing the gentler sections of the river could nicely fill a day (and the park makes an enjoyable **camping** place; ☎906-1020), but on a Saturday or Sunday you should devote part of the afternoon to the **Fort Foster Historic Site**, a reconstructed 1836 Seminole War fort only viewable with the **guided tour** (departures from the park entrance at 1pm, 2pm & 3pm; $2). Stemming from the US attempts to drive Florida's Seminole Indians out to reservations in the Midwest and make the state fit for the white man, the Seminole Wars waged throughout the nineteenth century and didn't end officially until 1937. Period-attired enthusiasts occupy the fort and recount historical details, not least the fact that more soldiers died from tropical diseases than in battle; over the river, the occupants of the Seminole camp unfurl a somewhat different account of the conflict: both sides make interesting listening.

CANOEING ON THE HILLSBOROUGH RIVER

To spend a half- or whole day gliding past the alligators, turtles, wading birds and other creatures who call the Hillsborough River home, contact *Canoe Escape*, 9335 E Fowler Avenue (☎986-2067), who have devised a series of novice-friendly routes along the tea-colored river. Cost is $24–28 for two people (extra person; $8), and you should make a reservation at least 72 hours in advance.

Eating

Choice and quality are features of Tampa **eating** with the exception of **downtown Tampa**, where street stands dispensing snacks to lunching office workers are the culinary norm. Nonetheless, *Peppercorns*, 102 S Tampa Street (☎221-4467), is a likely venue for a good sandwich or a salad; *Gladstone's Grilled Chicken*, 502 Tampa Street (☎221-2988), serves poultry like you've never tasted it before; and at the *New Soul Sandwich Shop*, 518 N Willow Avenue (☎251-3720), you can chow down on fried chicken, collard greens, black-eyed peas and other wholesome Southern staples. On a tour around the *Tampa Bay Hotel* (see "Downtown Tampa"), drop into the student-patronized *Rathskellar* for a cheap, light meal.

There's more choice elsewhere. In and around **Hyde Park**, budget breakfasts are found at *Café by the Bay*, 1350 S Howard Avenue (☎251-6659). Later, for lunch or dinner, *Storch & Sons Seafood*, 1713 S Lois Avenue (☎286-2993), offers low-cost seafood; *Ho Ho Chinois*, 720 Howard Avenue (☎254-9557), lays out a sizeable Chinese lunch buffet; and the *Cactus Club*, 1601 Snow Avenue (☎251-6897), has fiery Tex-Mex and delicious "Texas-style" pizzas.

In **Ybor City**, the *Café Creole & Oyster Bar*, 1330 Ninth Avenue (☎247-6283), excels in spicy cajun dishes, with the best value being the filling gumbo seafood soup; *Rough Riders* (☎248-2756), inside *Ybor Square* at 1901 Thirteenth Street, delivers sizzling burgers and ribs; the *Silver Ring*, 1831 E Seventh Avenue (☎248-2549), has been serving simple but authentic Cuban sandwiches for nearly fifty years; the *Columbia*, 2117 Seventh Avenue (☎821-0983), has been going even longer, its refined Spanish and Cuban food becoming a fixture on the tourist circuit (see "Ybor City"); and *Eighth Avenue Bistro*, 1906 Avenida de Cuba (☎248-8283), is a trendy stop for creative sandwiches and burgers. For a herbal tea pick-me-up and a muffin, dip into the *Three Birds Bookstore and Coffee Room*, 1518 Seventh Avenue (☎247-7041).

Nightlife

Tampa **at night** has always been strong on drinking and live rock music; of late, the cultural profile has been raised with regular high-quality shows in a state-of-the-art performance venue. For details of forthcoming arts and cultural events, phone the **Artsline** on ☎229-ARTS; general nightlife listings are available for free from **Nightlife** on ☎854-8000 (use your touch-tone phone to access the category – comedy clubs, sports bars, local bands and more – which interests you). For **tickets** to any major event, call *Ticketmaster*, ☎287-8844.

Drinking

Many live music venues and nightclubs (see below) have tempting **drink** reductions, although the most cost-effective way to booze, as ever, is at the **happy hours** taking place all over the city – just watch for the signs. For later drinking, head to Ybor City for the *Irish Pub*, 1721 E Seventh Avenue (☎248-2099), or the Gothic-inspired *Castle*, at the corner of Ninth Avenue and 15th Street (☎247-7547). If you like to yell at TV sport shows after downing a few, sample the city's biggest **sports bars**: *Sidelines Sports Emporium*, 11425 N Dale Mabry Highway (☎960-2398), and *Champions*, 1001 N Westshore Boulevard (☎286-2201).

Live music and nightclubs

Creative Loafing and *Tampa Tonight* (see "Information", above) have **live music** listings and local talent worth catching. Tampa's most dependable club is the blues- and reggae-dominated *Skipper's Smokehouse*, 910 Skipper Road (☎971-0666). You'll also find reggae at *Caribbean Jasmine*, 810 E Skagway Avenue (☎935-8988). Overall, though, it's no-nonsense hard rock that keeps Tampa jumping into the small hours: *Killans Lounge*, 4235 W Waters Avenue (☎884-8965), and *Kasey's Cove*, 2025 E Fowler Avenue (☎977-2683), are the places to hear it. Another place to hear live music – often featuring cult indie bands – is the *Ritz*, see below.

Of a bunch of average **nightclubs** (see *Tampa Tonight* for a full list), with varying drink specials, karaoke singalongs and theme nights, the *Green Iguana*, 4029 S Westshore Boulevard (☎837-1234), and *Hammerjax*, 901 N Franklin Street (☎221-JAXX), are the ones to try; cover varies from nothing to $8.

Major venues, the performing arts and theater

The big names in rock, jazz, funk and soul are becoming frequent visitors to Tampa's **major venues**: the *USF Sun Dome*, 4202 S Fowler Avenue (☎974-3002), and the *Tampa Stadium*, 4201 Dale Mabry Highway (☎872-7977). Another large and ultra-modern auditorium is the *Tampa Bay Performing Arts Center*, 1010 N MacInnes Place (☎221-1045), where **opera**, **classical music** and **ballet** programmes feature the top US and international names. Ticket prices for any big show are $10–45.

Oddly, given the weight placed on promoting the arts, the city has just one purpose-built **theater**: the *Ritz*, 1503 E Seventh Avenue, in Ybor City (☎247-PLAY), whose two stages see a mix of fringe and bigger-budget mainstream productions, costing $10–15, as well as live music (see above).

Film, comedy clubs and poetry readings

For a full list of **films** playing around the city, read the Friday edition of the *Tampa Tribune*. Foreign-language, classic or cult movies crop up only at the *Tampa Theatre*, 711 Franklin Street (see "Downtown Tampa"); pick up a schedule from the building itself or phone the 24-hour information line: ☎223-8981; tickets are $5. Tampa has one notable **comedy club**: *Comedy Works*, 3447 W Kennedy Boulevard (☎875-9129), where the cover charge is $4–12. If it's Thursday or Saturday, forsake the gags and get stuck into the **poetry readings** at the *Three Birds Bookstore and Coffee Room*, in Ybor City at 1518 Seventh Avenue (☎247-7041), a hangout for Tampa's coffee-drinking literary crowd.

Gay and Lesbian Tampa

Gay and lesbian life in Tampa is improving all the time, with constant additions to a number of established bars, clubs and resource centers. Get general information by calling the **Gay hotline** (☎229-8839) or the more radical **Queer Nation Tampa** (☎882-5783). Although their services are aimed at all women, lesbians can also pick up useful information by phoning the **women's information line** (☎656-77884) and by dropping into *Everywoman's Center*, 4202 E Fowler Street (☎974-3332). Ybor City's *Three Birds Bookstore and Coffee Room*, 1518 Seventh Avenue (☎247-7041), carries handouts for **events** of gay and lesbian interest in the city – and stocks a good range of gay- and lesbian-related literature.

Bars, clubs and restaurants

Easily the most popular, and most enjoyable, nightspot is *Tracks*, at 1430 E Seventh Avenue in Ybor City (☎247-2711), a predominantly gay-male disco with state-of-the-art lighting and cutting edge sounds. Of the exclusively or mainly **gay male bars**, *Carousel*, 1806 Platt Street (☎251-1019), and *Twenty Six-O-Six*, 2606 N Armenia Avenue (☎875-6993), are cruisey watering holes; *Baxter's*, 714 S Dale Mabry Highway (☎879-1161), is more relaxed and upmarket. Enjoyable **mixed bars and clubs** include; *Moody's*, 4010 Dale Mabry Highway (☎831-6537), a restaurant and bar with a Country & Western theme; and *Paradise*, 14802 N Nebraska Avenue (☎971-2132).

Listings

Airport Five miles northwest of downtown Tampa (☎870-8700); reach it with local bus #30, or the shuttle buses listed under "Arrival, information and public transportation".

Dentists For referral: ☎886-9040.

Doctor For referral: ☎870-4444.

Left luggage At the *Greyhound* station, 610 Polk Street; the train station, 601 Nebraska Avenue; and at the airport.

Local bus information ☎254/HART.

Pharmacy *Eckerd Drugs*, 11613 N Nebaska Avenue (☎978-0775), is open around the clock.

Police Emergencies ☎911. To report something lost or stolen: ☎223-1515.

Sport The city's professional football team, *Tampa Bay Buccaneers*, play at Tampa Stadium, 4201 Dale Mabry Highway (box office and match details: ☎879-BUCS); cheapest tickets are $15–35. Tampa's soccer team, the *Rowdies* (☎877-7800), play their outdoor matches at Tampa Stadium and indoor games at the Bayfront Center in St Petersburg, 400 First Street; tickets are $8–50.

Taxis Main operators are *United* (☎253-2424) and *Yellow* (☎253-8871).

Thomas Cook Nearest branch is in St Petersburg: Paragon Crossing, 11 300 Fourth Street North (☎577-6556).

Ticketmaster Branches around the city: ☎287-8844.

Weather ☎622-1212.

St Petersburg

Declared the healthiest place in the US in 1885, **ST PETERSBURG**, twenty miles from Tampa on the eastern edge of the Pinellas peninsula, wasted no time in attracting the recuperating and the retired to its paradisiacal climate, at one point putting five thousand green benches on its streets to take the weight of elderly backsides. By the early 1980s, few people under fifty lived in the town (which, incidentally, was named by a homesick Russian), and no one was surprised when it became the setting for the 1985 movie *Cocoon*, in which a group of local geriatrics magically regain the vigor of their youth. Right now, St Petersburg seems to be emulating them. The average age of its residents has been almost halved, the revamped pier is a great place for open-air socializing, and – most remarkably of all – the town has acquired the major collection of works by the controversial surrealist artist **Salvador Dali**: reason enough to be in St Petersburg, if only as a day's break from the beaches nine miles west on the Gulf coast (see the "St Petersburg Beaches").

Arrival and Information

The main route **by car** into St Petersburg is I-275; don't leave it before the "Downtown St Petersburg" exit or you'll face interminable traffic lights. The *Greyhound* **bus** station is centrally located at 180 Ninth Street (☎898-4455); the **train** station, 3601 31st Street, is two miles west of downtown St Petersburg – there are no trains between Tampa and St Petersburg, just an *Amtrak* bus link. You'll only need **local buses** (☎530-9911) to reach the St Petersburg beaches; though you can't always do this directly – see the "Buses between St Petersburg and the beaches" box on p.270. Most services arrive and depart from the Williams Park terminal, at the junction of First Avenue N and Third Street N, where an information booth gives route details.

Gather the usual tourist **information** and discount coupons from the **visitor center**, 100 Second Avenue N (Mon–Fri 9am–5pm; ☎821-4715), and look out for the free *Pinellas Tonight* for nightlife listings. The ground floor of the pier – see below – also has a well-stocked tourist counter.

The pier and around

Don't think you've arrived in a ghost town if the wide streets of downtown St Petersburg (around the junction of Central Avenue and Fourth Street) seem deserted: everyone gravitates to the quarter-mile-long **pier** jutting from the end of Second Avenue N, a few minutes' walk east. Browsable arts and crafts exhibitions often line the pier, and you'll find stacks of tourist information at the desk by the entrance of the inverted-pyramid-like building at its head, whose five storeys are packed with restaurants, shops and fast-food counters.

There's more to discover within a few blocks, starting at the foot of the pier with the **Historical and Flight One Museum** (Mon–Sat 10am–5pm; Sun 1–5pm; $4.50), a modest gathering recounting St Petersburg's early twentieth-century heyday as a winter resort – lasting until the wider and sandier Gulf coast beaches became accessible – and the world's first commercial airline, which made its inaugural flight from St Petersburg in 1914. There's documentation, too, on Weedon Island, five miles north of the town, once the base of a small film industry and where native American burial mounds yielded significant pottery finds until ransacked by looters in the 1960s. Now a state-protected wildlife refuge, the island's mostly used for fishing and doesn't merit a visit for any other purpose.

At the museum, pick up the free *Historic Downtown Walking Tour* brochure. Not all of the old buildings listed are much to look at, but at least walk along **Fourth Avenue**, passing the grandstands of the **Shuffleboard Court**, no. 536, spiritual home of the amazingly popular sport, and, directly across Fourth Avenue, the Mediterranean Revival facade of the **Coliseum Ballroom**, built in 1924 and still throbbing to big band sounds – see "Nightlife", below.

The Museum of Fine Arts and the Sunken Gardens

Another group of Mediterranean Revival buildings houses the **Museum of Fine Arts** at 255 Beach Drive NE (Tues–Sat 10am–5pm, Sun 1–5pm; donation $4; regular free guided tours). For years this has been one of the state's better art collections; now, however, given the giant strides made by newer museums elsewhere and the new rival Dali Museum (see below), it looks increasingly outmoded.

Inside, the main themes of painterly endeavor from the seventeenth century are represented usually by competent rather than imposing works, although Monet's *Houses of Parliament*, showing a London of silhouettes and misty blues, and Daumier's amusing *Connoisseur of Prints*, are two which shine – together with pre-Columbian pieces, and ceramics, glassworks and antiquities from Europe and Asia. Welcomingly fresher, the European moderns include drawings by Kandinsky, and the American contemporary room has some of Georgia O'Keeffe's blown-up flowers and George Luks' simple and emotive *The Musician*.

Anyone who isn't a fully fledged art buff will have more fun a mile north at the **Sunken Gardens**, 1845 Fourth Street (daily 9am–5.30pm; $8.95). Nearly seventy years ago, a water-filled sinkhole here was drained and planted with thousands of tropical plants and trees which now form the shady and sweet-scented gardens. For a crash-course in exotic botany, scrutinize the texts along the pathway, descending gently through bougainvillea, hibiscus and staghead ferns. Only the parrot shows and the depressingly small cages housing some of the resident animals dim an hour's unhurried pleasure.

The Dali Museum and Great Explorations

Few places make a less likely depository for the biggest collection of works by maverick artist Salvador Dali than St Petersburg, but this is exactly what's on show at the **Salvador Dali Museum**, 1000 S Third Street (Tues–Sat 9.30am–5.30pm, Sun noon–5pm; $5). It stores more than a thousand Dali works from the collection of a Cleveland industrialist who struck up a friendship with the artist in the Forties, bought stacks of his works and ran out of space to show them – until this purpose-built gallery opened in 1982.

Hook up with the **free tours**, which begin whenever sufficient people are mustered. These trace a fact-filled path around the chronologically arranged paintings (some shown on rotation), from early experiments with Impressionism and Cubism to the soft watches of the seminal surrealist canvas, *Persistence of Memory*, and on to Dali's "Classic" period from 1943: enormously complex, inventive works grappling with the fundamentals of religion, science and history. Some – such as the overwhelming *Discovery of America by Christopher Columbus*, and the multiple double-images of the *Hallucinogenic Toreador* – are so big they have been hung in a specially deepened section of the gallery.

Dali never visited the museum, although if he had it's easy to imagine him nipping across the street to spend hours working the hands-on exhibits of **Great Explorations**, 1120 Fourth Street (Mon–Sat 10am–5pm, Sun noon–5pm; $4.50), which is similar to Tampa's much larger Museum of Science and Industry in striving to make the rudiments of science accessible with inventive games. The technology of fun includes bubbles that can climbed inside, an elaborate test-your-fitness display and a chance to feel your way through a pitch-black tunnel – highly amusing, especially for kids whose parents are exploring the Dali collection.

Accommodation

Sleeping in St Petersburg can be less costly than doing so at the beaches; if you come for the day, it might pay to make a night of it. There are two **youth hostels**: *St Petersburg International Hostel*, 215 Central Avenue (☎822/4095), and the *St Petersburg AYH Hostel*, 326 First Avenue (☎822-4141); both charge members $12, others $15; the *AYH* hostel also offers single and double rooms from $32. **Motels** are plentiful and can be exceptionally cheap – under $30 during the summer, under $40 in winter. Of dozens along Fourth Street, the closest to the center are *Banyan* (no 610 N; ☎822-7072; ①), *Landmark* (no 1930; ☎895-1629; ①), and *Kentucky* (no 4246; ☎526-7373; ①).

Eating

The Eating Place, 320 First Avenue NE (☎894-3496), is the top spot for filling **breakfasts** and **lunches**, closely rivalled by the *Corner Coffee Shop*, 201 Third Street S (☎895-6018), and the very basic *Gold Coffee Shop*, 336 First Avenue (☎822-4922). For an excellent and inexpensive seafood lunch or **dinner**, head for *Fourth Street Shrimp Store*, 1006 Fourth Street N (☎822-0325), or the innovative *Seabar*, 4912 Fourth Street (☎527-8728), where you select your meal from the display and have it cooked to your desire. At the pier, you'll find a number of acceptable fast-food stands, and the *Columbia* (☎822-8000), providing high-quality Cuban and Spanish food for $10–15.

Nightlife

If you're at the pier, start the evening at the 4–7pm weekday **happy hour** at *Alessi's* (☎894-4659), then go up to the roof level for the free band playing at *Cha Cha Coconut's* (☎822-6655) – the cool ocean breeze and the night-time St Petersburg skyline making the lightweight rock sounds palatable. Elsewhere, a steady procession of **rock** bands appear at *Club Detroit*, 16 Second Street N (☎896-1244), and *The Big Catch*, 9 First Street (☎821-6444). For an evening with a difference, turn up with your own booze (there's no bar) and prepare your feet for one of the biggest dancefloors in the US, at the the *Coliseum Ballroom*, 535

BUSES BETWEEN ST PETERSBURG AND THE BEACHES

From the Williams Park terminal in St Petersburg, take bus #12, #29 or #35 to the Palms of Pasadena Hospital stop, just off Gulf Boulevard, where *Bats* buses (☎367-3086) cross the Corey Causeway **to St Petersburg Beach and Pass-a-Grille**; Mon–Sat 7am–6pm, Sun 7.45am–6.05pm. Bus #3 from the Williams Park terminal runs to the junction of Central Avenue and Park Street, where the *Treasure Island Dune Buggy* (☎360-0811) continues **to Treasure Island**, plying Gulf Boulevard between 79th and 125th avenues; hourly Mon–Sat 8.15am–4.15pm (except 12.15pm). There's a direct connection from Williams Park **to Madeira Beach and Indian Shores** with #71, and **to Clearwater** with #18 and #52, from where #80 continues **to Clearwater Beach**. For further transport details, see "Buses and boats around Clearwater and Clearwater Beach", p.273.

Fourth Avenue (☎892-5202), which has been a **big band** venue for decades; weekend cover is $9, less during the week.

The St Petersburg Beaches

Drab suburbs stretch west from St Petersburg, covering virtually all of the Pinellas peninsula, a bulky thumb of land poking between Tampa Bay and the Gulf of Mexico. Framing the Gulf side of the peninsula, a 25-mile chain of barrier islands form the **ST PETERSBURG BEACHES***, one of Florida's busiest coastal strips. When the famed resorts of Miami Beach lost their allure during the Seventies, the St Petersburg Beaches grew in popularity with Americans. More recently they've become a major destination for package-holidaying Europeans – English accents and the *Daily Mirror* are commonplace. The sands are broad and beautiful, the sea is warm and the sunsets are fabulous – but in no way is this Florida at its best or most diverse. Despite that, staying here can be very cost-effective (especially during the summer); a few of the islands have been kept in their pre-tourism state and deserve exploration; and it's quite feasible to combine lazing on the beach with day trips to the more interesting of the inland areas.

Beach area information

Several beach areas have **Chambers of Commerce** readily dispensing handy information: St Petersburg Beach, 6990 Gulf Boulevard (Mon–Fri 9am–5pm; ☎360-6957); Treasure Island, 152 108th Avenue (Mon–Fri 8am–4.30pm; ☎367-4529); Madeira Beach, 501 150th Avenue (Mon–Fri 9am–5pm; ☎391-7373). In Clearwater Beach, call at the **Welcome Center**, 40 Causeway Boulevard (Mon–Fri 9am–5pm; ☎446-2424). At any of the above, and in shops, restaurants and motels, look for **free magazines** such as *Beach Visitor*, *Guide Magazine* and *See*; if you want the latest nightlife listings, buy the Friday edition of the *St Petersburg Times*.

---

*A convenient name in the absence of an official collective title; each beach area has a name of its own, though you're likely to hear them branded "the Holiday Isles", or the "Pinellas County Suncoast".

The southern beaches

In twenty-odd miles of heavily touristed coast, just one section has the looks and feel of a genuine community: the slender finger of **PASS-A-GRILLE** at the very southern tip of the barrier island chain. One of the first beach communities on the West Coast, settled by fishermen in 1911, modern Pass-a-Grille is two miles of tidy houses, cared-for lawns, small shops and a cluster of bars and restaurants. On weekends, informed locals come to Pass-a-Grille's beach to enjoy one of the area's liveliest set of sands and unobstructed views of the tiny islands that dot the entrance to Tampa Bay.

A mile and a half north of Pass-a-Grille, you won't need a signpost to locate the **Don Cesar Hotel**, 3400 Gulf Boulevard (free guided tours on Fri at 11.30am; details on ☎360-1881), a grandiose pink castle with white-trimmed arched windows and vaguely Moorish turrets, rising above Gulf Boulevard and filling seven beachside acres. Conceived by a Twenties property speculator, Thomas J Rowe, the *Don Cesar* opened in 1928, but its glamor was short-lived. The Depression forced Rowe to use part of the hotel as a warehouse, and later drove him to allow the uncouth New York Yankees baseball team to make it their spring training base. After decades as a military hospital and then as federal offices, the building received a $15 million rejuvenation during the Seventies, and regained its hotel function – a vacation base for anyone with upwards of $150 a night to spare. The present interior bears little resemblance to Lowe's time, but you should stride past the marble columns and crystal chandeliers of the lobby into the lounge, where you can soak up the understated elegance from the depths of a sofa or, just outside, from the poolside – often in demand as a film set and used as a location for much of Robert Altman's satirical movie *Health*.

Just beyond the *Don Cesar*, Pinellas County Bayway cuts inland and makes a good route to take to Fort de Soto Park (see below). Keeping to Gulf Boulevard brings you into the main section of **ST PETERSBURG BEACH**, uninspiring rows of hotels, motels and eating places grouped along Gulf Boulevard and continuing for several miles. A very short break in the monotony is provided by a batch of pseudo-English shops around Corey Avenue. Further north, **TREASURE ISLAND** is even less varied tourist territory, culminating in the wood-walled, tin-roofed shops of **John's Pass Village**, 12901 Gulf Boulevard. Linked by a creaking boardwalk, the shops and the local fishing and pleasure-cruising fleet moored close by are mildly entertaining if you're at a (very) loose end. Immediately north, Gulf Boulevard crosses an arching drawbridge into **MADEIRA BEACH**, which is essentially more of the same – although, if you can't make it to Pass-a-Grille (see above), the local beach justifies a weekend fling.

Four miles north of Madeira Beach, at **INDIAN SHORES**, the **Suncoast Seabird Sanctuary**, 18328 Gulf Boulevard (daily 9am–sunset; donations requested; free guided tours on Tues at 2pm), offers a break from bronzing. The sanctuary is a respected treatment center for sick birds: convalescing pelicans, herons, turkey vultures and many other winged creatures bearing the brunt of human incursions into their natural habitat.

Fort de Soto Park

To soak up some history as well as the sunshine from the St Petersburg Beaches – provided you have a car – head across the Pinellas County Bayway, immediately north of the *Don Cesar*, and turn south along Route 679 to spend a day on the five islands comprising **Fort de Soto Park** (sunrise–sunset; free; 85¢ toll on approach road). The Spaniard credited with discovering Florida, Ponce de León, is thought to have anchored here in 1513, and again in 1521 when the islands' indigenous inhabitants inflicted on him what proved to be a fatal wound. Centuries later, the islands became a strategically important Union base during the Civil War, and in 1898 a fort was constructed to forestall attacks on Tampa during the Spanish-American War. The remains of the fort – which was never completed and never fired a shot in anger – can be explored on one of several walking trails, winding beneath Australian pines and oaks; typical features of an impressively untamed, thickly vegetated landscape. Three miles of swimmer-friendly beaches line the park, which in midweek possesses an intoxicating air of isolation – a far cry from the busy beach strips, and most effectively savored by **camping**, see "Accommodation" below.

The northern beaches

Much of the northern section of Sand Key, the longest barrier island in the St Petersburg chain, is lined by stylish condos and time-share apartments – this is one of the wealthier portions of the coast. It ends with the pretty **Sand Key Park**, where tall palm trees frame a scintillating strip of sand. The classic beach vista marred only by the nearby high-rises, which include the *Sheraton Sand Key Resort*, venue of the calamitous liaison between TV evangelist Jim Bakker and model Jessica Hahn in 1987, which led to the fall from grace of the media preacher and, for a time, greatly boosted the hotel's custom.

Sand Key Park occupies one bank of Clearwater Pass, across which a belt of sparkling white sands characterize **CLEARWATER BEACH**, yet another community devoted to the holiday industry – motels fill its side streets and European package tourists are everywhere – though one with an endearing small-town feel, and a pleasant place to spend a couple of days. A crucial plus for non-drivers are the regular bus links between Clearwater Beach and the mainland town of Clearwater – reached by a two-mile causeway – where you'll find connections to St Petersburg and Tarpon Springs, and a *Greyhound* station (see transport details, below).

Beyond its sands and two long piers, there's not much to do in Clearwater Beach: if the briny beckons, take the *Captain Memo* "pirate cruise" (two hours at sea for $25; ☎446-2587) from the marina just south of the causeway; or, more adventurously, make a day trip to the Caladesi or Honeymoon islands, a few miles north.

Honeymoon and Caladesi islands

In 1921, a hurricane ripped apart a five-mile-long island directly north of Clearwater Beach to create the aptly named Hurricane Pass and two islands which, now protected state parks, offer a chance to see the jungle-like terrain that covered the whole coast before the bulldozers arrived. Of the two, only **Honeymoon Island** can be reached by road; take Route 586 off Hwy-19 just north of Dunedin (or bus #83 from Clearwater). The condos which sprout from Honeymoon Island dent its natural impact – maintained in a wild pocket to the end of the road, viewable by a looping foot trail.

BUSES AND BOATS AROUND CLEARWATER BEACH

Clearwater Beach is good news for car-less travellers. **Around the beach strip**, the free *Clearwater Beach Trolley* runs half-hourly during the day between Sand Key (from the *Sheraton Sand Key Resort*) and Clearwater Beach (along Gulfview Boulevard, Mandalay Avenue and Acacia Street). **To the mainland**, bus #80 operates between Clearwater Beach and Clearwater's Park Street terminal (info: ☎530-9911). **Useful routes** from the terminal are: #83 to Honeymoon Island; #18 and #52 to St Petersburg; #68 to Tarpon Springs; and #200 (rush hours only) to Tampa.

Another way to get to the mainland is the *Clearwater Ferry* (☎442-7433), which makes 6–7 crossings a day between the *Sea Stone Suite Resort*, 445 Hamden Drive, on Sand Key, and the Recreation Center Park, in Clearwater Beach, to the Drew Street dock in Clearwater; one-way fare is $2. The same ferry company runs five trips a day (except Monday) between Drew Street and **Caladesi Island**, for $7.45 return, and to **Honeymoon Island** daily (except Sun) for $7.95 return; and has an outing to Tarpon Springs (see "Tarpon Springs") on Tuesday and Thursday for $18.95 one way (including lunch), $6 more for the return leg by boat or bus.

A third, much less frequent, mainland link is provided by two daily *Amtrak* buses, running from Tampa in lieu of trains; they stop in Clearwater at 657 Court Street, and at Clearwater Beach's Civic Center.

Clearwater's *Greyhound* **bus** station is at 2811 Gulf to Bay Boulevard (☎796-7315).

For a truer experience of untouched Florida make for **Caladesi Island**, just to the south. From a signposted landing stage beside Route 586, a **ferry** ($4 return) crosses between the islands daily between 10am and 6pm (hours are liable to vary, check on ☎734-5263); Caladesi Island can also be accessed from Clearwater Beach with the *Clearwater Ferry Service* (details below). Once ashore at Caladesi's mangrove-fringed marina, boardwalks lead to a beach of unsurpassed peacefulness: perfect for swimming, sunbathing, shell collecting and generally wasting a day. While here, though, summon up the strength to tackle the three-mile **nature trail**, cutting inland through saw palmetto and slash pines to an observation tower, before twisting back to the beach. Be certain to bring food and drink to the island; without them, the poorly stocked snack bar at the marina is the sole source of sustenance.

Accommodation

With the exception of camping, you're spoilt for choice when seeking **somewhere to sleep** around the beaches. **Hotels** are plentiful but tend to be filled with package tourists, and are always pricier than the **motels** that line mile after mile of Gulf Boulevard and the neighboring streets – typically $40–55 in winter, $10–15 less during the summer, though if you're staying long enough, many motels offer discounted weekly rates. Some have only a few standard rooms and will offer **efficiencies** for $5–10 above the basic room rate; if you don't need the kitchen, look elsewhere. Remember, too, that a room on the beach side of Gulf Boulevard costs $5–10 more than an identical room on the inland side.

Although savings over a motel room may be slim, Clearwater Beach also offers a **youth hostel**, at the *Sands Motel*, 606 Bay Esplanade (☎443-1211), with beds for $12.

Motels
Lack of competition causes prices in **Pass-a-Grille** to be around $10 higher than you might pay a few miles north – but the district makes an excellent base. The choices are the broadly similar *Keystone Motel*, 801 Gulf Way (☎360-1313; ②–③), and *Pass-a-Grille Beach Motel*, 709 Gulf Way (☎1-800/544-4184; ②–③). For a lengthy stay, opt for the cottages at *Gamble's Island's End Resort*, 1 Pass-a-Grille (☎360-5023; ④).

For the best deals in **St Petersburg Beach**, check out *Blue Horizon*, 3145 Second Street W (☎360-3946; ①–②); *Carlton House*, 633 71st Avenue (☎367-4128; ①–②); *Florida Dolphin*, 6801 Sunset Way (☎363-9853; ②); *The Lamp*, 7224 Coquina Way (☎360-4205; ①–②); or *Snug Harbor*, 13655 Gulf Boulevard (☎392-2743; ①–②).

Further north on **Treasure Island**, try *Beach House*, 12100 Gulf Boulevard (☎360-1153; ①–②); *Green Gables*, 11160 Gulf Boulevard (☎360-7794; ①–②); *Jolly Roger*, 11525 Gulf Boulevard (☎360-5571; ①–②); or *Sunrise*, 9360 Gulf Boulevard (☎360-9210; ①–②). In **Madeira Beach**, choose from *Beach Plaza*, 14560 Gulf Boulevard (☎391-8996; ①–②); *Gulf Stream*, 13007 Gulf Boulevard (☎391-2002; ①–②); and *Skyline*, 13999 Gulf Boulevard (☎391-5817; ①–②).

In **Clearwater Beach**, the lowest rates are with *Aqua-View*, 607 Bay Esplanade (☎447-6525; ①–②); *Bay Lawn*, 406 Hamden Drive (☎446-4529; ①–②); *Cyprus Motel Apts*, 609 Cyprus Avenue (☎442-3304; ①–③); and *Gulf Beach*, 419 Coronado Drive (☎447-3236; ①–③).

Hotels
Only a couple of **hotels** deviate far enough from the norms of the nationwide chains to be worth considering – if the rates aren't off-putting. For upwards of $150, bask in history and luxury at the *Don Cesar*, 3400 Gulf Boulevard (☎1-800/637-7200; ⑦) – described above – or sample the more affordable and fetchingly restored *Clearwater Beach Hotel*, 500 Mandalay Avenue (☎1-800/292-2295; ⑤).

Camping
There are no **campgrounds** along the main beach strip, although the nearest and nicest spot, at Fort de Soto Park (see above; ☎866-2662), is adjacent to sand and sea. The alternatives are inland: *St Petersburg KOA*, 5400 95th Street W (☎1-800/848-1094), five miles east of Madeira Beach; *Clearwater/Tarpon Springs KOA*, 37061 Hwy-19 (☎937-8412), six miles north of Clearwater, is handier for Clearwater Beach and surrounds – though neither site is much use without private transport.

Eating

It's easy to find a decent place to **eat** around the beaches. **From the south**, the *Hurricane Seafood Restaurant*, 807 Gulf Way (☎360-9558), sports a well-priced menu of the freshest seafood; the *Sea Horse*, 800 Pass-a-Grille (closed Tues; ☎360-1734), is strong on sandwiches; *Pep's Sea Grille*, 5895 Gulf Boulevard (☎367-3550), creates inspired matings of pasta and seafood; *Debby's*, 7370 Gulf Boulevard (☎367-8700), serves substantial breakfasts and lunches at insubstantial prices; *Doe-Al*, 85 Corey Circle (☎360-7976), knocks out gigantic platefuls of Southern favorites; and *O'Malley's Bar*, 7745 Blind Pass Way (☎360-2050), grills the thickest, juiciest burgers around.

If you're feeling wealthy, and inordinately hungry, on a Sunday, show up in smart attire for the lunchtime **buffet** at the *Don Cesar*, 3400 Gulf Boulevard (☎360-1881), which costs $30 per head.

In **Clearwater Beach**, *Alex*, 305 Coronado Drive (☎447-4560), and *Coca Cabana*, 669 Mandalay Avenue (☎446-7775), are good for cheap breakfasts; *Frenchy's Café*, 41 Baymont Street (☎446-3607), cooks up grouper burgers and shrimp sandwiches; *Seafood & Sunsets*, 351 S Gulfview Boulevard (☎441-2548), provides inexpensive seafood, ideally consumed while watching the sun sink. Larger appetites should be sated by the **dinner buffets** for under $10 spread out at the *Hilton Resort*, 715 S Gulfview Boulevard (☎447-9566).

Nightlife: drinking and live music

As you'd expect, most **nightlife** is aimed at tourists, though there are exceptions. Many hotel and restaurant bars have lengthy **happy hours** and lounges designed for watching the sunset while sipping a cocktail – look for the signs and ads in the free tourist magazines. For more cut-rate boozing, investigate *Jammin'z Dance Shack*, 470 Mandalay Avenue (☎442-5754), or the *Beach Bar*, 454 Mandalay Avenue (☎446-8866).

Bland pop bands are two-a-penny in the hotels. For better **live music**, aim for one of the following: the *Hurricane Seafood Restaurant*, 807 Gulf Way (☎360-9558), featuring some of the area's top jazz musicians; the *Harp and Thistle*, 650 Corey Avenue (☎360-4104), hosting Irish folksters most nights; *Bennigan's*, 4625 Gulf Boulevard, for the reggae bands on Saturday nights. In Clearwater Beach, there's **reggae** of fluctuating standards at *Cha Cha Coconuts*, 1241 Gulf Boulevard (☎569-6040), and at the *Tiki Deck*, part of the *Caribbean Gulf Resort Hotel*, 430 S Gulfview Boulevard (☎443-5714). Country music can be heard on Fridays and Saturdays at *Brassy's*, 138 Island Way (☎443-5493).

North of Clearwater: Tarpon Springs

Greek sponge-divers driven out of Key West by protectionist locals during the early 1900s resettled in **TARPON SPRINGS**, ten miles north of Clearwater off Hwy-19 (buses #19 and #68), the first of what became a sizeable Greek community in a town previously the preserve of wealthy wintering northerners. Demand for sponges was unprecedented during World War II (among other attributes, sponges are excellent for mopping up blood), but later the industry was devasted by a marine blight and the development of synthetic sponges. The Greek presence in Tarpon Springs remains strong, however, and is most evident in January when 40,000 participate in the country's largest Greek Orthodox Epiphany celebration. Each year an even greater number of tourists traipse around the souvenir shops lining the old sponge docks, largely neglecting the rest of the small town which – from restored buildings to weeping icons – has much more to intrigue.

The sponge docks

Along Dodecanese Boulevard on the banks of the Anclote River, the **sponge docks** are a disappointing conglomeration of one-time ships' supply stores turned into gift shops touting cassettes of Greek "belly-dancing music" and sponges ($2–3 for a small specimen). A boat departs every 45 minutes throughout the day on a

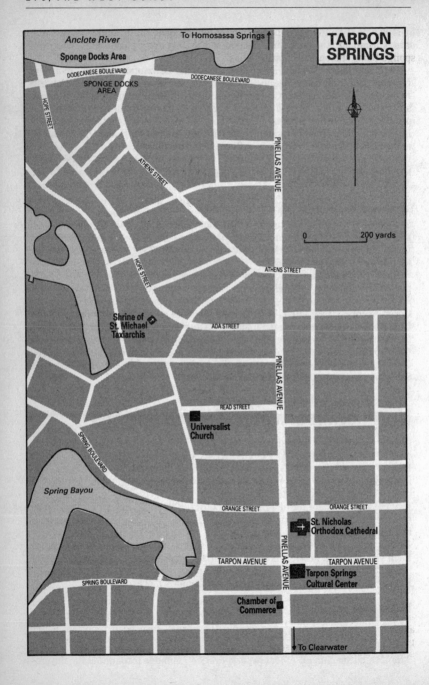

half-hour **sponge-diving trip** ($4) purely for the benefit of camera-toters; these days, shrimping is a more profitable pursuit than sponging and only a couple of sponge boats still operate commercially.

You'll pay less and learn more about the local community and the perils of sponge diving at the **Sponge Factory**, among a group of shops at 510 Dodecanese Boulevard, whose **Spongerama Exhibition** (daily 10am–6pm; free) traces the roots and growth of Tarpon Springs' Greek settlers, and the primitive techniques still used in the industry. Don't bother with the less satisfying **museum** (daily 10am–5pm; $2), down the street at the **Sponge Exchange**, where piles of freshly found sponges were once auctioned off (and a few still are early on Tuesday and Friday mornings) in an area that's become a dull Greek-themed shopping mall. Overall, you'd do well to give up on the docks and investigate the rest of the town.

The rest of Tarpon Springs
Symbols of the Greek community fill Tarpon Springs, by far the strongest being the resplendent Byzantine Revival **St Nicolas Orthodox Cathedral**, on the corner of Pinellas Avenue and Orange Street (daily 9am–5pm; free), partly funded by a half-percent levy on local sponge sales and finished in 1943. The full significance of the cathedral's ornate interior is inevitably lost on those not of the faith, though the icons and slow-burning incense create an intensely spiritual atmosphere.

After leaving the cathedral, drop into the neighboring **Tarpon Springs Cultural Center**, 101 S Pinellas Avenue (Tues–Sat 10am–4pm; free except for special events), which regularly stages imaginative exhibitions about Tarpon Springs' past and present. This Neoclassical building served as the city hall from 1915, a period when the adjacent Tarpon Avenue was a bustling commercial strip: butchers, bakers and grocers plied their trade from stumpy masonry structures, many of which still stand, several converted into curio-filled antique shops – good enough for a half-hour amble.

Walking west along Tarpon Avenue leads downhill to **Spring Bayou**, a crescent-shaped lake around which many homes of Tarpon Springs' pre-sponge-era residents – a mix of tycoons and artists – remain, their gabled roofs, shady porches and latticework decor an imposing sight from the lakeside path. Among the early residents was George Innes, a famed landscape painter, who rented a property eventually purchased by his son, George Jnr, also a noted landscape artist. George Jnr's primary legacy to the town can be viewed inside the nearby **Universalist Church**, 57 Read Street (Tues–Sun 2–5pm; free); the church, espousing utopian notions of peace, love and understanding, had its windows blown out by a hurricane in 1918 and George made six large-scale works to replace them. Take a look if the church is open but don't fret about missing them; size is their most impressive aspect.

Keeping to a religious theme, a few minutes' walk from the Universalist Church, the simple wooden form of the always-open **Shrine of St Michael Taxiarchis**, on Hope Street, belies the miracles said to have taken place in it. Erected by a local woman in gratitude for the unexplained recovery of her "terminally ill" son in 1939, numerous instances of the blind regaining their sight and the crippled throwing away their walking sticks after visiting the shrine have been reported: a free pamphlet has the full story. While here, study the icons closely for tear-tracks; several allegedly began crying – regarded as a bad omen – during 1989.

Practicalities

Collect general **information** from the **Chamber of Commerce** in the *Tarpon Arcade* building at 210 Pinellas Avenue (Mon–Fri 8.30am–5pm; ☎937-6109). Directly opposite is the town's least expensive place to eat: the *Last Drop Coffee Shop*, 217 Pinellas Avenue (☎942-1867); also in the *Tarpon Arcade*, the *Times Square Deli & Café* (☎934-4026) has sandwiches and snacks to eat in or take away. For a fuller sit-down meal, sample the inexpensive Greek dishes at *Costa's*, 510 Athens Street (☎938-6890), or *Plaka*, 769 Dodecanese Boulevard (☎934-4752); or try the pricier *Pappas* at 10 W Dodecanese Boulevard (☎937-5101).

Tarpon Springs makes a sensible **overnight stop** if you're continuing north. A number of motels dot the junctions with Hwy-19; more central are *Scottish Inn*, 110 Tarpon Avenue (☎937-6121; ②–③); *Sunbay Motel*, 57 W Tarpon Avenue (☎934-1001; ①–②); and the excellent-value bed and breakfast provided at the *Livery Stable*, 100 Ring Avenue (☎938-5547; ②).

THE NORTHWEST COAST: THE BIG BEND

Popularly known as the **Big Bend** for the way it curves towards the Panhandle, Florida's **northwest coast** is an oddity in as much as it has no beaches. Instead, thousands of mangrove islands form a fractured and almost unmappable shoreline, infrequently interrupted by snoozing villages, natural springs and – in one instance – an outstanding native American ceremonial site. Sand-crazy visitors miss it all by barrelling towards the Tampa Bay beaches on Hwy-19, the region's only major road, leaving the Big Bend one of the few sections of coastal Florida undisturbed by mass tourism – and one of the most rewarding for inquisitive visitors who want more from the state than a tan.

Homosassa Springs and around

Leaving the Tampa Bay area on Hwy-19, the roadside clutter of filling stations and used-car lots recedes north of New Port Richey, an uninteresting place of condos and time-share properties, and gives way to a more soothing – if often monotonous – outlook of hardwood and pine forests along with uncharitable expanses of swamp. After sixty-odd miles, watch out for the amusing dinosaur-shaped roof of *Harold's Auto Center* and, just ahead by the junction with Route 50, the "mermaids" of **Weeki Wachee** (daily, winter 9am–6pm, longer hours in summer; $15), who perform a thoroughly kitsch underwater choreography routine in one of the Big Bend's many natural springs.

As a nod to green concerns, Weeki Wachee has added a trip through a wildlife preserve as part of its entertainment, though any thirst for animals and (real) sea life is better sated twenty miles north at **HOMOSASSA SPRINGS** – the first community of any size on Hwy-19 – at the **Homosassa Springs State Wildlife Park** (daily 9am–5.30pm; $6.95), where squirrel-infested walking trails lead to another gushing spring, and an underwater observatory offers eye-to-gill sightings of the numerous fish and manatees swimming through it. To get a feel for the town, go a couple of miles west along the oak-lined Route 490, passing the crumbling walls and rusting machinery of the **Yulee Sugar Mill**, originally owned by David Yulee. Florida's first Congressman and financier of the 1860s Cedar Key to Fernandina Beach rail line (see "Cedar Key", below), he extended a section south to Homosassa Springs; the closest the place has ever been to civilization. With the railway long gone, the tranquil town's old wooden houses are finding favor with young artists: drop into the *Riverworks Gallery*, 10844 W Yulee Drive, to see some of the better work.

Crystal River and around

Seven miles further on Hwy-19, **CRYSTAL RIVER** is among the region's bigger centers despite a population of just four thousand, many of them retirees fearful of the crime in Florida's urban areas and unable to afford the more southerly sections of the coast. You'd never guess it from the drab Hwy-19, but quite a few arrivals are also drawn here by the sedate beauty of the see-through river from which the town takes its name. Manatees take a shine to it as well: during the winter, they're to be found in the numerous inlets of **Kings Bay**, a section of the river just west of Hwy-19. By snorkelling or scuba diving, you stand a fair chance of meeting one of these friendly, walrus-like creatures; **guided dives** are set up by *Bay Point Dive Center*, 300 NW Hwy-19 (☎904/563-1040), and several other dive shops in the vicinity, for around $20 a day.

Crystal River's present dwellers are by no means the first to live by the waterway; it provided a source of food for native Americans from at least 200 BC. To reach the center of their habitation, take State Park Road off Hwy-19 just north of the town, to the **Crystal River State Archeological Site** (daily 8am–sunset; cars $3.25, pedestrians and cyclists $1), where the temple, burial and midden mounds which they left are still very visible. Inside the **visitor center** (daily 9am–5pm), there's an enlightening assessment of the finds from the 450 graves discovered here, indicating trade links with tribes far to the north. Connections to the south, however, prove more fascinating: the site holds two *stelae*, or ceremonial stones, much more commonly found in Mexico, whose engravings – thought to be faces of Sun deities – suggest that large-scale solar ceremonies were conducted here. The sense of the past and the serenity of the setting make the site a highly evocative, as well a historically instructive, place – don't pass it by.

Practicalities

Other than diving and visiting the archeological site, Crystal River doesn't have much to justify a long stop, though if you're travelling by *Greyhound* (the station is at 200 N Hwy-19; ☎904/795-4445) it's a likely overnight break. The cheapest **accommodation** is provided by *Days Inn*, just north of the town on Hwy-19 (☎904/795-2111; ②–③); more expensive, but more relaxing, is the *Plantation Inn*, on Route 44 (☎1-800/632-6262; ④). If you're planning some diving and an overnight stay, check out the dive-and-accommodation packages, at around $60–70 per night, offered by the *Econo Lodge*, 614 NW Hwy-19 (☎904/795-3774; ③). The closest **campground** is *Sun Coast*, half a mile south on Hwy-19 (☎904/795-9049). For **food**, use the basic but dependable *Crystal Paradise Restaurant*, 508 Citrus

Avenue (☎904/563-2620). The **Chamber of Commerce**, 28 N Hwy-19 (Mon–Fri 8.30am–5pm; ☎904/795-3149), can supply general facts on Crystal River and around.

North from Crystal River: Yankeetown and around

Ten miles north of Crystal River, Hwy-19 spans the **Florida barge canal**, an attempt to provide a cargo link between the Gulf and Atlantic coasts conceived in the 1820s, started in the 1930s and – thanks to squabbling in high places and the efforts of conservationists – abandoned in the 1970s with just six miles completed. The bridge at least offers an unobstructed view of the Crystal River nuclear power station; the area's major employer and the reason why local telephone books carry hopeful instructions on how to survive a nuclear catastrophe.

Further on, taking any left turn off Hwy-19 will invariably lead to a tiny, eerily quiet community, where fishing on the local river is the only sign of life. One such place is **YANKEETOWN**, five miles west of Inglis on Route 40, reputedly named after some Yankee soldiers who moved here following the Civil War. To get the complete middle-of-nowhere effect, spend a night at the *Izaak Walton Lodge*, at the corner of Riverside Drive and 63rd Street (☎904/447-2311; ③), an angler's billet and restaurant since 1923 and still the fomenting place of local gossip.

The protected wildlife habitats of the **Wacassassa State Preserve** cover the salt marshes and tidal creeks on the coastal side of Hwy-19 as you travel on from Yankeetown. A breeding ground for deer and turkey, and sometimes visited by black bear and Florida panthers, these swampy lands are intended to allow the state's indigenous creatures to replenish their numbers: human accessibility is not a pressing concern, although there are periodic ranger-guided **canoe trips** through the area: details on ☎904/543-5567.

Cedar Key

One left turn you should unhesitatingly make is onto Route 24 at the hamlet of Otter Creek, continuing west for twenty miles until you run out of road in the center of **CEDAR KEY**. In the 1860s, the railroad from Fernandina Beach (see Chapter Four) ended its journey here, turning this isolated community – which occupies one of several small islands – into a thriving port. When ships got bigger and needed deeper harbors, Cedar Key stayed solvent by cutting down its cypress, pine and cedar trees to fuel a pencil-producing industry. Inevitably, the trees were soon all gone and by the turn of the century – not aided by a devastating hurricane – Cedar Key was all but a ghost town. The few who stayed eked out a living from fishing and harvesting oysters, as many of the thousand-strong population still do.

Only during the last ten years have there been signs of a revival: many decaying timber-framed warehouses have been turned into restaurants and shops, and more holiday homes are appearing. Given its remoteness, however, it's improbable that Cedar Key will ever be deluged with visitors – it's only at all busy during the October seafood festival, and the arts and crafts show during April – and it remains a fascinating example of old Florida: a great place for a day's visit, though frustratingly untouched by public transport.

Pass the time by strolling the ramshackle waterfront structures of Dock Street and the old wooden houses on and around Second Street, and be sure to drop into the **Historical Society Museum**, on the corner of D and Second streets (Mon–Sat 11am–4pm, Sun 1–4pm; $1), to scan the newspaper clippings attesting to the halcyon days of yore, and view the scraps of historical fallout – such as the long poles used in oyster harvesting – scattered about. More remains are stored a mile away at the **State Historical Museum**, at the end of Museum Drive (Mon & Thurs–Sat, times vary; 50¢), in an unprepossessing residential section of the town: you needn't feel uncomfortable about neglecting it. And, if possible, stick around long enough to admire the blazing sunset.

Practicalities

The **Chamber of Commerce**, inside the former city hall on Second Street (usually Mon, Tues, Thurs & Fri 9am–noon & 1–3pm; ☎904/543-5600), can supply the usual neighborhood information, and keep you up to date on the increasing number of **places to sleep** in the town. Bed and breakfast at the 130-year-old *Island Hotel*, corner of Second and B streets (☎904/543-5111; ④–⑤), is a great way to soak up the local atmosphere. For a standard room, try the *Beach Front Motel*, corner of First and G streets (☎904/543-5113; ②–③), *Faraway Inn*, corner of Third and G streets (☎904/543-5330; ②–③), or *Bayside Cottages*, half a mile out of the center on Route 24 (☎904/543-5141; ②). **Tents** can be pitched at *Sunset Isle*, three miles distant on Route 24 (☎904/543-5375).

Eating freshly caught seafood is a pleasurable way to stretch out the hours in Cedar Key: oysters, smoked mullet and fried trout are among the local specialities. Three likely spots to sample the goods are close to each other along Dock Street (and too conspicuous to have street numbers): *The Captain's Table* (☎904/543-5441), *Seabreeze* (☎904/543-5738) and the *Brown Pelican* (☎904/543-5428).

Continuing north towards the Panhandle

Back on Hwy-19, there's a featureless ninety-mile slog to the next noticeable town, **PERRY**, where only the **Forest Capitol State Museum**, 204 Forest Park Drive (Thurs–Mon 9am–noon & 1–5pm; $1), a celebration of the lumber industry which the place is famous for, breaks the journey towards the Panhandle, fifty miles distant. To reach Tallahassee, stick to Hwy-19 (from here also known as Hwy-27), or, for the Panhandle coast, branch west with Hwy-98. The Panhandle is fully detailed in Chapter Seven.

THE SOUTHWEST COAST

Flavoring the 150 miles of coast south of Tampa Bay are several individualistic towns with origins dating back to the early days of Florida's incorporation into the US, whose residents lead enviable lives away from the big city hurly-burly. Until recently they've had an easy job preserving their seclusion, but with newer nearby communities expanding at a colossal rate and large-scale tourism creeping steadily southwards, they're beginning to sense trouble. Despite the changes looming, the southwest coast is still one of Florida's most quietly absorbing sections: a fine balance of mainland sights and beaches begging for exploration, with the prize of the Everglades National Park at its end.

South from Tampa Bay

Taking I-275 south from St Petersburg (a preferable route to the lacklustre I-75 or Hwy-41 from Tampa), you'll soar over Tampa Bay on the **Sunshine Skyway bridge**, high enough to allow ocean-going ships to pass beneath and for the outlines of land and sea to become blurred in the heat haze. A phosphate tanker rammed one of the bridge supports during a storm in May 1980, causing the central span of the southbound section to collapse. With visibility down to a few feet, drivers on the bridge failed to spot the gap and 35 people, including the occupants of a *Greyhound* bus, plunged 250 feet to their deaths. The entire southbound section has been demolished; the bridge now carrying traffic in both directions was originally the northbound section. The tragedy was the worst of several fatal accidents on the Sunshine Skyway, which is also rife with tales of phantom hitchhikers: they thumb rides across, only to vanish into thin air before reaching the other side. For the dollar toll, it beats anything at Walt Disney World.

The Gamble Plantation

The bridge comes to earth about five miles north of Palmetto, a uninteresting dormitory community of Bradenton (see below). Without cause to rush ahead, veer east from Palmetto along Tenth Street (Hwy-301) to Ellenton, a riverside settlement where the the 1840s **Gamble Plantation**, 3708 Patten Avenue (grounds Thurs–Mon 9am–5pm; $2; free guided tours of the house on the hour 9–11am & 1–4pm), is one of the oldest homes on Florida's west coast and the only slave-era plantation this far south. Composed of thick tabby walls (a mixture of crushed shell and molasses) and girded on three sides by sturdy columns, the house belonged to a Confederate major, Robert Gamble, a failed Tallahassee cotton planter who ran a sugar plantation here before financial uncertainty in the run-up to the Civil War forced him to leave. An excellent showcase of wealthy (and white) Old South living, the house – stuffed to the rafters with period fittings – can only be seen on the guided tour, which, besides describing the building, its contents and owners, offers a thought-provoking Confederate view of the Civil War.

Bradenton

A major producer of tomato and orange juice, **BRADENTON**, across the broad Manatee River from Palmetto, is a hard-working town whose center comprises several unlovely miles of business buildings along the river's south bank. To see Bradenton at its best you need to travel eight miles west to the beaches, lining the northernmost of a chain of barrier islands running from here to Fort Myers – a better (if slightly longer) route by car to Sarasota than the inland options. It's inevitable, however, that you'll pass through Bradenton and, particularly if you've missed the Gamble Plantation (see above), you might find the town's historical collections briefly entertaining.

The historical collections – and towards the coast

In central Bradenton, the **South Florida History Museum**, 201 Tenth Street (Tues–Sat 10am–5pm, Sun 1–6pm; $5), takes a wide-ranging look at the region's past; its displays, dioramas and artefacts reflect every phase of habitation from native American civilization onwards – among them a credibility-straining re-creation of the sixteenth-century Spanish home of Hernando de Soto (see below). Further knowledge of turn-of-the-century settlers can be acquired at the **Manatee Village Historical Park**, corner of Sixth Avenue E and Fifteenth Street E (Mon–Fri 9am–5pm, Sun 2–5pm; free), which has a courthouse, church, general store and a cracker cottage, dating from Florida's rough-and-ready frontier days.

Five miles **west of central Bradenton**, the main route to the beaches, Manatee Avenue, crosses 75th Street W, at the northern end of which the **De Soto National Monument** (daily 8am–5.30pm; donations) is – very optimistically – believed to mark the spot where Spanish conquistador Hernando de Soto came ashore in 1539. The three-year de Soto expedition, hacking through Florida's dense subtropical terrain and wading through its swamps, led to the

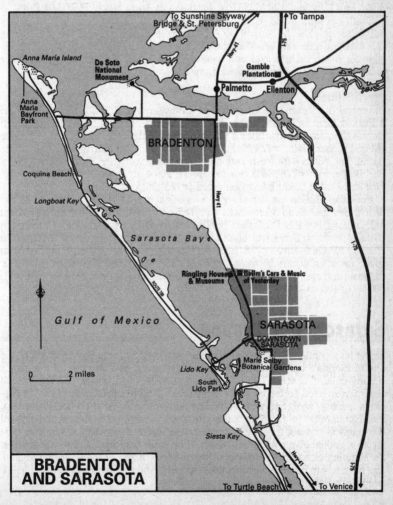

BRADENTON
AND SARASOTA

European discovery of the Mississippi River – and numerous pitched battles with native Americans. An exhibition records the key points of de Soto's trek, and, from December to April, park rangers dressed as sixteenth-century Spaniards add informative pointers to the lifestyles of Florida's first adventurers. For more about the de Soto expedition, see "History" in *Contexts*.

The Bradenton Beaches and on towards Sarasota

In contrast to central Bradenton's greyness, the ramshackle beach cottages, seaside snack stands and beachside bars on **Anna Maria Island**, onto which Manatee Avenue runs, are bright and convivial. From the end of Manatee Avenue, turn left along Gulf Drive for **Coquina Beach**, where the swimming is excellent and the weekend social life youthful and merry; with a quieter time in mind, turn right along Marina Drive for the calm **Anna Maria Bayfront Park**.

South of Anna Maria Island, **Longboat Key** is all about privacy: its pricey homes are shielded by rows of tall Australian pines, and, while all the sands along this nineteen-mile-long island are public property, access to them is almost impossible for non-residents. Not until you reach Lido Key, further south, are there more useable beaches – described below under "The Sarasota Beaches".

Practicalities

In central Bradenton, the **Chamber of Commerce**, 222 Tenth Street (Mon–Fri 8.30am–4.30pm; ☎748-3411), has the usual tourist information; better for beach facts is the **Anna Maria Island Chamber of Commerce**, 503 Manatee Avenue (Mon–Fri 9am–5pm; ☎778-1541). You should do your **eating** on Anna Maria Island. Top choices for fresh seafood lunches or dinners are *Rotten Ralph's*, 902 S Bay Boulevard (☎778-3953), *Harbor House*, 200 Gulf Drive N (☎778-5608), and *Fast Eddie's*, 101 S South Bay Boulevard (☎778-2251).

Accommodation on a budget is a problem within walking distance of the beach: *Sea and Sand Motel*, 2412 Gulf Drive (☎778-2231; ③–④), and the *Anna Maria Motel*, 806 Bay Boulevard (☎778-1269; ③–④), are possibilities. Costlier but cosier – and you'll need to book ahead – is bed and breakfast at the *Duncan House*, 1703 Gulf Drive (☎778-6858; ④). If beach prices are too high or there's no space (as often occurs between December and April), use one of the motels on the mainland approach roads, such as the *Bradenton Inn*, 2303 First Street E (☎1-800/447-6465; ②–③).

Sarasota and Around

Rising on a gentle hillside beside the blue waters of Sarasota Bay, **SARASOTA** is one of Florida's better-off and better-looking towns, and also one of the state's leading cultural centers: home to numerous writers and artists, and the base of several respected performing arts companies. Despite periodic conservative flappings (such as recent attempts to outlaw skimpy swimwear at the local beaches), the community is far less stuffy than its wealth, and the abundance of Neoclassical statues, fountains and manicured lawns decorating it, suggest. Save for an excellent grouping of bookshops, downtown Sarasota has less impact than the Ringling estate on the town's northern edge – home of the art-loving millionaire from whom modern Sarasota takes its cue – and the barrier island beaches, a couple of miles away across the bay.

The area code for the Sarasota area is ☎813

Arrival, Information and Getting Around

From the north, **Hwy-41** skirts the Ringling estate before running through down-town Sarasota, passing the main causeway to the islands. In downtown Sarasota, *Greyhound* **buses** stop at 575 N Washington Boulevard (☎955-5735), and the *Amtrak* bus from Tampa ends its trip at the local bus terminal – see below.

Local bus (information ☎951-5851 except Sun) routes radiate out from the downtown Sarasota terminal on Lemon Avenue, between First and Second streets. **Useful routes** are #2 or #10 to the Ringling estate; #4 to Lido Key; #18 to Longboat Key; and #11 to Siesta Key. If you're around for a week or more, a good way to explore the town and the islands is by **renting a bike** for around $20 per day from *Sarasota Bicycle Center*, 4048 Bee Ridge Road (☎377-4505); the *Village Bike Shop*, on Siesta Key at 5101 Ocean Boulevard (☎346-2111); or the *Backyard Bike Shop*, on Longboat Key at 5610 Gulf of Mexico Drive (☎383-5184).

For **information**, call at the **Visitors and Convention Bureau**, 655 N Tamiami Trail (Mon–Fri 9.30am–5pm, Sat 9am–noon; ☎1-800/522-9799), or the **Chamber of Commerce**, 1819 Main Street (Mon–Fri 9am–5pm; ☎955-8187). On **Siesta Key**, you'll find a Chamber of Commerce at 5263 Ocean Boulevard (Mon–Fri 9am–5pm; ☎349-3800). Besides the customary discount coupons and leaflets, look for the free magazines, *Sarasota Visitors Guide* and *See*, and the monthly entertainment guide, *SRQ*.

Northern Sarasota: the Ringling House and Museums

As you reach Sarasota from the north, don't fail to tour the house and art collec-tions of **John Ringling**, a multi-millionaire who not only poured money into the fledgling community from the 1910s but also gave it a taste for fine arts that it's never lost. One of the owners of the fantastically successful *Ringling Brothers Circus*, which toured the US from the 1890s, Ringling – an imposing figure over six feet tall and weighing nearly twenty stone – ploughed the circus's profits into railways, oil and land, acquiring a fortune estimated at $200 million by the Twenties. Charmed by Sarasota and recognizing its investment potential, Ringling built the first causeway to the barrier islands and made the town his circus's winter base – saving a fortune in northern heating bills and generating tremendous publicity for the town in doing so. His greatest gift to Sarasota, however, was a Venetian Gothic mansion – a combination of European elegance and American-millionaire extravagance – and an incredible collection of European Baroque paintings, displayed in a purpose-built museum beside the house. Gloom-stricken following the death of his wife, Mabel, in 1927, and losing much of his wealth through the Wall Street crash two years later, Ringling died in 1936, reputedly with just $300 to his name. The **Ringling house and museums**, three miles north of downtown Sarasota beside Hwy-41, are open daily from 10am to 5.30pm, on Thursdays between October and June until 10pm; admission is $8.50. The buildings are linked by pathways over a 66-acre site, though all are easy to walk between and clearly signposted. To get here from downtown Sarasota, use **buses** #2 or #10.

The Ringling House: Ca' d'Zan

Begin your exploration of the Ringling estate by walking through the gardens to the former Ringling residence, **Ca' d'Zan** ("House of John", in Venetian dialect), a gorgeous piece of work serenely situated beside the bay. Completed in 1925, reputedly at a cost of $1.5 million, the house was planned around an airy, two-storey-high living room marked on one side by a fireplace of carved Italian marble and on the other by a $50,000 organ belonging to the musically minded Mabel. The other rooms are similarly filled with expensive items, but unlike their mansion-erecting contemporaries elsewhere in Florida, John and Mable Ringling knew the value of restraint: their spending power never exceeded their sense of style, and the house remains a triumph of taste and proportion – and an excep-tionally pleasant place to walk around (take the **free guided tour** departing regu-larly from the entrance – then roam on your own).

The Art Museum

The mix of inspiration and caution that underpinned Ringling's business deals also influenced his art purchases. On trips to Europe to scout for new circus talent, Ringling became obsessed with **Baroque art** – then wildly unfashionable – and over five years, largely led by his own sensibilities, he acquired more than five hundred Old Masters; a gathering now regarded as one of the finest collections of its kind in the US. To display the paintings, many of them as epic in size as they were in content, Ringling selected a patch of Ca' d'Zan's grounds and erected a spacious **museum** around a mock fifteenth-century Italian palazzo, decorated by his stockpile of high-quality replica Greek and Roman statuary. As with Ca' d'Zan, the very concept initially seems absurdly pretentious but, like the house, the idea works: the architecture matching the art with great aplomb.

Five enormous paintings by **Rubens**, commissioned in 1625 by a Hapsburg archduchess, and the painter's subsequent *Portrait of Archduke Ferdinand*, are the undisputed highlights of the collection, though they shouldn't detract from the excellent canvases in succeeding rooms: a wealth of talent from Europe's leading schools of the mid-sixteenth to mid-eighteenth centuries. Watch out, in particular, for the finely composed and detailed *The Rest on the Flight to Egypt*, by Paolo Veronese, and the entertaining *Building of a Palace* from Piero de Cosimo. In contrast, recently acquired contemporary works include sculpture from Joel Shapiro and John Chamberlain, and paintings by Frank Stella and Philip Pearlstein.

The Circus Gallery and the Asolo Theater

The Ringling fortune may have its origins in the Big Top, but the **Circus Gallery** is an unworthy afterthought to the house and art museum: a dull bunch of leftovers – parade wagons, old costumes, a human-firing cannon – with only the antique illustrations of balancing tricks and, from a time when physical abnormal-ities were part and parcel of circus entertainment, some clothes and memorabilia from Tom Thumb, the celebrated nineteenth-century dwarf.

Elsewhere in the grounds, try the door of the *Asolo Theater* (sometimes locked) for a peek at what is – strange as it may seem – the interior of a genuine eighteenth-century Italian court playhouse. As well as plays it hosts lectures and art films – for a full programme of events phone ☎355-7115. Don't confuse this with the larger Asolo Center for the Performing Arts, 5500 Tamiami Trail, the present home of the *Asolo Theater Company* (see "Nightlife"), which was previously based here.

Bellm's Cars & Music of Yesterday
Only vintage car enthusiasts and devotees of old music boxes will derive any pleasure from **Bellm's Cars and Music of Yesterday**, across Hwy-41 from the entrance to the Ringling Estate (Mon–Sat 8.30am–6pm, Sun 9.30am–6pm; $7.50). Over 100 aged vehicles – a few Rolls Royces among them – are gathered together with hurdy-gurdies, cylinder discs and an enormous Belgian pipe organ, combining to make an awful racket.

Downtown Sarasota

The allure of the Ringling estate and the nearby beaches keep many visitors (except those travelling by public transport, who have no choice) away from **downtown Sarasota**, missing out on the restaurants, bars, boutiques and antique shops lining the strollable **Main Street**. Admittedly, other than eating and drinking, window shopping is the sole pursuit, although anyone bemoaning the lack of decent bookshops in Florida should take heart: here you'll find the biggest and most varied selection in the state. The best-filled shelves are at *Book Bazaar*, no 1532, *Charlie's News*, no 1341, and *Main Bookshop*, no 1962.

Away from Main Street, most of downtown Sarasota is an unrewarding mix of public buildings and offices, and you should head south, following the curve of the bay for half a mile, to the **Marie Selby Botanical Gardens**, 811 S Palm Avenue (daily 10am–5pm; $6). The walled perimeter bears little promise but inside the gathering of growths is small but startling, and time spent along the fragrant pathways can't fail to improve your mood.

The Sarasota Beaches

Increasingly the stamping ground of European package tourists spilling south from the St Petersburg Beaches, the powdery white sands of the **Sarasota beaches** – fringing two barrier islands, which continue the chain beginning off Bradenton – haven't been spared the attentions of property developers either, losing much of their scenic appeal to towering condos. For all that, the Sarasota beaches are worth a day of anybody's time – either to lie back and soak up the rays, or to seek out the few remaining isolated stretches. Both islands, Lido Key and Siesta Key, are reachable by car and buses from the mainland, though there's no link directly between them.

Lido Key
Financed by and named after Sarasota's circus-owning sugar daddy, the Ringling Causeway – take buses #4 or #18 – crosses the yacht-filled Sarasota Bay from the foot of Main Street to **Lido Key** and flows into **St Armands Circle**, a glorified roundabout ringed by upmarket shops and restaurants, and dotted by some of John Ringling's replica classical statuary – muscle-bound torsos surrealistically emerging from behind the palm fronds. Other than staging entertaining arts and crafts events on weekends and offering a safe place to stroll after dark, St Armands Circle has little to occupy anyone without a limitless budget and – after

a look around – you should continue south along Benjamin Franklin Drive. This route passes the island's most easily accessed beaches, fine in themselves though bearing a pronounced MOR holiday-maker bias. After two miles, it ends at the more attractive **South Lido Park** (daily 8am–sunset; free): a belt of dazzlingly bright sand beyond a large grassy park, with walking trails in the shade of Australian pines. Busy with barbecues and tanned bodies on Saturday and Sunday, the park is a delightfully subdued spot for a ramble on a weekday.

Away from the beaches, the only place of consequence on Lido Key is a mile north of St Armands Circle at City Island Park, just off John Ringling Parkway: the **Mote Marine Aquarium**, 1600 Ken Thompson Parkway (daily 10am–5pm; $5), the public offshoot of a marine laboratory studying the many ecological problems threatening Florida's sea life. Some of the work – such as research into the mysterious red tide, an unexplained algae which appears every few years, devastating sea life and causing sickness among people living along the coast – is outlined, and there's a great assortment of live creatures, from seahorses to sharks.

Siesta Key

The bulbous northerly section of **Siesta Key**, reached by Siesta Drive off Hwy-41 about five miles south of downtown Sarasota (bus #11), holds the bulk of the tadpole-shaped island's resident population on streets twisting around a complicated network of canals. Beach-lovers should hit **Siesta Key Beach**, beside Ocean Beach Boulevard, a wide and intensely white strand that can – and often does – accommodate thousands of partying sun-worshippers. To escape the crowds, continue south past Crescent Beach, which meets a second road (Stickly Point Road) from the mainland, and follow Midnight Pass Road for six miles to **Turtle Beach**, a small body of sand which has the islands' only campground; see below.

Accommodation

On the **mainland**, motels run the length of Hwy-41 between the Ringling estate and downtown Sarasota, typically charging $35–50. You can take your pick: *Sarasota Motor Inn* (no 7251; ☎1-800/282-6827; ②), *Cabana Inn* (no 2525; ☎955-0195; ②) and *Bel Air* (no 1088; ☎953-7544; ②) are as good as any.

At the **beaches**, prices are higher. Lowest rates on Lido Key are with the *Gulf Side Motel*, 138 Garfield Drive (☎388-2590; ③), and the *Lido Apartment Motel*, 528 S Polk Drive (☎388-9830; ②), with a few rooms for $25. Otherwise, be prepared to fork out substantially for a night at the *Harley Sandcastle*, 1540 Benjamin Franklin Drive (☎388-2181; ④–⑤), or the *Half Moon Beach Club*, 2050 Benjamin Franklin Drive (☎388-3694; ④–⑤). In general, Siesta Key is even more expensive, with many places renting out fully equipped apartments for a week in preference to motel rooms by the night. Two on Midnight Pass Road that do usually have plain inexpensive rooms, however, are *Surfrider Beach Apartments* (no 6400; ☎349-2121; ③–④) and *Gulf Sun Apartments & Motel* (no 6722; ☎349-2442; ③–④). The only budget alternative is the Turtle Beach **campground**, *Gulf Beach Travel Trailer Park*, 8862 Midnight Pass Road (☎349-3839), although it consists almost exclusively of RV sites; if you can get a tent site, be prepared to pay upwards of $20.

Eating

In **downtown Sarasota**, **eating** should be done along Main Street. The *New York Deli* (no 1371; ☎365-3188), delivers dependable omelettes and general diner food; *Coley's* (no 1355; ☎955-5627) does much the same but with a bigger selection, bigger portions and higher prices; *Guadalajara* (no 1377; ☎365-1742) serves inexpensive Mexican food in a 1950s American diner-like setting; and the *El Greco Café* (no 1592; ☎365-2234), carries extremely cheap Greek dishes besides the usual array of American breakfasts and lunches. For home-made food cooked to old-fashioned recipes, venture slightly further afield to one of the local Amish restaurants: *Sugar & Spice*, 1850 Tamiami Trail (☎953-3340), or *Der Dutchman*, 3710 Bahia Vista Street (☎955-8007).

Food is dearer at the **beaches**, especially on Lido Key. Around St Armands Circle, only *The Buttery*, 470 Ringling Boulevard (☎388-1523), offers round-the-clock respite from ritzy eating spots. Siesta Key is better news: *The Broken Egg*, 210 Avenida Madera (☎346-2750), is a favored locals' breakfast and lunch stop; *The Old Salty Dog*, 5023 Ocean Boulevard (☎349-0158), offers "English-style" fish and chips, alongside regular seafood and hot dogs; while *Turtles*, 8875 Midnight Pass Road (☎346-2207), and *Surfrider*, 6400 Midnight Pass Road (☎346-1199), both provide outstanding seafood dinners for under $15.

Nightlife

Some of the state's top small theatrical groups are based in Sarasota: **drama** devotees should scan local newspapers and the free *SRQ* for play listings or phone the theater directly. The major company, the *Asolo Theater Company*, based at the Asolo Center for the Performing Arts, 5555 N Tamiami Trail (☎351-8000), has a strong repertoire throughout the year (tickets $13–25). The other companies (tickets $5–15) stick to a winter season: *Florida Studio Theater*, 1241 N Palm Avenue (☎366-9796); *Golden Apple Dinner Theater*, 25 N Pineapple Avenue (☎366-5454); and *Players of Sarasota*, 838 N Tamiami Trail (☎365-2494).

Otherwise, Sarasota's **nightlife** is a bit limp. **Beer drinkers**, however, will find solace at the *Sarasota Brewing Company Bar & Grill*, 6607 Gateway Avenue (☎925-2337), which home-brews beers to traditional German specifications, and at *The Old Salty Dog* (address under "Eating", above), where a variety of British ales are sold by the pint. Elsewhere, there's **live music**: jazz and blues most nights at *Coley's* and at the *New York Deli* (see "Eating" for addresses). The *Animal House*, 1927 Ringling Boulevard (☎366-3830), is the most enjoyable of the local **discos**.

Inland from Sarasota: Myakka River State Park

Should your knowledge of Florida be limited to beaches and theme parks, broaden your horizons fourteen miles inland from Sarasota on Route 72, around the marshes, pinewoods and prairies forming **Myakka River State Park** (daily 8am–sunset; cars $3.25, pedestrians and cyclists $1), a great tract of rural Florida barely touched by human encroachment. On arrival, drop into the **interpretive center** to comprehend this fragile (and threatened) ecosystem and – if you're not equipped for hiking – explore the park on the numerous walking trails or by canoeing on the calm expanse of the Upper Myakka Lake. Patient **hiking** along the forty miles of trails through the park's **wilderness preserve** is a better way to get to close to the cotton-tailed rabbits, deer, turkey, bobcats and alligators who live in the park. Before commencing, register at the entrance office and get maps and weather conditions – be ready for wet conditions during the summer storms. Other than five basic campgrounds on the hiking trails, park **accommodation** (details and reservations: ☎361-6511) comprises two well-equipped **campgrounds**, and a few four-berth **log cabins** for $50 a night.

South from Sarasota: Venice and around

In the Fifties, the Ringling Circus moved its winter base twenty miles south from Sarasota to **VENICE**, a small town modelled on its European namesake: a place of broad avenues and Italianate architecture surrounded by water. Despite the circus's new show premiere each autumn (at 1410 S Ringling Drive; information on ☎484-9511) and the curiosity value of the world's only clown college, it's **beaches** that make the town. Utilized by a broad mix of sunbathers, water-sports enthusiasts and stooping beachcombers hunting for the fossilized shark's teeth commonly washed ashore, the best beaches flank the Venice Inlet, a mile west of Hwy-41.

Spending a night in this quiet community might seem an attractive proposition, although prices aren't low outside of summer: of the motels, try the *Kon Tiki*, 1487 Tamiami Trail (☎485-9696; ③–④), or the *Gulf Tide*, 708 Granada Avenue (☎484-9709; ③–④). For local **information** call at the **Chamber of Commerce**, 257 N Tamiami Trail (Mon–Fri 8.30am–5pm, Nov–March also Sat 9am–1pm; ☎488-2236).

Continuing south: towards Fort Myers

If you have personal transportation, explore around the underexploited coastline around Englewood, south of Venice on Route 775, pockmarked by small islands and creeks. Sooner or later, though, you'll have to rejoin Hwy-41, which, out of Venice, turns inland to chart an unremarkable fifty-mile course through retirement communities such as Punta Gunta and Port Charlotte, before reaching the far more appetizing Fort Myers.

Fort Myers

Lacking the elan of Sarasota, **FORT MYERS**, fifty miles south, is nonetheless one of the up-and-coming communities of the southwest coast, recently undergoing considerable expansion and looking set for a prosperous future. Fortunately, most of the growth has occurred on the north side of the wide Caloosahatchee River, which the town straddles, allowing the traditional center, along the waterway's south shore, to remain relatively unspoiled. The home and workplace of inventor Thomas Edison, who lived in Fort Myers for many years, provide the strongest interest in a town that otherwise relies on scenery – making the most of its riverside setting and the regimental lines of palm trees which decorate the main thoroughfares – to delay your progress towards the local beaches, fifteen miles south, or the islands of Sanibel and Captiva, a similar distance west.

Arrival and Information

Even without a car, Fort Myers is easy to get around. The mile between the downtown area and the Edison home is covered by **local buses** (☎939-1303) and a "trolley" (old-fashioned, single-carriage buses) service. To get from downtown Fort Myers to the beaches, take any bus to the Edison Square mall, then use #50 to Summerlin Square, from where a trolley continues to Estero Island and Carl Johnson Park. Note that there's no local public transport on Sundays. The *Greyhound* station is at 2275 Cleveland Avenue (☎334-1011), just south of downtown Fort Myers. Stacks of **information** await you at the **chambers of commerce** at 1365 Hendry Street (Mon–Fri 9.30am–5pm; ☎332-3634), and at the beaches at 1661 Estero Boulevard (Mon–Fri 8am–5pm; ☎1-800/782-WAVE).

Accommodation

Accommodation costs in and around Fort Myers are low between May and mid-December, when $10–20 is lopped of the standard rates given here. For a motel **in downtown Fort Myers**, look along First Street: *Sea Chest* (no 2571; ☎332-1545; ②–③), *Ta Ki-Ki* (no 2631; ☎334-2135; ②–③) and *Tides* (no 2621; ☎334-1231; ②–③). There are many more along Cleveland Avenue, though if you're driving, aim for the rustic cottages a mile east of Hwy-41 at *Rock Lake Motel*, 2930 Palm Beach Boulevard (☎334-3242; ①–②).

At the beaches, seek a room along the motel-lined Estero Boulevard and be prepared to spend $70. Midweek you may find cheaper deals at *Beacon*, (no 1240; ☎463-5264; ③), *Gulf* (no 2700; ☎463-9247; ③), *Laughing Gull* (no 2890; ☎463-1346; ③) or *Island*, 201 San Carlos Boulevard (☎463-2381; ③). Of the **campgrounds**, only *Red Coconut*, 3001 Estero Boulevard (☎463-7200), is an easy walk from the beach. Two others are a few miles inland: *Gulf Air Travel Park*, 17279 San Carlos Road (☎466-8100), and *San Carlos*, 18701 San Carlos Boulevard (☎466-3133).

Downtown Fort Myers

Once across the Caloosahatchee River, Hwy-41 (here called Cleveland Avenue) strikes **downtown Fort Myers**, picturesquely nestled on the river's edge, where the community first took root and now very much the commercial base. Aside from a few restored homes and storefronts around Main Street and Broadway, modern office buildings predominate and you'll need to look to the creditable exhibitions of the **Fort Myers Historical Museum**, 2300 Peck Street (Mon–Sat 9am–4.30pm, Sun 1–5pm; $2.50), for thorough insights into the past. These include the exploits of Doctor Franklin Miles, a Fort Myers inhabitant who developed *Alka Seltzer*. The invention of the world's great hangover cure was overshadowed, however, by the deeds of Thomas Edison, comprehensively recalled a mile west of downtown Fort Myers on McGregor Avenue – also the route to the Fort Myers beaches and the Sanibel Island causeway.

Along McGregor Boulevard

In 1885, six years after inventing the light bulb, workaholic **Thomas Edison** collapsed from exhaustion and was instructed by his doctor to find a warm working environment or face an early death. Vacationing in Florida, the 37-year-old

Edison noted a patch of bamboo sprouting from the banks of the Caloosahatchee River and bought fourteen acres of it, clearing a section to spend his remaining winters at what became the **Edison Winter Home**, 2350 McGregor Boulevard (guided tours every 30min; Mon–Sat 9am–3.30pm, Sun 12.30pm–3.30pm; $10) – and living to be 84.

A liking for bamboo was no idle fancy: Edison was a keen horticulturalist and often utilized the chemicals produced by plants and trees in his experiments. The **gardens** of the house, where the tours begin (get a ticket from the signposted office across McGregor Boulevard), provided Edison with much raw material: a variety of tropical foliage – from the extraordinary African sausage tree to a profusion of wild orchids nurtured by the inventor and intoxicatingly scented by frangipani. By contrast, Edison's **house** is an anticlimax: a palm-cloaked wooden structure with an ordinary collection of period furnishings glimpsed only through the windows. A reason for the plainness of the abode may be that Edison spent most of his waking hours inside the **laboratory**, attempting to turn the latex-rich sap of *solidago Edisoni* (a giant strain of goldenrod weed which he developed) into rubber – anticipating the shortage caused by the outbreak of World War II. A mass of test tubes, phials and tripods are scattered over the benches, unchanged since Edison's last experiment, performed just before his death in 1931.

Not until the tour reaches the **museum** does the full impact of Edison's achievements become apparent. A design for an improved ticker-tape machine provided him with the funds for the experiments which led to the creation of the phonograph in 1877, and financed research into passing electricity through a vacuum that resulted in the incandescent light bulb two years later. Scores of cylinder and disc phonographs with gaily painted horn-speakers, bulky vintage light bulbs, and innumerable spin-off gadgets, make up an engrossing collection; here, too, you'll see some of the ungainly cinema projectors derived from Edison's *Kinetoscope* – bringing the inventor a million dollars a year in patent royalties from 1907.

A close friend of Edison's since 1896, when the inventor had been one of the few people to speak admiringly of his ambitious car ideas, **Henry Ford** bought the house next door to Edison's in 1915, by which time he was established as the country's top automobile manufacturer. Unlike the Edison home, you can go inside the **Ford Winter Home** (tour hours as for Edison home; $10), though the interior, restored to the style of Ford's time but lacking the original fittings, hardly justifies the admission price: despite becoming the world's first billionaire, Ford lived with his wife in modest surroundings.

Before leaving the old homes, pause to admire the sprawling **banyan tree** outside the ticket office: grown from a seedling given to Edison by tyre-king Harvey Firestone in 1925, it's now the largest tree in the state.

The Fort Myers beaches

Still being discovered by the holidaying multitudes, the **Fort Myers beaches**, fifteen miles south of downtown Fort Myers, are appreciably different in character from the West Coast's more commercialized beach strips, with a cheerful seaside mood that's worth getting acquainted with. Accommodation (see below) is plentiful on and around Estero Boulevard – reached by San Carlos Boulevard, off McGregor Boulevard – which runs the seven-mile length of **Estero Island**;

the hubs of activity being the short fishing pier and the **Lynne Hall Memorial Park**, at the island's northern end.

Estero Island becomes quieter and increasingly residential as you press south, Estero Boulevard eventually swinging over a slender causeway onto the barely developed **San Carlos Island**. A few miles ahead, at the **Carl Johnson Park** (daily 8am–5pm; $1.50), a footpath picks a trail over a couple of mangrove-fringed islands and several mullet-filled creeks – a domain of weekend fishing enthusiasts – to **Lovers Key**, a spectacularly secluded beach where occasional washed-up drink cans are the only signs of human existence: a perfect base for stress-free beachcombing and sunbathing. If you don't fancy the half-mile walk, a free trolley-bus will transport you between the park entrance and the beach.

Inland from Fort Myers

Just as the beaches are kept in good condition, so much of the eastern perimeter of the town, verging on the open lands of central Florida, is protected by a series of parks: scenic spots for picnicking, with canoeing and walking trails often thrown in. For a more informative look at the local landscape, spend a couple of hours at the **Nature Center of Lee County**, 3450 Ortiz Avenue (Mon–Sat 9am–4pm, Sun 11am–4.30pm; $3), on boardwalk trails through cypress and pine woods; ideally doing so on the Sunday **free guided tour**, departing at 3pm. Cast an eye, too, around the aviary – where injured birds regain their strength before returning to the wild – and the indoor **museum**: alongside general geological and wildlife exhibits, you'll find a caged specimen of each of the state's four varieties of poisonous snake; the facial expressions of the mice, fed to each snake once a day, are not a sight for the faint-hearted.

Further inland, forty miles northeast of Fort Myers on Route 31, natural Florida rears up in even more decisive fashion with **Babcock Wilderness Adventures** (departures Tues–Sun at 9am, 11am, 1pm & 3pm; $17.50; reservations essential on ☎489-3911), which penetrate a section of a 90,000-acre ranch belonging to the phenomenally wealthy Babcock family (their fortune built on household supply stores). Turkey vultures circle overhead and buffalo roam in the distance as you sit aboard an open-top vehicle bumping around the rugged terrain, pausing to look for the rare Florida panther from a glass-fronted observation hut and to peer into a primordial cypress swamp. It's not a cheap tour, but it's probably as close as you'll get to the wildlands without a carefully planned expedition.

Eating

Inexpensive breakfasts, snacks and lunches are easily found in **downtown Fort Myers**: try the *The Snack House*, 2118 First Street (☎332-1808), or *Sam's Kitchen*, 2208 E First Street (☎332-3744), or pick up a fresh-baked goodie from *Mason's*, 1615 Hendry Street (☎334-4525). For a fuller lunch or dinner, use the *Victoria Pier*, 2230 Edwards Drive (☎334-4881), or, for prime steaks and ribs, *Smitty's*, 2240 W First Street (☎334-4415). **At the beaches**, the laid-back *Café du Monde*, 1740 Estero Boulevard (☎463-8088), produces tempting morsels from homemade recipes; *Top O' The Mast*, 1028 Estero Boulevard (☎463-9424), is a solid bet for seafood; with a massive appetite, go to *The Reef*, 2601 Estero Boulevard (☎463-4181), for all-you-can-eat nightly specials, ranging from catfish to frogs' legs.

Sanibel and Captiva Islands

When the Lee County authorities (who control the whole Fort Myers area) decided to link **SANIBEL ISLAND**, the most southerly of an island grouping around the mouth of the Caloosahatchee River, by road to the mainland in 1963, Sanibel's thousand or so occupants fought tooth and nail against the scheme, eventually losing a protracted legal battle. A decade later, they got their own back by seceding from the county, becoming a self-governing "city" and passing strict land-use laws to prevent their island sinking beneath holiday homes and hotels.

Those who remember the old days insist that the island has gone to the dogs: motels and restaurants are more numerous than ever before, and visitors always outnumber the present 7000 residents. But Sanibel is a credit to those who run it: high-rises have been kept out, the beaches are superb, and sizeable areas are set aside as nature preserves. Other than the complete lack of public transport from the mainland, there's no excuse not to visit the twelve-mile-long, two-mile-wide island: arrive for a few hours and you could find yourself staying several days.

North of Sanibel, a road continues to **CAPTIVA ISLAND**, even less populated, its only concession to modern-day economics being an upmarket holiday resort at its northern tip, from where boat trips make some of the neighboring islands accessible.

Sanibel Island

From the mainland, Causeway Boulevard ($3 outbound toll) – a continuation of Route 876, fifteen miles west from downtown Fort Myers and just north of the town's beaches – meets Periwinkle Way, the main route through the southern half of Sanibel Island. Erected in 1884, the undramatic **Sanibel lighthouse**, a mile to the left, is a relic most arrivals feel obliged to inspect (from the outside only) before spending a few hours on the presentable beach at its foot. More productively, retrace a course along Periwinkle Way and turn right into Dunlop Street, acknowledging the island's tiny city hall on the way to the **Island Historical Museum** (mid-Oct to mid-Aug Wed–Sat 10am–4pm; free): a century-old pioneer settler's home with furnishings and photos of early Sanibel arrivals – those who weren't seafarers tried agriculture until the soils were ruined by saltwater blown up by hurricanes – and displays on the pre-European dwellers, the Calusa Indians, most macabrely remembered by a thousand-year-old skeleton.

SHELLING ON SANIBEL AND CAPTIVA ISLANDS

Something Sanibel and Captiva share are **shells**. Literally tons of them are washed ashore with each tide, and the popularity of shell collecting has led to the bent-over condition known as "Sanibel Stoop". The potential ecological upset of too many shells being taken away has led to laws forbidding the removal of more than two live shells (ie one with a creature living inside) of a particular species per person, on pain of a $500 fine or a prison sentence. Novices and seasoned conchologists alike will find plenty to occupy them on the beaches; to identify your find, use one of the shell charts drawn in most of the giveaway tourist magazines – or watch the experts at work during the **Sanibel Shell Festival** in early March.

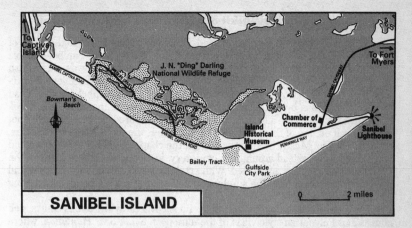

SANIBEL ISLAND

Continuing along Periwinkle Way, Tarpon Bay Road cuts west to the coast, passing the rampant vegetation of the **Bailey Tract**, a jungle-like rectangle of untamed land in the midst of a residential area: poorly marked trails will take you deeper in, among the alligators and the wildfowl – for the careful and courageous only. In either direction from the end of Tarpon Springs Road, resorts and tourists mark the beaches; turning left along Casa Ybel Road and Algiers Lane leads to the more promising **Gulfside City Park**, a slender sandy strip shaded by Australian pines and bordered by a narrow canal, with a nicely secluded picnic area. Before you leave, follow the bike path off Algiers Road for a few yards to a tiny **cemetery**, where a few wooden markers remember those who perished, some a hundred years ago, in their attempts to forge an existence on the then inhospitable island.

The J N "Ding" Darling Wildlife Refuge

In contrast to the smooth beaches along the Gulf side of the island, the opposite edge comprises shallow bays and creeks, a vibrant wildlife habitat under the protection of the **J N "Ding" Darling Wildlife Refuge** (daily except Fri sunrise–sunset; cars $4, cyclists and pedestrians $1), the main entance and **information center** just off the Sanibel–Captiva Road – chief artery of Sanibel's northern section. Alligators, brown pelicans and ospreys are usually easy to spy, but much of what you'll see at the refuge is determined by when you come: during the autumn, migrating songbirds are plentiful, thousands of wintering ducks show up in subsequent months, and in spring, graceful roseate spoonbills sweep by just before sunset.

The five-mile **Wildlife Drive** requires slow speeds and plenty of stops if you're to see the well-camouflaged residents by car. If you're cycling, take heed of the wind direction before entering: you'll usually keep the wind at your back and not in your face by pedalling north to south. You'd do better, though, to plod the four miles of the **Indigo trail**, beginning just beyond the information center. There's a second, much shorter, foot route close to the north end of Wildlife Drive: the **Indian Shell trail**, which twists between mangrove and buttonwood, and passes a few lime trees (remaining from the efforts to cultivate the island) to a native American **shell mound** – a hump in the ground, much less spectacular than you might hope.

Continuing north: Bowman's Beach and Captiva Island

One of Sanibel's loveliest swathes of sand, **Bowman's Beach**, lies to the north of the island; to reach it, watch for Bowman's Beach Road off the Sanibel–Captiva Road just prior to Blind Pass. Popular with the shell-hunting crowds, this is also an excellent spot for sunset-watching, and, in the more secluded sections, **naturists** perfect their all-over tans. Immediately north, the Sanibel–Captiva Road crosses Blind Pass by bridge and reaches Captiva Island, markedly less developed than Sanibel and inhabited only by a few hundred people. If you're not going to call on one of them, the sole site of note is the tiny **Chapel-by-the-Sea**, at 11580 Chapin. Mostly used for weddings, the chapel is unlikely to be open and you should walk instead around the **cemetery**, just opposite, where many of the island's orginal settlers are buried. With crashing waves a shell's throw away and the graves protected from the sun by a roof of seagrape, it's a fitting final resting place for an islander.

A few miles further, Captiva's northern tip is covered by the tennis courts, golf couses and Polynesian-style villas of the ultra-posh *South Seas Plantation*, where the cheapest beds are $150 a night. There's no point in hanging around here, except for the **boat trips** to the neighboring islands.

Beyond Captiva Island: Cabbage Key

Of a number of small islands just north of Captiva, **Cabbage Key** is the one to visit. Even if you arrive on the lunch cruise from Captiva (see the box above), skip the unexciting food in favor of prowling the footpaths and the small marina: there's a special beauty in the isolated setting and the views across Pine Island Sound. Do take a peep into the restaurant, though, to see the most expensive wallpaper in Florida: an estimated $25,000 worth of dollar bills, each one signed by the person who left it pinned up in observance of a Cabbage Key tradition. If you get the urge to stay longer, the inn has six simple rooms on offer at $65 and, more expensively, a few rustic cottages in the grounds; reserve on ☎282-2278 at least a month in advance.

Sanibel and Captiva facts

Your first stop on Sanibel should be the **Chamber of Commerce**, 1159 Causeway Boulevard (Mon–Sat 9am–7pm, Sun 10am–5pm; ☎472-1080), packed with essential **information** and numerous free publications. The only **public transport** is a "trolley" (info: ☎472-6374) operating from December to April between the Chamber of Commerce and the *South Seas Plantation*; one-day tickets are $2 for Sanibel and $4 to cover Sanibel and Captiva. If your stay on Sanibel is a brief one, you'll get a good sense of what makes the place tick from the **guided trolley tour** (Nov–April Mon, Wed & Fri at 10am & 12.30pm; $8).

Don't despair if the trolley isn't running; a better way to get about is by **bike**: *Finnimore's Cycle Shop*, 2353 Periwinkle Way (☎472-5577), and *The Bike Rental Inc*, 2330 Palm Ridge Road (☎472-2241), are the cheapest places to rent.

Accommodation

Accommodation on the islands is never as cheap as on the mainland, although from May to November room rates will be less than they are throughout the rest of the year (peak rates are listed here). *Kona Kai*, 1539 Periwinkle Way (☎472-

BOAT TRIPS FROM CAPTIVA ISLAND

Several organized boat trips begin from the docks at the *South Sea Plantation*. The best of them is the lunch cruise, departing at 10.30am and returning at 3pm, allowing two hours ashore at either Cabbage Key (see below) or at a gourmet restaurant on Useppa Island; cost is $27.50. A dinner cruise to the same destinations, departing at 6pm and returning at 10.30pm, costs $38. Neither price includes food while ashore – there's no obligation to eat once you land, but taking your own food on the boat isn't allowed. Other cruises include an hour-long breakfast voyage around Captiva, departing at 9am and costing $22 with a light meal provided; and an hour-long sightseeing cruise at 3.30pm for $16.50.

Whenever you sail, you're likely to see **dolphins**: many of them live in the warm waters around the islands, sometimes leaping above the water to turn somersaults for your benefit.

To get further **details** and to make **reservations** for all sailings, call ☎472-7549.

1001; ④–⑤), is among the least costly; if you'd rather be on the beach, use the cosy *West Wind Inn*, 3345 W Gulf Drive (☎1-800/282-2831; ⑤), or the functional *Jolly Roger*, 3201 W Gulf Drive (☎472-1700; ④). A good alternative to standard rooms are the wooden cottages, sleeping two to four people, at *Seahorse*, 1223 Buttonwood Lane (☎472-4262; ④). Sanibel also has a **campground**, *Periwinkle Trailer Park*, 1119 Periwinkle Way (☎472-1433).

Eating

You can get a two-dollar **breakfast** at *Bud's*, 1473 Periwinkle Way (☎472-5700); the *Lighthouse Café*, 362 Periwinkle Way (☎472-0303), serves good-value meals throughout the day; *Cheeburger Cheeburger*, 2413 Periwinkle Way (☎472-6111), has burgers in all styles. For a more substantial **lunch or dinner**, you'll find a wide selection of seafood at *The Mucky Duck*, Andy Rosee Lane (closed Sun; ☎472-3434), and at *Fast Eddie's*, 1975 Periwinkle Way (☎472-8445); alternatively, mouthwatering pasta and cajun dishes are a speciality of *The Jacaranda*, 1223 Periwinkle Way (☎472-1771).

South of Fort Myers

While Sanibel and Captiva islands easily warrant a few days of exploration, there's less to keep you occupied on the mainland on the seventy-mile journey south from Fort Myers towards the Everglades National Park. The towns you'll pass will carry less appeal than the nearby beaches, or the vistas of Florida's interior at the end of inland detours. Set aside a few hours, however, to examine one of the stranger footnotes to Florida's history: the oddball religious community of the Koreshans.

The Koreshan Historic Site

Around the turn of the century, some of the nation's radicals and idealists began viewing Florida as the last earthly wilderness; a subtropical Garden of Eden where the wrongs of modern society could be righted. Much to the amusement of hard-living Florida farmers, some of them came south to experiment with utopian ways, though few braved the humidity and mosquitoes for long. One of the more significant arrivals was also the most bizarre: the **Koreshan Unity** community, which came from Chicago in 1894 to build the "New Jerusalem" on a site now preserved as the **Koreshan State Historic Site**, 22 miles from Fort Myers, just south of Estero beside Hwy-41 (daily 8am–sunset; cars $3.25, pedestrians and cyclists $1).

The flamboyant leader of the Koreshans*, **Cyrus Teed**, was an army surgeon when he underwent the "great illumination": an angel appearing and informing him that the Earth was concave, lining the inner edge of a hollow sphere, at the center of which was the rest of the universe. Subsequently, Teed changed his name to "Koresh" and gained a following among Chicago intellectuals who, like him, were disillusioned with established religions and were seeking a communal, anti-materialistic way of life. Among the tenets of the Koreshan creed were celibacy outside marriage, shared ownership of goods, and gender equality. The aesthetes who came to this desolate outpost, reachable only by boat along the alligator-infested Estero River, quickly learned new skills in farming and house building, and marked out thirty-foot-wide boulevards which they believed would one day be the arteries of a city inhabited by ten million enlightened souls. In fact, at its peak in the three years from 1904, the community numbered just two hundred. After Teed's death in 1908, the Koreshans fizzled out, the last member – who arrived in 1940, fleeing Nazi Germany – dying in 1982.

The Koreshan library and museum

The Koreshan site will be a disappointment unless you first call at the **Koreshan library and museum**, 8661 Corkscrew Road (tours Mon–Fri at 1pm, 2pm, 3pm & 4pm; $1; four person minimum; details on ☎992-0311), for background on the Koreshans' beliefs, plus the chance to see numerous photos and portraits of Teed, some of his esoteric books and copies of the still-published Koreshan newspaper, *The American Eagle*. Along the broad thoroughfares at the neighboring **site**, several of the Koreshans' buildings have been restored. Among them are the Planetary Court, meeting place of the seven women – each named after one of the seven known planets – who governed the community; the home of Teed; and the the the Art Hall, where the community's cultural evenings were staged, where Koreshan celebrations (such as the solar festival in October and the lunar festival in April) still occur, and where the *rectilinator*, a device which "proved" the Koreshan theory of the concave Earth, can be seen.

Bonita Springs and the Corkscrew Swamp Sanctuary

A fast-growing residential community, **BONITA SPRINGS**, seven miles south of the Koreshan site, has negligible appeal besides providing access to **Bonita Beach**, along Bonita Beach Road, and the less impressive **Everglades Wonder Gardens**, on the corner of Terry Street and Hwy-41 (daily 9am–5pm; $5), keeping a multitude of the state's indigenous creatures in cramped confinement.

Make more of an effort and you'll get a better impression of natural Florida twenty miles **inland** on Route 846 (branching from Hwy-41 a few miles south of

---

* There is no link between the Koreshans and David Koresh, leader of the religious cult who barricaded themselves into their Waco, Texas, headquarters and battled with federal troops before they and their compound were incinerated in April 1993.

Bonita Springs) at the **Corkscrew Swamp Sanctuary** (daily, May–Nov 8am–5pm, otherwise 7am–5pm; $6.50), an enormous gathering of Spanish-moss-draped cypress trees rising through a dark and moody swamp landscape. Tempering the strange joy of the scene, though, is the knowledge that all of the much larger area presently safeguarded by the Big Cypress Swamp National Preserve (see "The Everglades", below) looked like this before uncontrolled logging scythed down the five-hundred-year-old trees, and severely reduced Florida's wood stork population, who nest a hundred feet up in the tree tops. The largest remaining wood stork colony in the country now inhabits the sanctuary, still threatened, as is the entire swamp, by falling water levels.

Continuing south: Naples and Marco Island

A place of million-dollar homes and $500-a-ticket costume balls, **NAPLES** has little to thrill the cost-conscious traveller except many miles of public **beaches**, that make the pervading social snobbishness bearable. You'll get the hang of the place on Fifth Avenue, where the boat yards from the town's fishing community origins have been turned into upmarket clothes shops, art galleries and restaurants – press on swiftly to **Lowdermilk Park**, about two miles north of the pier, which, on weekends, is the most gregarious of the local sands.

Greyhound buses do stop in Naples (at 2669 Davies Boulevard; ☎774-5660), but it's no great loss that they don't go anywhere near **MARCO ISLAND**, directly south, where artificial bald eagle nests are among the techniques dreamed up by property developers to bring back the wildlife their high-rise condos have driven away. At the northern end of the island, the old village of Marco has some charm, and **Tigertail Beach Park**, at the end of a boardwalk from Hernando Drive, is a fine place to relax – though neither really makes the journey (seven miles along Route 951 off Hwy-41) worthwhile. The Everglades, within easy striking distance, are a far superior target.

The Everglades

> *Nothing anywhere else is like them: their vast glittering openness, wider than the enormous visible round of the horizon, the racing free saltness and sweetness of their massive winds, under the dazzling blue heights of space. They are unique also in the simplicity, the diversity, the related harmony of the forms of life they enclose. The miracle of the light pours over the green and brown expanse of sawgrass and of water, shining and slow-moving below, the grass and water that is the meaning and the central fact of the Everglades of Florida. It is a river of grass.*
>
> Marjory Stoneman Douglas, *The Everglades: River of Grass*

Whatever scenic excitement you might anticipate from one of the country's more celebrated natural areas, no mountains, canyons nor even a signpost heralds your arrival in the **EVERGLADES**. From the straight and monotonous ninety-mile course of Hwy-41, the most dramatic sights are small pockets of trees poking above a completely flat sawgrass plain that stretches to the horizon. It looks dead and empty; you wonder what all the fuss is about. Yet these wide open spaces resonate with life, forming part of an immensely subtle and ever-changing ecosystem, evolved through a one-off combination of climate, vegetation and wildlife.

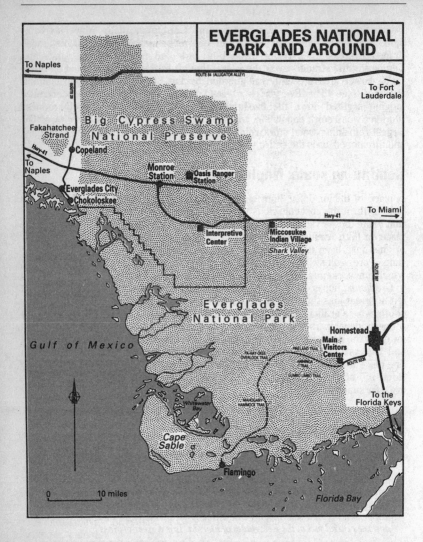

EVERGLADES NATIONAL PARK AND AROUND

Originally encompassing everything south of Lake Okeechobee, throughout this century the Everglades' boundaries have steadily been pushed back by urban development. It's important to remember that the **Everglades National Park** bestows federal protection to a comparatively small section around Florida's southeastern corner. It's in the park, where public access is designed to inflict minimum damage, that the vital links holding the Everglades together become apparent: the all-important cycle of wet and dry seasons; the ability of alligators to discover water and dig for it with their tails; the tree islands which provide sanctuaries for animals during the flood period; and the forces – such as human demands for farmland and fresh water – which threaten to tear them

EVERGLADES PRACTICALITIES

Orientation
A busy two-lane road, not the scenic drive you might expect, **Hwy-41** (the **Tamiami Trail**) runs east from Naples skirting the northern edge of the park, providing the only land access to the Everglades City and Shark Valley park entrances, and to Fakahatchee Strand, the Big Cypress National Preserve and the Miccosukee Indian Village. To reach the Flamingo entrance, touch the edge of Miami and head south. **No public transport** of any kind runs along Hwy-41 or to any of the park entrances, though day trips are available from Miami (see p.116). Between Naples and Fort Lauderdale, *Greyhound* buses use "Alligator Alley", the popular title for Route 84, twenty miles north of Hwy-41 and recently converted into a section of I-75.

When to visit
Though open all year, the park changes completely between its **wet** (summer) and **dry** (winter) seasons. The best time to visit is **winter** (Nov to April), when receding floodwaters cause wildlife, including migratory birds, to congregate around gator holes and sloughs (fresh water channels), ranger-led activities – such as guided walks, canoe trips and talks – are frequent, and the mosquitoes are bearable.

Throughout the **summer** (May to Oct), afternoon storms flood the sawgrass prairies and pour through the sloughs, with just the hammocks showing above the water. Food being plentiful, wildlife spreads throughout the park, the migratory birds have gone north, park activities are substantially reduced – and mosquitoes are a severe annoyance, rendering the backcountry campgrounds almost uninhabitable.

A clever compromise is a visit **between the seasons** (late April to early May or late Oct to early Nov), which avoids the worst of the mosquitoes and the winter tourist crowds, but reveals plenty of wildlife and the park's changing landscapes.

Entering the park and accommodation
Entering the park is free at Everglades City (although you can only see it by boat or canoe). At Shark Valley ($3) and Flamingo ($5) you **pay** per car; tickets are valid for seven days and can be used at either site (with a $2 supplement to use a Shark Valley ticket at Flamingo). Only Shark Valley closes for the night. With the exception of the wilderness waterway canoe trail between Everglades City and Flamingo, you can't travel from one section of the park into another.

Apart from the two organized campgrounds and hotel at Flamingo, park **accommodation** is limited to backcountry campgrounds. In most cases these are raised wooden platforms with a roof and chemical toilet, reachable by boat or canoe; to stay, you need a permit, issued free from the relevant visitor center. One backcountry site at Flamingo, Pearl Bay, is accessible to **disabled visitors**.

Practical tips
In the park, wear a hat, sunglasses and loose-fitting clothes with long sleeves and long trousers, and carry plenty of **insect repellent**. Besides the hazards of sunburn (there's very little shade) and mosquitoes, you need take no special measures for the walking trails, most of which are short trots along raised boardwalks.

Travelling and camping in the **backcountry** requires more caution. Most exploration is done by boat or canoe along marked trails with basic campgrounds available on the longer routes. Don't set off without ample provisions, including at least a **gallon of water** per person per day, and carry all supplies in **hard containers** – racoons are known to chew through soft ones. Carry a **compass**, and **maps** (available from visitor centers) and be sure to leave a **detailed plan** of your journey and its expected duration with a park ranger. Pay heed to the latest weather forecast, and note the tidal patterns if you're canoeing in a coastal area.

apart. None of this can be comprehended from a car window, or with a half-hour ride through the sawgrass on an airboat: noisy, destructive contraptions, touted all along Hwy-41 but banned inside the park.

Don't expect to fathom it all: the Everglades are a constant source of surprise, even for the few hundred people who live in them. Use the visitor centers, read the free material, take the guided tours and, above all, explore slowly. It's then that the Everglades begin to reveal themselves, and you'll realise you're in the middle of one of the natural world's most remarkable ecosystems.

Some geology and natural history

Appearing as flat as a table-top, the oolitic limestone (once part of the seabed) on which the Everglades stand actually tilts very slightly – by a few inches over seventy miles – towards the southwest. For thousands of years, water from summer storms and the overflow of Lake Okeechobee has moved slowly through the Everglades towards the coast. The water replenishes the sawgrass, growing on a thin layer of soil – or "marl" – formed by decaying vegetation on the limestone base, and gives birth to the algae at the foot of a complex food chain which sustains much larger creatures, most importantly alligators.

Alligators earn their "keepers of the Everglades" nickname during the dry winter season. After the summer floodwaters have reached the sea, drained through the bedrock or simply evaporated, the Everglades are barren except for the water accumulated in ponds – or "gator holes" – created when an alligator senses water and clears the soil covering it with its tail. Besides nourishing the alligator, the pond provides a home for other wildlife until the summer rains return.

Sawgrass covers much of the Everglades but where natural indentations in the limestone fill with marl, tree islands – or "hammocks" – appear, just high enough to stand above the flood waters and fertile enough to support a variety of trees and plants. Close to hammocks, wispy green-leafed willows often surround gator holes; smaller patches of vegetation, like small green humps, are called bayheads. In the few places where the elevation exceeds seven feet, you'll find pinewoods and, in drier areas, strands of dwarf cypress.

Human habitation and exploitation

Before dying out through contact with Europeans, several native American tribes lived hunter-gatherer existences in the Everglades; the shell mounds they built can still be seen in sections of the park. In the nineteenth century, Seminole Indians, fleeing white settlers from the north, also lived peaceably in the area (for more on them, see "Miccosukee Indian Village", below). By the late 1800s, a few white settlements – such as those at Everglades City and Flamingo – had sprung up, peopled by fugitives, outcasts and loners, who, unlike the Indians, looked to exploit the land rather than live in harmony with it.

As Florida's population grew, the damage caused by uncontrolled hunting, road building and draining the Everglades for farmland, gave rise to a significant conservation lobby.

In 1947, a section of the Everglades was declared a national park, but unrestrained commercial use of nearby areas continued to upset the Everglades' natural cycle; a problem acknowledged – if hardly alleviated – by the preservation of the Big Cypress Swamp, just north of the park, in the Seventies.

As human understanding increases, so the severity of the problems faced by the Everglades becomes ever more apparent. The 1500 miles of canals built to divert the flow of water away from the Everglades and towards the state's expanding cities, the poisoning caused by agricultural chemicals from the farmlands around Lake Okeechobee, and the broader changes wrought by global warming, could yet turn Florida's greatest natural asset into a wasteland – with wider ecological implications that can only be guessed at.

Everglades City and around

Purchased and named in the Twenties by an advertising executive dreaming of a subtropical metropolis, **EVERGLADES CITY**, thirty miles from Naples and three miles south off Hwy-41 along Route 29, has a population of under five hundred living around a disproportionately large city hall. Most who visit are solely intent on diminishing the stocks of sports fish living around the mangrove islands – the aptly titled **Ten Thousand Islands** – arranged like jigsaw puzzle pieces around the coastline.

For a closer look at the mangroves which safeguard the Everglades from surge tides, ignore the ecologically dubious tours advertised along the roadside and take one of the park-sanctioned **boat trips** (departures every 30min 9.30am–5pm; $9–12) from the dock on Chokoloskee, a blob of land – actually an Indian shell mound – marking the end of Route 29. The dockside **visitor center** (daily 8.30am–5pm; ☎695-3311) provides information on the cruises and the excellent ranger-led **canoe trips** (winter Sat at 10am). Anybody adequately skilled with the paddle, equipped with rough camping gear, and with a week to spare, should have a crack at the hundred-mile **wilderness waterway**, a marked trail through Whitewater Bay to Flamingo (see below) with numerous backcountry campgrounds.

Other than boat-accessed camping, there's no **accommodation** inside this section of the park. In Chokoloskee, though, you can rent an RV by the night for $45–60 at *Outdoor Resorts* (☎695-2881), or get a simple cottage in the grounds of the *Everglades Gun & Lodge Club*, 200 Riverside Drive (☎695-4211; ③).

Big Cypress Swamp National Preserve

The completion of Hwy-41 in 1928 led to the destruction of thousands of towering bald cypress trees – whose durable wood was highly marketable – lining the roadside sloughs. By the Seventies, attempts to drain these ecologically crucial acres and turn them into saleable residential plots had caused enough damage to the national park for the government to create the **Big Cypress Swamp National Preserve** – a massive chunk of protected land mostly on the northern side of Hwy-41. Sadly, neither the bald cypress trees nor the wood storks that once flourished here are present in anything like their previous numbers (a better place to observe both is the Corkscrew Swamp Sanctuary; see "Bonita Springs and the Corkscrew Swamp Sanctuary").

While it's not actually part of the national preserve, be sure to visit the nearby **Fakahatchee Strand**, directly north of Everglades City on Route 29: a water-holding slough giving life to dwarf cypress trees (much smaller than the bald cypress; grey and spindly during the winter, draped with green needles in summer), a stately batch of royal palms, and masses of orchids and spiky-leafed air plants. If possible, see it on a **ranger-guided walk**; details on ☎695-4593. Save for the awe inspired by its sheer size as you drive alongside it, the Big Cypress Swamp is less demanding of close attention and can only be traversed on a very rugged 29-mile hiking trail, beginning twenty miles east on Hwy-41 at the **Oasis Ranger Station** (Thurs–Mon 9am–4pm; ☎695-4111).

If your car's suspension is dependable, avoid the ranger station by turning right at Monroe Station, four miles west, onto a gravel road – potholed in parts and prone to sudden flooding – through cypress and pinewoods to Pinecrest, where an **interpretive center** makes sense of the varied terrains all around. The road rejoins Hwy-41 at Forty Mile Bend, just west of the Miccosukee Indian Village.

The Miccosukee Indian Village

Driven out of central Florida by newly arriving white settlers, several hundred Seminole Indians retreated to the Everglades during the nineteenth century to avoid forced resettlement in the Midwest. On hammocks, they lived in open-sided "chickees" built from cypress and cabbage palm, and traded, hunted and fished across the wetlands by canoe. Descendants of the Seminoles, and of a related tribe, the **Miccosukee**, still live in the Everglades, though the coming of Hwy-41 – making the land accessible to the white man – brought another fundamental change in their lifestyle as they set about grabbing their share of the tourist dollars.

Four miles east of Forty Mile Bend, the **Miccosukee Indian Village** (daily 9am–5pm) symbolizes their uneasy compromise. In the souvenir shop, good quality traditional crafts and clothes stand side-by-side with blatant tack, and in the "village" (entry $5), men turn logs into canoes and women cook over open fires: despite the authentic roots, it's such a contrived affair that anyone with an ounce of sensitivity can't help but feel uneasy – the arrow-shooting gallery and the awful alligator wrestling don't help. Since it's the only chance you're likely to get to discover anything of native American life in the Everglades, it's hard to resist taking a look; though a plateful of traditional pumpkin bread from the *Miccosukee Restaurant* (☎223-8388), across the road, and a read of the *Seminole Tribune* newspaper, describing present-day concerns, might serve you better. From the marina beside the restaurant, the tribe run **airboat rides** ($6) to another "village", set on a hammock about fifteen minutes away through the sawgrass – another chance to buy dismal souvenirs and not a lot else.

Shark Valley

In no other section of the park does the Everglades' "River of Grass" tag seem as appropriate as it does at **SHARK VALLEY** (daily 8.30am–6pm; cars $3, pedestrians and cyclists $1), a mile east of the Miccosukee Indian Village. From here, dotted by hardwood hammocks and the smaller bayheads, the tan-colored (in winter) sawgrass plain stretches as far as the eye can see. It's here, too, that the damage wrought by humans on the natural cycle can sometimes be disturbingly clear. The thirst of Miami coupled with a period of drought can make Shark Valley resemble a stricken desert.

Seeing Shark Valley

Aside from a few simple walking trails close to the **visitor center** (winter daily 8.30am–5.15pm; reduced hours during the summer; ☎305/221-8776), you can see Shark Valley only from a fourteen-mile loop road. Too lengthy and lacking in shade to be covered comfortably on foot, and off-limits to cars, the loop is ideally covered by renting a **bike** ($2.50 an hour; return by 4pm). Alternatively, a highly informative two-hour **tram tour** (winter departures hourly from 9am; summer departures at 9am, 11am, 1pm & 3pm; $6; reservations necessary March–July ☎305/221-8455) will get you around and stop frequently to view wildlife – but won't allow you to linger in any particular place, as you'll certainly want to do.

Set out as early as possible (the wildlife is most active in the cool of the morning), ride slowly and stay alert: otters, turtles and snakes are plentiful but not always easy to spot, and the abundant alligators often keep uncannily still. During September and October you'll come across female alligators tending their young; the brightly striped babies often sun themselves on the backs of their extremely protective mothers – watch them from a safe distance. More of the same creatures – and a good selection of bird life – can be seen from the **observation tower** overlooking a deep canal and marking the far point of the loop.

It may seem hard to believe but Shark Valley is only seventeen miles from the western fringes of Miami. To **see more of the park**, continue east on Hwy-41, turn south along Route 997, and head west for eleven miles along Route 9336 from Homestead to the park's Flamingo entrance.

Flamingo and Around

Everglades City has the islands and Shark Valley has the sawgrass, but the **FLAMINGO** section of the park – the entire southerly portion – holds virtually everything that makes the Everglades tick: spend a well-planned day or two here and you'll quickly grasp the fundamentals of its complex ecology. From the **park entrance** (always open; cars $5, pedestrians and cyclists $2), the road passes the **main visitor center** (daily 8am–5pm; ☎305/253-2241) and continues for 38 miles to the tiny coastal settlement of Flamingo, a one-time pioneer fishing colony now comprising a marina, hotel and campground. There's no compulsion to drive the whole way, and the short walking trails (none more than half a mile) on the route will keep you engaged for hours; sensibly, though, you should devote a day to walking and a second one to the canoe trails close to Flamingo.

Towards Flamingo: the walking trails

Apparently unimpressed by the multitudinous forms of nature and animal life throughout the Everglades, large numbers of park visitors simply want to see an alligator, and most are satisfied by walking the **Anhinga trail**, a mile from the main visitor center. Turtles, marsh rabbits and the odd raccoon are also likely to turn up on the route, but you should watch for the bizarre anihinga, a black-bodied bird resembling an elongated cormorant, which, after diving for fish, spends ages drying itself on rocks and tree branches with its white-tipped wings fully spread. Beat the crowds to the Anhinga trail and then peruse the adjacent but very different **Gumbo Limbo trail**, a hardwood hammock packed with exotic subtropical growths: strangler figs, gumbo limbos, royal palms, wild coffee and resurrection ferns – appearing dead during the dry season, these "resurrect" themselves in the summer rains to form a lush collar of green.

By comparison, the **Pinelands trail**, a few miles further by the Long Pine Key campground, offers an undramatic ramble through a forest of slash pine, though the solitude comes as a welcome relief after the busier trails: the hammering of woodpeckers is often the loudest sound you'll hear. More bird life – egrets, red-shouldered hawks and circling vultures among the readily identified species – is viewable six miles ahead from the **Pa-hay-okee Overlook trail**, emerging from a strand of dwarf cypress to face a great tract of sawgrass, a familiar sight if you've arrived from Shark Valley.

Although related to California's giant redwoods, the mahogany trees of the **Mahogany Hammock trail**, eight miles from the overlook – despite being the largest of the type in the country – are disappointingly small, and less of a draw than the colorful snails hanging from them and the golden orb spiders weaving webs around their branches. Continuing, you'll begin to see red mangrove trees – recognisable by their above-ground roots – rising from the sawgrass: a sure sign that you're approaching the coast.

Flamingo and Canoeing

A century ago, the only way to reach **FLAMINGO**, perched on Florida's southern tip, was by boat. This fact failed to deter – indeed it encouraged – a small bunch of settlers who spent their time fishing, hunting, smuggling and getting paralytic on moonshine whisky. Flamingo was so remote that it didn't have a name until the opening of a post office made one necessary: "The End of the World" was favored by those who knew the place, but Flamingo was chosen due to the abundant roseate spoonbills – pink-plumed birds which the locals failed to identify correctly as they killed them for their feathers. The completion of the road to Homestead in 1922 was expected to bring boom times to Flamingo: as it turned out, most people seized their chance and left. None of the old buildings remain and present-day Flamingo does a brisk trade servicing the needs of sports fishing fanatics. On land, the **visitor center** (daily 8am–5pm; ☎695-3101, ext 182) and the marina of the *Flamingo Lodge*, the park's only hotel, are the activity bases.

There are few short **walking trails** within reach, though the numerous **canoe trails** promise much more. Rent a canoe ($20 a day) from the marina, and get maps and advice from the visitor center. Obviously, you should pick a canoe trail that suits your level of expertise: a likely one for novices (though it's not advisable to try canoeing alone if you have no experience whatsoever) being the three-mile **Noble Hammock trail**, passing through sawgrass and around mangroves, using a course pioneered by bootleg booze-makers. For polished paddlers, the hundred-mile **wilderness waterway** to Everglades City (see above), lined by plentiful backcountry campgrounds, is the trip you've been waiting for.

If you lack faith in your own abilities, take one of the **guided boat trips** from the marina. The most informative, the **backwater cruise** (daily at noon & 3pm; $9; reservations on ☎305/253-2241), makes a two-hour foray around the mangrove-enshrouded Whitewater Bay, offering good views of Cape Sable, a strip of deserted beach and rough prairie hovering uncertainly between land and sea.

Accommodation

There are well-equipped **campgrounds** at Long Pine Key and Flamingo ($4), and many backcountry sites (free) on the longer walking and canoe trails. Reservations are not accepted for any of the campgrounds: spare space at Flamingo (which invariably fills first) or Long Pine Key can be checked on the board just inside the park entrance. If there is space and the visitor center is closed, you can use the site but should pay at the visitor center before 10am the following day. For the backcountry sites, you will, of course, need a permit: these are issued free at the visitor centers. The only **rooms** within the park are at *Flamingo Lodge* (☎695-3101 or ☎305/253-2241; ④–⑤) – you'll need to make a reservation months in advance if arriving between November and April.

travel details

Trains

From Tampa to Clearwater/Clearwater Beach (2 daily; 45min/1hr); St Petersburg/Treasure Island (2 daily; 30min/1hr); Bradenton/Sarasota (2 daily; 1hr 10min/1hr 40min); Lakeland/Kissimee/ Orlando/Winter Park/Sanford/DeLand/Palatka/ Jacksonville (2 daily; 32min/1hr 36min/2hr 16min/2hr 31min/2hr 54min/3hr 14min/4hr 1min/ 5hr 28min).

From St Petersburg to Tampa/Winter Haven (2 daily; 35min/2hr 45min); Treasure Island (1 daily; 30min).

Buses

From Tampa to Bradenton/Sarasota/Venice/Fort Myers/Naples/Fort Lauderdale/Miami (5 daily; 1hr/1hr 35min/2hr 10min/2hr 5min/4hr 5min/7hr 5min/8hr 55min); St Petersburg (15 daily; 35min); Clearwater (6 daily; 30min); Crystal River/ Tallahassee (3 daily; 3hr 13min/6hr 35min); Orlando (7 daily; 1hr 30min); Lakeland/Winter Haven/Lake Wales/Avon Park/Sebring/West Palm Beach (1 daily; 1hr/1hr 30min/1hr 55min/ 3hr 5min/3hr 30min/6hr).

From St Petersburg to Tampa (11 daily; 35min– 1hr); Clearwater (11 daily; 30min).

CHAPTER SEVEN

THE PANHANDLE

R ubbing hard against Alabama in the west and Georgia in the north, the long, narrow **Panhandle** has much more in common with the states of the Deep South than with the rest of Florida. Cosmopolitan sophisticates in Miami and Tampa have countless jokes lampooning the folksy life-styles of the people here – undeniably more rural and down-to-earth than their counterparts around the state – but the Panhandle has more to offer than many give it credit for; certainly, you won't get a true picture of Florida without seeing at least some of it.

Indeed, a century ago, the Panhandle *was* Florida. At the western edge, **Pensacola** was a busy port when Miami was still a swamp; fertile soils lured wealthy plantation owners south and helped establish **Tallahassee** as a high-society gathering place and administrative center – a role which, as the state capital, it retains; and the great Panhandle forests fuelled a timber boom which brought new towns and unrivalled prosperity. But the decline of cotton, the chopping down of too many trees and the coming of the East Coast railway eventually left the Panhandle high and dry.

The region today divides neatly in two. Much of the **inland Panhandle** still seems neglected: small farming towns that see few visitors despite the proximity of springs, sinkholes and the **Apalachicola National Forest**, perhaps the best place in Florida to disappear into the wilderness. The **coastal Panhandle**, on the other hand, is enjoying better times. Rows of hotels and condos mark the most popular, money-spinning sections, although much of its spectacular shoreline is shielded from developers, leaving many untainted miles of blindingly white sands. Each grain is almost pure quartz, washed down over millions of years from the Appalachian mountains – causing the beaches to squeak when you walk on them. Not to be outshone, the Gulf waters here are two-tone: emerald green close to the shore and deep blue further out.

Provided you're driving, **getting around** presents few problems. Across the inland Panhandle, **I-10** carries the through traffic and **Hwy-90** links the little places – and many of the natural sights – between Tallahassee and Pensacola. It's easy, too, to turn south off I-10 or Hwy-90 and get to the coast in under an hour. The main route along the coast is **Hwy-98**, although a number of smaller, scenic roads lead off it. Several daily *Greyhound* buses connect the bigger centers but

---

ACCOMMODATION PRICE CODES

All accommodation prices in this book have been coded using the symbols below. Note that prices are for the least expensive double rooms in each establishment. For a full explanation see p.26 in *Basics*.

①	up to $30	④	$60–80	⑦	$130–180
②	$30–45	⑤	$80–100	⑧	$180+
③	$45–60	⑥	$100–130		

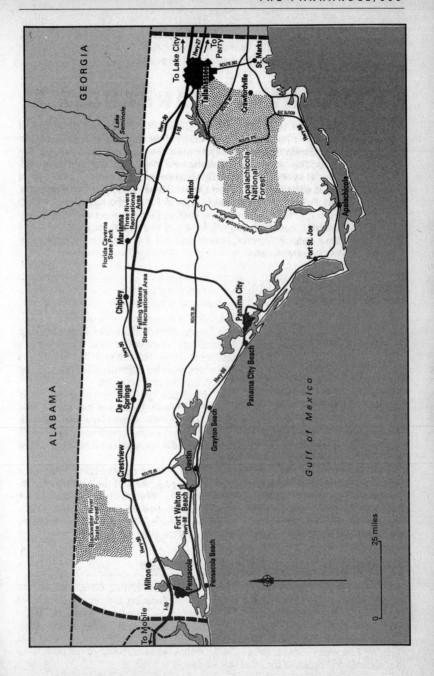

rural and coastal services are fewer, and some parts see no bus services at all. The Los Angeles–Jacksonville *Amtrak* service crosses the Panhandle, stopping once a day in each direction at Tallahassee and Pensacola.

THE INLAND PANHANDLE

Vast tracts of oak and pine trees, dozens of winding rivers and a handful of moderately sized agricultural bases make much of the **inland Panhandle** powerfully evocative of Florida in the days before mass tourism took hold. Despite the presence of the sociable state capital, **Tallahassee**, it's the insular rural communities strung along Hwy-90 – between Tallahassee and the busy coastal city of **Pensacola** – that set the region's true tone. These small towns, **Marianna**, **Chipley** and **De Funiak Springs**, which grew rich from the turn-of-the-century timber industry and now work the richest soils in Florida, generally offer little – beyond inexpensive accommodation and food – as you pass through to the area's more compelling natural features, which include the state's only explorable caverns, and two massive forests.

Tallahassee

State capital it may be, but **TALLAHASSEE** is a provincial city of oak trees and soft hills that won't take more than two days to explore in full. Briefcase-clutching bureaucrats set the mood around its small grid of central streets – where you'll find plentiful reminders of Florida's formative years – although the 25,000 students of Tallahassee's two universities are a more positive influence, brightening the mood considerably and keeping the city awake late into the night.

Though built on the site of an important prehistoric meeting place, Tallahassee's **history** really begins with Florida's incorporation into the US and the search for an administrative base between the former regional capitals, Pensacola and St Augustine. Once found, the local native Americans – the Tamali tribe – were unceremoniously dispatched to make room for the trio of log cabins in which the first Florida government sat in 1823.

The scene of every major wrangle in Florida politics, and the home of an ever-expanding white-collar work force handling the paperwork of the country's fourth fastest-growing state, Tallahassee's own fortunes through recent decades have been hindered by the lightning-paced development of south Florida. Oddly distanced from most of the people it now governs, the city remains a conservative place with a slow tempo – and a strong sense of the past.

Arrival, getting around and information

I-10 cuts across Tallahassee's northern perimeter; turning off along Monroe Street takes you past most of the budget accommodation and on into downtown Tallahassee, three miles distant. **Hwy-90** (known as Tennessee Street) and **Hwy-27** (Apalachee Parkway) are more central – arriving in or close to downtown Tallahassee. Coming by **bus** presents few problems: the *Greyhound* terminal is at 112 W Tennessee Street (☎222-4240), within walking distance of downtown Tallahassee and opposite the local bus station.

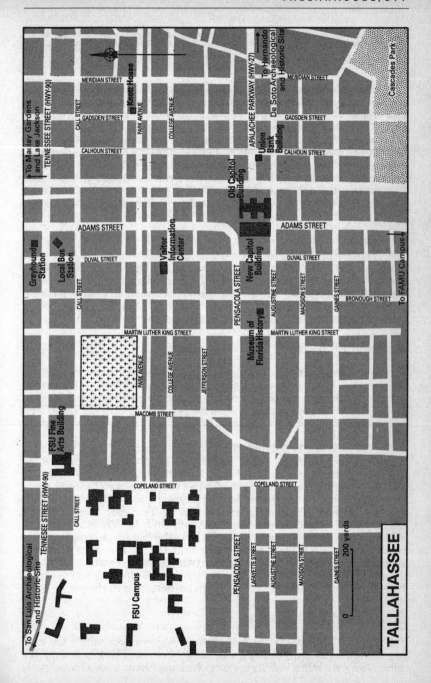

TALLAHASSEE

0   200 yards

FSU Campus

To San Luis Archaeological
and Historic Site

TENNESSEE STREET (HWY-90)

FSU Fine
Arts Building

Greyhound
Station

Local Bus
Station

To Maclay Gardens
and Lake Jackson

TENNESSEE STREET (HWY-90)

CALL STREET
GADSDEN STREET
CALHOUN STREET
ADAMS STREET
DUVAL STREET
CALL STREET
MARTIN LUTHER KING STREET
MACOMB STREET
COPELAND STREET

MERIDIAN STREET

Knott House

PARK AVENUE
COLLEGE AVENUE

Visitor
Information
Center

PARK AVENUE
COLLEGE AVENUE
JEFFERSON STREET

Museum of
Florida History

Old Capitol
Building

New Capitol
Building

PENSACOLA STREET
AUGUSTINE STREET
MADISON STREET
GAINES STREET

APALACHEE PARKWAY (HWY-27)

To Hernando
De Soto Archaeological
and Historic Site

MERIDIAN STREET
GADSDEN STREET
Union
Bank
Building
CALHOUN STREET

ADAMS STREET
DUVAL STREET

BRONOUGH STREET

MARTIN LUTHER KING STREET

COPELAND STREET

To FAMU Campus

Cascades Park

LAFAYETTE STREET
AUGUSTINE STREET
MADISON STREET
GAINES STREET
PENSACOLA STREET

The area code for Tallahassee, and the rest of the Panhandle area covered in this chapter, is ☎904.

Tallahassee's **airport** is twelve miles southwest of the city (☎891-7800); frustratingly, no public transport services link it to the town. A **taxi** to the center will cost around $15 (try *City Taxi*, ☎893-4111, or *Yellow Cab*, ☎222-3070); some motels offer a free pick-up service.

Downtown Tallahassee can be seen **on foot**, and **local buses** (☎891-5200) need only be used to reach outlying destinations. Collect a **route map and timetable** from the **bus station** (officially known as "Transfer Plaza") at the corner of Tennessee and Duval streets. You can get a **free ride** into downtown Tallahassee from the bus station with the **Old Town Trolley**, which runs to the Civic Center (near the New Capitol Building) and back at fifteen-minute intervals on weekdays between 7am and 6pm; hop on at any of the "Trolley Stop" signs.

Information

The **Chamber of Commerce**, 100 N Duval Street (Mon–Fri 8.30am–5pm; ☎224-8116), has stacks of leaflets relating to the city and the surrounding area. For material covering Tallahassee, the rest of the Panhandle and much of the rest of the state, use the **Tallahassee Area Visitor Information Center** (Mon–Fri 8am–5pm, Sat & Sun 8.30am–4.30pm; ☎1-800/628-2866) on the ground floor of the New Capitol Building – see "Downtown Tallahassee".

Accommodation

Finding **accommodation** in Tallahassee is only problematic during two periods: the sixty-day sitting of the state legislature from early April – if you're arriving then, try to turn up on a Friday or Saturday when the power-brokers have gone home – and on autumn weekends when the Seminoles (FSU's immensely well-supported football team) are playing at home. If you can't avoid these periods, book well ahead.

The cheapest **hotels** and **motels** are on N Monroe Street about three miles from downtown: the *Econo Lodge* (no 2681; ☎1-800/424-4777; ②), *Super 8* (no 2702; ☎386-8818; ②), and the *Days Inn* (no 2800; ☎1-800/325-2525; ②–③). Staying downtown is dearer, except during the summer when there are $28-a-night rooms on the FSU campus inside *Osceola Hall*, 500 Chapel Drive (☎222-5010; ①). Failing that, you're stuck with the *Holiday Inn*, 316 W Tennessee Street (☎1-800/HOLIDAY; ④), or the *Governors Inn*, 209 S Adams Street (☎1-800/342-7717; ⑤).

There are no **campgrounds** within the city. The nearest to accept tents are beside Lake Talquin to the west, the closest being *Coe Landing*, seven miles away off Route-20; the Public Works Department (☎488-9300) has details. Alternatively, the nearest **RV-only** sites are *Tallahassee RV Park* (☎878-7641), five miles east on Hwy-90, and *Bell's Campground* (☎576-7082), five miles west on Hwy-90.

Downtown Tallahassee

The soul of Tallahassee is the mile-square **downtown** area, where the main targets – the two Capitol Buildings, the State Museum of History and the two universities – are within walking distance of **Adams Street**, a peaceful and partly pedestrianized main drag whose restored Twenties storefronts more often than not conceal attorneys' offices. A day will cover everything with ease.

The Capitol Buildings and Around

A fifty-million-dollar eyesore dominates downtown Tallahassee – the vertical vents of the towering **New Capitol Building**, at the junction of Apalachee Parkway and Monroe Street (Mon–Fri 8.30am–5pm; Sat & Sun Visitor Information Center is open in lobby; free), make the seat of Florida law-making resemble a gigantic air-conditioning machine. The only way to escape from the irritating sight of the structure, unveiled to much outrage in 1977, is to go inside. The twenty-second-floor **observation level** provides an unobstructed view over Tallahassee and its environs – and if you're visiting during April or May, stop off at the fifth floor for a glance at the House of Representatives or the Senate in action, and mingle with the sharp-suited politicos striding purposefully around the corridors. Should you feel the need to learn more about the building's architecture and role, join the free 45-minute **guided tours** (on the hour, Mon–Fri 9–11am & 1–4pm, Sat & Sun 9am–3pm).

Florida's growing army of bureaucrats made the New Capitol Building necessary. Previously, they'd been crammed into the ninety-year-old **Old Capitol Building** (Mon–Fri 9am–4.30pm, Sat 10am–4.30pm, Sun noon–4.30pm; free; main entrance facing Apalachee Parkway) that stands in the shadow of its replacement. Designed on a more human and welcoming scale than its modern counterpart, with playful red and white awnings over its windows, it's hard to credit that the Old Capitol's walls once echoed with the decisions that shaped modern Florida. Proof is provided, however, by the political history contained within the side rooms: absorbing exhibits lifting the lid on the state's juiciest scandals and controversies.

Look along Apalachee Parkway from the Old Capitol's entrance to locate the nineteenth-century **Union Bank Building** (Tues–Fri 10am–1pm, Sat & Sun 1–4pm; free). The bank's past has been unsteady: going bust in the 1850s after giving farmers too much credit, re-opening to administer the financial needs of emancipated slaves after the Civil War, and later serving variously as a shoe factory, a bakery and a cosmetics shop. If the curator's on hand he'll deliver an enthusiastic account of the background, otherwise you'll need to make do with the pictures and texts, and the small collection of period furniture in the director's office.

The Museum of Florida History

For a more rounded history – easily the fullest account of Florida's past anywhere in the state – visit the **Museum of Florida History**, 500 S Bronough Street (Mon–Fri 9am–4.30pm, Sat 10am–4.30pm, Sun noon–4.30pm; free). Detailed accounts of Paleo-Indian settlements, and the significance of their burial and temple mounds – some of which have been found on the edge of Tallahassee (see "Out From The Center", below) – are valuable tools in comprehending Florida's prehistory, and the imperialist crusades of the Spanish, both in Florida and across South and Central America, are outlined with copious finds. Other than portraits of hard-faced Seminole chiefs, leaders of the native American tribes driven south into Florida's swamps and forests, however, there's disappointingly little on the nineteenth-century Seminole Wars – one of the sadder and bloodier skeletons in Florida's closet. There's plenty, though, on the turn-of-the-century railroads that made Florida a winter resort for wealthy northerners, and the subsequent arrival of "tin can tourists", whose nickname referred to the rickety

Ford campervans (forerunners of the modern Recreational Vehicles) they drove to what was by then called "the Sunshine State" – an ironic epithet for a region which had endured centuries of strife, feuding and almost constant warfare.

Tallahassee's Universities: FSU and FAMU

West from Adams Street, graffiti-coated fraternity and sorority houses along College Avenue line the approach to **Florida State University (FSU)**. This enjoys a strong reputation for its humanities courses, taught from the late 1800s in the Collegiate Gothic classrooms you'll see as you enter the wrought-iron gates, but has recently switched emphasis to science and business – which explains the newer, less characterful buildings on the far side of the campus. Shady oaks and palm trees make the grounds a pleasant place for a stroll, but there's little cause to linger. The student art of the **University Gallery and Museum** (Mon–Fri 9am–4pm; free), in the Fine Arts Building, might consume a few minutes, but you'd be better occupied rummaging around inside *Bill's Bookstore*, just across Call Street, whose large stock includes many student cast-offs at reduced prices.

The more interesting of Tallahassee's two universities, in spite of being financially much the poorer, is the **Florida Agriculture and Mechanical University (FAMU)**, about a mile south of the Capitol buildings: Florida's major black educational center since its founding in 1887. With leg-irons from slavery times and many small but revealing items from the segregation era, FAMU's **Black Archives Research Center and Museum** (Mon–Fri 9am–4pm; free) gives illuminating insights into the situation of black people in Florida and the US, and displays letters and memorabilia of those who helped bring about change, including Martin Luther King and Booker T Washington, and two Florida women who contributed to the rise of black awareness: educator and folklorist Mary McLeod Bethune (see "Daytona Beach", Chapter Four), and author Zora Neale Hurston (see "Books" in *Contexts*). The archives are in the center of the otherwise bleak campus, in an easily spotted nineteenth-century wooden building.

The Knott House

Another important landmark in Florida's black history, and one of the city's most evocatively restored Victorian homes, is the **Knott House Museum**, 301 E Park Avenue (Wed–Sat 10am–4pm; $3). It was built by a free black in 1843 and later became home to Florida's first black physician; Florida's slaves were officially emancipated in May 1865 by a proclamation read from the house's steps. The house takes its name, however, from the Knotts, a white couple who bought it in 1928. State treasurer during a period of economic calamity (Florida had been devastated by two hurricanes as the country entered the Depression), William Knott became one of Florida's most respected and influential politicians until his retirement in 1941. His wife, meanwhile, devoted her energies to the temperance movement (partly through her efforts, alcohol was banned in Tallahassee for a fifty-year period) and to writing moralistic poems, many of which you'll see attached to the antiques and furnishings which fill this intriguing relic.

Out from Downtown Tallahassee

Scattered around the fringes of Tallahassee, half a dozen diverse spots deserve brief visits: prehistoric mounds, archeological sites and lakeside gardens. All are easily accessible by car but most are much harder to reach by buses. With a bit more time to spare, venture twenty miles northwards and you're in Georgia, close to a well-preserved plantation home.

The Archeological Sites

Slowly being unearthed at the **San Luis Archeological and Historic Site**, 2020 Mission Road, about three miles west of downtown Tallahassee (bus #21), the village of San Luis de Talimali was a hub of the seventeenth-century Spanish mission system. Call at the **visitor center** (Mon–Fri 9am–4.30pm, Sat 10am–4.30pm, Sun noon–4.30pm; free) for a general explanation, and to see some of the finds – or join the hour-long **guided tour** (Mon–Fri at noon, Sat at 11am & 2pm, Sun at 2pm; free) to appreciate the importance of the place. On some weekends, period-attired individuals re-enact village life – it sounds tacky but it can be fun.

The historical associations may be more dramatic, but there's much less tangible evidence of the past – just a few holes in the ground, in fact, on a site which is closed to the public – at the **Hernando de Soto Archeological and Historic site**, two miles east of downtown Tallahassee at the corner of Goodbody Lane and Lafayette Street, thought to have been where Spanish explorer Hernando de Soto set up camp in 1540 and held the first Christmas celebration in North America. The de Soto expedition also saw the first European crossing of the Mississippi River: see "History" in *Contexts* for the full story.

Maclay State Gardens

For a lazy half-day, journey four miles northeast of downtown Tallahassee to **Maclay State Gardens**, 3540 Thomasville Road (daily 8am–sundown; Jan–April $3; May–Dec free). New York financier and amateur gardener Alfred B Maclay bought this large piece of land in the Twenties and planted flowers and shrubs intended to create a blooming season lasting from January to April. It worked: azaleas, camelias and pansies, framed by dogwood and redbud trees, are alive with fragrances and fantastic colors for four months each year. The gardens are worth visiting at anytime, however, if only to retire to the lakeside pavilion for a snooze as unconcerned lizards and squirrels scurry around your feet.

The admission fee charged during the blooming period also gets you into the **Maclay House** (closed during the rest of year), filled with the furniture of Alfred and his wife – and their countless books on horticulture. Bus #16 stops close by.

Lake Jackson and the Indian Mounds

Most boat-owning locals moor their vessels beside the sizeable **Lake Jackson**, five miles north of downtown Tallahassee. On an inlet known as Meginnis Arm are the **Lake Jackson Indian Mounds** (daily 8am–sunset; free), where rich finds, such as copper breastplates and ritual figures, suggest this eighty-acre site to have been an important native American ceremonial center. Other than large humps of soil and a sense of history, all that's here is an undemanding nature trail over a small ravine, and several picnic tables on which to enjoy a snack. By car, follow the signs off Monroe Street; on foot, the site's a three-mile trek from the #1 bus stop.

Museum of History and Natural Science

The **Tallahassee Museum of History and Natural Science** (Mon–Sat 9am–5pm, Sun 12.30–5pm; $5), three miles southwest of the city, off Lake Bradford Road (bus #15), is primarily aimed at kids, though it could fill an hour even if you don't have young minds to stimulate. The centerpiece is a working nineteenth-century-style farm, complete with cows and wandering roosters. Elsewhere, there's a short nature walk, a few cases of snakes and a couple of old buildings of moderate note – a 1937 Baptist Church and a vintage schoolhouse.

North from Tallahassee

The Georgia border is only twenty miles north of Tallahassee but the journey to it is a dour one. Twelve miles along Hwy-27, tiny **HAVANA** tries to lure drivers with several blocks of Olde Worlde antique shops and art galleries; further east, **Bradley's Country Store**, on Route 151, has been peddling Southern-style food for seventy years – country-milled grits, hogshead cheese and liver pudding among the delicacies on offer.

A more time-filling destination is just across the state line on Hwy-319, five miles south of Thomasville, where the **Pebble Hill Plantation** (Tues–Sat 10am–5pm, Sun 1–5pm, $2; hour-long guided tour of house, $5) remains from the times of cotton picking and slavery, and shows how comfortable things were for the wealthy whites who ran the show. Much of the original Pebble Hill burnt down in the Thirties, and what you see is a fairly faithful rebuilding of the sumptuous main house.

Eating

One of the few places to get **breakfast** in downtown Tallahassee is *Goodies*, 116 E College Avenue (☎681-3888), which also serves **lunch**, as does the stylish *Andrew's Adams Street Café*, 228 S Adams Street (☎222-3446). A couple of Chinese restaurants offer lunch and **dinner** buffets for $5–6: *Ouy Lin*, 220 W Tennessee Street (☎222-0896), and *China Garden*, 435 W Tennessee Street (☎561-8849). More appetizingly, and expensively, take an evening meal at the classy *Andrew's Second Act*, 102 W Jefferson Street (☎222-3446).

Out of downtown Tallahassee, *Mom and Dad's*, 4175 Apalachee Parkway (closed Mon; ☎877-4518), has delicious and affordable home-made Italian food; the *Wharf Seafood Restaurant*, 4141 Apalachee Parkway (☎656-2332), carries a great range of what its name suggests; there's more low-cost seafood – with a riotous atmosphere and live Fifties music – at *Barnacle Bill's*, 1830 N Monroe Street (☎385-8734); *The Mill*, 2329 Apalachee Parkway (☎656-2867) and 2136 N Monroe Street (☎386-2867), has burgers, sandwiches and exquisite pizzas to accompany its home-brewed beers.

Nightlife

Bolstered by its students, Tallahassee has a strong nightlife, with a leaning to social drinking and live rock music (see below). There's also **comedy** at the *Comedy Zone*, *Ramada Inn North*, 2900 N Monroe Street (☎386-5653), and *Coconuts*, at the *Econo Lodge*, 1355 Apalachee Parkway (☎942-NUTS); and a fair amount of **drama**, headed by the student productions at the *University Theater*, on the FSU campus (☎644-6500), and the *Tallahassee Little Theater*, 1861 Thomasville Road (☎224-8474). Find out **what's on** from the *Entertainments* section of the Friday *Tallahassee Democrat* newspaper, or, for live music details, listen to radio station *WUFS* on 89.7 FM.

Bars

On nights leading up to Seminole football matches, *The Phyrst*, 1415 Tymberlane Road (☎893-1088), is packed with clean-cut collegiate sports fans. Other strongly collegiate hang-outs are *Dudley's Pub*, 654 W Tennessee Street (☎599-6358), and *Poor Paul's Pourhouse*, 618 W Tennessee Street (☎222-2978).

Less student-dominated, *Calico Jack's*, 2745 Capitol Circle (☎385-6653), offers beer, oysters and stomping southern rock'n'roll records; *Halligan's*, 1700 Halstead Boulevard (☎668-7665), gets busy for its pool tables and chilled mugs of beer; and *Clyde's & Costello's*, 210 S Adams Street (☎224-2173), pulls a smart and very cliquey crowd, except on Thursdays when the four-for-one drinks strip away inhibitions.

Live Music and Clubs

Big name **live bands** appear at *The Moon*, 1020 E Lafayette Street (☎222-6666 for recorded info), or at the vast *Leon County Civic Center*, at the corner of Pensacola Street and Martin Luther King Jnr Boulevard (☎222-0400). More intimate, *The Warehouse*, 706 W Gaines Street (☎222-6188), mixes rockabilly, avant-garde music and performance art; *Andrew's Upstairs*, 228 S Adams Street (☎222-3466), hosts modern jazz combos; and there's rock and blues at the log-cabin-like *Bullwinkle's*, 620 W Tennessee Street (☎224-0651). The *Cow Haus*, 836 Lake Bradford Road (☎574-COWS), showcases known and unknown indie acts, while the best local indie groups are likely to be found at the *Milk Bar*, 826 W Gaines Street (☎561-3866)

Finally, *Club Park Avenue*, 115 E Park Avenue (☎599-9143), is the pick of the local **nightclubs**, with different themes on different nights – always good for a drink, dance or laugh.

Listings

Art galleries Tallahassee has a credible arts scene: around Railroad Square, close to the junction of Springhill Road and Gaines Street, near the FSU campus, are some innovative galleries, and several local artists have open studios there. Other contemporary art show-cases are *The Window on Gaines Street*, 1517 W Gaines St, and the *La Moyne Gallery*, 125 N Gadsden St.

Canopy roads The name applied to thoroughfares where oak-tree branches form an arch across the road, and you drive beneath a drooping fringe of Spanish moss. Miccossukee, Centerville, Old St Augustine, Meridian and Old Bainbridge roads are good examples.

Car rental Most companies have branches at the airport (see above), and at the following locations: *Alamo*, 1720 Capitol Circle (☎576-6134); *Avis*, 3300 Capitol Circle (☎331-1212); *Budget*, 1415 Capitol Circle (☎1-800/527-0700); *Lucky's*, 2539 W Tennessee St (☎575-0632); *Ugly Duckling*, 3120 W Tennessee St (☎575-0400).

Dentist Dental Information Service: ☎1-800/282-9117.

Hospital Non-emergencies: Capitol Medical Center ☎877-9018.

Pharmacy *Sullivan's Drugs*, 1330 Miccousukee Rd, is open until 10pm; later call ☎681-8657.

Sports Tickets for FSU baseball (March–May) and football (Sept–Nov) matches are on sale at the stadiums two hours before the games begin: ☎644-1073 and ☎644-1830 respectively. For info on FAMU sports teams, all known as the *Rattlers*, call ☎599-3200. There's a full fixture list in the local telephone book.

Western Union 460 W Tennessee St (☎224-4096); 1717 Apalachee Parkway (☎878-7990); 3111 Mahan Drive (☎877-0783).

South From Tallahassee

At weekends, many Tallahassee residents head south to the Panhandle's beaches (fully described under "The Coastal Panhandle"). If you're not eager to join them, make a slower trek south along **routes 363 or 61**, tracking down a few isolated pockets of historical or geological significance – or take **Hwy-319** and lose yourself in the biggest and best of Florida's forests.

One of the most enjoyable ways to explore is by **cycling** the 16-mile Tallahassee–St Marks Historic Railroad Trail, a flat and straight course through placid woodlands following the route of a long-abandoned railroad. Bikes can be rented from *Cyclelogical Bicycle Rentals*, 4780 Woodville Highway (☎656-0001).

The Natural Bridge Battlefield Site and St Marks

Ten miles southeast of Tallahassee, turning off Route 363 at Woodville leads to the **Natural Bridge Battlefield Site** (daily 8am–sunset; free) where, on March 4, 1865, a motley band of Confederates saw off a much larger group of Union soldiers, preventing Tallahassee falling into Yankee hands. Not that it made much difference – the war ended a couple of months later – but the victory is celebrated by a monument and an annual re-enactment on or close to the anniversary: several hours of shouting, loud bangs and smoke.

Twelve miles south of Woodville, Route 363 expires at the hamlet of **ST MARKS**, where the **San Marcos de Apalache Historic Site** (Thurs–Mon 9am–5pm, free; museum $1) offers decent pickings for students of Florida history – this sixteenth-century Spanish-built fort was visited by early explorers such as Pánfilo de Narváez and Hernando de Soto, and two hundred years later became Andrew Jackson's headquarters when he waged war on the Seminole Indians. Round off a visit at one of the nearby fishcamp eating places, such as *Posey's* (no phone), on Old Fort Drive.

Should wildlife appeal more than history – or eating – backtrack slightly along Route 363 and turn east along Hwy-98: at Newport you'll locate the main entrance to **St Marks National Wildlife Refuge** (daily sunrise–sunset; cars $3, pedestrians and cyclists $1), spreading over the boggy outflow of the St Marks River. Bald eagles and a few black bears are resident in the refuge, though you're more likely to spot otters, white-tailed deer, raccoons and a wealth of bird life from the various roadside look-out points and observation towers. Just inside the entrance, a **visitor center** doles out useful information (Mon–Sat 8am–4.30pm, Sun 10am–5pm).

Route 61: Wakulla Springs

Fifteen miles south of Tallahassee on Route 61, **Wakulla Springs State Park** (daily 9am–5.30pm; cars $3.25, pedestrians and cyclists $1), holds what is believed to be one of the biggest and deepest natural springs in the world, pumping up half a million gallons of crystal-clear pure water from the bowels of the earth every day – something that would be difficult to guess from the calm surface.

It's refreshing to **swim** in the cool liquid (do so only in the marked area), but to learn more about the spring, take the fifteen-minute narrated **glass-bottomed boat tour** ($4.50), and peer down to the swarms of fish hovering around the 180-foot-deep cavern through which the water comes. With the urge for more boat travel, join the half-hour **river cruise** ($4.50), bringing glimpses of some of the park's legged inhabitants: deer, turkeys, herons and egrets – and the inevitable alligators – among them. If *déjà vu* strikes, it may be because a number of movies have been shot here, including several of the early Tarzan flics and parts of *The Creature from the Black Lagoon*.

Don't leave without strolling through the **Wakulla Lodge**, a hotel built beside the spring in 1937 which retains many of its original features: Moorish archways, stone fireplaces and fabulous hand-painted Toltec and Aztec designs on the lobby's wooden ceiling. Pay respects, also, to the stuffed carcass of "Old Joe", one of the oldest and largest alligators ever known, who died in the Fifties measuring eleven feet long and was claimed to be 200 years old; he's in a glass case by the reception desk.

Spending a night at the lodge is comparatively cheap (☎224-5950; ③). It and its surrounds have an addictively relaxing air – and once the day-trippers depart you'll have the springs and wildlife all to yourself.

Further South: the Apalachicola National Forest

With swamps, savannahs and springs dotted liberally about its half-million acres, the **APALACHICOLA NATIONAL FOREST** is the inland Panhandle at its natural best. Several roads enable you to drive through a good-sized chunk, and many undemanding spots offer a rest and a snack, but to see more of the forest than its picnic tables and litter bins you'll have to make an effort: leaving the periphery and delving into the pristine interior, exploring unhurriedly and at length, following one of the hiking trails, taking a canoe on one of the rivers, or simply spending a night under the stars at one of the basic campgrounds.

Practicalities

The northeast corner of the forest almost touches Tallahassee's airport, fanning out from there to the edge of the Apalachicola River, about 35 miles west. Most of the northern edge is bordered by Hwy-20, the eastern side by Hwy-319, and to the south lies the gruesome no-man's-land of Tate's Hell Swamp (see below).

The main **entrances** are off Hwy-20 and Hwy-319, and three minor roads, Routes 267, 375 and 65, form cross-forest links between the two highways. **Accommodation** is limited to camping. With the exception of Silver Lake (see below), all the sites are free with basic facilities – usually just toilets and drinking water. The only place to **rent a canoe** near the forest is *TNT Hideaway* (☎925-6412), on Route 2 near Crawfordville, on Hwy-319.

One section of the forest, Trout Pond (open April–Oct only) on Route 373, is intended for **disabled visitors** and their guests, with a wheelchair-accessible lakeside nature trail and picnic area.

INFORMATION ON THE APALACHICOLA NATIONAL FOREST

Always get maps, a weather forecast and advice from a Rangers' Office before setting off on a hike or canoe trip through the forest (for more on how to travel in the backcountry safely, see *Basics*). The Ochlockonee River divides the forest into two administrative districts and the following offices are responsible for the west and east sides of the forest respectively:

Apalachicola Ranger District, Hwy-20, near Bristol; ☎643-2282.
Wakulla Ranger District, Route 6, near Crawfordville; ☎926-3561.

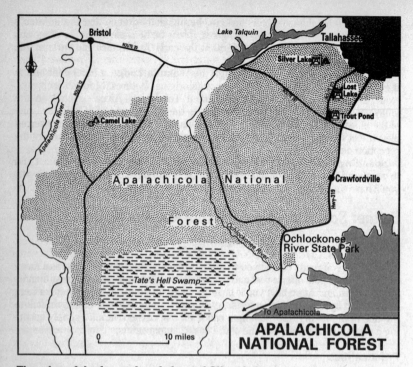

APALACHICOLA NATIONAL FOREST

The edge of the forest: Lost Lake and Silver Lake

For the merest taste of what the forest can offer, make for **LOST LAKE**, seven miles from Tallahassee along Route 373, where there's little except a few picnic tables beside a small lake. The area's well suited to a nibble and a waterside laze, and is less busy than the campervan-infested **SILVER LAKE**, nine miles east of the city, off Hwy-20. If you want swim or camp at Silver Lake, you'll have to pay ($1 and $4 respectively); anticipate the company of too many other people.

Deeper into the forest: hiking and canoeing

Several short, clearly marked **nature walks** lie within the forest but the major **hiking trail**, strictly for ardent and well-equipped backpackers, is the thirty-mile **Apalachicola trail**, which begins close to Crawfordville, on Hwy-319. This passes through the heart of the forest and includes a memorable (and sometimes difficult, depending on the weather conditions and water level) leg across the Bradwell Bay Wilderness, an isolated swamp. After this, the campground at Porter Lake, just to the west of the wilderness area, with its toilets and drinking water, seems the epitome of civilization.

The trail leads on to **CAMEL LAKE**, with its campground with drinking water and toilets, and the less demanding nine-and-a-half-mile **Camel Lake Loop trail**. By vehicle, you can get directly to Camel Lake by turning off Hwy-20 at Bristol and continuing south for twelve miles, watching for the signposted turn-off on the left.

Although there are numerous put-in points along its four rivers, **canoeists** can paddle right into the forest from the western end of Lake Talquin (close to Hwy-

20), and continue for a sixty-mile glide along the Ochlockonee River – the forest's major waterway – to the Ochlockonee River State Park, close to Hwy-319. Obviously, the length of trip means that to do it all you'll have to use the riverside **campgrounds**. Those with drinking water are at Porter Lake, Whitehead Lake and Mack Landing; be warned that these are often concealed by dense foliage, so study your map carefully.

South of the forest: Tate's Hell Swamp

Driving through the forest on Route 65, or around it on Hwy-319 (which merges with Hwy-98 as it nears the coast), you'll eventually pass the large and forbidding area believably called **Tate's Hell Swamp**. According to legend, Tate was a farmer who pursued a panther into the swamp and was never seen again. It's a breeding ground for the deadly water moccasin snake, and gung-ho locals sometimes venture into the swamp hoping to catch a few snakes to sell to the less reputable zoos; you're well advised to stay clear.

West from Tallahassee

To discover the social character of the inland Panhandle, take Hwy-90 **west from Tallahassee** all the way to Pensacola: 180 miles of frequently tedious rural landscapes and time-locked farming towns that haven't had much luck, or expansion, since the demise of the timber industry fifty years ago. When it gets too much to bear, you can easily switch to the speedier I-10, or cut south to the coast. But the compensations are the endless supply of rustic eating places, low-cost accommodation, several high-quality natural areas – and a chance to see a part of Florida that the travel brochures rarely reveal.

CROSSING THE TIME ZONE

Crossing the Apalachicola River, which flows north–south across the Inland Panhandle, roughly 45 miles west of Tallahassee, takes you into the **Central Time Zone**, an hour behind Eastern Time, and the rest of Florida. In the Coastal Panhandle, the time shift occurs about ten miles west of Port St Joe, on the boundary between Gulf and Bay counties.

Lake Seminole and the Three Rivers Recreational Area

Fifty miles out of Tallahassee, within spitting distance of the Georgia border, Hwy-90 reaches Sneads, a small town dominated by the large **Lake Seminole**, created by a Fifties hydroelectric project. On the lake's Florida side (other banks are in Georgia and Alabama), spend an enjoyable few hours in the **Three Rivers Recreational Area** (daily 8am–sunset; cars $3.25, pedestrians and cyclists $1), two miles from Sneads on Route 271. A mile-long **nature walk** from the park's **camping area** (☎482-9006) leads to a wooded, hilly section where squirrels and alligators are two-a-penny, and white-tailed deer and grey foxes lurk in the shrubbery. Primarily, though, the lake is popular for its massive catfish, bream and bass – none of which, it seems from the size of the average day's catch, can wait for the frying pan. To spend a night by the lake without camping, use the ten-room *Seminole Lodge* (☎593-6886; ②–③), at the end of Legion Road, just outside Sneads.

Marianna and the Florida Caverns State Park

Twenty-five miles further along Hwy-90, **MARIANNA** is one of the larger inland Panhandle settlements, despite having a four-figure population and only knowing excitement when the twice-monthly horse sale comes to town. There isn't much to commend the place, although the **Chamber of Commerce**, 2928 Jefferson Street (Mon–Fri 9am–4.30pm; ☎482-8061), will give you a walking-tour map of the town's elegant Old South homes (the Chamber of Commerce itself sits inside one), and there's a more-than-filling lunch buffet of Chinese and Vietnamese specialties at *Kim's*, 4157 Lafayette Street (☎482-2257). Inexpensive **lodgings** can be found at *Motel Sandusky*, 918 W Lafayette Street (☎1-800/238-2552; ②).

The best thing about Marianna is its proximity to **Florida Caverns State Park** (daily 8am–sunset; cars $3.25, pedestrians and cyclists $1), three miles north on Route 167, where hourly **guided tours** (9am–5pm; $4) venture through 65-foot-deep caverns filled by strangely shaped calcite formations. The caves are not new discoveries, they were mentioned in Spanish accounts of the area and used by Seminole Indians to hide from Andrew Jackson's army in the early 1800s – an unnerving experience in the days before electric lights illuminated the booming rock chambers. Back in the sun, the park has a few other features to fill a day comfortably. From the **visitor center** (☎482-9598) by the caverns' entrance, a **nature trail** leads around the floodplain of the Chipola River, curiously dipping underground for several hundred feet as it flows through the park. At the **Blue Hole Spring**, at the end of the park road, you can swim, snorkel or scuba-dive – and sleep at the **campground**.

Chipley and Falling Waters State Recreation Area

Continuing west, the next community of any size, **CHIPLEY**, 26 miles from Marianna, takes its name from William D Chipley, who put a railroad across the Panhandle in the mid-1800s to improve the timber trade, and gave rise to little sawmill towns such as Chipley. The railroad is still here (restricted locally to freight) but the boom times are long gone, and it's a smart idea to leave the town along Route 77 for **Falling Waters State Recreation Area** (daily 8am–sunset; cars $3.25, pedestrians and cyclists $1), three miles south, to inspect Florida's only waterfall. The so-called fall is in fact a 100-foot drop into a tube-like sinkhole topped by a viewing platform. A trail passes several other (waterfall-less) sinks, and another leads to a decaying oil well – remaining from an unsuccessful attempt to strike black gold in 1919. The park has a **campground** (☎638-6130), but for accommodation under a roof use *Wilburn's Motel*, 700 Hwy-90 (☎638-1850; ②), back in Chipley.

De Funiak Springs

The railroad that carried timber also brought the Panhandle's first tourists a century ago, many of them drawn to a large, naturally circular lake in **DE FUNIAK SPRINGS** (on Hwy-90, forty miles from Chipley) around which the Chautauqua Alliance – a benevolent religious society espousing free culture and education for all – had set up a winter base. With the death of its founders and the coming of the Depression, the alliance faded away, but the four-thousand-seat auditorium – which it built to stage the great speakers of the day – still stands beside the lake, one of several turn-of-the-century wooden structures whose Doric columns and raised balconies seem entirely at odds with the dozy character of the modern town. In all the grandeur, it's the smallest building that's most worth seeking out: at 100 Circle Drive, the **Walton-De Funiak Library** (Mon 9am–7pm, Tues, Wed & Fri 9am–6pm, Sat 9am–3pm; free) has been lending books since 1886, and more recently acquired the Panhandle's most unexpected sight – a small stash of medieval European weaponry, donated by a local collector.

Another unlikely find is the **Chautauqua Vineyards**, on Hwy-331 near the junction with I-10, whose diverse wines may not be the world's finest but have picked a few awards in their three years of existence and await your considered assessment (free tours and tastings, Mon–Sat 9am–5pm, Sun noon–5pm).

Stopping over in De Funiak Springs is a sound move if you're aiming for the more expensive coastal strip 25 miles south along Hwy-331. The *Econo Lodge*, 1325 S Freeport Road (☎892-6615; ②), has good rates but is closer to I-10 than the town; to stay in step with the historical mood, opt instead for **bed and breakfast** at the *Sunbright Manor*, 606 Live Oak Avenue (☎892-0656; ③). While in town, **eat lunch** amid the antiques at the *Busy Bee Café*, 2 N Seventh Street (☎892-6700).

The Blackwater River State Forest

Between the sluggish towns of Crestview and Milton, thirty miles west of De Funiak Springs, the creeks and slow-flowing rivers of **BLACKWATER RIVER STATE FOREST** are jammed each weekend with waterborne families enjoying what's officially dubbed "the canoe capital of Florida". In spite of the crowds, the forest is by no means overcommercialized, being big enough to absorb the influx and still offer peace, isolation and unruffled nature for anyone intrepid enough to hike through it. Alternatively, if you're not game for canoeing or hiking but just want a few hours' break, the **Blackwater River State Park** (daily 8am–sunset; cars $3.25, pedestrians and cyclists $1), within the forest four miles north of Harold off Hwy-90, has some very walkable trails.

From Milton, Hwy-90 and I-10 both offer a mildly scenic fifteen-mile drive over Escambia Bay to the hotels and freeways on the northern fringes of Pensacola, the city marking Florida's western extremity – see "Pensacola and around".

Accommodation in the forest

With the exception of the **cabins** at Tomahawk Landing (see below), which cost $29 to $69 depending on the comfort level, forest accommodation is limited to **camping**. There are fully equipped sites at the Krul Recreation Area (☎957-4201), near the junction of Forest Road 4 and Route 19, and at the Blackwater River State Park (see above; ☎623-2363). Free basic sites intended for hikers lie along the main trails.

Canoeing

Canoeing in the forest centers on *Adventures Unlimited* (☎623-6197 or 626-1669) at **Tomahawk Landing** on Coldwater Creek, twelve miles north of Milton on Hwy-87, where you can rent tubes, canoes and kayaks (around $6, $11 and $16 respectively per day). Two- and three-day trips, with overnight gear and food provided, can also be arranged for around $25 per person.

Hiking

Hardened **hikers** carrying overnight gear can tackle the 21-mile **Jackson trail**, named after Andrew Jackson who led his invading army this way in 1818, seeking to wrest Florida from Spanish control. On the way, two very basic shelters have handpumps for water. The trail runs between Karick Lake, off Hwy-189, fourteen miles north of Hwy-90, and the Krul Recreation Area. The shorter **Sweetwater trail** is a good substitute if your feet aren't up to the longer hike: an enjoyable four-and-a-half-mile walk, it leaves the Krul Recreation Area and crosses a swing-bridge and the Bear Lake dam before joining the Jackson trail.

THE COASTAL PANHANDLE

Lacking the glamor and international renown of Florida's other beach strips, the **coastal Panhandle** is nonetheless no secret to residents of the Southern states, who descend upon the region in their tens of thousands throughout the summer. Consequently, a few sections of the region's 180-mile-long coastline are nightmarishly overdeveloped: **Panama City Beach** revels in its "redneck riviera" nickname, and smaller **Destin** and **Fort Walton Beach** are only marginally more refined. By contrast, little **Apalachicola**, and the **South Walton beaches**, both easily reached (by car – they're inaccessible by bus) but out of the main tourist corridor, have much to recommend them: beautiful unspoilt sands, and off-shore islands where people are a rarer sight than wildlife.

Apalachicola and Around

A few miles south of the Apalachicola National Forest (see "The Inland Panhandle"), and the first substantial part of the coast you'll hit on Hwy-98 from central Florida, the **Apalachicola area** contains much of value. Mainland beaches may be few, but sand-seekers are compensated by the brilliant strands of three barrier islands, and the small fishing communities you'll pass through are untainted by the aggressive tourism that scars the coast fifty miles west.

Apalachicola

Now a tiny port with an income largely derived from harvesting oysters (nine out of every ten eaten in Florida are farmed here), **APALACHICOLA** once rode high on the cotton industry, which kept its dock busy and its populace affluent during the early 1800s. A number of stately columned buildings attest to former wealth; one, at 128 Market Street, is occupied by the **Chamber of Commerce** (Mon–Fri 9am–5pm; ☎653-9419), where you can pick up a map to find the others along an enjoyable half-hour's stroll.

To reach Apalachicola, Hwy-98 crosses the four-mile Gorrie Memorial Bridge, commemorating a man held in high regard by present-day Floridians. Arriving in the town in 1833, physician **John Gorrie** was seeking a way to keep malaria patients cool when he devised a machine to make ice (previously transported in large blocks from the north). Gorrie died broke before the idea took off, becoming the basis of the modern refrigerator and air-conditioning machine. The **Gorrie Museum** on Sixth Street (Thurs–Mon 9am–noon & 1–5pm; $1) remem-

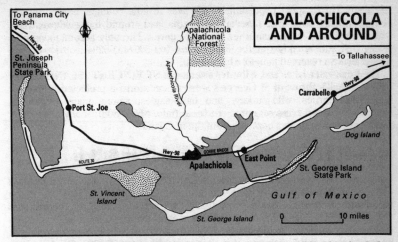

bers the man and his work, as well as the general history of Alpachicola. Only a replica of the cumbersome ice-making device stands here – the original is in the Smithsonian Institute in Washington DC.

Accommodation and eating

There isn't a lot to Apalachicola but the town makes a good base for visiting the barrier islands (see below). The crusty *Rainbow Inn*, 123 Water Street (☎653-8139; ②), has the least expensive rooms, and two inns – the *Pink Camellia*, 145 Avenue E (☎653-2107; ③), and the *Gibson Inn*, 57 Market Street (☎653-2191; ③–④) – offer **bed and breakfast**. The somewhat pricey restaurant in the latter is a good place to **eat**, as is the *Boss Oyster Bar*, 125 Water Street (☎653-8139), where you can tuck into fresh Apalachicola oysters.

The Barrier Islands: St George, Dog and St Vincent

A few miles off the coast, framing the Apalachicola Bay and the broad, marshy outflow of the Apalachicola River, the three Apalachicola **barrier islands** are well endowed with beaches and creatures – including thousands of birds who use them as rest stops during migration – and two of them hold what must qualify as the most isolated communities in Florida. Visit one if you have the chance: only the biggest, St George, is accessible by road.

Nine miles of powdery white sands and unobstructed ocean views are not the only reason to come to **ST GEORGE ISLAND**. Within a few strides, shady live oak hammocks and an abundance of osprey-inhabited pine trees add color to a day's lazy sunning. A few restaurants, beach shops and the eight-room B&B *St George Inn* (☎670-2903; ③–④) occupy the island's western section; the eastern sector is taken up by the raccoon-infested **St George Island State Park** (daily 8am–sunset; cars $3.25, pedestrians and cyclists $1), where a three-mile **hiking trail** leads to a very basic **campground** (there's a better-equipped site at the start of the hike). Get to the island along Route 1A, off Hwy-98 at Eastpoint.

A couple of miles east of St George, **DOG ISLAND**, only reachable by boat (signs advertising crossings are all over the marina in Carrabelle, on Hwy-98), has a small permanent population which lives in little cottages nestled among Florida's tallest sand dunes. Several footpaths lead around the windswept isle, which won't take more than a few hours to cover. The only accommodation is pricey bed and breakfast at the *Pelican Inn* (☎1-800/451-5294); obviously you should make a reservation before turning up.

The freshwater lakes and saltwater swamps of **ST VINCENT ISLAND**, almost within a shell's throw of St George's western end, form a protected refuge for loggerhead turtles, wild turkeys and bald eagles, among many others. In November **guided trips** set out to see them (info: ☎653-8808); at any other time, you'll have to negotiate a boat ride from the mainland.

St Joseph Peninsula State Park and Port St Joe

For a final taste of virgin Florida coast before hitting heavily commercial Panama City Beach, take Route 30 – eighteen miles from Apalachicola, off Hwy-98 – to the **St Joseph Peninsula State Park** (daily 8am–sunset; cars $3.25, pedestrians and cyclists $1). A long finger of sand with a short **nature trail** at one end and a spectacular nine-mile **hiking route** at the other, the park has rough **camping** at its northern tip and better-equipped sites and **cabins** (☎227-1327; ④) about half-way along near Eagle Harbor.

The peninsula wraps a protective arm around **PORT ST JOE** on the main-land, another dot-on-the-map fishing port that has seen better days. One such came in 1838 when a constitution calling for statehood (which Florida didn't acquire until seven years later) and liberal reforms was drawn up here*, only to be deemed too radical by the legislators of the time. At the **Constitution Convention State Museum** (Mon–Sat 9am–noon & 1–5pm; $1), signposted from Hwy-98 as you enter the town, daft, battery-powered waxworks re-enact the deed, alongside more credible mementoes of the town's colorful past, which go to show how it earned the title "wickedest city in the Southeast" during its early years.

Panama City Beach

An orgy of motels, go-kart tracks, mini-golf courses and amusement parks, **PANAMA CITY BEACH** is entirely without pretensions, capitalizing as blatantly as possible on the appeal of its 27-mile beach. The whole place is as commercial as hell, but with the shops, bars and restaurants all trying to undercut one another, there are some great bargains to be found – from air-brushed T-shirts and cut-price sunglasses to cheap buffet food. With everybody out to have a good time, there's some damn fine cruising to be done, too; not least during the Spring Break months of March and April when thousands of students from the Deep South states arrive to drink and dance themselves into oblivion. As vulgar and crass as it often is, Panama City Beach cries out to be seen. Come here once, if only as a voyeuristic day trip – you might well be adequately smitten by its tacky charm to stay longer.

---

*Strictly speaking, the constitution was drawn up in the town of St Joseph (later devastated by yellow fever, two hurricanes and a fire), whose site Port St Joe now occupies.

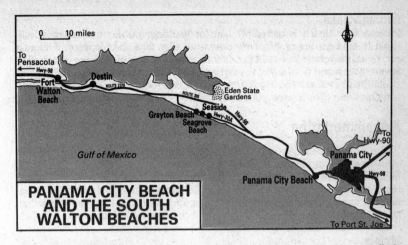

0 ___ 10 miles

To Pensacola ← Hwy-98

Fort Walton Beach

Destin
ROUTE 77B

ROUTE 395

Eden State Gardens

Seaside

Grayton Beach
Seagrove Beach
Hwy-304

Hwy-98

To Hwy-90

Gulf of Mexico

Panama City

Panama City Beach

Hwy-98

**PANAMA CITY BEACH
AND THE SOUTH
WALTON BEACHES**

To Port St. Joe

Seasons greatly affect the mood. Throughout the lively **summer** (the so-called "100 Magic Days"), accommodation costs are high and advance bookings essential. In **winter**, prices drop and visitors are fewer; most are Canadians and – increasingly – northern Europeans, who have no problems sunbathing and swimming in the cool (typically around 65°F) temperatures.

What Panama City Beach doesn't have is any **history** worth mentioning. It began as an offshoot of **Panama City**, a dull place of docks and paper mills eight miles away over the Hathway Bridge (which Hwy-98 crosses), which grew with the timber industry and was named as a result of being on the same latitude as the Panama Canal. Today there's little love lost between the two communities; they have nothing in common besides a name.

Arrival, Information and Getting Around

Panama City Beach being essentially a very long beach, **getting your bearings** could hardly be simpler, even if the lack of landmarks, except for two similar piers (City Pier to the west, County Pier to the east), can cause confusion. **Front Beach Road** (part of Hwy-98A, which starts at the foot of the Hathway Bridge) is the main track, a two-lane highway, often called "the Strip", that's very much the place to cruise at crawling pace on weekends. The speedier, four-lane **Middle Beach Road** loops off Front Beach Road for a few blocks around County Pier from the junction with **Thomas Drive** (which links the eastern extremity of the beach). If you don't want to see gaudy Panama City Beach at all, **Back Beach Road** (Hwy-98) will take you straight through its anonymous residential backside.

Greyhound **buses** pick up and drop off at the Exxon station, 17325 W Hwy 98, leaving a fifteen-minute walk to the nearest motels. Travelling by bus, however, you may well end up in Panama City (917 Harrison Avenue; ☎785-7861), rather than Panama City Beach, and you'll need to use one of the four daily *Greyhound* services linking them.

For free newssheets, magazines and discount coupons, drop into the **Visitors and Convention Bureau**, 12015 Front Beach Road (Mon–Fri 8am–5pm; ☎1-800/ PCBEACH).

Getting around

Panama City Beach is incredibly bad for **walking**; **public transport** is non-existent and **taxis** are prohibitively expensive, even for a short journey. Without a car, rent a **bicycle** (around $12 per day) or a **scooter** (around $25 per day; driving licence necessary) from any of the myriad beach shops: *Beach Things*, 13226 Front Beach Road (☎234-0520), *Uncle Harvey's*, 17280 Front Beach Road (☎235-9963), and *California Cycle Rentals*, 8906 Thomas Drive (☎230-8080), among them.

Accommodation

Visitors to Panama City Beach outnumber residents and **places to stay** are everywhere – but fill with amazing speed, especially on weekends. **Prices** are higher than you'll pay elsewhere in the Panhandle – $50–60 for a basic motel room in summer – so if you're counting the bucks, stay inland and drive to the beach. Camping is the only way to cut costs; sites are rarely more expensive than their equivalents elsewhere, although only a couple are good for tents.

Motels

As a very general rule, **motels** at the eastern end of the beach are smarter and slightly pricier than those in the center, and those at the western end are quiet and family-oriented. That said, you're unlikely to find much to complain about at the first place that takes your fancy – or use one of the following.

To the **east**: *Bay Villa*, 4501 W Hwy-98 (☎785-8791; ③); *Lagoon*, 5915 N Lagoon Drive (☎235-1800; ③); or *Pana Roc*, 5507 Thomas Drive (☎234-2775; ③).

In the **center** on Front Beach Road: *Barney Gray* (no 10901; ☎234-2565; ③), *Beachside* (no 10710; ☎234-3997; ③), *Driftwood Lodge* (no 15811; ☎234-6601; ③), or *Siesta* (no 9113; ☎234-2510).

To the **west** on Front Beach Road: *Blue Dolphin* (no 19919; ☎1-800/541-2583; ③–④), *Desert Palms* (no 17729; ☎234-2140; ③),s *Impala* (no 17751; ☎234-6462; ③); or *Sea Witch* (no 21905; ☎234-5722; ③–④).

Campgrounds

Several large and busy **campgrounds** cater mainly to campervans: the most central are *Miracle Strip RV Resort*, 10510 W Hwy 98 (☎234-3833), and *Raccoon River*, 12405 Middle Beach Road (☎234-0181). Quieter, and better for **tents**, are *Magnolia Beach*, 7800 Magnolia Road (☎235-1581), and the *St Andrews State Recreation Area*, 4415 Thomas Drive (☎234-5140).

Around the beach

Getting a tan, running yourself ragged at beach sports and going hammer-and-tongs at the nightlife are the main concerns in Panama City Beach – you'll be regarded as a very raw prawn indeed if you go around demanding history, art and culture.

If you remain dissatisfied, try go-karting (around $5 for ten laps), visiting one of the amusement parks (usually $12 for a go-on-everything day ticket), going on a fishing trip (take your pick of the party boats on the Thomas Drive marina, around $25 a day) or scuba-diving (several explorable shipwrecks litter the area; details from any of the numerous dive shops). Otherwise, the following provide the only variation.

Gallery of Crime and Punishment

8500 Thomas Drive. Daily 9am–6pm; $2.50.

With an electric chair, a guillotine, mugshots of mass murderers and much more purporting to document America's unending struggle against crime, this gory collection can only be described as sensationalist.

Gulf World Marine Park

15412 Front Beach Road. Daily 9am–7pm; $10.95.

A cramped marine park, which offers performing sea lions and dolphins, sharks being fed and stingrays ripe for petting. Mildly more unusual is the "parrot show", featuring a roller-skating parrot and a high-wire-walking parakeet.

Museum of Man in the Sea

17314 W Hwy-98. Daily 9am–5pm; $5.

All you ever needed to know about diving: enormous eighteenth-century under-water helmets, bulky airpumps and matching bodysuits, deep-sea cutting devices, torpedo-like propulsion vehicles, among a large collection. A separate display documents *Sealab*, the US Navy's underwater research vessel, the first of which was fitted out in Panama City and now stands outside the museum. This enter-taining stop makes an ideal prelude to a day's snorkelling.

St Andrews State Recreation Area

4405 Thomas Drive. Daily 8am–sunset; cars $3.25, pedestrians and cyclists $1.

Get here early and you'll spot a variety of hopping, crawling and slithering wildlife by following one of the nature trails around the pine forest and salt marshes within the park. By noon the hordes have arrived to swim, fish and prepare picnics. If you're with kids, they'll enjoy splashing in the shallow lagoon sheltered by an artificial reef known as The Jetties.

Shell Island

Half an hour by ferry from the Capt. Anderson Marina, foot of Thomas Drive. Boat departures at 9am, 1pm & 3.45pm; round trip $8.

This seven-mile strip of sand is a haven for shell collectors and sun worshippers alike. With little shade on the undeveloped island, dark glasses are essential; the glare off the sands can be blinding. Most trips include a break for feeding the dolphins (not an ecologically sound practice) that frequently bask in the area.

Zoo World

9008 Front Beach Road. Daily 9am–dusk; $8.95.

A small but enjoyable – assuming you're not opposed to seeing animals subjected to any kind of incarceration – gathering of lions, tigers, orang-utangs and other creatures. Many of the inmates prefer to sleep through the midday heat, so try to time your visit for early morning or late afternoon.

Eating

With an emphasis on basic wholesome cooking, and lots of it, the cheapest places to **eat** are the **buffet** restaurants, charging $4–10 for all you can manage. Try *Bishop's Family Buffet*, 12628 Front Beach Road (☎234-6457), for substantial meals three times daily; the *Golden Anchor*, 11800 Front Beach Road (☎234-1481), for sizeable seafood lunches and dinners; or *Seven Seas*, at 8317 & 15928 Front Beach Road (☎234-7173 and 235-1918), offering an especially good-value $4 breakfast.

Wherever you can get a buffet it's also possible to order from the menu, but if that's your intention you're better off having **lunch or dinner** at one of the places below.

Hamilton's, 5711 N Lagoon Drive (☎234-1255). Serves blackened alligator nuggets among the more regular dishes.

Hickory Key Smoked BBQ, 4106 Thomas Ave (☎234-2717). Known for its barbecued meats, but also putting together a formidable seafood platter.

Mikato, 7724 Front Beach Rd (☎234-1388). Japanese food prepared by knife-throwing chefs.

Mike's Diner, 17554 Front Beach Rd (☎234-1942). Honest-to-goodness coffee shop that opens early, closes late and is great value throughout the day.

Shuckum's Oyster Pub & Seafood Grill, 15618 W Hwy-98 (☎234-3214). Cheap oysters in many styles, including fried in a sandwich.

Sweet Basil's, 11208 Front Beach Rd (☎234-2855). Classy Italian food combined with the freshest seafood.

The Treasure Ship, 3605 Thomas Drive (☎234-8881). A seafood restaurant built to resemble a wooden sailing ship, with pirates hopping around the tables.

Nightlife

Even if you only stay a few minutes, you should visit one of the two beachside **nightlife** fleshpots: *Club La Vela*, 8813 Thomas Drive (☎234-3866), or *Spinnaker*, 8795 Thomas Drive (☎234-7822). Each has dozens of bars, several discos, live bands and a predominantly under-25 clientele looking eagerly forward to the weekend bikini and wet T-shirt contests, and to the thrice-weekly "hunk shows". Both clubs are open from 10am to 4am, have free entry and, because competition between the two is so intense, there'll often be free beer in the early evening. During the day, the action is by the clubs' open-air pools, where you're over-dressed if covering anything more than your genitalia.

Everywhere else is tranquil by comparison. Although they may also have live music, a number of **bars** are worth a call simply for a drink. Check out *Sharky's*, 15201 Front Beach Road (☎235-2420), a massive tiki bar right on the beach; *Schooner's*, 5121 Gulf Drive (☎234-9074), for its ocean-view beachside tables; or the small and dimly lit *Shamrock Lounge*, 15600 Front Beach Road (☎234-6563), which, believe it or not, used to be the city hall.

West from Panama City Beach

West of Panama City Beach, motels eventually give way to a more rugged, less developed outlook: the **beaches of South Walton County***, comprising fifty miles of some of Florida's best-kept coast. With a few exceptions, accommodation here is in resort complexes with sky-high rates, but it's a great area to spend a day gliding through. **Route-30A** links the region's small beach communities – a superior course to Hwy-98 (also known as Route 30), which takes an inland route.

*It makes no difference to travellers, but for official purposes the South Walton Beaches don't include Fort Walton Beach, which is in adjoining Okaloosa County.

For **general information** on the South Walton beaches and surrounding area, phone the *South Walton Development Council*: ☎1-800/822-6877.

Along Route 30A: Seaside and Grayton

A exception to the casual, unplanned appearance of most South Walton beach towns, **SEASIDE**, forty miles from Panama City Beach, is an experiment in urban architecture begun in 1981 by a rich, idealistic developer called Robert Davies. The theory is that Seaside's pseudo-Victorian cottages foster village-like good neighborliness and instil a sense of community: in reality, they do nothing of the sort. The silly picket fences and pastel paintwork of the cottages (available for summer rental at around $350 per night; call ☎231-4224 if you're interested), and the aseptic red-brick streets – on which it seems antisocial to leave so much as a footprint – make for a place too expensive and exclusive to ever feel a part of.

Fortunately, the antidote to Seaside's sterility is just a few miles further along Route 30A at **GRAYTON**, whose secluded position (hemmed in by protected land) and ramshackle wooden dwellings have taken the fancy of a number of artists, who now reside here. Some of their work is regularly on show at the beachside *Gallery at Grayton* (Mon–Thurs 9.30am–5pm). Make a call, too, at the open-air workshop of **Joe Elmore**, on Route 283, unsignposted amid an impossible-to-miss batch of shops and galleries. Elmore is a wood sculptor who works with a chainsaw; his remarkably detailed creations (priced from $200 to $2000) can be admired here – as can several of his chainsaws.

Many who come to Grayton skip straight through to the **Grayton Beach State Recreation Area** (daily 8am–sunset; cars $3.25, pedestrians and cyclists $1), just east of the village. Walled by sand dunes and touching the banks of a large brackish lake, a night at the park's **campground** leaves plenty of time for a slow exploration of the village and its natural surrounds. Route 30A rejoins Hwy-98 seven miles west of Grayton.

Inland: Eden State Gardens

Away from the coast road, only **Eden State Gardens** (daily 8am–sunset; free), reached by Route 395 from Seagrove Beach a mile east of Seaside, justifies a visit. Their peace now disturbed only by the buzz of dragonflies, the gardens were once the base of the Wesley Lumber Company, which helped decimate Florida's forests during the turn-of-the-century timber boom. Impressed with the setting, the company boss pinched some of the wood to build himself a grandiose two-storey plantation-style home, the **Wesley house** (guided tours on the hour, Mon–Thurs 9am–4pm; $2), rife with period architectural details and stuffed with the eighteenth-century antiques and curios of a later owner.

If you're hungry, drive a few miles west along Hwy-98 from the junction with Route 395 to *LeBleau's Cajun Kitchen* (usually closing at 9pm, sometimes earlier; ☎267-3724), a local legend for its cajun food at giveaway prices – unparalleled value compared to the tourist traps around Destin, twenty miles further.

Destin and Around

Once a small fishing village and a cult name among anglers for the fat marlin and tuna waiting to be caught in an undersea canyon a few miles offshore, the towering condos of **DESTIN** emerge through the heat haze as you approach on Hwy-

98, proof that two decades of unrestrained exploitation have stripped away much of the town's character. Further evidence of Destin's sudden expansion can be found amid the fading photos of earlier days inside the **Old Destin Post Office Museum** (Mon & Wed 1.30–4.30pm; free), opposite the town library on Stahlman Avenue, while the **Fishing Museum**, on Mareno Plaza (Tues–Sun 11am–4pm; donation $1), with its mounted record-breaking catches, and thousands of pics of landed fish with their grinning captors, is proof of Destin's high esteem among hook-and-line enthusiasts. Pick up tourist information at the **Chamber of Commerce** (Mon–Fri 9am–5pm; ☎837-6241), signposted to your right as you arrive on Hwy-98. If you fancy **staying** in the area, you'll do best to base yourself about four miles east, on Route 2378.

East of Destin

It's worth heading **east of Destin** to enjoy the area's enticing white sands and to escape the condo overkill. Lined by unobtrusive motels and beach shops, **Route 2378** (also known locally as Beach Road or Old Hwy-98) makes a coast-hugging loop off Hwy-98, starting about four miles from Destin: the adjacent beach is family territory, but it offers relaxation, excellent sea swimming and classic Gulf-coast sunsets. While here, resist any temptation to visit the **Museum of the Sea and Indian**, at 4801 Beach Drive (daily, winter 8am–5pm, summer 8am–7pm; $4.50), a vile place where you're loaned a cassette player and pointed to a dull batch of sea creatures and shells, and an equally uninspired ragbag of native American pieces.

Eating and Nightlife

At the foot of Destin Bridge (see below), *Fred's Breakfast Shop* (☎837-9277) does a traditional breakfast fry-up for $3; later in the day, there's a buffet at the *Seafood Factory*, 21 Hwy-98 (☎837-0991), and imaginative Caribbean specials at *Cockatoo's*, in the *Shore Line Village Mall* at 900 E Hwy-98 (☎654-1800). Along Route 2378 you can munch a fish sandwich or shrimp salad at *Captain Dave's* (no 3769; ☎837-2627), while gazing over the ocean, and at *The Back Porch* (no 1740; ☎837-2020), a delicious vegetable platter complements the usual seafood dishes. When hunger strikes in the middle of the night, head for the 24-hour *Destin Diner*, 1038 Hwy-98 (☎654-5843), which serves breakfasts, burgers and frothy milkshakes in surrounds of neon and chrome.

Destin's **nightlife** has little vigor: a few of the beachside bars and restaurants offer nightly drink specials – look for the signs – or you can drink to the accompaniment of undistinguished rock bands at the *Hog's Breath Saloon*, 1239 Siebert Street (☎244-2199).

Accommodation

You'll seldom find accommodation under $60 a night among the monolithic hotels in central Destin, so head east to the **motels** along Route 2378. The lowest rates are with *Sun'n'Sand* (no 4080; ☎837-6724; ②–③), *Crystal Beach Motel* (no 2931; ☎837-4770; ②–③) and *Surf High* (no 3000; ☎837-2366; ②–③). For several people planning a **long stay**, *Surfside* (no. 4701; ☎837-4700), a high-rise **hotel** with two- and three-bedded rooms with kitchens, can be extremely cheap: around $1000 a month in winter.

Of the **campgrounds**, only two accept tents: *Destin KOA*, on Route 2378 (☎837-6215), and, in central Destin, *Destin Campground*, 209 Beach Drive (☎837-6511).

Okaloosa Island and Fort Walton Beach

Hwy-98 leaves Destin by rising over the **Destin Bridge**, giving towering views of the two-tone ocean and intensely white sands, before hitting the crazy golf courses and amusement parks of **OKALOOSA ISLAND**. The island's **beaches**, immediately west, are a better sight, kept in their raw state by their owner – the US Air Force – and making a lively weekend playground for local youth and high-spirited beachbums.

A mile west, the neon motel signs that greet arrivals to **FORT WALTON BEACH** offer no indication that this was the site of a major religious and social center during the Paleo-Indian period; so important were the finds made here that the place gave its name to the "Fort Walton Culture" (see "History", in *Contexts*, for more). A sizeable temple mound stands incongruously beside the busy highway, and the small **Indian Temple Mound Museum** (June–Aug Mon–Sat 9am–4pm, otherwise Mon–Sat 11am–4pm; 75¢), at the junction of Hwy-98 and Route 85, is crammed with elucidating relics.

These days, however, it's military culture which dominates Fort Walton Beach, the town being the home of **Eglin**, the country's biggest Air Force base. The first guided missiles were put together here in the Forties, and work on developing and testing (non-nuclear) airborne weaponry has continued unabated ever since. The **Air Force Armament Museum** (daily 9.30am–4.30pm; free), six miles north of Fort Walton Beach on Route 85, has a large stock of what the base is famous for: guns, missiles and bombs – and the planes that carry them.

Aside from a few crewcuts and topless bars, you'll see little evidence of the base close to Hwy-98, and much of Fort Walton Beach has a more downbeat and homely feel than Destin – and slightly lower prices. The local **Chamber of Commerce**, 34 SE Miracle Strip Parkway (Mon 9am–5pm, Tues–Fri 8am–5pm; ☎244-8191), has abundant information on eating and accommodation.

Eating

Impressive for quantity if not quality, *Shoney's*, 201 Miracle Strip Parkway (☎244-3101), offers a mountainous **breakfast buffet**; later there are good-value **lunch and dinner buffets** at *The Kettle*, 1200 Hwy-98 (☎243-9701). More healthily, *Mother Earth's Good Time Café*, 422 Eglin Parkway (☎863-5484), uses nothing but fresh natural ingredients and country recipes, and *Sitar*, 238 Parkway Plaza, off Eglin Parkway (☎864-3033), serves an excellent Indian lunch buffet.

Fort Walton Beach **nightlife** amounts to little more than the usual **beachfront bars**, mostly on Okaloosa Island, with some good happy hours. The best are *Pandora's*, 1120 Santa Rosa Boulevard (☎244-8669), drawing tourists and locals to its nightly specials; *Jamaica Joe's*, 785 Sundial Court (☎244-4137), a giant tiki bar; and *Jeremiah's*, 203 Brook Street (☎664-6666), on stilts under the Brooks Bridge.

Accommodation

The cheapest **motels** are along Miracle Strip Parkway (the local section of Hwy-98): *Americana* (no 333; ☎244-4999; ②–③), *Budget Host* (no 209; ☎244-5137; ②–③), *Days Inn* (no 135; ☎1-800/325-2525; ②–④), and *Greenwood*, 1340 Hwy-98 (☎244-1141; ②–③). The nearest **campground** is the RV-only *Playground RV Park*, four miles north on Hwy-189 (☎862-3513); campers with **tents** should make for *Gulf Winds Park*, ten miles west on Hwy-98 (☎939-3593), or, slightly further on, *Navarre Beach Family Campground* (☎939-2188), just outside Navarre.

West to Pensacola by car or bus

If you're driving, travel **west from Fort Walton** along Santa Rosa Boulevard, which continues (as Route 399) for sixty scenic miles along **Santa Rosa Island** to the Gulf Island National Seashore, near Pensacola Beach (see "Pensacola and around"). The parallel route, Hwy-98, is much duller, but is the one the daily *Greyhound* **bus** takes from the station at 68 N Beal Parkway (☎243-1940).

Pensacola and Around

Tucked away at the western end of the Panhandle, you might be inclined to overlook **PENSACOLA**, built on the northern bank of the broad Pensacola Bay and five miles inland from the nearest beaches, particularly as its prime features are a naval aviation school and some busy dockyards. Pensacola is, however, an historic center: occupied by the Spanish from 1559 – only the hurricane which ended their settlement prevented it becoming the oldest city in the US – it repeatedly changed hands between the Spanish, French and British before becoming the place where Florida was officially ceded by Spain to the US in 1821. Enough evidence of the seesawing past remains around the city's oak-lined central streets to give substance to a short visit; to justify a longer stay, cross the Bay Bridge to the coast, where Pensacola Beach neighbors the wild, protected beaches of the Gulf Island National Seashore.

Arrival, Information and Getting Around

Unless you're arriving from the inland Panhandle on I-10 or Hwy-90, aim to take the scenic route to Pensacola, along Santa Rosa Island on **Route 399** (also known here as Via De Luna). Doing this, you'll first strike Pensacola Beach, from which Pensacola Beach Road swings north, crossing the Santa Rosa peninsula and joining **Hwy-98** before crossing the three-mile-long Pensacola Bay Bridge into the city. At the foot of the bridge, on the city side, is the **visitor information center** (daily 8am–5pm; ☎1-800/343-4321), packed with the usual worthwhile handouts.

Unusually, the **Greyhound** station is far from central, being seven miles north of the city center at 505 W Burgess Road (☎476-4800); bus #10 links it to Pensacola proper. **Local buses** (info: ☎436-9383) serve the city but not the beach; the main terminal is at the junction of Gregory and Palofax streets. To get from the city to the beach without personal transport, take a **taxi** (*ABC* ☎438-8650, or *Yellow* ☎433-3333): the fare will be roughly $9.

Accommodation

Plenty of **budget chain hotels**, all $30–50 a night, with unmissable billboards, line N Davis Boulevard and Pensacola Boulevard, the main approach roads from I-10. **Central** options are more limited: cheapest is the *Seville Inn*, 221 E Garden Street (☎1-800/277-7275; ②); the *Civic Inn*, 200 N Palofax Street (☎1-800/962-0130; ②), and *Days Inn*, 710 N Palofax Street (☎438-4922; ②), are slightly dearer. A few miles west of the center is the *Mayfair Motel*, 4540 Mobile Highway (☎455-8561; ①). **At the beach**, the lowest prices are at *Barbary Coast*, 24 Via De Luna (☎932-2233; ③–④), *Gulf Aire*, 21 Via de Luna (☎932-2319; ②–③), and *Tiki House*, 17 Via de Luna (☎934-4447; ①–③).

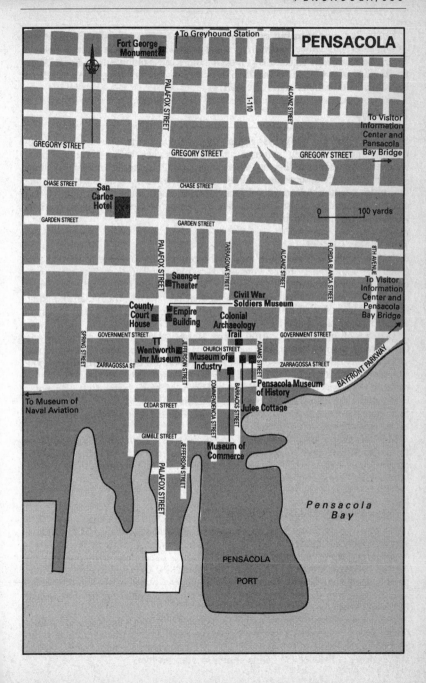

PENSACOLA

To Greyhound Station

Fort George
Monument

I-110

ALCANIZ STREET

PALAFOX STREET

GREGORY STREET

GREGORY STREET

GREGORY STREET

To Visitor
Information
Center and
Pensacola
Bay Bridge

CHASE STREET

San
Carlos
Hotel

CHASE STREET

GARDEN STREET

GARDEN STREET

0   100 yards

TARRAGONA STREET

ALCANIZ STREET

FLORIDA BLANCA STREET

8TH AVENUE

PALAFOX STREET

Saenger
Theater

Civil War
Soldiers Museum

To Visitor
Information
Center and
Pensacola
Bay Bridge

County
Court
House

Empire
Building

Colonial
Archaeology
Trail

SPRING STREET

GOVERNMENT STREET

GOVERNMENT STREET

BAYFRONT PARKWAY

Wentworth
Jnr. Museum

ZARRAGOSSA ST

JEFFERSON STREET

CHURCH STREET

Museum of
Industry

ADAMS STREET

ZARRAGOSSA STREET

COMMENDENCIA STREET

BARRACK'S STREET

Pensacola Museum
of History

To Museum of
Naval Aviation

CEDAR STREET

Julee Cottage

GIMBLE STREET

JEFFERSON STREET

Museum of
Commerce

PALAFOX STREET

*Pensacola
Bay*

PENSÁCOLA

PORT

The closest **campground** is the *Fort Pickens Campground* (☎932-5018) on the Gulf Islands National Seashore, a few miles west of Pensacola Beach (see below). Two others are further out: *Big Lagoon*, ten miles southwest on Route 292A (☎492-1595), and *Circle G* (☎944-1096) on the city's forested fringe, near Exit 2 off I-10, about twelve miles from the center.

The City

Pensacola's past was much livelier than its present and virtually everything worth seeing, chiefly restored buildings and museums, lies within three adjoining districts in the center of the city, where only a small number of offices and shops – and surprisingly few people – suggest that time has moved on. Elsewhere, just the **naval aviation museum** – the city's major single tourist attraction – offers any inducement to delay heading out to Pensacola Beach for some serious sunbathing and nature exploration.

The Palofax District

Already a booming port by the turn of the century, the opening of the Panama Canal was expected to boost Pensacola's fortunes still further. The many new buildings which appeared in the **Palofax District**, around the southerly section of Palofax Street, in the early 1900s – with their delicate ornamentation and attention to detail – reflected the optimism of the era. The surge in wealth never came, but the structures remain.

Take a look first at the **County Court House**, at the junction of Palofax and Government streets, which has also seen service as a customs house, a post office and tax offices, besides its legal function; and the **Empire Building**, opposite, whose slender form and vertically aligned windows exaggerate the height of what, in 1909, was the tallest building in Florida. A block further, at 118 Palofax Place, is the Spanish Baroque **Saenger Theater**, now the base of the Pensacola Symphony Orchestra; if the door's open, go in – the interior is twice as evocative as the outside.

Also meriting a look, the **Civil War Soldiers Museum**, 108 S Palofax Place (Mon–Sat 10am–4pm; $4) assembles uniforms, weaponry and many unsettling medical tools – all of which saw action in the Civil War – and uses them to illustrate soldiers' conditions during the conflict between the States.

North Hill

Between 1870 and 1930, Pensacola's professional classes took a shine to the area just across Wright Street from the Palofax district called **NORTH HILL**, commissioning elaborate homes in a plethora of fancy styles. Strewn across the tree-studded fifty-block area are pompous Neoclassical porches, cutesy-pie Tudor-Revival cottages, low-slung California bungalows and the rounded towers of the finest Queen Anne homes. Being private residences, none are open to the public, and the best way to see them is by driving around Palofax, Spring, Strong and Brainerd streets.

The clamor to build houses in this fashionable neighborhood led to the ruin of **Fort George**, which once barracked two thousand British troops and fell to the Spanish at the Battle of Pensacola in 1781. Only an imitation cannon and a plaque at the corner of Palofax and LaRua streets locates the spot.

The Seville District: Historic Pensacola Village

As a commercial center, Pensacola kicked into gear from the late 1700s, with a cosmopolitan mix of native Americans, early settlers and seafaring traders gathering to swap, sell and barter on the waterfront of the **SEVILLE DISTRICT**, about half a mile east of Palofax Street. Those who did well took up permanent residence and many of their homes remain in fine states of repair, forming – together with several museums – the **Historic Pensacola Village** (daily 10am–4pm; $5.50). Paying once gets you into all of the museums and former homes (and you should see them *all*, the effect of the whole is far greater than the sum of its parts) in an easily navigated four-block area.

Start at the **Museum of Commerce**, on the corner of Zaragoza and Tarragona streets, an entertaining indoor re-creation of Palofax Street in its turn-of-the-century heyday, with many of the storefronts and shop fittings of the time. Much of the prosperity of Pensacola was based on the timber industry, a point celebrated by a noisy, working sawmill in the **Museum of Industry**, just across Zaragoza Street, where there's also an immense pile of fishing tackle and other reminders of how the city stayed on its uppers for many years.

To catch up on earlier local history, cross Church Street to the sedate **Colonial Archeology trail**, where bits of pottery and weapons suggest the lifestyles of the city's first Spanish inhabitants, and a marked path leads around the site of the British-era Government House, an outpost of empire which collapsed in the 1820s. Virtually next door, the 1809 **Julee Cottage** belonged to Julee Panton, a "freewoman of color" – a euphemism for being black and not a slave – who had her own land and business, and even her own slave: the building's exhibits record her life and deeds, and the achievements of later black people with Pensacola associations.

Other **restored homes** in the vicinity signify the mishmash of architectural styles, from Creole to Greek Revival, which were the taste of wealthier Pensacolions in the late 1800s. Filled with period furnishings, they make for an enjoyable browse – despite the somewhat twee attendants who sit in them, dressed in period costume.

If you don't have the energy or the inclination to visit all the museums and old homes of the Historic Village, head instead to the **Pensacola Historic Museum** (Mon–Sat 9am–4.30; $2), inside the Old Christ Church at 405 S Adams Street, easily spotted by its sturdy masonry tower. Built in 1832, the church now keeps an imposing clutter, from fossils and native American pottery to cut-glass ornaments owned by the well-to-do settlers of the early 1900s, which helps make Pensacola's complicated history comprehensible.

Similar historical detritus can be found inside the **T T Wentworth Jnr Museum** on Plaza Ferdinand (Mon–Sat 10am–4pm; $5; free admission with Historic Pensacola Village ticket), a yellow-brick Renaissance affair built as the city hall in 1907. Its arched corridors and rooms are filled with photos, maps and markers to the city's past, while the upper floor has a room with hands-on exhibits to amuse restless kids. It was in Plaza Ferdinand, incidentally, that Florida was officially accepted into the US – a statue to Andrew Jackson, the state's first governor, salutes the fact.

The Museum of Naval Aviation

You don't have to be a military fanatic to enjoy the **Museum of Naval Aviation** (daily 9am–5pm; free; ID must be shown), inside the US naval base on Navy

Boulevard, about eight miles southwest of central Pensacola (bus #14), although harboring *Biggles* fantasies will help: many of the full-sized training cockpits can be climbed into and their controls tugged and pulled.

The main purpose of the museum, however, is to collect and display US naval aircraft, from the first flimsy seaplane acquired in 1911 to the Phantoms and Hornets of more recent times. Among them are a couple of oddities: a small Vietnamese plane which carried a Vietnamese family onto a US carrier during the Fall of Saigon, and the Command Module from the first Skylab mission – whose crew were naval pilots. Possible anti-military objections apart, it's all quite viewable, and underlines Pensacola's role as the home base of US naval aviation, training ground for thousands of new pilots each year.

Around Pensacola

On the other side of the bay from the city, the glistening beaches of Santa Rosa Island (the barrier island that runs sixty miles from Fort Walton) are ideal for sunbathing, and two protected areas – a dense prehistoric forest and a long line of windswept sand dunes – demand investigation. The area doesn't lack history either, holding the well-preserved remains of a nineteenth-century fort, erected to guard Pensacola from hostile forces. Put all this together and you have a convincing argument for not spending all your time in Pensacola itself.

Gulf Breeze

Before reaching Santa Rosa Island – which holds Pensacola Beach – you'll pass through **GULF BREEZE** on the Santa Rosa peninsula, a well-scrubbed, well-off community that's going all-out to attract homebuyers. The only reason to give it more than a passing thought is the **Naval Live Oaks Reservation** (daily 8am–sunset; free), about a mile east along Hwy-98. In the 1820s, part of this live oak forest was turned into a tree farm, intended to ensure a supply of shipbuilding material for years to come. Incredible as it may seem, precise calculations were made as to how many trees would be needed for a particular ship, and the requisite number of acorns then planted – followed by a fifty-year wait. Problems were plentiful: the oak was too heavy for road transportation, wood rustlers cut down trees and sold them to foreign navies, and the final blow for the farm was the advent of iron-built ships.

The **visitor center** (daily 8.30am–5pm), near the entrance, has exhibits and explanatory texts on the intriguing forest, where fragments from native American settlements dated to 1000 BC have been found. To escape the glare of the sun for an hour or so, take one of the short but shady **forest trails**, which include a two-mile section of what was, in the early 1800s, Florida's major roadway, linking Pensacola and St Augustine.

Pensacola Beach and the Gulf Islands National Seashore

PENSACOLA BEACH has everything you'd want from a Gulf coast beach: mile after mile of fine white sands, rental outlets for beach and water-sports equipment, a fisherman-lined pier and a sprinkling of motels, hotels, beachside bars and snack stands. It's hard to beat for uncomplicated oceanside recreation, but while sunning yourself, don't ignore what lies a short way west – at the **GULF ISLANDS NATIONAL SEASHORE**, on Fort Pickens Road (9am–sunset; cars $3, pedestrians and cyclists free). Here, vibrant white sands are walled by a nine-mile stretch

of high, rugged dunes and the only reminder of civilization – other than the road –
is a foliage-encircled campground. Hoofing over the dunes is strictly forbidden but
several tracks lead from the road to the beach, and you'll find plenty of space and
seclusion once you get there. To learn more about the dunes, and the curious ecology of the island, join one of the frequent **ranger-led walks**; for details call ☎934-
2600, or read *The Barnacle*, a free newssheet handed out at the entrance.

Fort Pickens

Within the national seashore area, at the western tip of Santa Rosa Island, are the
substantial remains of **Fort Pickens** (daily 9am–5pm; free), slave-built in the
early 1800s to protect Pensacola from seaborne attack. The **free guided tours**
(daily in summer 11am & 2pm; rest of the year Mon–Fri at 2pm, Sat & Sun at
11am & 2pm) are worth catching, though plenty can be gleaned by walking
around the fort's creepy passageways and cellar-like rooms on your own. A small
museum explains the origins of the structure, details the flora and fauna of the
national seashore area, and records the travails of the seventeen Apache Indians
who were imprisoned here in 1886. Among their number was a chief, Goyahkla,
better known as **Geronimo**, who, depending on which account you believe,
served his sentence chained to the walls being yelled at by locals in boats – or
roaming the sands, unable to swim and afraid of water. The Apaches, whose
tribal lands covered much of the southwestern US, were one of the last native
American tribes to surrender to the advancing white settlers, signing a peace
treaty with the sympathetic General Crook in 1886. Soon after, the higher-
ranking General Sheridan reneged on the terms of the surrender and locked up
Geronimo and his fellows. Crook resigned from the army in protest.

Beside the fort, some crumbling concrete walls remain from another fort
erected in the Forties, which, together with the pillboxes and observation posts
that litter the area, is a reminder that the fort's defensive function lasted until the
end of World War II, only becoming obsolete with the advent of guided missiles.

Eating and Entertainment

There's a dearth of restaurants in **central Pensacola**, but *Elise's*, 11 S Palofax
Street (☎432-5100), has inexpensive breakfasts and lunches, as does *EJ's*, 232 E
Main Street (☎432-5886), with well-priced daily specials and a big salad bar; *Hall's
Catfish & Seafood*, 916 E Gregory Street (☎438-9019), has fish-laden dinner
buffets. You'll find more choice at **Pensacola Beach**: *Butler's*, 27 Via de Luna
(☎932-6537), and the *Sundeck Sidewalk Café*, 12 Via de Luna (☎932-0835), do well-
priced breakfasts and lunches, while *Boy on a Dolphin*, 400 Pensacola Beach
Boulevard (☎932-7954), and *Flounder's Chowder & Ale House*, 800 Quietwater
Beach Road (☎932-2003), both offer hearty seafood dinners.

Nightlife

In **central Pensacola**, avoid the *Seville Quarter*, 130 E Government Street (☎434-
6201), a tourist-aimed bar and disco decked out to reflect Pensacola's history, but
too expensive and contrived to be fun. Better is *McGuire's Irish Pub*, 600 E Gregory
Street (☎433-6789), which serves home-brewed ale. At **Pensacola Beach** the
action centers on *Flounder's Chowder & Ale House* (see above), which draws as
many drinkers as diners and has live music about once a week, and *The Dock*
(☎934-3314), beside the pier, which is packed every Friday and Saturday night.

travel details

Trains

From Tallahassee to Jacksonsville (1 daily; 4hr 20min); Pensacola (1 daily; 4hr 15min).

From Pensacola to Jacksonsville (1 daily; 8hr 50min); Tallahassee (1 daily; 4hr 15min).

Buses

From Tallahassee to Marianna (5 daily; 35min); Chipley/De Funiak Springs (1 daily; 1hr 30min/2hr 25min); Panama City Beach (2 daily; 2hr 30min); Pensacola (5 daily; 2hr 35min); Jacksonsville (5 daily; 3hr 40min); Gainesville (5 daily; 2hr 40min); Miami (5 daily; 11hr 55min); Tampa (5 daily; 5hr); Orlando (4 daily; 6hr 30min); Thomasville (1 daily; 1hr 5min); New Orleans (6 daily; 8hr 30min).

From Panama City Beach to Panama City (2 daily; 30min); Destin (2 daily; 50min); Fort Walton Beach (2 daily; 1hr 10min); Pensacola (2 daily; 2hr 15min).

From Pensacola to Tallahassee (5 daily; 4hr 25min); Fort Walton Beach (2 daily; 1hr 5min); Destin (2 daily; 1hr 25min); Panama City Beach (2 daily; 2hr 15min); Mobile (8 daily; 1hr); New Orleans (6 daily; 4hr 15min).

PART THREE

THE

CONTEXTS

THE HISTORICAL FRAMEWORK

Contrary to popular belief, Florida's history goes back far beyond Walt Disney World and motel-lined beaches. For thousands of years, its aboriginal inhabitants lived in organized social groupings with contacts across a large section of the Americas. During the height of European colonization, it became a Spanish possession and, for a time, was under British control. Only in the nineteenth century did Florida become part of the US: the beginning of a period of unrestrained exploitation and expansion and the start of many of the problems with which the state continues to grapple today.

ORIGINS OF THE LAND

Over billions of years, rivers flowing through what's now **northern Florida** carried debris from the Appalachian mountains to the coast, their deposits of fine-powdered rock forming the beaches and barrier islands of the Panhandle. Further south, the highest section of a seabed plateau – the **Florida peninsula** – altered in shape according to the world's ice covering. The exposed land sometimes measured twice its present size; during other periods, the coastline was far inland of its current position, with wave action carving out still-visible bluffs in the oolitic limestone base. In the

present era, beginning about 75 million years ago, rotting vegetation mixed with rainfall to form acid that burned holes in the limestone, and natural freshwater springs emerged; the underground water accumulated from heavy rains which preceded each Ice Age. Inland forests of live oak and pine became inhabited 20,000 years ago by mastodons, mammoths and saber-toothed tigers, thought to have travelled – over many generations – across the ice-covered Bering Strait from Siberia.

FIRST HUMAN HABITATION

Two theories exist regarding the origins of Florida's **first human inhabitants**. It's commonly held that the earliest arrivals followed the same route as the animals from Siberia, crossing North America and arriving in northern Florida around 10,000 years ago. A minority of anthropologists take the alternative view that the first Floridians were the result of migration by aboriginal peoples in South and Central America. Either way, the **Paleo** (or "Early") **Indians** in Florida lived hunter-gatherer existences – the spear tips they used are widely found across the central and northern parts of the state.

Around 5000 BC, social patterns changed: settlements became semi-permanent and diet switched from meat to shellfish, snails and molluscs, which were abundant along the rivers. Travelling was done by dugout canoe and periodically a community would move to a new site, probably to allow food supplies to replenish themselves. Discarded shells and other rubbish were piled onto the **midden mounds** still commonly seen in the state.

Though pottery began to appear around 2000 BC, not until 1000 BC was there a big change in lifestyle, as indicated by the discovery of **irrigation canals**, patches of land cleared for **cultivation**, and cooking utensils used to prepare grown food. From the time of the Christian era, the erection of **burial mounds** – elaborate tombs of prominent tribespeople, often with sacrificed kin and valuable objects also placed inside – became common. These suggest strong religious and trading links across an area stretching from Central America to the North American interior.

Spreading east from the Georgian coastal plain, the **Fort Walton Culture** became prevalent from around 200 AD. This divided society into a rigid caste system and people lived in villages planned around a central plaza. Throughout Florida at this time, approximately 100,000 inhabitants formed several distinct tribal groupings: most notably the **Timucua** across northern Florida, the **Calusa** around the southwest and Lake Okeechobee, the **Apalachee** in the Panhandle and the **Tequesta** along the southeast coast.

EUROPEAN DISCOVERY AND SETTLEMENT

After Christopher Columbus located the "New World" in 1492, Europe's great sea powers were increasingly active around the Caribbean. One of them, Spain, had discovered and plundered the treasures of ancient civilizations in Central America, and all were eager to locate other riches across these and neighboring lands. The **first European sighting** of Florida is believed to have been made by John and Sebastian **Cabot** in 1498, when they set eyes on what is now called Cape Florida, on Key Biscayne in Miami.

In 1513, the **first European landing** was made by **Juan Ponce de León**, a Spaniard eager to carve out a niche for himself in the expanding empire and previously employed as governor of Puerto Rico, a Spanish possession. Although searching for Bimini, Ponce de León sighted land during *Pascua Florida*, the Spanish Festival of the Flowers, and named what he saw *La Florida* – or "Land of Flowers". After putting ashore somewhere between the mouth of the St John's River and present-day St Augustine, Ponce de León sailed on around the Florida Keys, naming them *Los Martires*, for their supposed resemblance to the bones of martyred men, and *Las Tortugas* (now the Dry Tortugas), named for the turtles he saw around them.

Sent to deal with troublesome natives in the Lower Antilles, it was eight years before Ponce de León returned to Florida, this time with a mandate from the Spanish king to **conquer and colonize** the territory. Landing on the southwest coast, probably somewhere between Tampa Bay and Fort Myers, Ponce de León met a hostile reception from the Calusa Indians and was forced to withdraw, eventually dying from an arrow wound received in the battle.

Rumors of gold hidden in Apalachee, in the north of the region, stimulated several Spanish incursions into Florida, all of which were driven back by the aggression of the indigenes and the ferocity of the terrain and climate. The most successful undertaking – even though it ended in death for its leader – was the **Hernando de Soto expedition**, a thousand-strong band of war-hardened knights and treasure seekers which landed at Tampa Bay in May 1539. Recent excavations in Tallahassee have located the site of one of de Soto's camps, where the first Christmas celebration in North America is thought to have taken place before the expedition continued north, later making the first European crossing of the Mississippi River – for a long time marking Florida's western boundary.

Written accounts of the expeditions became the source of most that's known about the aboriginal life of the period, though anthropology was not a major concern of the Spanish and the news that Florida did not harbor stunning riches caused interest to wane. Treasure-laden Spanish ships sailing off the Florida coast between the Americas and Europe were of interest to pirate ships, however, many of them British and French vessels hoisting the Jolly Roger. The Spanish failure to colonize Florida made it a prime base for attacks on their vessels, and a small group of **French Huguenots** landed in 1562, building Fort Caroline on the St John's River.

The French presence forced the Spanish into a more determined effort at settlement. Already commissioned to explore the Atlantic coast of North America, **Pedro Menéndez de Avilés** was promised the lion's share of whatever profits could be made from Florida. Landing south of the French fort on August 28, 1562, the day of the Spanish Festival of San Augustín, Menéndez named the site **St Augustine** – founding what was to become the longest continuous site of European habitation on the continent. The French were quickly defeated, their leader **Jean Ribault** and his crew massacred after being driven ashore by a hurricane; the site of the killing is still known as Matanzas, or "Place of Slaughter".

THE FIRST SPANISH PERIOD (1565–1763)

Only the enthusiasm of Menéndez held Florida together during the early decades of Spanish rule. A few small and insecure settlements were established, usually around **missions** founded by Jesuit or Franciscan missions bent on Christianizing the Indians. It was a far from harmonious setup: homesick Spanish soldiers frequently mutinied and fought with the Indians, who responded by burning St Augustine to the ground. Menéndez replaced St Augustine's wooden buildings with "tabby" (a cement-like mixture of seashells and limestone) structures with palm-thatched roofs, a style typical of early European Florida. While easily the largest settlement, even St Augustine was a lifeless outpost unless a ship happened to be in port. Despite sinking all his personal finances into the colony, Menéndez never lived to see Florida thrive, and he left in 1571, ordered by the king to help plan the Spanish Armada's attack on Britain.

Fifteen years later, as war raged between the European powers, St Augustine was razed by a naval bombardment led by **Francis Drake**, a sign that the **British** were beginning to establish their colonies along the Atlantic coast, north of Florida. Aware that the Indians would hold the balance of power in future colonial power struggles, a string of Spanish missions were built along the Panhandle from 1606; besides seeking to earn the loyalty of the natives, these were intended to provide a defensive shield against attacks from the north. By the 1700s the British were making forages into Florida ostensibly to capture Indians to sell as slaves. One by one, the missions were destroyed, and only the timely arrival of Spanish reinforcements prevented the fall of St Augustine to the British in 1740.

With the French in Louisiana, the British in Georgia and the Spanish clinging to Florida, the scene was set for a bloody confrontation for control of North America. Eventually, the **1763 Treaty of Paris**, concluding the Seven Years' War in Europe, settled the issue: the British had captured the crucial Spanish possession of Havana, and Spain willingly parted with Florida to get it back.

THE BRITISH PERIOD (1763–1783)

Despite their two centuries of occupation, the Spanish failed to make much impression on Florida. It was the British, already developing the colonies further north, who grafted a social infrastructure onto the region. They also divided Florida (then with only the northern section inhabited by whites) into separate colonies: **East Florida** governed from St Augustine, and **West Florida** governed from the growing Panhandle port of **Pensacola**.

By this time, aboriginal Floridians had largely died out through contact with European diseases, to which they had no immunity, and Florida's Indian population was becoming composed of disparate tribes arriving from the west, collectively known as the **Seminoles**. Like the Spanish, the British acknowledged the numerical importance of the Indians and sought good relations with them. In return for goods, the British took Indian land around ports and supply routes, but generally left the Seminoles undisturbed in the inland areas.

Despite attractive grants, few settlers arrived from Britain. Those with money to spare bought Florida land as an investment, never intending to develop or settle on it, and only large holdings – **plantations** growing corn, sugar, rice and other crops – were profitable. Charleston, to the north, dominated sea trade in the area, though St Augustine was still a modestly important settlement and the gathering place of passing British aristocrats and intellectuals. West Florida, on the other hand, was riven by political factionalism and often the scene of skirmishes with the Seminoles, who received worse treatment than their counterparts in the east.

Being a new and sparsely populated region, the discontent which fuelled the **American War of Independence** in the 1770s barely affected Florida, except to bring British Royalists fleeing into St Augustine, many of them moving on to the Bahamas or Jamaica. Pensacola, though, was attacked and briefly occupied in 1781 by the Spanish who had been promised Florida in return for helping the American rebels defeat the British. As it turned out, diplomacy rather than gunfire signalled the end of British rule in Florida.

THE SECOND SPANISH PERIOD (1783–1821)

The **1783 Treaty of Paris**, with which Britain recognized American independence, not only returned Florida to Spain but also gave it Louisiana and the prized port of New Orleans. Spanish holdings in North America were now larger than ever, but with Europe in turmoil and the Spanish colonies in Central America agitating for their own independence, the country was ill-equipped to capitalize on them. The British and smaller numbers of ethnically diverse European settlers remaining in the region, together with the increasingly assertive Seminoles (now well established in fertile central Florida, and often joined by Africans escaping slavery further north), made Florida a complex melting pot, impossible for a declining colonial power to govern.

As fresh European migration slowed, Spain was forced to **sell land to US citizens**, who bought large tracts confident that Florida would soon be under Washington's control. Indeed, in gaining Louisiana from France in 1800 (to whom it had been ceded by Spain), and moving the Georgia border south, it was clear the US had Florida in its sights. Fearful of losing the commercial toehold it still retained in Florida and aligned with Spain through the Napoleonic wars, Britain landed troops at Pensacola in 1814. In response, a US general, **Andrew Jackson**, used the excuse of an Indian uprising in Alabama to march south, killing hundreds of Indians and pursuing them – unlawfully and without official sanction from Washington – into Pensacola, declaring no quarrel with the Spanish but insisting that the British depart. The British duly left, and Jackson and his men withdrew to Mobile (a Floridian town that became part of Alabama as the Americans inched the border eastwards), soon to participate in the Battle of New Orleans, which further strengthened the US position on the Florida border.

THE FIRST SEMINOLE WAR

Jackson's actions in 1814 had triggered the **First Seminole War**. As international tension heightened, Seminole raids (often as a result of baiting on the US side) were commonly used as excuses for US incursions into Florida. In 1818, Jackson finally received what he took to be presidential approval (the "Rhea Letter", thought to have been authorized by President Monroe) to march again into Florida on the pretext of subduing the Seminoles but with the actual intention of taking outright control.

While US public officials were uneasy with the dubious legality of these events, the American public was firmly on Jackson's side. The US government issued an ultimatum to Spain, declaring that either it police Florida effectively or relinquish its ownership. With

little alternative, Spain formally **ceded Florida to the US** in 1819, in return for the US assuming the $5 million owed by the Spanish government to American settlers in land grants (a sum which was never repaid). Nonetheless, it took the threat of an invasion of Cuba for the Spanish king to ratify the treaty in 1821; at the same time Andrew Jackson was sworn in as Florida's first American governor.

TERRITORIAL FLORIDA AND THE SECOND SEMINOLE WAR

In territorial Florida it was soon evident that the East and West divisions were unworkable, and a site midway between St Augustine and Pensacola was selected as the new administrative center: **Tallahassee**. The Indians living on the fertile soils of the area were rudely dispatched towards the coast – an act of callousness that was to typify relations between the new settlers and the incumbent native Americans for decades to come.

Under Spanish and British rule, the Seminoles, notwithstanding some feuding between themselves, lived peaceably on the productive lands of northern central Florida. These, however, were precisely the agriculturally rich areas that US settlers coveted. Under the **Treaty of Moultrie Creek** in 1823, most of the Seminole tribes signed a document agreeing to sell their present land and resettle in southwest Florida. Neither side was to honor this agreement: no time limit was imposed on the Seminole exodus, and those who did go found the new land to be unsuitable for farming; the US side, meanwhile, failed to provide promised resettlement funds.

Andrew Jackson spent only three months as territorial governor, though his influence on Florida continued from the White House when he became US president in 1829. In 1830 he approved the **Act of Indian Removal**, decreeing that all native Americans in the eastern US should be transferred to reservations in the open areas of the Midwest. Two years later, James Gadsen, the newly appointed Indian commissioner, called a meeting of the Seminole tribes at Payne's Landing on the Oklawaha River, near Silver Springs, urging them to cede their land to the US and move west. Amid much acrimony, a few did sign the **Treaty of Payne's Landing**, which provided for their complete removal within three years.

THE SECOND SEMINOLE WAR (1821–1842)

A small number took what monies were offered and resettled in the west, but most Seminoles were determined to stay and the **Second Seminole War** ensued, with the Indians repeatedly ambushing the US militiamen who had arrived to enforce the law, and ransacking the plantations of white settlers, many of whom fled and never returned. Trained for set-piece battles, the US troops were rarely able to deal effectively with the guerrilla tactics of the Seminoles. It was apparent that the Seminoles were unlikely to be defeated by conventional means and in October 1837, their leader, **Osceola**, was lured to St Augustine with the promise of a truce – only to be arrested and imprisoned, eventually to die in jail. This treachery failed to break the spirit of the Seminoles, although a few continued to give themselves up and leave for the west, while others were captured and sold into slavery.

It became the policy of the US to drive the Seminoles steadily south, away from the fertile lands of central Florida and **into the Everglades**. In the Everglades, the Seminoles linked up with the long-established "Spanish Indians" to raid the Cape Florida lighthouse and destroy the white colony on Indian Key in the Florida Keys. Even after bloodhounds were – controversially – used to track the Indians, it was clear that total US victory would never be achieved. With the Seminoles confined to the Everglades, the US formally **ended the conflict** in 1842, when the Seminoles agreed to stay where they were – an area earlier described by an army surveyor as "fit only for Indian habitation".

The six-year war crippled the Florida economy but stimulated the growth of a number of **new towns** around the army forts. Several of these, such as Fort Brooke (Tampa), Fort Lauderdale, Fort Myers and Fort Pierce, have survived into modern times.

STATEHOOD AND SECESSION (1842–1861)

The Second Seminole War forestalled the possibility of Florida **attaining statehood** – which would have entitled it to full representation in Washington and to appoint its own administrators. Influence in Florida at this time was split between two camps. On one side

were the wealthy slave-owning plantation farmers, concentrated in the "cotton counties" of the central section of the Panhandle, who enjoyed all the traditions of the upper rung of Deep South society. They were anxious to make sure that the balance of power in Washington did not shift towards the non-slave-owning "free" states, which would inevitably bring a call for the abolition of slavery. Opposing statehood were the smallholders scattered about the rest of the territory – many of whom were Northerners, already ideologically against slavery and fearing the imposition of federal taxes.

One compromise mooted was a return to a divided Florida, with the West becoming a state while the East remained a territory. Eventually, based on a narrowly agreed **constitution** drawn up in Port St Joseph on the Panhandle coast (on the site of present-day Port St Joe), Florida **became a state** on March 3, 1845. The arrival of statehood coincided with a period of material prosperity: the first railroads began spidering across the Panhandle and central Florida; an organized school system became established; and Florida's 60,000 population was doubled within twenty years.

Nationally, things were less bright. The issue of slavery was to be the catalyst that led the US into civil war, though it was only a part of a great cultural divide between the rural Southern states – to which Florida was linked more through geography than history – and the modern industrial states of the North. As federal pressure intensified for the abolition of slavery, Florida formally **seceded from the Union** on January 10, 1861, aligning itself with the breakaway Confederate States in the run-up to the Civil War.

FLORIDA IN THE CIVIL WAR (1861–1865)

Inevitably, the **Civil War** had a great effect on Florida, although most Floridians conscripted into the Confederate army fought far away from home, and rarely were there more than minor confrontations within the state. The relatively small number of Union sympathizers generally kept a low profile, concentrating on protecting their families. At the start of the war, most of Florida's **coastal forts** were occupied by Union troops as part of the blockade on Confederate shipping. Lacking the strength to mount effective attacks on the forts, those Confederate soldiers who remained in Florida based themselves in the interior and watched for Union troop movements, swiftly destroying whatever bridge, road or railroad lay in the invaders' path – in effect creating a stalemate which endured throughout the conflict.

Away from the coast, Florida's primary contribution to the war effort was the **provision of food** – chiefly beef and pork reared on the central Florida farms – and the transportation of it across the Panhandle towards Confederate strongholds further west. Union attempts to cut the supply route gave rise to the only major battle fought in the state, the **Battle of Olustee**, just outside Live Oak, in February 1864: 10,000 participated in an engagement which left 300 dead and both sides claiming victory.

The most celebrated battle from a Floridian viewpoint, however, happened in March 1865 at **Natural Bridge**, when a youthful group of Confederates defeated the technically superior Union troops, preventing the fall of Tallahassee. As events transpired, it was a hollow victory; following the Confederate surrender, the war ended a few months later.

RECONSTRUCTION

Following the cessation of hostilities, Florida was caught in an uneasy hiatus. In the years after the war, the defeated states were subject to **Reconstruction**, a rearrangement of their internal affairs determined by, at first, the president, later by a much harder-line Congress intent on ensuring the Southern states would never return to their old ways.

The Northern ideal of free-labor capitalism was an alien concept in the South, and there were enormous problems. Of paramount concern was the future of the **freed slaves**. With restrictions on their movements lifted, many emancipated slaves wandered the countryside, often unwittingly putting fear into all-white communities that had never before had a black face in their midst. Rubbing salt into the wounds, as far as the Southern whites were concerned, was the occupation of many towns by black Union troops. As a backlash, the white-supremacist **Ku Klux Klan** became active in Tennessee during 1866 and its race-hate, segregationist doctrine soon spread into Florida.

Against this background of uncertainty and trepidation, Florida's **domestic politics** entered a period of unparalleled chicanery. Suddenly, not only were black men allowed to vote, but there were more black voters than white. The gullibility of the uneducated blacks and the power of their votes proved an irresistible combination to the unscrupulous and power hungry. Double dealing and vote-rigging were practised by diverse factions united only in their desire to restore Florida's statehood and acquire even more power. Following a constitution written and approved in controversial circumstances, Florida was **re-admitted to the Union** on July 21, 1868.

Eventually, in Florida as in the other Southern states, an all-white, **conservative Democrat government** emerged. Despite emancipation and the hopes for integration outlined by the Civil Rights Act passed by Congress in 1875, blacks in Florida were still denied many of the rights reasonably regarded as basic. In fact, all that distanced the new administration from the one which led Florida into secession was awareness of the power of the federal government and the need to at least appear to take outside views into account. It was also true that many of the former slave-owners were now the employers of freed blacks, who remained very much under their white masters' control.

A NEW FLORIDA TAKES SHAPE (1876–1914)

Florida's bonds with its neighboring states became increasingly tenuous in the years following Reconstruction. A fast-growing population began spreading south – part of a gradual diminishing of the importance of the Panhandle, where ties to the Deep South were strongest. Florida's identity became forged by a new **frontier spirit**. Besides smallholding farmers, loggers came to work the abundant forests and a new breed of wealthy settler started putting down roots, among them Henry DeLand and Henry S Sanford, who each bought large chunks of central Florida and founded the towns that still bear their names.

As northern speculators invested in Florida, they sought to publicize the region, and a host of articles extolling the virtues of the state's climate as a cure for all ills began to appear in the country's newspapers. These early efforts to promote **Florida as a tourist destination** brought the wintering rich along the new railroads to enjoy the sparkling rivers and springs, and naturalists arrived to explore the unique flora and fauna.

With a fortune made through his partnership in Standard Oil, **Henry Flagler** opened luxury resorts on Florida's northeast coast for his socialite friends and gradually extended his Florida East Coast Railroad south, giving birth to communities such as **Palm Beach** and making the remote trading post of **Miami** an accessible, expanding town. Flagler's friendly rival, **Henry Plant**, connected *his* railroad to **Tampa**, turning a desolate hamlet into a thriving port city and a major base of cigar manufacture. The **citrus industry** also got into top gear: Florida's climate enabled oranges, grapefruits and other fruits to be grown during the winter and sold to an eager market in the cooler north. The **cattle farms** went from strength to strength, Florida becoming a major supplier of beef to the rest of the US: cows were rounded up with a special wooden whip which made a gunshot-like sound when used – hence the nickname **"cracker"**, which was applied to rural settlers.

One group who didn't benefit from the boom years were the blacks: many were imprisoned for no reason, and found themselves on chaingangs building the new roads and railroads; punishments for refusing to work included severe floggings and hanging by the thumbs. Few whites paid any attention, and those who were in a position to stop the abuses were usually too busy getting rich. There was, however, the founding of **Eatonville**, just north of Orlando, which was the first town in Florida – and possibly the US – to be founded, governed and lived in by black people.

FLORIDA AND THE SPANISH-AMERICAN WAR

By the 1890s, the US was a large and unified nation itching for a bigger role in the world. As the drive in **Cuba** for independence from Spain gathered momentum, an opportunity to participate in international affairs presented itself. Florida already had long links with Cuba – the capital, Havana, was just ninety miles from Key West, and several thousand Cuban migrants were employed in the Tampa cigar factories. During 1898, tens of thousands of US troops – the Cuban Expeditionary Force – arrived in the

state, and the **Spanish-American War** was declared on April 25. As it turned out, the fighting was comparatively minor; Spain withdrew and on January 1, 1899, Cuba attained independence (and the US a big say in its future). But the war was also the first of several major conflicts that were to prove beneficial to Florida. Many of the soldiers would return as settlers or tourists, and improved railroads and strengthened harbors at the commercially significant ports of Key West, Tampa and Pensacola did much to boost the economy.

THE BROWARD ERA

The early years of the 1900s were dominated by the progressive policies of **Napoleon Bonaparte Broward**, state governor from 1905. In a nutshell, Broward championed the small man against corporate interests, particularly the giant land-owning railroad companies. Among Broward's aims were an improved education system, a state-run commission to oversee new railroad construction, a tax on cars to finance road building, better salaries for teachers and the judiciary, a state-run life assurance scheme, and a ban on newspapers – few of which were well-disposed towards Broward – knowingly publishing untruths. Broward also enacted the first **conservation laws**, protecting fish, oysters, game and forests; but at the same time, in an attempt to create new land to rival the holdings of the rail barons, he conceived the drainage programme that would cause untold damage to the Everglades.

By no means all of Broward's policies became law, and he departed Tallahassee for a US Senate seat in 1910. Nonetheless, the forward-thinking plans of what became known as the **Broward Era** were continued through subsequent administrations – a process that went some way to bringing a rough-and-ready frontier land into the twentieth century.

WORLD WAR I AND THE FLORIDA LAND BOOM

World War I continued the tradition of the Spanish-American War by giving Florida an economic shot in the arm, as the military arrived to police the coastline and develop sea-warfare projects. Despite the influx of money and the reforms of the Broward years, there was little happening to improve the lot of Florida's blacks. The Ku Klux Klan was revived in Tallahassee in 1915, and the public outcry which followed the beating to death of a young black on a chaingang was answered only by the introduction of the sweatbox as punishment for prisoners considered unruly.

Typically, most visitors to Florida at this time were less concerned with social justice than with getting drunk. The coast so vigilantly protected from advancing Germans during the war was left wide open when **Prohibition** was introduced in 1919; the many secluded inlets became secure landing sites for liquor from the Caribbean. The illicit booze improved the atmosphere in the new resorts of **Miami Beach**, a picture-postcard piece of beach landscaping replacing what had been a barely habitable mangrove island just a few years before. Drink was not the only illegal pleasure pursued in the nightclubs: gambling and prostitution were also rife, and were soon to attract the attention of big-time **gangsters** such as Al Capone, initiating a climate of corruption that was to scar Florida politics for years.

The lightning-paced creation of Miami Beach was no isolated incident. Throughout Florida, and especially in the southeast, new communities appeared almost overnight. Self-proclaimed architectural genius **Addison Mizner** raised the "million dollar cottages" of Palm Beach and began fashioning **Boca Raton** with the same mock-Mediterranean excesses, on the premise: "get the big snob and the little snob will follow"; visionary **George Merrick** plotted the superlative **Coral Gables** – now absorbed by Miami – which became the nation's first pre-planned city and one of the few schemes of the time to age with dignity.

In the rush of prosperity that followed the war, it seemed everyone in America wanted a piece of Florida, and chartered trains brought in thousands of eager buyers. The spending frenzy soon meant that for every genuine offer there were a hundred bogus ones: many people unknowingly bought acres of empty swampland. The period was satirized by the Marx Brothers in their first film, *Cocoanuts.*

Although millions of dollars technically changed hands each week during the peak year of 1925, little hard cash actually moved: most deals were paper transactions with buyers paying a small deposit into a bank. The inflation inherent in the system finally went out of control in 1926: with buyers failing to keep up

payments, banks went **bust**, quickly followed by everyone else. A **hurricane** devastated Miami the same year – the city's house-builders never thought to protect the structures against tropical storms – and an even worse hurricane in 1928 caused Lake Okeechobee to burst its banks and flood surrounding communities.

With the Florida land boom well and truly over, the **Wall Street Crash** in 1929 proceeded to make paupers of the millionaires, such as Henry Flagler and Sarasota's **John Ringling**, whose considerable investments had helped to shape the state.

THE DEPRESSION, WORLD WAR II AND AFTER

At the start of the **Thirties** even the major railroads that had stimulated Florida's expansion were in receivership, and the state government only avoided bankruptcy with a constitutional escape clause. Due to the property crash, Florida had had a few extra years to adjust to grinding poverty before the whole country experienced the **Depression**, and a number of recovery measures – making the state more active in citizens' welfare – pre-empted the national **New Deal** legislation of President Roosevelt.

No single place was harder hit than **Key West**, which was not only suffering the Depression but hadn't been favored by the property boom either. With a population of 12,000, Key West was an incredible $5 million in debt, and had even lost its link to the mainland when the Overseas Railroad – running across the Florida Keys between Key West and Miami – was destroyed by the 1935 Labor Day hurricane.

What saved Key West, and indeed brought financial stability to all of Florida, was **World War II**. Once again, thousands of troops arrived to guard the coastline – off which there was an immense amount of German U-boat activity – while the flat inland areas made a perfect training venue for pilots. Empty tourist hotels provided ready-made barracks, and the soldiers – and their visiting families – got a taste of Florida that would bring many of them back.

In the immediate **postwar period**, the inability of the state to plan and provide for increased growth was resoundingly apparent, with public services – particularly in the field of education – woefully inadequate. Because of the massive profits being made through illegal gambling, corruption became endemic in public life. State governor **Fuller Warren**, implicated with the Al Capone crime syndicate in 1950, was by no means the only state official suspected of being in cahoots with criminals. A wave of attacks against blacks and Jews in 1951 caused Warren to speak out against the Ku Klux Klan, but the discovery that he himself had once been a Klan member only confirmed the poison flowing through the heart of Florida's political system.

A rare upbeat development was a continued commitment to the conservation measures introduced in the Broward era, with $2 million allocated to buying the land that, in 1947, became the **Everglades National Park**.

FLORIDA IN THE FIFTIES AND SIXTIES

Cattle, citrus and tourism continued to be the major components of Florida's economy as, in the ten years from 1950, the state soared from being the twentieth to the tenth most populous in the country, home to five million people. While its increased size raised Florida's profile in federal government, within the state the demographic changes – most dramatically the shift from rural life in the north to urban living in the south – went unacknowledged and **reapportionment** of representation in state government became a critical issue, one only resolved by the **1968 constitution** which provided for automatic reapportionment in line with population changes.

The fervent desire for growth and the need to present a wholesome public image prevented the state's conservative-dominated assembly from fighting as hard as their counterparts in the other Southern states against **de-segregation**, following a ruling by the federal Supreme Court on the issue in 1956. Nonetheless, blacks continued to be banned from Miami Beach after dark, from swimming off the Palm Beach coast, and were subject to segregation in restaurants, buses, hotels, schools – and barely represented at all in public office. As the **Civil Rights** movement gained strength during the early Sixties, bus boycotts and demonstrations took place in Tallahassee and Daytona Beach, and a march in St Augustine in 1964 resulted in the arrest of the movement's leader, Martin Luther King Jnr. The

success of the Civil Rights movement in ending legalized discrimination did little to affect the deeply entrenched racist attitudes among much of Florida's longer-established population. Most of the state's blacks still lived and worked in conditions that would be intolerable to whites: a fact which, in part, accounted for the **Liberty City riot** in August 1968, the first of several violent uprisings in Miami's depressed areas.

The ideological shift in Florida's near-neighbor, **Cuba** – declared a socialist state by its leader Fidel Castro in 1961 – came sharply into focus with the 1962 **missile crisis**, which triggered a tense game of cat and mouse between the US and the USSR over Soviet missile bases on the island. After world war was averted, Florida become the base of the US government's covert anti-Castro operations. Many engaged in these activities were among the 300,000 **Cuban migrants** who had arrived following the Castro-led revolution. The Bay of Pigs fiasco in 1961 proved that there was to be no quick return to the homeland, and while not all of the new arrivals stayed in Florida, many went no further than Miami, where they were to totally change the social character – and eventually the power balance – of the city.

Another factor in Florida's expansion was the basing of the new civilian space administration, **NASA**, at the military long-range missile testing site at Cape Canaveral. The all-out drive to land a man on the moon brought an enormous influx of space industry personnel in the early Sixties – quadrupling the population of the region soon to become known as the **Space Coast**.

Although it didn't open until 1971, **Walt Disney World** got off the drawing board in the mid-Sixties and was to have terrific impact on the future of Florida. The state government bent over backwards to help the Disney Corporation turn a sizeable slice of central Florida into the biggest theme park complex ever known. Throughout its construction, debate raged over the commercial and ecological effects of such a major undertaking on the rest of the region. Undeterred, smaller businesses rushed to the area, eager to capitalize on the anticipated tourist influx, and the sleepy cow-town of **Orlando** suddenly found itself the hub of one of the state's fastest-growing population centers – soon to become one of the world's best-known holiday destinations.

CONTEMPORARY FLORIDA

The great commercial success of Walt Disney World, and a fortuitous set of circumstances – American fears of terrorism reducing foreign travel and price-wars between tour operators and airlines encouraging overseas visitors – have helped solidify Florida's place in the **international tourist market**: directly or indirectly, one in five of the state's twelve million inhabitants now makes a living from tourism. Simultaneously, the general swing from heavy to **high-tech industries** has resulted in many American corporations forsaking their traditional northern bases in favor of Florida, bringing their white-collar workforces with them.

Behind the optimistic facade, however, lie many problems. Taxes kept low to stimulate growth have reduced funding for public services, leaving the apparently booming state with appalling levels of adult illiteracy, infant mortality and crime. Efforts to **raise taxes** during the late Eighties met incredible resistance and forced a U-turn by the state governor, Bob Martinez. A further cause for concern is the broadening **gap** between the relative liberalism of the big cities and the arch-conservatism of the bible-belt rural areas. While Miami is busy promoting its modernity and multicultural make-up (glossing over some severe inter-ethnic conflicts in doing so), the Ku Klux Klan holds picnics in the Panhandle, a children's storybook is removed from a north Florida school's reading list for containing the words "damn" and "bitch", and in Pensacola, a doctor is shot dead by anti-abortion activists.

GUNS AND DRUGS

Contradictions are also apparent in efforts to reduce crime. In 1976, Florida became the first state to **restore the death penalty**, declaring it the ultimate deterrent to murder; yet the state's **gun laws** remain notoriously lax. Some districts impose a "cooling off" period of a few days while the background of a potential gun purchaser is checked; but in most, firearms can be bought over the counter on production of the flimsiest ID.

The multi-million-dollar **drugs trade** active in the state shows few signs of abating. Geographically highly convenient for the exporters of Latin America, estimates suggest that at least a quarter of the cocaine entering the US arrives through Florida. In Miami, around ninety separate drug-law enforcement agencies are operative, but fear of corruption causes them to act alone and not pool information. Ironically, a recent switch of emphasis from capturing dealers to clamping down on **money-laundering** (the filtering of illegal profits through legitimate businesses) has begun to threaten many of Miami's financial institutions, built on – and it's an open secret – the drugs trade.

RACIAL ISSUES – AND CONSERVATION

Racial issues continue to be vexed. Black–white relations are often strained, and many Anglo-Americans are rueful of the powerful positions attained by Cubans who've steadily worked their way up the system since the Sixties. At the other end of the scale, large-scale immigration – legal and otherwise – into south Florida from the poor and unstable countries of Latin America and the Caribbean has put considerable pressure on the state's social services (such as they are), and played into the hands of right-wingers, who favor strict measures to curtail the influx and advocate a hardening of attitudes towards the state's ethnic minorities.

Increased protection of the state's **natural resources** has been a more positive feature of the last decade. Impressive amounts of land are under state control and, overall, wildlife is less threatened now than at any time since white settlers first arrived. Most spectacular of all has been the revival of the state's alligator population. On the downside, the Everglades – and its dependent animals – could still be destroyed by south Florida's ever-increasing need for drinking water.

VIOLENCE AGAINST TOURISTS

Repeated incidents of violence against European tourists, including the murders of German and British holiday makers, earned the state much adverse publicity. Governor Lawton Chiles (a liberal successor to Martinez, and elected against the odds in November 1990) responded in February 1993 by creating the Task Force on Tourist Safety. The task force launched pilot schemes in Miami and Orlando which entailed improved road signs (to show more clearly routes to major attractions), new tourist information centers at key arrival points, and an ending of the giveaway "Y" and "Z" licence plates on rental cars.

While the task force is a step forward, nobody seriously thinks that crime against the Florida tourist can ever be completely eradicated – particularly as many European visitors fail to heed the routine safety procautions (outlined in *Basics*) which most Americans take for granted. As state officials are swift to point out, however, European visitors are statistically much more likely to become victims of crime in their home countries than in Florida.

HURRICANE ANDREW

In August 1992, **Hurricane Andrew** brought winds of 168mph tearing through the southern regions of Miami (blowing down the radar of the National Hurricane Center in the process). Although the hurricane was no surprise – scores of potential hurricanes develop off Florida's shores each year between June and November and are closely observed; most die out well before striking the coast – roofs were ripped off homes, supermarkets were gutted, 150,000 were left homeless or living in ruins, 230,000 more had no power supply, and the cost of damage was estimated at $30 billion.

Governor Chiles declared the stricken region a disaster area, deployed 1500 National Guardsmen to stem looting, and warned that Florida would be bankrupt if left to foot the bill alone. As criticism of the sluggishly paced and disorganized federal response to the emergency mounted, then-president Bush made two child-hugging tours of the devastated area and eventually deployed 20,000 marines, and a naval convoy, in what became the biggest relief operation ever mounted.

Even a year after the hurricane struck, signs of its handiwork were apparent. Homestead was dotted by gutted supermarkets and abandoned homes, and on Key Biscayne – drenched by the hurricane's saltwater storm – none of the hotels had re-opened at the time of writing.

While older Floridians may remember the series of hurricanes that hit the state in the Twenties and Thirties, and recall their destructive power, it's been a common trait of recent arrivals to play down the threat of hurricanes, with few people bothering to stock emergency provisions or take heed of evacuation warnings. Post-Andrew, however, this attitude has dramatically changed and hurricane preparedness events – which give tips on preparing for and surviving a hurricane – now attract very big crowds indeed.

NATURAL FLORIDA

The biggest surprise for most people in Florida isn't the size of the state lottery but the abundance of undeveloped, natural areas throughout the state and the extraordinary variety of wildlife and vegetation within them. From a rare hawk that eats only snails to a vine-like fig that strangles other trees, natural Florida possesses plenty that you've probably never seen before, and which – due to drainage, pressures from the agricultural lobby, and the constant need for new housing – may not be on view for very much longer.

BACKGROUND

Many factors contribute to the unusual diversity of **ecosystems** found in Florida, the most obvious being **latitude**: the north of the state has vegetation common to temperate regions, which is quite distinct from the subtropical flora of the south. Another crucial element is **elevation**: while much of Florida is flat and low-lying, a change of a few inches in elevation drastically affects what grows, due in part to the enormous variety of soils.

THE ROLE OF FIRE

Florida has more thunderstorms than any other part of the US, and the resultant lightning frequently ignites **fires**. Many Florida plants have adapted to fire by developing thick bark, or the ability to regenerate from stumps. Others, such as cabbage palmetto and sawgrass, protect their growth bud with a sheath of green leaves. Fire is necessary to keep a natural balance of plant species – human attempts to control naturally ignited fires have contributed to the changing composition of Florida's remaining wild lands.

FORESTS AND WOODLANDS

Forests and woodlands aren't the first thing people associate with Florida, but the state has an impressive assortment, ranging from the great tracts of upland pine common in the north to the mixed bag of tropical foliage found in the southern hammocks.

PINE FLATWOODS

Covering roughly half of Florida, **pine flatwoods** are most widespread on the southeastern coastal plain. These pine species – longleaf, slash and pond – rise tall and straight like telegraph poles. The Spanish once harvested products such as turpentine and rosin from Florida's flatwood pines, a practice which continued during US settlement: some trees still bear the scars on their trunk. Pine flatwoods are airy and open, with abundant light filtering through the upper canopy of leaves, allowing thickets of shrubs such as saw palmetto, evergreen oaks, gallberry and fetterbrush to grow. **Inhabitants** of the pine flatwoods include white-tailed deer, cotton rats, brown-headed nuthatches, pine warblers, eastern diamondback rattlesnakes and oak toads. Although many of these creatures also inhabit other Florida ecosystems, the **fox squirrel** – a large and noisy character with a rufous tinge to its undercoat – is one of the few mammalian denizens more or less restricted to the pine flatwoods.

UPLAND PINE FORESTS

As the name suggests, **upland pine forests** – or high pinelands – are found on the rolling sand ridges and sandhills of northeastern Florida and the Panhandle; conditions which tend to keep upland pine forests dryer and therefore even more open than the flatwoods. Upland pine forests have a groundcover of wiregrass and an overstorey of (mostly) longleaf pine trees, which creates a park-like appearance. Red-headed woodpeckers, eastern bluebirds, Florida mice, pocket gophers (locally called "salamanders", which is a distortion of "sand mounder") and gopher tortoises (an amiable sort which often shares its burrow with gopher frogs) all make the high pine country their home. The latter two, together with scarab beetles, keep the forest healthy by mixing and aerating the soil. The now-endangered red-cockaded woodpecker is symbolic of old-growth upland pine forest; logging and repression of the natural fire process have contributed to its decline.

HAMMOCKS

Wildlife tends to be more abundant in hardwood **hammocks** than in the associated pine forests and prairies (see below). Hammocks consist of narrow bands of (non-pine) hardwoods growing transitionally between pine-lands and lower, wetter vegetation. The make-up of hammocks varies across the state: in the south, they chiefly comprise tropical hardwoods (see the "South Florida Rocklands", below); in the north, they contain an overstorey of oaks, magnolia and beech with a few smaller plants – red-bellied woodpeckers, red-tailed and red-shouldered hawks and barred owls nest in them, and you can also find eastern wood rats, striped skunks and white-tailed deer.

SCRUB AND PRAIRIE

Scrub ecosystems once spread to the southern Rocky Mountains and northern Mexico but climatic changes reduced their distribution and remnant stands are now found only in northern and central Florida. Like the high pines, scrub occurs in dry hilly areas. The vegetation, which forms an impenetrable mass, consists of varied combinations of drought-adapted evergreen oaks, saw palmetto, Florida rosemary and/or sand pine. The **Florida bonamia**, a morning-glory with pale blue funnel-shaped blossoms, is one of the most attractive plants of the scrub, which has more than a dozen plant species offi-cially listed as endangered. Scrub also harbors some unique animals, which include the Florida mouse, the Florida scrub lizard, the sand skink and the Florida scrub jay. The **scrub jay** has an unusual social system: pairs nest in cooperation with offspring of previous seasons, who help carry food to their younger siblings. Although not unique to scrub habitat, other inhabitants include black bear, white-tailed deer, bobcats and gopher tortoises.

Some of Florida's inland areas are covered by **prairie**, characterized by love grass, broom-sedge and wiregrass – the best examples surround Lake Okeechobee. In keeping with the popular image, herds of **bison** roamed Florida's prairies some two hundred years ago, only to be destroyed by settlers. Bison are now being reintroduced to some state parks. A more diminutive prairie denizen is the **burrowing owl**: most owls are active at night, but burrow-ing owls feed during the day and, equally unusually, live in underground dens and bow nervously when approached – earning them the nickname the "howdy owl". Eastern spotted skunks, cotton rats, black vultures, eastern meadowlarks and box turtles are a few other prairie denizens. Nine-banded **armadillos** are

also found in prairie habitats and in any non-swampy terrain. A recent invader from Texas, the armadillos usually feed at night on insects and forage. Due to poor eyesight, they often won't notice a human's approach until the last minute, when they will leap up and bound away noisily.

THE SOUTH FLORIDA ROCKLANDS

Elevated areas around the state's southern tip – in the Everglades and along the Florida Keys – support either pines or tropical hardwood hammocks on limestone outcroppings collec-tively known as the **south Florida rocklands**. More jungle-like than the temperate hardwood forests found in northern Florida, the **tropical hardwood hammocks** of the south tend to occur as "tree islands" surrounded by sparser vegetation. Royal palm, pigeon plum, gumbo limbo (one of the most beautiful of the tropical hammock trees, with a distinctive smooth red bark) and ferns form dense thickets within the hammocks. The **pine forests** of the south Florida rocklands largely consist of scraggly-looking slash pine. Wet prairies or mangroves surround the hammocks and pine forests.

EPIPHYTIC PLANTS

Tropical hammocks contain various forms of **epiphytic plants** – which use other plants for physical support, but don't depend on them for nutrients. In southern Florida, epiphytes include orchids, ferns, bromeliads (**Spanish moss** is one of the most widespread bromeliads, hang-ing from tree branches throughout the state and forming the "Canopy Roads" in Tallahassee, see Chapter Seven). Seemingly the most aggressive of epiphytes, **strangler figs**, after germinating in the canopy of trees such as palms, parasitise their host tree: they send out aerial roots that eventually reach the soil and then tightly enlace the host, preventing growth of the trunk. Finally, the fig produces so many leaves that it chokes out the host's greenery; the host dies leaving only the fig.

OTHER PLANTS AND VERTEBRATES

The south Florida rocklands support over forty plants and a dozen vertebrates found nowhere else. These include the crenulate lead plant, the Key tree cactus, the Florida mastiff bat, the Key deer and the Miami black-headed snake. More common residents include **butterflies and spiders** – the black and yellow yeliconia butterflies, with their long paddle-shaped wings and a distinctive gliding flight pattern, being particularly elegant. Butterflies need to practise careful navigation as hammocks are laced with the meter-long webs of the banana spider. Other wildlife species include sixty species of land snail, green treefrogs, green anoles, cardinals, oppossums, raccoons and white-tailed deer. Most of these species are native to the southeastern US, but a few West Indian bird species, such as the mangrove cuckoo, gray kingbird and white-crowned pigeon, have colonized the south Florida rocklands.

FRESHWATER SWAMPS AND MARSHES

Although about half have been destroyed due to logging, peat removal, draining, or sewage outflow, **swamps** are still found all over Florida. Trees found around swamps include pines, palms, cedars, oaks, black gum, willows and bald cypress. Particularly adapted to aquatic conditions, the **bald cypress** is ringed by knobby "knees", or modified roots, providing oxygen to the tree which would otherwise suffocate in the wet soil. Epiphytic orchids and bromeliads are common on cypresses, especially in the southern part of the state. Florida's official state tree, the **sabal palm**, is another swamp/hammock plant: "heart of palm" is the gourmet's name for the vegetable cut from its insides and used in salads.

Florida swamps also have many species of **insectivorous plants**, with sticky pads or liquid-filled funnels that trap small insects which are then digested by the nitrogen-hungry plant. Around the Apalachicola National Forest is the highest diversity of carnivorous plants in the world, among them pitcher plants, bladderworts and sundews. Other swamp-dwellers include dragonflies, snails, clams, fish, bird-voiced tree frogs, limpkins, ibis, wood ducks, beavers, raccoons and Florida panthers.

Wetlands with relatively few trees, **freshwater marshes** range from shallow wet prairies to deep-water cattail marshes. **The Everglades** form Florida's largest marsh, most of which is sawgrass. On higher ground with good soils, sawgrass (actually a sedge) grows densely; at lower elevations it's sparser, and often an algal mat covers the soil between its

plants. Water beetles, tiny crustaceans such as amphipods, mosquitoes, crayfish, killifish, sunfish, gar, catfish, bullfrogs, herons, egrets, ibis, water rats, white-tailed deer and Florida panthers can all be found. With luck, you might see a **snail kite**: a brown or black mottled hawk with a very specialized diet, entirely dependant on large apple snails. Snail and snail kite numbers have drastically fallen following the draining of marshes for agriculture and flood control: so far, 65 percent of the Everglades has been irreversibly drained.

WETLAND DENIZENS: ALLIGATORS AND WADING BIRDS

Alligators are one of the most widely known denizens of Florida's wetlands, lakes and rivers. Look for them on sunny mornings when they bask on logs or banks. If you hear thunder rumbling on a clear day, it may in fact be the bellow of territorial males. Alligators can reach ten feet in length and primarily prey on fish, turtles, birds, crayfish and crabs. Once overhunted for their hides and meat, alligators have made a strong comeback since protection was initiated in 1973; by 1987, Florida had up to half a million of them. They are not usually dangerous – in the fifteen years from 1973 there were only four fatal attacks. Most at risk are people who swim at dusk and small children playing unattended near water. To many creatures, alligators are a life-saver: during the summer, when the marshes dry up, they use their snouts, legs and tails to enlarge existing pools, creating a refuge for themselves and for other aquatic species. In these "Gator Holes", garfish stack up like cordwood, snakes search for frogs, and otters and anhingas forage for fish.

Wading birds are conspicuous in the wetlands. Egrets, herons and ibis, usually clad in white or grey feathers, stalk frogs, mice and small fish. Turn-of-the-century plume-hunters decimated these birds to make fanciful hats, and during the last few decades habitat destruction has caused a 90 percent reduction in their numbers. Nonetheless, many are still visible in swamps, marshes and mangroves. Cattle egrets, invaders from South America, are a common sight on pastures, where they forage on insects disturbed by grazing livestock. Pink waders – roseate spoonbills and, to a much lesser extent, flamingoes – can be also found in southern Florida's wetlands.

LAKES, SPRINGS AND RIVERS

Florida has almost 8000 freshwater **lakes**. Game fish such as bass and bluegill are common, but the waters are too warm to support trout. Some native fish species are threatened by the introduction of the **"walking" catfish**, which has a specially adapted gill system enabling it to leave the water and take the fish equivalent of cross-country hikes. A native of India and Burma, the walking catfish was released into southern Florida canals in the early Sixties and within twenty years had "walked" across twenty counties, disturbing the indigenous food chain. A freeze eliminated a number of these exotic fish, though enough remain to cause concern.

Most Florida **springs** release cold fresh water but some springs are warm and others emit sulphur, chloride or salt-laden waters. Homosassa Springs (see Chapter Six), for example, has a high chloride content, making it attractive to both freshwater and marine species of fish.

Besides fish, Florida's extensive **river** system supports snails, freshwater mussels and crayfish. Southern river-dwellers also include the lovable **manatee**, or sea cow, which inhabits bays and shallow coastal waters. The only totally aquatic herbivorous mammal, manatees sometimes weigh almost a ton but only eat aquatic plants. Unable to tolerate cold conditions, manatees are partial to the warm water discharged by power plants, taking some of them as far north as North Carolina. In Florida during the winter, the large springs at Crystal River (see Chapter Six) attract manatees, some of which have become tame enough to allow divers to scratch their bellies. Manatees have few natural enemies but are on the decline, often due to power-boat propellers injuring their backs or heads when they feed at the surface.

THE COAST

There's a lot more than sunbathing taking place around Florida's **coast**. The sandy beaches provide a habitat for many species, not least the sea turtles which creep ashore after dark to lay their eggs. Where there isn't sand, you'll find the fascinating mangrove forests, or wildlife-filled salt marshes and estuaries. Offshore, coral reefs provide yet another exotic ecosys-

tem, and one of the more pleasurable to explore by snorkelling or diving.

SANDY BEACHES

Waves bring many interesting creatures onto Florida's **sandy beaches**, such as sponges, horseshoe crabs and the occasional sea horse. Florida's **shells** are justly famous – fig shells, moon snails, conches, whelks, olive shells, red and orange scallops, murex, cockles, pen and turban shells are a few of the many varieties. As you beachcomb, beware of stepping barefoot on purplish fragments of **man-o-war** tentacles: these jellyfish have no means of locomotion, and their floating, sail-like bodies often cause them to be washed ashore – their tentacles, which sometimes reach to sixty feet in length, can deliver a painful sting. More innocuous beach inhabitants include wintering birds such as black-bellied plovers and sanderlings, and nesting black skimmers.

Of the seven species of **sea turtle**, five nest on Florida's sandy beaches: green, loggerhead, leatherback, hawksbill and olive ridley. From February to August, the female turtles haul out at night, excavate a beachside hole and deposit a hundred-plus eggs. Not many of these will survive to adulthood: raccoons eat a lot of the eggs, and hatchlings are liable to be crushed by vehicles on the coastal highways when they become disoriented by their lights. Programmes to hatch the eggs artificially have helped offset some of the losses. The best time to view sea turtles is during June – peak nesting time – with one of the park-ranger-led walks offered along the southern portion of the northeast coast (see Chapter Four).

MANGROVES

Found in brackish waters around the Florida Keys and the southwest coast, Florida has three species of **mangrove**. Unlike most plants, mangroves bear live young: the "seeds", or propagules, germinate while still on the tree; after dropping from the parent, the young propagule floats for weeks or months until it washes up on a suitable site, where its sprouted condition allows it to put out roots rapidly. Like bald cypress, mangroves have difficulty extracting oxygen from their muddy environs and solve this problem with extensive aerial roots, which either dangle finger-like from branches or twist outwards from the lower trunk. Various fish species, such as the mangrove snapper, depend on mangroves as a nursery; other **mangrove inhabitants** include frogs, crocodiles, brown pelicans, wood storks, roseate spoonbills, river otters, mink and raccoons.

SALT MARSHES AND ESTUARIES

Like the mangrove ecosystem, the **salt marsh and estuary** habitat provides a nursery for many fish species, which in turn fodder larger fish, herons, egrets and the occasional dolphin. **Crocodiles**, with narrower and more pointed snouts than alligators, are seldom sighted, and confined to salt water at the state's southernmost tip. In a few southern Florida salt marshes, you might find a **great white heron**, a rare and handsome form of the more common great blue heron. Around Florida Bay, great white herons have learned to beg for fish from local residents, each of these massive birds "working" a particular neighborhood – striding from household to household demanding fish by rattling window blinds with their bills or gutturally croaking. A less appealing salt marsh denizen is the **mosquito**: unfortunately, the more damaging methods of mosquito control, such as impounding salt water or spraying DDT, have inflicted extensive harm to the fragile salt marshes and estuaries.

THE CORAL REEF

A long band of living **coral reef** frames Florida's southeastern corner. Living coral comes in many colors: star coral is green, elkhorn coral is orange and brain coral is red. Each piece of coral is actually a colony of hundreds or thousands of small, soft animals called **polyps**, related to sea anemones and jellyfish. The polyps secrete limestone to form their hard outer skeletons and at night extend their feathery tentacles to filter seawater for microscopic food. The filtering process, however, provides only a fraction of the coral's nutrition – most is produced via the photosynthesis of algae that live within the polyp's cells. In recent years, influxes of warmer water, possibly associated with global warming, have killed off large numbers of the algal cells. The half-starved polyp then often succumbs to disease, a phenomenon known as "bleaching". Although this has been observed throughout the Pacific, the damage in Florida has so far been moderate: the impact of the tourist industry on the reef has been more pronounced, though reef destruction for souvenirs is now banned.

Coral reefs are home to a kaleidoscopic variety of brightly colored fish – beau gregories, porkfish, parrot fish, blennies, grunts and wrasses – which swirl in dazzling schools or lurk between coral crevices. The **damselfish** is the farmer of the reef: after destroying a polyp patch, it feeds on the resultant algae growth, fiercely defending it from other fish. Sponges, feather-duster worms, sea fans, crabs, spiny lobsters, sea urchins and conches are among the other thousands of coral reef species.

BOOKS

Florida's perennial state of social and political flux has always promised rich material for historians and journalists eager to pin the place down. Rarely have they managed this, although the picture of the region's unpredictable evolution which emerges can make for compulsive reading. Many established fiction writers spend their winters in Florida, but few have convincingly portrayed its characters, climate and scenery. Those that have, however, have produced some of the most unique and gripping literature to emerge from any part of the US.

HISTORY

Edward N Akin *Flagler: Rockefeller Partner & Florida Baron* (Kent State University). Solid biography of the man whose Standard Oil fortune helped build Florida's first hotels and railroads.

Howard Kleinberg *The Way We Were* (Surfside). Oversized overview of Miami's history: colorful archival photos and text by a former editor-in-chief of the city's newspaper of 92 years, *The Miami News*.

Helen Muir *Miami, USA* (The Pickering Press). An insider's account of how Miami's first developers gave the place shape during the land boom of the Twenties.

John Rothchild *Up for Grabs: A Trip Through Time and Space in the Sunshine State* (Penguin). Irreverent look at Florida's chequered career as a vacation spa, tourist trap and haven for scheming ne'er-do-wells.

Charlton W Tebeau *A History of Florida* (University of Miami). The definitive academic tome, but not for casual reading.

Garcilaso de la Vega *The Florida of the Inca* (o/p). Comprehensive account of the sixteenth-century expedition led by Hernando de Soto through Florida's prairies, swamps and aboriginal settlements; extremely turgid in parts, overall an excellent insight into the period.

Lawrence E Will *Swamp to Sugarbowl: Pioneer Days in Belle Glade* (Great Outdoors). A "cracker" account of early times in the state, written in first-person redneck vernacular. Variously oafish and offensive – but never dull.

NATURAL HISTORY

Jon L Dunn & Eirik A T Blom *Field Guide to the Birds of North America, Second Ed.* (National Geographic Society). The best country-wide guide, with plenty on Florida and excellent illustrations throughout.

Harold R Holt *Lane's "A Birder's Guide to Florida"*. Detailed accounts of when and where to find Florida's birds, including maps and seasonal charts. Aimed at the expert but excellent value for the novice bird-watcher.

Ronald L Myers and John J Ewel *Ecosystems of Florida* (University of Central Florida Press). Technical yet highly readable treatise for the serious ecologist.

TRAVEL AND IMPRESSIONS

T D Allman *Miami: City of the Future* (Atlantic Monthly Press). Excellent, incisive look at modern Miami that becomes bogged down when going further back than *Miami Vice*.

William Bartram *Travels* (o/p). The lively diary of an eighteenth-century naturalist rambling through the Deep South and on into Florida during the period of British rule. Outstanding accounts of the indigenous people and all kinds of wildlife.

Edna Buchanan *The Corpse had a Familiar Face* (Charter Books/Bodley Head). Sometimes sharp, often sensationalist account of the author's years spent pounding the crime beat for the *Miami Herald*: five thousand corpses and gore galore. The subsequent *Vice* is more of the same.

Joan Didion *Miami* (Pocket Books/Penguin). A rivetting though ultimately unsatisfying voyage around the impenetrably complex and wildly passionate *el exilio* politics of Cuban Miami.

Marjory Stoneman Douglas *The Everglades: River of Grass* (Mockingbird). Concerned conservationist literature by one of the state's most respected historians, describing the nature and beauty of the Everglades from their beginnings. A superb work that contributed to the founding of the Everglades National Park.

Lynn Geldof *Cubans* (Bloomsbury). Passionate and rambling interviews with Cubans in Cuba and Miami, which confirm the tight bond between them.

Henry James *The American Scene* (St Martin). Interesting waffle from the celebrated novelist, including written portraits of St Augustine and Palm Beach as they thronged with wintering socialites at the turn of the century.

Norman Mailer *Miami and the Siege of Chicago* (DI Fine/Penguin o/p). A rabid study of the American political conventions of 1968, the first part frothing over the Republican Party's shenanigans at Miami Beach when Nixon beat Reagan for the presidential ticket.

Roxanne Pulitzer *The Prize Pulitzer: The Scandal that Rocked Palm Beach* (Ballantine/Headline). A small-town girl who married into the jet-set lifestyle of Palm Beach describes the mud-slinging in Florida's most moneyed community when she seeks a divorce.

David Rieff *Going to Miami: Exiles, Tourists and Refugees in the New America* (Penguin Viking/Bloomsbury). An exploration of Miami through the minds of its conservative Cubans, its struggling blacks and Haitians, and its resentful Anglos – but with too many sexist musings to be credible.

John Williams *Into the Badlands: A Journey through the American Dream* (Paladin). The author's trek across the US to interview the country's best crime writers begins in Miami, "the city that coke built", its compelling strangeness all too briefly revelled in.

ARCHITECTURE AND PHOTOGRAPHY

Barbara Baer Capitman *Deco Delights* (E P Dutton). A tour of Miami Beach's Art Deco buildings by the woman who championed their preservation, with definitive photography.

Laura Cerwinske *Miami: Hot & Cool* (Clarkson N Potter). Coffee-table tome with text on high-style south Florida living and glowing, color pics of Miami's beautiful homes and gardens. By the same author, *Tropical Deco: The Architecture & Design of Old Miami Beach* (Rizzoli) delivers a wealth of architectural detail.

Donald W. Curl *Mizner's Florida: American Resort Architecture* (Architectural History Foundation/The Massachusetts Institute of Technology). An assessment of the life, career and designs of Addison Mizner, the self-taught architect responsible for the "Bastard Spanish Moorish Romanesque Renaissance Bull Market Damn the Expense Style" structures of Palm Beach and Boca Raton.

Hap Hatton *Tropical Splendor: An Architectural History of Florida* (Knopf). A readable, informative and effectively illustrated account of the wild, weird and wonderful buildings that have graced and disgraced the state over the years.

Alva Johnston *The Legendary Mizners* (Farrar, Straus & Giroux). A racy biography of Addison Mizner and his brother Wilson, telling how they wined, dined and married into the lifestyles of the rich and famous of the Twenties.

Gary Monroe *Life in South Beach* (Forest & Trees). A slim volume of monochrome photos showing Miami Beach's South Beach before the restoration of the Art Deco district and the arrival of globetrotting trendies.

FICTION

Pat Booth *Miami* (Century). It had to happen: best-selling author uses the glitz-and-glamor of Miami's South Beach as a backdrop to a pot-boiling tale of seduction and desire.

Edward Falco *Winter in Florida* (Soho Press/Bellew). Flawed but compulsive story of a cossetted New York boy seeking thrills on a central Florida horse farm – and finding them.

Ernest Hemingway *To Have and Have Not* (MacMillan/Penguin). Hemingway lived and drank in Key West for years but set only this moderate tale in the town, describing the woes of fishermen brutalized by the Depression.

Zora Neale Hurston *Their Eyes Were Watching God* (Harper Collins/Virago). Florida-born Hurston became one of the bright lights of the Harlem Renaissance in the Twenties. This novel describes the founding of Eatonville – her home town and the state's first all-black town

– and the laborers' lot in Belle Glade at the time of the 1928 hurricane. Equally hard to put down are *Jonah's Gourd Vine* (Virago) and the autobiography, *Dust Tracks on a Road* (Virago).

David A. Karfelt *American Tropic* (Poseiden Press). Overblown saga of passion and power set during several key eras in Florida's history; just the job for idle hours on the beach.

Peter Matthiessen *Killing Mister Watson* (Vintage/Collins Harvill). Thoroughly researched story of the early days of white settlement in the Everglades. Slow-paced but a strong insight into the Florida frontier mentality.

Thomas McGuane *Ninety-Two in the Shade* (Minerva). A strange, hallucinatory search for identity by a young man of shifting mental states who aspires to become a Key West fishing guide – and whose family and friends are equally warped. By the same author, *Panama* (Minerva) is also set in Key West.

Theodore Pratt *The Barefoot Mailman* (Mockingbird). A Forties account of the long-distance postman who kept the far-flung settlements of pioneer-period Florida in mail by hiking the many miles of beach between them.

John Sayles *Los Gusanos* (Harper Collins/Hamish Hamilton). Absorbing, if long-winded novel set around the lives of Cuban exiles in Miami – written by a cult film director.

Daniel Vilmure *Life in the Land of the Living* (McGraw/Faber). Only the vigor of the writing lifts this purposeless story of two brothers rampaging through an unnamed Florida port town on a blisteringly hot Friday night.

CRIME FICTION

Edna Buchanan *Nobody Lives Forever* (Random/Mysterious). Tense, psycho-killer thriller played out on the mean streets of Miami. See also "Travel and impressions".

Liza Cody *Backhand* (Chatto & Windus). London's finest female private investigator, Anna Lee, follows the clues from Kensington to the West Coast of Florida – highly entertaining.

James Hall *Under Cover of Daylight; Squall Line* (each Mandarin); *Hard Aground* (Heinemann). Taut thrillers with a cast of crazies that make the most of the edge-of-the-world landscapes of the Florida Keys.

Carl Hiaasen *Double Whammy* (Warner Books/Pan). Ferociously funny fishing thriller that brings together a classic collection of warped but believable Florida characters; among them a hermit-like ex-state governor, a cynical Cuban cop and a corrupt TV preacher. By the same author, *Skin Tight* (Pan) explores the perils of unskilled plastic surgery in a Miami crawling with mutant hitmen, bought politicians and police on gangsters' payrolls, and *Native Tongue* (Pan) delves into the murky goings-on behind the scenes at a Florida theme park.

Elmore Leonard *Stick; La Brava; Gold Coast* (each Avon/Penguin). The pick of this highly recommended author's Florida-set thrillers, respectively detailing the rise of an opportunist black through the money, sex and drugs of Latino Miami; low-life on the seedy South Beach before the preservation of the Art Deco district; and the tribulations of a wealthy gangster-widow alone in a Fort Lauderdale mansion.

Charles Willeford *Miami Blues* (Ballantine/Futura). Thanks to an uninspired film, the best-known but not the best of a highly recommended series starring Hoke Mosely, a cool and calculating, but very human, Miami cop. Superior titles in the series are *The Way We Die Now* (Ballantine/Futura), *Kiss Your Ass Goodbye* (McMillan/Gollancz) and *Sideswipe* (Ballantine/Gollancz).

INDEX

THE ROUGH GUIDES

Title	ISBN	Price
Amsterdam	1858280184	£6.99
Australia	1858280354	£12.99
Barcelona & Catalunya	1858280486	£7.99
Berlin	1858280338	£8.99
Brazil	0747101272	£7.95
Brittany & Normandy	1858280192	£7.99
Bulgaria	1858280478	£8.99
California	1858280575	£9.99
Canada	185828001X	£10.99
Crete	1858280494	£6.99
Cyprus	185828032X	£8.99
Czech & Slovak Republics	185828029X	£8.99
Egypt	1858280753	£10.99
Europe	1858280273	£12.99
Florida	1858280109	£8.99
France	1858280508	£9.99
Germany	1858280257	£11.99
Greece	1858280206	£9.99
Guatemala & Belize	1858280206	£9.99
Holland, Belgium & Luxembourg	1858280036	£8.99
Hong Kong & Macau	1858280664	£8.99
Hungary	1858280214	£7.99
Ireland	1858280516	£8.99
Italy	1858280311	£12.99
Kenya	1858280435	£9.99
Mediterranean Wildlife	0747100993	£7.95
Morocco	1858280400	£9.99
Nepal	185828046X	£8.99
New York	1858280583	£8.99
Nothing Ventured	0747102082	£7.99
Paris	1858280389	£7.99
Peru	0747102546	£7.95
Poland	1858280346	£9.99
Portugal	1858280222	£7.99
Prague	185828015X	£7.99
Provence & the Côte d'Azur	1858280230	£8.99
Pyrenees	1858280524	£7.99
St Petersburg	1858280303	£8.99
San Francisco	0747102589	£5.99
Scandinavia	1858280397	£10.99
Sicily	1858280370	£8.99
Spain	1858280079	£8.99
Thailand	1858280168	£8.99
Tunisia	1858280656	£8.99
Turkey	1858280133	£8.99
Tuscany & Umbria	1858280559	£8.99
USA	1858280281	£12.99
Venice	1858280362	£8.99
West Africa	1858280141	£12.99
Women Travel	1858280710	£7.99
Zimbabwe & Botswana	1858280419	£10.99

The complete series of Rough Guides is available from all good bookshops but can be obtained directly from Penguin by writing to:
Penguin Direct, Penguin Books Ltd, Bath Road, Harmondsworth, West Drayton, Middlesex UB7 ODA; or telephone our credit line on 081 899 4036 (9am–5pm) and ask for Penguin Direct. Visa, Access and Amex accepted. Delivery will normally be within 14 working days.

The availability and published prices quoted are correct at the time of going to press but are subject to alteration without prior notice.
Penguin Direct ordering facilities are only available in the UK.

See the world...

Reserve Worldwide

- Reserve 6 months ahead
- Immediate confirmation
- Pay in local currency

Secure your accommodation now!